Income Planning

4th Edition

CCH
a Wolters Kluwer business

CCH Canadian Limited
300-90 Sheppard Avenue East
Toronto Ontario
M2N 6X1
1 800 268 4522
www.cch.ca

Published by CCH Canadian Limited

Important Disclaimer: This publication is sold with the understanding that (1) the authors and editors are not responsible for the results of any actions taken on the basis of information in this work, nor for any errors or omissions; and (2) the publisher is not engaged in rendering legal, accounting or other professional services. The publisher, and the authors and editors, expressly disclaim all and any liability to any person, whether a purchaser of this publication or not, in respect of anything and of the consequences of anything done or omitted to be done by any such person in reliance, whether whole or partial, upon the whole or any part of the contents of this publication. If legal advice or other expert assistance is required, the services of a competent professional person should be sought.

For CCH Canadian Limited

Editor: Hyun Joo Kim

National Library of Canada Cataloguing in Publication

Towers Watson
Canadian Pensions and Retirement Income Planning

4th ed.: edited by Towers Watson
Includes index.
ISBN: 978-1-55496-100-9

1. Income tax — Canada — Deductions — Retirement contributions. 2. Pension — trusts — Taxation — Law and legislation — Canada. 3. Pensions — Taxation — Law and legislation — Canada. I. Towers Watson (Firm)

HJ4662.A45C364 2010 343.7105'23 C2010-905267-0

Typeset by CCH Canadian Limited.
Printed in the United States of America.

ACKNOWLEDGEMENTS

Towers Watson would like to acknowledge the contribution of the Canadian associates who have helped to develop and update content, research issues, and review this book from both a technical and qualitative perspective. Special recognition is extended to Cindy Boates as Editor in Chief and associates: Paul Timmins, Graham Abell, Dean Taylor, Alison Fairey, Peter Miodonski, Lori Satov, Moira Graham, Doug Chandler, Karen DeBortolig, and Dan Morrison, as well as Sonia Massicotte of PBI Actuarial Consultants Ltd. for their invaluable assistance and patience in researching, reviewing, and editing. A special thanks also goes to Joyce Lee, whose word processing skills are indispensable.

Towers Watson is a leading global professional services company that helps organizations improve performance through effective people, risk, and financial management. With 14,000 associates around the world, we offer solutions in the areas of employment benefits, talent management, rewards, and risk and capital management.

For more information, visit us online at **towerswatson.com**.

TOWERS WATSON

FOREWORD

This book has been produced at this time primarily to:

- update the 3rd edition of this book written by Watson Wyatt and Company and published by CCH Canadian Limited in order to incorporate revisions to the *Income Tax Act* (Canada) and the Income Tax Regulations, as well as to reflect our understanding of newer policies, rules, and practices at the Canada Revenue Agency;
- assist retirement plan sponsors, tax advisers, pension consultants, and other interested individuals in understanding some of the complex tax rules that affect how Canadians save for their retirement;
- assist plan administrators in understanding the requirements for the registration of pension plans and deferred profit sharing plans;
- assist plan sponsors and plan administrators in understanding how to determine pension adjustments, past service pension adjustments and pension adjustment reversals and to provide information on reporting requirements; and
- provide a general perspective of legislative, professional, and administrative requirements for running pension and other retirement schemes in Canada.

This book primarily covers three areas:

- registered retirement savings plan (RRSP) contribution rules;
- pension adjustments (PAs), past service pension adjustments (PSPAs), pension adjustment reversals (PARs); and
- registration rules for registered pension plans (RPPs) and deferred profit sharing plans (DPSPs).

We have not attempted to explain in detail the government's goals underlying the changes, nor how successfully these goals have been met. Rather, our intention has been to describe the rules that apply from 1990 (and, where relevant, the rules prior to 1990) and to present strategies, which both employers and individual taxpayers can follow, in order to maximize any tax advantages offered by these rules.

This book reflects the provisions of the Income Tax Act *(Canada) and the Regulations in effect as of March 1, 2010, together with our understanding of any proposed changes and administrative rules of which we have been made aware as of the time of writing this book.*

Current Era

The era of significant change and transition that the Canadian retirement environment has undergone for over 20 years is now over and the major changes to the taxation system that were first proposed in 1984 have now been fully in place for several years. Increased contribution and benefit limits have been put in place for the years up to 2009, and, starting in 2010, these limits will be indexed in accordance with increases in the average wage.

Over this same time period, the federal government and most provinces introduced significant changes to improve the minimum standards applicable to registered pension plans. Changes in minimum standards are ongoing with many jurisdictions continuing to make further revisions to legislation that was already substantially improved 15 or more years ago. Concurrently, professionals who assist plan sponsors in managing their pension plans continue to broaden and redefine their own professional guidelines. For the actuarial profession, much research and training has been put into revising methodologies for setting appropriate long-term economic and demographic assumptions and in determining commuted values of pension benefits. Changes are forthcoming in the accounting profession for proper and consistent determination of pension expense for financial reporting purposes.

And while the era of big change is over, the retirement system continues to be modified and adjusted as Canadian employers face new and different challenges. Legislators continue to make changes while several jurisdictions have taken a full step back, with various discussion papers and commissions, to review how more significant changes to the minimum standards legislative framework might be able to provide secure and affordable retirement for Canadian employees. All the while, plan sponsors are grappling with growing defined benefit liabilities and increasing volatilities at the same time as they try to maintain their competitiveness in the global marketplace. Increasingly, plan sponsors are turning to defined contribution programs to maintain their competitiveness with other jurisdictions where defined contribution is more prevalent, while at the same time, continuing to be concerned about the ability of defined contribution programs to provide adequate retirement income for their employees. New and innovative plan designs will continue to be developed in response to these dual pressures.

Contents and Organization

The text of this book has been split into eight parts, as follows:

- Chapters 1 and 2 provide the background that is needed to understand current retirement programs in Canada, including a definition of terms;
- Chapters 3 and 4 set out the details of the RRSP contribution rules;
- Chapters 5 to 9 lay out the detailed rules for determining pension adjustments for different types of pension plans;
- Chapters 10 to 12 provide details regarding past service pension adjustments and pension adjustment reversals;
- Chapters 13 to 15 provide additional framework on retirement savings programs in Canada, including background on minimum standards pension legislation, details on the various tax-sheltered retirement savings vehicles that are available, and an overview of pension plan funding and accounting issues;
- Chapters 16 to 21 set out registration rules for pension plans and deferred profit sharing plans;
- Chapters 22 covers reporting requirements for registered pension plans; and
- Chapter 23 covers some of the special considerations regarding some of the ways in which Canadian organizations provide retirement benefits that are in excess of the benefits that may be provided by a registered plan.

Four appendices are also included:

- Appendix 1 contains information regarding various transitional and other rules that were in effect but no longer apply — they have been placed in the appendix for historical purposes;
- Appendix 2 contains a summary of most of the relevant tax forms and includes samples of the more important forms;
- Appendix 3 contains charts of government benefits, interest rates, and other reference data; and
- Appendix 4 contains tables of cross-references between Chapters 4 to 12 and Chapters 16 to 22 of this book and the *Income Tax Act* (Canada) and its Regulations.

TABLE OF CONTENTS

¶100 OVERVIEW

¶105 Background on Canadian Retirement Savings Tax Reform

It is not surprising that the federal government has devoted so much time and effort to studying the taxation of retirement savings. The tax dollars involved are very significant, as is the impact on the Canadian economy of the pools of Canadian assets held in registered retirement savings plans (RRSP) and private pension plans. For example, the amount that was contributed to RRSPs in 2008 was over $33 billion, representing just under 6.3 million contributors. In 2007, over $40 billion was contributed to trusteed registered pension plans (RPP), with further amounts being contributed to insured pension plans.

The first attempts at making significant changes to the existing decades-old system of rules and laws covering contributions to RPPs and personal RRSPs occurred in the May 1985 federal Budget. Although those initial proposals were heavily criticized and subsequently withdrawn, further proposals occurred over the next four-and-a-half years, resulting in the system that was eventually implemented in 1990.

In developing the current retirement tax system, the Department of Finance had four major concerns with the previous system.

First, the system treated individuals in different circumstances inconsistently and inequitably. There were three main categories of individuals, each treated differently within the previous system:

- employees who belonged to defined benefit pension plans;
- employees who belonged to other types of employer-sponsored registered retirement plans, such as defined contribution pension plans and deferred profit sharing plans (DPSP); and
- employees who fell into neither of the above categories, including those who were self-employed.

The total amount of money that could be tax sheltered on behalf of a person under the previous system could vary dramatically, depending on which of the above three categories the individual belonged to. For example, using 1989 rules, the maximum contribution which could be made to an RRSP by a self-employed individual was $7,500. By comparison, an employee who belonged to a defined contribution pension plan could contribute a combined total of $3,500 to the plan and RRSP, and the employer could contribute up to $3,500 to the pension plan for that individual, resulting in an overall maximum of $7,000. On the other hand, a defined benefit plan providing the maximum benefit of 2% of best average earnings (or $1,715 of annual pension, if less) for a particular year of service could provide benefits of far greater value than $7,000; in addition, the individual could contribute $3,500 to an RRSP if the defined benefit plan did not require employee contributions.

Second, some provisions in the previous system could be used by individuals and their employers to increase the amount of tax-sheltered income over and above what the Department of Finance intended. These loopholes (including techniques known as "double-dipping" and "flip-flopping") do not exist under the current system.

Third, there was a concern that the previous system for RRSPs was not flexible enough. For example, if an individual was unable to make an RRSP contribution in a particular year, the ability to make and deduct that contribution was lost forever. The introduction of the RRSP carry-forward alleviated this problem.

Finally, the registration requirements for pension plans were set out in an Information Circular (first introduced in 1972). Since this circular did not have the force of law, Revenue Canada (as the Canada Revenue Agency was then known) could modify these administrative guidelines to suit a particular set of circumstances. The federal government preferred these rules to be embodied in legislation.

Based on these concerns, the Department of Finance developed specific goals for the reform of the retirement savings tax system, as outlined below:

- To increase the equity in the tax system without introducing excessive compliance costs. The total amount of income that can be tax sheltered on behalf of any individual will not be considered a function of his or her employment status, or of the type of RPP or DPSP offered by the employer.
- To increase flexibility in the timing of individual RRSP contributions through the RRSP carry-forward system.
- To encourage individual savings for retirement. As "baby boomers" reach retirement age, the large number of pensioners will put considerable stress on the government-sponsored retirement system (primarily Old Age Security and the *Canada Pension Plan/Quebec Pension Plan*). It will be important for future generations that today's younger generation be relatively financially independent after retirement.
- To provide increased incentives for profit sharing, through higher deductible contribution limits to DPSPs.
- To increase the amount of information available to the federal government on levels of retirement savings and the relative utilization of different tax-assisted retirement savings vehicles.
- To codify many of the pension plan registration requirements previously set out in Information Circular 72-13R8. This codification ensures the consistency of application of these rules with the new system of pension and contribution levels and limits the flexibility which the Canada Revenue Agency (CRA) previously had in administering the *Income Tax Act* (Canada) and the federal government policy as it relates to RPPs.

The legislation discussed in this book has had a significant impact on how Canadians save for their retirement and how organizations structure their retirement savings programs. The registration rules are comprehensive and complex and the reporting requirements for pension adjustments (PA), pension adjustment reversals (PAR) and past service pension adjustments (PSPA) have increased the workload for pension plan administrators.

We are now at the end of a 20-year period of change that has produced the current system for taxation of retirement savings programs: a system that has increased the level of benefits that may be provided from an RPP through higher limits on benefits, that allows higher levels of contributions to all forms of plans, including personal RRSPs, and that has, to some degree, evened out many of the differences between the various types of retirement savings vehicles in terms of the overall amount of tax-sheltered retirement savings permitted. Further, various loopholes and administrative interpretations of the pre-existing rules have been eliminated, resulting in a more even-handed treatment in the application of the rules.

During this same period, other forces have exerted pressure on the employer pension plan, primarily impacting the practicality and attractiveness of the traditional defined benefit plan.

The federal government and most provinces introduced significant changes to improve the minimum standards applicable to RPPs. Changes in minimum standards are ongoing, with some jurisdictions making further revisions to legislation that was already substantially improved 15 or more years ago. Actuaries have been revising methodologies used to set appropriate long-term assumptions in light of changes in demographics, the economic environment and funding policies. Accountants have established rules for consistent determination of pension expense for financial reporting purposes. A major shift towards a "mark to market" world is anticipated in light of the decision by the Canadian Institute of Chartered Accountants to adopt the standards of the International Accounting Standards Board for publicly traded Canadian companies around the year 2011. Precedent-setting court decisions in a number of high profile cases have also altered the pension landscape.

In addition to professional and legislative changes, the general financial situation in the economy in the recent past has resulted in significant underfunding in defined benefit plans, with the long era of contribution holidays, generous early retirement incentives and regular benefit improvements, at least for now, a thing of the past.

¶110 Historical Timelines

A number of dates in Canadian history have been significant in the development of private pension plans and individual savings plans:

1919	Employee contributions to RPPs first become deductible for income tax purposes under the *Income War Tax Act*.

1947	The federal government introduces a requirement for a pension plan trust to provide that any surplus would be applied equitably for the increased benefit of plan members, with no reversion to the employer. This requirement was later removed; however, in the late 1980s this provision came back to haunt many employers with mature pension plans.
1957	First availability of RRSPs — the plans are designed primarily to allow self-employed taxpayers the opportunity to make tax-deferred contributions towards their retirement income.
1961	The *Income Tax Act* (Canada) is amended to allow employers to make contributions on behalf of employees to DPSPs on a tax-deferred basis.
1965	Introduction of the Ontario *Pension Benefits Act* — the first provincial legislation in Canada to require such items as minimum funding standards, minimum vesting, and locking-in requirements. This legislation is implemented primarily for the protection of pension plan members. Over time, most other provinces followed suit with legislation similar to Ontario's.
1966	Introduction of the *Canada Pension Plan* and the *Quebec Pension Plan*, which significantly affects the design of most private pension plans.
1972	Revenue Canada releases Information Circular 72-13, which explains in some detail the requirements for a pension plan to achieve favourable tax status by becoming registered. This Information Circular has been updated frequently since 1972, the most recent (and last) version being 72-13R8, dated December 16, 1988.
1976	The first increase in the contribution limits to RPPs, RRSPs, and DPSPs. In addition, the maximum pension under defined benefit plans increases from $1,143 to $1,715 per year of pensionable service.

1981	Saskatchewan becomes the first province to depart dramatically from the generally uniform pension legislation which had been passed by most of the provinces and the federal jurisdiction. Saskatchewan's new legislation includes reforms on minimum interest rates to be credited to employee contributions, minimum benefits under contributory defined benefit pension plans, and more generous vesting requirements.
1984	Manitoba introduces even broader reforms to pension legislation, some of which come into effect on January 1, 1984.
1986	The RRSP contribution limit for individuals not in an RPP increases from $5,500 to $7,500. In addition, Saskatchewan introduces the *Saskatchewan Pension Plan*, a money purchase plan available to residents of Saskatchewan to enable them to save towards their retirement. It is primarily designed to assist homemakers and employees of businesses that do not have pension plans. Significant revisions are announced in 1992.
January 1, 1987	The effective date of new minimum standards legislation under the federal *Pension Benefits Standards Act* and the Alberta *Employment Pensions Plans Act.*
January 1, 1988	The effective date of Ontario's and Nova Scotia's *Pension Benefits Acts*, incorporating new minimum pension standards. Many provisions in Ontario's Act are retroactive to January 1, 1987.
January 1, 1990	The effective date of Quebec's amended *Supplemental Pension Plans Act*, adopting new minimum pension standards.
June 27, 1990	Royal Assent granted to the legislation implementing the new tax rules for retirement savings.
June 27, 1991	Royal Assent granted for British Columbia's *Pension Benefits Standards Act* implementing minimum standards reform.

December 31, 1991	The effective date of new minimum standards under New Brunswick's *Pension Benefits Act*.
January 15, 1992	Regulations to the *Income Tax Act* (Canada) published in the *Canada Gazette*.
February 25, 1992	The federal Budget proposals deferring increases to the dollar limits affecting RPPs and RRSPs by one year.
June 19, 1992	Notice of Ways and Means Motion tabled, containing draft amendments to the *Income Tax Act* (Canada) and an accompanying Appendix of draft amendments to the Regulations.
August 28, 1992	Royal Assent granted for major revisions to Saskatchewan's *Pension Benefits Act*, intended to bring this legislation more into line with that of other jurisdictions.
October 30, 1992	Revenue Canada announcement of a delay in the filing deadline for amendments to plans registered before January 15, 1992 that contain a defined benefit provision.
December 18, 1992	Draft legislation released, containing draft amendments to the *Income Tax Act* (Canada) and Income Tax Regulations, relating primarily to unregistered pension plans, including foreign plans.
February, 1994	The federal Budget includes an announcement of a review of programs relating to Canada's aging population, including the tax treatment of the retirement savings system.
February 10, 1994	Release of new pension plan supervision policy by the Québec Régie with a focus on "selective plan supervision".
March 17, 1994	Introduction of federal Regulation SOR/94-246 to make the Home Buyers' Plan a permanent program, allowing first-time home buyers to withdraw funds from RRSPs tax-free to purchase a home.
June 2, 1994	Effective date of Quebec's regulations dealing with simplified pension plans.

January 11, 1995	Passage of amendments to the federal Income Tax Regulations, which include provisions governing PAs, PSPAs, and registration rules governing pension plans, RRSPs, and DPSPs.
March 26, 1995	Royal Assent given to *An Act to Amend the Income Tax Act and the Income Tax Application Rules*, which implements measures from the 1994 federal Budget, including the Home Buyers' Plan.
June 30, 1995	Royal Assent given to Manitoba's *Maintenance Enforcement (Various Acts Amendment) Act*, which allows the garnishment of pension credits of active and former members when family maintenance payments are in arrears.
July 19 & 20, 1995	Release of draft provisions of the *Income Tax Act* (Canada) and Regulations incorporating changes to retirement savings limits and Old Age Security benefits announced in the 1995 federal Budget. Provisions modify contribution limits on RRSPs and pension plans and reduce the lifetime penalty-free excess contribution limit for RRSPs from $8,000 to $2,000 for 1996 and subsequent tax years. The Budget also eliminates the $2,000 per year of service rollover of retiring allowances to RRSPs for years of service after 1995.
March 6, 1996	The federal Budget contains modified limits for money purchase pension plans and profit sharing plans. The RPP limits are reduced from $14,500 in 1997 and $15,500 in 1998 to $13,500 for both years, and the RRSP limits for 1998 and 1999 are reduced to $13,500 from $14,500 and $15,500, respectively. All limits are frozen for a further four years. The Budget eliminates the seven-year limit on carry-forward of unused RRSP contribution room and reduces the age limit for maturity of RPPs, RRSPs, and DPSPSs from age 71 to age 69.

November 25, 1996	Release of newsletter of flexible pension plans by Revenue Canada, which sets out the conditions that plans that provide for optional ancillary contributions and benefits must meet in order to be registered.
January 1, 1997	Effective date of Newfoundland's *Pension Benefits Act, 1996*. With its passage, Prince Edward Island becomes (and remains) the only province without pension legislation in force.
February, 1997	Federal Budget introduces a PAR to restore lost RRSP contribution room for individuals who leave RPPs or DPSPs before retirement.
April 8, 1997	Quebec Bill 102, *An Act to Facilitate Phased Retirement and Early Retirement*, introduces significant changes to how retirement is traditionally viewed and permits payment of part of an individual's pension in a lump sum and partial receipt of retirement pension while in employment. Royal Assent received on June 5, 1997. Regulations effective January 1, 1998.
June 26, 1998	Release of draft regulations by the federal government relating to PARs and other pension-related measures from the 1995 and 1996 federal Budgets.
April 30, 1999	Effective date of Manitoba Regulation 81/99, which amends the Pension Benefits Act Regulation to incorporate more comprehensive solvency rules and to bring Manitoba's pension legislation in line with that of other jurisdictions.
July 15, 1999	Effective date of British Columbia Bill 58, *The Pension Benefits Standards Amendment Act*, which contains provisions relating to flexible pension plans, surplus, and vesting, provides a new definition of spouse that recognizes same-sex partners and provided enhanced responsibilities for plan administrators and fund holders.

November 30, 1999	Release of a package of draft technical amendments to the *Income Tax Act* (Canada), which includes amendments relating to the amount of an employee's pension contributions and RPP transfers.
February 7, 2000	Release of Foreign Service Newsletter Update No. 00-01 by the Registered Plans Division increases the number of years of foreign service that may be recognized in a Canadian registered pension plan to five years from three years.
February 28, 2000	The federal Budget includes an increase in the permissible foreign content limit for investments in RPPs and RRSPs to 25% for 2000 and 30% for 2001 and subsequent years. The foreign property rule is eliminated altogether in the February 2005 federal Budget.
March 1, 2000	Effective date of Alberta Bill 30, the *Employment Pension Plans Amendment Act*, and the related Regulation, which contains substantial amendments to the *Employment Pension Plans Act*.
March 3, 2000	Effective date of Ontario Bill 27, the *Pension Benefits Statute Law Amendment Act*, which contains measures to permit access to locked-in retirement accounts in situations of hardship and shortened life expectancy and to harmonize and streamline pension administration and regulation. Associated Regulations released March 3, 2000 and April 25, 2000.

March 16, 2000	Introduction of Quebec Bill 102, *Act to Amend the Supplemental Pension Plans Act*, which adds 60 sections to the *Supplemental Pension Plans Act* and amends, repeals, or replaces 195 existing sections. It is the biggest revision since the *Supplemental Pension Plans Act* came into force in 1990. Effective date for new legislation is January 1, 2001. Significant provisions include indexing through the additional benefit, phased retirement benefits, and the elimination of partial wind-up provisions.
April 18, 2000	Release of a package of draft technical amendments by the federal government, primarily relating to the RPP provisions of the Income Tax Regulations. The more important amendments include a change to the timing of when PSPAs for certain individuals reduce RRSP contribution room and modified bridging amendments to accommodate provisions in Quebec's *Supplemental Pension Plans Act*. The Regulations were finalized and took effect January 30, 2001.
June 29, 2000	Royal Assent given to federal Bill C-23 and B.C. Bill 21, extending pension benefits and obligations to same-sex partners. All couples who have been cohabiting in a conjugal relationship for at least one year are eligible for benefits.
July 1, 2000	Introduction of proposed changes to locked-in retirement funds in Newfoundland. Claimants will be entitled to temporary pension income or the withdrawal of small balances from locked-in retirement funds.
September 1, 2000	The Registered Plans Division, the government department within the CRA responsible for enforcing the RPP rules set out under the *Income Tax Act* (Canada), is reorganized and renamed the Registered Plans Directorate.

October 18, 2000	Federal mini-budget offers CPP and QPP deductions for self-employed individuals. Self-employed individuals will be entitled to deduct the portion of CPP or QPP deductions that represent the employer's share.
October 20, 2000	Federal Bill C-24 receives Royal Assent. The Bill improves the application of the goods and services tax and harmonized sales tax (GST/HST) to multi-employer pension plans (MEPPs). Under Bill C-24, MEPPs receive a rebate equal to 33% of the GST/HST incurred on expenses related to the administration of the plan.
November 29, 2000	Quebec Bill 102 passes through the Quebec Legislative Assembly. Most new provisions come into effect January 1, 2001. Draft Regulations are not introduced until September 26, 2002. Final Regulations introduced on March 7, 2002 and most provisions effective on March 21, 2002.
March 27, 2001	Amendments to Nova Scotia's *Pension Benefits Act* issued. Bill 9 extends pension plan eligibility, revises issues with respect to life income funds and introduces new requirements for registration of pension plans.
April 23, 2001	Canada Customs and Revenue Agency releases new Form T920E(1), Application to Amend a Registered Pension Plan. The new form requires additional information when requesting acceptance of an amendment, including the business number of the plan sponsor, contact information for the plan administrator, and information about the plan's consultant.
June 14, 2001	Release of regulations amending the Regulations to the federal *Pension Benefits Standards Act, 1985*. Amendments include changes to surplus withdrawal regulations and a new average formula for the collection of fees by the Office of Superintendent of Financial Services.

October 2, 2001	In response to internationally binding measures in United Nations Security Council Resolution 1373 and the events of September 11, 2001, the federal government introduces regulations amending the Regulations to the federal *Pension Benefits Standards Act, 1985* on reporting requirements for Canadian financial institutions and pension plan administrators. The intent of the regulations is to prevent the collection of funds for use in terrorist activities.
April 1, 2002	Effective date of introduction of amendments to the Pensions Benefits Regulations in Saskatchewan. The new regulations offer greater flexibility to retirement planners by recognizing registered retirement income funds as a pension choice and allowing for the transfer of funds from life income funds (LIF) and locked-in retirement income funds (LRIF) into registered retirement income funds (RRIF).
April 16, 2002	Amendments to the Regulations to New Brunswick's *Pensions and Benefits Act* introduced. The amendments deal with vesting requirements, changes with respect to the commutation of benefits, and the distribution of surpluses. The amendments receive Royal Assent on June 2, 2002. Some provisions are retroactive to December 31, 1991 and December 1, 2000, and the remainder come into force December 1, 2003.
February 18, 2003	The federal Budget increases RRSP dollar limits, money purchase RPP limits, and maximum pension limits. Limits for money purchase RPPs increase to $15,500 for 2003, $16,500 for 2004, and $18,000 for 2005. RRSP dollar limits increase to $14,500 for 2003, $15,500 for 2004, $16,500 for 2005, and $18,000 for 2006. Maximum pension limits increase to $1,833.33 for 2004 and $2,000.00 for 2005. Thereafter, all limits are to be indexed to increases in the average wage. A subsequent federal Budget (2005) set fixed limits through to 2009, with indexation of the limits occurring thereafter.

April 30, 2003	The Ontario government Throne Speech makes plans for the abolishment of mandatory retirement.
May 14, 2003	The Alberta government issues regulations allowing for the withdrawal of funds from locked-in RRSPs, locked-in retirement accounts (LIRA), RIFs, and LRIFs in the event of financial hardship.
May 17, 2003	Release of a package of draft technical amendments to the Income Tax Regulations, which include amendments to increase funding ratios for shared-cost defined benefit pension plans, changes to the rules for tax-free transfers between money purchase plans, and to permit member funding of an unfunded liability in a pension fund.
February 27, 2004	The release of draft amendments to the Income Tax Regulations dealing with defined benefit plans, defined contribution plans, and investment rules. Among the changes are amendments dealing with PSPA exclusions for increases in the maximum pension limit and new rules for RRIF-type payouts from money purchase plans.
July 29, 2004	The Supreme Court of Canada releases its decision in the case of *Monsanto Canada Inc. v. Ontario (Superintendent of Financial Services)*. The Supreme Court holds that subsection 70(6) of Ontario's *Pension Benefits Act* requires the distribution of surplus on a partial pension plan wind up.
February 1, 2005	New Standards of Practice for Determining Pension Commuted Values implemented by the Canadian Institute of Actuaries. Quebec adopts the new standard effective April 14, 2005. In all other jurisdictions the new standard is effective from February 1, 2005.

February 23, 2005	The federal Budget eliminates the foreign content restrictions for pension plans and RRSPs and also increases RRSP dollar limits, money purchase RPP limits, and maximum pension limits. Limits for money purchase RPPs increase to $19,000 for 2006, $20,000 for 2007, $21,000 for 2008, and $22,000 for 2009. RRSP dollar limits increase to $18,000 for 2006, $19,000 for 2007, $20,000 for 2008, $21,000 for 2009, and $22,000 for 2010. Maximum pension limits increase to $2,111.11 for 2006, $2,222.22 for 2007, $2,333.33 for 2008, and $2,444.44 for 2009. Thereafter, all limits are to be indexed to increases in the average wage. Amendments to the *Income Tax Act* (Canada) Regulations receive Royal Assent on June 29, 2005.
April 19, 2005	Effective date of most provisions in Manitoba's Bill 10, which amends the *Pension Benefits Act*. Amendments include changes to participation standards, vesting, locking in, survivor pensions and death benefits, normal retirement age, funding standards, and governance and investment standards. Of the date of writing this book, this Bill is expected to be proclaimed on May 31, 2010.
June 1, 2005	Effective date of Saskatchewan Bill 47, which contains amendments to the Saskatchewan *Pension Benefits Act, 1992*. The Bill contains provisions with respect to vesting on the death of a beneficiary, the right to waive an entitlement to a death benefit, and new definitions for "optional ancillary contributions" and "optional ancillary benefits" designed to accommodate flexible pension plan designs.

June 2, 2005	Alberta's *Pension Plans Amendment Act, 2005*, and the Regulations receive Royal Assent in 2005 but do not come into force until August 10, 2006. The amendments include unlocking of up to 50% of locked-in pension funds in certain conditions, new funding, reporting and disclosure requirements, the ability to pay defined contribution benefits from the plan fund, changes to LIFs, and the discontinuance of LRIFs. The unlocking becomes available as of November 1, 2006.
December 12, 2005	Ontario passes legislation abolishing mandatory retirement in that province. Most provisions of Bill 211 come into effect on December 12, 2006. This makes Ontario the first province to eliminate mandatory retirement since Manitoba and Quebec abolished it in the early 1980s (with the exception of Nova Scotia, which abolished it only for public servants in 2003).
March 28, 2006	Quebec Bill 194 proposes amendments to the *Supplemental Pension Plans Act* in order to establish a pension benefits guarantee fund. This is a private member's Bill that has not yet been passed.
October 4, 2006	The Ministry of Finance announced that Regulations removing the requirement to convert federally regulated LIFs to life annuities at age 80 has come into force as of September 21, 2006.
November 3, 2006	In a move intended to provide over $1 billion of tax relief annually, the federal Minister of Finance announces that Canadian residents in receipt of pension income will be able to allocate up to half of that income to their resident spouse or common-law partner each tax year, beginning in 2007.

November 6, 2006	The Government of Saskatchewan introduces Bill 9, the *Saskatchewan Human Rights Code Amendment Act, 2006*. The legislation proposes to amend the definition of "age" in paragraph 2(1)(*a*) of the *Saskatchewan Human Rights Code* by removing the restriction that such protection expires at age 65.
November 7, 2006	The federal Department of Finance announces the release of final solvency relief regulations (Solvency Regulations) for federally-regulated defined benefit pension plans. The Solvency Regulations provide plan sponsors with four temporary funding relief measures to help federally regulated defined benefit plans. The regulations were first proposed in the May 2, 2006 federal Budget and introduced on June 2, 2006. The measures expire on February 1, 2019.
November 9, 2006	Ontario extends the application of section 8 of the Regulations to the *Pension Benefits Act, 1990* to December 31, 2009. Section 8 is the "surplus sharing regulation" requiring that no distribution of surplus be made to an employer on full or partial wind-up unless there is a written agreement. Section 8 was intended as a temporary three-year measure when it first came into force on December 18, 1991 but has continually been extended since that time.
November 9, 2006	Ontario announces creation of an Expert Commission on Pensions. The Commission is given a mandate to "examine the legislation that governs the funding of defined benefit pension plans in Ontario, the rules relating to pension deficits and surpluses, and other issues relating to the security, viability and sustainability of the pension system in Ontario".
November 20, 2006	The Government of Newfoundland and Labrador announced that pensioners in the province will be able to split eligible pension income for provincial income tax purposes.

November 23, 2006	The Legislative Assembly of Nova Scotia gave Royal Assent to Bill 68, *An Act to Amend the Pensions Benefit Act* (PBA). The Bill contains measures to permit access to locked-in retirement assets in situations of financial hardship.
December 12, 2006	Finances Québec announces that couples resident in the province will be able to split their retirement income beginning January 1, 2007 for provincial tax purposes. Legislation providing for this is introduced on May 8, 2008.
December 13, 2006	The Government of Quebec passes Bill 30, *An Act to amend the Supplemental Pension Plans Act, particularly with respect to the funding and administration of pension plans*. The Bill is designed to protect pension benefits for plan members and beneficiaries by improving pension plan funding, enhance the governance of pension plans, and better define the scope of the responsibilities of pension plan administrators.
February 14, 2007	The Quebec government adopts regulations permitting the establishment of member-funded pension plans (MFPP). The purpose of the regulation is to facilitate the establishment of "member-funded" defined benefit pension plans, at the request of workers' associations or workers.
March 22, 2007	Ontario Budget provides for a number of pension-related proposals, including the introduction of a new LIF that features an optional one-time unlocking of 25% of locked-in funds. The Budget also proposes allowing for pension income splitting.

March 29, 2007	Nova Scotia introduces Bill 163, *An Act Respecting the Elimination of Mandatory Retirement*. The Act amends the *Human Rights Act* and *Labour Relations Code* to remove mandatory retirement provisions.
April 19, 2007	The Government of Alberta announces it will introduce pension income splitting for seniors in order to allow higher-income earning seniors to transfer up to 50% of their eligible pension income to their spouse. The measure is effective as of January 1, 2007.
April 25, 2007	The Government of British Columbia introduces legislation eliminating mandatory retirement. Bill 31, the *Human Rights Code Mandatory Retirement Elimination Amendment Act* ends mandatory retirement, extending protection from age discrimination to those 65 and over. The legislation takes effect on January 1, 2008.
June 22, 2007	The federal government gave Royal Assent to Bill C-52, *An Act to implement certain provisions of the budget tabled in Parliament on March 19, 2007*. Bill C-52 implements a number of amendments proposed in the March 19, 2007 federal Budget, including an increase to the age limit for maturing RRSPs, RPPs, and DPSPs from 69 to 71 years of age, and the introduction of pension income splitting for pensioners, both effective beginning in 2007.
June 26, 2007	The Government of New Brunswick gives Royal Assent to Bill 66, *An Act to Amend the Pension Benefits Act*. The amendments will require employers to eliminate any existing solvency liabilities in their sponsored plans within five years of plan wind-up.

July 25, 2007	Ontario makes a number of important changes to the rules governing locked-in accounts. The changes include the introduction of a new LIF which allows for more flexible payments and the opportunity for owners to make a one-time 25% withdrawal in the new LIF; an option to directly transfer money from a locked-in account to an unlocked vehicle, an RRSP, or a RRIF depending on the situation; and, effective January 1, 2008, owners of locked-in accounts who are non-residents of Canada, may apply two years after departure from Canada to withdraw the money in their accounts. In addition, as of July 27, 2007, owners of LIFs are no longer required to purchase an annuity by the end of the year in which they reach 80 years of age.
August 24, 2007	The Ontario government amends the funding rules for MEPPs in the province. The key changes introduced in the regulations are the introduction of temporary solvency funding relief for Specified Ontario multi-employer pension plans (SMEPPs), and further clarification of the funding requirements for MEPPs.
October 2, 2007	Federal Finance Minister Jim Flaherty releases draft legislation designed to implement tax measures proposed in the March 19, 2007 federal Budget. Of particular note, the draft legislation contains provisions regarding phased retirement.

October 19, 2007 — The Finance Ministers of Alberta and British Columbia announce the creation of a Joint Expert Panel on Pension Standards (Joint Panel) to review Alberta's *Employment Pension Plans Act* and British Columbia's *Pension Benefits Standards Act*. The Joint Panel is to consult with stakeholders and present their findings and recommendations to the provincial finance ministries. Key issues to be examined by the Expert Panel include the role of pensions in attracting and retaining the future workforce while ensuring fairness for both employees and employers; balancing risks and rewards; encouraging the establishment and maintenance of employee pension plans; changes that will continue making both provinces attractive jurisdictions for investment; and removing barriers to the creation and maintenance of pension plans in the two jurisdictions.

November 17, 2007 — Saskatchewan's Bill 9 revises several statutes to eliminate mandatory retirement, specifically, removing the upper age of 65 from the definition of "age" in the *Human Rights Code*. Mandatory retirement may still be permitted in certain situations, based on *bona fide* occupational requirements. All provinces have now eliminated mandatory retirement.

November 23, 2007 — Nova Scotia Labour introduces Bill 4 to amend the Nova Scotia *Pension Benefits Act*. Bill 4 will require companies to fully fund plans on wind up, with the exception of MEPPs. Bill 4 includes a requirement for full funding of grow-in benefits on wind up; however, employers will not have to include the cost of grow-ins when determining solvency liabilities. The Bill is eventually proclaimed on January 15, 2008 and is retroactive to May 1, 2007.

November 29, 2007	The Alberta Employment Pension Plans Regulation 35/2000 is amended to permit letter of credit financing for pension plan solvency deficiencies.
December 14, 2007	The Joint Alberta–British Columbia Expert Panel on Pension Standards(Joint Panel) issues the discussion paper *A Better Pension System for the Future: Finding a Balance*.
January 15, 2008	Nova Scotia proclaims into law Bill 4, amending the *Pension Benefits Act* to require pension plans to be fully funded on wind up. The amendment is retroactive to May 1, 2007.
February 14, 2008	Nova Scotia becomes the fourth jurisdiction (after Ontario, Alberta, and British Columbia) to announce the creation of a Pension Review Panel to review the province's pension legislation.
February 26, 2008	The federal government tables the 2008 federal Budget. Among the proposals is the creation of a new tax-free savings account (TFSA) beginning in 2009. Canadian residents age 18 or older will be able to contribute up to $5,000 a year in after tax funds to the account. Any unused contribution room is carried forward. This maximum contribution will be indexed to inflation (rounded to the nearest $500).
April 17, 2008	British Columbia's Bill 33, the *Miscellaneous Statutes Amendment Act, 2008*, receives first reading. Bill 3 includes amendments to the province's *Pension Benefits Standards Act* (PBSA) allowing plan sponsors to offer phased retirement, as well as a number of other changes to the Act.
May 8, 2008	The federal Department of Finance announces changes to the rules governing LIFs that will allow for a one-time 50% unlocking for LIFs and unlocking for financial hardship.

May 8, 2008	Quebec government introduces Bill 79, *An Act to amend the Taxation Act, the Act respecting the Quebec sales tax and other fiscal legislative provisions*. Bill 79 amends the *Taxation Act* to make amendments allowing Canadian residents receiving "eligible pension" income to allocate up to half of that income to their resident spouse or common-law partner each tax year. These provisions were first announced on December 12, 2006.
June 4, 2008	The Government of Newfoundland and Labrador gave Royal Assent to Bill 21, *An Act to Amend the Pension Benefits Act, 1997*. The Act requires pension plan sponsors to fully fund solvency deficiencies on plan wind up.
June 12, 2008	Newfoundland and Labrador implements Regulation 30/08 providing temporary solvency funding relief for defined benefit pension plans that have filed actuarial valuation reports completed between January 1, 2007 and January 1, 2009.
June 20, 2008	Quebec's Bill 68, *An Act to amend the Supplemental Pension Plans Act, the Act respecting the Québec Pension Plan and other legislative provisions* receives Royal Assent. Bill 68 proposes to amend the phased retirement provisions of the *Supplemental Pension Plans Act* to coordinate with new phased retirement provisions under the *Income Tax Act*.
July 17, 2008	The Government of British Columbia introduces amendments to the Pension Benefits Standards Regulations which will permit the use of letters of credit to fund solvency deficiencies in pension plans registered in the province.

November 20, 2008	The Ontario Expert Commission on Pensions released its final report, *A Fine Balance: Safe Pensions, Affordable Plans, Fair Rules*. The report makes 142 wide-ranging recommendations for reforming Ontario's system of pension regulation. Proposals address funding, the changing economy, plan failures, regulation and governance, and the future of the pension system.
December 2, 2008	The Joint Panel releases its final report, *Getting Our Acts Together*. The report makes 130 distinct recommendations on subjects such as regulation and harmonization, funding, governance and investment, and unlocking.
December 9, 2008	British Columbia proclaims portions of Bill 33, the *Miscellaneous Statutes Amendment Act*. The legislation received Royal Assent May 29, 2008 and includes amendments to section 38 of the PBSA to accommodate the new phased retirement provisions under the *Income Tax Act*.
January 15, 2009	The Government of Quebec passes Bill 1, *An Act to amend the Supplemental Pension Plans Act and other legislative provisions in order to reduce the effects of the financial crisis on plans covered by the Act*. The Bill introduces a number of measures designed to offer solvency relief for Quebec pension plans.
January 27, 2009	The Nova Scotia Pension Review Panel releases their final report, *Promises to Keep*. The Report makes recommendations on a number of topics, including new plan design, partial wind ups, solvency funding, amortization periods, and the introduction of a province-wide pension plan.

January 29, 2009	The Financial Institutions Commission of British Columbia (FICOM) releases Bulletin PEN-09-001, *Guidelines for Requests for Solvency Extensions for Defined Benefit Pension Plans*. While the provincial PBSA generally requires that solvency deficiencies be amortized over five years, section 6 of the PBSA allows the Superintendent of Pensions to extend this amortization period.
February 18, 2009	Alberta announces the release of a regulation designed to offer temporary solvency relief to defined benefit plans in the province.
March 13, 2009	The governments of British Columbia, Alberta, and Saskatchewan hold their inaugural joint cabinet meeting. The provinces agreed jointly to work on developing a new regional voluntary pension plan option for workers who do not have an employer-based plan. Such a plan will build on the *Saskatchewan Pension Plan*, which has been in place since 1986. The report of the Joint Panel also recommended that the provinces establish the ABC Plan, a pension plan that would be open to all employers and workers in both provinces.
March 23, 2009	The Government of British Columbia introduces Bill 11, the *Pension Benefits Standards Amendment Act, 2009*. Bill 11 contains technical changes to the *Pension Benefits Standards Act* that will allow for the creation of a new private sector defined contribution pension plan that would be available to all employers, employees, and self-employed persons in the province.
April 30, 2009	Nova Scotia's Minister of Labour and Workforce Development introduces Bill 249, the *Pension Benefits Amendment Act*. Bill 249 amends the *Pension Benefits Act* to allow plans to offer phased retirement benefits.

May 6, 2009	The Quebec government publishes draft regulations with options for solvency relief in Quebec.
May 26, 2009	Saskatchewan announces amendments to the Pension Benefits Regulations that will provide temporary solvency relief for defined benefit pension plans registered in the province.
June 12, 2009	The federal government releases final text of the Solvency Funding Relief Regulations, 2009, which provide temporary solvency funding relief to federally registered defined benefit (DB) pension plans. As of the date of writing this book, permanent or temporary relief measures have been introduced in all provinces except Nova Scotia, where such measures are still under consideration.
June 23, 2009	The Ontario government publishes Regulation 239/09 amending the Pensions Benefits Regulation to offer three temporary solvency relief options for defined benefit plans. The Regulation also makes a number of changes to Ontario's rules regarding locked-in accounts, introducing a number of one-time unlocking opportunities for LIFs and LRIFs.
July 1, 2009	Mandatory retirement ends in Nova Scotia as a valid reason for age discrimination with the introduction of Bill 163, *An Act Respecting the End of Mandatory Retirement*.
August 7, 2009	Supreme Court of Canada releases its decision in *Nolan v. Kerry (Canada) Inc.* The decision allows plan expenses to be paid for from the pension fund, contribution holidays to be taken for both the defined benefit and defined contribution components, and allows the plan sponsor to fund the defined contribution component of the plan from the defined benefit surplus.

September 1, 2009	Canadian Association of Pension Supervisory Authorities (CAPSA) issues a revised Agreement Respecting Multijurisdictional Pension Plans. The Agreement discusses the rationale for the introduction of a new multi-jurisdictional plan agreement and sets out a clear framework for the administration and regulation of multi-jurisdictional pension plans.
September 2, 2009	The British Columbia government introduces amendments to subsection 40(2) of the *Pension Benefits Standards Act* clarifying the process and conditions under which a pension plan member may elect to unlock their pension funds owing to shortened life expectancy.
October 21, 2009	The Quebec government releases a revised version of the Regulation to amend the Regulation respecting supplemental pension plans. The Regulation includes measures dealing with actuarial valuations, the use of letters of credit, revisions to the formula for the Provision for Adverse Deviation, and the partition of pension benefits following marriage breakdown.
October 22, 2009	Nova Scotia introduces Bill 48, *An Act to Amend Chapter 340 of the Revised Statutes, 1989, the Pension Benefits Act*. Bill 48 amends the province's *Pension Benefits Act* to permit pension plans to offer phased retirement to plan members by permitting payments of up to 60% of an accrued pension to be paid to eligible members without plan members retiring or reducing work hours.
October 27, 2009	The federal government releases plans for the reform of the legislative and regulatory framework governing federal private pension plans. Proposed measures include requirements for full funding on plan wind up, limits on contribution holidays, the adoption of immediate vesting, new solvency funding rules, limited use of letters of credit, and changes to investment rules.

November 4, 2009	Nova Scotia announces funding relief for private pension plans to allow plans to amortize certain solvency deficiencies over 10 years as opposed to the regular five-year period.
November 11, 2009	The Quebec government releases regulations to provide temporary solvency relief measures for defined benefit plans.
December 9, 2009	Ontario introduces Bill 236, *The Pensions Benefits Amendment Act, 2009*. Bill 236 clarifies the benefits of plan members affected by lay-offs and eliminates partial wind ups, facilitates plan restructuring while protecting benefit security, increases transparency and access to plan information, enhances regulatory oversight, and improves plan administration. Most provisions will come into effect January 1, 2012.
January 1, 2010	2010 marks the first year that maximum limits under the *Income Tax Act* (Canada) are increased in accordance with increases in the average wage. Until now, limits on maximum pensions, money purchase RPP limits, and RRSP dollar limits were set by Regulation.

¶115 Advantages of Tax-Sheltered Retirement Plans

The primary advantage of the tax sheltering that is provided for certain retirement plans is the fact that investment income is sheltered from taxation until the benefits are ultimately paid out to individuals. The compounding effect of the tax-sheltered investment earnings over a period of many years is quite significant. Numerous studies have shown that the benefits received on an after-tax basis from an arrangement where the investment income is tax sheltered are higher than those benefits payable from an arrangement whose investment income is taxed as it is earned.

There are two other important advantages:

- The individual's contributions, where permitted, are tax deductible.
- Employer contributions to an RPP or DPSP are generally tax deductible by the employer within limits and do not confer an immediate taxable benefit on the individual.

The following sections provide a high-level overview of the types of retirement programs that are typically offered in Canada as well as some commentary regarding how these plans have changed with the introduction of the tax rules detailed in this book.

¶120 The Defined Benefit Plan

Before the current decade, defined benefit plans had enjoyed a long period of good investment returns and a labour surplus, which at one time or another led to contribution holidays, regular benefit improvements and early retirement programs.

However, over the past decade or more, there has been a steady decline in defined benefit pension coverage, and the decline has not been matched by a commensurate increase in coverage by money purchase arrangements, especially when viewed in terms of the level of benefit provided.

Although the system of PAs in Canada has somewhat disadvantaged the defined benefit plan when compared to a money purchase arrangement (as discussed at ¶715), especially for younger pension plan members, the substantive changes to the retirement tax system have been only one factor contributing to the decline in defined benefit coverage, which has been a global phenomenon. The relative disadvantages of defined benefit plans, however, have been lessened by the current low-interest environment and an aging workforce.

Towards the end of the period when the tax rules were being implemented, defined benefit plans began to feel pressures from other fronts as employers became eager to make changes to the plan structure to make it less costly, less volatile, more tax effective or, more radically, to abandon the defined benefit plan altogether in favour of a defined contribution arrangement. This has dramatically accelerated as a result of a significant percentage of pension plans being in deficit positions in recent years. However, with the significant amount of contributions being directed towards those deficits, this situation had begun to reverse by 2006 only to be worsened again by the economic crisis of 2008 and 2009. The current funded status of many defined benefit plans has led most minimum standards jurisdictions to introduce temporary funding relief measures to help cash-stricken employers.

Despite these pressures, defined benefit plans still hold significant appeal for many employees and employers. It is not clear yet whether money purchase arrangements are going to be able to provide an adequate level of retirement benefit for those who prefer such arrangements, unless employers contribute a significant amount or the employees either make significant personal contributions to their RRSPs or other non-registered investments, or delay retirement. However, employers who sponsor defined benefit plans, no matter how generous the plan may be, will still face employees who would prefer to maximize their RRSP contributions rather than participate in the defined benefit plan and receive a PA that, in many cases, overstates the value of the benefit being earned under the plan. Employees, particularly younger ones, may not be swayed by the usual counter-arguments, which include an explanation that the PAR will restore some of the RRSP contribution room foregone by participation in the pension plan should the member terminate prior to retirement, and perhaps more importantly, that a member who does not wish to participate in the defined benefit pension plan will not receive any employer contribution towards retirement if the employer has no retirement savings vehicle other than the defined benefit plan.

Employers have made significant efforts over the years since the tax rules were introduced in order to introduce new features and provisions to make the defined benefits more tax-effective and attractive to all employees.

Making the Benefit Formula More Tax-Effective

The most obvious change to lower the PA so as to maximize RRSP contribution room is to reduce the lifetime benefit under the defined benefit plan and increase the value of the ancillary benefits correspondingly (such as post-retirement death benefits or survivor benefits or to add indexation). While this may lower the PA, thus providing more RRSP contribution room, it will keep the commuted value of the benefit roughly the same. This is appealing for employees who expect to terminate employment prior to retirement. It will not likely appeal to employees who are older or who anticipate staying through to retirement as they generally tend to value the lifetime pension more than the ancillary benefits. However, retirees would generally appreciate indexing even when inflation seems to be very low.

There is a disadvantage of enhancing ancillaries at the expense of the initial pension, on account of the solvency funding rules. Generous early retirement benefits and indexing can lead to higher solvency liabilities relative to growing concern liabilities, thus potentially creating volatile contributions, as solvency deficits usually have to be paid off over relatively short periods.

Choice of Defined Benefit and Money Purchase

Other measures include allowing existing defined benefit plan members to opt out and, instead, to participate in a defined contribution pension plan (or a group RRSP or DPSP).

Typically, a money purchase arrangement (whether a group RRSP, a defined contribution pension plan, or a DPSP) will not appeal to the older plan members, since it is likely that they would receive better benefits from the defined benefit plan. This drawback can be alleviated to some degree by arranging for any employer contributions that are made to the money purchase arrangement to increase with length of service. (Note, however, that making contributions that increase solely with the employee's age may be subject to challenge as age discrimination under human rights legislation, but a contribution formula based on the sum of age plus service is generally considered acceptable.)

Younger employees who do not know how long they will stay with their employer or who prefer to maximize their RRSP contributions, or who want more control over their retirement investments, may appreciate the opportunity to opt out of (or not be required to join) their employer's pension plan and to have an employer contribution made to a money purchase vehicle instead.

It is important to have an effective communication program for employees who are offered the option to opt out of the defined benefit plan, so that employees have enough knowledge of the risks and benefits to make informed choices.

Hybrid Plans

Another alternative is a hybrid plan which is a registered pension plan that provides benefits under more than one type of benefit provision. Typically, the hybrid plan combines a defined benefit provision with a money purchase component (through an RRSP, a defined contribution pension plan, or a DPSP). Chapter 20 discusses different types of hybrid plans and the special registration rules under the *Income Tax Act* (Canada) that have been put in place to accommodate these types of plans.

The possible variations of these plan types are as different as the diverse types of employees that are being covered under the plans: some organizations may match or partially match employee contributions to the money purchase component and others do not; some may offer different levels of defined benefit; and some may offer the ability to switch back and forth between a defined benefit and a defined contribution component.

Hybrid plans would appear to offer the best of both worlds to the employee in terms of providing a core defined benefit accrual for all employees and permitting additional money purchase contributions for those who wish to enhance their retirement pensions. To the employer, however, while meeting the needs of various employee groups, the administration requirements are increased.

Flexible Pension Plans

Another plan design change which increases the flexibility and tax-effectiveness of a defined benefit plan is the "flexible pension plan" that has been developed specifically with the current tax rules in mind. Under this approach, the employer provides a defined benefit plan and the employee may elect to make contributions, on a tax-deductible basis, in order to purchase enhanced ancillary benefits that do not affect the PA, such as post-retirement indexation, improved early retirement benefits, spousal benefits after retirement, or an enhanced definition of final average earnings.

This type of plan can be "cost neutral" to the sponsoring organization, as the cost of the enhancements, at the time of conversion, is exactly equal to the value of the employee contributions with interest. The cost of administration and employee communication, however, will increase.

One important condition imposed on flexible pension plans is the so-called "use it or lose it" condition. If the cost of the allowable supplementary benefits at retirement is less than the flexible contribution balance, the unused contributions are to be forfeited — they cannot be refunded to the member or applied to purchase additional lifetime benefits. (Note, however, that certain minimum standards jurisdictions require that the employer reimburse the employee for the forfeited amount, resulting in a payment outside the pension plan to ensure that the employee receives full value for the accumulated contributions.) This can happen, for example, if an employee, early in his or her career, anticipates retiring early and makes significant flexible contributions anticipating the purchase of enhanced early retirement benefits plus bridging benefits. If this employee stays until normal retirement, the balance in the flexible account may be too high and there may not be enough other ancillary benefits left to entirely use up the accumulated account balance. Careful planning is therefore required to minimize forfeiture of contributions. The employer must be able to assist members on an ongoing basis in determining whether any loss of contributions is possible or likely. The employer could consider establishing an unregistered supplemental employee retirement pension plan (SERP) to compensate for any "loss" of contributions under the "use it or lose it" rules.

It is interesting to note, however, that when an employee group is offered a flexible pension plan arrangement, the participation rate in the voluntary contributions is typically relatively low, say 15% or less. While employees may want the flexibility to make more tax-sheltered contributions towards retirement, many of them do not actually take maximum advantage of the opportunity to do so.

If there is likely to be a relatively low take-up among the plan sponsor's full employee group, the plan sponsor could consider minimizing the administrative and communication challenges attached to a flexible pension plan by only offering it to groups of employees (such as executives or other high earners) who are most likely to have the disposable income to make the additional contributions.

¶125 Phased Retirement

Canadian employers face increasing challenges as they attempt to match the supply and demand for skilled labour. Canada, along with other countries, will be forced to deal with a shrinking workforce and its related demographic bulge as baby boomers retire. An improvement of living standards at a desired steady rate of 1.85% per year will likely lead to a labour shortage of one million workers in 2016, and close to three million in 2026. Employers in other countries can be expected to adopt strategies that will heighten the international level of competition for talent — potentially exacerbating Canada's brain drain and diminishing the potential influx of skilled immigrants.

Further, employers are feeling the effects of years of buyouts and early retirement packages that have left shortages of experienced, skilled workers. In addition, many defined benefit plans contain generous early retirement provisions providing for unreduced early retirement at age 60 or even earlier, with the end result that employees plan for retirement at those key dates rather than considering staying to normal retirement.

It is becoming an increasingly high priority to employers to consider ways to permit and in fact, encourage, older workers to continue to make active contributions to the workforce. The Organisation for Economic Co-operation and Development released a policy paper in June 2006 noting that governments in many countries are now considering ways to slow the expected exodus of retiring baby boomers. Further, they state that "public early retirement schemes should be gradually phased out, and public and private pensions as well as other welfare systems reformed so as to remove incentives for early labour market exit".

What this will mean to the next generation of retirees is the gradual reduction in early retirement incentives and bridging benefits from their defined benefit plans and the introduction of late-retirement incentives.

The abolishment of mandatory retirement has occurred in several provinces and/or various employment sectors, most notably with Ontario abolishing mandatory retirement in late 2005, in order to give workers the right to continue to work beyond age 65, should they wish to do so.

However, the elimination of mandatory retirement, on its own, is not likely to do much to encourage employees to continue to work.

If older workers are to be encouraged to remain at work, more flexibility will be needed to find ways to allow the worker to continue to work, perhaps on a reduced work schedule, as long as there are assurances that their pension benefits are not negatively impacted. When older, experienced employees who are approaching early or normal retirement age work a reduced schedule for a period before finally retiring, this is usually referred to as phased retirement.

Early forms of phased retirement were done on an informal and individual basis, whereby an employer would allow an employee to retire, begin receiving his or her defined benefit pension, and then return to work on a part-time contract basis. However, the resulting loss of seniority, job security, active member benefits (e.g., medical and dental) and discontinued pension accrual makes this a less than ideal employment situation.

However, phased retirement in the form of a program whereby the employee remains an active employee and defers retirement can cause problems if the employee is a member of a defined benefit plan with generous early retirement provisions.

Often the availability of a subsidized unreduced early retirement pension is an incentive to take full retirement at an early date. By deferring the commencement of this pension as a result of continuing to work, the value of the employer subsidy diminishes over time, so the employer must develop a strategy of counteracting this effect in order to persuade the employee to continue to work.

There were two key impediments under the Regulations to the *Income Tax Act* (Canada). First, as noted at ¶1775, the Regulations require that either accruals under the defined benefit provision cease if the member is in receipt of a pension from the plan, or that no pension may be paid if the individual is accruing a defined benefit pension. Cessation of accruals is often unpalatable to the employee as he or she will not then receive a full pension in respect of all service upon full retirement. Cessation of accruals may also be prohibited under minimum standards pension benefits legislation. The employee may feel that the only way to both receive a subsidized pension and accrue a pension is to move to another employer, in which case the above restriction under the Regulations would not apply.

Second, as noted at ¶1675, the Regulations require that defined benefit lifetime pensions must be paid in equal periodic amounts, which hinders one of the objectives of a phased retirement model where increasing pension amounts are paid as an individual gradually reduces his or her working hours.

Although these two impediments in the Regulations were resolved in October 2007 when draft Regulation changes were introduced to accommodate more beneficial phased retirement provisions, certain jurisdictions had already introduced innovative ways to more or less achieve a phased retirement.

Quebec was the first jurisdiction to develop an approach to deal with the barriers by amending the SPPA to allow a phased retiree to continue to accrue a pension based on actual earnings while receiving a series of lump-sum payments from the pension plan rather than a monthly pension. There were certain restrictions in terms of the amount that may be received early from a pension plan in this manner. Alberta made similar changes to its pension legislation. Manitoba had also included similar provisions in its updated 2005 legislation. New Brunswick introduced a program that applied narrowly to the nursing sector in that province.

Yet Quebec's innovative lump-sum approach had a very low take-up rate. There are several reasons for this, but the major reason is that the individual lost any early retirement subsidies that would have otherwise been available had full early retirement been chosen instead of electing to work part-time. The individual would select lump sums that are received annually during the phased retirement period and a pension of equivalent actuarial value is later offset against the normal retirement pension accrued to the date of final retirement. In a plan with a generous early retirement provision, this represented a huge potential loss.

The 2007 federal Budget and Economic Statement announced changes to federal legislation to overcome the existing impediments to phased retirement, thus providing employers and employees with better options for developing and implementing phased retirement programs.

The changes to the Regulations under the *Income Tax Act* (Canada) allow defined benefit registered pension plans to permit qualifying employees to receive temporary bridging benefits on a stand-alone basis or to receive up to 60% of their accrued pension while continuing to accrue additional benefits under the plan. The 60% limit will be based on the amount of lifetime pension benefit (and bridging benefits) that the employee would receive if he or she were instead taking full retirement.

To complete the picture, however, changes were also required to each jurisdiction's minimum standards pension legislation to accommodate these new Regulation changes. The first pension jurisdiction to introduce the necessary changes was the federal *Pension Benefits Standards Act*. The changes in that jurisdiction included:

- Phased retirement benefits could be offered to plan members who have reached normal retirement age or who qualify for early retirement under the terms of the pension plan;
- The plan member must enter into a written agreement with an employer who contributes to the plan from which the phased retirement benefits will be paid;
- The member continues to accrue a pension benefit during the phased retirement period. Pension benefits accrued during the phased retirement period are treated as vested without regard to conditions as to age, period of membership in the pension plan, or period of employment. The amount of the phased retirement benefit received is not taken into account when determining the immediate pension benefit to which the plan member is entitled or eligible to receive upon full retirement. This will ensure that the amount and value of the pension payable on complete retirement is not reduced or diminished because of the earlier phased retirement;
- Employees will still be considered plan members during a phased retirement period, will not be considered "retired" under the *Pension Benefits Standards Act*, and will be deemed not to be receiving an immediate pension benefit;
- The 50% minimum employer contribution rule (as discussed in greater detail at ¶ 1314) does not apply at the time of commencing a phased retirement period. Since the member on phased retirement is not considered to have retired, the 50% rule in a contributory plan would not apply until the member ceased employment with the employer;
- The phased retirement benefit can be paid to the member only and there is no requirement to pay the benefit in a joint and survivor form if the member has a spouse when the phased retirement benefits begins;
- A member who passes away during the phased retirement period will be deemed to have retired for the purposes of the survivor benefit and to have chosen a joint and 60% survivor form of pension. As a result, the surviving spouse of that person will be entitled to the 60% survivor benefit commencing as of the death of the member; and
- Retirees may also take advantage of the phased retirement provisions provided that in the case of a retiree receiving a pension in the form of a joint and survivor pension, the spouse or common-law partner in question consents in writing to the cessation of the payment of the benefit. This ensures that the spouse or

common-law partner does not lose any rights to such joint and survivor pension without input. Once the phased retirement agreement is finished, there is no return to the formerly agreed upon joint and survivor pension benefit. The initial election is rendered void and the retiree is required to make a new decision regarding any further pension benefits payable.

The above conditions are only relevant to federally regulated entities such as banks, telecommunication companies and airlines. Provincially regulated pension plans can only take advantage of the phased retirement rules once the relevant pension standards legislation is amended to accommodate the new phased retirement provisions now permitted under the *Income Tax Act* (Canada).

Quebec has since made changes to its prior phased retirement provisions to coordinate with the Regulation changes. Alberta has not made any formal amendments to its legislation as it believes that its legislation currently permits the Regulation-phased retirement changes. Other jurisdictions are in the process of making similar changes, or, where legislative changes are not formally needed, issuing policy statements about the application of the phased retirement provisions within the jurisdiction. This includes British Columbia, Nova Scotia, and Saskatchewan. Eventually it is expected that other jurisdictions will follow suit.

Phased retirement can serve as a useful tool for employers to help keep older workers who possess expertise, knowledge, and skills that are in high demand. The introduction of provisions amending the federal *Pension Benefits Standards Act* in order to define phased retirement and provide the framework for its implementation is an important step in the introduction of phased retirement in all Canadian jurisdictions.

Without phased retirement programs, employees who continue to work despite being eligible to receive reasonably generous early retirement pensions often end up working for substantially less than the wages received, when the value of missed pension payments is taken into account. By permitting the continued accrual of a defined benefit pension while allowing for receipt of a portion of the unreduced pension, the new measures will reduce the likelihood of this loss of income. Under the *Income Tax Act* (Canada) changes, the employee in this situation can collect on the value of the early retirement pension by receiving as much as 60% of that pension and still accrue more at the same time.

Employees will have to ensure that phased retirement is the correct option for them. Since only 60% of the pension can be received, it remains to be seen whether the 60% pension with continued accrual will be sufficient to entice employees to remain at work instead of collecting 100% of the pension and working elsewhere or for the same employer as a contract employee. And while the option of returning to work and recommencing to accrue a pension may be an attractive one to some retirees (if, for example, the entire pension can be recalculated with more favourable reductions upon subsequent retirement), they will need to seriously consider the pros and cons of stopping the pension payments in order to begin a phased retirement period.

Finally, employers will need to consider all the ramifications of offering a phased retirement program, to ensure that it succeeds in its objective of encouraging key employees to stay a bit longer rather than tempting employees to reduce working hours earlier than intended. It appears that federally regulated employers will be permitted to offer phased retirement on a selective basis, employee by employee, although it is not certain whether the package terms can differ from person to person depending on their circumstances. For other jurisdictions in Canada, until the required amendments are made to pension standards legislation, it will remain unclear whether an employer will be able to offer phased retirement on a selective basis or whether it will have to be made available to broad-based membership.

This is an issue that needs to be resolved. If it is certain that different members can be treated in different ways (such as the degree of generosity of the pension offering, or the ability to refuse to offer phased retirement to some members based on individual circumstances, without risk of being deemed to be discriminating or using plan assets to benefit some members and not others), then the pension plan route may prove advantageous. Otherwise, employers will likely continue to create phased retirement packages for individuals based on current pension plan provisions, and will instead use cash or other financial and non-financial rewards to entice the employee to continue working.

The alternative to a pension solution being used for a phased retirement package is to use other means of reward. One can design a cash compensation package that is sufficiently large (when compared to the early retirement pension otherwise available) that there is an incentive to continue working.

Whatever means of compensation are used, whether cash or non-cash, it is important not to make the phased retirement package appear so generous that those employees continuing to work full-time (despite being eligible for an early retirement pension) do not generally find the phased retirement package to be especially attractive. Otherwise, a solution that is designed to keep older workers in the workforce may backfire with too high a take-up rate for the phased retirement.

Canada Pension Plan and Quebec Pension Plan

In addition to the employer pension issue, there is also the question of how the benefits payable under the *Canada Pension Plan/Quebec Pension Plan* are impacted by phased retirement. Under the *Canada Pension Plan* (CPP), there is an obstacle, in that, in order to receive CPP benefits early from age 60, the employee must either be not working or, if continuing to work, must be earning less than the maximum CPP benefit (i.e., less than $934.17 per month for 2010). Once the CPP benefits commence, the employee can continue to work again, but cannot make any additional contributions to CPP so no further CPP benefits can accrue. Quebec has addressed this by changing the *Quebec Pension Plan* (QPP) so that employees can continue to accrue QPP benefits based on their full salary rather than their reduced salary during a phased retirement period. In addition, employees aged 60 to 65, who reduce their work hours so that their salary is reduced by at least 20%, can receive an early QPP pension while continuing to work part-time.

¶130 The Money Purchase Plan

The increasing complexity of the tax regime, accounting disclosures, and pension standards legislation has reduced the attractiveness of defined benefit plans. In addition, there have been a number of other forces, as discussed at ¶ 120, which have caused many employers to review the continued appropriateness of using a defined benefit approach. Many employers have considered turning to a money purchase arrangement, some have made the switch, abandoning the defined benefit plan altogether, while other employers have used a money purchase arrangement for new hires only or for future service for all employees.

A money purchase plan is considered a lower risk to the employer since it removes the volatility of pension expense, contribution levels, and funding deficits. However, it introduces the risk of inadequate levels of pension for cohorts of retirees who retire at a time when markets are down or annuity costs are up. This, in turn, can cause employees to delay their retirement. Some of these employees will not be productively engaged and others may have to be discharged by their employers at substantial cost.

Money purchase is definitely a higher risk to the older employee, as the employee is now responsible for making important, long-term investment decisions about his or her retirement income in order to ensure that a sufficient level of income is accumulated to provide for retirement. Unless the employee purchases an annuity at retirement, investment risks and responsibilities will continue after retirement as well.

It is unlikely that a pure defined contribution arrangement will be able to provide an adequate level of retirement income, unless it has a very high level of employer contribution or is augmented by an employee's own personal RRSP contributions (using RRSP contribution room freed up by the elimination of the defined benefit PAs).

Where an employer is choosing between a defined benefit plan and a money purchase arrangement, there are some advantages and disadvantages to consider.

The main advantages of money purchase arrangements over defined benefit plans, from an employer's perspectives, are as follows:

1. Cost Control

By defining its contribution to a money purchase arrangement, the employer establishes control over its funding costs. The employer does not run the risk of unfunded liabilities or accelerated solvency payments that are inherent in the funding of defined benefit plans. Nor does the employer risk the impact of wide fluctuations that can occur from one year to the next in the pension expense reported on the company's financial statements. Conversely, however, the employer will not benefit from experience or investment gains that might reduce future contribution requirements.

2. Employee Communication and Education

The employer's role in employee communications is usually simpler with a money purchase arrangement than with a defined benefit plan. Most employees are used to the concept of money purchase arrangements through their familiarity with bank savings accounts and RRSPs. However, because employees are making important, long-term decisions that will impact on their future retirement income, employers must make sure that they have taken all reasonable steps to ensure that employees have been educated about the available investment options to enable them to make appropriate decisions to maximize and protect their retirement funds. In addition, employees must constantly monitor their investment choices, both before and during retirement and make appropriate adjustments on a regular basis. Typically, however, many employees do not spend a lot of time managing this process and change investments only infrequently or make investment decisions that are too conservative and will not produce adequate retirement income. Therefore, the employer must ensure that the employees have the information and assistance needed to make proper investment decisions. If the employer does not provide adequately in this area, the employer could potentially be faced with litigation and its associated costs. In May 2004, the Joint Forum of Financial Regulators released its Guidelines for Capital Accumulation Plans (CAP Guidelines) which sets out industry best practices and lays out a framework for good governance of capital accumulation plans such as money purchase retirement programs in order to assist plan sponsors in managing the risk associated with money purchase plans. The CAP Guidelines are discussed in greater detail at ¶ 140.

3. Administration

The administration of a money purchase arrangement is generally simpler than that required to operate a defined benefit plan. Many of the same financial institutions that offer individual RRSP products and administration also offer state-of-the-art, employee online administration services for money purchase arrangements. In addition, the consulting and legal fees involved in operating a money purchase arrangement can often be lower than for a defined benefit plan since the management and operation of these types of plans is typically much less complex. However, the investment management expenses in such plans must be watched carefully, as these can be high depending on the type of investments offered and selected by the employees. It is easy for the plan sponsor to be unconcerned about these expenses since they are borne by the plan member, but they should not be overlooked and, in fact the CAP Guidelines (as discussed at ¶ 140) require the plan sponsor to take an active role in offering and monitoring appropriate investment options.

The main disadvantages of money purchase plans over defined benefit plans, from a plan member's perspective, are as follows:

1. Investment Risk

The employer bears the full investment risk under a defined benefit plan. Under a money purchase arrangement, the employee, of course, bears the investment risk. The individual's pension is totally dependent on investment returns earned in the working years, and, if the funds are to be used to purchase an annuity, on annuity rates prevailing at retirement or date of purchase. If an annuity is not purchased at retirement, as is increasingly the case with the LIF options that are now available as an alternative to an annuity purchase, then the employee must continue to invest, and bear the investment risk, long after retirement and perhaps long after the retired employee feels comfortable making these decisions. Corporations are generally in a better position to bear this risk than employees, particularly older employees.

2. Predictability of Benefit Payout

The ultimate benefit payable from a defined benefit plan is predictable. Predictability is an advantage to both employees and employers. Employees can build their retirement planning around a known benefit. Employees are reasonably good at estimating future salary increases and future earnings potential, and with a defined benefit plan can reasonably predict the amount of retirement income. Defined benefit plan annual statements will often contain projected retirement income (based on the assumption of no salary increase) or at the very least, the annual statement gives enough information to allow the employee to easily calculate this and see the impact that events such as early retirement will have on retirement income. Predicting and projecting retirement income with money purchase plans is very sensitive to the rates of return that are expected to be earned as well as to the annuity rates that may prevail at retirement. Employers run the risk where a dissatisfied pensioner might discover that, through lower than expected investment yields and annuity rates, the pension is lower than anticipated — for example, falling investment returns can play havoc with retirement planning for members of money purchase arrangements, who are approaching retirement age. This can have a negative effect on the company's productivity as employees who should be retiring, either fully or partially, may be forced to stay on the company's payroll because they do not have the means to retire.

¶135 Money Purchase Plan Options

Where an employer has decided to consider a money purchase arrangement as a retirement savings vehicle, the employer must choose between three vehicles: a group RRSP, a DPSP, or a defined contribution pension plan, as discussed below.

Group RRSP

A group RRSP provides a convenient way for employees to save additional funds for their retirement. Under a group RRSP, an employer can make contributions on the employees' behalf. This approach is simple and easy to communicate and does not require registration with any minimum standards jurisdiction. On the other hand, there are some disadvantages relative to DPSPs and defined contribution pension plans. For example:

- Vesting is immediate, since the employer is essentially making an RRSP contribution on behalf of the employee. The amount of the contribution is included in the employee's taxable income and the employee will receive a tax receipt for the contribution made to the RRSP from the RRSP financial institution as if the employee had made the contribution directly.
- The employer contributions will attract the provincial health payroll tax levy (where applicable) and, since they represent additional income to the employee, Employment Insurance (EI) premiums and CPP/QPP contributions will have to be made on the basis of this additional income (unless the maximum EI premium or CPP/QPP contribution is already being made for the year). In addition, these contributions may affect the employer assessment for workers' compensation and the level of benefits provided under other employer

programs, such as life insurance and long-term disability, which in turn may increase employer or employee costs (depending on who is paying the premiums).

- Although many employers who contribute to an RRSP on behalf of an employee restrict the employee's ability to cash out the RRSP while still employed, employers cannot easily prohibit the employee from cashing out the RRSP after termination of employment. Thus, there is no guarantee that the employer contributions will ultimately be used to provide a retirement income.
- Since RRSP contribution room is based on earned income, for those employees who may be disabled or on leaves of absence (such as parental or maternity leave) and have no (or reduced) earned income, there is little ability to ensure that individuals under these circumstances are not losing out on retirement savings. This can be a significant drawback for employees who are on long-term disability leave, receiving benefits under an employee-pay-all plan, and cannot accumulate any retirement income because they have no earned income for many years.
- The maximum permitted RRSP contribution is based on both the previous year's earned income and the PA, if any. Since earned income is not limited to employment income, employers are not in a position to be able to determine an individual's RRSP contribution room. For example, a pension plan member with low earned income in the previous year (due to making large alimony payments, for example) may have no RRSP contribution room at all. Therefore, the employer may not be able to make a contribution to the RRSP without putting the employee in a penalty tax situation. Further, the employer will not even be aware that the employee is in a penalty tax situation as the employer does not typically have knowledge of a particular employee's personal tax situation. A special problem arises in the first and second years of employment if the employee was a member of the registered pension plan or DPSP of his or her previous employer. This problem has been alleviated somewhat with the introduction of the relief for contributions to a "qualifying group RRSP". These changes, introduced for the 1996 tax year, apply to non-elective contributions to a group RRSP and raise the level of contributions that are permitted before the penalty tax applies.

Since the proceeds from the RRSP may be taken in cash or may be used to buy a life or term certain annuity or to purchase a RRIF, a group RRSP gives the employee more flexibility in tax and retirement planning (although many jurisdictions have introduced more flexibility to pension plans in the form of LRIFs and amendments to the *Income Tax Act*

(Canada) — refer to the section below on defined contribution pension plans). In addition, if the employer so chooses, the employee could be allowed to divert some or all of the employer contribution to the employee's spousal RRSP, thus taking advantage of possible income splitting opportunities.

DPSP

A DPSP may have some attraction as a vehicle for employer contributions. It is especially suitable in circumstances where the employer wishes to have the monies invested primarily in company stock. By having part of their retirement capital invested in their employer's company, the employees have a vested interest in the success of the organization. In addition, employer contributions to a DPSP do not attract the provincial health payroll tax levy, nor do they increase the amount of EI or CPP/QPP contributions or workers' compensation assessments payable. Furthermore, the amount of employer contributions to the DPSP for a particular year will depend upon the profits of the company and the benefits that can be made subject to a two-year vesting requirement.

Like a group RRSP, the funds in a DPSP may be locked-in during employment, but not after termination of service. Therefore, there is no guarantee that the funds will ultimately be used to provide retirement income. However, a significant difference between DPSPs and other money purchase vehicles is the level of contribution permitted: employees are not permitted to contribute and as a result, the maximum employer contribution is one-half of the money purchase limit.

Since employee contributions are not permitted under a DPSP, employers will often offer a group RRSP for the employee contributions in conjunction with the DPSP.

Defined Contribution Registered Pension Plan

Unlike a group RRSP or DPSP, a defined contribution registered pension plan falls under the jurisdiction of the minimum standards pension regulators. As a result, such an arrangement ensures that the employer monies will be used to provide retirement income once the plan member has satisfied the minimum standards locking-in requirements. However, the terminating employee often sees this locking-in as a disadvantage. Many of the jurisdictions have introduced the ability for employees to convert their pension entitlements into a RRIF, subject to additional restrictions. This more restrictive arrangement is known as an LIF or an LRIF. (Refer to Chapter 14 for more information on LIFs and LRIFs.) Members of pension plans therefore have more flexibility at retirement than in the past. It must be noted, however, that the typical provision links the maximum annual withdrawal permitted under an LIF or LRIF to an annuity purchase rate based on current rates of interest on long-term bonds. At interest rates prevalent at the time of writing, the degree of flexibility in the allowable annual withdrawal is small. Some jurisdictions are now offering even more flexibility — in 2002, Saskatchewan introduced a prescribed RRIF which is a non-locked-in vehicle into which locked-in funds can generally be transferred after age 55. And in 2003, the *Income Tax Act* (Canada) was amended to allow for "variable benefits" to be paid from a defined contribution plan, which essentially allows a plan member to leave the bulk of the assets in the defined contribution pension plan at retirement, and draw out periodic amounts in a "RRIF-like" manner. Refer to ¶1660 for additional details on variable benefits. Various jurisdictions have also introduced one-time unlocking of a portion of locked-in funds.

There are other advantanges to a defined contribution plan over a group RRSP or DPSP, such as:

- the fact that the contribution limit is based on the current year's earnings from the employer which avoids the difficulties associated with the one-year lag in determining RRSP room as discussed above under the group RRSP section (however, it should be noted that DPSP contributions are also based on current-year earnings, so this advantage applies only to defined contribution plans compared to group RRSPs);
- the employer can contribute to a member's account based on deemed earnings during periods of unpaid absence which is not possible for a group RRSP or DPSP (see ¶1625 regarding prescribed compensation for further details);
- employer contributions are not subject to the various payroll levies; and
- member accounts are protected from creditors.

Although there can be additional costs associated with operating a defined contribution plan, when compared to a group RRSP or DPSP, mostly involving the minimum standards registration requirements, some employers will consider that the features offset the disadvantages.

¶140 Capital Accumulation Plan Guidelines

As discussed at ¶130, in May 2004, the Joint Forum of Financial Regulators released their CAP Guidelines.

The employer risk in managing money purchase arrangements is recognized in the CAP Guidelines, which sets out industry standard best practices and lays out a framework for managing and structuring good governance practices for such plans. However, the CAP Guidelines do not provide a safe harbour; following them may not protect the plan sponsor from a lawsuit.

There are specific guidelines dealing with setting up and maintaining a capital accumulation plan, investment and decision-making tools for CAP members, ongoing communication with members, and terminating a CAP.

The CAP Guidelines contain recommendations in four key categories: requirements for setting up a new plan, provision of investment information and decision-making tools, requirements for initial and ongoing communication and disclosure, and plan maintenance criteria.

Some of the key recommendations include the following:

- Information, documentation, and decision-making tools provided to members should be in a format that assists in readability and comprehension.
- Sponsors should select, offer, and monitor a diversified range of investment options to members, although available options may be limited by legislative requirements.
- Members should be allowed a reasonable opportunity, at least quarterly, to transfer among available investment options, with the costs of these transfers chargeable to members.
- Sponsors should have a policy outlining what happens if a member does not select an investment option (a default option) and this policy must be communicated prior to any action being taken by the plan sponsor.
- Sponsors should provide advance notice to members of significant changes in investment options where plan activity may be suspended or disrupted.
- Sponsors may, but are not required to, enter into arrangements with service providers to provide investment advice to members. If no arrangement is entered into, the sponsor should recommend that plan members seek advice from qualified investment advisers.
- Sponsors who choose a service provider to provide investment advice to members should monitor their performance in the same manner that any other service provider would be assessed.
- Sponsors should establish criteria for the periodic review of all service providers including the criteria used to select the service provider and the frequency and/or triggering events for the review.

- Sponsors must clearly document the roles and responsibilities of all parties involved in the plan, document which activities can and will be performed in-house and which will be outsourced, and establish procedures for proper maintenance of records and appropriate records-retention policies.

Most sponsors of CAP plans, in all likelihood, had in place procedures and policies dealing with many of the recommendations set out in the CAP Guidelines. However, it is significant that these recommendations have been formalized and made consistent across all types of money purchase plans (including non-retirement plans such as registered education savings plans (RESP)) where previously there was not a consistent set of guidelines that applied for all such plans.

It also highlights the heavy responsibility for ongoing communication that lies with the plan sponsor to ensure that plan members are provided with as much information as possible to allow them to make appropriate and informed decisions with respect to their plan assets. In fact, some of the CAP Guidelines in essence reduce some of the employee's risk inherent in CAP plans by requiring the plan sponsor to be highly involved in the selection and monitoring of the investment vehicles.

¶145 Present System for Taxation of Retirement Savings

The current retirement savings tax system is comprised of sections of the *Income Tax Act* (Canada), Regulations to the Act, as well as various forms and guides to assist plan sponsors in complying and administering the rules. These sections of the Act set out the foundation for the system and contain elements which can only be changed by the House of Commons through a new Bill. The Regulations set out details which have been changed (and will continue to be changed) by the Department of Finance from time to time to accommodate policy and regulatory changes. The Regulations deal primarily with the rules for determining PAs, PSPAs, and PARS and set out the provisions that a registered pension plan must contain in order to continue to be registered under the Act.

The role of the Department of Finance is to formulate federal government policy on financial, economic, and fiscal matters. The role of the CRA is to carry out this policy as it relates to taxation. Although the current system was developed by the Department of Finance, officials from the CRA were consulted throughout, since they were to be responsible for administering the system. The Department of Finance continues to provide input on any policy-related matters. The Province of Quebec has brought its retirement savings tax rules into line with those of the federal government.

The responsibilities imposed on retirement plan sponsors, particularly those who sponsor a defined benefit plan, are seen by some as quite onerous. The difficulty of complying increases with plan complexity. A fair degree of expertise is needed in order to comply with all aspects of the legislation. Unintended errors or misinterpretations have occurred, and will likely continue to occur, from time to time. It should be noted that the *Income Tax Act* (Canada) provides that offenders are liable for a fine of not less than $1,000 and not exceeding $25,000, and for imprisonment for up to 12 months, if they fail to comply with the Regulations or do not administer a pension plan in accordance with the terms of the plan as registered. In addition, the Act and Regulations provide the regulators with a very persuasive compliance tool: the ability to revoke the registration of the plan in the event that a plan sponsor does not comply with the requirements of the Act and the Regulations. If a plan's registration is revoked, the plan is retroactively treated as a retirement compensation arrangement (RCA), with all the less favourable tax-treatment accorded such an arrangement.

¶200 DEFINITIONS

¶205 Definitions

The following definitions and terms are used consistently throughout this book. The relevant reference in the *Income Tax Act* (Canada) or the Regulations, or, where appropriate, the section in this book where the definition is used, appears at the end of the definition.

Accrued pension is the pension credited to a plan member according to his or her service, earnings, etc., up to a given time.

Active member is an employee actively employed by an employer and currently earning benefits in the employer's registered pension plan or deferred profit sharing plan. *Regs 8500(1)*

Actuary is an individual who is a Fellow of the Canadian Institute of Actuaries (CIA), or a firm, provided at least one of the employees is a Fellow of the CIA. *Act 147.1(1)*

Additional voluntary contribution (AVC) is an optional contribution made on a money purchase basis to an RPP by an active member. *Act 248(1)*

Administrator is the person who has ultimate responsibility for administering the plan; typically the administrator is the employer or a board of trustees established to administer the plan. *Act 147.1(1)*

After-tax savings plan, also known as an **employee savings plan**, is a generic term for company sponsored non-registered employee savings plan in which employees can save for retirement or other financial purposes. It is often offered in conjunction with a tax deferred savings arrangement such as a **group RRSP**, **DPSP** or a **defined contribution pension plan**. Employer contributions are not required, but are permitted. Employee contributions are not tax-deductible, employer contributions are taxable income in the year they are made, and investment earnings in the after-tax savings plan are not tax-sheltered.

Ancillary benefit is a benefit other than the regular lifetime pension benefit, paid under an RPP on a member's retirement, on the death of a member or a pensioner, on a member's termination of employment or disability, or in the form of increases in pension payments to pensioners.

Annuity is a contract with an insurance company licensed to do business in Canada in which provides for a periodic stream of payments to be made to the annuitant for life or for a fixed period in exchange for a lump-sum payment. An annuity can be deferred, meaning that the stream of payments will commence at some point in the future, or immediate. There are various types of annuities available depending on the source of funds used to purchase the annuity (registered or non-registered) and the tax treatment of the payments depends on the type of annuity purchased.

Arm's length and **non-arm's length** refers to the closeness of the business relationship between two persons or tax entities; if a person or tax entity is seen to be beneficially interested in the tax entity, then the person is deemed to not be dealing at arm's length; the *Income Tax Act* (Canada) provides that, where a member is considered to be non-arm's length, certain benefits cannot be provided to or contributions made in respect of that member. *Act 251*

Average Consumer Price Index for a calendar year is $1/12$ of the sum of the Consumer Price Indices for the 12 months ending September 30 of the immediately preceding calendar year. *Regs 8500(1)*

Average wage for a calendar year is the amount that is obtained by dividing the aggregate of all amounts by 12, each of which is the **wage measure** for a month in the 12-month period ending on June 30 of the immediately preceding calendar year. The average wage information for the years 1984 through 2010 is set out in Appendix 3. *Act 147.1(1)*

Beneficiary of an individual who is a member of an **RPP** or other **tax-sheltered retirement savings vehicle**, means a person who has a right to receive benefits under the pension plan or retirement savings vehicle after the death of the individual. *Regs 8500(1)*

Benefit accrual for a particular year is the annual pension that a member of a defined benefit plan has earned in respect of credited service in that year, determined using special rules. It is the difference between the **normalized pensions** calculated at the end and the beginning of the calendar year (see ¶710).

Benefit entitlement for a particular year is the portion of a defined benefit plan member's **benefit accrual** that is attributable to the member's employment with a particular employer who is participating in the plan. If, for example, the individual works for two such employers in a particular year, the total of the two benefit entitlements for that year will equal the individual's benefit accrual for that year (see ¶ 710).

Bridging benefit is a temporary benefit provided to employees who retire prior to age 65 (i.e., prior to the time when Old Age Security (OAS) and CPP/QPP benefits are normally available), in order to supplement their pension income until their government benefits commence. Registered pension plans which provide these bridging benefits either do so as an add-on to the lifetime pension otherwise payable from the plan, or express the pension formula as a pension payable from the retirement date until a specified date (usually age 65), at which point the pension is reduced by an amount that reflects the actual or estimated benefits payable under OAS or the CPP/QPP. In both situations, the difference between the full pension payable before the age at which the pension reduces and the amount of pension payable after that reduction occurs is defined as the "bridging benefit". In this book, the term "bridging benefit" does not include a situation where it is paid for by the retiree, at the retiree's option, through an actuarial reduction in the individual's lifetime pension. *Regs 8500(1)*

Commuted value is the amount of an immediate lump-sum payment equal to the actuarial value of a future series of benefit payments.

Compensation is the salary, wages, and other amounts received by an individual in respect of his or her employment that are required (by sections 5 and 6 of the *Income Tax Act* (Canada)) to be included in the individual's income for a particular calendar year. Under certain circumstances, additional amounts are prescribed to be included in compensation for the purposes of allowing the individual to accrue benefits under an RPP during periods of reduced remuneration due to disability, leave of absence, or part-time employment without violating the pension adjustment limits. *Act 147.1(1)*

Connected person is, in general terms, a person who, together with other **non-arm's length** persons, owns at least 10% of the employer's shares, or a person who does not deal at **arm's length** with the employer. *Regs 8500(3)*

Consumer Price Index for a particular month is the national Consumer Price Index for the month as published by Statistics Canada. Note that this definition is not the same as **Average Consumer Price Index**, and the two may be used for different purposes depending on the section of the *Income Tax Act* (Canada) referenced. *Regs 8500(1)*

Contributory plan is a pension plan which requires employees to make contributions by payroll deduction in order to qualify for benefits under the plan (see the definition of **non-contributory plan** for comparison).

CRA is the Canada Revenue Agency, the government agency formerly known as Canada Customs and Revenue Agency and prior to that, as Revenue Canada. The CRA administers tax laws for the Government of Canada and for most provinces and territories and also administers various social and economic benefit and incentive programs delivered through the tax system. In particular, the Registered Plans Directorate within the CRA is responsible for registering and monitoring compliance under the *Income Tax Act* (Canada) for retirement savings programs such as **RPP**s, **RRSP**s, **RIF**s and **DPSP**s.

Deferred pension is a specified pension determined at the time of termination of employment or termination of a pension plan, but not payable until some later date (usually the **normal retirement age** as specified in the pension plan).

Deferred pensioner is a terminated employee who remains entitled to a **deferred pension**.

Deferred profit sharing plan (DPSP) is a savings vehicle as defined in section 147 of the *Income Tax Act* (Canada), to which employer contributions are made from profits, or determined in accordance with profits. It often forms part of an employee savings plan. *Act 147(1)*

Defined benefit limit is equal to 1/9 of the **money purchase limit** for a particular calendar year and is one of the limits on the maximum amount of pension that may be paid out of a defined benefit pension plan in respect of a year of **pensionable service** (the other limit being 2% of the **highest average indexed compensation**). Since the money purchase limit is indexed in accordance with the **average wage** after 2009, so too is the defined benefit limit. For 2010, the defined benefit limit is $2,494.44. The defined benefit limits for the years 1990 through 2010 appear in Appendix 3. *Regs 8500(1)*

Defined benefit pension plan is an RPP that promises a certain level of pension income at retirement according to a predetermined formula. The main types of defined benefit pension plans are:

- A **final average pension plan**, which bases the benefits on a percentage of **pensionable earnings** averaged over a relatively short period of time prior to retirement, multiplied by the years of **pensionable service**;

- A **career average pension plan**, which provides a benefit that is usually expressed as a percentage of each year's **pensionable earnings** over an employee's career; and
- A **flat benefit pension plan**, which provides a specific dollar amount of benefit for each year of **pensionable service**.

Defined benefit provision is a provision within an **RPP** that provides one of the above types of benefits to members. In fact, the *Income Tax Act* (Canada) defines it as any plan provision under which benefits are determined in a way other than under a **money purchase provision**. *Act 147.1(1)*

Defined contribution pension plan (also known as a **money purchase pension plan**) is an **RPP** under which employer contributions and, if applicable, employee contributions are individually allocated to the credit of the employees and provide whatever pension the accumulated contributions and investment earnings will provide at retirement. The amount of contributions is usually determined by reference to a percentage of **pensionable earnings**.

Dependent of a member of a **registered pension plan** is a parent, grandparent, brother, sister, child, or grandchild who was dependent on the member for support at the relevant date and who must be:

- under age 19;
- a full-time student; or
- dependent by reason of mental or physical infirmity. *Regs 8500(1)*

Designated factor is the factor used to determine the minimum payment required from the member's defined contribution account balance if the benefits under a **defined contribution pension plan** are payable from the pension plan after retirement. The factor is the same factor used to determine the minimum payment under a **RRIF** (see ¶1660). *Regs 8506(5)*

Designated plan is a defined benefit **RPP** which, throughout a calendar year, is not maintained pursuant to a collective bargaining agreement and in which the total of the **pension credits** for **specified individuals** exceeds 50% of the total of the **pension credits** for all members. *Regs 8515(1)*

Disabled, in respect of a member of an **RPP**, means having a physical or mental impairment that prevents the member from performing the duties of employment in which the individual was engaged before the commencement of the impairment. (See the definition of **totally and permanently disabled** for comparison.) *Regs 8500(1)*

Earned income is the income on which RRSP contribution limits are based (see ¶ 405). *Act 146(1)*

Eligible period of reduced pay is a period of an individual's employment in which remuneration is less than what the individual could normally expect to receive, based on the remuneration of the individual prior to the period of reduced pay, and provided that the individual was not connected with the employer and had been employed by the employer for at least 36 months. Examples of periods of reduced pay would be a temporary reduction of hours or phased-in retirement. It does include a period of **disability**. *Regs 8500(1)*

Eligible period of temporary absence is a period within the period of employment of an individual in which he or she does not render services. Examples of periods of temporary absence are leave of absence, lay-off, strike, lock-out or any other circumstance acceptable to the Minister. It does not include a period of **disability** or any period after 1990 during which the individual was a connected person. *Regs 8500(1)*

Eligible survivor benefit period of a dependent of a member of an RPP is the period from the death of the member to the end of the year in which the dependant attains age 18, or when the dependant ceases to be a full-time student, if later. If the person is a dependant by virtue of a physical or mental infirmity, the period extends throughout the full period of such infirmity. *Regs 8500(1)*

Employees Profit Sharing Plan (EPSP) is an arrangement that allows an employer to share profits with all, or a designated group of, employees. Under an EPSP, amounts are paid to a trustee to be held and invested for the benefit of the employees who are beneficiaries of the plan. Each year, the trustee is required to allocate to such beneficiaries all employer contributions, profits from trust property, capital gains and losses, and certain amounts in respect of forfeitures. These allocated amounts, with certain exceptions, are included in computing the taxable income of the beneficiaries for the year in which they are allocated and are not subject to tax when actually received by the beneficiaries.

Excess money purchase transfer is an amount which is used in the **PSPA** calculation for post-1996 terminations and represents the amount transferred to tax-sheltered retirement savings vehicle in respect of the terminating defined benefit member that is in excess of the combined total of the **PA**s and **PSPA**s attributable to the member's post-1989 service. It is used in certain circumstances if this same service is later credited again to the individual (see ¶ 1036). *Regs 8303(7.1)*

Existing plan is an **RPP** (RPP) that was an RPP on March 27, 1988, or an RPP for which an application for registration had been made by that date. The definition of an existing plan is normally relevant only for a **defined benefit plan**. (See the definition of **grandfathered plan** for comparison.) *Regs 8500(1)*

Flexible pension plan is a type of **defined benefit pension plan** that allows members to make additional contributions to acquire or improve **ancillary benefits** that are provided in connection with basic pension benefits accruing under the plan (see ¶ 120).

Forfeited amount (also known as a **forfeiture** or a **non-vested forfeiture**) is an amount under a money purchase provision to which a member no longer has any rights (other than amounts that have been paid out as death benefits or upon a marriage or relationship breakdown). A forfeited amount normally arises upon the termination of a member before becoming entitled to any vested benefits. *Regs 8500(1)*

Government-sponsored retirement arrangement is a type of unregistered plan that provides retirement income to individuals who are paid from public funds but are not employees of a public service organization. *Regs 8308.4(1)*

Grandfathered plan is an **existing plan** that, on March 27, 1988, contained a **defined benefit provision**. (See the definition of **existing plan** for comparison.) *Regs 8500(1)*

Grossed-Up PSPA means the amount of the provisional PSPA determined with respect to a past service event, before taking into account any qualifying transfers, money purchase transfers and excess money purchase transfers. The grossed-up PSPA, therefore, measures the full PA value of the past service benefit being provided. *Regs 8304.1(7)*

Group RRSP is an umbrella program covering individual **RRSPs** offered by an employer to its employees, allowing payroll deduction for employee contributions. Investment decisions may be made either by the employees or the employer. Sometimes employers contribute to these arrangements. An employer contribution confers a taxable benefit on the employee.

Highest average indexed compensation is the average of the best three non-overlapping 12-month periods of indexed compensation. For this purpose, monthly compensation is indexed to increases in the **average wage** from the calendar year in which the compensation was paid to the year of pension commencement. Highest average indexed compensation is used in determining the highest **lifetime retirement benefit** that may be paid from a **defined benefit pension plan** (see ¶ 1710) *Regs 8504(2)*

Hybrid plan (also known as a **combination plan**) is the combination of a **defined benefit pension plan** with one or more of the following: a **defined contribution plan** (either as a separately registered pension plan or as a provision within the same registered pension plan), a **deferred profit sharing plan** (as a separately registered plan), or a facility to permit **additional voluntary contributions** within the same registered pension plan (see Chapter 20).

Indexing is the periodic adjustment of a benefit amount (usually after retirement), according to a formula which is usually based on a recognized index of price or wage levels, e.g., the **Consumer Price Index** or the **Average Wage**.

Information Circular 72-13R8 is the final version of the series of Circulars covering rules regarding the treatment of benefits and contributions under the *Income Tax Act* (Canada) as they applied to **RPPs** submitted for registration prior to March 28, 1988; the rules set out in the Information Circular generally continue to apply to benefits provided in respect of service before 1991 under defined benefit provisions.

Integration is the provision in a pension plan in which plan contributions and/or benefits are defined by reference to those of a government pension program such as the CPP/QPP.

Letter of credit (LOC) is an agreement between a financial institution such as a bank and a sponsoring organization which provides for security of certain employee benefits. The organization pays premiums to the bank in exchange for the bank agreeing to pay the organization the face value of the LOC in the event of certain specified triggering events (such as defaulting on benefit payments or a change of control). LOCs are used to provide security of benefits without fully prefunding the benefits. LOCs are used in SERP programs and are also permitted to be used to secure funding requirements for solvency deficiencies in RPPs in certain minimum standards pension jurisdictions.

Lifetime retirement benefits are periodic payments that are paid for the lifetime of a registered pension plan member, unless suspended or commuted before the member's death. (See the definition of **bridging benefit** for comparison.) *Regs 8500(1)*

Locking-in is the provincial or federal legislative requirement that pension contributions or benefits cannot be withdrawn or otherwise forfeited if the employee has attained a certain age and/or has completed a certain period of service or plan membership on termination of employment, death, retirement, or on plan termination. If an active member terminates employment and transfers his or her locked-in entitlement to an **RRSP** (or other eligible **tax-sheltered retirement savings vehicle**), the fund's custodian must agree to administer the assets in accordance with the terms of applicable **minimum standards legislation**. Chapter 14 covers the various maturity options available for locked-in funds.

Maximum PA rule stipulates that the **PA** in respect of benefits accruing and contributions being made under a **hybrid plan** during a year may not exceed the maximum contribution that could be made to a **defined contribution pension plan**. This maximum is the lesser of 18% of the year's **compensation** and the **money purchase limit**. *Act 147.1(8)*

Member-funded pension plan is a type of defined benefit pension plan permitted by Quebec's SPPA. In an MFPP, the employer contributions are fixed at a pre-determined rate. The member contributions to the plan may vary, depending on the rate of return the plan fund receives. An MFPP essentially reverses the funding roles of the employer and the plan members from those in a traditional defined benefit plan.

Minimum standards legislation refers collectively to the pension legislation issued by each of the provinces (and the federal jurisdiction for employees who are subject to federal employment standards) and which sets out the rules covering individual employee rights under **RPP** and the administration and financing of such plans (see Chapter 13).

Money purchase arrangement is an arrangement whereby contributions to a **tax-sheltered retirement savings vehicle** are paid on behalf of a member or by a member on a money purchase basis. Money purchase arrangements include a **defined contribution pension plan**, **DPSP**, **RRSP**, and **additional voluntary contributions**.

Money purchase basis describes the process whereby contributions are credited with investment earnings, and on termination of employment, retirement, or death, the accumulated value is used to purchase a life annuity, is withdrawn in cash, or is transferred to another registered vehicle.

Money purchase limit is the maximum total contribution that may be made in a calendar year to a **defined contribution pension plan**.

The money purchase limit for each calendar year is set out at ¶1616 and in Appendix 3. *Act 147.1(1)*

Money purchase pension plan (also known as a **defined contribution pension plan**) is an **RPP** under which employer contributions and, if applicable, employee contributions are individually allocated to the credit of the employees and provide whatever pension the accumulated contributions and investment earnings will provide at retirement. The amount of contributions is usually determined by reference to a percentage of **pensionable earnings**.

Money purchase provision is a provision within an **RPP** that provides benefits to members on a **money purchase basis**. *Act 147.1(1)*

Money purchase transfer is variable C in the modified **PSPA** calculation formula and is the amount of monies that are transferred out of the exporting plan to a **tax-sheltered retirement savings** vehicle on behalf of the plan member who is transferring **pensionable service** from one RPP to another RPP under a **reciprocal transfer agreement** or **portability arrangement**. The money purchase transfer does not transfer to the importing plan and is not used to fund the benefits to be provided under the importing plan. The money purchase transfer measures the extent to which the benefit provided under the former provision exceeds the "reduction" in the **PA** value of benefits that occurs in moving from the former provision to the new provision. *Regs 8304(5)*

Multi-employer pension plan is an **RPP** covering employees of more than one employer, where it is reasonable to expect that no more than 95% of the active members of the plan are employed by a single **participating employer** or participating employers who do not deal with each other at **arm's length**. Multi-employer pension plans are subject to special treatment with respect to the reporting of **PAs** (see Chapter 9) **PSPAs** and **PARs** (see Chapter 12), and with respect to the registration rules (see Chapter 21). A plan that may otherwise be considered a multi-employer plan will not be so considered if the main reason for having more than one **participating employer** is to take advantage of these special rules. *Act 147.1(1)*

Non-contributory plan is a pension plan which does not require any employee contribution in order to qualify for benefits (see the definition of **contributory plan** for comparison).

Normal retirement age is the age specified in an RPP at which employees are expected or entitled to retire. Often it is the age at which pensions are first paid without reduction.

Normalized pension is an individual's **accrued pension**, calculated using special rules that are applicable to the determination of **PAs** in a **defined benefit pension plan** (see ¶710 and ¶735). *Regs 8303(5)*

PA transfer amount means variable D in the **PAR** calculation formula and is generally used only in **reciprocal transfer agreement** or **portability arrangement** situations where an individual is credited with past service under an **RPP** for service that was previously credited under another RPP. It is equal to the lesser of the grossed-up **PSPA**s under the importing plan and the **PA**s originally reported under the exporting plan. *Regs 8304.1(10)*

Participating employer in relation to an **RPP** is an employer who is required to make contributions to the plan. *Act 147.1(1)*

Past service event is any circumstance or situation that gives rise to a benefit improvement in respect of post-1989 service that requires the calculating and reporting of a **PSPA** in respect of that improvement. The benefit improvement can take the form of a change in the manner of providing benefits in respect of service already credited or in the crediting of new periods of service not previously credited. *Regs 8300(1)*

Past service pension adjustment is the amount of reduction in an individual's **RRSP contribution room** due to the granting of certain additional past service benefits by an employer in a **defined benefit pension plan** (see Chapters 10 and 12). *Regs 8303(1)*

Pension adjustment is the deemed value that, for tax purposes, is placed on the benefit accruing under an **RPP** or **deferred profit sharing plan** in a particular year (see Chapters 5 to 9). *Regs 8301(1)*

Pension adjustment reversal is an amount which restores **RRSP contribution room** to individuals terminating from an **RPP** or **DPSP** after 1996 for whom a lump-sum payment is made in respect of the benefits accrued under the **RPP** or **DPSP**. **RRSP contribution room** is restored to the extent that the lump-sum provided to the individual in respect of post-1989 service is less than the sum of the **PAs** and **PSPAs** reported in respect of that service (see Chapters 11 and 12). *Regs 8304.1(1)*

Pension benefits supervisory authorities are the federal and provincial bodies that administer pension benefits standards legislation. All pension benefits supervisory authorities are members of the CAPSA.

Pension credit has two meanings. The principal meaning, in this book, relates to individual components of the **PA** calculation in a hybrid plan; the total of all pension credits under the plan equals the **PA** which is reported to the CRA. A pension credit is also a term used when describing the splitting of pensions upon marriage breakdown; this is known as pension credit splitting. *Regs 8301*

Pensionable earnings are the portion of an individual's total earnings used in calculating the pension entitlement under an RPP, as defined in the plan document; in addition to basic salary, pensionable earnings may or may not include bonuses, overtime payments, taxable benefits, or other components of earnings.

Pensionable service (also known as **credited service**) is the period of employment that is used in determining the amount of a pension that may be received by an individual. Periods of service which may be included in pensionable service for purposes of the registration rules are discussed at ¶1745. *Regs 8500(1)*

Period of disability is a period throughout which the member is **disabled**. *Regs 8500(1)*

Portability refers to the ability to transfer the **commuted value** of a **deferred pension** to an **RRSP**, another RPP, or an insurance company for the purchase of an annuity when an individual terminates employment, dies, or retires, or upon the termination of a pension plan (see ¶1313).

Pre-reform service/post reform service refers generally to periods of **pensionable service** in **defined benefit pension plans** for which registration rules are set out in either **Information Circular 72-13R8** or under the Income Tax Regulations. Pre-reform service means pre-1991 service for all plans except **grandfathered plans**. Pre-reform service for **grandfathered plans** means all service prior to January 1, 1992 and the effective date of the amendment made to the plan to comply with the Regulations, but in no event earlier than January 1, 1991. All service after those dates is post-reform service. Pre-reform benefits are benefits that accrue in respect of a period of pre-reform service. All other benefits are post-reform benefits.

Prescribed compensation refers to notional amounts that may be included in a member's compensation in order to allow contributions to be made to an RPP in respect of eligible periods of temporary absence and reduced pay. Without this prescribed compensation, contributions would exceed the PA limits and the plan's registration would become revocable. *Regs 8507(1)*

Provisional PSPA means the sum of the **pension credits** with respect to the **past service event**, offset by any transfers of tax-sheltered assets that will be used to reduce the **PSPA**. The provisional PSPA is the **PSPA** that is reported to the **CRA** and will be either deducted automatically from the plan member's **RRSP contribution room** (in the case of an exempt PSPA) or certified prior to being deducted from the plan members's **RRSP contribution room** (in the case of a non-exempt PSPA). *Regs 8303(3)*

Public safety occupation is one of the following occupations: firefighter, police officer, corrections officer, air traffic controller, or commercial airline pilot. **Registered pension plans** are permitted to allow members in public safety occupations to retire with an unreduced pension earlier than other members. *Regs 8501(1)*

Qualifying transfer is an amount that an individual transfers directly to a defined benefit plan from an **RRSP**, **DPSP**, **RPP**, or **SMEP** to be used to fund post-1989 past service benefits provided to the individual. A qualifying transfer reduces the amount of the PSPA that must be reported in respect of the additional benefits being provided. *Regs 8303(6)*

Qualifying withdrawal (also known as prescribed withdrawal) is an amount which an individual must remove from his or her personal **RRSP** in order to be able to be provided with additional past service benefits following the reporting of a **PSPA**. A qualifying withdrawal does not reduce the amount of the **PSPA** and is included in income in the year in which it is withdrawn. *Regs 8307(6)*

Reciprocal transfer arrangement or **portability arrangement** is an agreement that permits a plan member to accept service or benefits previously credited under another RPP in the current employer's plan in return for the individual giving up entitlement to such service or benefits under the former plan (see ¶1055).

Registered pension plan is a **defined contribution pension plan** or a **defined benefit pension plan** accepted by the **CRA** for registration under the *Income Tax Act* (Canada). *Act 248(1)*

Registered retirement income fund means a registered arrangement between a carrier and an individual, into which funds are transferred from an individual's RRSP at maturity, and from which varying amounts are withdrawn each year by the individual, subject to certain minimum amounts in accordance with specific formulae. The individual remains responsible for investing the funds until they are exhausted. *Act 146.3(1)*

Registered retirement savings plan is a vehicle available for individual tax-sheltered savings. *Act 146(1)*

RRSP contribution room or **RRSP deduction limit** available to an individual in any one year represents the amount of contributions that may be made in that year by the individual to an **RRSP** on a fully tax-deductible basis. Alternatively, it is the amount that an individual may deduct from taxable income in the year that relates to an **RRSP** contribution made by the individual in a previous year that the individual could not deduct, or chose not to deduct, from taxable income in that previous year. *Act 14(1)*

RRSP dollar limit for a particular year is the **money purchase limit** for the preceding year (with some historical exceptions as set out in Appendices 1 and 3). *Act 146(1)*

Retirement compensation arrangement is an arrangement whereby an employer may set aside monies on a tax-deductible basis to prefund a retirement arrangement that is not registered with the **CRA** as an **RPP**. *Act 248(1)*

Retiring allowance is a payment or series of payments to an individual upon loss of office or employment or on/after retirement in recognition of long service. *Act 248(1)*

Simplified pension plan is a money purchase plan that combines elements of defined contribution RPPs, group RRSPs and DPSPs and was designed to respond to the needs of small businesses. Although originally introduced in Quebec under Quebec minimum standards pension legislation, the *Income Tax Act* (Canada) implemented some Regulation changes with additional restrictions on such plans outside Quebec.

Specified beneficiary means the **spouse** of a member of a **defined contribution pension plan** who has been so designated by the member for the purpose of determining the minimum payment required from the member's defined contribution account if the benefits are payable from the pension plan after retirement (see ¶1660). *Regs 8506(8)*

Specified distribution is the lump-sum **commuted value** of a benefit paid to an individual upon his or her exit from a **defined benefit provision** (inclusive of excess contributions under the 50% cost-sharing rule or other lump-sums) in respect of the individual's post-1989 benefits under an **RPP**. The lump-sum may be paid in cash or transferred to an **RRSP** or other **tax-sheltered retirement savings vehicle** and is used in calculating the **PAR**. *Regs 8304.1(8)*

Specified individual is an individual **connected** with a **participating employer** at any time during a particular calendar year or whose total remuneration during the year from **participating employers** exceeds 2½ times the **year's maximum pensionable earnings (YMPE)** for the year. *Regs 8515(4)*

Specified multi-employer plan (SMEP) is a particular type of **MEPP** that is governed by special rules under the *Income Tax Act* (Canada) (see ¶910.) *Act 147.1(1)*

Specified retirement arrangement is a partially-funded or unfunded **RCA** maintained by a tax-exempt employer. *Regs 8308.3(1)*

Specified shareholder is an employee of a corporation who does not deal at **arm's length** and who is entitled, either directly or indirectly, to at least 10% of the assets of the corporation. *Act 248(1)(d)*

Spouse of a particular individual means a person who:

(a) is married to the individual, including a marriage that is voidable or void; or

(b) is cohabiting with the individual in a conjugal relationship and

(i) has so cohabited for a period of at least one year, or

(ii) is a parent of a child of whom the individual is also a parent.

If the parties cease to cohabit in the conjugal relationship, coverage as a spouse under (b) above ceases, unless the point of measurement is less than 90 days following the breakdown of the conjugal relationship. *Act 252(3)*; *Regs 8500(5)*

Supplemental Executive Retirement Plan or **Supplemental Employee Retirement Plan** is the general term for a retirement program that provides lifetime retirement benefits that are in excess of the benefits that may be paid from an **RPP** due to restrictions on registered benefits under the *Income Tax Act* (Canada).

Tax-free savings account is a new tax-sheltered account (introduced for the 2009 taxation year) into which all Canadians age 18 and older may contribute up to $5,000 per year in after tax funds. The maximum contribution will increase in future years in accordance with inflation.

Tax-sheltered retirement savings vehicle is one of a number of different types of funds offered by financial institutions to permit tax-sheltering of the fund's assets. Certain tax-sheltered retirement savings vehicles are designed specifically to hold assets transferred from an **RPP** upon the termination, retirement, or death of a plan member, or upon termination of the plan (see Chapter 14).

Totally and permanently disabled describes an individual who suffers from a physical or mental impairment that prevents the individual from performing any occupation for which the individual is reasonably suited by virtue of his or her education, training, or experience and for which there is no reasonable expectation of the individual recovering from the impairment. An individual who is totally and permanently disabled may receive certain enhanced benefits under an **RPP** upon retirement. (See the definition of **disabled** for comparison.) *Regs 8500(1)*

Vesting is a status whereby an employee becomes irrevocably entitled to benefits under an **RPP** or a **DPSP** as a result of achieving a specified age and/or length of service or plan membership. Employees are always vested in their own contributions, but there may be a certain period of time until they become vested in any employer contributions or other specified benefits (see ¶ 1312).

Wage measure is the monthly measure of the average weekly wages and salaries of the industrial aggregate in Canada as published by Statistics Canada. Of all the aggregates that Statistics Canada compiles, the one that corresponds to wage measure is the monthly industrial aggregate in Canada representing the average weekly earnings for all employees, including overtime. Statistics Canada publishes the monthly industrial aggregate in Catalogue 72 002 called Employment, Earnings and Hours. *Act 147.1(1)*

Year's maximum pensionable earnings is a term used in both the CPP and QPP. It refers to the maximum employment earnings on which CPP and QPP contributions are calculated after deduction of the year's basic exemption (which is equal to $3,500 each year), or on which CPP and QPP benefits are calculated. The YMPE increases each year according to a formula based on increases in **average wage** levels — in 2010 it equals $47,200. *Regs 8500(1)*

Chapter 3

¶300 CONCEPTUAL OVERVIEW OF RRSP CONTRIBUTION RULES

¶305 Introduction

The major goal of the retirement savings tax system is to treat all taxpayers equitably. This means that the maximum amount of money that may be contributed to any registered plan on behalf of an individual, and deducted from taxable income by the individual or the employer, should be (more or less) the same, regardless of the exact circumstances of the individual or the registered vehicle being used to provide the retirement income.

The concept of RRSP contribution room is at the heart of the system. The maximum amount of tax-deductible RRSP contribution room available in a year is 18% of the previous taxation year's earned income, up to certain dollar maximums. This may be contributed in full to an RRSP, and deducted from taxable income, if the taxpayer does not belong to an RPP or DPSP. If he or she does belong to an RPP or DPSP, the RRSP contribution room is reduced by the deemed value of the benefits accrued under the RPP or DPSP in the prior taxation year. This deemed value is known as the PA — the more generous the RPP or DPSP, the larger the PA, and the lower the RRSP contribution room in the following year. This effect is illustrated on the following page.

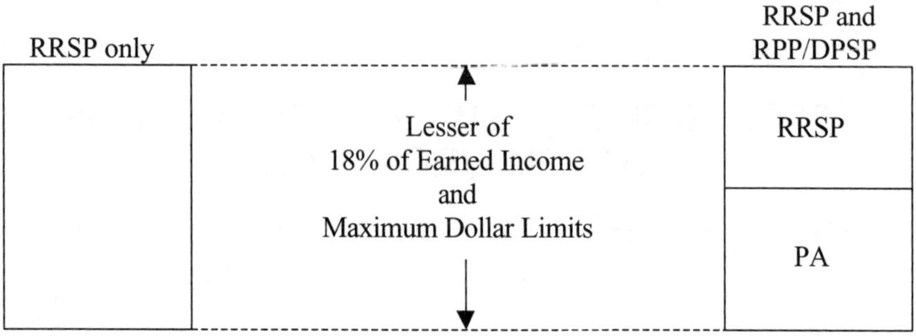

For defined contribution pension plans and DPSPs, the PA is quite straightforward. Generally, it is the total of the employer and employee contributions made to the defined contribution pension plan or DPSP in that year on the individual's behalf.

However, for defined benefit pension plans, one major complication in the process is the difficulty of placing a current value on the pension earned. The funding of defined benefit plans is quite complex, but it can easily be demonstrated that a greater contribution by the employer is required to provide the same dollar amount of benefit at retirement for an older individual than a younger one — for a younger individual, there is a longer period of time for the funds to generate investment earnings under the RPP to fund the benefit. There are added complexities due to the different types of defined benefit plans that provide, not only different levels of retirement benefits, but also a variety of ancillary benefits, such as indexing, special early retirement benefits, or death benefits. These ancillary benefits do not increase the deemed value of the retirement benefit and do not increase the PA.

Ideally, the value of the "defined benefit" earned by each plan member should be calculated individually to reflect the level of benefits, the type of plan, and the individual's age, gender, and marital status. This, of course, would be very difficult to do efficiently. Consequently, the retirement savings tax system defines a factor that, for tax purposes, converts the amount of "defined benefit" being earned by the employee in a year to a current lump sum. This is the "factor of 9". The factor of 9 used in the PA calculation is a factor which is multiplied by the "defined benefit" being earned by an employee in a particular year, to convert it to an amount that is deemed (for tax purposes) to be comparable to a contribution made to a defined contribution plan. This amount, with certain modifications, is the PA for the year.

The factor of 9 was chosen to tie together the limits on the pension payable from a defined benefit plan and the contribution limits to an RRSP or a defined contribution plan. Using the factor of 9 to place a deemed value on the benefits under a defined benefit plan, the maximum pension under a defined benefit plan is then deemed to have the same value as the maximum contribution to an RRSP or a defined contribution plan. The reason for selecting 9 as the factor is discussed at ¶715.

For 2010, the dollar limit on pensions payable from a defined benefit plan (i.e., the current maximum defined benefit limit of $2,494.44) corresponds to the maximum money purchase limit of $22,450 per year ($2,494.44 × 9 = $22,450). The earnings-related limit under a defined benefit plan, namely 2% of the highest average compensation for each year of service, corresponds to the money purchase limit of 18% of earnings (2% × 9 = 18%).

For an individual who belongs to the most generous defined benefit plan or defined contribution plan, the maximum earnings that can effectively be covered are $124,722 (i.e., $2,494.44 divided by 2%, or $22,450 divided by 18%). In 2010, this represents approximately 2.6 times the average wage.

¶310 Timing — The "One-Year Lag"

One other practical element comes into play when determining RRSP contribution room — timing. Ideally, an employee's deductible RRSP contribution limit in a particular year should reflect the benefits earned by that employee in that same calendar year under a pension plan or DPSP. In other words, ideally the RRSP contribution limit should be reduced by that year's PA, rather than the previous year's PA. However, this would prevent taxpayers from determining their RRSP contribution limit for a particular year until well into the following calendar year, since the PA for the year generally is only reported by the employer to the CRA after the calendar year end.

Similarly, the 18% RRSP contribution limit is based on earned income in the previous calendar year, to allow the CRA sufficient time to determine taxpayers' RRSP contribution room and advise them as to how much they may contribute to an RRSP that year.

Consequently, the retirement savings system is based on a one-year lag — that is, the amount of money an employee may contribute to his or her RRSP for a calendar year is a function of the earned income and the PA, if any, for the previous calendar year.

This one-year lag does have its consequences. RRSP contribution room is created based on earned income in the previous calendar year of employment. However, even though RRSP contribution room has been created in that first year after retirement, and may be carried forward until age 71 (the last year in which retirement funds may be fully tax sheltered), the individual's taxable income in retirement is probably significantly lower than while employed, and he or she may have insufficient taxable income against which to deduct that RRSP contribution. On the other hand, there may be tax-planning techniques available to ensure that taxable income is available in at least one of the post-retirement years.

The one-year lag does allow for a practical reporting system. Employers integrate the reporting of PAs with the T4 reporting process. The PA for the previous calendar year appears on the employee's T4 slip and on the T4 Summary, which are then filed with the CRA. The CRA receives the individual's tax return for the previous year, enabling it to determine the individual's earned income for that previous year. The CRA will then be in a position to notify each individual as to how much he or she may contribute to an RRSP for that same year. This notification is provided on the individual's notice of assessment, which is provided to the individual subsequent to filing his or her income tax return.

The retirement savings system permits individuals to defer making an RRSP contribution in respect of a particular year until a later year when it may be more advantageous to do so. This is known as the "RRSP carry-forward". This flexibility recognizes the possibility that other financial considerations may take priority over making RRSP contributions in certain years.

Since the amount of RRSP contribution room available to a member of an RPP or DPSP in a particular year depends on the PA for the previous year, and since that PA is only reported at the end of February in that year, there is a two-month period at the beginning of every year when such an individual does not know what his or her RRSP contribution room is for the coming year. There is, therefore, the potential for errors to be made by RRSP contributors. In view of this, the threshold of excess RRSP contributions above which a penalty tax will apply is established at $2,000 on a lifetime basis. Thus, in general terms, an individual may, over the course of his or her lifetime, contribute as much as an additional $2,000 in excess of the tax-deductible RRSP contribution limits, without incurring the penalty tax of 1% per month on excess RRSP contributions. The $2,000 is reduced when an individual has negative RRSP room (which may be due to a prior PSPA). In addition, if an individual is younger than 18 years of age at any time during the calendar year, he or she would not qualify for the additional $2,000 amount.

¶315 Past Service Upgrades

The PA takes away RRSP contribution room as benefits are granted for current service. The PSPA takes away RRSP contribution room if certain past service upgrades are granted under a defined benefit plan for post-1989 service. The PSPA calculation and reporting process is the most complex feature of this system. It has resulted in significant changes in the way plan sponsors make improvements to their pension plans. An important part of any plan design or union negotiation process is to examine the impact of the benefit improvement on members' RRSP room in order to avoid or minimize the impact of PSPAs. Fortunately, many types of past service upgrades will not generate a PSPA (discussed in greater detail at ¶1015).

¶320 Restoring RRSP Contribution Room

The PAR completes the picture. The PAR restores RRSP contribution room in situations where a pension plan member terminates employment and elects to receive a lump-sum in lieu of monthly pension payments at retirement. If the lump sum payment in respect of post-1989 service is less than the sum of the PAs reported since 1990, then a PAR is reported. The PAR is the difference between the lump-sum payment and the sum of the reported PAs and PSPAs. The plan member is then permitted to make additional tax-deductible contributions to his or her RRSP equal to the PAR. The PAR has the greatest impact with younger employees who terminate from defined benefit plans.

¶325 RRSP Contribution Room

Every year, the CRA reports to each taxpayer who is entitled to contribute to an RRSP (i.e., who had earned income in the previous year) the amount that the taxpayer will be able to contribute to an RRSP on a tax-deductible basis in the current year. The CRA reports this RRSP contribution limit on the notice of assessment form which also confirms the individual's tax liability for the previous year.

The amount of RRSP contribution room in a calendar year is broadly determined as follows (discussed in greater detail at ¶415):

(a) unused RRSP contribution room that has been carried forward from a previous calendar year; plus

(b) new RRSP contribution room for the calendar year (not less than zero) equal to:

- the lesser of 18% of earned income in the previous calendar year and the flat dollar overall limit for the current calendar year, reduced by
- the total of all PAs for the previous calendar year, less

  a. any PSPAs for the year, net of certain qualifying interplan transfers or RRSP withdrawals, plus

  b. any PARs for the year, less

  c. certain other adjustments that apply in special cases (see ¶415).

The result of the above calculation is the amount of RRSP contribution room available for the calendar year. To the extent that it is not fully utilized through tax-deductible RRSP contributions in respect of that year, or through taking a tax deduction in respect of an RRSP contribution made in a previous year but not deducted at that time (discussed in detail at ¶420), the RRSP contribution room may be carried forward and added to the new RRSP contribution room in a subsequent year.

¶400 DETAILED RRSP CONTRIBUTION RULES

¶405 Definition of Earnings for RRSP Purposes

The level of earnings on which RRSP contribution limits are based is referred to as "earned income". The components of earned income are summarized in the following table:

Components of Earned Income

Aggregate of:	
— Net income from an office or employment (in accordance with section 5 of the *Income Tax Act* (Canada)), before reduction on account of deductions under clergy's residence and deductions for registered pension plan contributions and retirement compensation arrangement contributions	Yes
— Income from self-employment if engaged in business alone or as an active partner	Yes
— Superannuation and pension benefits, CPP/QPP retirement pensions, and OAS	No
— CPP/QPP disability pensions	Yes
— Amounts received out of RRSP or RRIF	No
— Taxable payments from DPSP or revoked plan	No
— Employee profit sharing plan allocations	Yes
— Eligible retiring allowances	No
— Amounts received out of RCA	No
— Taxable benefits from wage loss replacement plan (e.g., disability benefits)	Yes
— Death benefits	No

— Alimony and maintenance receipts (taxable)	Yes
— Royalties for work or invention if taxpayer was author or inventor	Yes
— Supplementary unemployment benefits	Yes
— Research grants net of certain related expenses	Yes
— Net rental income on real property	Yes
— Canadian-source business or employment income while a non-resident	Yes
— Canadian-source income (or loss) while a non-resident (except business or employment income)	No
Less Aggregate of:	
— Employment Insurance premiums	No
— CPP/QPP and RPP contributions	No
— Eligible lump-sum transfers to RPP, RRSP, RRIF, DPSP, or annuity	No
— Periodic RPP or DPSP transfers to spousal RRSP	No
— Deductible contributions to RCA	No
— Refunds of salary, wages, and research grants	Yes
— current year net rental losses on real property	Yes
— current year losses from carrying on a business	Yes
— Deductible alimony and maintenance payments made	Yes
— Estate tax deducted with respect to inherited property	No

It should be noted that the first item in the above table (net income from an office or employment) is net of certain deductions, such as union dues and automobile expenses, which, therefore, act as a reduction in earned income for RRSP purposes.

¶410 New RRSP Contribution Room for the Year

The current system for determining RRSP contribution room came into effect for 1991. New RRSP contribution room is created each calendar year equal to the lesser of 18% of the previous calendar year's earned income and a dollar limit. The schedule of dollar limits is as follows (indexing of the limits is scheduled to take effect from 2011):

Year	RRSP Dollar Limit	Year	RRSP Dollar Limit
1991	$11,500	1995	$14,500
1992	$12,500	1996	$13,500
1993	$12,500	1997	$13,500
1994	$13,500	1998	$13,500

Year	RRSP Dollar Limit	Year	RRSP Dollar Limit
1999	$13,500	2006	$18,000
2000	$13,500	2007	$19,000
2001	$13,500	2008	$20,000
2002	$13,500	2009	$21,000
2003	$14,500	2010	$22,000
2004	$15,500	2011*	$22,450
2005	$16,500		

For individuals who accrue a benefit under an RPP or DPSP, the above limit is reduced by the PA in respect of the previous calendar year. Therefore, the amount of new RRSP contribution room created in 2010 equals 18% of the 2009 earned income, or $22,000 if less, minus the 2010 PA. The 2009 PA represents the deemed value of the benefits that accrued under a defined benefit pension plan or the sum of all contributions received under a defined contribution pension plan or a DPSP during 2009. The detailed rules for determining PAs are set out in Chapters 5 to 9.

Although an RRSP must mature by the end of the calendar year in which an individual attains age 71, new RRSP contribution room continues to be created after age 71 if the individual has earned income, following the same rules as for younger taxpayers. Any RRSP contribution room after age 71 may be used for three purposes:

- To make a contribution to a spousal RRSP if the spouse has not yet reached age 71, or has turned 71 in the year, as discussed at ¶425;
- To deduct from taxable income any previously undeducted RRSP contributions made by the individual, as discussed at ¶420 and ¶435; and
- To cover a PSPA that arises under a defined benefit pension plan due to a pensioner's former employer granting a pension increase that exceeds the rate of inflation.

* 2011 is the first year in which the limits increase in the average wage.

¶415 RRSP Contribution Limit and Carry-forward

The concept of RRSP contribution room was discussed at ¶325. New RRSP contribution room is created each year, as discussed at ¶410. This amount then has to be adjusted by any PSPAs and PARs, as well as any contribution room carried forward from an earlier year.

The RRSP contribution room available at any point in time is determined as follows:

(a) unused RRSP contribution room that has been carried forward from earlier calendar years; plus

(b) new RRSP contribution room for the calendar year, equal to 18% of earned income in the previous calendar year (or the dollar limit for the current calendar year, if less) minus the total of all PAs reported for the previous calendar year, as well as any prescribed amount in connection with participation in a foreign pension plan, as outlined at ¶555, under a government-sponsored retirement arrangement (GSRA) as outlined at ¶550, and any PA arising from participation in a specified retirement arrangement, as outlined at ¶545; (if the calculation causes the new contribution room for the year to be negative, the new contribution room equals zero); plus

(c) any PAR reported during the current year (refer to Chapter 11 for details regarding PARs); less

(d) any PSPA that has become effective during the current year. The amount by which RRSP contribution room is reduced is net of any qualifying interplan transfers that are applied towards the cost of those additional past service benefits (these transfers are netted against the PSPA when the PSPA is calculated), and also net of any RRSP withdrawals that are required in order to cover the PSPA resulting from certain past service improvements. (The rules regarding the date when a PSPA becomes effective during the year, and the impact of qualifying transfers and RRSP withdrawals on the PSPA, are discussed in detail in Chapter 10); less

(e) any contributions made to a provincial pension plan established for a province's residents. (The *Saskatchewan Pension Plan* continues to be the only provincial plan in this category); less

(f) for "connected persons" who joined an RPP or recommenced accruing benefits under an RPP in the current calendar year, and who did not have a positive 1990 PA, an amount equal to (b) above (i.e., the new RRSP contribution room for the year, less any PA offset), subject to a maximum of $11,500 (or 18% of 1990 earned income, if less). The CRA becomes aware of this situation when the employer completes Form T1007(E), the Connected Person Information Return. Note that for all years after the year of joining the plan, these individuals' RRSP contribution room is reduced by PAs in the usual way.

The existence of RRSP contribution room serves three purposes:

- It allows an individual to make a new contribution to his or her own RRSP, or to a spousal RRSP, and to deduct this amount from taxable income;
- It allows an individual to take a new deduction in respect of an RRSP contribution made in a previous calendar year that has not previously been deducted from taxable income (see ¶420 for further details); and
- It allows a defined benefit pension plan sponsor to make improvements for a prior year (after 1989), which generates a PSPA.

If an RRSP contribution is made by an individual, the effective date on which it reduces the individual's RRSP contribution room is the date on which the CRA first receives notice that the tax deduction is being taken.

Having determined the individual's RRSP contribution room at the end of the year, this is then reduced by any RRSP contributions for which a tax deduction is being taken. Where an RRSP contribution was made in an earlier year (post-1990), but not deducted in that earlier year, RRSP contribution room may also be utilized to deduct that contribution from taxable income. The balance of RRSP contribution room may then be carried forward to be utilized in a future calendar year.

Normally, the amount of RRSP contribution room carried forward into a subsequent year is greater than zero (or zero, if maximum RRSP contributions are being made). However, it is possible for RRSP contribution room to be negative. This can occur if an improvement in past service benefits under a defined benefit pension plan has resulted in a PSPA that was greater than the available RRSP contribution room in the year in which the past service improvement took place (see Chapter 10). In these circumstances, the amount of RRSP contribution room that is carried forward would be negative, and this would gradually increase to a positive amount as new RRSP contribution room is created in subsequent years. Only when RRSP contribution room is, again, greater than zero, may the individual make a tax-deductible RRSP contribution.

¶420 RRSP Tax Deduction and Carry-forward

In addition to the carry-forward of unused RRSP contribution room (discussed at ¶415), the retirement savings system permits the carry-forward of RRSP tax deductions. The taxpayer could, for example, make an RRSP contribution in 2009, but then not report the tax deduction on the 2009 tax return. Therefore, the individual's RRSP contribution room carried forward into 2010 remains intact. In some future year, the individual can utilize any available RRSP contribution room to take the tax deduction in respect of that 2009 contribution.

This feature is beneficial to individuals who have low taxable income in a particular year but who have RRSP contribution room and have enough cash with which to make an RRSP contribution. If the individual believes that he or she will have higher taxable income in a future year, and will therefore be subject to a higher marginal tax rate, it may be worthwhile for the individual to delay taking the tax deduction. Rather than waiting to make the RRSP contribution until that future year, the individual may wish to make the RRSP contribution in the year of low taxable income in order to tax shelter the investment income under the RRSP for a longer period.

For example, an individual who left Canada for a temporary period of time could make an RRSP contribution in the first year outside Canada based on the previous year's Canadian earned income, but delay the tax deduction until a later year when the individual returns to work in Canada.

There are two potential disadvantages to this strategy:

- There is no guarantee that the individual's taxable income will be higher in a future year. For example, the individual's income may decrease significantly due to disability or unemployment (although if such a significant drop in income occurs, the individual could reopen his or her last tax return in respect of an earlier year where there was higher income and claim the tax deduction there).
- If a PSPA arises before the individual has taken the tax deduction, the PSPA may utilize all of the RRSP contribution room available at the time of the past service improvement. Therefore, there may be no RRSP contribution room available to utilize as a tax deduction for any undeducted RRSP contributions made in earlier years.

Although age 71 is a limiting age for the purpose of making an RRSP contribution under one's own RRSP, it is not a limiting age for the purpose of taking a tax deduction for an RRSP contribution made in a previous year. Such tax deductions may be carried forward beyond age 71.

If the tax deduction has not been taken by the time the individual dies, the tax deduction may be taken in the tax return for the final "tax year" (the year starting on January 1 of the year of death and ending at the date of death).

This feature does not necessarily give an individual the opportunity to contribute large amounts to an RRSP in the hope that the corresponding tax deductions eventually may be taken — an excess RRSP contribution may lead to a penalty tax, as discussed at ¶ 435.

¶ 425 Spousal RRSP Contributions

Instead of contributing to one's own RRSP, one may choose to contribute to a spousal RRSP. The RRSP contribution is based on the contributing individual's earned income in the previous calendar year and is deductible from the contributor's taxable income in the calendar year in which the contribution is made (or in the previous calendar year if made within the first 60 days of the year). Alternatively, this tax deduction may be carried forward to a future year, as described at ¶ 420. The contribution uses up part or all of the contributor's RRSP contribution room at the time that it is deducted from the contributor's taxable income.

The advantage of a spousal RRSP contribution is that, although the contributor deducts the contribution from his or her taxable income, the benefits payable from the spousal RRSP are included in the spouse's taxable income, provided the funds remain in the spousal RRSP for at least two calendar years (see Special Attribution Rule at ¶ 430). Thus, this is a useful income-splitting technique if the spouse's marginal tax rate is likely to be lower than the contributor's.

Once a contribution has been made to a spousal RRSP, the monies belong to the spouse, not the contributor. If a PSPA arises in a subsequent year and the individual is given the opportunity to deregister RRSP assets to cover the PSPA (see ¶ 1065 for details), the assets of a spousal RRSP cannot be used for this purpose.

For purposes of a spousal RRSP, the definition of "spouse" includes certain common-law relationships as well as same-sex partners living in a common-law relationship.

Because an RRSP must mature by age 71, individuals may not contribute to an RRSP in their own name beyond the end of the calendar year in which they reach age 71. However, if an individual has unused RRSP contribution room available and has a younger spouse, the unused RRSP contribution room may be utilized as a contribution to a spousal RRSP until the end of the year in which the spouse attains age 71 regardless of the contributor's age.

¶430 Special Attribution Rule

As mentioned at ¶425, a contribution to a spousal RRSP is advantageous, provided the funds remain in the spousal RRSP for a certain number of years. However, if the spousal RRSP is deregistered soon after the contribution has been made, a special attribution rule applies. Under this rule, if the spousal RRSP is deregistered prior to a specified date, the resulting refund is included in the contributor's taxable income, not the spouse's, even if the tax deduction corresponding to that contribution has not yet been taken because it has been carried forward to a later year (see ¶420). This specified date is the January 1 following the two calendar years after the end of the calendar year in which the contribution was made.

For example, a contribution made to a spousal RRSP in February 2008 would be subject to the attribution rule if it is withdrawn on or before December 31, 2010 (even if that contribution was made in respect of 2007). In fact, even if this contribution were withdrawn after 2010, it could possibly still be subject to the attribution rule if a further spousal RRSP contribution had been made in 2009 or 2010 — the attribution rule continues to apply to that 2008 contribution until all later contributions are no longer subject to the rule. In other words, there is a "last-in/first-out" approach in determining whether the attribution rule applies.

To minimize the chance of the attribution rule applying, it is important for the spousal RRSP contributions to be segregated from any RRSP assets that result from the spouse's own contributions. Consider an individual whose contributions to his or her spouse's RRSP were not segregated from the spouse's own RRSP contributions. If the spouse chooses to deregister some RRSP assets while spousal contributions to the RRSP are still subject to the attribution rule, these deregistered assets will be included in the contributor's taxable income. The CRA will assume that the assets that have been deregistered are the spousal RRSP assets, not the monies contributed directly by the spouse to his or her own RRSP.

Exceptions to the attribution rule are permitted if, at the time of payment or deemed receipt:

- the spouses are living separate and apart by reason of a marriage breakdown;
- the contributor or his or her spouse is a non-resident of Canada for tax purposes;
- the contributor is deceased or dies within the calendar year;
- the spouse transfers the monies directly to purchase an annuity that cannot be commuted for at least three years;

- the spouse transfers the monies to a RRIF and does not withdraw more than the minimum amount; or
- the spouse transfers the monies directly to an RPP and does not commute any of the monies within the three-year attribution period.

¶435 Excess RRSP Contributions

For excess contributions made to an RRSP the penalty tax in respect of a particular month equals 1% of the "cumulative excess amount" determined as at the end of that month. The cumulative excess amount is defined as:

(i) the amount of any undeducted RRSP contributions, including any RRSP contributions made during the year (because these have not yet been shown as a tax deduction in the individual's tax return for the year), reduced by any amounts received out of an RRSP or RRIF that are included in taxable income; less

(ii) the available RRSP contribution room, if any; less

(iii) a penalty-tax-free lifetime allowance of $2,000, which is applicable unless the individual is under the age of 18 at any time during the calendar year (this stipulation is intended to discourage non-deductible contributions being made to RRSPs of the taxpayer's children).

The $2,000 lifetime margin reduces the likelihood of the penalty tax being applied where earnings fluctuate and RRSP contributions are made on the basis of a fixed percentage of current earnings (as is often the case with contributions to a group RRSP). However, there is still a chance that an excess contribution will be made to an RRSP and will not be covered by the $2,000 lifetime margin. If such an excess contribution is made due to reasonable error, and if reasonable steps are taken to remove the excess contribution, one may apply to the Minister of National Revenue to waive the penalty tax.

If an RRSP contribution is made in excess of the deductible limit, the taxpayer may wish to remove the excess from the RRSP by deregistering it, because the individual wishes either to limit RRSP contributions to amounts that are tax-deductible or to minimize the penalty tax. This refund is included in the taxpayer's taxable income in the year withdrawn. However, provided the refund occurs within a specified period and is not being used to certify a non-exempt PSPA (see ¶1065), an offsetting tax deduction is available unless it is shown that:

- the taxpayer did not reasonably expect to be able to deduct the corresponding contributions in the calendar year in which the contributions were made (or in the preceding calendar year if the contributions were made in the first 60 days of the calendar year); and
- the taxpayer made all or part of the corresponding contribution with the intent of subsequently withdrawing it.

The specified period (previously mentioned) for withdrawing an RRSP contribution that was made in error is the year of the contribution or the following year; the year in which the contributor receives the CRA's notice of assessment (typically the year after the contribution was made); or the year following receipt of the assessment. This effectively gives a three-year window in which to remove the inadvertently made excess without incurring double taxation.

It should be noted that the RRSP carrier is required to withhold tax on any amounts withdrawn from an RRSP, even if those amounts represent RRSP contributions that had inadvertently been made in excess of the deductible limits, unless a properly completed and approved Form T3012A has been provided to the RRSP carrier.

If an individual chooses to utilize the $2,000 penalty tax-free lifetime allowance deliberately, any amount withdrawn from his or her RRSP corresponding to this excess contribution will be taxable with no offsetting tax deduction, even though the excess contribution was not tax deductible. Although this represents double taxation, this may be a useful strategy if the excess contributions remain in the RRSP for many years. This is because the investment income on those excess contributions remains tax sheltered — provided the 1% penalty tax is not invoked. The tax sheltering of that investment income may more than offset the effect of the double taxation, due to compounding of tax-sheltered investment income over a period of many years. The period during which the excess contribution must remain in the RRSP to make this a viable strategy depends on the RRSP's investment return and the individual's marginal tax rate at the time of the overcontribution and at the time of the subsequent withdrawal. The break-even period can vary considerably (from a few years to over 30 years).

On the other hand, even though it may not be possible to deduct the excess contribution from taxable income at the time it is made, the taxpayer may be able to arrange to deduct it from taxable income in some future year, when sufficient new RRSP contribution room has been created, by fully or partially suspending future RRSP contributions. In the same way, if an excess contribution has been made, and it has not been possible to deduct it from taxable income prior to the end of the year of attaining age 71, the undeducted excess may still be able to be deducted from taxable income after age 71, if new RRSP contribution room is created after age 71. (For example, the individual may have employment or rental income, or may be receiving alimony payments, which are all sources of earned income for RRSP purposes.)

It should be noted that the $2,000 penalty-tax-free lifetime allowance is eroded by any subsequent PSPAs, to the extent that those PSPAs create negative RRSP contribution room. Thus, when RRSP contribution room becomes negative, not only may no new RRSP contributions be made on a tax-deductible basis, but in addition, the $2,000 penalty-tax-free lifetime allowance is reduced by an amount equal to the negative RRSP contribution room. This could have the effect of applying the 1% per month penalty tax earlier than would have been the case if the PSPA had not arisen.

As a final note, the introduction of the TFSA on January 1, 2009, eliminates the need to make a $2,000 excess contribution as a deliberate investment strategy in order to access the tax sheltering. The TFSA permits contributions to be made from after tax income, the income is tax sheltered and no tax is deducted when the contributions are removed.

¶440 Deregistered RRSP Assets

There is only one circumstance in which funds that are withdrawn from an RRSP (i.e., deregistering an RRSP) help to create additional RRSP contribution room. This circumstance is where a non-exempt PSPA has arisen and the individual is given the opportunity of deregistering RRSP assets in order to provide additional RRSP contribution room to cover the PSPA (see ¶ 1065 for further details). In no other circumstance does the withdrawal of funds from an RRSP create extra RRSP contribution room.

¶445 Transfer of Retiring Allowance to RRSP or RPP

A retiring allowance is broadly defined under the *Income Tax Act* (Canada) as a payment in respect of a loss of office or employment or a payment upon or after retirement in recognition of long service. Payments by an employer that qualify as a retiring allowance will continue to be eligible to be transferred to the individual's RRSP (not to a spousal RRSP) or to an RPP, without eroding the individual's RRSP contribution room, up to a certain limit. The limit effective for retiring allowances paid in a calendar year equals:

- $2,000 multiplied by the number of calendar years prior to 1996 that the individual was employed with that employer (or a related employer); plus

- $1,500 multiplied by the number of calendar years (up to and including 1988) in respect of which no employer contributions to a pension plan (whether registered or not) or DPSP have vested in the individual at the time that the retiring allowance is paid.

Note that if there are any pre-1989 years in which the employee bought back and paid both the employee and employer share of the buy-back, such years are considered to be years in which the employer made contributions for the purposes of determining whether the addition $1,500 applies to such years.

Since years of service after 1995 no longer count in determining the rollover amounts, the rollover of retiring allowances will gradually be phased out, as future departing employees will have increasingly fewer years of employment before 1996.

Suppose the individual had been credited with extra years of pre-1996 service in respect of employment with a prior employer (typically, where the current and prior employers had a reciprocal agreement to allow credits of past service when an employee moves from one employer to the other). In this case, those extra years may be counted for both the $2,000 and the $1,500 rollover provisions, to the extent that those years of service were not already counted for the purpose of a transfer of a retiring allowance that the individual may have received when he or she left the prior employer.

In calculating the individual's calendar years of employment with the employer, a partial calendar year is counted as a full year for the purpose of determining the eligible amount for rollover.

Consider an individual who was hired in October 1985 and joined the employer's pension plan in November 1987. Service is credited under the pension plan from November 1987. The individual terminated service in October 2009, having belonged to the pension plan continuously up to that date, and was fully vested under the plan's provisions. The total amount of any retiring allowance that may be transferred to the individual's RRSP or to an RPP is determined as follows:

2 × $1,500	= $ 3,000	(for 1985 and 1986)
11 × $2,000	= $22,000	(for 1985 to 1995, inclusive)
	= $ 0	(for 1996 to 2009, inclusive)
	$25,000	

In this example, there were 11 calendar years prior to 1996 (1985 through 1995) counting towards the $2,000 rollover per year of service, and two calendar years (1985 and 1986) in respect of which the individual did not accrue any vested pension entitlement and which count towards the $1,500 rollover per year of service. The year 1987 does not count towards the $1,500 rollover provision, because the individual accrued vested benefits under the pension plan in the last two months of that year. The years 1996 through 2009 do not count towards any rollover amount.

The transfer of a retiring allowance into an RRSP or RPP may be direct, meaning that the transfer goes directly from the employer to the individual's RRSP, or indirect, meaning that the individual first receives the payment and then deposits it into the RRSP. Tax will be withheld if the transfer is indirect, but this tax will be later refunded when the individual files a tax return for the calendar year, identifying the eligible amount of tax-free rollover.

If an employer pays an individual an amount that qualifies as a retiring allowance, and the amount exceeds the maximum that may be transferred to an RRSP or RPP, the balance will be reported as severance pay. As a result, the excess amount would qualify as earned income for the purpose of a regular RRSP contribution, which would not be the case for the amount reported as a retiring allowance.

When a transfer of a retiring allowance takes place, it is usually made to an RRSP. However, as mentioned, it is also possible for the transfer to be made to an RPP. Some employees may feel that there is an advantage to this alternative, in that it may be perceived that the employer is able to earn a higher investment return within the RPP than the employee would be able to achieve within his or her own RRSP. However, few employers permit a transfer into the employer's RPP.

¶450 Adjustment to RRSP Contribution Room Upon Marriage Breakdown

Where pension credits are split upon a marriage breakdown, there is no restoration of RRSP contribution room to the party giving up the RRSP payment and, similarly, no penalty to the party receiving such RRSP payment.

¶455 RRSP Contribution Following Death

An individual's final "tax year" is the year starting on January 1 of the year of death and ending at the date of death. On behalf of the deceased, the executor is permitted to make a contribution from the individual's estate to his or her RRSP or to a spousal RRSP, the objectives being to enable a final tax deduction to offset the deceased's taxable income in the year of death and to enable the surviving spouse to tax shelter the RRSP contribution and any resulting investment income.

The first objective — creating a tax deduction in respect of the RRSP contribution — may only be achieved if the individual has sufficient RRSP contribution room to cover the deduction. This means that the executor must determine the amount of RRSP contribution room that is available at the date of death. The deadline for making a contribution for a deceased individual is 60 days after the calendar year of death. The executor should consider several points:

- Even if death occurs early in the year, there may still be a significant amount of new RRSP contribution room created for the year of death, based on the deceased's earned income in the previous year. However, if the deceased was a "connected person" and had joined an RPP earlier in the year of death, there would be no new RRSP contribution room for the year, as noted at ¶415.
- RRSP contribution room is not simply the amount of new contribution room created in the year of death. It also includes RRSP contribution room carried forward from previous years that has not yet been used.
- The individual may have made an RRSP contribution in an earlier year but delayed the corresponding tax deduction, as discussed at ¶420.
- The CRA will be able to inform the executor how much RRSP contribution room the deceased had, but this amount will only be as up-to-date as the information that the CRA had received at that time. For example, if death occurs before the CRA has received the deceased's tax return in respect of the tax year prior to the year of death, it will not yet be aware of any RRSP deductions being taken for that year. In addition, the deceased's new RRSP contribution room for the year of death is net of any PA for the previous year. But if death occurs very early in the year, that PA will only be reported when the deceased's employer issues the T4 slip for the previous year (this is usually done near the end of February). As another example, the executor should check with the deceased's employer whether a PSPA has recently been reported to the CRA, or is expected to be reported shortly. Since responsibility for reporting a PSPA rests with the pension plan administrator rather than the employer, and since the administrator of some pension plans (such as multi-employer plans) is not the same entity as the deceased's employer, the executor will have to determine whether it is necessary to approach the plan administrator to obtain any information on PSPAs that may have arisen.
- If the deceased has a significant amount of RRSP contribution room available at the date of death, and the executor believes that there is insufficient cash available to fully utilize that contribution room, there may still be life insurance proceeds forthcoming and it may be possible to obtain or borrow funds in advance of those proceeds being received which could be contributed to the deceased's RRSP.

Chapter 5

¶500 INTRODUCTION TO PENSION ADJUSTMENTS AND GENERAL PA RULES

¶505 Introduction

For readers who are not familiar with pension plan terminology or with how PAs fit in with the overall retirement savings system, Chapters 2 and 3 should be read before reading Chapters 5 to 9.

It should be noted that the detailed PA rules in Chapters 6 to 9 concentrate on the PA rules as they currently apply. Any special PA transition or historical rules that applied in earlier years are described in Appendix 1.

The PA is the deemed value that, for tax purposes, is placed on the benefit accruing under an RPP or DPSP in a particular calendar year. The more generous the RPP or DPSP, the larger the PA.

With defined contribution pension plans and DPSPs, the PA is the sum of the actual contributions made to the plan in a particular calendar year and is therefore a realistic representation of the value of plan participation to the individual. However, with defined benefit pension plans, the PA bears little relation to the true value of the benefits being earned under the plan during the year. This inequity is especially true for individuals who leave a defined benefit pension plan before retirement. In an attempt to alleviate this inequity, PARs form a part of the retirement savings system. PARs restore an individual's RRSP room that would otherwise be permanently lost upon termination, if termination benefits fall below the aggregate of the PAs reported while the individual was a plan member. Chapter 11 covers PARs in greater detail.

A PA must be reported for members of an RPP or DPSP who accrue benefits in a year, even if the member has not yet vested in the employer contributions or the benefits earned. There is no exemption for RPPs where the employer contributions are being funded out of surplus. Where an employer sponsors a group RRSP for its employees, no PA is reported for any employer or employee contributions made to the group RRSP.

¶510 Use of a Pension Adjustment

The PA for a particular year is used by the CRA for three major purposes:

1. To determine the amount of RRSP contribution room available in the following calendar year.

2. To limit the maximum permissible contributions and benefits under an RPP or DPSP, or a combination of RPP provisions and/or DPSP provisions. The PA in respect of the benefits accruing and the contributions being made under a hybrid arrangement during a year, may not exceed the maximum contribution that could be made to a defined contribution pension plan — this is known as the "maximum PA rule". This maximum is the lesser of 18% of that year's compensation (as defined in Chapter 2) and a dollar limit. The current schedule of dollar limits is as follows (indexing of the limits commenced to take effect in 2010):

Year	**Maximum RPP Money Purchase Contribution**	**Maximum DPSP Contribution**
2007	$20,000	$10,000
2008	$21,000	$10,500
2009	$22,000	$11,000
2010	$22,450	$11,225
2011	Indexed in accordance with increases in the average wage	

A complete schedule of RRSP contributions for earlier years appears in Appendix 3.

Note that since plan members may not contribute to a DPSP, there is a limit to the amount that the employer may contribute to a DPSP alone — namely, half of the dollar limits for defined contribution pension plans.

Employee required contributions to a defined benefit pension plan and employee optional ancillary contributions made to flexible pension plans to purchase ancillary benefits do not form part of the PA. However, an employee's additional voluntary contributions to a defined benefit pension plan or employee required contributions to the defined contribution portion of a hybrid plan do form part of the PA. Refer to Chapter 8 for additional information on calculating PAs for hybrid plans. Refer to ¶ 120 for a discussion regarding flexible pension plans.

It should be noted that where the PA for an individual is less than what would be permitted under the maximum PA rule, the difference may not be carried forward to be used as additional plan contribution room in a subsequent year. The only carry-forward permitted is the carry-forward of RRSP contribution room. If an individual's PA is lower than the maximum permitted for the year, this will generally lead to some new RRSP contribution room being created in the following year, which could then be carried forward.

3. To determine the maximum employee current service contribution to a defined benefit provision. These contributions are limited each year to the lesser of 9% of compensation and a limit based on the PA for the year under that defined benefit provision (discussed in more detail at ¶ 1805) — the higher the PA, the higher the limit on employee contributions. If the PA is zero in the year (for example, if the employee has reached a maximum service limit under the plan), the formula for determining the limit on employee current service contributions leads to a limit of $1,000 for the year.

¶515 PA Reporting

In almost all cases, the PA for a particular year is reported on the T4 slip for that year (in Appendix 2 for the T4 Slip, Box 52). That T4 slip must be provided to the employee by the end of February of the following year, and a copy is sent by the employer to the CRA within the same deadline.

The registration number of the RPP or DPSP to which an employee belongs in the year must also be inserted in Box 50 on the employee's T4 slip. If contributions on behalf of an employee are made to more than one plan sponsored by the same employer, the registration numbers of all the plans must appear in Box 50.

If an employee participates in an RPP or DPSP but no PA is reportable (see ¶530 for circumstances where this may occur) or if the PA is calculated as zero, Box 52 should be left blank.

If a member of an RPP or DPSP terminates service during a particular year, having earned a benefit entitlement in respect of that partial year, a PA must be determined for that year and reported on the individual's final T4 slip by the end of February of the following year.

No PA is reported for a person who died during the year.

Where an employer splits its T4 slips by province of employment, and a particular employee worked for that employer in more than one province in a particular year, the CRA prefers that the individual's PA for that year be split, province by province, on the T4 slips, with a partial PA appearing on each T4 slip for the individual. We understand that if the employer chooses not to prorate in this manner, it is permissible for the employer to instead report the full year's PA on one of the T4 slips.

If a T4 slip would not otherwise be required (for example, if the individual works abroad or is disabled for the whole year and accrues a pension under an RPP), the CRA will permit an employer to use a T4A slip for reporting the PA, rather than a T4 slip (see Appendix 2 for the T4A slip). However, this is not the case in certain multi-employer plan situations (as discussed at ¶915).

Generally, it is the employer's responsibility to report PAs. Therefore, even if several employers participate in one pension plan, and there is a common plan administrator who generally performs all pension administration tasks on behalf of the employers, it is still the responsibility of each employer to report the PA. These employers and the plan administrator must co-ordinate their PA reporting. There are only two exceptions where the administrator is given responsibility for PA reporting (see ¶910 and ¶915 for more details):

- in the case of a multi-employer defined benefit plan in respect of individuals who are experiencing a period of reduced pay or temporary absence or disability, but only if the plan administrator has applied to the CRA to take responsibility for this reporting; and

- in the case of a "specified multi-employer plan" in respect of members who make contributions directly to the administrator.

In some cases the employer or employee contributes to an RPP indirectly through a union or employer association. There are two special rules in this situation:

- if the employer's contributions to the union or association include contributions for another purpose (such as benefit plans), the union or association is required to notify the employer or plan administrator of the amount of the contribution that has been contributed to the RPP, no later than January 31 of the year following the year in which the employer or employee made the contribution; and

- the PA rule for defined contribution plans, whereby employer contributions that are made and allocated in respect of a particular year by the end of February of the following year are included in the particular year's PA (as set out at ¶610), is modified so that such contributions form part of the following year's PA.

If an employee belongs to two or more RPPs or DPSPs of a particular employer during a year, either simultaneously or consecutively, these PAs (actually known as pension credits in this case, as discussed at ¶520) must be totalled and reported as a single PA on one T4 slip. This may not be practical for an employer with multiple payrolls, in which case it is permitted to split the PA between two or more T4 slips; however, the total of such PAs for the individual must equal the PA that would apply if it were reported on only one T4 slip.

Special prorating rules apply in the situation where an employee is employed by two or more employers who participate in the same RPP (for example, if an employee moves from one subsidiary of an employer to another during the year) — see ¶920 for details.

Where a member of an RPP changes employment in a year and joins the new employer's RPP in that year, the PA that the new employer reports in respect of service in the second part of the year is determined independently of the PA that the previous employer reports in respect of service in the first part of the year. In this situation, the sum of the PAs may exceed the PA limit without penalty, nor does the individual have to reduce his RRSP contribution room to accept the higher pension benefit. However, there is one exception. As noted at ¶795, if the change in employment is the result of a sale of a company or division, and the new employer's RPP provides benefits that are identical to those under the previous employer's RPP, the new employer may co-ordinate that year's PA reporting with the PAs reported by the previous employer for that year, subject to obtaining CRA approval. The advantages and disadvantages of following this co-ordinated PA approach are discussed at ¶795.

In addition to PA reporting each February, the plan administrator must file an annual information return. Historically, this was a separate form filed with the CRA; however, all jurisdictions have now harmonized this annual filing with the minimum standards annual information return, and the plan sponsor now files just one return with the minimum standards jurisdiction, within the time frames required by that jurisdiction's filing requirements. The minimum standards jurisdiction forwards information collected from the return to the CRA. The type of information collected by the CRA includes certain details on whether the plan was terminated during the year, the actuarial liabilities, plan membership, the number of connected persons, and whether past service benefits that would give rise to PSPAs have been provided to members.

¶520 Pension Credit

A "pension credit" is an important feature of the PA rules. Where a retirement savings arrangement is a combination of a number of defined benefit, defined contribution, and/or DPSP provisions, a pension credit is determined in respect of each such provision using the usual PA rules that would apply if that provision were the only provision under which the member is accruing benefits for the year. For example, an individual who belongs to a defined benefit pension plan may be making additional voluntary contributions on a money purchase basis; an employee may belong to an RPP which provides the sum of a defined benefit provision and a defined contribution provision; or an individual may belong to both an RPP and a DPSP. In such cases, the PA reported on the T4 slip for the individual is the total of the pension credits in respect of each such provision.

Since the term "PA" is more widely used than "pension credit", we have generally used "PA" in Chapters 6, 7, and 9, even though technically we are calculating pension credits. However, we use the correct terminology in Chapter 8 (Hybrid Plans), Chapter 10 (PSPAs), and Chapter 12 (PSPAs and PARS for Multi-Employer Plans), since pension credits are particularly relevant in these situations.

¶525 Rounding

Pension credits and PAs are rounded to the nearest dollar. If a pension credit or PA equals a number of dollars plus 50 cents (or as the Regulations words it, if it is equidistant from two consecutive multiples of one dollar), it should be rounded to the next higher dollar.

¶530 Circumstances Where No Pension Credit Arises

There are a number of circumstances where one might erroneously believe that a pension credit has arisen and, therefore, a PA should be reported. Some of these circumstances are set out below:

- No PA is reported in respect of the year in which an individual dies. Of course, if an individual moves from one employer to another during a year and dies later that year, the first employer will still probably report a PA since that employer is unlikely to know that the individual has died. In this situation, the CRA will ignore the PA, because RRSP contribution room in the year after death is irrelevant.
- If a member of a defined benefit plan has reached a maximum credited service limit that exists under the plan, and is no longer accruing any benefits under the plan, no PA arises for calendar years after the year in which the maximum service limit is reached, even if the employee is still required to contribute to the plan.
- If a member of a defined benefit pension plan postpones retirement beyond the normal retirement age, and the pension plan provides for the member's pension to be actuarially increased in recognition of the delayed retirement (with no further accruals of pensionable service), no PA arises.
- An amount transferred to an RPP directly from another RPP, an RRSP, or DPSP, or the portion of a retiring allowance that is within the tax-free rollover (described at ¶445), that is transferred to an RPP, is not included when determining the PA.

¶535 PA Upon Re-Employment After Downsizing

As discussed at ¶1780, certain additional pension benefits may be provided when an employer initiates an "approved downsizing program". However, the provision of these additional benefits is restricted when an individual, who terminated service under the program, is later re-employed by the employer. Basically, no additional service may accrue until the individual has sufficient service such that the total pension to which the individual would have been entitled, had the additional downsizing benefits not been provided (i.e., based on the plan's usual pension formula and based on all service with the employer), has increased to a level equal to the enhanced pension that was provided as a result of the downsizing program, ignoring the period after re-employment. Further, no PA will be determined in respect of the re-employed individual until the additional service results in an increased pension.

¶540 First Year PA for a Connected Person

A connected person is someone who:

- directly or indirectly owns 10% or more of the issued shares of any class of the capital stock of the employer or any related corporation;
- does not deal at arm's length with the employer; or
- is a specified shareholder of the employer.

Also, a person may be a connected person if shares of the employer or a corporation related to the employer are owned by:

- someone related to the person;
- a trust of which the person is a beneficiary; or
- a partnership of which the person is a member.

If an individual who is, or was at any time after 1989, a connected person, and such individual joins an RPP (or starts to accrue benefits under an RPP following a period in which no benefits accrued), then the individual's RRSP room for the year in which the individual joins the plan is reduced by a prescribed amount.

The prescribed amount will be equal to one of the following amounts, whichever is less:

- 18% of the connected person's 1990 earned income for RRSP purposes; and
- $11,500.

Further, when such connected person joins an RPP, the employer must file Form T1007(E), Connected Person Information Return, within 60 days of the date that the individual joins the plan. Similarly, the employer has to file Form T1007(E) within 60 days of the date that such an individual starts to accrue benefits under the plan following a period in which no benefits accrued.

For all years after the year of joining the plan, the PA for the connected person is determined in the usual way.

¶545 PA for a Specified Retirement Arrangement (SRA)

An "SRA" is an arrangement whereby an employee has a right to benefits that are receivable after retirement or termination of service, and at least a portion of the benefits are amounts that may be received after reaching age 71 (or, if later, more than five years after retirement or termination). The arrangement must be an RCA or it must be such that it would fall within the definition of an RCA if the employer were contributing towards it (thus, RPPs and salary deferral arrangements are excluded). However, if the arrangement is an RCA that is funded substantially in the same manner as if it were an RPP subject to minimum standards legislation, it is also excluded.

Where, at the end of a year, an individual is employed by, or holds office with, a tax-exempt employer, and has a right to benefits earned under an SRA for the year, a special PA is to be reported.

Further, if an individual belongs to an SRA, but also has a PA from another plan that he or she belongs to (whether an RPP, DPSP, or foreign pension plan), the special PA reported is the difference between the calculations set out below and the actual PA reported from the other plan.

For years after 2003, the following amount is first determined:

the lesser of:

- 18% of the individual's compensation from that employer less the PA offset; or

- money purchase limit for the year less the PA offset.

If the PAs reported with respect to other plans is less than 85% of this calculated amount, then the SRA PA is equal to this amount less the actual PA reported under the other plan(s). If, for example, the SRA is supplemental to an RPP that provides benefits at, or close to, the maximum permissible level, the PA is not increased at all to reflect the SRA.

If, the PA is greater than zero in respect of the SRA, the PA that the employer will then report on the individual's T4 slip will be the total of the special PA for the SRA and any other PA relating to the individual's membership in an RPP or DPSP of that employer.

If the employer prefers to calculate the special PA for the SRA in a manner that is more consistent with the PA rules applicable to RPPs, the employer may apply to the Minister of National Revenue for permission to do so.

There were adjustments to this methodology for years prior to 2003. Refer to Appendix 1, section 3C for further details.

PSPAs can also arise if past service benefits under an SRA are improved. As with PAs, alternative methods of calculation may be used, subject to the approval of the Minister of National Revenue.

¶550 Prescribed Amounts for a GSRA

A further reduction is prescribed for a GSRA, which is an unregistered arrangement for paying retirement income from public funds established to benefit individuals who provide professional services that are paid for out of public funds (federal or provincial). GSRAs have amounts prescribed by the Regulations that reduce the amounts an individual can contribute to their RRSP. The prescribed amount for a GSRA is equal to the preceding year's money purchase limit.

¶555 Prescribed Amounts and PAs for Foreign Registered Pension Plans

There are two situations that can arise that restrict the ability of individuals who are considered Canadian residents for tax purposes to contribute to their RRSPs even if they do not belong to a Canadian RPP or DPSP.

If the Canadian resident provides services in Canada, or is primarily connected to a business that is carried on in Canada, but who belongs to a foreign pension plan, the individual's PA treatment will depend in part on whether contributions are made to the foreign plan, and whether the foreign plan is treated as an RCA for Canadian tax purposes. Further information on the calculation of the PA in this situation can be found at ¶646.

If the Canadian resident was primarily employed outside Canada by a foreign employer and continued to be entitled to a benefit under the foreign employer's pension plan, an amount is prescribed that reduces the amount of RRSP contribution room available. The prescribed amount is discussed further at ¶647.

¶560 Amending an Earlier PA

There are two main situations where a PA that was reported for a previous year is to be corrected:

- the employer realizes that an error was made when calculating the earlier year's PA, either in the methodology followed or in an employee's pension information (such as incorrect salary or service information); and
- an employee returns from a leave of absence within a certain time frame (as discussed at ¶635, ¶778, and ¶779).

An amended PA does not have to be reported if the difference between the previously reported PA and the amended PA is less than $50.

However, this administrative rule does not apply if an employee wants his or her PA to be accurately reported or the CRA requests that the amended PA be reported.

When an amended PA arises, a new T4 (or T4A) slip must be produced, showing the amended PA as well as repeating all other information that appeared on the original T4 slip. The T4 slip is to be marked "Amended". The amended T4 slips should be accompanied by a letter explaining that the amended T4 slip has been produced because of the need to report an amended PA, and explaining the circumstances that gave rise to the amended PA, including the taxation year to which the amended PA applies.

A different procedure must be followed where the amended PA is in respect of a tax year that is more than four years ago. For example, if, in 2010, the employer needs to report an amended PA in respect of the tax year 2005 or earlier, or if the amended PAs are in respect of a combination of years that are more than four years ago as well as more recent years, a different process is required. In these cases, the CRA requires that a spreadsheet be provided for each reporting employer, showing the employer name, address, RPP number and contact information, and, for each member for whom an amended PA is being reported, set out the following information (one line per member):

- plan member name;
- social Insurance Number;
- for each year in which an amended PA is being reported, the previously reported PA and the amended PA; and
- the total change in PA value (whether positive or negative) should be the final column in the spreadsheet.

All members for whom there is an overall positive change in PA value should be included together on one spreadsheet and all members for whom there is an overall negative change in PA value should be set out in a separate spreadsheet. Further, if any of the years where an amended PA is being reported are years in which the plan member was on a pensionable leave of absence, maternity leave, or disability leave where compensation is prescribed (as discussed further at ¶1625), or a period of foreign service, this should be indicated on the spreadsheet.

If there are some members for whom amended PAs are required only in respect of the most recent four tax years, they should not be included in this spreadsheet. These should be reported in the normal way, through amended T4 or T4A slips.

The completed spreadsheets should be sent to the following address:

CRA-IRPPD
ARAD, Pension & Partnership Projects Section
Attn: Pension Program Officer
875 Heron Rd., A-200
Ottawa, Ontario K1A 1A2

An amended PA can potentially impact the individual's previously filed tax returns. For example, suppose an individual made an RRSP contribution of $7,000 in 2008, representing the full amount of RRSP contribution room available that year, and deducted the entire contribution from his or her 2008 taxable income. Late in 2009 the employer discovers that the individual's 2007 PA was *understated* by $1,500. This means that the 2008 RRSP deduction exceeded the deductible limit by $1,500 and, therefore, insufficient tax was paid for 2008. The individual must file a T1 adjustment form with the CRA, together with payment of the additional tax on the $1,500 for 2008.

In addition, the individual may now be in a penalty tax situation with the RRSP if the excess $1,500 contribution cannot be covered by the $2,000 penalty tax-free allowance discussed at ¶435. The individual should use Form T1-OVP (Individual Tax Return for RRSP Overcontributions) for the appropriate tax year to determine the amount of tax owed. There are various tax relief provisions that can be used by the individual, including obtaining a waiver on tax on undeducted RRSP contributions that are withdrawn and taken into income (using Form T3012A) or requesting a waiver of tax on RRSP overcontributions by submitting a written letter to the local tax service office.

As another example, consider an individual who had made an excess RRSP contribution in 2009, in an amount that was not covered by the $2,000 penalty tax-free allowance (see ¶435). Therefore, the individual had paid a penalty tax on a portion of the excess contribution. Subsequently, the employer realizes that the 2008 PA was *overstated*. This means that the penalty tax paid by the individual in 2009 was overstated, since the amount of the excess contribution has now been reduced. The individual may now claim a tax refund using a T1 adjustment form.

Chapter 6

¶600 PENSION ADJUSTMENTS FOR DEFINED CONTRIBUTION RPPs AND DPSPs

¶605 Introduction

This chapter sets out the general PA rules specific to defined contribution pension plans, followed at ¶655 by the rules specific to DPSPs.

¶610 General PA Rules for Defined Contribution RPPs

The PA for a defined contribution RPP for a year equals the total of:

- all employer contributions made during the year, or made in respect of the year, by the end of February of the following year;
- all required or voluntary employee contributions made during the year, whether withheld from remuneration or contributed directly to the RPP by the employee;
- non-vested forfeitures that are reallocated (discussed in further detail at ¶620); and
- amounts of surplus that are allocated, where the surplus resulted from the conversion of a defined benefit RPP to a defined contribution RPP.

A question arises as to how to treat a contribution in respect of a previous fiscal year of an employer, if that fiscal year is not the calendar year. Consider a company that sponsors a profit sharing money purchase pension plan, and whose fiscal year end is October 31. The company makes its contribution to the plan in February 2010 in respect of the fiscal year ending October 31, 2009. Effectively, $\frac{1}{6}$ of that contribution is in respect of the last two months of 2008, and the remaining $\frac{5}{6}$ is in respect of the first 10 months of 2009. In this situation, however, the portion of the contribution that relates to the last two months of 2008 is to be included in the 2009 PA, rather than issuing a corrected PA for 2008. Therefore, the whole of the February 2010 contribution is included in the 2009 PA. A consistent approach would then be followed for subsequent years.

Where an employee contribution is withheld from remuneration in the last week of December 2009, for example, and is only paid into the pension fund in early January 2010, this contribution forms part of the 2009 PA if it is included with the 2009 employee contributions for tax reporting purposes on the 2009 T4 slip. However, where the employer instead includes these employee contributions on the 2010 T4 slip, these contributions should form part of the 2009 PA.

Similarly, if an employee's contribution is withheld from pay on, for example, January 6, 2010, and is based on compensation for the two weeks since the last payday, the portion of that contribution that relates to compensation in December 2009 should be included in the 2010 PA, if it is reported for other purposes on the 2010 T4 slip.

¶620 Reallocations of Non-Vested Forfeitures

If a defined contribution RPP reallocates forfeitures among other active plan members (i.e., reallocates amounts that are forfeited by plan members who terminate service before becoming vested in employer contributions), the amount of any forfeiture allocated to an individual plan member must be included in that member's PA for the year in which it is reallocated, together with investment earnings attributable to the forfeiture that are included in the allocation. This does not apply if the reallocated forfeiture is paid to the member in cash (and therefore taxed).

It should be noted that the inclusion of forfeited amounts, together with related investment earnings, may create a record-keeping problem for some employers or their third-party administrators, since the employer must ensure that the members have sufficient RRSP contribution room (i.e., 18% of earnings) to accept the forfeiture. Therefore, before making a policy decision for the plan to reallocate forfeitures and deposit them into member accounts (instead of paying in cash or refunding to the employer as discussed at ¶ 1618), the employer should review whether this policy will cause a record-keeping problem.

¶625 Expenses

The plan administrator's fees are generally charged against investment earnings, charged against the members' account balances, or paid directly by the employer. These fees may not be deducted directly from the contributions, because there is a registration rule that states that all contributions made to a defined contribution RPP must be allocated to members (see ¶ 1675, Item 8). This rule should not present a problem where the other alternatives are being used.

Notwithstanding how expenses are paid, they may not be netted against the contributions when determining the PAs.

¶630 Timing of Contributions

Most defined contribution RPPs make contributions on a monthly or more frequent basis. The rule that requires the plan sponsor to include employer contributions that are made by the end of February in respect of the previous year in that previous year's PA may create some practical difficulties for certain defined contribution RPPs (such as profit sharing pension plans) where the employer contributions are not regularly made on a monthly or more frequent basis. Suppose an employer's payroll department needs to know the 2009 PA amounts by, for example, February 17, 2010, in order to include the PAs on the 2009 T4 slips by the February 28, 2010 deadline. In this case, it may not be advisable for the employer to make any contributions in respect of 2009 during the period from February 17 to February 28, 2010, since this requires the employer to provide the payroll department with an advance listing of the contributions it is going to make during that period (in order for the payroll department to be able to process the 2009 PAs) — any errors will require a corrected 2009 PA and, therefore, a corrected T4 slip. Such an employer may be advised to either make all of its 2009 contributions before the February 17, 2010, payroll cut-off date or delay the balance of any 2009 contributions until after February 28, 2010.

It should be realized that if, for example, the employer contribution in respect of 2009 is only made in March 2010, but the 2010 contribution is made in February 2011, then the 2010 PA would include both the 2009 and 2010 employer contributions. Since the maximum PA permitted for 2010 is 18% of 2010 taxable compensation, the maximum PA rule (discussed at ¶ 510) could be broken if the 2009 and 2010 contributions were relatively large. In that case, the plan's registration would be revocable. In this situation, if there is a likelihood that employer contributions will exceed 9% of taxable compensation each year (or less, if the employee also contributes to the plan), missing the cut-off date for including the 2009 contribution in the 2009 PA could mean that the employer is forced to delay all successive years' contributions until after February 28 of the following year.

¶635 Contributions to Defined Contribution RPP Following Leave of Absence

Some defined contribution RPPs provide for retroactive contributions to be made after the end of a particular year in respect of a period of reduced pay or temporary absence during that year. If such retroactive contributions, in respect of a particular year, are paid by the end of February of the following year, they automatically form part of the particular year's PA.

There is a special rule that states that if the employer or employee makes a retroactive contribution in respect of a previous year on or before the last day of April of a particular year, and the period of reduced service completely ended during the immediately preceding year, the retroactive contribution forms part of the PA for the year(s) in respect of which the contribution was made. In this situation, if the employer or employee makes a retroactive contribution during March or April of a particular year, then these PAs must be redetermined and reported to the CRA within 60 days of the date of the retroactive contribution. This will require reissuing the T4 slip with a note on the T4 slip that it is a replacement.

Consider an individual who returns from a leave of absence that covered two calendar years and belongs to a defined contribution plan that provides for retroactive contributions. No contributions were made to the plan during the leave of absence. Suppose that the individual becomes entitled to employer contributions of $3,000 for each year upon returning from the leave. Provided these contributions for those two years are made by the end of April of the year following the second year of leave, a redetermined PA of $3,000 is reported for each of the two years of leave. Each of these redetermined PAs retroactively reduces (or could even eliminate) the new RRSP contribution room that arose in the year following each of the two years. Of course, if this new RRSP contribution room was zero because the individual had no earned income during the leave of absence, the redetermined PAs will have no effect on RRSP contribution room.

Another special rule concerns the situation where the employee enters into a written commitment with the employer whereby the employee will make a retroactive contribution in respect of a previous year of reduced pay or temporary absence. Under this agreement, it may be that the employer will also make a retroactive contribution conditional on the employee making a contribution. If this written commitment is entered into before the last day of April of a particular year, and the period of reduced service completely ended during the immediately preceding year, the contributions are to be treated as if they were made on the date when the written commitment was entered into. Therefore, they would form part of the PA for years in respect of which the contributions were made. The amended T4 slips must be filed within 60 days of the date on which the commitment is entered into.

The above special rules are designed to prevent the PA for a particular year from exceeding the maximum limit permitted under the maximum PA rule (discussed at ¶510). This problem can still arise if the retroactive contribution is made, or the written commitment is entered into, after the last day of April following a period of reduced service that ended during the immediately preceding year or an earlier year. In this case the retroactive contributions form part of the PA for the year in which the contributions are made, together with any other contributions that normally are included in that year's PA. It can be seen that there is a risk of this total PA exceeding the allowable limit, especially if the employee terminates service in that year.

¶640 Employees Borrowed from Another Employer

Consider an employee who is borrowed from another employer but is paid by the borrowing employer. If the lending employer has a defined contribution RPP and continues to make contributions to the plan on behalf of the employee (based on the employee's compensation paid by the borrowing employer), PA reporting is the responsibility of the borrowing employer for the period of the loan. In this situation, the lending employer must co-operate by providing all relevant information to the borrowing employer to enable the borrowing employer to calculate the PA based on the lending employer's plan provisions.

In the case of an employee who is paid partly by one employer and partly by another, both employers are responsible for reporting a PA. The lending employer calculates its PA using the contribution based on compensation paid directly by that employer. Similarly, the borrowing employer bases its PA on the compensation it pays the employee. This could occur in either of two situations:

- in the year in which the loan takes place, as well as in the year in which the employee returns to work with the lending employer; or
- in a year where the employee receives compensation simultaneously from both employers.

In the first situation, the contributions in respect of the two portions of the year must be split between the two employers. Thus, each of the two employers has to report a PA for a partial year of service, with the total of these two PAs equal to what the PA would have been had the lending employer been responsible for reporting it for the whole year.

¶645 Employees Working Abroad and Foreign Pension Plans

If an employee transfers abroad and receives compensation (as defined in subsection 147.1(1) of the *Income Tax Act* (Canada)) from the Canadian employer, and if the Canadian employer continues to contribute to its defined contribution RPP on behalf of the employee, the Canadian employer is responsible for reporting PAs as usual.

If the foreign employer pays the employee's compensation and does not participate in the RPP, any contributions to the defined contribution RPP made on behalf of the employee for the period of employment with the foreign employer must be attributed to the employer who participates in the plan for PA purposes. Therefore, it is the employee's compensation from the participating employer, rather than from the foreign employer, that must be determined. Thus, compensation can only be included to the extent that it is permitted to be prescribed in accordance with the rules for prescribing compensation for eligible periods of leave of absence or to the extent that it is accepted by the CRA. Further information regarding benefits that can be provided in respect of employment outside Canada can be found at ¶1755 and Registered Plans Directorate Newsletters 93-2 (Foreign Service Newsletter), and 00-1 (Foreign Service Newsletter Update).

The balance of ¶645 to ¶647 deals with foreign pension plans that are prefunded and that are not registered as RPPs. The impact of membership in such a plan on an individual's RRSP contribution room is linked to the tax treatment of contributions being made to the plan, and the issues involved are quite complex. The rules are described below. For these purposes, residency is considered in a tax context — a Canadian resident means an individual who is taxed as a Canadian resident. Some individuals who only live temporarily in Canada may not be considered to be Canadian residents for tax purposes.

Apart from pension plans for athletes, an RCA that is maintained primarily for the benefit of non-residents in respect of services rendered outside Canada is excluded from the definition of an RCA by virtue of paragraph (l) of the RCA definition in subsection 248(1) of the *Income Tax Act* (Canada). Such an arrangement is defined as a "foreign plan" for the purpose of ¶646 to ¶647. As far as non-resident members of such plans are concerned, no PAs are reported.

For Canadian residents, however, there are two sets of rules. One set of rules (discussed at ¶646) covers services rendered primarily in Canada, or primarily in connection with a business carried on in Canada. The other set of rules (discussed at ¶647) covers services rendered outside Canada where the employment does not relate to a business carried on in Canada.

¶646 Services Primarily in Canada or Primarily With a Business in Canada

Consider an organization that employs a Canadian resident who renders services primarily in Canada, or primarily in connection with a business carried on in Canada. If the individual belongs to a foreign pension plan, the individual's PA treatment depends in part on whether contributions are made to the foreign plan and whether the foreign plan is treated as an RCA for Canadian tax purposes.

Suppose the employee accrues benefits under the foreign plan in a particular year and remains entitled to benefits under the plan at the end of the year. If no contributions are made to the plan in the year in respect of the individual (for example, if the plan is a defined benefit plan with an actuarial surplus that is being used to fund the benefits accruing to this individual), PAs are to be reported.

However, if a contribution is made in the year in respect of the employee, it is necessary to investigate the nature of the contribution. There are three categories of contribution. The description of these three categories, and the tax treatment of contributions, is as follows:

(1) Suppose the employee was a member of the foreign plan before becoming a Canadian resident and, at the start of the period of service in respect of which the contribution is being made, has not been a Canadian resident for more than 60 of the last 72 months. In this case, the foreign plan is considered to be an "employee benefit plan" — no RCA taxation is involved with respect to the contribution, but PAs must be reported. For the purpose of this rule, a contribution that covers a period of service during which the individual attains 60 months of residence in the last 72 months must be partitioned into a contribution for the pre-60-month period and a contribution for the post-60-month period. The pre-60-month portion is then a category 1 contribution, and the balance then falls into categories 2 or 3, as appropriate.

(2) If the contribution is a "prescribed contribution", it is also not subject to RCA taxation, but PAs must be reported. To be classified

as a "prescribed contribution" and obtain this tax treatment, several conditions must be met (described below). One of these conditions is that the employer must make a certain election. The election must be made no later than the last day of February following the first year in which a contribution is made on behalf of any employee that would otherwise be classified as a "resident's contribution" (see category 3 below); however, the Minister of National Revenue has the discretion to accept a late election. If the election is not made within that time frame, the contribution is then considered to be a "resident's contribution" (as are all contributions made to the foreign plan in later years on behalf of any Canadian residents who render services primarily in Canada, or primarily in connection with a business carried on in Canada, other than those in category 1 above).

(3) If the contribution does not fall into categories 1 or 2 above, it is then a "resident's contribution". In this case, the portion of the foreign plan that relates to such contributions is considered to be an RCA — these contributions, as well as any related investment income, are then subject to the refundable 50% RCA tax, but no PA needs to be reported. If a foreign organization is liable for withholding such RCA taxes and if the individual is an employee of a Canadian-resident subsidiary corporation, the subsidiary will be jointly and severally liable to pay the taxes if the parent organization does not remit them.

Prescribed Contribution — Conditions

The conditions that such a contribution must meet to be classified as a "prescribed contribution" depend on the year in which the contribution is made. For contributions made since 1991, two sets of conditions are stipulated:

- for contributions made in 1992, 1993, or 1994; and
- for contributions made after 1994.

The conditions for contributions made in 1992, 1993, and 1994 are described in Appendix 1. The rules below apply to contributions made after 1994.

Some of the conditions are aimed at foreign non-profit organizations, which are defined as non-profit organizations that have their main place of management outside Canada and that carry on their activities primarily outside Canada.

A contribution is classified as a "prescribed contribution" if the following conditions are satisfied:

(a) the contributions were paid to a "qualifying entity" (a non-resident trust, corporation, or other entity that is tax-exempt or is permitted a reduced rate of tax or other favourable tax treatment in the country in which it is resident and whose principal purpose is to provide benefits under a retirement plan or other employee benefit plan);

(b) the employer has elected to have all such contributions treated as "prescribed contributions" (i.e., the employer has elected to make the foreign plan exempt from taxation as an RCA). This election must be made in writing to the Minister of National Revenue, in the form of a signed letter from the employer, within the time frame described earlier (under the description for the second category of contribution). The employer may, with the Minister's permission, revoke any such election at any time, in which case future contributions will fall into categories 1 or 3 above (if the circumstances remain as described in the first paragraph of ¶ 646);

(c) if the employer is a foreign non-profit organization, either:

(i) the individual has no PA for the year in respect of the employer, apart from the PA arising in connection with the foreign plan, or

(ii) the individual's PA, including the amount in respect of the foreign plan, does not exceed the lesser of the money purchase limit for the year and 18% of the individual's "compensation" (as defined below) for the year from the employer;

(d) if the individual is granted a leave of absence or a period of reduced pay by an employer and is loaned to a foreign non-profit organization during that period, the individual's PAs are determined based on the rules described at ¶ 640 (these are the PA rules for employees borrowed from another employer); and

(e) if the employer is not a foreign non-profit organization:

(i) the individual was a non-resident person at some point before the contribution was made,

(ii) the individual became a member of the foreign plan before the end of the month after the month in which the individual became a Canadian resident, and

(iii) the individual is not a member of an RPP or a DPSP in which the employer or a related employer participates.

For the purpose of condition (c) above, "compensation" means compensation as defined in subsection 147.1(1) of the *Income Tax Act* (Canada), but without including prescribed amounts and amounts in respect of periods of non-residency that are permitted by the Minister to be included in compensation for other purposes.

PA Rules

Having decided whether the contributions to a foreign plan on behalf of Canadian resident employees are to be subject to RCA taxation, the employer is then in the position to determine any PAs. Suppose that

(i) the employee earned benefits under the foreign plan in a particular year in respect of services rendered to the employer while a Canadian resident;

(ii) the employee remains entitled to benefits under the foreign plan at the end of the year; and

(iii) at least one contribution made in the year in respect of the employee was not subject to the RCA tax or, alternatively, no contributions were made in the year on behalf of the employee.

The PA, therefore, exclusive of any PA otherwise determined for the employee by virtue of membership in any RPP or DPSP with which the employer is involved, equals to the lesser of two amounts:

- the money purchase limit for the year (as defined at ¶205), minus the PA offset of $600; and
- 18% of the individual's "compensation" (as defined earlier) for the year from the employer, minus the PA offset of $600.

If the employer adopts this "default PA" calculation method, no PSPA can arise in the future if benefits are retroactively increased.

If the employer prefers to calculate a PA in a different manner (for example, in a manner that is more consistent with the PA rules applicable to RPPs), the employer may write to the Minister of National Revenue — the Minister's approval is effective only if it is in writing.

Since the PA is not inclusive of any PA that is otherwise determined for the individual by virtue of membership in any RPP or DPSP with which the employer is involved, that PA must be added to the foreign plan PA to obtain the total PA that the employer must report on behalf of the individual.

It should be noted that if benefits for post-1991 service are retroactively increased in a later year, the use of an alternative PA calculation method may mean that PSPAs will have to be reported, as noted at ¶1085.

It should also be noted that for the period from 1996 to 2003, there was another adjustment in the PA calculation to take into account the delay in the retirement savings system reaching full maturity (i.e., the delay in the maximum RRSP contribution reaching $15,500). This adjustment is described in Appendix 1.

Consider a foreign non-profit organization that employs an individual who was not a member of a foreign plan before becoming a Canadian resident or who has been a Canadian resident for more than 60 of the last 72 months. If the total PA for the individual after 1994 exceeds the limit set out in condition (c), described earlier, then that condition is not met and any contribution would no longer be classified as a "prescribed contribution" — it would therefore become a "resident's contribution", resulting in RCA treatment. It would also remove the requirement to report a PA in respect of the employee's membership in the foreign plan, except for a year in which the employee accrued benefits under the foreign plan but for whom no contribution is made to the plan that year.

Example

Consider a foreign plan covering some Canadian resident employees who all belonged to the foreign plan before becoming Canadian residents, who have not been Canadian residents for more than 60 of the last 72 months, and who are being credited with service under the plan. Since any contribution made on behalf of these individuals is not subject to RCA taxes (because it falls under category 1, mentioned earlier), PAs are to be reported. In fact, PAs need to be reported even if no contribution is made on their behalf. Note that the employer does not have to be concerned yet with the election that needs to be made for a contribution to be a "prescribed contribution".

Now consider what happens when the first of these Canadian-resident members has been a Canadian resident for more than 60 of the last 72 months. For RCA taxes to be avoided on all future contributions made on behalf of these employees from the time that their Canadian residency has lasted more than 60 of the last 72 months, the employer must elect "prescribed contribution" status soon after the next contribution is made on behalf of this first individual. PAs can only be avoided for this individual if the employer makes contributions that are classified as "resident's contributions" and are, therefore, taxed as an RCA. But if the employer allows the foreign plan to be treated in that manner and, therefore, chooses not to elect to have contributions classified as "prescribed contributions" within the time frame set out earlier in this section, the employer has effectively prevented itself from ever electing "prescribed contribution" status, and all such employees will be subject to RCA taxation. As a result, no PAs would ever have to be reported on behalf of these employees while their circumstances remain unchanged, except with respect to an employee who continues to earn benefits under the foreign plan in a particular year but for whom no contribution is made to the plan that year.

¶647 Services Outside Canada, Not Related to a Business in Canada

Canadian resident employees who participate in a foreign plan may have to report an amount similar to a PA that will reduce their RRSP deduction limit in the following year. The purpose is to reduce the amount of RRSP contribution room available to members of foreign pension plans so that their tax-assisted savings for retirement is equivalent to that available to Canadian resident employees who are members of RPPs.

The reduction applies for a particular calendar year, if

(i) the Canadian resident rendered services outside Canada at any time in the particular year;

(ii) the individual's employment did not relate to a business carried on in Canada; and

(iii) the individual continued to be entitled, either absolutely or contingently, to benefits under the foreign plan at the end of that particular year.

This reduction in RRSP contribution room is not achieved through the use of PAs, and employers are not required to report the amount of the reduction. Instead, each individual taxpayer is responsible for ascertaining whether their RRSP contribution room is to be reduced on account of participation in the foreign plan.

The first year for which RRSP contribution room was affected in this manner was 1994, based on participation in a foreign pension plan in 1993. Special rules were in place for calendar years from 1994 to 2004 inclusive. These rules are set out in Appendix 1.

For calendar years after 2004, the prescribed reduction for a year is the lesser of two amounts:

(a) the money purchase limit for the particular year, minus $600 (the PA offset); and

(b) 10% of the portion of the individual's "compensation" (as defined at ¶646) for the year the services were rendered outside Canada.

The amount prescribed for a year in respect of an individual is subtracted from the individual's new RRSP contribution room for the year, in exactly the same way as if it were a PA. Thus, if the prescribed amount exceeds the new RRSP room for the year (for example, if the individual has relatively low earned income for RRSP purposes), no new RRSP room is created that year — but there is no impact on any unused RRSP room carried forward from the previous year.

¶650 Back Pay or Bonus Included in Pensionable Earnings

Consider an employer that retroactively increases an employee's compensation in respect of an earlier year. As a result, an extra contribution is made in respect of that additional compensation. In this situation, an extra PA may arise.

For example, suppose that, in February 2010, the individual's rate of salary since July 1, 2009 is retroactively increased, and the increase is paid as a lump sum that February. If the lump sum is considered to be pensionable earnings under the defined contribution RPP and the additional contribution in respect of that lump sum is paid into the plan before March 1, 2010, the 2009 PA must include the additional contribution, as noted at ¶630. On the other hand, if that additional contribution is paid into the plan on or after March 1, 2010 it forms part of the 2010 PA, even if no PA would otherwise be reported for 2010 (for example, if the individual terminated service towards the end of 2009).

The same approach applies if a pensionable bonus is paid after the end of a calendar year. The contribution in respect of that bonus forms part of the previous year's PA if the contribution is made before March 1, but it forms part of the PA for the year of the contribution if made on or after that date.

¶655 General PA Rules for DPSPs

The PA for a DPSP for a particular year equals the total of:

- all employer contributions made during the year, or made in respect of the year by the end of February of the following year; and
- non-vested forfeitures that are reallocated (see ¶620).

Suppose a company has a fiscal year of February 1, 2009 to January 31, 2010, and it contributes to a DPSP by February 28, 2010, in respect of that fiscal year. A question arises as to whether the 2009 PA should equal the amount of that contribution or whether only $^{11}/_{12}$ of that contribution should be included in the 2009 PA on the grounds that $^{1}/_{12}$ of that contribution is in respect of January 2010. It appears that either approach may be taken, provided that all contributions make their way into a PA; however, it would be best to adopt a consistent approach from year to year.

As another example, consider a company whose fiscal year end is October 31. Suppose the company contributes to the DPSP in February 2010 in respect of the fiscal year ending October 31, 2009. One-sixth of that contribution is in respect of the last two months of 2008, but the 2008 PA has already been reported. It appears that the entire February 2010 contribution should be included in the 2009 PA.

The comments contained at ¶ 620, ¶ 625, ¶ 630, ¶ 640, and ¶ 650 that are applicable to defined contribution RPPs apply equally to DPSPs. However, for DPSPs the maximum PA rule that was discussed in the last paragraph of ¶ 630 must be modified if, for example, the employer contributes to a DPSP in March 2010 and a member terminates service in, for example, April 2010. The March 2010 contribution forms part of the 2010 PA, but the 2010 PA is limited to 18% of 2009 compensation (or a dollar limit). Since the 2010 compensation with that employer is only received for the period up to the date of termination, the March 2010 contribution could exceed the maximum 2010 PA permissible. In this situation, the maximum PA is modified so that the 18% limit is based on the larger of the compensation in the year of termination and the compensation from that employer in the previous year. In most situations this will increase the maximum PA permitted and will remove this problem.

Note that ¶ 635 does not apply to DPSPs because employer contributions may not be made to a DPSP during an unpaid leave of absence. With respect to an employee working abroad, the employer may only continue to contribute to a DPSP if the Minister of National Revenue so permits. If such a contribution is permitted, it is reported as a PA in accordance with the usual rules.

Chapter 7

¶700 PENSION ADJUSTMENTS FOR DEFINED BENEFIT PLANS

Page

¶705 Introduction

This chapter begins with the basic rules for determining the PA for a member of a defined benefit RPP who belongs to that plan throughout the calendar year. Later sections of this chapter describe some variations based on different ancillary provisions, more complex plan designs and partial years of service. Finally, a number of miscellaneous PA rules are covered. Examples of PA calculations appear throughout the chapter.

Chapter 8 (at ¶800) covers PAs for combination or hybrid plans. Chapter 9 (at ¶900) covers PAs for multi-employer plans and other plans where several employers participate. Chapters 7, 8, and 9 are intended to cover the majority of situations that will be encountered in practice. Due to the complex nature of some pension plans, it is impossible to cover all unusual situations here.

As discussed at ¶520, the legislation refers to "pension credits" as well as PAs. Since the term PA is used more widely used than "pension credit", we have generally used PA in this chapter, even though technically we are calculating pension credits.

¶710 Basic PA Rules

The formula for determining the PA for a defined benefit plan is deceptively simple:

PA = (9 × benefit entitlement) - $600

If the above calculation produces a negative amount, as might happen in a relatively poorly defined benefit plan or if an individual only belongs to a plan for a small portion of the year, a PA of zero is reported.

Chapter 9 sets out the PA rules for pension plans where several employers participate. At ¶920 we explain the difference between the benefit entitlement in respect of a particular employer and the benefit accrual. Essentially, if an individual works for two employers in a particular year, the individual earns a benefit accrual for the entire year, and this benefit accrual is split into the various benefit entitlements in respect of each of the participating employers for whom the individual worked during the year. In the case of a pension plan with only one participating employer, the benefit accrual and the benefit entitlement are the same. Accordingly, we will use the term "benefit entitlement" in the balance of this book, except in Chapter 9 where we refer to benefit accruals as well.

The rules for determining the benefit entitlement can be quite complex, depending on the situation. The balance of the chapter is concerned primarily with how to determine the benefit entitlement in various situations.

Essentially, the benefit entitlement for an individual in a particular calendar year is the portion of the individual's "normalized pension" under the defined benefit provision at the end of the year that can reasonably be considered to have accrued in respect of the year. Typically, this can be determined as the difference between the normalized pension at the end of the year and the normalized pension at the start of the year.

The "normalized pension" at a particular time represents the employee's annual accrued lifetime pension that would be paid as if the individual were retiring at the end of the calendar year at age 65 (or, in the case of an employee who actually started to receive a pension during the year, the annual lifetime pension determined as if the employee's age was 65, if the actual pension commencement age was less than 65), based on credited service to date, but modified in a number of ways. For example, when determining the normalized pension at the start and the end of a particular calendar year in a defined benefit plan whose formula is based on earnings, both normalized pensions are effectively based on the individual's pensionable remuneration in the year and, where applicable, that year's YMPE under the CPP/QPP. This is because the rules state that, when calculating this normalized pension, the individual's earnings and the YMPE in all prior years are assumed to be equal to the current year's earnings and YMPE.

The earnings figure that is used must be determined in accordance with the plan's definition of pensionable earnings (e.g., salary only; salary plus bonus; all T4 earnings except for overtime; salary in excess of the YMPE; T4 earnings capped at $100,000; etc.).

The actual rules for determining a normalized pension are contained in Regulation 8302(3). However, it should be noted that if an employer considers that the usual PA rules are not appropriate, bearing in mind the terms of the pension plan or the way in which it is administered, the employer may write to the Minister of National Revenue to request approval for a different approach, because the Regulations give the Minister the power to accept an alternative formula.

For the vast majority of employees, taking the difference between the normalized pension at the end of the year and the normalized pension at the start of the year is an unnecessarily long process. This is because, for most employees, this calculation produces a benefit entitlement that is simply equal to the benefit rate or rates applicable under the plan, applied to the individual's pensionable earnings in the year, or in the case of a flat benefit plan, the flat benefit formula multiplied by the portion of the year for which service has been credited. Accordingly, it is not common for literature on this subject to refer to the normalized pension approach.

Nevertheless, it is important to understand the basic rules involving normalized pensions, because there are certain situations where this more complex method of calculating the PA must be used. Typically, this applies when there is a "career limit" under the plan, such as a 35-year cap on credited service, or, for example, a maximum pension of 70% of final average earnings for long service employees. These "career limit" rules are set out in detail at ¶ 735. Until we reach ¶ 735, we will follow the more straightforward approach of simply determining the benefits that have arisen during the year.

The benefit entitlement considered to arise during a particular calendar year, for PA purposes, is essentially equal to the lifetime retirement benefit accruing during the year, based on the benefit formula that would be applicable if the individual were to retire at age 65 at the end of the year, fully vested, with a pension commencing to be paid at the start of the following year. There are other assumptions that are made, which will be detailed in the rest of this chapter. Accordingly, it can be seen that this benefit entitlement for PA purposes is not necessarily equal to the benefits that have actually accrued during the year or the benefits that might appear on the individual's annual benefit statement. This benefit entitlement for PA purposes is an artificial number in most cases.

When calculating the PA, the amount of an employee's required contributions to the defined benefit plan is ignored as is the amount of employee optional ancillary contributions made to flexible pension plans to purchase ancillary benefits. However, an employee's additional voluntary contributions to a defined benefit pension plan or employee required contributions to the defined contribution portion of a hybrid plan do form part of the PA. Refer to Chapter 8 for additional information on calculating PAs for hybrid plans. Refer to ¶120 for a discussion regarding flexible pension plans.

Other ancillary benefit provisions are also ignored, such as any early retirement subsidies, bridging benefits, pre-retirement death benefits, post-retirement indexing provisions, and the "50% rule" (discussed at ¶1314).

For individuals who have a full year of credited service in an earnings-related defined benefit plan, the PA is the same regardless of whether the formula is based on final average earnings, best average earnings, or career average earnings. As mentioned, it is the individual's pensionable earnings in the year that are utilized when determining the benefit entitlement for PA purposes; the employer is not required to average earnings over a period of years or to project them into the future. However, where the individual only has a partial year of credited service in a particular year, the treatment of earnings in the PA formula can depend on whether the formula is based on final average, best average, or career average earnings, as discussed at ¶730.

The rules for determining the benefit entitlement are modified for pension plans in which two or more employers participate. These rules are detailed in Chapter 9 at ¶900. In some situations involving more than one employer, the $600 offset that appears in the PA formula is modified, as noted at ¶795 and ¶915. These are the only situations where the $600 offset is modified, except for one special case: where an individual works for an employer with two or more defined benefit plans and the individual belongs to more than one of these plans in a particular year, the total offset under all of these plans may not exceed $600 for that year. For example, if an employee belongs to both the defined benefit plan for salaried employees and the defined benefit plan for executive employees and is accruing benefits under both plans, either of the two plans may apply the $600 offset to the pension credit under the plan (see ¶ 520 for a description of pension credits), or the $600 offset could be split between the two plans.

Examples of how to determine PAs for a full or partial year of service are set out at ¶ 725 and ¶ 730.

¶715 Factor of 9

The factor of 9, used in converting the annual benefit entitlement accruing under a defined benefit plan into a value that could be compared to money purchase contributions was one of the very early concepts in the long development of the current system of PAs, PARs, and PSPAs. It was first introduced in the February 1984 government proposals, which stated:

> Actuarial calculations show that $9 of contributions should be enough to buy each $1 of target pension for a representative individual over an earning career. This factor of 9 provides more deduction entitlement than is required for target pension accumulation during the earlier years of an individual's career, but less deduction entitlement than required in later years. As the excess in earlier years just offsets the deficiency in later years, the funding factor of 9 yields the right amount of contribution for the target pension over a full career.

In order to determine the factor of 9, certain assumptions had to be made:

- the individual retires at age 63 with an unreduced pension, after 35 years of plan membership;
- the pension is indexed in line with the Consumer Price Index less 1%;
- the pensioner has a spouse, and the pension reduces on first death to 60% of the initial benefit; and
- although not specifically stated, we understand that the factor of 9 was also based on the assumption that the maximum benefit limit of $1,722.22 per year of service and other related limits would be indexed in line with increases in the average wage.

There are certain flaws with these assumptions which impact on the relative attractiveness of defined benefit plans over other retirement schemes, as it produces an overstated PA for a typical defined benefit plan (and therefore provides less RRSP contribution room):

- few pension plans guarantee indexing after retirement; many defined benefit plans provide *ad hoc* increases to pensioners, but relatively few do so to the extent of the increases in the Consumer Price Index less 1%;
- although provincial pension reform has required that a survivor pension be provided on death after retirement, in the majority of defined benefit plans this survivor pension is financed by the retiree through a reduction in the initial pension; however, the factor of 9 assumes that the survivor pension will be provided at the employer's expense;
- many employees who retire as early as age 63 are not entitled to an unreduced pension; and
- there has been a multiple year delay in the scheduled automatic indexation of the $1,722.22 maximum pension (originally scheduled to commence increasing in accordance with the average wage beginning in 1995 but the first such increase actually occurred in 2004); in addition, not all plan sponsors choose to automatically index the maximum.

On the other hand, the factor of 9 does not allow for more generous subsidized early retirement benefits that are provided under some pension plans, through bridging benefits and unreduced early retirement pensions.

Even if one accepts that the factor of 9 is a reasonable approximation for most long service employees, it is not the factor that is actually used in determining the amount of a lump-sum transfer to an RRSP for a vested employee terminating from a defined benefit plan. In many of these situations, the actual present value calculation will be based on a factor less than 9 — significantly less in many cases. In fact, depending on current age, interest rates, expected retirement age, and the extent of indexing and survivor benefits, the factor could vary from less than 1 to over 30.

Concerns that the factor of 9 is overstated for most defined benefit pension plan participants is addressed by the PAR. When a pension plan member receives a lump-sum benefit entitlement from the defined benefit pension plan, a PAR is calculated. In general terms, the PAR is equal to the total of all PAs reported after 1989, offset by the post-1989 portion of any lump-sum payment made to the exiting plan member. Thus, the role of the PAR is to reinstate RRSP room that is lost by virtue of the PAs being overstated.

However, the PAR is only determined once a plan member ceases to be entitled to a benefit under the particular defined benefit provision, which most typically happens at termination of employment or retirement. Thus, while the PAR goes a long way to overcome the "factor of 9" concerns, the resulting additional RRSP room may not become available to the plan member until later in the plan member's career. PARs are described in more detail in Chapters 11 and 12.

¶720 Special PA Transition Rules for Higher Income Employees Prior to 2005

For the years 1990 through 1994, there were some PA transition rules in place for higher income employees which provided consistency between lower and higher income employees during the early transition years. These rules are set out in detail in Appendix 1.

However, for years after 1994, there were further modifications to the rules, introduced in subsequent federal budgets, which delayed the complete transition into the new system until 2004, when the maximum RRSP contribution room finally reached $15,500.

As a result of these delays, for years after 1994 until the system matured in 2004, there were situations for high earners where the calculated PA was actually higher than the maximum RRSP dollar limit for the following year. As discussed at ¶510, the CRA required that the higher PA be reported; however, there was no impact on RRSP contribution room by the reporting of a PA higher than the maximum RRSP contribution limit, since new RRSP contribution room generated in a particular year can never be less than zero (as indicated at ¶325). It should be noted that for the calculation of the PAR, the administrator must ensure that the lower of the reported PA and the relevant maximum dollar limit be used, as discussed further at ¶1130. However, unlike the situation just described for PARs, the actual reported PA, regardless of the fact that it exceeds the maximum RRSP contribution room, is used in the calculation of a PSPA.

¶725 PA Examples for a Full Year of Credited Service

Example 1 — Flat Benefit Plan

With flat benefit plans, it is important to determine the portion of a year for which service has been credited. Consider a flat benefit plan with a pension formula of $55 per month per year of credited service, where a full year of service is credited if an individual works 1,800 hours in a calendar year. Therefore, an individual who, for example, is hired on February 15, 2010, and who works more than 1,800 hours for the balance of 2010, is credited with a full year of 2010 service under this plan.

This individual's 2010 benefit entitlement equals $55 × 12, or $660, because the benefit entitlement for PA purposes is to be expressed as an annual pension rather than a monthly pension. Therefore, the 2010 PA is as follows: (9 × $660) - $600 = $5,340.

Example 2 — Flat Benefit Plan with Negotiated Increases

Suppose a union has negotiated benefit improvements under a flat benefit plan, whereby individuals retiring or terminating in 2010 will receive a pension based on a benefit formula of $55 per month per year of service; for those leaving in 2011, it will be based on a formula of $56 applied to all years of service; and for those leaving in and after 2012, it will be based on a formula of $59 for all years of service.

It might be thought that the 2010 PA for most employees should be based on the $59 formula, because that is the formula that will apply when they reach retirement age. However, as noted at ¶ 710, the formula that is to be adopted is the formula applicable as if the individual were to retire at the end of the current year.

Therefore, in this case, the pension formula that is used for the 2010 PA is $55, $56 for the 2011 PA, etc.

As the benefit level increases in 2011 and 2012, it is necessary to take into consideration the possibility of PSPAs arising (i.e., a PSPA is a "catch-up" PA that is determined at the time of an increase in benefits). Refer to Chapter 10 for details on PSPAs.

Example 3 — Earnings-Related Formula

The PA for a straightforward earnings-related defined benefit plan for a full year of credited service is quite simple. Consider a defined benefit plan whose formula is 1% of pensionable earnings per year of credited service.

If an individual has pensionable earnings of $75,000 in 2010 and receives a full year of credited service in 2010, the benefit entitlement for PA purposes is 1% × $75,000, or $750, and the 2009 PA is as follows: (9 × $750) - $600 = $6,150.

As mentioned at ¶ 710, it does not matter whether this plan's formula is based on the final average, best average, or career average earnings, in the case of an individual with a full year of credited service — the PA is the same.

Example 4 — Earnings-Related Formula/High Earner

For the same pension plan as described in Example 3, consider another individual whose pensionable earnings are $250,000 and who has a full year of credited service in 2010.

Following the logic from Example 3, the 2010 benefit entitlement would be 1% × $250,000, or $2,500 and the 2010 PA would be determined as follows: (9 × $2,500) - $600 = $21,900.

However, the maximum defined benefit PA for 2010, as shown in Appendix 3, Table 1, is $21,850. Thus, the maximum PA that is to be reported for 2010 is $21,850.

Another way of illustrating how the maximum PA is derived is to take note of the maximum defined benefit pension of $2,494.44 for 2010 (also shown in Table 1 of Appendix 3). Although the benefit formula under the plan in this example is 1% of pensionable earnings per year of credited service, there is a cap on the maximum pension that can be earned in the year equal to the maximum defined benefit pension.

Thus, the benefit entitlement is really the lesser of 1% of pensionable earnings ($2,500) and $2,494.44, or $2,494.44. The PA is therefore (9 × $2,494.44) - $600 = $21,850, which is also the maximum defined benefit PA for 2010.

Example 5 — Earnings-Related Formula/Indirect Integration

Consider a defined benefit plan whose formula is integrated with benefits from the CPP/QPP. There are two types of integration — indirect and direct. This example deals with indirect integration (direct integration is dealt with at ¶ 740).

A defined benefit plan provides a pension per year of credited service of:

- 0.8% of pensionable earnings below the YMPE; plus
- 1.4% of pensionable earnings above the YMPE.

Consider an individual whose 2010 pensionable earnings are $75,000 and who has a full year of credited service during 2010. Based on the 2010 YMPE of $47,200, the 2010 benefit entitlement is: 0.8% × $47,200 + 1.4% × ($75,000 - $47,200) = $766.80.

Therefore, the 2010 PA is: (9 × $766.80) - $600 = $6,301.20 (this is rounded to $6,301).

Again, since a full year of credited service is involved, it makes no difference whether the formula is based on the final average, best average, or career average earnings.

For this particular pension plan, the following chart shows the 2010 PAs and the 2011 RRSP contribution room for a range of pensionable earnings, in the case of individuals with a full year of credited service in

2010. This table assumes that earned income for RRSP purposes equals pensionable earnings:

2010 Pensionable Earnings	2010 PA	2011 RRSP Contribution Room
$ 30,000	$ 1,560	$3,840
50,000	3,151	5,849
75,000	6,301	7,199
90,000	8,191	8,009
110,000	10,711	9,089
130,000	13,231	9,219
150,000	15,751	6,699
170,000	18,271	4,179
198,400 or higher	21,850	600

As you can see from the above table, 2011 RRSP contribution room increases as earned income (which we have assumed to be equal to pensionable earnings) increases. At earned income levels above $110,000 (in fact, at $124,724), RRSP contribution room begins to decline, since the maximum RRSP dollar limit of $22,450 begins to cap total RRSP contribution room. At pensionable earnings levels of $198,400 and above, the PA itself is capped at $21,850, since the pension plan formula itself is subject to the maximum pension limitation of $2,494.44 per year of service (refer to ¶1710 for details regarding the maximum pension limitation under a defined benefit pension plan). Accordingly, at earnings levels of $198,400 and above, 2010 RRSP contribution room is capped at $600.

Note that if the individual's earned income for RRSP purposes includes such items as bonuses and overtime, the RRSP contribution room could be increased considerably if these types of compensation are not included in pensionable earnings. Alternatively, the RRSP contribution room could be reduced if the individual is making large alimony payments or incurs rental losses, because these reduce earned income but do not affect pensionable earnings. Thus, it is not true in all situations to state that individuals who belong to the most generous defined benefit plan have only $600 of RRSP contribution room (since 2004, RRSP contribution room cannot be less than $600); it could be more than that, depending on their personal circumstances.

¶730 PA Rules and Examples for a Partial Year of Credited Service

Consider a member of a defined benefit plan who is credited with less than a full year of service in a particular calendar year — for example, he or she joins the plan partway through the year, terminates service or retires during the year; works part-time and is credited with less than a full year of service; reaches a service cap that exists under the plan; or is on a non-pensionable leave of absence during part of the year. The benefit entitlement for the year is then reduced, as compared to the benefit entitlement for an individual with a full year of credited service.

For flat benefit plans, the determination of the benefit entitlement for a partial year of credited service is quite simple. The annual lifetime pension, payable as if the individual were retiring at the end of the year at age 65, is simply multiplied by the proportion of the year for which service has been credited. For example, consider a flat benefit plan whose formula is $55 per month per year of credited service. This must first be expressed as an annual pension of $660 (i.e., $55 × 12). If an individual has five months of service during 2010 and if the plan credits service on the basis of years and months employed (as opposed to crediting service on the basis of hours worked), the 2010 benefit entitlement is $660 × $^5/_{12}$, or $275. Therefore, the 2010 PA is: (9 × $275) - $600 = $1,875.

However, for earnings-related defined benefit plans the rules are less straightforward. A different approach is taken, depending on whether the plan "annualizes" earnings in a partial year of service. To decide whether the plan annualizes earnings, one must consult the pension plan document, but unfortunately the answer is not always immediately obvious. Even if the plan document shows that earnings are not annualized, but the plan has generally been administered on the basis of annualizing earnings, the plan must be assumed to annualize earnings for PA purposes. It is likely that the majority of earnings-related plans annualize earnings in a partial year of service.

One way of deciding whether earnings are annualized is to consider how the actual pension would be determined if a plan member were to leave with, for example, 10 complete calendar years plus six months of credited service. How would the pension in respect of that final half year of credited service be determined? If it would be determined by calculating an average annual earnings figure, using this in the plan's benefit formula and then multiplying by 0.5 to reflect the half year's service, then for PA purposes the plan effectively annualizes earnings in a partial year. On the other hand, if the pension in respect of that final half year of credited service is determined by reference to actual earnings during that half year, without multiplying the resulting benefit by 0.5, then for PA purposes the plan does not annualize earnings.

In almost all final or best average earnings plans, earnings are annualized in a partial year for benefit calculation purposes, in which case this approach would be taken for PA purposes as well.

Consider the following three examples. In the first example, the pension formula is 1% of the best average earnings per year of credited service. In this type of plan, one first determines the best average earnings, which invariably involves taking the average of several annual earnings figures. Alternatively, it might involve taking the average of, for example, 36 consecutive months of earnings and multiplying by 12 to make it into an average annual earnings figure. In either case, this average annual earnings figure is used in the plan's benefit formula and the resulting benefit per year of service is then multiplied by the member's years of service. Therefore, the earnings in that final half year are said to be annualized.

As a second example, consider a plan where the employee contributes 3% of pay up to the YMPE and 5% of pay in excess of the YMPE. The pension equals 40% of the employee's contributions. This is effectively a career average plan, since the pension formula in respect of a particular year of service can be expressed as 1.2% of earnings up to the YMPE in that year (i.e., 3% × 40%), plus 2% of that year's earnings in excess of the YMPE (i.e., 5% × 40%). Typically, the pension earned in respect of the final half year of credited service is equal to 40% of the employee's contributions made during that six-month period. Suppose the employee's contributions at the start of each calendar year are 3% of earnings until the employee's earnings in the year reach an amount equal to the YMPE, and then for the rest of the year the contribution rate becomes 5% of earnings. In this case, the benefit earned in a year during which an individual terminates service before his or her earnings have reached the YMPE is equal to 1.2% of that partial year's earnings, and therefore this plan does not annualize earnings for PA purposes. On the other hand, suppose the employee's contributions as determined at the start of a calendar year are based on the employee's projected earnings for the year. If the individual is projected to earn more than the YMPE that year, his or her contributions for a particular month equal 1/12 of the sum of 3% of projected annual earnings up to the YMPE and 5% of projected annual earnings in excess of the YMPE. Effectively, this plan is annualizing earnings in a partial year, and therefore earnings would be annualized for PA purposes.

As a third example, consider a career average plan whose pension formula is 1% of earnings up to the YMPE plus 2% of earnings in excess of the YMPE. In the case of a member who terminates service or retires part-way through a year, the pension in respect of the final calendar year of employment might be equal to 1% of his or her actual earnings in the year up to that year's annual YMPE figure, plus 2% of the actual earnings in the year in excess of the annual YMPE figure. In this case, the plan is not annualizing earnings for PA purposes. However, if the pension for that final partial year of service is instead determined by calculating 1% of annualized earnings up to the YMPE plus 2% of annualized earnings in excess of the YMPE, and then multiplying this result by the portion of the year for which service has been credited, then earnings are considered to be annualized for PA purposes.

Having determined whether the plan annualizes earnings or not, one can then determine the benefit entitlement for the year in which a partial year of credited service occurs.

Example 6 — Earnings Annualized

Consider a defined benefit plan whose pension per year of credited service equals:

- 0.8% of final average salary below the YMPE; plus
- 1.4% of final average salary above the YMPE.

The plan annualizes earnings for benefit calculation purposes, and credited service is based on years and fractional months of service as a plan member (a different approach would have to be followed if credited service were based on years and completed months of service, as discussed at ¶765).

Consider an individual whose annualized rate of salary in 2010 is $75,000, and for whom service is credited from April 15 to December 31, 2010.

The 2010 benefit entitlement is: [0.8% × $47,200 + 1.4% × ($75,000 - $47,200)] × 8.5/12 = $543.15.

Therefore, the 2010 PA is: (9 × $543.15) - $600 = $4,288.35 (this is rounded to $4,288).

Example 7 — Earnings Not Annualized

Now consider a pension plan that does not annualize earnings for benefit calculation purposes. The pension formula is:

- 0.8% of salary up to the YMPE; plus
- 1.4% of salary above the YMPE.

Consider an individual who belongs to this career average earnings plan from January 1 to September 15, 2010, and whose earnings during that period are $53,125.

The 2010 benefit entitlement equals [0.8% × $47,200 + 1.4% × ($53,125 - $47,200)] or $460.55.

Accordingly, the 2010 PA equals: (9 × $460.55) - $600 = $3,544.95 (this is rounded to $3,545).

It can be seen that this PA is lower than the PA of $4,323 in Example 6 for the individual earning $75,000, even though the percentage of earnings used in the pension formula and the individual's credited service and annual rate of pay are identical ($53,125 over the 8.5-month period is equivalent to an annual salary of $75,000). This is because this particular plan does not annualize earnings in a partial year, and, as a result, a smaller portion of the individual's pensionable earnings in the year is based on the 1.4% formula, compared to the final average earnings situation in Example 6. This is not intended to suggest that it is in the individual's best interests for the plan not to annualize earnings. Although this can lead to a reduced PA, it can also reduce the actual benefits payable in respect of the year in which the individual terminates service or retires.

Example 8 — Pensionable Earnings Include Overtime

Consider a pension plan whose formula is 2% multiplied by the best average annual pensionable earnings multiplied by the years of credited service up to 35 years. In this particular plan, pensionable earnings include all taxable earnings that appear on the T4 slip, rather than being limited to salary only.

Consider an individual who is a plan member continuously from July 1, 2010, but who has been employed with that employer throughout 2010. The individual's T4 earnings for 2010 include only salary and overtime. The salary and overtime paid during the first six months of 2010 are, respectively, $34,000 and $2,000. During the second half of 2010, salary and overtime are, respectively, $35,000 and $4,000. Therefore, total T4 earnings for 2010 amount to $75,000 (comprising $69,000 in salary and $6,000 in overtime).

This particular plan annualizes earnings in a partial year. Accordingly, we begin by determining the 2010 pensionable earnings figure on which the benefit entitlement is based. There are two possibilities. One is to use the actual T4 earnings figure of $75,000; the other is to annualize the T4 earnings of $39,000 for the second half of the year and utilize an annualized pensionable earnings figure of $78,000.

Strictly speaking, the answer to the question of which figure to select should lie in the pension plan document, which should define whether all employment earnings or just earnings during the pensionable service period are used. If the individual were to retire at the end of that year at age 65, how would the pension for that six months of credited service be determined, assuming the individual was vested? If the pension would be 2% × $75,000 × 0.5 years, then that would be the formula for the 2010 benefit entitlement. However, if the actual July to December T4 earnings of $39,000, annualized to $78,000, were to be used in this formula instead, then it would also be used in determining the 2010 benefit entitlement.

As a practical matter, it is probably easier to use the January to December T4 earnings figure of $75,000 in this example.

Now consider another individual who only joined this employer as a full-time employee on July 1, 2010, and was a member of the plan from that date. This individual's salary and overtime for the second half of 2010 are, respectively, $35,000 and $4,000. While it may be easy to accept the requirement that the six-month salary be doubled to produce an annualized figure for PA purposes, it is questionable whether it is reasonable and logical to do the same for the overtime payments.

According to the CRA, in this situation (full-time employee; pensionable earnings not limited only to salary; partial year of credited service involved; earnings to be annualized for PA purposes; insufficient evidence of what the pensionable earnings would be had a full year of service been credited that year), only the salary figure is to be annualized; the other components of T4 earnings that are counted as pensionable earnings are not annualized. However, if the employee works part-time and belongs to the plan throughout the entire year, and the partial year of credited service is only due to the employee being part-time, all earnings are to be annualized for PA purposes.

The employee in our example works full-time, so the annualized pensionable earnings for PA purposes would be $74,000 (i.e., 2 × $35,000, plus $4,000).

¶735 Situations Requiring the Calculation of Normalized Pensions

As discussed at ¶710, the benefit entitlement for an individual in a particular calendar year is the portion of the individual's "normalized pension" under the defined benefit provision at the end of the year that can reasonably be considered to have accrued in respect of the year. For most situations, it is possible to follow the more straightforward approach of simply determining the benefit accrual that has arisen during the year (this was the approach followed in ¶725 and ¶730).

However, there are certain situations where a more complex method of calculating the PA must be used; this involves determining the difference between the normalized pension at the end of the year and the normalized pension at the beginning of the year.

When determining the normalized pension based on credited service to the beginning or end of the year, the pensionable earnings and the

YMPE in all previous years are assumed to equal the pensionable earnings and the YMPE for the current year. However, there is a special rule if the individual is not working on a full-time basis in the current year, or did not work on a full-time basis in some previous year. This rule is particularly complex and is discussed at the end of this section.

The situations where the more complex method of PA calculation is to be used usually involve a "career limit" under the plan. The simplest example is a 35-year cap on credited service, which is common in generous final or best average earnings plans. Consider a pension plan whose formula is 2% of final average earnings per year of credited service up to 35 years. In the case of an individual whose credited service to January 1, 2010 is 34.5 years and whose pensionable earnings for the full 12 months of 2010 are $75,000, we first determine the normalized pension at January 1, 2010 based on the entire 34.5 years of credited service to date. Since a partial year is involved (due to the 35-year service cap), we must determine whether earnings are annualized for PA purposes. In this case, we assume that they are.

Therefore, the normalized pension at January 1, 2010 is: 2% × $75,000 × 34.5 years = $51,750.

The normalized pension at the end of 2010, allowing for the 35-year cap on credited service, is: 2% × $75,000 × 35 years = $52,500.

Therefore, the 2010 benefit entitlement equals $52,500 less $51,750, or $750. Of course, this could have been determined instead by realizing that only six months of service is credited during the year, and accordingly by determining the 2010 benefit entitlement using the simpler method: 2% × $75,000 × 0.5 = $750.

A more complex situation arises where the normal pension formula under a plan is limited to a maximum formula that incorporates a cap on service. The most typical situation is the maximum pension permitted under the *Income Tax Act* (Canada), which, in its application to some private sector pension plans, features a 35-year service cap. (As discussed at ¶1710 and Appendix 1, section 10A, the CRA permits service after January 1, 1992, which is in excess of 35 years, to be used in determining the maximum pension; however, some plans have retained the 35-year cap.) Essentially, these pension plans provide the lesser of two pension formulae: the usual pension formula under the plan and the maximum formula. Again, one determines the normalized pension at the beginning of the year, which is the lesser of the normalized pensions using the two different formulae. One does the same at the end of the year and the benefit entitlement for the year is equal to the difference.

Example 9 — Cap on Pensionable Service

Consider a defined benefit plan whose formula is 1.8% of best average earnings per year of credited service. The maximum pension under the plan is 2% of best average earnings per year of credited service up to 35 years. Both of these formulae annualize earnings for a partial year of service.

Consider an individual whose 2010 pensionable earnings are $75,000 and who belongs to the plan throughout the year. The individual joined the plan on July 1, 1971 and therefore has 38.5 years of credited service to January 1, 2010.

The normalized pension at January 1, 2010 is the lesser of:

(i) 1.8% × $75,000 × 38.5 = $51,975; and

(ii) 2% × $75,000 × 35 = $52,500.

Therefore, the normalized pension at January 1, 2010 equals $51,975. The normalized pension at December 31, 2010 is the lesser of:

(i) 1.8% × $75,000 × 39.5 = $53,325; and

(ii) 2% × $75,000 × 35 = $52,500.

Therefore, the normalized pension at December 31, 2010 equals $52,500.

The 2010 benefit entitlement is the difference between these two normalized pensions, i.e., $52,500 - $51,975, or $525.

Therefore, the 2010 PA equals: (9 × $525) - $600 = $4,125.

By following this same approach in 2011 and assuming that this individual continues in the pension plan throughout 2011, the normalized pension at both the beginning and the end of the year will be based on the maximum pension formula under the plan, and therefore the two normalized pension figures will be identical. This leads to a PA of zero in 2011. This is the case even though the individual's actual accrued pension may be increasing as a result of the increase in the best average earnings (due to the individual's earnings increasing from year to year).

Example 10 — No Service Cap on Basic Formulae/Service Cap on Maximum

This example shows the impact on the normalized pension when there is a cap on the maximum service that a member may accrue for the purposes of determining the maximum benefit payable from the plan.

Consider a career average earnings plan whose formula up to December 31, 1991 had been 1.4% of salary up to the YMPE, plus 2% of salary in excess of the YMPE. Subsequent to that date, the formula changed to 1.8% of salary up to the YMPE, plus 2% of salary in excess of the YMPE. When determining the normalized pension at a particular point in time, it is sometimes necessary to allow for the different benefit formulae or different definitions of pensionable earnings that may have applied in earlier years under the pension plan.

With career average earnings plans, the accrued pensions become eroded by inflation over time, since they are based on earnings in prior years (unlike final or best average earnings plans). Accordingly, this particular employer has updated the pensions earned up to December 31, 1997 to be based on the 1997 salary and the 1997 YMPE. The pensions for service up to December 31, 1997 have therefore been increased to the sum of A and B, where:

> **A** is 1.4% of the 1997 salary up to the 1997 YMPE, plus 2% of the 1997 salary above the 1997 YMPE, multiplied by the years of credited service up to December 31, 1991; and
>
> **B** is 1.8% of the 1997 salary up to the 1997 YMPE, plus 2% of the 1997 salary above the 1997 YMPE, multiplied by the years of credited service from January 1, 1992 to December 31, 1997.

For credited service from January 1, 1998, the usual career average formula applies, namely, 1.8% of salary up to the YMPE, plus 2% of salary above the YMPE.

Under this particular plan, pensionable earnings are not annualized for calculating benefits for a partial year of credited service.

There is also a career limit under this particular plan, namely 2% of best average T4 earnings per year of credited service up to 35 years. (Technically, the CRA generally only applies this 35-year service cap to the pension earned up to December 31, 1991, but this employer has chosen to continue to apply it to the total pension.)

Now, consider a full-time employee whose credited service under the plan began on July 1, 1968 and ceased on June 30, 2010, due to retirement. The individual's salary in the first six months of 2010 equals $38,000 (i.e., an annual rate of salary of $76,000). The individual also received overtime payments of $3,000 in that same six-month period and did not receive any other T4 earnings.

When determining the normalized pension at the beginning and the end of the year, we must take into account the old pension formula that applied for credited service up to December 31, 1991 for reasons that may not be immediately obvious. We also ignore the salary and YMPE history for years prior to 2010, because the legislation states that, for PA purposes, the annual rate of pensionable earnings in all years prior to 2010 is assumed to equal the annual rate of pensionable earnings in 2010.

As of January 1, 2010, the individual has 41.5 years of credited service. As such, the benefit entitlement for PA purposes under the normal plan formula in each of those 41.5 years is based on an annualized earnings figure of $76,000. Overtime payments are not considered part of pensionable earnings for the purpose of the normal plan formula.

Accordingly, the first component in the calculation of the normalized pension of January 1, 2010, based on the normal plan, is:

(1.4% × $47,200 + 2% × ($76,000 - $47,200)) × 23.5 years, plus

(1.8% × $47,200 + 2% × ($76,000 - $47,200)) × 18 years = $54,725.60

This must be compared with the normalized pension at January 1, 2010, which takes into account the maximum pension formula that is stipulated in the plan document. Since a cap of 35 years is applied when determining this maximum, the normalized pensions at both the start and the end of 2010 are based on 35 years of credited service. The earnings figure utilized in this normalized pension calculation includes overtime payments, because this particular plan's maximum pension formula is based on T4 earnings, which include overtime. Following the approach set out at the end of ¶ 730, the salary is annualized but the overtime payments are not. Therefore, the T4 earnings for PA purposes are $79,000 (i.e., 2 × $38,000, plus $3,000).

Therefore, using the maximum pension formula under the plan, the second component in the calculation of the normalized pension at January 1, 2010 is: 2% × $79,000 × 35 years = $55,300.

The normalized pension at January 1, 2010 is the lesser of these two components, i.e., $54,725.60. It can be seen that, at this stage of the calculation, the "career limit" has had no effect.

The normalized pension under the normal plan formula at December 31, 2010 is effectively the same as the normalized pension at the date of retirement of June 30, 2010, because that is the date on which service ceased to be credited under the plan formula. We must therefore include an extra portion of normalized pension in respect of the first six months of 2010. For this purpose, the earnings figure of $38,000 is used, because this plan does not annualize earnings in respect of a partial year. Accordingly, the normalized pension at December 31, 2010 equals the lesser of:

(i) \$54,725.60 (as calculated earlier) plus (1.8% × \$38,000*) = \$55,409.60;

and

(ii) 2% × \$79,000 × 35 years = \$55,300.

Therefore, the normalized pension at December 31, 2010 equals \$55,300.00. It can be seen that the career limit has now had an impact on the normalized pension.

Taking the difference between the normalized pension at the beginning and the end of 2010 (\$55,300.00 - \$54,725.60), we obtain the 2010 benefit entitlement of \$574.40. As a result, the 2010 PA is (9 × \$574.40) - \$600 = \$4,569.60 (this is rounded to \$4,570).

It is interesting to note how this calculation would have differed had the maximum pension under this particular pension plan been set out in the plan document as "the maximum pension permitted under the *Income Tax Act* (Canada) and Regulations". As mentioned, in most situations the CRA applies its 35-year service cap to service up to December 31, 1991 only.

In this example, the plan member had completed 35 years of credited service as of July 1, 2003. As such, the additional seven years of credited service from July 1, 2003 to June 30, 2010 (the date of retirement) may count for the purpose of determining the maximum pension limit. When determining the normalized pension at December 31, 2010, using the maximum pension formula in the above example, we would have to use: 2% × \$79,000 × 42 years = \$66,360.00.

In that case, the "career limit" would have no impact at all on the normalized pensions, both at the beginning and at the end of 2010. Therefore, the 2010 benefit entitlement would be the difference between \$55,409.60 and \$54,725.60, or \$684. This is higher than the benefit entitlement of \$574.40 that was determined in the first part of this example.

It is interesting to note that this benefit entitlement of \$684.00 is the same as the benefit entitlement that would have been obtained had we used the more straightforward method set out at ¶725 and ¶730. That approach concentrated only on the benefits accruing during 2010, for which the 2010 benefit entitlement would have been: 1.8% × \$38,000 = \$684.00.

This example illustrates the importance of examining the plan document carefully. One must consider such issues as:

- any previous formula that apply;

* Since earnings are not annualized.

- different definitions of pensionable earnings that may have applied to service credited in previous years; and
- the definition of pensionable earnings for both the normal plan formula and the *Income Tax Act* (Canada) maximum (or any other career limits under the plan).

There are other situations that require the use of the normalized pension approach, such as those set out in Examples 12 and 13 at ¶742.

¶740 Government Benefits Offsets

As discussed under Example 5 at ¶725, there are two methods of integrating the benefits under a defined benefit plan with the benefits from the CPP/QPP — indirect (implicit) and direct (explicit). The method of dealing with indirect integration was covered in Example 5.

This section deals with direct integration, where the formula under the plan calls for benefits from the CPP/QPP to be directly offset against the plan's pension. In this situation, the CPP/QPP retirement benefit is deemed, for PA purposes, to be equal to 25% of pensionable earnings up to the YMPE annualized for a partial year of service or for a part-time employee.

When a direct CPP/QPP offset applies, most pension plans prorate it according to service. This is primarily due to minimum standards legislation in most of the pension jurisdictions, which generally require that if the CPP/QPP benefits are to be offset directly, they must accrue over a period of at least 35 years. Thus, a typical offset would equal $1/35$ of the CPP/QPP retirement benefits per year of credited service up to 35 years. For PA purposes, this offset would therefore become $1/35 \times 25\%$ of pensionable earnings up to the YMPE (i.e., 0.7143% of pensionable earnings up to the YMPE). As a reasonable alternative, one could simply round this figure to 0.7%.

Consider a defined benefit plan whose formula is 2% of final average earnings per year of credited service, reduced at age 65 by $1/35$ of CPP/QPP retirement benefits per year of credited service up to 35 years. Since, for PA purposes, the offset is equivalent to 0.7143% of pensionable earnings up to the YMPE, the defined benefit formula with respect to each of the first 35 years of credited service is equivalent to: 1.2857% of earnings below the YMPE, plus 2% of earnings above the YMPE. The factor of 1.2857% could be modified to 1.3% as a reasonable alternative.

For credited service beyond 35 years, the formula is simply 2% of earnings, since the offset no longer applies.

Example 11 — Direct Integration

Consider a defined benefit plan whose formula per year of credited service is 2% of final average salary, reduced at age 65 by $^1/_{70}$ of the C/QPP retirement benefit.

This particular plan annualizes earnings for benefit calculation purposes for a partial year of service (see ¶730 for the rules for partial years of service). We will assume that there is no career limit under the plan.

Consider an individual who was hired before 2010 but whose service under the plan is only credited from July 1 to December 31, 2010. The individual's salary for the 12 months of 2010 is $75,000.

Converting the offset into the formula to be used for PA purposes, the offset is determined to be 25% × $^1/_{70}$ = 0.35714%, and therefore, the formula becomes 1.64286% of salary up to the YMPE plus 2% of salary in excess of the YMPE.

Since this plan annualizes earnings for a partial year of service, the earnings figure to be used is $75,000. Therefore, the 2010 benefit entitlement is: [(1.64286% × $47,200) + 2% × ($75,000 - $47,200)] × 0.5 = $665.71.

This could alternatively be expressed as (2% × $75,000 - $^1/_{70}$ × 25% × $47,200) × 0.5, which leads to the same answer.

The 2010 PA becomes (9 × $665.71) - $600 = $5,391.39 (this is rounded to $5,391).

¶742 CPP/QPP Offset Not Prorated

In a few pension plans, the CPP/QPP retirement benefits are offset in full, without regard to the length of credited service. For example, this approach is still permitted for federally regulated pension plans that fall under the federal *Pension Benefits Standards Act*.

For PA purposes, unless the Minister of National Revenue decrees otherwise, this CPP/QPP retirement benefit offset is to be treated in the same way as set out above, except that the normalized pension approach would be used. This is because the offset is not based on credited service. Therefore, for the early years of an individual's membership in a plan, the CPP/QPP benefit offset eliminates the benefit entitlement for PA purposes. Note that, in view of the fact that this method may produce zero PAs in the early years of membership, it is possible that the Minister may dictate an alternative approach, using the powers granted to the Minister in the Regulations.

Example 12 — CPP/QPP Offset Not Integrated

Consider a defined benefit plan whose formula is 2% of final average salary per year of credited service, reduced at age 65 by the maximum CPP/QPP retirement benefits.

Consider an individual whose 2008 salary was $72,000 and who had seven years of credited service at December 31, 2008. The 2008 YMPE was $44,900. The normalized pension at December 31, 2008 was: 2% × $72,000 × 7 years - 25% × $44,900 = -$1,145.

Since the normalized pension at the end of 2008 was negative, and was even more negative at the start of 2008 (i.e., 2% × $72,000 × 6 years - 25% × $44,900 = -$2,585), there was no benefit entitlement for 2008, and therefore the 2008 PA was zero.

In 2009, suppose the individual's salary has increased to $73,000. The 2009 YMPE was $46,300. Now, the normalized pension at January 1, 2009 is: 2% × $73,000 × 7 - 25% × $46,300 = -$1,355.

The normalized pension at December 31, 2009 is : 2% × $73,000 × 8 - 25% × $46,300 = $105.

Therefore, the amount of the normalized pension at the end of 2009 which has arisen during 2009 is $295, which becomes the 2009 benefit entitlement. Therefore, the 2009 PA is (9 × $105) - $600 = $345.

In this example, for years 2010 and later, assuming the plan's integration formula is not changed, it might be thought that there would be no need to follow the normalized pension approach, since the normalized pension at the end of 2009 is greater than zero. If this were the case, it would be possible to follow the more straightforward approach set out at ¶725 and ¶730, which would lead to a benefit entitlement for 2010 of 2% of the 2010 salary. However, this is not necessarily true. For example, suppose the individual's salary remains at $73,000 in 2010. The 2009 YMPE is $46,300. The normalized pension at January 1, 2010 is: 2% × $73,000 × 8 years - 25% × $47,200 = -$120.

The normalized pension as at December 31, 2010 is: 2% × $73,000 × 9 years - 25% × $47,200 = $1,340.

The 2010 benefit entitlement will then equal $1,340, which is less than 2% of the 2010 salary (2% × $73,000 = $1,460).

Example 13 — Integrated Grandfathered Formula

In this final example illustrating how the normalized pension approach works, consider a plan with a pension formula of 1.4% of salary up to the YMPE, plus 2% of salary in excess of the YMPE.

When the employer first introduced the above pension formula, employees who were covered under the previous plan were "grandfathered" by being allowed to retire on the formula under the old plan, based on all past and future years of credited service, if that produces a higher pension than the formula under the new plan. The formula under the old plan was 2% of final average salary per year of credited service, offset at age 65 by the full CPP/QPP retirement benefit.

The maximum pension that an individual is permitted to receive under this plan is 2% of the best three-year average salary per year of credited service up to 35 years.

Consider an individual whose credited service began on January 1, 1968, who has a full year of credited service in 2010 and who earns a salary of $73,000 in 2010. The normalized pension at January 1, 2010 is the lesser of A and B, where:

A is the greater of:

(i) (1.4% × $47,200 + 2% × ($73,000 - $47,200)) × 42 years = $49,425.60; and

(ii) 2% × $73,000 × 42 years - 25% × $47,200 = $49,520; and

B is 2% × $73,000 × 35 years = $51,100.

Therefore, the normalized pension at January 1, 2010 is $49,520.

The normalized pension at December 31, 2010 is calculated by changing the 42 years shown in the above plan formula to 43. In this case, the normalized pension at December 31, 2010 is again based on the grandfathered plan formula with the CPP/QPP offset, and equals $50,980 (i.e., 2% × $73,000 × 43 years - 25% × $47,200).

Therefore, the 2010 benefit entitlement is $50,980 - $49,520, or $1,460, which is also equal to 2% × $73,000. In this case, the results of the normalized pension approach show that it is the grandfathered plan formula which applies to this individual for 2010, rather than the current plan formula or the maximum pension formula.

¶744 Offset Based on Old Age Security Benefits

The above approach can similarly be applied in those few pension plans where the offset is based on the benefits payable from OAS at age 65. Again, these would only be plans registered under the federal *Pension Benefits Standards Act*; as such integration is no longer permitted in any other jurisdiction (including Prince Edward Island, once that province's legislation is proclaimed). The only difference from the methodology set out under ¶742 is that one must determine the actual

OAS benefits that would be payable in the year for which the PA is being calculated, as if the individual was actually receiving maximum OAS benefits that year. Since the OAS benefit increases quarterly, this involves determining the total of the 12 months of OAS payments for that year, allowing for the quarterly increases during the year.

¶745 Adjustments Due to Special Normal Forms and Optional Forms of Pension

Where the amount of an individual's lifetime retirement benefit depends on either the form of benefits provided (whether at the option of the individual) or other circumstances that affect the form of benefits, the form of benefits or the circumstances that are taken into account in the PA calculations must be such as to maximize the amount of the individual's lifetime retirement benefit payable at the time of commencement of payment.

Typical variations in the form of benefits that are contemplated here include an increase in the initial lifetime pension resulting from the election of:

- lower post-retirement death benefits; or
- lower post-retirement indexing of benefits.

In these situations, for PA purposes, the individual is assumed to elect the option that leads to the highest lifetime retirement benefits payable from age 65.

Examples 14 to 18 will help explain the operation of this rule and illustrate the permissible exceptions.

Example 14 — Unreduced Joint and Survivor Normal Form

Consider a defined benefit plan whose normal form of pension is joint and survivor, where this form of pension is not financed by the retiree through a reduction in the initial pension that would otherwise be applicable if the retiree were single. Thus, the normal form provides the same amount of initial pension at retirement regardless of whether the individual has a spouse or is single. For individuals with a spouse, a percentage of the pension continues to be paid to the surviving spouse after the retiree's death.

Suppose retirees with a spouse are allowed under the plan to elect a higher single life pension (i.e., a pension without survivor protection, where, by foregoing the survivor protection, the initial pension is increased). In this case, for PA purposes, one must assume that all members who have not yet retired will have a spouse at retirement and will elect this higher single life pension (even for members who currently have no spouse). This approach applies even when determining the final PA for a member who has retired during the year and who did not elect that higher pension.

The only exception to this rule is where the election of the higher single life pension is only available under the plan if the spouse has a shortened life expectancy.

Note that if the plan document states that any optional form that is permitted by the CRA may be elected by the retiree, then one must assume for PA purposes that every retiree will elect the highest amount of lifetime pension possible (usually a single life pension with no guarantee).

Keep in mind, however, that the election of a higher single life pension is not permitted to lead to a higher pension than the maximum pension formula (that is, both the 2% limit and the defined benefit limit — i.e., $2,494.44 for 2010), according to the registration rules. This maximum limit will have to be taken into account in the PA calculation in a plan with this type of optional form of pension.

If this optional form provision exists, some reasonable assumption regarding the typical age difference between retirees and their spouses must be made in order to determine the PAs for all plan members. For example, it might be reasonable to assume that female spouses are on average four years younger than male spouses and, by determining the relative proportions of male and female members, derive an average increase in the initial pension for typical retirees who elect the higher single life pension.

In this situation, the increase in the PA could be significant. The existence of this optional form of pension in the plan could be quite unpopular with many employees if they realize that their PAs are being artificially increased due to the existence of the option. Accordingly, serious consideration should be given to amending the pension plan to eliminate this option.

Example 15 — Special Exemption for 10-Year Guarantee

Consider a defined benefit plan whose normal form of pension is a single life pension guaranteed for more than 10 years and in which retirees are allowed to elect a higher initial pension with a lower guarantee or with no guarantee. Again one must assume that all retirees will elect the highest possible initial pension in this situation.

However, if the normal form of pension is guaranteed for 10 years or less, a special exemption allows one not to increase the PAs in this manner, even if retirees may elect a higher initial pension with a lesser guarantee or no guarantee.

Example 16 — Increase in Pension Due to Spouse's Age

Consider a pension plan whose normal form of pension is joint and survivor, but the initial pension is increased automatically by 1% for each year that the spouse is more than 10 years older than the retiree. For example, if the spouse is 12 years older than the retiree, the initial pension is increased by 2%.

Reading the Regulations literally, one must assume that the circumstances will be such that the retiree will be entitled to the highest initial pension possible (subject, of course, to the maximum pension limits). Theoretically, one would therefore have to assume that all retirees will have a spouse aged around 110, because this maximizes the initial pension payable.

Although this is the literal interpretation of the Regulations, in fact it is probably reasonable to assume that spouses are not more than 10 years older than retirees, and therefore one could ignore this increase in the initial pension. Strictly speaking, this employer should contact the CRA to obtain approval to use this approach.

Example 17 — Choice Between Two Formulae

Suppose a pension plan permits retirees to choose either a non-indexed pension of 2% of earnings per year of service or an indexed pension of 1.8% of earnings per year of service. If the choice is made by the individual at his or her retirement date, then the 2% formula must be used for determining the PA, because it is assumed that the individual will select the highest possible initial pension.

Similarly, suppose the plan is structured so that the individual must choose to be covered by one of the two pension formulae during his or her career. However, the plan states that if an individual switches from the 1.8% indexed formula to the 2% non-indexed formula at some stage, all accrued benefits to the date of the switch will be based on the 2% non-indexed formula. Again, individuals who have chosen to be covered by the 1.8% indexed formula should be assumed to switch to the 2% non-indexed formula at some stage before reaching retirement age, and the PAs would be based on the 2% formula.

On the other hand, suppose the plan states that when an individual switches from the 1.8% formula to the 2% formula, the benefits earned to the date of the switch are still based on the 1.8% indexed formula. In that case, the PAs up to the date of the switch are based on the 1.8% formula, and PAs following the switch simply move to being based on the 2% formula instead of the 1.8% formula.

Example 18 — Level Income Option

Many defined benefit plans allow an individual to elect a bridging option (also known as a level income option). This allows a higher pension to be paid from a retiree's early retirement date and the pension then reduces, usually at age 65, by an amount equal to the benefits under the CPP/QPP. Thus, where the retiree has elected this option, the pension payable after age 65 is lower than what the pension would be if the bridging option were not elected. Because the election of this option lowers the lifetime retirement benefits that are payable from age 65, the availability of this option has no impact on PAs.

¶750 Normal Retirement Age Less Than 65

If the normal retirement age under a defined benefit plan is less than 65, there may be a requirement to increase the PAs for all members of the plan. This depends on how the plan deals with employees who remain employed beyond their normal retirement date.

There are two methods commonly used for increasing the pension for an individual who remains employed beyond the plan's normal retirement date and postpones commencement of the pension, in recognition of the fact that the individual is not receiving a pension that would otherwise be due to him or her. The first method, the "actuarial increase method", involves an actuarial increase in the pension determined at normal retirement date, based on credited service to the normal retirement date. Generally speaking, Quebec requires this method as a minimum for postponed retirements, with additional benefits if the member is required to continue contributing after the normal retirement date.

The other method, the "continued accrual method", involves the crediting of additional years of service beyond the normal retirement date until the individual finally starts drawing a pension. This approach must be offered to late retirees in the other jurisdictions in Canada.

Where a pension plan has a normal retirement age earlier than age 65 and where the plan provisions state that individuals who postpone their pension commencement date beyond the normal retirement date will have an actuarial increase in the pension accrued to their normal retirement date, the PAs for all active plan members who have not yet reached the normal retirement age are to be based on the pension that would be payable at age 65 as if they were to remain employed until that age. Thus, some reasonable actuarial increase factor must be determined and incorporated in the benefit entitlements for all members who have not yet reached their normal retirement date. This is also true for those who reach their normal retirement date in the year for which the PA is being calculated, except of course that this PA is based on a partial year of credited service. For years after the year in which the individual reaches his or her normal retirement date, no PA is reported, as discussed at ¶755, unless extra pension amounts are accruing in respect of the additional years of service.

On the other hand, if the continued accrual method is used under the plan provisions for postponed retirements, no such increase in the PAs is required for members who have not yet reached their normal retirement date. However, for members still employed beyond their normal retirement date, continuing accrual of service will lead to continued PA reporting, as discussed at ¶755.

Some pension plans provide for the actuarial increase method for members in certain provinces and the continued accrual method for members in other provinces. For example, consider a pension plan with a normal retirement age of 60. Under this plan, members who postpone their pension commencement date beyond age 60 get an actuarial increase if they are employed in Quebec, but get continued accrual of credited service if they are employed in other provinces. In addition, the plan states that an employee who moves to Quebec becomes entitled to the actuarial increase method for all benefits, including those benefits that were earned in respect of service while in other provinces. In this case, using the principles stated at ¶745, we understand that the employer must assume that all employees in provinces other than Quebec will end up moving to Quebec. Accordingly, an actuarial increase factor from age 60 to 65 must be incorporated in the benefit entitlement for all employees for PA purposes, regardless of whether employees are likely to move from province to province. Note that if the employer prefers instead to report a PSPA when an employee moves to Quebec, it may be worthwhile trying to convince the CRA to accept this approach.

The above rule should not be confused with a pension plan whose normal retirement age is less than 65 and which guarantees indexing after retirement. Consider a pension plan with a normal retirement age of 62, which guarantees indexing after retirement in line with increases in the Consumer Price Index. One might think that the above rule means that, when calculating the benefit entitlement for PA purposes for all employees, one should add an assumed three years of inflationary increases to the pension payable at age 62. However, this is not the case. The PA calculation assumes that the plan member has attained age 65 and is retiring at the end of the year. Therefore, the PA calculation ignores the post-retirement guaranteed indexing provision in this plan; however, an actuarial increase factor from age 62 to 65 would have to be incorporated if this plan provides for actuarial increase upon retirement after age 62.

¶755 Adjustments for Members Still Employed Beyond Normal Retirement Age

As discussed, the PA calculation for a member of a defined benefit plan involves determining what the normalized pension would be if the individual were retiring at the end of the year as if he or she was age 65. Where an employee is already beyond the plan's normal retirement age, PAs must continue to be reported in the usual manner if additional pension amounts are accruing based on continuing service. On the other hand, if the pensions earned by late retirees up to their normal retirement date are actuarially increased in recognition of the postponed retirement and no additional pension amounts are accruing based on continuing service, no PA is required to be reported beyond the individual's normal retirement date. In the calendar year containing the normal retirement date, the PA would be determined using the rules applicable to a partial or full year of credited service, as the case may be.

¶760 Minimum Benefits

Where a plan provides that the accruing benefits will not be less than a specified minimum, that minimum must be taken into account for PA purposes. For example, if the plan formula was changed in some previous year, and employees covered by the previous plan formula were grandfathered by being promised benefits based on the greater of the old and the new formula (with this grandfathering being applied to service after the date of the change as well as before), the PAs for those grandfathered employees must be based on the larger of the two formulae (as illustrated in Example 13 at ¶742).

As another example, consider a plan whose benefit is the larger of a career average earnings formula and a final average or best average earnings formula. Typically, the career average earnings formula is a larger percentage of earnings than the final/best average earnings formula, the latter acting as protection for plan members in case the plan sponsor does not regularly upgrade the accrued benefits under the career average earnings formula to reduce the impact of inflation. The benefit entitlement for PA purposes is based on the greater of the two pension formulae, even though members may be retiring under the other formula. (Note that there was a special interim rule for determining 1990 and 1991 PAs, which lowered the PAs in some cases (as described in Appendix 1), but this no longer applies.

Another situation where a minimum benefit is provided under a plan is found in flat benefit plans that provide a minimum benefit for individuals retiring with long service. Consider a flat benefit plan whose formula is $40 per month per year of service, but where individuals who retire after 30 or more years of service will receive a minimum benefit of $1,360 per month. The PA is to be based on the assumption that the individual will retire at the end of the year. Therefore, in the case of an individual who has not yet reached 30 years of service, the $1,360 minimum benefit would not apply if the individual were to retire at the end of the year, and therefore the PAs for that individual would be based on the regular benefit of $40 per month per year of service.

When that same individual attains 30 years of service, theoretically a past service event arises at that time, potentially leading to a PSPA, because the individual's accrued benefit of $1,200 per month immediately increases to $1,360 per month. However, the PSPA may turn out to be zero, because the flat benefit formula for post-1989 past service is allowed to be increased in line with the increase in the average wage (or even higher), as discussed at ¶1017. Then, for the next four years of service there would be no PAs until the accrued benefit first exceeds $1,360 per month.

Now consider an individual who has already attained 34 or more years of service. Here, the minimum benefit is no longer relevant because the accrued pension exceeds $1,360 per month, and this individual is subject to PAs based on the formula of $40 per month per year of service.

For members with between 30 and 34 years of service, their accrued benefit is essentially $1,360 per month. Until these individuals attain 34 years of service, they are not actually accruing any further pension for PA purposes, and would therefore have PAs of zero until the year in which they attain 34 years of service.

¶765 Credited Service Based on Completed Months

Some defined benefit plans base the credited service on completed months of service. Strictly speaking this requires an adjustment to the PA rules and a PSPA at the beginning of every calendar year, unless the completed months coincide with calendar months (i.e., unless all plan members' credited service began on the first day of a calendar month).

Consider a defined benefit plan where credited service is based on completed months of service (not completed calendar months). An individual joins the pension plan on April 15, 2010, and remains a member of the plan throughout 2010. Although the individual has belonged to the pension plan for 8.5 months in 2010, only eight months of service have been credited as of December 31, 2010. Theoretically, only eight months of service should be counted when determining the 2010 benefit entitlement for PA purposes. However, in this case, if the individual remains a member of the plan until January 15, 2011, an additional month of service becomes credited to the individual on that date, of which half is in respect of service in 2010 (that is, service from December 15 to December 31, 2010). Since this effectively represents an additional period of credited service for a previous year, the extra half month of 2010 credited service should be reported as a 2011 PSPA. For 2011, the PA would only cover 11.5 months of credited service (from January 1 to December 14), and another PSPA arises on January 15, 2012.

In this situation, most employers would probably prefer to count 8.5 months of credited service in determining the 2010 benefit entitlement for PA purposes and not have to report a PSPA every year. Since this is not strictly in accordance with the Regulations, the employer should obtain the Minister of National Revenue's approval before following this simpler approach.

¶770 Back Pay and Bonuses

Consider an employer that retroactively increases an employee's pensionable earnings where the situation is such that an earlier year's PA would have increased had it been based on the higher level of pensionable earnings that is now applicable for that earlier year. In this situation, the extra benefits based on that increase in pensionable earnings form part of the benefit entitlement for the year in which the back pay is actually paid.

A slightly modified approach applies where back pay is paid in the year after the calendar year of termination or retirement, in the situation where it forms part of pensionable earnings. In this situation, one is effectively required to recalculate the PA in respect of the final calendar year of employment as if the back pay had formed part of pensionable earnings in that year, and then determine the difference between that recalculated PA and the PA that was actually reported for that year. This difference would then be reported as a PA for the year in which the back pay has actually been paid. (In fact, if the back pay was retroactive to an even earlier year, that earlier year's PA would also be recalculated and the difference between that recalculated PA and the PA actually reported for that year would also be included when determining the PA for the year in which the back pay is actually paid.)

The above rules are also applied if a pensionable bonus for a particular year is paid after the end of the year.

¶775 Pensionable Leaves of Absence and Disability

When an individual takes a leave of absence from an employer or becomes disabled, there is a rule for determining how many years of leave may be counted as credited service (as discussed at ¶1746). Where, in accordance with this rule, a leave of absence or a period of disability does form part of credited service under the employer's defined benefit plan, there are three different situations to consider.

¶777 Service Automatically Credited During the Leave

Where service is credited automatically under the pension plan while the individual is on a leave of absence or on disability, PAs must be reported during the leave. The benefit entitlement for PA purposes during the leave must be based on the benefits actually accruing under the plan.

If the plan's formula is based on earnings, an earnings figure is needed for the duration of the leave in order to determine the PAs. For this purpose, one is required to determine the amount that it is reasonable to consider would have been the individual's remuneration in the year for which the PA is being determined had the individual rendered services on a regular basis in that year. In other words, one is required to estimate how much the individual might have been paid had he or she not been on the leave of absence. This applies even if the individual is on an extended leave of absence (e.g., on disability), where it may be difficult to determine how much the individual might have been paid had he or she still been employed. For example, the job that the individual was performing prior to becoming disabled may no longer exist and there may therefore be no pay scale applicable to that job.

Where service is credited automatically while on a leave of absence or during a period of disability, PAs still have to be reported on a T4 slip. However, as mentioned at ¶515, in the case of a period where the employer is not otherwise required to complete a T4 slip, a T4A slip may be used instead.

Service may only be credited automatically in this situation if it complies with the definition of pensionable service (see ¶1746). As noted at ¶1747, there is a limit to the benefit accruals that may be subject to PA reporting during a leave of absence.

¶778 Service Credited After the Leave, Contingent on Returning to Work

Where credited service is granted in respect of a leave of absence (and meets the definition of pensionable service, as discussed at ¶1746) but is contingent on the individual returning to work, corrected PAs are reported in respect of the period of leave (provided the leave of absence does not extend beyond the "five-year/three-year" limit, as discussed below). These corrected PAs must be reported to the CRA within 60 days of the date on which the credited service has been granted in respect of the leave of absence.

A corrected PA following a leave of absence can have the effect of causing an individual to lose the tax deduction already taken in respect of RRSP contributions made during the leave of absence, and even to have to pay a penalty tax on excess RRSP contributions. Consider an individual who takes a leave of absence for two calendar years. The individual receives earned income from another source during those two years, resulting in new RRSP contribution room of $2,500 in each of the two years. No PA is reported during that period. The individual contributes the maximum to an RRSP in each of those years.

When the individual returns to work, the two years are then automatically credited as service under the terms of the pension plan. A corrected PA arises for each of the two years in the amount of $3,000 per year, for example, which has the effect of eliminating the new RRSP contribution room that arose in each of the two years. The result is that the individual loses the tax deduction on the RRSP contributions that were made. Further, it now turns out that the individual contributed a total of $5,000 while no RRSP contribution room was being created. Unless the individual had some RRSP contribution room carried forward at the start of the leave of absence, $500 of the first year's RRSP contribution and $2,500 of the second year's RRSP contribution become excess contributions with effect from the date on which the contributions were made ($2,000 of the total $5,000 RRSP contributions is not subject to the penalty tax, as discussed at ¶435). This figure of $3,000 would be higher if part of the penalty-tax-free allowance had already been used up prior to making this contribution. Therefore, it is possible that the individual will be subject to the 1% per month penalty tax with effect from the date on which the excess contribution was made, unless the Minister of National Revenue waives the penalty tax.

As noted at ¶435, one can apply to the Minister to waive the penalty tax if: (a) the excess arose because of reasonable error; and (b) reasonable steps are taken to remove the excess. Thus, if the employee in this example could somehow prove that he or she had no idea that the automatic granting of two years of credited service at the end of the leave of absence could create a penalty tax situation and if the individual also takes steps to remove the $3,000 excess, it may be possible to obtain the Minister's waiver of the penalty tax. Even if the employee knew that the crediting of service at the end of the leave could create the situation described above, it may still be possible to avoid the penalty tax by arguing that he or she only decided to return to employment with the same employer some time after the second year's RRSP contribution was made.

As noted at ¶1747, there is a limit to the amount of service that may be credited following a leave of absence and may be subject to PA reporting. In general terms, this limit is five years of full-time service, plus an additional three years in respect of periods of parenting. After this "five-year/three-year" limit is reached under a defined benefit RPP, any additional service that is credited in respect of a leave of absence and that complies with the definition of pensionable service would be subject to PSPA reporting instead.

These types of leaves of absence will clearly require personal attention by the employer. The individual involved should understand, in advance, all of the implications of the leave and the subsequent return to work.

¶779 Service Granted Retroactively (Not Automatically) After Returning to Work

Where service is credited retroactively, but not automatically, after a leave of absence, the reporting treatment depends on the timing involved. If the decision to credit that retroactive service is made after April 30 of the year following the calendar year in which the leave of absence ended, a PSPA is involved. However, if the decision to retroactively credit that service is made on or before April 30 of the year following the calendar year in which the leave of absence ended, a corrected PA is involved, and must be reported within 60 days after the date on which the retroactive service has been credited. This situation might arise, for example, if the employee is given the option of buying back that service by making additional contributions after returning to work.

This same treatment (either corrected PAs or a PSPA, depending on when the service is retroactively credited) also applies when service is credited upon recovering from a disability and returning to work. For example, suppose a plan member receives a disability pension from a defined benefit plan and then recovers and is credited with the service in respect of the period of disability. If the service is credited upon returning to work, corrected PAs must be reported. However, if the decision to retroactively credit that service is delayed until after April 30 of the year immediately following the calendar year in which the member returns to work, a PSPA is reported instead.

¶780 Employees Borrowed from Another Employer

Consider an employee who is borrowed from another employer but is paid by the borrowing employer. If the lending employer has a defined benefit plan and continues to credit service under the plan on behalf of the employee, PA reporting is the responsibility of the borrowing employer for the period of the loan. In this situation, the lending employer must co-operate by providing all relevant information to the borrowing employer to enable the borrowing employer to calculate the PA based on the lending employer's plan provisions.

In the case of an employee who is partly paid by one employer and partly paid by the other, both employers are responsible for reporting a PA. The lending employer calculates its PA based on the pensionable earnings paid directly by that employer; similarly, the borrowing employer bases its PA on the pensionable earnings it pays the employee. This could occur in either of two situations:

- the employee receives compensation simultaneously from both employers; or
- in the year in which the loan takes place, as well as in the year in which the employee returns to work with the lending employer, the employee receives a partial year of compensation from both employers.

In either situation, the benefit entitlement must be prorated between the two employers in proportion to the remuneration received by the employee in the year from each employer. The $600 PA offset must also be prorated. Generally, this will mean that the total of the two PAs is the same as the PA that the lending employer would report if the employee had not been loaned to the other employer.

¶785 Employees Working Abroad and Foreign Pension Plans

If an employee works abroad, but accrues pensionable service under a defined benefit RPP in Canada, the PA treatment depends on whether the individual is employed by the Canadian employer.

If the employee continues to be employed by a participating employer in the Canadian plan, then the amount of service that can be credited is not limited (other than any plan limitation and the usual *Income Tax Act* (Canada) limitations) and the PAs are calculated and reported in the normal way.

However, where the member is working outside Canada while employed by a non-resident participating employer, a non-participating employer connected with the participating employer or a non-participating employer under a special arrangement with a participating employer, up to five years of service may be credited under the Canadian plan. Refer to ¶1755 for the conditions under which the individual may accrue the five years of service. If the service is considered eligible foreign service, then the *Income Tax Act* (Canada) permits the remuneration received by the employee to be used as "compensation" in order to calculate and report PAs each year of the leave.

Of course, if the individual has no earned income in Canada for RRSP contribution purposes, the PAs will have no impact on the individual's RRSP contribution room, since no new contribution room is being created.

If a Canadian resident employee participates in a foreign pension plan that is not registered as an RPP in Canada, the PA treatment is as set out at ¶646 and ¶647.

¶790 Crediting Extra Service

There are three situations covering extra service that is credited under a defined benefit plan for which special PA rules exist. These are discussed at ¶791, ¶792, and ¶1025.

¶791 Waiting Period with Automatic Crediting of Past Service

The first situation is where a pension plan has a waiting period for joining the plan and, when an employee joins, past service is automatically credited back to the date of hire. In this situation, the employer may choose to report PAs during the waiting period, even though the individual does not actually belong to the plan during that time. (Although this choice is not specifically referenced in the Regulations, it is permitted by the CRA.) However, the employer could instead choose to report a PSPA in respect of the individual once he or she joins the pension plan (this issue is discussed further at ¶1025).

The above approach has to be modified in the rare situation where membership in a defined benefit plan is optional, but where past service is granted back to the date of hire when an employee finally decides to join the plan. Where membership is conditional on an election to be made at some unknown later date, a PSPA would have to be reported at the time the employee finally joins the pension plan and is actually credited with the past service.

¶792 Reciprocal Transfer Agreement

If an individual transfers in 2010, for example, from a defined benefit plan of one employer to a defined benefit plan of another employer under a reciprocal transfer agreement situation, the importing employer determines a 2010 PA based only on service that is credited under the importing employer's plan subsequent to the date of the transfer. The importing employer is not required to co-ordinate the 2010 PA calculation with the amount of the 2010 PA that the exporting employer must report in respect of 2010 pensionable service prior to the transfer. Any 2010 service that is credited under the importing employer's plan in respect of the period prior to the transfer is then taken into account in a PSPA that would be determined using the rules set out at ¶1055, but reduced to reflect any amounts transferred to the importing employer's plan from the individual's RRSP or from a defined contribution RPP to fund the past service benefits.

¶793 Future Years of Service Credited at Retirement

The third situation arises where additional years of future service are granted to an individual who is retiring early, due to a downsizing that complies with the special "downsizing rules" (see ¶1780), where the additional years are granted in respect of the period from the individual's actual retirement date to age 65, for example. The additional years of credited service beyond the year of retirement are not subject to PA reporting.

If the situation does not comply with the CRA's definition of "downsizing", the extra years of future service may not be credited.

¶795 Sale of a Company or Division

In the event of a sale of a company or division, there is a situation where the buyer is allowed to co-ordinate its PA reporting with that of the seller in order to facilitate PA reporting for both the buyer and seller. This situation arises if the purchaser's defined benefit RPP has identical benefits to those of the seller's RPP. This might occur, for example, if the purchase–sale agreement requires the buyer to set up a defined benefit plan that is identical to the plan to which the transferring employees had belonged prior to the sale.

If the PA co-ordination process is not followed, and if the two employers operate at arm's length from each other, the PAs that the buyer must report in respect of the part of the year after the sale would be determined independently of the PAs that the seller reports in respect of the earlier part of the year. Thus, a transferring employee's total PA for the year normally will have been reduced twice by the $600 PA offset, since this offset is applied separately by both the seller and the buyer. This process will benefit employees whose RRSP limit is based on 18% of earned income, rather than on the dollar limit (i.e., everyone but high earners).

However, if the buyer wishes to co-ordinate that year's PA reporting with the seller, the buyer may apply to the Minister of National Revenue to report a PA that is determined as if the buyer was the transferring employee's employer prior to the sale. Thus, the PA that the buyer determines for a particular employee is based on the employee's total pensionable service with both employers in the year of the sale, reduced by the PA that the seller reports in respect of the first part of the year. In fact, under this arrangement the seller has the option of not reporting any PA at all for the year.

Separate reporting will benefit employees affected by the sale since it will generally result in an additional $600 of new RRSP contribution room being available in the year after the sale.

As an example, consider a sale that was effective July 1, 2010, and assume that both employers have identical defined benefit plans whose pension formula is 1.75% of earnings for each year of service. Assume that both employers follow the annualized earnings approach when determining PAs for a partial year of service (as discussed at ¶730). Suppose a particular employee had annualized pensionable earnings of $75,000 at each company in 2010 and had six months of pensionable service under each employer's pension plan that year. If the PA co-ordination process is not followed, each employer will report a 2010 PA that is determined as follows:

- 2010 benefit entitlement is: 1.75% × ($75,000 × 6/12) = $656.25; and
- 2010 PA reported by each employer equals: (9 × $656.25) - $600 = $5,306.25 (rounded to $5,306).

Therefore, the total 2010 PA for this individual is $5,306 × 2 = $10,612.

On the other hand, if the PA co-ordination process is followed, the 2010 benefit entitlement is: 1.75% × $75,000 = $1,312.50.

The 2010 PA is then: (9 × $1,312.50) - $600 = $11,212.50 (rounded to $11,213).

Thus, if the PA co-ordination process is followed, this individual has 2011 RRSP contribution room of $2,287 (i.e., 18% × $75,000 - $11,213), assuming earned income is equal to pensionable earnings. If the two PAs are calculated and reported separately, the 2011 RRSP contribution room is $2,888 (i.e., 18% × $75,000 - $10,612). Therefore, in this example, the employee is worse off (that is, has less RRSP contribution room in 2011) if the PA co-ordination process is used.

In the example above, if the member's earnings are $150,000, then the 2011 benefit entitlement determined by each employer is the lesser of:

- 1.75% × ($140,000 × 6/12), or $1,312.50; or
- $2,494.44* × 6/12 or $1,247.22.

Each employer then reports a PA of $10,624.98 (i.e., 9 × $1,247.22 - $600, rounded). The total PA reported for the individual is, therefore, $21,250. However, the individual's available RRSP contribution room for 2011 (before the PA offset) is equal to the lesser of 18% of earnings of $150,000 (or $27,000) and the 2011 dollar limit of $22,450, leaving new RRSP contribution room in 2011 equal to $1,200 ($22,450 less the reported PAs of $21,250). In this situation, separate reporting of the PAs is again, more beneficial than co-ordinated reporting of the PAs, which will result in only $600 of RRSP contribution room in 2011, since the $600 offset is used only once in the co-ordinated reporting approach.

It should be noted that if the benefit formulae under the two employers' pension plans are not identical, the co-ordination process may not be used.

* The defined benefit limit for 2010, since the benefit is limited to the maximum pension.

¶800 PENSION ADJUSTMENTS FOR COMBINATION PLANS AND HYBRIDS

¶805 Introduction

There are two types of hybrid plans (also known as combination plans) for which special PA rules apply:

1. A stacked plan which provides a combination of a defined benefit tier and a money purchase tier (see ¶810).
2. An integrated plan where the benefit is based on the greater of a defined benefit formula and a benefit provided by a defined contribution accumulation (see ¶815).

¶810 Two-Tiered Plans

Where a plan provides a combination benefit of a defined benefit provision plus a defined contribution provision or a DPSP, a pension credit must be determined in respect of each element, using the usual PA rules that would apply if that provision were the only provision under which the member is accruing benefits for the year, as discussed at ¶520. The PA is the total of the pension credits in respect of the employee.

Typical examples of two-tiered plans are as follows:

- A pension plan with both a defined benefit tier and a defined contribution tier.
- A defined benefit plan in combination with a DPSP. In this situation, the DPSP often forms part of an employee savings plan — it may not be readily apparent that the employer contributions to the savings plan are in fact being directed to a DPSP.

- A defined benefit plan to which employees make additional voluntary contributions on a money purchase basis.

It should be noted that where an employer provides both a defined benefit plan and a group RRSP, this is not a combination plan for PA purposes, since PAs are not reported in respect of the group RRSP. For this type of arrangement, the amount of available RRSP room at the beginning of the year is known since it is based on accumulated RRSP contribution room, earned income for the previous year and the PA for the defined benefit plan for the previous year. Thus, the special rules and issues for combination plans do not arise with this type of arrangement.

It should also be noted that for combination plans, although only one PA is reported on the T4, employers should track separately the two pension credits comprising the PA, for the following reasons:

- If the defined benefit provision is later improved, it may be necessary to report a PSPA.
- When members terminate, a PAR may be reported in respect of the defined benefit provision.
- PSPAs and PARs can arise in reciprocal transfer and portability situations and it may be necessary to access the defined benefit and defined contribution pensions separately.

A two-tiered plan can have the effect of completely eliminating RRSP contribution room for employees. Suppose the pension credit under the defined benefit tier is sufficiently large that, in the absence of any money purchase tier, the individual would have only $600 of RRSP contribution room in the following year. If a contribution of $600 is made that year to the money purchase tier on behalf of the employee, and is therefore included in the PA for the year, then that contribution could eliminate the employee's RRSP contribution room in the following year.

In fact, in these hybrid plans, care must be taken throughout the year not to exceed the "maximum PA rule" (discussed at ¶630 and ¶655). This can happen if the combination of the defined benefit formula and the required money purchase contributions together produce a total PA that exceeds the limits permitted. In situations like this, typically the money purchase contributions must be cut off at some point during the year in order to avoid an excessive PA at the end of the year. This may present quite a challenge if the elements are relatively generous, as well as in the case of higher-income employees whose defined benefit pension credit is high. Monitoring when the money purchase contributions should cease may have to be done on a person by person basis, since money purchase contributions are not likely to cease in such situations at the same time for each affected member.

For example, consider the following two-tiered pension plan:

- defined benefit tier: 1.8% of earnings per year of credited service; and
- defined contribution tier: employee contribution of 3% of earnings, accumulating on a money purchase basis, which is required as a condition of plan membership.

Consider a member whose 2010 pensionable earnings are $130,000 and whose 2010 T4 earnings are $140,000. The pension credit under the defined benefit tier is based on a Benefit Entitlement of: 1.8% × $130,000 = $2,340.00. Therefore, the 2010 defined benefit pension credit is: (9 × $2,340.00) - $600 = $20,460. The maximum defined benefit PA for 2010 is, from Appendix 3, Table 1, $21,850 and the money purchase limit for 2010 is $22,450.

Using the "maximum PA rule", the maximum 2010 combined PA for this employee is the lesser of 18% of $140,000 (i.e., $25,200) and $22,000. Therefore, while the defined benefit pension credit on its own does not exceed the maximum permitted of $21,400, the plan contribution room available for the defined contribution tier in 2010 is limited to: $22,450 - $20,460, or $1,990.

Therefore, although the plan requires a contribution of 3% of $130,000, or $3,900, to the defined contribution tier, unless a lower defined benefit formula is utilized that year, the required employee contribution will have to be reduced to $1,990 in 2010. This represents only 51% of the contribution otherwise required. If the employee contributes at the rate of 3% of earnings from the start of 2010, the PA limit will probably be reached sometime during July 2010, assuming the full defined benefit pension credit of $20,460 applies that year (i.e., assuming the individual remains a member of the plan throughout the year). If the employee continues to contribute beyond July 2010, and the employer only realizes later in the year (or in the following year when PAs are being calculated) that the maximum PA rule has been breached, the employer will have to take immediate steps to refund the excess contributions to the employee. The approval process to remove the excess contributions from the plan varies from jurisdiction to jurisdiction, but will generally require obtaining a letter from the CRA confirming that the plan's registration is in jeopardy and the plan is in a revocable position in order to obtain permission from the relevant pension supervisory authority to remove the excess contributions. The excess contributions should not be included in the PA. Normally, any amount paid out of an RPP is included in income even though the contribution may not have been tax-deductible when made to the plan due to exceeding the contribution limits (i.e., "double taxation"). However, if it can be shown that the excess contributions were made due to reasonable error, and the problem is identified and steps are taken to remove the excess contributions from the plan as quickly as possible, then an administrative exception can be made and the employee's excess contributions that are refunded out of the plan will not be included in income nor included in the PA. However, there is no such administrative exception for any excess employer contributions; excess contributions refunded to the employer are included in the employee's taxable income and are not tax-deductible to the employee.

¶815 Greater of Defined Benefit and Defined Contribution Formula

The Regulations do not allow an RPP to provide a benefit based on the greater of a defined benefit formula and a benefit provided by a defined contribution accumulation. Instead, this type of formula must be expressed as the sum of the defined contribution provision and the pension under the defined benefit provision which is calculated as the amount determined under the defined benefit formula less the pension generated under the defined contribution provision. However, the combination of the two tiers still amounts to taking the larger of the defined benefit formula and the benefit under the defined contribution formula.

The method of calculating PAs for this type of pension plan in 1990 and 1991 was particularly complicated, as discussed in Appendix 1, section 6A.

The PA is generally equal to the larger of the pension credit under the defined benefit formula and the pension credit under the defined contribution formula. In fact, the legislation reflects the structure described above. The Regulations separate the PA calculation into two parts:

(a) the defined contribution pension credit; plus

(b) a defined benefit pension credit calculated using a benefit entitlement in which the defined benefit is offset by 1/9th of the defined contribution pension credit.

However, a complex transitional rule applied for each year up to and including 1999. This rule appears in Appendix 1, section 6B.

Example

Consider a defined contribution plan to which the employee and employer each contribute 5% of salary. Benefits under the plan are subject to a minimum defined benefit guarantee equal to 1.5% of the final average salary per year of credited service. (Although, as mentioned earlier, the

Regulations require that this minimum be expressed as a second tier that is provided in addition to the defined contribution first tier.)

Consider an individual whose 2010 salary is $75,000. The individual belongs to the pension plan throughout 2010.

The 2010 pension credit under the defined contribution provision equals 10% of salary, i.e., $7,500.

The 2010 benefit entitlement under the defined benefit formula is: 1.5% × $75,000 less 1/9 of $7,500, or $291.67.

The 2010 pension credit in respect of the defined benefit is: (9 × $291.67) - $600 = $2,025.

The 2010 PA is equal to the sum of the pension credit under the defined contribution formula ($7,500) and the adjusted pension credit under the defined benefit formula (i.e., $2,025). Therefore, the 2010 PA equals $9,525.

For the same reasons as noted at ¶810, employers should separately track the two pension credits comprising the PA in these "greater of" two formulae situations, even though only one PA is reported on the T4.

Chapter 9

¶900 PENSION ADJUSTMENTS FOR PLANS WITH SEVERAL PARTICIPATING EMPLOYERS

¶905 Introduction

There are three situations where more than one employer participates in one RPP. Each of these situations is governed by its own special rules:

- specified multi-employer plans (SMEPs) — see ¶910;
- multi-employer plans (MEPs) other than SMEPs — see ¶915; and
- pension plans with several participating employers that do not fall under the definition of an MEP or an SMEP — see ¶920.

As discussed at ¶520, the legislation refers to "pension credits" as well as PAs. Since the term "PA" is more widely used than "pension credits", we have generally used "PA" in this chapter, even though technically we are calculating pension credits.

¶910 Specified Multi-Employer Plans

If an individual belongs to an SMEP, the PA is generally determined using the simpler rules applicable to defined contribution pension plans. From the employer's viewpoint, this is one of the primary advantages of being classified as an SMEP.

To qualify as an SMEP in a particular calendar year, the pension plan must fall within one of the following three categories:

- Category 1 — a plan that satisfies all of the following conditions at the beginning of the year:

  (i) there are a number of participating employers in the plan, but it is reasonable to expect that no more than 95% of the active members in the year are employed by any single participating employer or by participating employers who are related;

  (ii) it is reasonable to expect that either at least 15 unrelated employers will participate in the year or at least 10% of the active plan members will be employed in the year by at least two of the unrelated participating employers;

  (iii) substantially all (generally at least 90%) of the participating employers are not exempt from taxation under Part I of the *Income Tax Act* (Canada). Examples of employers who are exempt from taxation include labour organizations, municipalities, corporations owned by the Crown, and registered charities;

  (iv) participation in the plan is pursuant to a collective bargaining or similar agreement and contributions are made according to a negotiated formula under the agreement;

  (v) the plan administrator is a board of trustees (or similar body) that is not controlled by representatives of the employers;

  (vi) employer contributions are determined to some extent by reference to the hours worked by employees (or some other employee-specific measure) and are made in accordance with a negotiated or fixed schedule of rates, with no variation being permitted by reference to the plan's financial experience; and

  (vii) the plan administrator has the power to determine benefits under the plan, whether or not that power is subject to the terms of a collective bargaining agreement.

- Category 2 — a plan that has been designated by the Minister of National Revenue as an SMEP, following application by the administrator. Typically, this is where the plan satisfies most of the conditions in Category 1 and would face serious difficulties in reporting PAs if it were not designated as anSMEP.

- Category 3 — a plan that was a Category 1 SMEP in the preceding year. This prevents the plan from no longer being an SMEP in a subsequent year simply because one of the conditions in Category 1 is no longer satisfied. For an MEP to no longer be treated as an

SMEP, the Minister must have given written notice to the plan administrator to this effect, following application by the administrator. This notice will only be given if the Minister is satisfied that participating employers will be able to report PAs on a defined benefit basis correctly and within the required deadlines.

To summarize in more general terms, an SMEP is a defined benefit plan with several participating employers, not all related to each other, where employer contribution rates are negotiated and, based on those agreed-upon contribution rates, the board of trustees is empowered to determine benefits that would be supported by those contributions, at least until the next set of negotiations.

These pension plans are often set up through the collective bargaining process. Since both the benefits and the contributions are defined, it resembles both a defined benefit plan and a defined contribution plan.

There are some situations where a plan administrator may prefer that the plan not be treated as an SMEP, even though the plan qualifies under the above-mentioned rules. For example, if the employees are relatively old or if a large portion of the contribution is related to an unfunded past service liability, many of the employees' PAs could possibly be reduced if the PA reporting were based on the plan's benefit formula — in other words, by using defined benefit PA rules rather than defined contribution PA rules. For the plan not to be treated as an SMEP in a particular year, the administrator must have obtained the Minister's approval before the beginning of the year.

However, for the Minister to allow an MEP, that would normally qualify as a SMEP, to be treated instead in accordance with the rules for multi-employer plans other than SMEPs (as described at ¶915), the plan administrator must convince the Minister that the participating employers generally will have little difficulty in complying with the defined benefit PA rules. In the vast majority of cases this will be difficult or impossible to do. Furthermore, in order to confirm this application, the Minister must receive the participating employers' consents to the proposal. Therefore, in most of these situations, the plan will likely end up being treated as an SMEP.

Where an MEP qualifies as an SMEP, the PA is treated using the rules set out in Chapter 6 for defined contribution plans, with two exceptions:

- any employee contributions made to the plan in a particular calendar year in respect of pensionable service for that year or in respect of pensionable service for a plan year ending in that year, and any employee contributions made in January of the year in respect of service in the immediately preceding year, are to be included in the PA for the calendar year in which the contribution is made; and

- any funds representing non-vested forfeitures that are left in the plan after members terminate service without vesting are ignored.

To be able to determine the PA as if the plan were a defined contribution plan, all employer contributions must be attributed to individual members. Any lump-sum contribution made by a participating employer that is not determined by some measure specific to individual plan members (such as being based on a "cents per hour per employee" formula) must be allocated to plan members in proportion to the members' share of the member specific contributions made by the employer.

With an SMEP, the participating employers are responsible for reporting PAs in all situations, except where employees are purchasing additional pensionable hours in a year during which they do not work on a full-time basis (see ¶2105). In this limited circumstance, the plan administrator is responsible for reporting the portion of the employee's PA that is in respect of these employee contributions; the employer remains responsible for reporting the balance of that year's PA. Special rules apply if an employer or employee contributes to an SMEP indirectly through a union or employer association (see ¶515).

¶915 Multi-Employer Plans Other Than SMEPs

If a pension plan has several participating employers, where it is reasonable to expect that no more than 95% of the active members are employed by a single participating employer or by participating employers who are related, the plan qualifies as an MEP.

Typically, these situations are found in the public sector where, for example, a province sets up a pension plan for teachers and the participating employers are the individual school boards.

Care should be taken in these situations with respect to the definition of "employer". In the example of the provincial pension plan for teachers, the plan generally would qualify as an MEP if the individual school boards are regarded as the employers; but if the provincial government is regarded as the employer of all teachers in that province, the plan may not qualify as an MEP — instead, it may be a single employer plan.

Without any special rules applicable to MEPs, the PA calculations would be particularly difficult in the circumstance where an employee switches between participating employers during the year. For example, if a teacher leaves one school board in June of a particular year and starts at another school board in the same province in September of that year, the first school board may not find out that the employee has returned to work for another school board later in the year and is, therefore, still a member of the same pension plan. Without the special rule noted below, the two school boards would have to co-ordinate their PA calculations, in order to ensure that the $600 PA offset and the benefit accrual in respect of credited service under the plan for the year are correctly prorated. For practical purposes, this co-ordination would be very difficult, if not impossible, given the annual PA reporting deadlines.

Where a plan qualifies as n MEP and is not an SMEP, the following special PA rules apply for each employer, unless approval is obtained from the Minister of National Revenue to follow a different approach:

- Each employer determines the PA for an individual as if the individual were not employed by any other participating employer during the year — thus, each of the two school boards in the above example would use the PA rules applicable to a partial year of service.
- If the member has not been employed with the employer on a full-time basis throughout the year, the $600 PA offset is to be prorated in the ratio of the individual's actual credited service in the year to his or her total potential credited service as a full-time employee in the year. This prorating would therefore be required if, for example, the individual joins or leaves a participating employer in mid-year, is a part-time employee, or is on a non-pensionable leave of absence.
- If an individual takes a leave of absence in a year, the portion of that year's PA relating to pensionable service granted during that leave may be determined independently from the portion relating to benefits credited while the individual was actually employed by a participating employer during the year.

With MEPs, the participating employers are responsible for reporting PAs in all situations except, if the Minister so consents, in respect of pensionable leaves of absence (for which the plan administrator would then be responsible for PA reporting). If this consent has been granted, the administrator may request written permission to use a T4A slip instead of a T4 slip when reporting PAs in respect of members on a pensionable leave of absence.

¶920 Several Participating Employers

Consider an individual who works during the year for two or more employers who participate in the same pension plan, and assume that the plan does not qualify as an MEP or an SMEP. For example, the individual may have begun the year with one of the employers and then switched to one of the other participating employers in the same year. Also consider an individual who works during a year for two or more related employers, each of whom sponsors a separate pension plan to which the individual belongs.

In the above situations, the employee's benefit accrual for PA purposes in the year must be prorated between the employers. As discussed at ¶ 710, the benefit accrual is the total of the benefit entitlements that the individual has earned in the year in respect of employment with each participating employer that year. The benefit accrual is calculated in the same way as one calculates a benefit entitlement for a pension plan with only one participating employer, and is then split into the portion in respect of each participating employer for whom the member worked in the year. Each of these portions is known as the benefit entitlement in respect of that employer, and each employer calculates a PA based on the benefit entitlement attributable to that employer. Separate PAs must then be reported by each employer. In addition, the total defined benefit PA offset by all employers in the year in respect of the employee may not exceed $600 — each employer could prorate this offset, or the employers could agree that the entire offset be utilized by just one of the employers in the year.

These situations can present significant difficulties in PA reporting and require the co-ordination of information between the employers.

¶925 Union Considered to be a Single Employer

A union and all of its locals and branches are considered a single employer for the purposes of the maximum PA rule (as well as for the definition of an MEP and the exemption of foreign plans from the RCA rules). This prevents members from doubling up on benefits payable from an RPP.

Chapter 10

¶1000 PAST SERVICE PENSION ADJUSTMENTS

¶1005 Introduction

The concept of the PSPA was introduced to ensure equitable access to tax-assisted retirement savings and to ensure equity within the PA system. Equity requires measurement. The PA measures the value, for tax purposes, of the benefit accruing in the current calendar year, whereas the PSPA measures the degree to which past PAs are undervalued when certain benefit improvements are made retroactively. The PSPA is one of the more complicated aspects of the current retirement tax system as there are complex rules for applying, calculating, and reporting PSPAs.

In the tax system as it applied to 1989 and earlier years, it was possible for certain individuals to "double-dip" — that is, to have greater access to tax assistance than others. The most common example of this was an individual who was not a member of an RPP or DPSP and who made maximum contributions to an RRSP each year. If this individual's employer then set up a pension plan that provided past service benefits, then this individual has doubly benefited — by being able to make maximum RRSP contributions and then potentially receiving a maximum pension benefit in respect of those same years of service. From 1990 onwards, individuals participating in employer-sponsored benefit plans cannot tax shelter more money than those outside of such plans.

This chapter discusses the rules for calculating and reporting PSPAs. The actual methodology for calculating the PSPA is set out in ¶1035. It describes the rules to be used since the introduction of the PAR (see Chapter 11 regarding the PAR). There are two different methodologies used to calculate PSPAs: the basic approach and the modified approach. The appropriate methodology to use depends on when the past service event occurred and whether it occurred in conjunction with a portability or reciprocal transfer situation.

As noted at ¶1105, the tax system did not originally include provisions for a PAR. When the PAR was introduced in 1997, the rules surrounding the calculation of the PSPA were changed further to accommodate the introduction of the PAR, with additional modifications added in 1998 and 2000. The old rules that were in place prior to the introduction of the PAR, along with the modifications that were added in 1998 and 2000, appear in Appendix A.

The PSPA applies only to defined benefit pension plans and only to benefits that relate to pensionable service after 1989. When certain types of retroactive plan improvements are made on behalf of an individual or when additional years of past service are credited, a revised pension credit (as defined at ¶520) is calculated, based on the new benefit formula, for each year after 1989 for which benefits are to be improved or provided. The total increase in the pension credits for all affected years becomes the individual's PSPA. In effect, the PSPA is a "past service PA" — hence, the name. The PSPA reduces RRSP contribution room in much the same way as a PA. However, unlike the PA, which can only reduce (or eliminate) new RRSP contribution room that arises in the year, the PSPA reduces (or eliminates) any RRSP carry-forward an individual may have and can cause RRSP contribution room to become negative. The PSPA may even lead to the member having to make a choice between deregistering some RRSP assets or not receiving the benefit improvement.

There are two general scenarios under which PSPAs are generated. The first occurs when a pension plan retroactively credits additional periods of past service after 1989. In this circumstance, the plan administrator must calculate the PAs that would have been reported had the benefits been earned in the year for which the service has been granted. The sum of these "simulated" PAs constitutes the PSPA. Common PSPA situations include an employee who "buys back" one or more years of post-1989 service by contributing extra amounts to the pension plan; or an employee who quits in 1990 or later, returns to the same employer after a few months or years, and wishes to have the earlier period of post-1989 service reinstated as pensionable service.

The other scenario occurs when benefits are retroactively improved, but only where the improvement would have affected the calculation of an earlier year's PA had the improvement been in effect in that year. For example, consider a plan where the benefit formula is 1.5% of earnings for each year of service — the PA would have been based on this benefit level. If the formula is improved to 2% of earnings for each of those years of service, then the PSPA is the sum of the differences between what the PAs would have been had the higher benefit formula been in place throughout the period and what the PAs actually were.

A PSPA may need to be "certified", as described in general terms at ¶1010, when an individual transfers to a new employer from another employer under a reciprocal transfer agreement or portability arrangement, i.e., service is credited under the new employer's pension plan in respect of employment with an unrelated employer. Under this circumstance, when the new employer's pension plan credits part or all of the service with the previous employer, a PSPA is generated if the new employer's pension formula leads to higher PAs than the previous employer's. Certification means pre-approval by the CRA that the individual has sufficient RRSP contribution room to permit the service to be credited.

Fortunately, there are many types of past service improvements that are excluded from PSPA calculations or generate a zero PSPA. In particular, there are major exceptions for improvements to flat benefit plans. These exceptions are outlined at ¶1017.

The balance of this chapter deals with the calculation of PSPAs under defined benefit plans (other than MEPs) and the associated reporting mechanisms. PSPAs for MEPs are discussed in Chapter 12.

¶1010 The General Process

In contrast to the reporting of the PA being the responsibility of the employer (see ¶515), it is the plan administrator's responsibility to calculate and report PSPAs. In most single-employer pension plans, the plan administrator is the employer; however, in Quebec, the plan administrator is a pension committee and in MEPs, the administrator is generally a different body from any of the participating employers.

There are two types of PSPAs:

- Certifiable: when the past service benefit improvement applies to a small number of members (or a single member) of a pension plan, a PSPA is required to be certified for that member (or members) by the CRA before the improved benefits are provided (see ¶1065); this type of PSPA is also called "non-exempt";

- Reportable: when in general terms, the past service improvement applies to most of the plan members, of whom relatively few are highly paid, then the PSPAs for the whole group need to be reported to the CRA but no certification is required; these PSPAs are "exempt" — i.e., exempt from having to be certified (see ¶1060).

The certification process is such that the administrator calculates the PSPA for the affected individual and reports that amount to the CRA on a special form (T1004). The CRA compares the amount of the PSPA for the individual to his or her amount of available RRSP contribution room. If the PSPA is less than the amount of the individual's RRSP contribution room (or no more than $8,000 greater than the amount of available contribution room), the PSPA is certified. The individual would then be entitled to the past service improvement and his or her RRSP contribution room is reduced by the amount of the PSPA. This process could result in negative RRSP contribution room (up to $8,000 is permitted). On the other hand, if the individual's RRSP contribution room would be made deficient by more than $8,000 as a result of the PSPA, the CRA allows him or her to deregister an appropriate amount of RRSP assets (and pay tax on those assets) in order to bring the deficiency at or below $8,000 and, therefore, qualify for the past service credit.

Obviously, there is an administration cost associated with this certification process. The plan administrator must keep track of every individual's past service benefit as certified by the CRA and must keep note of those employees for whom the past service improvement was not certified.

The certification process is most often used for one-off and individual situations. Where the past service improvement applies to most plan members, the "exempt PSPA" process is used, which streamlines the CRA's workload and alleviates the administrative workload associated with the certification process. Under the exempt PSPA approach, if the situation meets specific requirements, the plan administrator is exempt from having to obtain individual by individual approval, and instead, all individuals immediately have their RRSP contribution rooms reduced by the amounts of the PSPA and are granted the past service improvements (provided, of course, that the improvements comply with the CRA's plan registration rules).

With the exempt approach, individuals will not be given any opportunity to deregister RRSP assets to create additional RRSP contribution room to cover the PSPA. The exempt PSPA can result in the employees having a deficiency with respect to their RRSP contribution room of greater than $8,000 — in fact, there is no limit on the size of the deficiency for an exempt PSPA (but it is indirectly limited by constraints imposed on the benefit improvement that generates the exempt PSPA). However, the individual may not make additional RRSP contributions until he or she generates enough new RRSP contribution room in future years to make the balance positive again. As noted earlier, negative RRSP contribution room can also result from a non-exempt PSPA, in which case, the same comments apply with respect to making additional RRSP contributions, but in the non-exempt case, the individual is given the "opportunity" to deregister enough RRSP assets to bring the balance back up to zero again immediately.

¶1012 Precise Use of Terminology

The PSPA rules are prescribed in specific terms defined in the *Income Tax Act* (Canada) and Regulations. The most important concept is the "past service event". This means any transaction, event, or circumstance that causes retirement benefits for post-1989 service to be retroactively improved in a defined benefit plan. All PSPAs are generated by past service events. The nature and the date of a past service event are key factors in determining which type of PSPA is applicable and how it should be calculated.

When a PSPA is first calculated, it is called a "provisional PSPA". The "accumulated PSPA" in a particular year is the sum of the provisional PSPAs for the year that were exempt from certification and the provisional PSPAs that have already been certified in the year by the CRA. The "PSPA" is the "accumulated PSPA" for the individual, in respect of an employer, determined at the end of a calendar year. A "grossed up PSPA" is the total value of pension credits in respect of the improved benefits. It is equal to the provisional PSPA before its reduction by any qualifying transfers, money purchase transfers, and excess money purchase transfers.

Generally, for ease of communication, we will use the term "PSPA" and only use the terms "provisional PSPA" or "accumulated PSPA" where the context requires clarification.

¶1014 Effective Date

PSPAs only arise when a "past service event" occurs after 1989. The effective date of the event is not necessarily the effective date of the amendment to the plan. It is the date of the official decision to improve the past service benefits (for example, the date of the board resolution amending the plan, or the date on which the employee and employer agree that the employee will buy back an earlier period of service).

The following past service events have effective dates as follows:

- where a new pension plan providing past service benefits is introduced — the effective date of registration of the plan;
- where benefits are retroactively improved — the date on which the plan sponsor's decision is taken to improve the benefits (for example, the date on which the plan sponsor's board of directors passes a resolution to amend the plan or the date on which a collective agreement is ratified);
- where the benefit is scheduled to increase at a specific future date, when an employee meets required conditions to be eligible for an increased benefit, or when benefits automatically increase — the date when the benefit increase becomes effective; and
- where an employee chooses to purchase past service benefits — the date of the election.

¶1015 Circumstances Where PSPAs are Nil

Generally, PSPAs are generated when there is a past service event. Some PSPAs are exempt from certification, whereas others are required to be certified. However, not all past service events result in the calculation or reporting of a PSPA. There are many circumstances where benefits under defined benefit plans may be improved in respect of prior service where either there are special rules that permit part or all of the benefit improvement to be excluded from the PSPA calculation or where the PSPA is equal to zero. These circumstances are outlined at ¶1016 to ¶1034.

¶1016 Pre-1990 Service

Because the system is prospective in nature, improving benefits for service prior to 1990 does not result in a PSPA. The first PAs were in respect of calendar year 1990, so, therefore, PSPAs can only impact service after 1989.

However, there are other restrictions that may apply in the situation where benefits for pre-1990 service are improved. This is discussed further at ¶1715 and ¶1746.

¶1017 Excluded Benefits — Flat Benefit Plans

In an earnings-related defined benefit plan, PAs are based on the current year's pensionable earnings and the pension formula in effect. Thus, when the pension plan provides benefits based on best average earnings, the calculation of the PA amount implicitly includes indexing for future inflation until the pension commences. The reduction in the RRSP contribution room in any year on account of the previous year's PA is based on the previous year's pensionable earnings, not the highest average earnings or any other earnings base that may be used in calculating the actual pension benefit at the time the benefit is payable.

A similar concept is applied to flat benefit pension plans. Consider a pension plan which provides a level dollar amount per month for each year of service. These types of programs are most commonly found in negotiated pension plans. Under certain conditions as set out below, as long as the pension benefit is increased at a rate no greater than the change in the average wage over a specific time period, PSPAs generated by such an increase for all plan participants are nil. To determine the specific time period, the employer selects any base year (no earlier than 1984), and the benefit formula that was in effect in that base year becomes the formula against which the increase will be measured in respect of post-1989 service. There is also another exemption that permits benefits to increase by up to $1.50 per month without generating a PSPA.

The conditions that must apply in order to be able to take advantage of these exemptions are as follows:

- the benefit increase is of the type that would lead to a PSPA that would be exempt from certification (as set out at ¶1060);
- the pension is determined using only one flat benefit rate; and
- the new flat benefit per year of service is not greater than 40% of the defined benefit limit for that year (i.e., 40% of $2,494.44 for 2010).

If these conditions are met, a PSPA is created but equal to zero if the past service event does not cause the flat benefit rate to increase beyond the greater of the following two amounts:

- the benefit rate just prior to the increase plus $1.50 per month multiplied by the number of years (including fractions) from the day on which the current rate was first effective (or January 1,

1984, if later) to the day of the increase (see the example at ¶ 1052); and

- any flat benefit rate that was effective on or after January 1, 1984, increased by the change in the average wage from that year (the "base year") to the year of the increase.

The amount determined above would be compared to the new benefit level and any increase in the benefit up to this amount can be excluded in determining the PSPA. Thus, if the above amount were greater than the new benefit level, there would be a nil PSPA, since the benefit increase is less than the maximum exempt increase. But, if the new benefit level exceeds the above amount, the amount of the excess would generate a non-zero PSPA.

The condition that only one flat benefit rate applies means that one flat rate must be used for all periods of service. This means that for some members, the amount of the increase in the benefit level may not be able to be excluded while, for others, it may be excluded. For example, if the plan provided for a benefit of $25 per month for service up to 2000 and $35 per month for service after 2000, the benefit increase for active members who joined the plan before or during 2000 cannot be excluded whereas the benefit increase for members who joined after 2000 can be excluded.

¶ 1018 Excluded Benefits — Increases in Flat Rates (Including Increases in the Flat Dollar Maximum Pension)

The benefit rate may be increased by the one-year increase in the average wage with a zero PSPA. These increases can be applied to the first flat benefit rate increase each year prior to the member's retirement as well as for the first flat benefit rate increase after the member retires. For a flat benefit plan, the benefit rate is the amount of the flat benefit payable. Thus, if the flat benefit plan does not meet the conditions set out for the exemptions in ¶ 1017, the benefit rate may still be increased by the one-year increase in the average wage and the PSPA generated is nil.

This rule also accommodates an increase in the defined benefit limit when that limit is increasing in accordance with increases in the average wage — no PSPA is required to be reported for members whose benefits are limited by this flat rate. After retirement, the defined benefit limit can be increased in accordance with increases in the Consumer Price Index (CPI), as discussed at ¶ 1028.

However, for the period from 2004 to 2010, the defined benefit limit has increased faster than the increase in the average wage. The defined benefit limit was $1,722.22 per year of service from 1990 up until December 31, 2003. Since then, the defined benefit limit has increased, as follows:

Year	*DB Limit*	*% increase over prior year*	*% increase in average wage over prior year*
2004	$1,833.33	6.45	2.77
2005	$2,000.00	9.09	2.80
2006	$2,111.11	5.56	3.05
2007	$2,222.22	5.26	3.41
2008	$2,333.33	5.00	3.34
2009	$2,444.44	4.76	3.73

Note that the defined benefit limit in 2010 is, for the first time, based on the defined benefit limit for the prior year, increased by the increase in the average wage.

Thus, the increase in the defined benefit limit for the years 2004 through 2009 have all exceeded the increase in the average wage over the same period.

When the above increases were introduced as a result of budgetary measures in 2003 and 2005, a new regulation was also introduced to provide a special exemption under certain conditions from the PSPA reporting that would be required because the actual increases were expected to exceed the increases in the average wage in each year from 2004 to 2009.

Some plans provide for a maximum pension that is based on the defined benefit limit in effect at the particular time. These plans need not be amended to take into account the higher limits set out in the table above as the plan implicitly allows the higher benefits. No PSPA is created since there has not been a past service event.

However, some plans state a specific maximum pension dollar limit (i.e., specifically state that the maximum benefit payable under the plan is $1,722.22 per year of service, for example). If such plans are now amended in order to allow the higher limits, a past service event will be created.

The new regulation provides that where benefits in the plan are based on the lesser of a percentage of remuneration and a fixed rate per year of service and the plan is amended to increase the fixed amount, then certain benefits arising from the increase will be excluded from a PSPA.

However, if the fixed benefit rate has not been adjusted annually to reflect the annual increases in the defined benefit limit, a PSPA exclusion will only be available if the following conditions are met:

- there are 10 or more active plan members under the particular provision;
- the plan is not a designated plan; and
- the Minister has provided written approval of the exclusion.

Note that the regulation does not provide for an exclusion in the case of past service purchases.

As an example, consider a plan which provides a benefit of 2% of final average earnings per year of service, but is subject to a maximum flat benefit of $1,722.22. On January 1, 2010, the plan sponsor decides to amend the plan so that the maximum flat benefit will be the defined benefit limit rather than the flat $1,722.22. Consider a plan member with eight years of service and, for simplicity, assume the member's earnings are $130,000 in each of the last eight years. Thus, this member's benefit has always been limited by the $1,722.22 flat benefit.

Consider the benefit that the member is entitled to at January 1, 2010, for each of the eight years of credited service, after the amendment to increase the flat benefit maximum. The new regulation permits the portion of the benefit increase that is related to the increase in the defined benefit limit to be excluded from the PSPA calculation.

For Benefit Accruing in Respect of:	*Defined Benefit Limit*	*Plan's Flat Benefit Prior to Amendment*	*Plan's Flat Benefit After Amendment*	*Increase in Benefit*	*Portion of Benefit Increase Subject to PSPA*
2002	$1,722.22	$1,722.22	$2,494.44	$772.22	$ 0.00
2003	$1,722.22	$1,722.22	$2,494.44	$772.22	$ 0.00
2004	$1,833.33	$1,722.22	$2,494.44	$772.22	$111.11
2005	$2,000.00	$1,722.22	$2,494.44	$772.22	$277.78
2006	$2,111.11	$1,722.22	$2,494.44	$772.22	$388.89
2007	$2,222.22	$1,722.22	$2,494.44	$772.22	$500.00
2008	$2,333.33	$1,722.22	$2,494.44	$772.22	$611.11
2009	$2,444.44	$1,722.22	$2,494.44	$772.22	$722.22
2010	$2,494.44				

Therefore, in the above example, the benefit accrued as at January 1, 2010 for the year 2007 (after the plan amendment to increase the flat benefit maximum) is $2,494.44, a benefit increase of $772.22.

However, of this increase, $272.22 can be excluded since this represents the "normal" increase in the defined benefit limit from 2007 to 2010 (from $2,222.22 to $2,494.44). Thus, the PSPA in respect of the 2007 increase is based on the $500 increase from $1,722.22 to $2,222.22, since this increase has not yet been captured in the PA previously reported for 2007, which would have been based on the $1,722.22 flat maximum that was in effect at that time. Thus, the PSPA in respect of 2007 is equal to $9 \times \$500 = \$4,500$.

In these situations, where the plan has not been amended annually as the increases to the defined benefit limit have occurred, it is unlikely that the Minister will grant an exclusion if it appears that the purpose of the delay was to allow members to gain additional RRSP contribution room.

However, if the reason for the delay was due to funding or co bargaining considerations, the Minister may approve a PSPA exclusi

Another exclusion was introduced at the same time in the case o defined benefit plans or combination or hybrid plans with both a defined benefit and defined contribution component, in which the defined benefit accrual rate is stated as a fixed ratio of the defined benefit limit for the current year. A PSPA exclusion is allowed if the Minister approves and if it is reasonable to conclude that the fixed rate is set each year as a proportion of the defined benefit limit, that the ratio of the fixed rate to the defined benefit limit has been and will remain constant since 1989, the plan is not a designated plan and the member for whom the exclusion will apply is not in receipt of a pension under the plan.

¶1019 Job Category or Rate-of-Pay Change Resulting in Benefit Increase

Sometimes, an organization has a flat benefit plan for hourly staff with two or more job categories, each with its own benefit level within the plan. When a plan member is promoted to a higher job category, the pension benefit for all years of service becomes based on the higher flat benefit for that job category. When this occurs, a zero PSPA is created if the increase in the flat benefit level is in proportion to the increase in salary that the member receives as a result in the change in job category. The benefit level is permitted to increase, without generating a PSPA, as long as the ratio of benefits to earnings does not increase by more than 10%. This exemption may be applied on a group basis. The average income for those eligible for one level of benefit may be compared to the average income for those eligible for a higher level.

¶1020 Updating the Pensionable Earnings Base

In an earnings-related defined benefit plan, the PA is based on the plan formula and the individual's pensionable earnings in that year and does not necessarily reflect the actual average earnings base used in calculating the pension benefit. A defined benefit plan that has a benefit formula of 1% of career average earnings generates the same PA as a plan that has a benefit formula of 1% of the highest three-year average earnings.

Therefore, if the plan sponsor improves benefits by changing the earnings base on which benefits are calculated (for example, from career average to average earnings near retirement or from a highest ten-year average to a highest five-year average), there would have been no effect on the calculation of the PA, and, therefore, a zero PSPA arises. This means that sponsors of career average plans may update past service benefits to more recent earnings levels without reporting a PSPA, as long as the benefit formula is not changed at the same time.

t the plan sponsor should be careful if the earnings to include items in earnings that were previously ssed at ¶ 1057, this could give rise to a PSPA.

can also be excluded if they are related to s or increases in a general measure of salaries and average wage increases). For example, instead of s base on which a career average benefit is determined, a plan sponsor may choose instead to increase each year's accrual by a fixed percentage. This can be accommodated provided the fixed percentage increase used for a particular year is related to cost-of-living or average wage increases. However, the plan sponsor must apply in writing to the CRA for permission to exclude such increases.

¶ 1021 Ancillary Benefits

Ancillary benefits generally have no impact on the calculation of the PA. Therefore, providing or improving benefits by introducing retroactive indexation, early retirement subsidies, death benefits, or bridging benefits (all in accordance with the prescribed maximums) will not cause a PSPA to be created. However, introducing an optional form of pension, whereby retirees may elect a higher initial lifetime pension with less generous survivor benefits, can sometimes lead to a non-zero PSPA, in the same way as this option can increase the PAs (see ¶ 745).

¶ 1022 Increases in Benefits as a Result of Retirement after Age 65

In certain situations, a pension plan will provide that benefits payable upon postponed retirement (typically retirement after age 65) will be actuarially increased upon commencement. Although most minimum standards pension jurisdictions provide for continued accrual of benefits if a member remains employed and a member of the plan after age 65, it is possible (most notably in Quebec) that the postponed retirement benefit is an actuarial increase in the benefit accrued to age 65. No PSPA arises as a result of such actuarial increase.

¶ 1023 Breaks in Service

As discussed at ¶ 778, when a break in service occurs (such as maternity leave) and where credited service is automatically granted if the individual returns to work, the employer reports an amended PA rather than a PSPA.

Of course, if the entire leave of absence takes place within one calendar year, the PA would be reported as usual on the T4 slip for that year. However, in the case of a break in service that includes a year end, the employer would recalculate the PA when the individual returns to work and report the amended PA to the CRA in the same way as the employer would report any other adjustment to an individual's T4 slip. Amending the PA triggers the amendment to the RRSP room for the previous year and may lead to an RRSP excess contribution, with an imposition of a penalty tax (i.e., the employee made a maximum RRSP contribution in the previous year based on the RRSP room before the amendment of the PA).

Similarly, an amended PA (rather than a PSPA) is reported if, in a particular year, service is credited retroactively for a leave that ended in the previous calendar year, where such service is not automatically credited under the terms of the plan, provided the decision to credit the retroactive service is made before April 30 of the particular year. This usually occurs when an individual is given an option of "buying back" the break in service as pensionable service by making the appropriate required contribution. However, as noted at ¶779, if the decision is made after April 30, a PSPA is reported instead.

¶1024 Past Service in the Current Year

Where post-1989 benefits are being improved or additional years of post-1989 service are credited or where the member terminated from a defined benefit provision after 1996 and the same service is later reinstated under either the same or another defined benefit provision, current service for the year of the past service event is not included in the PSPA calculation but instead is included in the PA that is determined at the end of the calendar year. PSPAs that arise under these circumstances follow the "basic approach" for calculating the PSPA, as described in detail at ¶1036. Therefore, there is no PSPA in respect of the year of the past service event.

However, where past service benefits are provided in respect of a period of service in the current year and none of the service being credited was pensionable service under the provision immediately prior to the past service event or where the member terminated prior to 1997 and the same service is being reinstated under the same or another defined benefit provision (that is, the "modified approach", as described at ¶1037, is being used for the calculation of the PSPA), that current year past service is included in the PSPA calculation. However, it is possible to submit a written request to the CRA for permission to include that current year past service with the other employer in the PA for the current employer instead of calculating and reporting a PSPA.

¶1025 Waiting Periods

Many pension plans have a waiting period before an employee can become a member. As noted at ¶791, when an employee has reached the end of that waiting period, in some of these plans, the period is then counted as credited service. In this case, the CRA allows the employer to report a PA for the employee during the waiting period. If the employer makes this election, no PSPA would be reported for the employee upon joining the plan.

The choice of how to handle this situation is up to the plan sponsor. If the employer reports PAs during the waiting period, all employees who terminate employment before becoming members of the plan would temporarily lose some RRSP contribution room until their PARs are reported.

If, on the other hand, the employer chooses not to report PAs, but asks the pension administrator to report PSPAs for each employee upon becoming a member of the plan, then the plan administrator must follow the more administratively complex non-exempt PSPA certification process, as discussed at ¶1065. The employer may not contribute to the plan in respect of the waiting period until the plan administrator has applied for PSPA certification, and may not pay out the benefit in respect of the waiting period, should an employee terminate or retire with rights to these benefits, until certification is received. Moreover, some of the plan members may not be able to accept the waiting period benefits due to lack of sufficient RRSP room. The plan administrator also has to keep track of individuals whose PSPAs are not certified and, therefore, may not be able to have the waiting period treated consistently for all employees as pensionable service.

If membership is voluntary and an employee may choose to join at any time, with service during the waiting period becoming pensionable service upon joining, no PA would be reported during the waiting period because of the uncertainty of the timing as to when an employee will join the plan. Instead, a PSPA would be calculated when an individual joins the plan and the benefits for the past service would be provided only after that PSPA is certified by the CRA.

¶1026 Reciprocal Transfers Between Similar Plans

It is quite common in the public sector, and occasionally in the private sector, for employers to establish reciprocal transfer agreements or portability arrangements, whereby an employee terminating employment with one employer and joining another can transfer his or her pensionable service from the former employer's plan to the new employer's plan. Reciprocal transfer agreements and portability arrangements are discussed in greater detail at ¶1055. Generally, no PSPA is created, if:

- the benefit formula under the new employer's plan is no greater than that under the former employer's plan; and
- there are no transfers on behalf of the employee out of the former employer's plan into the new employer's plan as a money purchase amount or into the employee's RRSP.

Under a reciprocal transfer agreement or portability arrangement, there will typically be a direct transfer of assets from the former employer's plan to the new employer's plan — this amount usually represents the value (or a portion of the value) of the liabilities being transferred from one plan to the other. Since there are no assets being transferred on a money purchase basis in this situation (i.e., either to the new employer's plan or into the employee's RRSP), the amount of direct transfer into the plan does not have any impact on the PSPA because it is being used only to provide defined benefits under the new employer's plan.

However, as discussed at ¶ 1055, a PAR, could arise in respect of the amount of transfer from the former employer's plan and the amount of the PAR can only be determined once the PSPA is calculated.

¶ 1027 Plan Subdivisions

If an organization sells a division and the new employer sets up a pension plan providing essentially the same benefits as before (i.e., the same benefits from a PA point of view) and assets are transferred from the former plan to the new plan in respect of benefits under the former plan that are now being provided under the new plan, there is no need for the new employer to report PSPAs, even though the new employer's pension plan is crediting past service benefits.

If the buyer does not accept the past service benefits and does not provide past service benefits under the new pension plan, the past service benefits remain in the seller's pension plan. Depending on the requirements of the minimum standards jurisdiction, it is possible that the plan could be wound up in respect of the transferring employees and the benefits paid out to the transferring employees. However, no past service event has occurred and, therefore, there is no PSPA.

¶ 1028 Increases to Pensions in Payment and Increases in Pensions during Deferral Period

Pensions in payment can generally be increased in line with increases in the CPI (on a cumulative basis), or alternatively, in accordance with a fixed rate up to 4% *per annum*, without PSPA consequences.

An increase greater than the increase permitted may result in PSPAs to be reported for pensioners. If such increases are provided at the same time as a benefit increase for the active members of the plan, this may ensure that PSPAs generated for pensioners are exempt — i.e., required only to be reported but not certified. The PSPAs for pensioners are calculated only on the portion of pension that accrued for post-1989 service. Increasing pensions paid entirely for pre-1990 service are not subject to the PSPA rules. Refer to ¶ 1056 for a discussion on PSPAs for retired members.

During a deferral period (i.e., after an individual has terminated employment or terminated from the defined benefit provision but prior to when the individual commences to receive pension payments), pensions may be increased in line with increases in the average wage without generating a PSPA.

¶1029 Additional Pension Provided by 50% Rule and Quebec's Additional Benefit

Under minimum standards pension legislation, a plan member is not required, in a contributory plan, to pay for more than 50% of the benefit accruing. Typically, this applies only to benefits accruing and contributions made on and after the relevant reform date. In other words, the plan sponsor is required to pay for at least 50% of the benefit payable to the member. Any contributions made by the member in excess of 50% of the value of benefits are returned to the member. Refer to ¶1314 for further discussion regarding the 50% rule.

Typically the excess contributions are paid to the member in a lump-sum. However, some minimum standards jurisdictions provide that the excess contributions may remain in the plan to be used to provide additional lifetime benefits at retirement. In these situations, although additional benefits are being provided to the former member, no PSPA arises, as a result of these additional benefits.

As noted in ¶1319, under Quebec's minimum standards pension legislation, an additional benefit is provided to terminating members representing the value of partial indexation on the benefit accruing on and after January 1, 2001. The amount of indexation that is provided is equal to 50% of the increase in the CPI between the member's age at termination of employment and age 55. If the member elects a deferred pension, the additional benefit may be payable in the form of an increased lifetime pension which is then added to the pension accrued under the regular lifetime pension formula. Thus, since the pension payable to the member increases, it may be thought that there would be a PSPA required to reflect the additional benefit being provided.

However, since it is permissible to increase a pension during the deferral period by increases in the average wage without incurring a PSPA (as discussed at ¶1028), then an additional pension provided in accordance with Quebe'c partial indexing rules will similarly be able to be provided without incurring a PSPA as long as the additional benefit does not exceed the increase in the average wage from the termination date to the retirement date. Since the Quebec partial indexing rules only require indexation at 50% of the increase in the CPI up to age 55, it would be highly unlikely that the additional benefit provided could increase the formula benefit to a level higher than what would be determined by applying full average wage indexing from the member's date of termination to the member's pension commencement age, even if the pension commencement age were as early as age 55. Although Quebec's indexing is based on increases in the CPI and the tax rules permit increases during the deferral period in accordance with the average wage, in practical terms, these two indexing measures are typically quite similar (with average wage increases typically being slightly higher than CPI increases).

¶1030 Beneficiaries

The beneficiaries of deceased plan members (usually surviving spouses) may be the recipients of increases in survivors' benefits. Under these circumstances, no PSPA is created.

¶1031 PSPA = Zero

A benefit improvement can yield a zero PSPA in certain circumstances. For example, for a plan member with very high earnings, if his or her PA for a particular year was limited by the defined benefit pension limit (i.e., $2,494.44 per year of service for 2010), a later improvement in the benefit formula in respect of service in that year will have no effect, as far as PSPA rules are concerned, because the benefit entitlement is still limited by the defined benefit limit.

¶1032 Special Downsizing

Sometimes an employer will provide additional pension benefits to employees who are retiring due to workforce downsizing. If the benefits qualify as special downsizing benefits (as described at ¶1780) any qualifying lifetime benefits will not generate a PSPA.

¶1033 Increase in Foreign Service from Three to Five Years

Under certain conditions, where a member renders services outside Canada and remains a member of the Canadian plan, such period of service could be included in pensionable service for a period of up to five years. The five-year limit came into effect in 2000. Previously, only three years was permitted to be credited. The conditions under which this service may be credited is discussed at ¶1755.

Thus, qualifying individuals may be able to be credited with up to an additional two years of past service under this change. The CRA has indicated that on a case by case basis, they will determine whether the additional period of service can be excluded in calculating the individual's PSPA.

¶1034 Less than $50 PSPA

A PSPA does not have to be reported for a plan member if it is calculated to be less than $50. Also, an amended PSPA does not have to be reported for a plan member when the difference between a previously reported PSPA and the amended PSPA is less than $50. However, this less than $50 tolerance is cumulative, so it applies to the total of:

- the difference between a previously reported PSPA and an amended PSPA; and
- PSPA(s) calculated since the last reported PSPA.

This is an administrative rule and, therefore, does not apply if an employee or the CRA requests that a PSPA be accurately reported.

Refer to ¶1070 for further information on how to report an amended PSPA.

¶1035 Calculating the PSPA

The rules that appear below are the rules to be used to calculate PSPAs after 1997 — after the introduction of the PAR. The PAR was intended to be included in the retirement tax system when it was originally introduced, but was eliminated at the last minute, only to be reintroduced in 1997. As a result, modifications were required to the rules for calculating both PAs and PSPAs. The changes required to the PSPA rules primarily take into account the change in the PA rules with respect to the "year of termination" rule that was in effect prior to 1997 (see Appendix 1, section 3B, and variable B in the modified PSPA calculation rules at ¶1037) and also to introduce the concept of the "negative PAR", which is variable D in the basic PSPA calculation at ¶1036).

The rules that applied prior to the introduction of the PAR appear, for historical purposes, in Appendix 1, section 7C. Changes to the PA rules as a result of the introduction of the PAR appear at Appendix 1, section 8B. Chapter 11 covers the rules for PARs.

Under both the old and new rules, there is a basic calculation method (as set out at ¶1036) and a modified calculation method (as set out at ¶1037). Although similar to the old rules, the new rules have changed as have the circumstances under which the basic or modified method must be used. The new rules apply for past service events that occur after 1997. The rules in place for past service events prior to 1997 appear in Appendix 1, section 7C.

As noted at Appendix 1, section 5A, the PA offset for years after 1996 was decreased from $1,000 to $600 as a result of the introduction of the PAR. The offset for years before 1997 remains at $1,000. If PAs for the years 1990 to 1996, inclusive, are being recalculated in order to calculate PSPAs, plan administrators should continue to use the appropriate offset for the year in which the PA is being recalculated.

Note that there are different rules to follow if the plan is an SMEP. Refer to ¶1210 for information on how to calculate PSPAs for SMEPs.

¶1036 The Basic Calculation Method

The basic calculation method is used to calculate PSPAs, when crediting a member with past service benefits under a defined benefit plan in the following situations:

- post-1989 benefits are improved;
- additional years of post-1989 service are credited; or
- the member terminated from a defined benefit provision after 1996 (i.e., a PAR was reported) and the same service is later reinstated under the same provision or another defined benefit provision. If a member terminated prior to 1997 and no PAR was reported, then the PSPA for the reinstatement must be calculated using the modified rules as described at ¶1037.

The basic rules take into account the PA value of the additional benefits being provided or reinstated and is reduced by the amount, if any, of assets transferred from an individual's RRSP or other tax-sheltered savings vehicle to fund the benefits being provided. The amount of this reduction is known as the "qualifying transfer" and is discussed in greater detail later in this section (under variable C in the basic PSPA formula).

In addition, the basic rules take into account any lump-sum benefit transferred from the former plan to a tax-sheltered retirement savings vehicle which is in excess of the PAs and PSPAs reported in respect of the former plan. This is necessary to ensure that the member does not tax shelter more than his or her RRSP room.

The PSPA under the basic formula is determined as follows:

A - B - C + D

where **A**, **B**, **C**, and **D** are defined as follows:

A is the recalculated (or "calculated" in the case of benefits being provided for the first time) pension credit determined as at the time of the past service event for the past service being provided. This amount is essentially the sum of the pension credits (each rounded to the nearest dollar) that should have been reported, covering all prior years of post-1989 credited service but excluding the year of the past service event, had the benefit improvement always been in place. For the year of the past service event, the benefit provided for the part of the past service period within the current calendar year is ignored, as discussed at ¶1040, and is instead included in the PA that is reported at the end of the calendar year.

B is the sum of the pension credits (i.e., the PAs and PSPAs) that were reported in respect of the benefits that were in effect immediately prior to the past service event. Again, ignore the benefit provided for the part of the past service period within the current calendar year as the PA value of this benefit will be captured when the PA is reported at the end of the calendar year. If service is being credited for the first time, variable B will be zero. If the years were previously pensionable and there was a money purchase transfer after 1996 (i.e., a PAR was reported), B will also be zero.

C is the amount of any "qualifying transfer" that the individual has made to the plan to fund the additional benefits being provided to that individual.

A "qualifying transfer" is an amount of money that the member transfers to the defined benefit provision from a defined contribution RPP (or a defined contribution provision of an RPP, such as an additional voluntary contribution), an RRSP, or a DPSP. A transfer from a defined benefit plan can be classed as a qualifying transfer only if the defined benefit plan is an SMEP or if the defined benefit plan is the spouse's plan and the transfer is occurring as a result of death or marriage breakdown. The amount transferred is being used as a source of financing of the defined benefit being granted — it is not being treated as an additional voluntary contribution or other money purchase amount. A qualifying transfer acts as a direct offset to an amount that would otherwise be reported as a PSPA and, therefore, will reduce the PSPA that is reported and deducted from the individual's RRSP contribution room. If the individual gives an irrevocable direction to make the asset transfer within 90 days of certification, the amount can be treated as a qualifying transfer even though the transfer has not actually occurred at the date on which the PSPA is determined. Qualifying transfers will normally be required or permitted in situations, such as service buy-backs, resulting in PSPAs that must be certified before the service can be credited. Typically in these situations, the individual agrees to make a payment (or series of payments) into the plan to fund part or all of the past service. The payment will typically be a qualifying transfer or could be in the form of tax-deductible cash contributions or a cash lump-sum. Only qualifying transfers (i.e., assets that are already tax sheltered and have been "accounted for" from a PA point of view) serve to reduce the PSPA.

Further, only that portion of the transfer that can reasonably be considered to be required or used to fund post-1989 benefits is considered as a qualifying transfer. This prevents plan members from using the entire amount transferred into the pension plan to reduce the PSPA regardless of whether that transfer is actually used to fund both pre-1990 and post-1989 benefits. Other amounts can be transferred directly into the plan to fund pre-1989 benefits, but they cannot be used to reduce the amount of the PSPA.

A situation may arise whereby the amount of the qualifying transfer exceeds the amount required to be transferred in order for the PSPA to be certified. Refer to ¶ 1065 for information about the certification process. This would occur, for example, if an error was made in the initial calculation of the PSPA. In such situations, there is no provision in the *Income Tax Act* (Canada) for the funds to be returned back to where they were transferred from. The Registered Plans Directorate advises that in such situations the amount must be removed from the plan and paid out to the member and the funds are to be included in the member's income for the year for tax purposes. However, the Registered Plans Directorate may consider requests for alternative treatment on a case by case basis. For example, they may consider allowing the excess funds to remain in the plan and to be treated as additional voluntary contributions.

As noted, any amounts paid by the individual in cash to fund part or all of the benefits being provided do not represent a "qualifying transfer" for the purpose of reducing the PSPA. In this case, these are treated as employee contributions and the limits on the tax-deductibility of these contributions are discussed at ¶ 1810.

D is the amount of any "excess money purchase transfer". An excess money purchase transfer is an amount that arose in respect of an individual's prior period of employment and is equal to the excess of the amount provided to the terminating member over the combined total of the PAs and PSPAs attributable to the member's post-1989 service. In other words, it is a measure of the degree to which a member has received tax sheltering in excess of the amounts reflected in the reported PAs and PSPAs. Generally, this variable will only be used in post-1996 terminations only in circumstances where the same service is later credited again to the individual. In a sense, it can be considered a "negative PAR". As described in Chapter 11, when a member terminates from a plan and the sum of the reported PAs and PSPAs exceeds the lump-sum benefit provided to the member, a PAR is reported and RRSP room is restored. But, if the sum of the reported PAs and PSPAs is *less* than the lump-sum provided, then this is an excess money purchase transfer situation, but no PAR is actually reported. However, if this service is later reinstated, the PSPA calculation must take into account this "negative PAR" to recognize that the member has already received tax sheltering of retirement benefits greater than the RRSP room determined each year using those PAs and PSPAs and to ensure that the member does not receive additional tax sheltering in respect of the same service.

Note that this variable **D** essentially requires that a plan sponsor keep track of all excess money purchase transfers for all members indefinitely in case the situation arises where service is reinstated for a particular member. Even if the plan provisions do not currently permit such reinstatement, it is possible that the plan could be changed in the future to allow reinstatement of previously credited service.

If the above formula (**A - B - C + D**) results in an amount greater than zero, this is the amount of the PSPA. If the amount is less than zero, then the PSPA is nil.

Note that in situations where additional years of post-1989 service is being credited, the basic methodology can result in a PSPA for high earners where one might not be expected, as the exclusions discussed at ¶ 1018 do not apply in such situations. Consider a member who, in 2010, is purchasing a year of 2006 service that was not previously considered pensionable. The defined benefit limit in 2006 was $2,111.11 and the PA that would have been reported had the service been considered pensionable in 2006 would have been $18,400 (9 × $2,111.11 - $600) leaving the member with $600 of RRSP room in 2007. If the plan member purchases this year of service in 2010, when the defined benefit limit is $2,494.44), the PSPA will be $21,850 (9 × $2,494.44 - $600). This results in the situation where the "cost" of this benefit, in terms of "RRSP room" used in respect of 2006 is $21,850, whereas the total amount of RRSP contribution room that the member actually earned in respect of 2006 was only $19,000 (assuming the member was not a member of any other registered plan). Thus, the RRSP room "cost" to purchase the benefit in 2010 compared to 2006 is equal to $2,850, which may or may not be greater than the investment earnings accumulated on the RRSP assets over the same period.

¶ 1037 The Modified Calculation Method

Modifications to the basic approach are required in certain situations. The modified method is used most typically in reciprocal transfer agreement or portability situations where the relative differences in the PAs under the former and new plans must be taken into account as well as the impact of an asset transfer from the former plan to the new plan to partially or fully fund the benefits being granted under the new plan.

The modified rules are also used in a non-reciprocal transfer situation when an individual is applying for reinstatement of benefits that have already been foregone and no PAR was reported at the time of the initial termination of employment (i.e., a termination prior to 1997).

Modifications are necessary to recognize that there could be a duplication of benefits and ability to excess tax shelter in reciprocal transfer and reinstatement situations, and as a result, appropriate modifications are made to the basic formula to avoid double-dipping.

Note also that the modified calculation method takes into account pensionable service up to the date of the past service event, whereas the basic calculation method only includes pensionable service to the end of the calendar year immediately preceding the past service event. Further, the modified calculation method takes into account the special "year of non-vested termination" rule that existed for terminations prior to 1997 (in variable B).

Thus, the modified method is used to calculate PSPAs for past service events that occur after 1996 in the following situations:

- an individual transfers from one defined benefit provision of an RPP to another defined benefit provision of a different RPP and relinquishes entitlement to the benefits accrued under the first provision in order to receive benefits under the second provision; or

- an individual terminated from a defined benefit provision prior to 1997 (i.e., a PAR was not reported) and the same service is later (i.e., after 1997) reinstated under the same provision or credited under another defined benefit provision.

The PSPA under the modified formula is determined as follows:

A + B + C - D

where **A**, **B**, **C**, and **D** are defined as follows:

A is equal to variable A minus variable B in the basic PSPA formula but modified to include the past service provided in the current year. As discussed at ¶ 1040, in contrast to how variables A and B are determined in the basic PSPA formula, past service being provided in the current year is included up to the date of the past service event. This necessitates calculating the PA for the current year up to the date of the past service event much earlier in the year than the PA is normally calculated. As a result, not all information required to calculate the pension credit for that part year may be available (for example, commissions or bonus data); moreover, the PSPA is to be calculated by the plan administrator of the new pension plan while the PA calculation for the current year is the responsibility of the previous employer and the plan administrator of the new plan may be unable to obtain the required information in respect of the ex-employee within a reasonable time frame. If this is the case, the plan administrator is allowed to make reasonable assumptions in order to facilitate the calculation of the PSPA. If variable A minus variable B (with the appropriate adjustments discussed above) is negative, then variable A under the modified formula is zero. This could occur in a reciprocal transfer situation if the benefits under the former plan were more generous than the benefits under the new plan.

B is an adjustment that must be made in respect of the "year of non-vested termination" rule. As discussed at Appendix 1, section 3B, this is a rule that was in effect prior to 1997 (prior to the introduction of the PAR) such that the PA in the year of non-vested termination is calculated as the lesser of the pension credit determined as if the individual were vested and the member's contributions for the year. If this rule had been applied to the individual when his or her PA was determined for a year that is part of the period covered in variable A, the PSPA now being determined must be increased by the amount by which that PA was actually reduced because of the application of the "year of non-vested termination" rule.

For example, if the individual should have had a PA of $1,200 in the earlier year of termination had he or she been vested at that time, but only $700 was reported as the PA because this was the employee contribution in the year of termination and the employee was not vested, then an additional $500 must be added to the PSPA as the special non-vested PA adjustment.

Obviously, variable B will disappear in the future as it is greater than zero only if service from a pre-1997 termination is being recredited.

C is the "money purchase transfer" associated with the service being provided that has been, or remains to be, provided to the individual in respect of post-1989 service that is not being transferred to the new provision to fund the new benefits and such amount will be, or has been, transferred to an RRSP, a money purchase provision of an RPP, or a defined benefit provision of an SMEP. Numerically, variable C is equal to the amount that has been paid or will be paid in respect of the former provision minus the amount by which variable B in the basic formula exceeds variable A in the basic formula. Variable C is a measure of the extent to which the benefit provided under the former provision exceeds the "reduction" in the PA value of benefits that occurs in moving from the former provision to the new provision.

D is the amount of any "qualifying transfer" that the individual has made to the plan to fund the additional benefits being provided. Refer to the discussion under variable C in the basic formula for further information regarding qualifying transfers.

If the above formula (**A** + **B** + **C** - **D**) results in an amount greater than zero, this is the amount of the PSPA. If the amount is less than zero, then the PSPA is nil.

Note that normally, the calculation of A under this modified calculation method is equal to variable A (new PAs) less variable B (old PAs), as described at ¶ 1036 for the basic calculation method, and that the PAs and PSPAs used in determining variable B are normally the actual PAs and PSPAs previously reported in respect of the benefits in effect immediately prior to the past service event (taking into account that for past service in the current year, the PA may not yet have been reported). In situations involving high-earners, the actual reported PAs would have reflected the defined benefit limits in effect for the year for which the PA was reported.

If the plan sponsor strictly followed this methodology, this would result in PSPAs being created for members whose benefits are capped by the defined benefit limit both before and after the past service event.

For example, if a past service event in 2010 improved benefits earned in respect of the year 2006, when the defined benefit limit was $2,111.11, variable A for a particular high earner is $2,494.44 and variable B might be assumed to be $2,111.11, resulting in a PSPA of $3,450 (9 × ($2,494.44 - $2,111.11)). However, generally, PSPAs are not created in situations where the benefit has increased solely due to increases in the defined benefit limit. Therefore, the appropriate method to calculate the PSPA in such situations is to use the current defined benefit limit in **both** variable A and variable B. This, therefore, means that variable B must be recalculated using appropriate earnings and other plan information rather than using the PAs that were already reported. This will result in a nil PSPA for a member limited by the defined benefit limit both before and after the past service event.

Finally, it should also be noted that for certain years when the reported PA was actually higher than the maximum RRSP dollar limits for the following years (as discussed at ¶ 720), the actual reported PA is used in the calculation of the PSPA regardless of the fact that it exceeds the maximum RRSP contribution room.

¶ 1038 Approximation if Previous Years' Pensionable Earnings Information is Unavailable

A plan administrator may need information from the plan member's previous employer in order to calculate the PSPA. A written request for such data requires a response within 30 days. Failure to comply is subject to a penalty of $100 to $2,500 per request. Such a request typically arises in a reciprocal transfer or portability situation between non-related employers or when an employee purchases previously non-pensionable service with the same large employer but a different division/agency.

If pensionable earnings information is not available for previous years, the administrator may have no other choice than to use an estimate. Since this is not specifically provided for in the Regulations, the CRA's permission to do this must be requested. One method for estimating previous years' pensionable earnings might be to project current pensionable earnings backwards in line with changes in the average wage during the corresponding period.

¶1039 Past Service Conditional on Future Employee Contributions

A past service event occurs when an employee makes an irrevocable decision to purchase the past service by a series of instalments. Suppose the individual cannot fulfil his or her commitment to continue contributing (for example, because the person is terminated) and, in accordance with the plan provisions, the employer then takes away some of the years of past service that were granted under the deal. In this situation it is advisable to write to the CRA and ask for permission to cancel the PSPA previously certified because the irrevocable decision of the employee to buy the past service cannot be fulfilled. The specific reasons should be outlined in the letter to the CRA. With the cancellation of the previous PSPA, an amended PSPA should be submitted for certification, reflecting only the past service purchased to date. Refer to ¶1070 for additional information on amending a PSPA.

However, if, under the terms of the buy-back agreement, a few additional months or years of past service are granted for each occasion on which the individual elects to make a further contribution, a PSPA arises on each occasion on which the individual is scheduled to make a contribution. This approach solves the problem of RRSP contribution room loss that arises when an individual commits to a full past service buy-back but later does not fulfil that commitment. Usually such an individual is required to make an irrevocable commitment and pay via payroll deductions — the only occasion when he or she cannot fulfil the commitment to make the contributions is because he or she terminates employment. However, it increases the administration involved in the buy-back, since a series of PSPAs may have to be reported on behalf of the individual. If such contributions are being made by payroll deductions over several years (i.e., in some cases, up to the date of retirement or even beyond), certifying a PSPA after each contribution being made is simply not feasible.

¶1040 Mid-Year Past Service Event

Where a past service event does not occur on January 1 of the year, a decision must be made as to how the benefit improvements that relate to the service in the year of the past service event are to be treated — will they form part of the PA for the current year or the PSPA?

It should be noted that if an improvement is made in January or February of a year, causing the previous year's PA to be understated, it is a PSPA that is created, not an adjusted PA in respect of the previous year (even though the T4 slip showing the previous year's PA may not yet have been prepared).

Generally, where the basic approach is used to calculate the PSPA, benefits that are earned in the year of the past service event are included in that year's PA, as mentioned at ¶1036 and benefit improvements in respect of all years up to the end of the prior year are reflected in the PSPA.

Therefore, in the following three circumstances, for example, the benefits earned in the year of the past service event would not be included in the PSPA (but instead are incorporated in the PA for the year):

- Where the benefits being provided to the member are replacing those he or she has already earned under a defined benefit provision or a money purchase provision of a pension plan or a DPSP provided by the same employer. No benefits may continue to accrue under the old provision and no amounts may be transferred to any other money purchase arrangement from the old plan.
- When the past service period in the current year had never been pensionable service in any RPP nor service in a DPSP to which contributions have been made in that period.
- Where benefits were previously provided in respect of a past service period in the current year and for which no amount was transferred to an RRSP or other money purchase provision when those benefits were no longer provided; this is a less common situation which would result if benefits are being reinstated in the same year.

Otherwise, in most other situations where the service may have been pensionable service at some point but is not pensionable service in the plan immediately prior to the past service event (i.e., situations requiring the modified calculation method), pensionable service in the current year is included in the PSPA calculation up to the date of the past service event. This requirement may be waived by the Registered Plans Directorate upon written request, in which case the current year past service benefit would be included in the current year PA.

¶1045 The PA Offset

As noted at Appendix 1, section 5A, the PA offset for years after 1996 was decreased from $1,000 to $600 as a result of the introduction of the PAR. The offset for years before 1997 remains at $1,000. If PAs for the years 1990 to 1996, inclusive, are being recalculated in order to calculate PSPAs, plan administrators should continue to use the appropriate offset for the year in which the PA is being recalculated.

¶1050 Examples of Circumstances Where PSPAs are Created

PSPAs most often arise in situations where a plan is amended to retroactively improve benefits in respect of pensionable service prior to the current year or where a plan did not previously recognize certain periods of past service for pension purposes and commences to recognize those periods of service.

However, there are many other situations that give rise to PSPAs and some of these are discussed below.

¶1051 PSPA Calculation for Earnings-Related Plans

The following is an example of a PSPA calculation in respect of a change in benefit formula that retroactively increases the percentage benefit rate under an earnings-related defined benefit plan. This example follows the basic PSPA approach, not the "modified" approach:

- benefit rate is to be increased in 2010 from 1% to 1¼% of earnings for each year of past service;
- the 2009 PA of $5,250 has already been reported to the CRA;
- pensionable earnings in 2010 = $65,000;
- PA for 2009 *should* have been: 9 × 0.0125 × $65,000 - $600 = $6,712; and
- additional pension credit for 2009 service = $6,712 - $5,250 = $1,462.

This exercise is repeated for each year after 1989 to which the new benefit rate applies. For each such year, the calculation is based on the actual pensionable earnings of the individual in that year. The sum of the additional pension credits for each post-1989 year is the PSPA.

If the past service event in this example occurred on July 1, 2010, the PSPA would only be calculated reflecting the post-1989 calendar years through 2010. The 2010 PA would reflect the 1¼% formula for the entire year.

¶1052 Flat Benefit Plans — Special Treatment

As discussed at ¶1017, flat benefit plans are allowed to increase their benefits retroactively within certain limits with a zero PSPA.

Special treatment is accorded to increases in flat benefit plans that are larger than the percentage change in the average wage if:

- the benefit increase is of the type that would lead to a PSPA that would be exempt from certification;

- the pension is determined using only one flat benefit rate. (In this context, one flat benefit rate must apply to all service for a particular individual. If the benefit formula consists of several different rates applying for different periods of time, then this would not be considered to be the type of benefit for which the plan administrator would be able to use this special treatment; see ¶ 1017 for additional discussion regarding the meaning of one flat benefit rate); and

- the new flat benefit per year of service is not greater than 40% of the defined benefit limit for that year (i.e., 40% of $2,494.44 for 2010).

Consider an example where no improvement has been made since the plan's inception in 2003 and where the annual benefit entitlement is increasing from $600 to $700 per year of service in 2010. For the portion of the benefit exclusion calculation that is based on the increase in the average wage, the earliest possible "base year" is selected for measuring the increase in the average wage, because the benefit exclusion minimizing the PSPA is the largest of calculated amounts. In this case, 2003 is, therefore, selected as the base year and the increase in the average wage is then calculated for the period since that base year.

The average wage is defined at ¶ 205; however, also refer to the discussion of the average wage measure that appears in Appendix 3. The average wage has increased by 23.16% (from $663.28 to $816.88) from 2003 to 2010. The following process is then followed:

- Calculate the benefit exclusion. This is the amount by which the benefits can be increased with zero PSPA. Rather than increase the previously reported PAs, the approach involves reducing the new benefit formula by the amount of this benefit exclusion. The benefit exclusion is the greater of:

  (a) 23.16% of $600 = $138.96; and

  (b) $1.50 × 12 × 6 years = $108.

  The exclusion is, therefore, $138.96;

- As a result, the full benefit improvement of $100 is excluded and the corresponding PSPA is nil. This calculation shows that improving the benefit rate even further — up to $738.96 per year of service — would not have PSPA consequences, which may be taken into account when the new rate is negotiated.

Instead, now assume that the annual benefit increases by $150, from $600 to $750, in the same set of circumstances:

- Calculate the benefit exclusion. It is still the greater of:

  (a) 23.16% of $600 = $138.96; and

  (b) $1.50 × 12 × 6 years = $108.

  The exclusion is, therefore, still $138.96;

- In this case, the amount of the exclusion is less than the actual benefit increase.

The redetermined benefit entitlement is equal to $750 less the benefit exclusion of $138.96, or $611.04. Therefore, the PSPA is based on a benefit increase of $11.04 (i.e., $611.04 - $600). If an individual has two years of credited service, the PSPA would be $199, determined as follows:

(a) 2 × (9 × $611.04 - $600) = $9,799; less

(b) 2 × (9 × $600 - $600) = $9,600.

Note that this calculation can be simplified as follows: 2 × (9 × $11.04) = $199.

Note that the date of the increase in the annual benefit entitlement can be anytime in 2010 and there will be no impact on this calculation nor on the PSPA for this past service event. Since the basic PSPA approach can be followed, service up to December 31, 2009 only is taken into account. The increase in the benefit for service in 2010 from January 1, 2010 up to the date of the past service event is later taken into account in the PA calculation for 2010.

Now suppose that the 2010 benefit rate of $750 is next increased in 2012 and that the administrator is determining the amount of the PSPA in 2012. Again, the administrator is free to choose any base year from 1984 (or a later year if the plan's effective date was after 1984, as in our example), the objective being to determine the highest possible amount of exclusion. Unlike the above example, where it was obvious that the earliest possible year (2003) should be selected for this purpose, the administrator should now also examine what the benefit exclusion would be if 2010 is instead selected as the base year, since a new benefit entitlement was established in 2010. The administrator would then use the following process:

- Increase the 2003 flat benefit rate by the percentage increase in the average wage from 2003 to 2012;

- Increase the 2010 flat benefit rate by the percentage increase in the average wage from 2010 to 2012; and

- Select the higher of the two above amounts. Unless the result of the calculation of the "$1.50 exclusion" leads to a higher amount, this is then the amount of the benefit exclusion that is used in calculating the redetermined benefit entitlement for PSPA purposes.

The actual base year selected for the above purpose is merely a step in the calculation of the benefit exclusion. The base year selected is not an important item for any other purpose — it does not have to be disclosed, nor is it important in a later year to remember which base year was selected.

Flat benefit rate plan increases, such as those described in these examples, are typically seen in union-negotiated plans. Typically, the negotiation process occurs every two or three years, with benefit rates being agreed upon for the subsequent period until the next set of negotiations. Thus, in order to minimize the impact of PSPAs, it is advisable to space out the benefit increases over the negotiated period to take advantage of the "zero PSPA" exclusions rather than a large increase at the beginning or end of the period and very small increases in between.

¶1053 Escalating Flat Dollar Benefits

A common situation in negotiated pension plans occurs where the collective agreement and the plan document stipulate an escalating benefit formula, depending upon the year of retirement. For example, employees who retired in 2008 received a pension of $55 per month for all years of service, those who retired in 2009 received a benefit of $57 per month for all years of service, and those retiring in 2010 will receive a benefit of $60 per month for all years of service. Assume that the plan became effective on January 1, 2008, and that the subsequent benefit changes all occurred on July 1 of the relevant year.

The 2008 PA would have been based on the $55 benefit formula for all employees. The 2009 PA would have been based on the $57 formula, and the 2010 PA is based on $60.

Assume also that, as described at ¶1017, this situation is eligible for the larger exclusion — i.e., in addition to being less than 40% of the defined benefit limit, the pension is determined using only one flat benefit rate and the PSPA is exempt from certification.

First, determine whether a PSPA is reportable in 2009. The maximum amount by which the benefit may be increased without creating a PSPA is calculated by first determining the amount of benefit that can be excluded due to increases in the average wage and then by determining how much can be excluded due to the $1.50 exclusion:

(a) $55 × ($800.37* ÷ $771.60*) = $57.05; or

(b) $1.50 × 1.5 years + $55 = $57.25.

* From Appendix 3, Table 2.

The maximum amount to which the benefit could be increased is the greater of (a) and (b) above, or $57.25. As this amount is greater than the $57 to which the benefit actually increased in 2009, there is no PSPA in 2009.

The analysis is different in 2010. The additional decision that has to be made is what base year should be used for applying the change in the average wage. In this case we have the choice of either 2008 or 2009, as follows:

(a) 2008 base year: $55 × ($816.88* ÷ $771.60*) = $58.23, or,
2009 base year: $57 × ($816.88* ÷ $800.37*) = $58.18; or

(b) $1.50 × 1 year + $57 = $58.50.

We would still select 2008 as the base year because it produces the greater number. However, neither of these base-year choices gives an exclusion that is greater than the exclusion provided by the $1.50 rule; therefore, we will use $58.50. The 2010 PSPA would, therefore, be based on the increase from $58.50 to $60.

Assume an individual joined the plan when it was first effective (January 1, 2008) and, therefore, has 2.5 years of service in the plan as of July 1, 2010 (the effective date of the improvement to $60). The PSPA would be calculated as follows, based on the individual's two years of past service:

- ($60.00 - $58.50) × 12 × 9 = $162;
- Therefore, the portion of the PSPA relating to 2008 service is $162 and the portion relating to 2009 service is also $162; and
- PSPA = 2 × $162 = $324.

Following the logic set out at ¶1036, the 2010 PA would reflect the benefit increase for the entire year.

¶1054 Transfers from Flat Benefit Plan to Earnings-Related Plan

Another common situation is where an organization has a flat benefit plan for hourly staff and an earnings-related plan for salaried staff. When an individual transfers from hourly to salaried status, and if the salaried employees' plan applies its formula to all years of service and uses the accrued flat benefit pension as an offset, a special rule must be followed to determine if there is a PSPA. To calculate what the pension credits would have been had the individual always been in the salaried plan and to reduce these by the reported PAs and PSPAs would likely lead to an overstatement of the amount of the PSPA. The correct procedure is as follows:

1. Calculate the redetermined pension credits at the time of the past service event. The date of the past service event occurs when the

individual becomes a member of the salaried plan. Here, the employer must calculate the pension credits for each year of past service as if the individual had always been in the salaried plan, using actual pensionable earnings. Each year's pension credit is rounded to the nearest dollar;

2. Calculate the redetermined pension credits at the time immediately before the past service event. The redetermined pension credits in this case would be based on the benefit formula under the hourly plan immediately prior to the change in status. Normally, the flat benefit formula under an hourly plan increases every two or three years, depending on the collective bargaining cycle. If the flat benefit formula had always increased at a rate less than the increase in the average wage, or within the $1.50 exclusion, then the individual has never been subject to a PSPA under the hourly plan. To simply use the sum of the reported PAs and PSPAs (which we are assuming are nil) overstates the PSPA being calculated, because the flat dollar benefit under the hourly plan may have been increasing periodically without ever incurring a PSPA. Therefore, this step allows for the recalculation of pension credits as if the plan had always provided benefits at the most recent flat dollar level. Again, each pension credit is rounded to the nearest dollar; and
3. The excess of 1 over 2 above, if any, represents the PSPA.

If the hourly plan's benefit formula had not increased over the years to the maximum extent possible without leading to a PSPA, there is a potential to reduce the above PSPA amount by first increasing the past service benefits under the hourly plan to the maximum possible while not leading to a PSPA. This technique would require appropriate wording in the hourly plan provisions, but it may not be feasible in some jurisdictions where minimum standards legislation places restrictions on granting a benefit improvement for only one individual. The PSPA associated with this past service event would require certification by the CRA.

¶1055 Transfers Between Pension Plans

As set out in ¶1746, pensionable service under one pension plan can be credited under another unrelated pension plan as long as the individual is no longer entitled to such service under the first plan. This transfer of service and benefits directly from one plan to the pension plan of an unrelated employer occurs in reciprocal transfer or portability situations. It can also occur if the benefits are first transferred to an RRSP or another tax-sheltered vehicle before then being transferred to the second pension plan.

Reciprocal transfer agreements (RTA) and portability arrangements are agreements between an employer and a plan member to accept service or benefits previously credited under another RPP in the current employer's plan in return for the individual giving up entitlement to such service or benefits under the former plan.

An RTA is a two-way arrangement that permits assets to be transferred based on a pre-agreed calculation basis that does not necessarily match the actuarial valuation basis used by either the importing or the exporting plan or the Canadian Institute of Actuaries Standards of Practice for Determining Pension Commuted Values. The objective usually is to transfer an amount close to the full funding liability from one plan to the other, but in situations where the funding actuarial valuation basis differs between the two plans, the basis to be used is negotiated so that neither plan gains nor loses significantly. The RTA is an adjunct to each pension plan document and is usually signed by parties to each of the plans. RTAs typically appear in public sector plans but they do also exist to a much lesser degree between private sector plans (or between a public sector and a private sector plan).

A portability arrangement, on the other hand, is typically a much less formal arrangement than an RTA and it is generally not "two-way". Portability arrangements tend to cover one-off situations to accommodate specific needs of both the employer and employee in certain situations, such as hiring a mid-career senior level employee where past service pension benefits with another employer are to be transferred to the new employer's plan.

Under both an RTA and a portability arrangement, the possibility of PSPAs arises unless both the exporting and the importing plans are identical. PSPA calculations in RTA, or portability arrangements are subject to the "modified" approach to calculating PSPAs (discussed at ¶1037) when both the importing and the exporting plan are defined benefit plans. The "basic" approach described at ¶1036 is used when the exporting plan is a defined contribution plan or where the defined benefit has already been transferred to an RRSP or other money purchase arrangement. When the exporting plan is a hybrid plan with both defined contribution and defined benefit elements, separate PSPAs must be calculated using either the modified approach or the basic approach, as appropriate.

In the case of a transfer between defined benefit plans, it is important to distinguish between the calculation of the PSPA, which measures the difference in the PA value of the benefit being transferred from one plan to the other, and the determination of the appropriate amount of assets that transfers from one plan to the other to fund the benefit. The two amounts can be very different, the latter ranging from zero to something close to or higher than the PA value of the benefits being provided under the new plan. The asset transfer is stipulated by the basis set out in the RTA or the portability arrangement, depending on the terms of the RTA or the portability arrangement. Once the assets are transferred into the new plan, a reconciliation may be done to determine whether any additional contributions are required to be paid by the transferring plan member and an appropriate payment schedule is established with the deductibility of such contributions determined as discussed in ¶ 1810. It is more likely under a portability arrangement that additional contributions will be required to fund the benefit since it is a termination benefit being transferred, whereas the amount being transferred under an RTA often will be closer to the value required to fund the past service being transferred.

"Qualifying transfers", on the other hand, represent amounts that are transferred from a defined contribution provision (meaning from a defined contribution plan or provision within a plan, additional voluntary contributions, RRSP assets, amounts from a DPSP, or a defined benefit SMEP) and these do factor into the PSPA calculation (in variable C in the basic calculation method or as variable D in the modified calculation method).

Co-Ordination Between Employers and Pension Plan Administrators

Since a PSPA can arise when a plan member is granted past service that was previously provided under a different pension and a PAR can arise when a plan member terminates or otherwise ceases to be entitled to benefits, reciprocal transfer and portability situations require co-ordination between employers and pension plan administrators, on both sides of the transfer, in order to accurately determine the amount of any PSPA or PAR.

A PSPA may arise if the member is being provided with more generous benefits under the new plan than was provided under the former plan. Similarly, a PAR may arise if the transferring plan member receives less generous benefits under the new plan compared to the former plan and as a result, receives a benefit payout that reflects the extent to which funds in the former plan are not required to be transferred to the new plan (and are instead paid to the transferring member directly).

As a result, the PAR calculation and the PSPA calculation become linked and one cannot be calculated without the other. The importing plan must determine whether a PSPA arises as a result of the transfer and the exporting plan must determine whether a PAR has arisen as a result of the transfer. However, the exporting plan cannot calculate the PAR until certain information is provided by the importing plan. And the importing plan cannot calculate the PSPA until certain information is provided by the exporting plan. This requires both importing plan and exporting plan employers and plan administrators to co-operate fully in the necessary transfer of information. This can become administratively complex, especially in the case of MEPs or large plans covering many locations and divisions/agencies.

The exporting plan must first provide the importing plan with enough information regarding the benefits provided under the exporting plan (including any transfer with respect to the post-1989 past service made or to be made) so that the importing plan can determine variable C in the modified PSPA formula described at ¶1037.

The importing plan administrator then can calculate the modified PSPA, which will also take into account qualifying transfers as per the formula described at ¶1037. The "PA transfer amount" is then reported by the importing plan to the exporting plan. The PA transfer amount is variable D in the PAR formula as described at ¶1130. The PA transfer amount recognizes that the PSPA under the importing plan may be significantly decreased to zero as a result of the transfer of the PA value of the benefits from one plan to the other. Therefore, it would be inappropriate to include the full amount of the PAs in respect of the exporting plan when determining the PAR under the exporting plan.

The importing plan administrator must report the PA transfer amount to the exporting plan administrator within 60 days of the past service event if the PSPA is exempt from certification. However, more typically, this type of PSPA would not be exempt from certification. Thus, the importing plan administrator reports the PA transfer amount to the exporting plan administrator within 60 days of receiving certification of the PSPA.

The exporting plan PAR can then be determined. As described at ¶1165, the exporting plan administrator must calculate and report the PAR by the later of 60 days after the end of the calendar quarter in which the transfer occurred and 60 days after the exporting plan administrator receives notification of the PA transfer amount from the importing plan administrator.

Even if the importing employer's plan provisions are less generous than the exporting employer's plan provisions, there is still a need to co-operate fully as the modified PSPA formula takes into account the money purchase transfer in respect of the benefits under the former provision.

Although the exporting employee may be able to provide the historical PA information to the importing employer, the PA for the final partial year of service may not have been calculated by the exporting employer by the time the importing employer's plan administrator wishes to calculate the PSPA. If the importing plan administrator is not willing or not able to delay the PSPA reporting until that final year's PA is available (notwithstanding the fact that there is no deadline for reporting a non-exempt PSPA), the importing plan administrator will have to estimate that final year's PA based on the other employer's plan provisions (or ask the exporting employer to provide the final year PA amount for use in determining the PSPA). In this situation, if the PA that the importing plan administrator has estimated differs from the actual PA that the exporting employer subsequently reports for that final year, no adjustments are made by either party.

Method of Apportioning Service

Unusual situations can arise when credited service is transferred between two employers' defined benefit plans under a reciprocal transfer agreement or portability arrangement. Consider an individual who is transferring from one employer's plan to another's through a reciprocal transfer agreement, and assume that Plan A (the exporting plan) has a lower benefit formula than Plan B (the importing plan). Suppose that the transfer date is December 31, 2009, and the individual has three years of pensionable service under Plan A, but the transfer value in respect of this service will only cover two years of pensionable service under Plan B, due to Plan B's higher benefit formula.

In this situation, under Plan B, there are three methods of apportioning the service over the three years of original pensionable service from Plan A, each method leading to a different PSPA. One can count service from the earliest possible year (i.e., years 1 and 2) or one can use the most recent service (i.e., years 2 and 3). Alternatively, one can spread the two years of import plan service over the three-year export plan service period, so that two-thirds of a year of service has accrued in each of the three years: 2007, 2008, and 2009.

In each case, the PSPA will be determined by comparing the PAs using the Plan A and Plan B formulae (in total) for the relevant post-1989 period (i.e., 2007 and 2008, 2008 and 2009, or all three years where only two-thirds of a year of service is being credited in each year under Plan B). The resulting PSPA will be different in each case. The plan document and/or reciprocal agreement should spell out the method of apportionment of the service in these situations.

The decision on how to apportion service becomes more critical if pre-1990 service is involved. Crediting of pre-1990 service does not give rise to a PSPA but all other implications of providing the earliest service first need to be reviewed carefully (for example, different benefit provisions may be in place for pre-1990 *versus* post-1989 service).

Most defined benefit plans that allow reciprocal transfers or portability situations include a provision that would allow the individual to "buy back" any extra service, such as the one year that was foregone in the example above. If this is the case, and if the individual chooses to proceed with the buy-back of all of the extra service immediately upon entry to Plan B, the total PSPA in respect of the transferred service and the "buy-back" service can be reported in one sum. In this case, the total PSPA will be the same, regardless of the method of apportionment of the transferred service. The fact is, however, that some individuals in this situation will never buy back the extra service or will choose to do so (if the plan allows) at a later date. It is, therefore, necessary to ensure that mechanisms are in place to handle the PSPAs that will arise only in respect of the transferred service and to ensure that the PSPA accurately reflects the correct partial or full years of service being bought back.

¶1056 PSPAs for Retired Members

As noted at ¶1028, pensions in payment can be increased in line with increases in the CPI on a cumulative basis. They can sometimes even be increased by amounts higher than the increase in the CPI, provided the plan provides for automatic increases in the pension after commencement following one of the alternative adjustment methods described at ¶1770, should any of those methods result in pension increases higher than that warranted by the CPI.

Most plans that provide for automatic increases in pensions payable provide for an increase aligned with the full or a portion of the increase in the CPI since the retirement date. Also, companies that offer *ad hoc*, or non-guaranteed, increases to pensions in payment typically align the increase with the CPI as well.

Sometimes, however, there are situations that arise, whereby an employer would like to provide an increase that is higher than that permitted to be granted, and this would give rise to a PSPA. An example of such a situation would be where the company wants to keep increases for retirees in a flat benefit plan in line with the increases provided for active members for a period of time after retirement (for example, as part of an early retirement incentive program). Another example would be a situation where an employer wants to provide a CPI-related increase but with a minimum dollar amount of increase payable. Both of these situations would give rise to PSPAs.

The granting of additional benefits for retired members is somewhat different than for active members since the retired member is likely no longer generating new RRSP contribution room, and may no longer have RRSP contribution room (or RRSP assets, for that matter, if the retired member has attained age 71 and has collapsed the RRSP) from which to deduct the PSPA.

Further, the calculation of the PSPA may not be obvious, especially in a situation where pensions are to be increased by a percentage of the pension or where there is a minimum increase payable. In these situations, in order to determine the PSPA (as the difference between PAs under the new benefit and the PAs under the original benefit), it is necessary to "redefine" the benefit formula that is underlying the original benefit formula in such a way that the resulting increase in pension represents the desired increase in the pension payment. For example, suppose the original plan benefit was 1.5% of final average earnings. If increasing the benefit to, say, 1.55% of final average earnings would achieve the amount of pension increase that is desired, then the PSPA would be calculated on the difference between the redefined 1.55% benefit and the original 1.5% benefit. Similar pension increases in subsequent years would have to be tracked, as a subsequent increase would be redefined from the new underlying 1.55% benefit. However, in no event can the underlying benefit be increased above the maximum benefit permitted of 2% of final average earnings. Different increases in formula may be required for different plan members; the plan amendment supporting the increases would have to be worded carefully and the history of all such increases would have to be tracked separately, by each individual, to determine if or when the retiree's "redefined benefit" reaches 2% of final average earnings.

If the increase takes place at a time when increases are provided for all plan members, then the PSPA could be considered exempt from certification, in which case, RRSP room can become infinitely negative without impacting on the ability for the member to receive the benefit increase. It is of no consequence whether the retired member can no longer make contributions to an RRSP or no longer has RRSP assets.

Alternatively, if the increase can be structured to take into account only pre-1990 service, no PSPA is created; further, the pre-1990 restrictions discussed at ¶ 1715 and the proportionality conditions discussed at ¶ 1746 must be kept in mind.

However, the situation is more likely to be that pre-1990 service cannot be improved and the PSPA is not considered exempt. For a plan member who does not have sufficient RRSP contribution room to accept the PSPA or who no longer has RRSP assets (by virtue of reaching age 71 and collapsing the RRSP), then no additional benefit may be granted to that person from the pension plan. Assets cannot be required to be withdrawn from a RIF since RIF withdrawals are not qualifying withdrawals.

However, regardless of whether the PSPA is exempt or non-exempt, the above calculations and the future tracking of these, on an individual by individual basis, are administratively complex for what might be relatively small PSPAs. To avoid this, companies may opt to pay the excess pension payments from general revenues or to provide a lump-sum to retirees representing the commuted value of the increase that is to be provided.

¶ 1057 PSPA with No Change in Benefit Formula

There are some unusual situations where one might think that no PSPA is created, because the actual benefit formula has not changed, and yet a PSPA must still be reported.

For example, suppose service is being transferred under a reciprocal transfer agreement between two plans with identical benefit formulae, but the importing plan's normal form of pension is a 15-year post-retirement guarantee and the plan allows members to opt for an actuarially increased pension payable for life only. As discussed in Example 14 at ¶745, this provision results in higher PAs, and thus, a PSPA will arise equal to the difference between the importing plan PAs and the exporting plan PAs, even though the benefit formulae are the same.

A similar situation arises where the importing plan has a normal retirement age below 65 and provides for actuarial increases to the pension payable on postponed retirement. Again, this type of provision increases the importing plan's PAs, as discussed at ¶750. Assuming the exporting plan has an identical benefit formula but a normal retirement age of 65, a PSPA will arise when service is transferred to the importing plan.

Another situation arises if the definition of pensionable earnings in a final average earnings plan is changed to include bonuses where such component of earnings was not previously included. A PSPA will arise in this situation since, had bonuses been included in pensionable earnings in prior years, the reported PAs would have been higher.

Even if the plan provisions under both employers' plans are identical, a PSPA can arise if the importing plan is an MEP (as defined at ¶205) but the exporting plan is not. This is because the PA offset must be prorated under the importing plan in the ratio of the individual's actual credited service in the year of transfer to his or her total potential credited service as a full-time employee in the year, as discussed at ¶915. However, the PA offset is applied in full under the exporting plan, since it is not an MEP.

¶1060 Exempt PSPA Approval Process

To be exempted from the case by case certification process, the administrator must prove to the CRA that the past service improvement meets given criteria, as follows:

1. The plan must have at least 10 active members who are earning benefits under the plan.
2. In the case of a benefit improvement, substantially all of the active members who are earning benefits under the plan's defined benefit provision are receiving the improvement.
3. The improvements in benefits are not more advantageous for inactive members than for active members.
4. No more than 25% of the active members affected by the improvement are "specified active members" — i.e., those who are "connected persons" or who are expected to earn more than 2.5 times the YMPE in the year of improvement.

5. Improvements are not provided disproportionately to "specified active members".

In addition, there are further limitations when a new plan or provision is being established and past service benefits are being provided. The PSPA will not be exempt from certification for any member who is a "specified active member", nor in the case where a member's PSPA is greater than 3.5 times the money purchase limit for the year in which the past service event occurs. Also, if the individual is not an active member, his or her PSPA will not be exempt if the individual was connected with the participating employer in any of the five years prior to the past service event or earned over 2.5 times the YMPE with participating employers in any year over the same period.

Where these conditions are not fully met, one may nevertheless apply to the Minister of National Revenue for exemption from the certification process. The Minister may grant the exemption if the conditions are substantially satisfied.

In essence, the exemption from the certification process applies to employer-funded plan amendments that affect a material number of individuals, where almost all of the individuals are receiving the plan improvement and where the improvement is not biased in favour of highly paid or connected individuals.

The exempt process is as follows:

- The administrator submits the amendment to the CRA for approval, calculates PSPAs for all affected individuals and, if greater than zero, submits a T215 Summary, along with individual PSPA forms (T215 Supplementary), within 120 days of the past service event. The T215 Summary provides the totals of each of the amounts on the forms for all of the affected employees — i.e., those employees who were eligible for exempt PSPAs. The 120-day deadline became effective May 18, 2005; previously this form was required to be filed within 60 days of the past service event but was extended to allow employers more time to obtain all the information required for the forms.
- If the CRA is satisfied that the improvement is indeed exempt (i.e., it meets the required qualifications set out above), each individual's RRSP contribution room is reduced in the year following the year of the past service event by the amount of the PSPA. As noted in Appendix 1, section 7E, originally, the RRSP room was reduced effective on the date of the past service event but an April 18, 2000 technical amendment to the Regulations changed the timing for past service events after 2000.
- If the employee had no RRSP contribution room or even a negative balance, the benefits could still be provided. However, the employee

would not be allowed to contribute to an RRSP until he or she has generated enough new RRSP contribution room to eliminate the negative balance.

An individual close to retirement who receives a benefit improvement, and whose resulting RRSP room is negative, may never have the opportunity of generating enough new RRSP contribution room to eliminate the negative balance. The individual has, however, benefited from an employer-paid pension improvement and the tax sheltering of his or her own RRSP contributions. Although the individual will no longer be able to make RRSP contributions, the individual faces no other negative consequences as a result of the negative balance.

With exempt PSPAs, because the approval process is "automatic", individuals who terminate employment or retire shortly after the improvement is made may immediately be provided with the benefit improvements.

Notwithstanding this impact on RRSP contribution room, the plan amendment supporting the benefit improvement still has to be approved by the CRA and an actuarial cost certificate supporting any additional required contributions must be filed. This approval process does not mean that the employer must hold back making contributions in respect of the past service improvement (once the cost certificate has been filed), nor that the extra benefits may not be paid out as individuals terminate employment or retire. However, if the CRA refuses to approve the plan amendment or if it is not approved by the minimum standards regulator, the process would have to be reversed and there may be a problem in recovering any extra benefits that have been paid out.

¶1065 Non-Exempt PSPA Approval Process

If an employer is making past service improvements and the resultant PSPAs are not "exempt", they must be certified by the CRA before the benefits may be provided. Contributions required to fund the additional benefits, however, can commence to be paid as soon as an application for certification has been filed (and as long as there is an actuarial certification supporting such contributions, if required) but must cease immediately if certification is denied.

When a pension plan is amended to improve past service benefits or where a pension plan allows past service credits to be granted without requiring a plan amendment (if, for example, the plan already permits past service buy backs or reinstatements of previous service) and, as a result, the reporting of non-exempt PSPA amounts is required, the administrator must first calculate a provisional PSPA for each affected employee.

The administrator then submits the individual PSPA forms (T1004) for each affected member to the CRA. If the pension plan does not already provide for the additional benefits, an executed plan amendment supporting the plan change must also be submitted, but not necessarily at the same time as the PSPA forms are submitted. The CRA will then compare each PSPA amount to each employee's available RRSP contribution room. The back of one of the copies of form T1004 features a worksheet that may be used to determine if the CRA will certify the PSPA. A copy of this worksheet also appears in Appendix 2.

If, taking into account any "qualifying withdrawals" (as defined earlier in this chapter), an individual's available RRSP contribution room is greater than his or her PSPA, the RRSP contribution room is reduced by the "net PSPA" (i.e., the PSPA net of any qualifying withdrawals). Unlike an exempt PSPA in which RRSP room is reduced in the year after the past service event, in the case of a non-exempt PSPA, RRSP room is reduced in the year that the PSPA is certified by the CRA.

If, instead, the individual's available RRSP contribution room is only slightly deficient (i.e., the "net PSPA" exceeds the RRSP contribution room by no more than $8,000), the CRA will approve the full past service upgrade, but will still subtract the "net PSPA" from the individual's RRSP contribution room. The individual will be allowed to increase the resulting negative RRSP contribution room to as much as zero by proving that he or she made an RRSP withdrawal out of previously deducted RRSP funds in that same calendar year or in the two preceding calendar years. Withdrawals from a spousal RRSP do not count for this purpose. These withdrawals, in effect, create extra RRSP contribution room as part of the PSPA certification process, but of course, RRSP assets have been depleted in order to accomplish this. The member must also submit form T1006, which describes the transaction.

On the other hand, suppose the "net PSPA" exceeds the available RRSP contribution room by more than $8,000. The CRA will then write to the employee to explain that if he or she wishes to receive the full past service upgrade, the employee will have to make a special RRSP withdrawal (again, only from funds derived from previously deducted contributions and not from a spousal RRSP) in order to restore sufficient RRSP contribution room to allow the past service upgrade to be approved. In fact, the employee could increase the negative RRSP contribution room balance back to zero by deregistering further RRSP assets. However, deregistering RRSP assets merely to create extra RRSP contribution room for use in a later year may only be a useful strategy if the individual's marginal tax rate is expected to increase in a subsequent year. This transaction requires the use of form T1006, as described in the preceding paragraph. For example, if the available RRSP contribution room prior to the PSPA is $10,000 and the "net PSPA" is $21,000, a special RRSP withdrawal of $3,000 (i.e., $21,000 - ($10,000 + $8,000)) is required. This would lead to negative RRSP contribution room of $8,000 (i.e., $10,000 +

$3,000 - $21,000). A further RRSP withdrawal of $8,000 would allow the RRSP contribution room to become zero.

The employee is given 30 days in which to decide whether to make the RRSP withdrawal (or prove that a withdrawal was made within that calendar year or the two preceding years) and file form Tl006 with the CRA. The employee must either enclose form T4RSP issued by the RRSP issuer or have the issuer certify the withdrawal in Part IV of form Tl006. The CRA will have a default position in the event that the individual does not respond in time; the default position will be to not certify the PSPA. It must be noted that the denial will apply to the whole amount of the PSPA and the whole period of past service and not only the portion in deficiency.

The employer and the plan administrator have no involvement in this process at this stage and it is between the employee and the CRA to resolve whether the employee has made the appropriate RRSP withdrawal in order to be able to be provided with the benefit improvement. Therefore, it may be in the plan administrator's best interests to explain the process to the employee in advance of the reporting of the PSPA in order to try to determine whether it will be possible to provide the desired benefit improvement to the employee.

As mentioned earlier, a "qualifying withdrawal" is the actual removal of monies from an individual's RRSP to enable a PSPA to be certified. It must come from the individual's own RRSP, not a spousal RRSP. The amount withdrawn constitutes, of course, taxable income and will be subject to withholding tax upon withdrawal and possibly additional tax when the individual later files a tax return for the year in which the monies are withdrawn.

Note that a "qualifying withdrawal" is different from a "qualifying transfer". A qualifying transfer, as described at ¶ 1036, is a transfer from certain registered vehicles into a defined benefit plan, as a source of financing of the defined benefit being granted. It acts as an offset when the administrator is calculating the PSPA itself, unlike a qualifying withdrawal, which is used by the CRA in the PSPA certification process.

The qualifying withdrawal is designated as such on form T1006 and must be an amount that has been withdrawn from the individual's RRSP during the year before the date on which the T1006 is filed or in either of the two immediately preceding calendar years.

In the event that the individual had already been affected by another past service event earlier in the year, the following approach is used. Certification is given when the PSPA in respect of the current past service event, when added to the accumulated PSPA (i.e., total PSPAs in the year but excluding the current PSPA), does not exceed $8,000, plus any RRSP contribution room at the end of the preceding year, plus the current qualifying withdrawal, plus any "PSPA withdrawal". A "PSPA withdrawal" is defined as the sum of all qualifying withdrawals made in the same year but before the current "past service event".

Qualifying withdrawals made in error can be recontributed to an RRSP without adverse tax consequences. This could occur where a withdrawal has been made and the PSPA is then not certified.

There is no set deadline for applying for certification of a provisional PSPA if it is "non-exempt". However, there is little point in delaying the application, since the employer may not make any contributions to the plan in respect of the additional benefits that have been granted until the administrator has applied for certification (provided there is an actuarial certification supporting such contributions, if required), and the additional benefits may not be paid to the employee until certification has been received.

As noted earlier, the effective date on which RRSP contribution room is reduced by virtue of a non-exempt PSPA is the date on which the PSPA is certified.

Because of this process, some employers may be hesitant to give the same past service upgrade to all or a significant number of employees where the non-exempt process must be followed. For example, some employees may find RRSPs so attractive that they are not interested in minor past service upgrades. They may, therefore, prefer no upgrade at all, rather than lose some RRSP contribution room. There are also situations where an employee cannot receive the full past service upgrade because the employee has insufficient RRSP assets to cover the required withdrawal (even after allowing for the $8,000 cushion described above). Examples of such a situation are where:

- the employee's contributions had been made to a spousal RRSP and, therefore, the employee has no personal RRSP assets to withdraw;
- the employee has been divorced and part of his or her RRSP assets have been split with the ex-spouse; again, the employee may not have enough RRSP assets to withdraw;
- the employee has already withdrawn RRSP assets for other reasons; or
- the employee has suffered a significant capital loss within the RRSP.

Once the above process is complete, the CRA will notify the administrator which PSPAs have been certified and which have not. In the case of employees whose PSPAs were not certified, the CRA will not tell the plan administrator the amount of the shortfall, because this is considered to be personal and private information known only to the employee. Thus, the plan administrator will not know how much of an upgrade could result in the PSPA being certified, unless the employee is willing to divulge full information on his or her RRSP contribution room. The plan administrator must decide whether it is practical or administratively feasible to credit only partial improvements to some employees.

The employer and/or the employee are not permitted to make contributions towards the cost of the benefit improvement until application for certification of the PSPA is made (provided there is actuarial certification supporting the additional contributions). However, if certification is later denied, contributions must cease immediately and steps must be taken to refund the contributions to the employer and/or the employee.

Some employers may wish to provide past service upgrades to a large number of plan members (assuming the upgrade does not qualify for exempt status) where some of the members will not be able to accept the full upgrade due to the PSPA not being certified. The employer may not wish to permit partial past service upgrades for those who cannot accept the full upgrade and may prefer no upgrade at all for those employees whose PSPA would not be certified if they were to get the full upgrade. This situation would have to be clearly set out in the plan amendment that covers the upgrade. In that event, when an individual does not have sufficient RRSP contribution room, it must be made clear to the employee that if sufficient RRSP assets are not withdrawn, no past service upgrade at all will be received.

Plan administrators must notify their plan members about the PSPA event within 60 days of certification by giving them a certified copy of form T1004. It is recommended, however, that this process be carefully and fully communicated to plan members well before making an application to the CRA.

¶1070 Correcting, Amending, or Deleting a Previously Reported PSPA

The process for reporting PSPAs is set out in ¶1060, ¶1065, and ¶2237.

If a PSPA has been incorrectly reported and the plan administrator wants to correct the PSPA, the appropriate approach depends on whether the PSPA was exempt or non-exempt.

For an exempt PSPA, a new T215 slip must be filed, showing the corrected PSPA (or showing zero if the purpose is to delete the PSPA). A T215 Summary must also be completed and both forms should be marked as amendments by checking off "amended return" on the T215 Summary and answering "yes" in Box 5 on the T215 slip. All other information from the original T215 should be reproduced on the replacement.

If there is another error other than the amount of the PSPA (for example, the past service event date was incorrectly reported), the error should be corrected by writing a letter of explanation to the CRA. At the time of writing of this book, the address to send the replacement forms to is:

Ottawa Technology Centre
875 Heron Road
Ottawa, Ontario
K1A 1A2
Fax: (613) 739-1147

For a non-exempt PSPA, a letter of explanation should be sent to the CRA at the above address, detailing the situation, including the information in Form T1004 and providing the corrected PSPA amount.

If the difference between the previously reported PSPA and the amended PSPA is less than $50, an amended PSPA does not have to be reported. However, this less than $50 tolerance is cumulative, so it applies to the total of:

- the difference between a previously reported PSPA and an amended PSPA; and
- PSPA(s) calculated since the last reported PSPA.

However, this is an administrative rule and, therefore, does not apply if an employee or the CRA requests accurate reporting of the PSPA.

¶1075 PSPAs for Specified Retirement Arrangements

As discussed at ¶545, under certain circumstances, PAs are to be reported for benefits accruing under SRAs.

Therefore, if past service benefits under an SRA are improved, then it is possible that PSPAs can also arise. Each situation should be carefully reviewed to determine whether a PSPA arises. However, if the SRA is supplemental to an RPP that provides benefits at, or close to, the maximum permissible level, the PA is not increased at all to reflect the SRA and benefit improvements may be able to be made without any additional PSPA implications. As with PAs, alternative methods of calculation may be used, subject to the approval of the Minister of National Revenue.

¶1080 PSPAs for Government-Sponsored Retirement Arrangements

As discussed at ¶550, PAs may be reported for a GSRA, which is an unregistered arrangement for paying retirement income from public funds established to benefit individuals who provide professional services that are paid for out of public funds (federal or provincial).

GSRAs have amounts prescribed by the Regulations that reduce the amounts an individual can contribute to their RRSP. Therefore, if past service benefits under a GSRA are improved, then it is possible that PSPAs can also arise. Each situation should be carefully reviewed to determine whether a PSPA arises. Again, however, if the prescribed amount for the GSRA is already a "maximum PA", then benefit improvements to the GSRA will have no impact.

¶1085 PSPAs for Foreign Pension Plans

The PA rules for various foreign pension plan situations are described at ¶645 to ¶647.

In foreign pension plan situations where PAs are to be reported, PSPAs can also arise if an individual's benefits for post-1991 service are retroactively increased. However, a non-zero PSPA can only occur if the employer adopted an alternative PA calculation method instead of the "default PA" formula set out at ¶646, which calls for the reporting of a maximum PA.

¶1090 Employee Contributions To Purchase Past Service

If the employee is required under the terms of the RPP (or under the terms of an amendment to the RPP providing for the benefit improvements) to make contributions to fund the new benefits being provided, the tax deductibility of such employee contributions depends on whether the service being purchased by the employee is pre-1990 or post-1989.

Any employee contributions that are required to fund the new post-1989 benefits will be fully deductible in the year in which they are made and will have no additional effect on the level of unused RRSP contribution room.

Since pre-1990 past service does not require the reporting of PSPAs and, therefore, does not impact on an individual's RRSP contribution room, there are stricter rules regarding the level of contribution that may be made to the plan and tax deducted by the individual. This is discussed further at ¶1810.

¶1100 PENSION ADJUSTMENT REVERSALS

¶1105 Introduction

As we have seen in earlier chapters, the PA measures the value, for tax purposes, of an employee's participation in a registered pension plan or DPSP. The PA directly reduces the amount that an employee may contribute to an RRSP in the following year. The greater the PA, the less personal RRSP room an employee has. The PA calculation itself, for defined benefit plans, takes into account a number of assumptions that are not representative for any particular pension plan or member. When a plan member terminates employment or retires prior to the normal retirement age, the value of the actual benefit received will not be equal to the PAs reported. If the benefit received is considerably less than the PAs reported, then the member has been disadvantaged from an RRSP contribution point of view since the member has had RRSP room reduced. This "lost" RRSP room has not been replaced by receipt of a tax-sheltered benefit from a pension plan.

Until the introduction of the PAR, this was the unfortunate consequence of terminating early from a defined benefit pension plan. The PAR is the remedy for this situation: if the PAs reported exceed the value of the post-1989 benefit received at termination, the individual will be credited with a PAR. The PAR will permit the individual to contribute additional amounts to an RRSP which were lost by the reporting of the PAs.

Although the PAR was not introduced until the February 1997 federal Budget, the concept was not new. When the system of determining PAs was developed in the late 1980s, an important part of the proposed system was the PAR. The purpose of the PAR is to recognize that the PAs are overstated for many members of defined benefit plans (i.e., the "factor of 9" used in the PA calculation is often too high) as well as for members of defined contribution pension plans or DPSPs who terminate before becoming fully vested in the employer contributions. While it was considered an integral part of the retirement savings system, in finalizing the rules, it was ultimately decided to eliminate the PAR, in the belief that the new system of PAs and PSPAs was complex enough.

The decision to eliminate the PAR resulted in much discussion about the inequity this created for members of defined benefit plans, given that the original intent of the new RRSP system was to create equal opportunity for retirement savings for all employees, regardless of the type of retirement savings plan(s) in which they participated. The concession at the time for the elimination of the PAR was to change the offset under the PA formula for defined benefit plans to $1,000 from the originally contemplated $600. When the PAR was introduced in 1997, the offset was changed from $1,000 back to the original $600.

PARs are reported to the CRA quarterly by the plan administrator on behalf of those plan members who cease to be entitled to benefits under the defined benefit provision during that calendar quarter. More details regarding the timing and forms to be used for this reporting are discussed at ¶1160.

As a result of the introduction of the PAR, there were modifications made to the way in which PAs and PSPAs are calculated. Modifications to the PA rules are discussed in Appendix 1, section 3B and Appendix 1, section 8B and modifications to the PSPA rules are discussed in Chapter 10 and Appendix 1, section 7C.

¶1110 When is a PAR Calculated?

When an individual participates in an RPP or DPSP, the employer reports a PA each year to the CRA. The PA is the total of the individual's pension credits for the year under any DPSP or RPP benefit provision of which the individual is a member. The PA, briefly, is:

- for a DPSP, the total of all contributions and non-vested forfeitures allocated to the plan member in the year;
- for a money purchase provision of an RPP, the total of all contributions, non-vested forfeitures, and surplus allocated to the plan member in the year;
- for a defined benefit provision of an RPP, the amount determined by following the formula set out at ¶710, which determines the value, for tax purposes, of benefits accruing to the plan member under the provision in the year.

An individual's PA for a year reduces RRSP deduction room for the following year. Further, as discussed in Chapter 10, when benefits are provided to an individual under a defined benefit provision of an RPP on a past service basis, the individual's RRSP deduction room is reduced by the PSPA associated with those benefits.

A PAR is calculated whenever an individual ceases entitlement to a benefit under a provision of the RPP or DPSP after 1996, for which PAs and/or PSPAs were originally reported. Thus, a PAR is to be calculated and reported under the following situations:

- The member elects to receive the commuted value of his or her defined benefit entitlement or the lump-sum value from his or her defined contribution benefit as a cash payment, or transfer to another savings vehicle of a money purchase nature. Note that the member could have terminated prior to 1997, but if he or she did not receive the commuted value until after 1996, then a PAR may arise.
- If a member was not vested at the date of termination, in the case of a non-contributory plan, the PAR would be triggered on the individual's termination date, since no payment or settlement is due. In a contributory plan, a PAR would be triggered when the member is refunded his or her contributions.
- A PAR must be calculated if the member's defined benefit entitlement is converted to a money purchase benefit and the member is no longer entitled to a benefit under the defined benefit provision; however, the PAR is not reportable until regulatory approval of the conversion is received.
- If a defined benefit plan is being wound up and benefits are fully commuted, a PAR must be calculated even when the question of surplus ownership is still unresolved; if surplus is subsequently used to provide additional post-1989 lifetime benefits and a PSPA has been reported, any subsequent commutation of these additional

benefits would be considered as another termination and result in another PAR calculation (refer to ¶1145 for additional details).

- If the member's defined benefit entitlement is transferred directly to another defined benefit plan through a reciprocal transfer agreement or portability arrangement, a PAR may arise to reflect the extent to which the PA value of the benefits under the exporting plan exceed the PA value of benefits being provided under the importing plan (refer to ¶1155 for additional details).

Note that an individual does not necessarily have to cease employment in order to receive a PAR; he or she simply has to cease being entitled to all benefits under the particular provision.

If an individual ceases to be entitled to benefits from a DPSP or from a money purchase provision of an RPP before becoming vested, the individual's entitlement to amounts allocated under the plan or provision (other than the individual's own contributions plus earnings) is forfeited. The individual's PAR will restore the RRSP deduction room previously given up on account of the allocation of the amounts that are now being forfeited.

If an individual ceases to be entitled to benefits from a defined benefit provision of an RPP, the termination benefit paid from the plan could be less than the total pension credits and PSPAs reported while the individual was a plan member. Generally, a PAR will increase the individual's RRSP deduction room by the amount of the shortfall, thereby restoring RRSP deduction room that would otherwise be lost permanently.

It should be noted that a PAR is not reported under the following circumstances:

- If a plan member dies.

- For certain SMEPs, in order to maintain consistency with respect to the special rules for calculating PAs for these types of plans. When a member forfeits benefits on termination from a defined benefit SMEP, the plan funds supporting those benefits can be used to augment the benefits of other plan members without increasing the pension credits of those members. It would be inappropriate, therefore, to allow the forfeited amounts also to give rise (through a PAR) to additional RRSP deduction room for the terminating member. The exception for defined benefit SMEPs also reflects the practical difficulties in determining PARs in plans where active membership may often be episodic. PARs and PSPAs for multi-employer plans are discussed in Chapter 12.

- If a terminating plan member elects a deferred or immediate pension, since pension plan membership has not terminated under this situation.
- If the plan member receives an interest in an annuity contract in full or partial satisfaction of the plan member's entitlement to benefits under a defined benefit plan (other than an annuity contract acquired by way of first transferring to an RRSP or RRIF), no PAR is reported as the individual is deemed not to have terminated.
- If a member retires under the plan and receives a pension from the plan, again, since pension plan membership has not terminated.
- When a pension is split on marriage breakdown and payments from a pension plan are made to the non-member former spouse, a PAR is not reported; the member's PAR is only calculated at the time of his or her termination (refer to ¶ 1150 for additional details).
- If a plan member participates in more than one defined benefit provision of an RPP where benefits provided to the individual under one of the provisions are supplemental to, or otherwise dependant on, benefits provided to the individual under the other provisions, a PAR is not calculated until he or she is no longer a member with respect to all of the related provisions (refer to ¶ 1140 for additional details). Note that a defined benefit provision that appears to be dependent on a defined contribution provision does not fall into this category. An example of this would be a defined benefit provision that has as an offset the benefit that can be provided by a defined contribution benefit within the same plan. Such a plan would be considered a hybrid or combination plan and the PARs for each of the defined benefit and the defined contribution provisions can be calculated and reported independently.
- If a plan is being wound up, surplus remains after basic benefits have been paid out and that surplus is later used to provide only ancillary benefits after basic benefits have been paid out (i.e., no increase in the lifetime retirement benefit); in this situation, no PAR is calculated when the ancillary benefits are paid out since there were no PAs or PSPAs associated with providing these ancillary benefits (refer to ¶ 1145 for additional details).

¶1115 Basic PAR Rules

The PAR is a measure of the extent to which an individual's RRSP deduction room has been reduced on account of membership in an RPP or DPSP, where other tax-sheltered benefits were not provided. Conceptually, the method for calculating the PAR is deceptively simple:

Total of PAs and PSPAs reported

less

lump-sum benefit paid in respect of post-1989 benefits.*

The PAR is rounded to the nearest dollar.

Generally, a PAR is calculated independently in respect of each benefit provision to which the member is entitled upon termination of membership in the provision. There are, however, situations where a PAR is not calculated until the member has terminated from *all* provisions. Refer to ¶ 1140 for further details on these types of situations.

For defined benefit provisions, the Regulations refer to the lump-sum benefit paid indicated in the above formula as the "specified distribution". Refer to ¶ 1120 for more details regarding the calculation of the specified distribution.

For many pension plans, the calculation of the PAR will be relatively straightforward. However, in situations where the defined benefit formula has a money purchase offset, where PSPAs have been previously reported, where a plan member is transferring from one defined benefit provision to another defined benefit provision (such as a reciprocal transfer or portability situation) or where benefits that were previously provided to a member are being reinstated, the calculation of the PAR is more complex.

For members of defined contribution RPPs and DPSPs, the above formula amounts to the total of the PAs reported that are not vested in the individual. Under the minimum standards vesting requirements for RPPs and the *Income Tax Act* (Canada) vesting rules for DPSPs, PARs will not arise very often in these types of plans and generally these PARs will not be significant amounts.

For defined benefit RPPs, a PAR can arise under various other situations in addition to a non-vested termination. The following is an example of a PAR calculation for a defined benefit RPP.

Suppose an individual has belonged to a defined benefit plan since January 1, 2005. The formula under the defined benefit plan is 1% of average earnings for each year of membership. When the individual terminated on July 1, 2010 at age 40, he or she was entitled to a commuted value of $13,000 and elected to transfer this to a LIRA. The individual's earnings have ranged from $65,000 *per annum* in 2004 to $75,000 *per annum* at the termination date. The total of the PAs reported equals $25,215. The PAR is calculated as follows:

* Since PAs and PSPAs were not reported prior to 1990

Total of PAs reported: $25,200 *less*

lump-sum benefit paid: $13,000

PAR = $25,200 - $13,000

= $12,200.

Thus, it can be seen that for a relatively modest final average formula, for an average aged individual at a mid-range level of earnings who belonged to a pension plan for a relatively short period of time, the additional RRSP room provided by the PAR is not insignificant.

The relative size of the PAR is determined in part by the interest rate used to calculate the commuted value. Generally, during periods when interest rates are higher, the PAR will be higher since the commuted value will be lower. Also, note that although the PAR restores lost RRSP room, there is no compensation for the time value of interest foregone had the plan member had access to the RRSP room at an earlier time.

Another determining factor in the size of the PAR is the plan member's age at the date of termination, as this, along with the interest rate, is a significant factor in the size of the commuted value. The following is an example of the relative size of the PAR for an individual who belongs to a 1½% final average earnings defined benefit plan. The individual joined the plan on January 1, 2001 and terminated employment on December 31, 2008. The pension plan provides a non-indexed pension, payable from age 65 and guaranteed for five years. The following illustrates the relative variance in the PAR by age and final average earnings at termination:

Age at Termination	PAR if Final Earnings = $75,000	PAR if Final Earnings = $100,000
30	$47,000	$68,000
40	$33,000	$50,000
50	$10,000	$19,000

As this example shows, the PAR is significant for terminations at younger ages and less significant at older ages. However, even for an individual terminating at age 50, the plan member as shown above would be entitled to additional RRSP contribution room.

Some modifications apply to the basic PAR calculation in certain defined benefit situations and these will be discussed and numerical examples provided later in this chapter. The following are the most notable:

- In determining the amount of a PSPA that is to be included in a PAR, certain adjustments will be made to ensure that the PA value of past service benefits is not understated. This is referred to as using the "grossed-up" PSPA. The "grossed-up" PSPA is the measure of the full PA value of the past service being provided. What this means is that the PSPA used should be the PSPA before there were any offsets applied in the PSPA calculation. In particular, where a PSPA had been reduced by an amount transferred from an RRSP or money purchase provision of an RPP to fund past service benefits (i.e., a "qualifying transfer"), that reduction will be disregarded. Or if, by virtue of the modified PSPA rules (as discussed at ¶1037), a PSPA had been reduced by the PA value of defined benefits previously provided to the individual, that reduction will also be disregarded.

- An amount transferred between defined benefit provisions under a reciprocal transfer agreement or portability arrangement will not reduce the PAR determined for the individual under the exporting plan. However, there will be a reduction in the individual's PAR to reflect the extent to which the PA value of benefits provided to the individual under the exporting plan reduces the individual's PSPA under the importing plan; this reduction is known as the "PA transfer amount" and must be reported to the exporting plan in order to be able to calculate the PAR under the exporting plan.

¶1120 The Specified Distribution

The post-1989 portion of a lump-sum paid upon a plan member's exit from a defined benefit provision of an RPP plan is more formally referred to as the "specified distribution".

In general terms, a specified distribution is the commuted value of the benefit or any lump-sums (including excess contributions under the 50% cost-sharing rule and any amounts payable in cash resulting from the *Income Tax Act* (Canada) limits on transfers from defined benefit plans, as discussed at ¶1743) paid to the individual, or transferred to an RRSP or other money purchase type of registered plan, including any interest thereon, in respect of the individual's post-1989 benefits under the provision.

Amounts paid in respect of benefits for periods prior to 1990 are not included in the PAR calculation. Thus, if an individual ceases entitlement under a given plan provision in respect of service prior to 1990, the specified distribution used in the PAR calculation is that portion of the total benefit that can reasonably be attributed to post-1989 service.

The Regulations do not specify how the administrator is to determine the portion of distributions to be attributed to pre-1990 and post-1989 service. Prorating is one possibility where benefit accruals have been "uniform". The CRA has indicated in its Pension Adjustment Reversal Guide that it is acceptable to simply prorate the benefit to determine the post-1989 portion if the benefit formula is reasonably uniform for the whole period.

However, a more careful estimation of the post-1989 benefit must be done where the benefit accrued in respect of each year is not uniform. Some examples of non-uniform benefit accruals are:

- if the formula has changed during the period and such change was not retroactive for the entire service history;
- where the benefit formula is a career average formula (for the period where earnings have not been updated);
- where there is a 50% rule refund payable in respect of certain years but not all years of service; and
- where the commuted value for a Quebec member includes the value of the additional benefit (as discussed in ¶ 1319) for post-January 1, 2001 service.

There is another non-uniform situation that could arise if the benefit accrual is uniform, but different actuarial factors were used to determine commuted values of benefits during different time periods. This situation could occur where, for example, minimum standards jurisdictions require or the plan sponsor has chosen to value different periods of benefits (i.e., pre- and post-minimum standards reform) differently in aspects such as the use of unisex mortality or differing pre-retirement death benefits. In jurisdictions such as Ontario, whose minimum standards reform date is January 1, 1987, it might therefore be reasonable to prorate the post-January 1, 1987 benefit to arrive at the post-1989 lump-sum payment. However, the CRA has indicated that it is acceptable to treat the entire benefit as uniform for these purposes if it is not practical to determine the split more accurately.

Clearly, since there are no definitive guidelines on how to determine the post-1989 lump-sum payment, the onus is on the plan administrator to use a method that is reasonable, and a methodology that would result in an inappropriately low specified distribution (and therefore an inappropriately high PAR) would not be acceptable.

While pre-1990 amounts are not included in the specified distribution, certain other amounts in respect of post-1989 are also not considered specified distributions. For example, the following are not included in the specified distribution:

- An amount that is transferred to another defined benefit provision of an RPP (other than an SMEP) in order to fully or partially fund the past service benefits being provided under the other defined benefit provision.

- An amount that is a cash payment of actuarial surplus (i.e., surplus is not used to provide additional lifetime or ancillary benefits).

- A return of contributions with interest to a member where such return of contributions results from an amendment to the plan that also reduces or eliminates future member contributions.

- An amount that is a payment of benefits for a period when the plan was a SMEP (refer to ¶910 for further information when a plan is considered to be an SMEP and how to calculate PAs for SMEPs).

- An amount that is related to past foreign service that did not generate a PSPA (refer to ¶1033 for additional information about situations where the foreign service will not generate a PSPA).

- An amount that represents only a partial payment of the benefit. In some situations a member may take only a portion of his or her benefit out of the plan and leave the remainder in the plan. This would occur, for example, in situations where a plan is underfunded and the full commuted value cannot be paid to the terminating plan member immediately upon termination. In these situations, the plan sponsor may choose not to "top-up" the commuted value to 100% of the member's entitlement and as a result, the member will receive the remainder of the benefit within a five-year period from termination. This could also occur in some legislative jurisdictions or plans that permit partial portability in certain situations. In another situation, a member may only choose to receive the excess contributions arising from the 50% cost-sharing rule and may leave the rest of his or her benefit in the plan. In all these cases, the member has not ceased entitlement and is therefore not entitled to a PAR at this time. If, in the future, the member does receive in a lump-sum, or transfer out, the remainder of their entitlement, a PAR will be triggered and the earlier payment(s) (without interest to the PAR date) will form part of the specified distribution.

¶1125 PARs for Defined Contribution Plans and DPSPs

If a member terminates from a DPSP or defined contribution provision, a PAR must be calculated and reported if:

- the member is not vested;
- the payment of the termination benefit occurred after 1996;
- the termination is not because of the individual's death;
- periodic retirement benefits have not been made from the plan in respect of the individual (for example, where a member terminating from a DPSP elects to receive payout of the entitlement over a period of time rather than in a lump-sum); and
- no annuity has been purchased by the plan for the individual.

If all of the above conditions are satisfied, the amounts included in an individual's PAR are those employer contributions made in respect of the plan member, and those amounts forfeited by other plan members and reallocated to the plan member, which are subsequently forfeited by the plan member.

This means that a terminating plan member will have a PAR under a DPSP or a defined contribution provision of an RPP only when the member is not fully vested on termination.

Investment or other earnings on contributions and other allocated amounts are not taken into account in the calculation of the PAR, nor is there any provision for a restoration of RRSP deduction room to compensate for a negative rate of return.

An amount allocated to and subsequently forfeited by the member (including employer contributions), under a DPSP or defined contribution provision in the year in which the member terminates from the plan, is included in the pension credit for the year for the purposes of computing a PA. (Prior to 1997, however, as discussed in Appendix 1, section 3B, in the year of termination, the PA of non-vested members in a DPSP or a defined contribution provision consisted only of employee contributions.)

The PAR in respect of the partial year of termination will effectively cancel out the PA reported for that same year. However, due to differences in timing for the reporting of the PAR and the PA, the PAR will generally be reported prior to the PA being reported and the member will appear to have been granted additional RRSP contribution room before the reporting of the PA will cancel it out.

When an individual terminates from a DPSP or a money purchase RPP and subsequently rejoins the plan, any PA amounts associated with the first termination are ignored when there is a subsequent termination (and potential subsequent PAR). This is the case regardless of whether the member transfers his or her money purchase assets back into the pension plan. There is no PSPA associated with such an individual rejoining the plan (since no "past service benefits" can be credited to the member) and therefore, no need to re-examine whether inappropriate tax sheltering is being provided.

¶1130 PARs for Defined Benefit Plans

If a member terminates or otherwise ceases to be entitled to a defined benefit provision, a PAR is reportable once the final payment is made under the provision, or if the provision is non-contributory and the individual has not satisfied the vesting requirements, when the employee terminates.

A PAR is then determined if the following conditions are met:

- the payment of the entire termination benefit occurred after 1996 or, if the member was not vested, if the termination occurred after 1996;
- the termination is not because of the individual's death;
- periodic retirement benefits have not been or will not ever be made from the plan in respect of the individual; and
- no annuity has been purchased by the plan for the individual.

The formula for the PAR for a defined benefit provision is as follows:

A + B - C - D

where **A**, **B**, **C** and **D** are defined as follows:

A is the sum of the member's pension credits in respect of the provision. For high earners, the pension credit used in A is the lesser of the actual pension credit and the RRSP dollar limit for the following year, as discussed at ¶720. This will ensure that the PAR in respect of those years in which the pension credit reported exceeded the maximum RRSP room that could be generated in the following year, is not inappropriately high. This could have happened for high earners for the years from 1995 to 2002 inclusive, as a result of various delays in the complete transition to the new retirement savings system. For example, for the year 2002, even though the member's pension credit could have been as high as $14,900 (for a single defined benefit provision) and a PA of $14,900 was reported, the maximum new RRSP room that could have been created in 2003 prior to the PA offset was $14,500. The excess PA over the maximum RRSP dollar limit of $14,500 for 2003 is disregarded in calculating the PAR. This process is followed for PAs for the years 1995 through 2002 inclusive in order to ensure that the PAR does not restore more RRSP room than was originally impacted by the PA. The maximum RRSP contribution room reached $15,500 in 2004, offset by the PA for 2003, which was capped at $14,900. Thus, capping the PA for PAR purposes has not been required since 2003, as the maximum PA for the years 2003 onward has been less than available RSSP contribution room for the years 2004 and onward. Table 1 in Appendix 3 shows the maximum PA for the purposes of the PAR calculation from 1990 onwards.

B is the sum of the "grossed-up PSPAs" associated with any past service benefits granted to the plan member during the period of plan membership. Variable B takes into account the PA value related to past service benefits and serves to increase the PAR to reflect the resultant loss of RRSP room. The term "grossed-up PSPA" refers to the pure PSPA calculation prior to its reduction, to take into account any qualifying transfers that were used to fund the past service benefit (and reduce the PSPA at the same time). It is necessary to use the grossed-up PSPAs to ensure that the PAR accurately reflects the degree to which benefits under the pension plan have reduced RRSP contribution room. For example, if the member transfers assets from his or her RRSP to fund additional past service benefits, thereby reducing the PSPA by the amount of RRSP assets transferred into the plan, then it is not appropriate to use the reduced PSPA in the PAR calculation since the calculated PAR would not take into account that the member had given up RRSP room in order to receive the past service benefits.

C is the amount of the specified distribution. Refer to ¶ 1120 for further information on the specified distribution.

D is the member's PA transfer amount. The PA transfer amount will generally be used only in situations of portability or reciprocal transfer where an individual is credited with past service benefits for periods of defined benefit pensionable service under an RPP that were previously credited as pensionable service under another RPP or in situations where benefits under an RPP are being replaced by benefits under another RPP of the same employer. Numerically, the PA transfer amount is equal to the lesser of variable A in the basic PSPA formula (i.e., the PA value of the past service benefits under the new provision) and variable B in the basic PSPA formula (i.e., the PA value of benefits provided under the former provision). Refer to ¶ 1036 for a full description of these two variables. In reciprocal transfer and portability situations, a provisional PSPA is calculated using the modified PSPA rules (as described at ¶1037) so that the PSPA under the new provision is offset by the sum of the PAs and PSPAs under the previous provision. Under the modified PSPA rules, the PSPA measures the extent to which a transferring plan member receives more generous benefits under the new plan compared to the benefits provided under the former plan. It then follows that a PAR will arise if a transferring plan member receives less generous benefits under the new plan compared to the former plan.

Refer to ¶1155 and ¶1165 for additional information on the timing of reporting PARs in situations where variable D is required for the determination of the PAR. Paragraph 1155 also sets out some examples of PAR situations where a PA transfer amount applies.

It should be noted that, due to differences in timing for the reporting of the PAR and the PA, the PAR will generally be reported prior to the date the PA, in respect of the year of termination, is reported (i.e., at the end of a calendar quarter *versus* by February 28 of the following year). Thus, the member must be aware that even though he or she has terminated and received additional RRSP contribution room, some of that RRSP room will be reduced in the following year once the PA for the year of termination is reported.

It should also be noted that this timing difference means that the plan administrator must effectively calculate the final year PA at the time of termination (since it is required in order to determine the PAR) instead of waiting until the end of the year when PAs for all members are determined. However, normally that final year PA would not actually be reported until the end of the year, along with the regular PA reporting.

The PAR calculation for defined benefit plans will be more complex for the following situations:

- the individual is changing jobs and transferring past service benefits under an RTA or portability arrangement (this is discussed in greater detail at ¶1155);
- the individual's benefits under the terminating provisions are being replaced with benefits under another defined benefit provision of an RPP maintained by the same employer(s) (also discussed in greater detail at ¶1155);
- where the plan does not have uniform accrual of benefits;
- where there is related provision (i.e., where benefits provided to an individual under one defined benefit provision are dependent on

benefits provided under one or more other defined benefit provisions, discussed in greater detail at ¶1140); or

- when the plan is a hybrid or combination of defined benefit and defined contribution provisions (discussed in greater detail at ¶1135).

As noted at ¶1110, PARs are not determined when an individual terminates from a defined benefit provision of an SMEP. However, since a plan that is currently classified as an SMEP may not have been an SMEP for all years, PARs may still arise for the period of time that a plan was not considered an SMEP. The PAR formula then deems pension credits for years in which the plan was an SMEP to be zero. Refer to Chapters 9, 12, and 21 for further discussion regarding SMEPs.

¶1135 PARs for Hybrid or Combination Plans

A hybrid or combination plan is one that contains elements of both defined benefit and defined combination provisions. A typical combination plan is one in which the member belongs to two tiers that are independent of each other, such as a defined benefit core formula plus a defined contribution tier to which the member and/or the plan sponsor make contributions on a money purchase basis.

In some hybrid plans, the benefit payable is a defined benefit formula that is offset by a money purchase provision (either a defined contribution benefit or a DPSP benefit). As an example, an employer may maintain a defined contribution plan for all employees and a supplementary defined benefit plan for executives. Benefits under the defined benefit executive plan are offset by benefits that can be purchased at retirement from the executive member's defined contribution account.

A DPSP or money purchase provision is considered to be an "offset provision" in relation to a defined benefit provision, if the individual's pension credits under the plan or provision have been taken into account in determining the individual's pension credits under the defined benefit provision. Refer to ¶815 for further details on calculating pension credits under these types of provisions.

Under both types of hybrid or combination plans, a member may terminate membership in one provision, but not in both. However, the PARs may be calculated and reported independently. For example, a member may elect to purchase an annuity from an insurance company with the defined contribution entitlement but elect to transfer the entitlement under the defined benefit provision to a locked-in retirement account. In this situation, a PAR can be determined in respect of the defined benefit provision even though the member is not considered to have terminated from the defined contribution provision (by virtue of the annuity purchase).

¶1140 PARs for Defined Benefit Plans with Related Provisions

In some situations, benefits provided to an individual under one defined benefit provision are dependent on benefits provided under one or more other defined benefit provisions. For example, consider the situation where a member transferred from the hourly plan to the salaried plan of the same employer. The member retains a frozen hourly pension in the hourly plan. As per the terms of the salaried plan, the member's salaried plan benefit will be calculated using the salaried plan formula and will include the service while the member was in the hourly plan. However, the hourly frozen pension will be offset from the salaried plan pension and paid separately from the hourly plan. This is not an uncommon treatment for transfers and is known as a "wrap-around".

In this situation, because the two provisions (hourly and salaried) are related as a result of the offsetting nature, a PAR will not be triggered until the member ceases entitlement in both plans. This would mean that the member would have to transfer both his hourly and salaried pensions to his or her LIRA in order to receive a PAR. One pension could not remain as a deferred pension while the other is transferred out.

In these situations, the plan member is not considered to have terminated under the provision unless he or she has also terminated under all of the related provisions.

Further, any benefits provided or amounts paid under one of the provisions are also considered to be benefits provided or amounts paid under each of the other related provisions. Thus, a specified distribution from one provision is considered to be a specified distribution under each of the other provisions. The purpose of this additional provision is to ensure that the sum of the PARs reported in respect of each of the provisions does not exceed the PAR that would have been reported if all the provisions were considered to be a single provision.

However, if in a particular situation, the opposite result occurs — that is, the sum of the PARs under each of the provisions is less than the PAR that would have been reported had all the provisions been considered as a single provision — then the CRA will, on a case by case basis, waive this method of deeming the specified distribution from one provision to be a specified distribution under each of the other provisions.

For this purpose, the condition that the termination from both plans must occur after 1996 is disregarded.

Wrap-around type benefit provisions between two unrelated employers sometimes arise through purchase–sale situations. An organization may acquire a division from another organization but may not want to take on all past service defined benefits accrued to transferring employees and as a result, the past service benefits remain frozen in the seller's plan. However, in order that these past service pensions not be eroded over time (since growth in final average earnings is frozen as well), the purchaser may be willing to "wrap" its benefit around the frozen benefit by providing a benefit based on all service and final average earnings with the purchaser, less the frozen benefit remaining in the seller's plan.

Consider the PAR calculation for this situation. Suppose that a member had 10 years of service in total, with the first seven years as a member of Company A's plan and the last three years with Company B's plan, as a result of Company B acquiring a division of Company A at that time. Company A's plan provides a benefit of 1½% of final average earnings. Company B provides a wrap-around so that the pension from Company B's plan is based on all 10 years of service, less the frozen benefit remaining in Company A's plan, as agreed at the time of the acquisition. The member's final average earnings with Company A at the time of the acquisition was $55,000 and by the end of the 10 years of service, final average earnings with Company B is $61,000.

The member is now terminating employment. Assume the commuted value factor for both plans is seven. The frozen benefit payable under Company A's plan is $5,775 *per annum* (i.e., $55,000 x 1.5% × 7 years), with a value at termination of $40,425. Total PAs reported during those first seven years are $45,885.

For the final three years, the sum of the PAs reported are $22,905 and the benefit under Company B's plan, taking into account the wrap-around, is determined as follows:

$61,000 × 1.5% × 10 years *less* frozen benefit from Company A's plan

= $9,150 *less* $5,775

= $3,375.

The commuted value of the Company B plan benefit is $23,625.

In the absence of any related provision considerations, Company A would calculate and report a PAR as follows:

Total of PAs reported: $45,885

Specified Distribution: $40,425

PAR = $45,885 - $40,425 = $5,460.

Company B would calculate and report a PAR as follows:

Total of PAs reported: $22,905

Specified Distribution: $23,625

PAR = $0, since the sum of the PAs reported is less than the value of the benefits.

Therefore, the total PARs reported on behalf of this member is $5,460.

However, consider what the PAR would be, had Company B not acquired Company A. Assume the member would have had the same stream of earnings. The pension on behalf of all 10 years of service would be $9,150 (i.e., $61,000 × 1½% × 10 years) and the commuted value would be $64,050. The PAR on behalf of all 10 years of service would be determined as follows:

Total of PAs reported: $45,885 + $22,905 = $68,790

Specified Distribution: $64,050

PAR = $68,790 - $64,050 = $4,740.

Thus, the separate calculating and reporting of the PAs results in a PAR that exceeds the PAR if the related provisions were considered to be a single provision. Instead, the related provision rules require that the specified distribution under one provision be considered to be a specified distribution under the related provision.

Application of this rule in this example would result in splitting the Company B plan benefit into two time periods: the first seven years and the last three years. The benefit for the last three years is $61,000 × 1.5% × 3 = $2,745, with a value of $19,215. Therefore the value of the "wrap-around" benefit for the first seven years is $4,410 (i.e. $23,625 - $4,410). If this part of the specified distribution is considered to be part of the specified distribution for the Company A plan PAR calculation, then the Company A PAR becomes:

Total of PAs reported: $45,885

Specified Distribution: $40,425 + $4,410 = $44,835

PAR = $45,885 - $44,835 = $1,050.

And the Company B PAR becomes:

Total of PAs reported: $22,905

Specified Distribution: $19,215

PAR = $22,905 - $19,215 = $3,690.

And the total PARs reported on behalf of this individual is $4,740 (= $1.050 + $3,690), which is the PAR that would be reported if all provisions were considered to be a single provision.

Clearly, this related provision rule, as it applies to unrelated companies, will require coordination and sharing of information, in order that the two organizations do not, collectively, report a PAR that is too high (or too low).

¶1145 PARs and Surplus Distributions

Generally, when a defined benefit RPP is terminated (either fully or partially), provision must be made for handling any surplus assets that exist as at the date of the partial or full wind-up. A surplus distribution can also arise at the time of a plan conversion from defined benefit to defined contribution.

If part or all of the surplus assets are to be distributed to plan members, there are a number of possible scenarios that can occur that will impact on how and when the PAR calculation is determined.

If surplus is paid out along with the basic benefit entitlement under the provision, it could be paid in one of the following formats:

- paid in a lump-sum cash payment;
- paid in the form of additional lifetime benefits or ancillaries which can then be commuted and transferred to another tax-sheltered vehicle — this payment may either be made at the same time as the basic benefit entitlement or a later date; or
- a combination of the above.

If surplus is paid in a lump-sum cash payment, it is not considered a specified distribution and therefore is not taken into account when calculating a PAR. No additional pension benefit (either as a lifetime pension or an ancillary) is being provided and therefore, no specified distribution occurs.

If surplus is paid in the form of additional lifetime benefits or ancillaries at the same time that the basic benefit is paid, the additional benefit provided may give rise to a PSPA, which must first be calculated and reported to take into account the additional PA value of any benefits to be received. Thus, once used in this manner, the surplus becomes part of the commuted value and therefore, as with any other PAR, the entire transfer value would be prorated for pre- and post-1989 service. The post-1989 portion would be considered a specified distribution for the purpose of variable C in the PAR formula. Then, once the total benefit is paid to the member, inclusive of any additional benefits provided from the surplus allocation, the PAR is calculated in the usual manner, taking into account the historical PAs reported and the PSPA reported and splitting the benefit into pre-1990 and post-1989 portions (either by prorating or another appropriate method as discussed at ¶1120).

However, often surplus ownership is in dispute and the payment of the surplus is deferred until the basic benefit entitlements have been paid out. Thus there is a time lag between the payment of the basic entitlement and the eventual payment of the surplus, which again could be either in the form of a cash payment or additional lifetime or ancillary benefits. An individual's right to surplus under a defined benefit provision of an RPP is not considered to be a right to benefits until the surplus is used to provide benefits to the individual.

If surplus is subsequently used to provide additional benefits, any subsequent commutation of these benefits would be considered another termination from the provision and result in another determination of a PAR, without regard for anything that happened during the individual's period of membership.

In these situations, a special rule applies so that if an individual terminates membership in all ways except for the payment of surplus, the individual is treated as though he or she has no entitlement to the surplus until it is actually allocated. This permits the PAR to be calculated and reported in the usual manner and within the usual time frames after the payment of the basic benefit entitlement, even though there is the possibility that surplus may later be used to provide additional benefits.

However, in situations where surplus is distributed in the form of additional benefits after the termination has occurred and the PAR reported, the surplus can only be used to provide ancillary benefits for periods prior to 1990. In this situation, it is therefore not considered part of the specified distribution and, as a result, does not give rise to another PAR.

At the same time, it should be noted that since the associated lifetime retirement benefits have already been commuted, normally the ability to transfer the commuted value of the ancillary benefit would be hampered by the fact that there is no lifetime pension foregone (and therefore the maximum transfer value would be nil (refer to ¶1743 for a discussion regarding maximum transfer values). That would mean that the commuted value would have to be paid to the individual in cash.

However, the individual can use previously unused maximum transfer value amounts to accommodate a rollover of the commuted ancillary benefits. Thus, if an individual's maximum transfer value at the date of termination was $50,000 (determined by applying the maximum transfer value factors to the lifetime pension foregone) and the initial termination benefit, before the surplus distribution was $30,000, up to $20,000 of surplus could be transferred subsequently (provided, of course, that this surplus was used to provide pre-1990 ancillary benefits).

As a final note, as time passes, the ability of an employer to use surplus to provide pre-1990 ancillaries and to permit employees to tax shelter that surplus will diminish as the number of plan members with sufficient pre-1990 service on which to provide ancillary benefits decreases.

¶1150 PARs and Marriage Breakdown

A special rule applies in the situation where a plan member ceases to have rights to all or a part of his or her benefits before terminating from the provision as a result of marriage breakdown where the benefits for-gone are paid to the spouse. The special rule is required in order to ensure that the PAR calculation is not inappropriately large, which would be the case if the PAR calculation only took into account the actual payment to the plan member alone. Also, since the benefit paid to the spouse may continue to be tax sheltered, this rule prevents the PAR from inappropriately restoring too much RRSP contribution room.

If the spouse receives a single payment from the plan before the member terminates employment, the calculation of the member's PAR (calculated when the member ceases entitlement) must include the amount paid to the spouse as part of the total specified distribution. Although the amount paid to the spouse may actually have been paid several years earlier, the member's specified distribution includes the exact amount paid to the spouse, without any adjustment to take into account interest or differences in interest rates used to determine the lump-sum paid to the spouse.

However, if the spouse does not receive the benefit until after the member terminates employment, the present value (determined as at the date of termination of employment) of the benefits the member is forfeiting is included in the specified distribution in the calculation of the PAR. This would be the situation, for example, where the spouse is provided with or elects to receive a deferred pension instead of a lump-sum.

If, on marriage breakdown, an individual's former spouse acquires rights to an amount allocated to the individual under a DPSP or defined contribution RPP, the allocated amount is taken into account in determining the individual's PAR in connection with any subsequent termination from the plan.

Thus, while the member does not recover any RRSP room associated with the benefit foregone, neither is there a PAR reported on behalf of the spouse, since an individual who has rights to a benefit from the provision or plan because of another individual's participation in the provision or plan is not considered a member.

¶1155 PARs and PSPAs and RTAs

As a result of the introduction of PARs, the reporting and calculation of PSPAs has been modified (as discussed at ¶1035). The methodology to be used in calculating the PSPA now depends on when the termination of employment occurred and whether the PAR is being calculated in combination with a reciprocal transfer agreement or portability arrangement in which the individual becomes entitled to service or pension benefits under a new pension plan upon ceasing to be entitled to benefits under the former pension plan.

In these situations, it must be determined whether a PAR is to be reported as a result of the cessation of membership in the former plan and whether a PSPA arises as a result of the service becoming credited under the new plan. In fact, it is possible that there could be both a PAR under the former plan and a PSPA under the new plan, depending on the differences between the plans, the amount to be transferred to fund the benefits and the commuted value payable under the former plan.

The PAR under the former plan is calculated using the formula set out at ¶1130. Variable D in the PAR formula is the PA transfer amount. A PAR will arise in a transfer situation where the transferring plan member receives less generous benefits under the new plan compared to the former plan and as a result, receives a benefit payout that reflects the extent to which funds in the former plan are not required to be transferred to the new plan (and are instead paid to the transferring member directly). Refer to ¶1165 for information on the timing requirements for obtaining this information from the new plan.

A PSPA under the new plan may arise if the PA value of the benefits being provided under the new plan is greater than the PA value of benefits being relinquished under the former plan. The methodology of calculating PSPAs in reciprocal situations follows the modified calculation rules set out at ¶1037.

The following are examples of situations in which PA transfer amounts apply.

Suppose an individual transferred his or her benefit entitlement from Employer A to Employer B under an RTA. The total PAs reported by Employer A (from the date of plan entry in 1996 to the individual's termination date) was $45,000. The individual received $10,000 in cash as a refund of excess contributions. The commuted value was transferred directly to Employer B's plan to fund the benefits transferred.

Employer B has an identical plan to Employer A. Therefore the PSPA actually reported by Employer B was zero. However, the "grossed-up" PSPA (i.e., before any reductions for PAs previously reported by Employer A) equals $45,000. This grossed-up PSPA forms the PA transfer amount that Employer A must use in the PAR to ensure that the PAR is not overstated.

The PAR from Employer A will therefore be calculated as follows:

A + B - C - D, where

A = sum of PAs reported by Employer A = $45,000

plus

B = sum of PSPAs reported by Employer A = $0

less

C = Specified Distribution* = $10,000

less

D = PA Transfer Amount provided by Employer B = $45,000.

Therefore, the PAR equals $0 in this example. This makes sense because the benefits provided under both plans have the same PA value, so the member has not foregone any benefits — they are being completely replaced (from a PA point of view) under the new plan.

As another example, consider an individual who changes jobs and elects under a RTA to transfer the defined benefit entitlement under the defined benefit plan with Employer A into the defined benefit plan with Employer B. The benefit formula under Employer B's plan is less generous than the benefit formula under Employer A's plan, giving rise to lower PAs using the new formula, compared to the former formula. The total pension credits under Employer A's plan equal $75,000 and the total pension credits for the same years of service under Employer B's plan equal $85,000. The administrator for Employer A's plan reports a nil PSPA (refer to ¶1055 for more details on calculating PSPAs in reciprocal transfer situations). The administrator for Employer A's plan also advises Employer B that the PA transfer value is $75,000, the lesser of the pension credits under Employer A's plan and Employer B's plan.

The PAR is, therefore calculated using the formula **A + B - C - D**, where:

A = sum of PAs reported by Employer A = $85,000

plus

B = sum of PSPAs reported by Employer A = $0

less

C = Specified Distribution = $0

less

D = PA Transfer Amount provided by Employer B = $75,000.

Therefore, the PAR equals $10,000, which represents the extent to which the individual has given up PA value under Employer B's plan compared to Employer A's plan.

Note that the actual commuted value of the member's benefit under Employer A's plan is not used in the determination of the PAR. It is

* Only the excess contributions paid form part of the specified distribution. The commuted value transfer to the new employer is not part of the specified distribution.

assumed that, under the terms of the reciprocal transfer agreement, the full commuted value is required to be transferred to Employer B's plan to fund the benefit to be provided. If the commuted value of the individual's benefit under Employer A's plan exceeds the commuted value of the benefit under Employer B's plan, the reciprocal transfer agreement would likely provide that the excess of the commuted value of the benefit under Employer A's plan over the commuted value of benefit under Employer B's plan be paid out to the member from Employer A's plan. That amount would then become the specified distribution in the PAR calculation. Suppose in our earlier example that the commuted value of the benefits under Employer A's plan is $74,000 and the commuted value of the benefits under Employer B's plan is $68,000. The amount transferred to Employer A's plan is $68,000, leaving a remaining termination benefit of $6,000 to be paid to the individual.

The PAR is, therefore, calculated using the formula **A + B - C - D**, where:

A = sum of PAs reported by Employer A = $85,000

plus

B = sum of PSPAs reported by Employer A = $0

less

C = Specified Distribution = $6,000

less

D = PA Transfer Amount provided by Employer B = $75,000.

Therefore, the PAR equals $4,000, which makes logical sense since, while the PA value of benefits under Employer B's plan is lower than the PA value of benefits under Employer A's plan, the individual has not fully "lost" the $10,000 of tax sheltering given up by moving from Plan A to Plan B.

¶1160 Reporting Requirements

PARs are reported by the plan administrator, which is generally the employer for most single employer plans, but could instead be a pension committee (for example, in Quebec). In the case of DPSPs, PARs are reported by the plan trustee. However, in this latter situation, the employer can be deemed to be a trustee for the purpose of reporting the PAR.

PARs are required to be reported on a quarterly basis, as follows:

For members who cease entitlement during:	**To be reported to the CRA by:**
January 1 – March 31	May 30
April 1 – June 30	August 29
July 1 – September 30	November 29
October 1 – December 31	January 30

Note that, for terminations in the first three quarters of each year, the PARs are to be reported within 60 days of the end of the calendar quarter. However, for the final quarter, PARs are to be reported within 30 days of the end of that quarter in order to give individuals the opportunity to make additional RRSP contributions before the RRSP deadline and to deduct the contributions from taxable income arising in the previous calendar year.

If there have been no terminations during a quarter that give rise to a PAR, then the plan administrator/DPSP trustee need not report anything for that calendar quarter.

All PARs are rounded to the nearest dollar. Separate PARs must be reported for each RPP/DPSP involved.

If the calculation of the PAR results in a nil PAR (which would occur if the specified distribution is greater than the total of all relevant PAs and PSPAs previously reported in respect of the distribution), then there is no PAR reported.

Further, if the PAR to be reported is less than $50, there is no need to report the PAR. This could arise in two situations:

- the actual PAR calculates to be less than $50; or
- a PAR is being amended as a result of more accurate information or correction of an error and the resultant difference between the original and amended PARs is less than $50.

However, the terminating plan member has the right to request that the PAR be reported accurately, in which case, the administrator/trustee is obligated to do so.

PARs are reported on the T10 return form, consisting of:

- a T10 summary;
- T10 slips; and
- in certain situations, where there are more than 300 T10 slips to be reported, T10 segment forms where each group of T10 slips is grouped together into groups of 300.

There is no requirement to file the T10 forms electronically, as there is with the filing of PSPA T215 forms (as discussed in ¶2237).

A copy of the T10 form is forwarded to both the CRA and the affected plan member. The plan administrator/DPSP trustee fulfils his or her obligations by mailing the T10 form for the plan member to the individual's last known address. If the form is returned due to a change of address and the new address is unknown to the administrator/trustee, there is no further obligation on the part of the administrator/trustee since the CRA is also provided with a copy of the T10 and will advise the employee of the increased RRSP room in the next notice of assessment.

There is a late-filing penalty that may be levied, which is equal to the greater of:

- $100; and
- $25 for each day late, to a maximum of 100 days, late (i.e., $2,500).

If a PAR is to be amended, then another T10 slip is to be filed for the plan member and the Box 5 "Amendment" should indicate "yes". The amended T10 slip should contain the full amount of the revised PAR, not simply the difference between the original and revised PAR amounts. As noted above, if the calculation of the amended PAR is within $50 of the original PAR, there is no need to report a revised PAR amount.

The PAR system is not designed to accept more than one PAR in a calendar year under a particular RPP or DPSP in respect of a single individual (other than an amendment to a previously reported PAR). Therefore, if the unusual situation arises where a member is hired and terminates twice in a calendar year, which would normally lead to the reporting of two separate PARs, the administrator/trustee should report one PAR comprising the sum of both PARs. If the first PAR has already been reported by the time the second PAR is known, then an amended PAR is reported comprising the sum of both PARs.

¶1165 Special Timing Issues When There is a PA Transfer Amount

If variable D is used in the calculation of the PAR (as defined at ¶1130), there are some additional reporting considerations to follow. Variable D is the PA transfer amount and may arise in portability or reciprocal transfer situations. Generally, the importing plan administrator will calculate the PA transfer amount and provide it to the exporting plan administrator. The exporting plan administrator needs to know if there is to be a PA transfer amount as a result of the transfer and requires the amount of the PA transfer amount in order to properly calculate the PAR. The importing plan administrator is required to advise the exporting plan administrator within 30 days of the transfer that there will be a PA transfer amount to be reported. The importing plan administrator must then report the PA transfer amount to the exporting plan administrator within 60 days of the past service event, if the PSPA is the type of PSPA that is exempt from certification. Otherwise, the importing plan administrator reports the PA transfer amount to the exporting plan administrator within 60 days of receiving certification of the PSPA. Refer to ¶1010 for discussion of when a PSPA is considered exempt or non-exempt.

The exporting plan administrator must then calculate and report the PAR by the later of 60 days after the end of the calendar quarter in which the transfer occurred and 60 days after the exporting plan administrator receives notification of the PA transfer amount from the importing plan administrator.

Refer to ¶1055 for additional information on this process from the PSPA perspective.

¶1170 Reporting Requirements for "Negative PARs"

In some situations, the sum of the PAs and PSPAs reported for the member may be lower than the specified distribution, thus resulting in a "negative PAR" in the PAR calculation. In this situation, no PAR is reported. However, the administrator should store this negative amount on the employee's file, in case it is needed for a future PSPA that may be reported either by this employer or another employer. This "negative PAR" amount is more appropriately known as the "excess money purchase transfer" and forms part of the PSPA formula. Refer to the description of variable D in the basic PSPA calculation formula at ¶1036 for more details regarding this "negative PAR".

¶1175 PARs and Partial Payouts of Commuted Values

Under minimum standards legislation, if a defined benefit RPP is not fully funded on a solvency, or plan termination basis at the time when a member terminates, it may not be possible to payout the full commuted value to the terminating member at the time of termination. The amount paid to the plan member at termination is that portion of the benefit that is fully funded (i.e., the total benefit multiplied by the solvency ratio). Any remaining amounts are to be paid to the member within five years. The full commuted value can, however, be paid to the plan member at termination if the plan sponsor is willing to make an immediate contribution to the plan to make up the shortfall. There are some exceptions to this rule for small amounts of shortfall. The objective is to ensure that the payout of one member's entitlement does not adversely affect the solvency of the plan in respect of all other plan members.

These requirements create particular problems in the timing of the reporting of the PAR. The PAR is to be calculated and reported when the final payout is made to the former plan member. However, in situations where the payments are being made over a five-year period, the terminating plan member is disadvantaged in several ways:

- it could be up to five years before the balance of the commuted value plus interest is paid out;
- the PAR that is ultimately received will be considerably reduced by interest accumulating on the balance of the commuted value which may not be paid out for up to five years; and
- the RRSP room restored by the PAR will be restored up to five years later with significant loss of opportunity to earn investment income.

Due to the recent downward turn in the financial markets, underfunded pension plans are more common so it is likely that more plan sponsors will be paying out benefits over a five-year period and plan members will need to wait longer to receive their PARs and subsequent restoration of RRSP contribution room. This time delay also arises when a defined benefit plan sponsor decides to terminate the pension plan and the plan is underfunded. Minimum standards legislation permits the plan sponsor to fund the deficit over a five-year period. In this situation, no commuted value is payable to the members under the wind-up until the plan is fully funded, resulting in a delay in reporting the PAR until the plan is fully funded and the benefit is paid out.

¶1180 Data Issues

The calculation of the PAR requires PA and PSPA data dating back to 1990. The employer and plan administrator are required to take reasonable steps to have this information available. However, it was recognized that there are situations where such information is not readily available, for example, in divestiture situations where there is a new employer and the PA/PSPA data is no longer easily accessible or may even have been destroyed. Thus, where the required information is not available, the CRA accepts "a reasonable reconstruction" of the missing information.

In collecting historical PA information, the administrator should be aware of a situation that exists for PAs for high earners for the years 1995 to 2002, inclusive, as a result of various delays in the complete transition to the new retirement saving system. Depending on the plan provision, it is possible for a member's PA for a particular year to have exceeded the RRSP dollar limit for the following year. While the higher PA was actually reported, this had no effect on the member's RRSP contribution room as new RRSP room created in a particular year can never be negative. However, in the PAR calculation, the administrator must restrict the PA for these years to be the RRSP dollar limit, regardless of whether the higher PA was originally reported. This rule ensures that the PAR for high earners is not inappropriately high in situations where the PA reported exceeded the RRSP dollar limit.

It should be noted that, due to differences in timing for the reporting of the PAR and the PA, the PAR will generally be reported prior to the date the PA, in respect of the year of termination, is reported (i.e., at the end of a calendar quarter *versus* by February 28 of the following year). This timing difference means that the plan administrator must effectively determine the final year PA at the time of termination (since it is required in order to determine the PAR) instead of waiting until the end of the year when PAs for all members are determined.

It should also be noted that the plan administrator or the plan trustee (in the case of DPSPs) is responsible for reporting the PAR whereas it is the responsibility of the employer to report the PA. Thus, in situations where the plan administrator is not the employer, this will require co-ordination between the two parties to ensure that the PAs and PARs are accurately calculated and reported.

Chapter 12

¶1200 PSPA AND PAR FOR MULTI-EMPLOYER PLANS

¶1205 Introduction

As discussed in Chapter 9, there are certain special rules related to the calculation of PAs for SMEPs and MEPs. For much the same reasons, special rules exist with respect to the calculation of PSPAs and PARs under these plans.

¶1210 Specified Multi-Employer Plans

For PA purposes, an SMEP is treated much like a money purchase plan. However, for PSPA and PAR purposes, SMEPs are treated quite differently from all other plans.

Under an SMEP, a PSPA only arises in the situation where a member makes a contribution in respect of post-1989 past service benefits (i.e., the individual is purchasing additional years of credited service under the SMEP). Accordingly, a PSPA equal to the amount of the post-1989 past service contribution made in the particular year is to be reported. This PSPA is non-exempt, and will require certification by the CRA before the past service benefits can be paid.

With respect to PARs, SMEPs are unique in that when a member terminates, no recognition is given to pension credits (PAs and PSPAs) in respect of benefits accrued under the SMEP for PAR calculation purposes. PARs are not even calculated when the member terminates and is not vested under SMEP provisions, since the plan funds supporting the non-vested benefits can be used to augment the benefits of other plan members without increasing the PAs of those members. Thus, members of SMEPs give up PARs and the restoration of RRSP room upon termination in exchange for generally smaller PAs being reported, much as in a money purchase plan.

¶1215 Multi-Employer Plans Other Than SMEPs

PSPAs arising under MEPs are generally determined in the same manner as single employer RPPs. In most cases, the PSPA will involve a single employee, arising from the employee's desire to "buy back" service or through a transfer under an RTA or portability arrangement, and the PSPA will therefore require certification. It is not common for MEPs to have an across-the-board improvement that would give rise to exempt PSPAs.

There is one situation that merits special attention. It results from one of the unique aspects of PAs for MEPs other than SMEPs in that the $600 offset in the PA formula is prorated if the member is earning less than a full year of pensionable service in the year with an employer.

Consider an example where, under an RTA, a member is transferring service at the end of a calendar year into an MEP from a single employer RPP and where the two plans have exactly the same benefit formula. Suppose that, in the last year of service under the single employer RPP, the member was on a non-pensionable leave of absence and only has six months of pensionable service that year. In addition, assume that the benefit entitlement for that half-year of service is $800. Under single employer RPPs, the PA for that year would be $6,600 ($800 × 9 - $600); however, under the MEP, the PA for that year equals $6,900 ($800 × 9 - ($600 × 6/12)). Accordingly, a PSPA of $300 arises in this situation, and also in respect of any other partial year of service that is transferred to the MEP (such as service during the first calendar year of membership in the single employer plan, if this service occurred after 1989). A PSPA would not, however, arise in this situation if both plans were MEPs or if both plans were single employer RPPs.

PARs arising under MEPs are determined in the same manner as single employer RPPs as described in Chapter 11. Special attention should be used in the PAR calculation and the reporting on the T10 forms for situations such as in the above example, marriage breakdown and in the case of the existence of supplemental defined benefit provisions, to ensure that the appropriate PAs and PSPAs are included.

Chapter 13

¶1300 INTRODUCTION TO MINIMUM STANDARDS LEGISLATION FOR RPPS

¶1305 Introduction

In addition to following the rules set out in the previous chapters requiring the reporting of PAs, PARs, and PSPAs, RPPs are required to comply with registration rules outlined in the *Income Tax Act* (Canada) and its Regulations. Many of these registration rules exist in the Regulations to harmonize the requirements with the rules relating to contribution limits for RRSPs and generally serve to limit the amount of benefits that can be paid from an RPP. Chapters 16 through 21 cover these registration rules in detail.

The rules for registration of a pension plan cover every type of provision that might appear in an RPP. Strictly speaking, the rules as currently written apply to benefits accrued under "new" plans and benefits accrued since January 1, 1992 under "grandfathered plans" (broadly speaking, a grandfathered plan is a plan that existed on March 27, 1988 and had a defined benefit provision at that time). Benefits accrued prior to January 1, 1992 under grandfathered plans continue to be administered at the discretion of the Minister of National Revenue in accordance with Information Circular 72-13R8.

However, every RPP is registered not only under the *Income Tax Act* (Canada), but also with the pension regulator in the province in which there is the plurality of plan members. Further, certain individual member entitlements follow the minimum standards pension legislation for the province in which the employee works. Therefore, the *Income Tax Act* (Canada) registration rules must be considered in conjunction with minimum standards legislation applicable in the relevant minimum standards pension jurisdiction. To help the reader put the registration rules in some context, we summarize some of the more important minimum standards legislation in this chapter.

Minimum standards legislation is continually evolving as governments review and update legislation. The next few years will likely see another round of minimum standards reform. As of the date of writing this book, Ontario and federal jurisdictions have announced significant changes to their legislation with several other jurisdictions undergoing a substantive review.

¶1310 Minimum Standards Legislation

A full discussion of federal and provincial minimum standards legislation is beyond the scope of this book. However, highlights of some of the more important minimum standards follow.

¶1311 Jurisdiction

Pension plans covering employees who are subject to federal employment standards (those who work primarily in the banking, communication, and transportation industries, or who work in the Yukon, Northwest Territories, or Nunavut, or who are members of aboriginal groups) are subject to the federal *Pension Benefits Standards Act* (PBSA).

Other employees are covered by provincial employment standards, and their pension benefits and rights are subject to the minimum standards legislation of the province in which they report to work or are deemed to report to work, if such legislation exists. The administration and financing of pension plans are subject to the legislation of the province in which the plurality of the plan members report to work or are deemed to report to work. Accordingly, an employer operating across the country could have its pension plan subject to as many as nine different provincial pension benefits Acts, as well as the PBSA if the plan also covers federally regulated employees. All provinces, except Prince Edward Island, have legislation covering minimum standards legislation. Prince Edward Island's legislation is still awaiting proclamation at the time of writing this book.

The effective dates of these various Acts are set out in the table below, together with the effective dates of the most recent round of major legislative reforms:

Effective Dates of Legislation

	Original Act	*Reform Date(s)**	*Most Recent Changes***
British Columbia	January 1, 1993	January 1, 1993	March 31, 2009
Alberta	January 1, 1967	January 1, 1987 and January 1, 2000	August 10, 2006
Saskatchewan	January 1, 1969	July 1, 1981 and January 1, 1993	June 1, 2005
Manitoba	January 1, 1976	January 1, 1985	April 19, 2005***
Ontario	January 1, 1965	January 1, 1987	March 3, 2000
Quebec	March 1, 1966	January 1, 1990 and January 1, 2001	June 20, 2008
New Brunswick	December 31, 1991	December 31, 1991	June 7, 2002
Nova Scotia	January 1, 1977	January 1, 1988	May 1, 2007
Prince Edward Island	passed (not proclaimed) ****		
Newfoundland	January 1, 1985	January 1, 1997	June 4, 2008
Federal (PBSA)	October 1, 1967	January 1, 1987	March 31, 2009

* *Reform Dates, in this context, are critical dates where major provisions under the legislation were changed and service and benefits accruing prior to the Reform Date are generally treated differently than service and benefits accruing after the Reform Date.*

** *Most Recent Changes, in this context, is the effective date of significant amendments to the legislation, but not necessarily a date that is considered a Reform Date, as described above.*

*** *Manitoba passed new pension legislation on April 19, 2005 and it is expected to be proclaimed on May 31, 2010.*

**** *Effective date is expected to be one year after proclamation*

Generally speaking, the minimum standards governing pension benefits that accrued in respect of service before the date of the legislative reforms ("pre-reform benefits") are less generous to the employee than those governing pension accruals in respect of service after the reform date ("post-reform benefits").

As at the date of writing this book, the only pension plans that are not subject to any minimum standards legislation are those whose members all report to work in Prince Edward Island and who are subject to provincial employment standards — pension legislation in Prince Edward Island received Royal Assent on April 26, 1990, but that legislation has yet to be proclaimed.

Generally, the types of plans that are governed by minimum standards legislation are plans in which the employer is required to make contributions. These are plans that are typically, but not necessarily, limited to RPPs (i.e., plans that are registered for tax purposes with the CRA). There is a divergence as to how provincial jurisdictions deal with pension vehicles that are not RPPs. In virtually all jurisdictions, supplemental pension plans, defined as a pension plan in which the initial and continuing membership in the plan is subject to first having membership in another plan or a plan that provides a benefit or contributions in excess of the *Income Tax Act* (Canada) maximums, are not subject to pension standards legislation

Retiring allowances, as defined in the *Income Tax Act* (Canada), are also virtually universally exempt from pension standards legislation, as are DPSP and employee profit sharing plans. Other retirement vehicles that are specifically exempted from pension standards legislation, in at least some jurisdictions, include RCAs and group RRSPs (or more specifically, group RRSPs in which all benefits are provided by member contributions).

In Nova Scotia, the superintendent has taken the position that group RRSPs may, in fact, be a pension plan. "Structured" group RRSPs that prohibit employees from withdrawing any of the RRSP funds while they are employed and require that "employer" contributions be used to provide a pension at retirement must be registered under the province's pension benefits act.

Provincial employment standards legislation, workers compensation legislation, and human rights legislation may also affect certain pension plan provisions.

¶1312 Vesting and Locking In

Each minimum standards pension Act has its own minimum vesting schedule. Benefits are also locked in at the same point as they are vested; locking in refers to the inability of the pension benefit to be paid as a cash amount to the terminating or retiring member — instead it must remain in the pension plan or may be transferred to one of several different types of tax-sheltered retirement savings vehicles that have been created for the purposes of holding locked-in pension money. Chapter 14 covers the locked-in vehicles that are available in each jurisdiction.

In most jurisdictions, post-reform benefits must be vested after an individual has been a plan member for no more than two years. Two jurisdictions, however, base the minimum vesting period on years of employment. Post-reform benefits must be fully vested after no more than five years of continuous employment in New Brunswick and after no more than two years of continuous employment in Saskatchewan.

Manitoba's minimum vesting schedule is the earliest of two years continuous service or two years of continuous plan membership.

In Alberta, a member will vest after two years of continuous membership. The vesting applies only to the membership period on and after January 1, 2000. The five-year continuous service rule continues to apply to service from January 1, 1987 to December 31, 1999.

In British Columbia, a member is vested after two years of continuous plan membership. Vesting for benefits between the reform date of January 1, 1993 and January 1, 1998, however, is based on completion of five years of continuous service.

Finally, in Quebec, vesting for all service occurs immediately upon becoming a member. Manitoba, as well, has eliminated the service requirements for vesting in legislation passed in April 2005 and expected to be proclaimed on May 31, 2010.

There are various exemptions to the requirement to have benefits locked in. All jurisdictions have minimum thresholds under which benefits are not required to be locked in but can instead be paid in cash. Each jurisdiction has a different threshold or combination of threshholds varying from annual pensions payable of 2%, 4%, or 10% of the YMPE or commuted values of 4%, 10%, or 20% of the YMPE. New Brunswick has a complex rule to determine what is not required to be locked in, based on the member's commuted value and age. Several jurisdictions permit a percentage of pre-reform benefits to be unlocked at termination. Certain jurisdictions permit unlocking in situations of shortened life expectancy or financial hardship. All jurisdictions require unlocking where the commuted value of benefits exceeds the amounts that may be transferred on a tax-sheltered basis (as set out at ¶1743).

Chapter 14 also outlines various situations where funds transferred to a locked-in vehicle at termination may later be unlocked.

¶1313 Portability

Portability is the right to transfer, on a locked-in basis, the value of the vested benefits to another registered retirement savings arrangement, such as an RRSP or another RPP. In general, this right does not need to be offered if an individual is eligible for an immediate pension, although the plan may still offer it, provided the pension plan document permits it. The amount to be transferred is the current value of the benefit accrued to the date of transfer, normally calculated using the Canadian Institute of Actuaries' recommendations for the determination of commuted values of pensions.

There are three options with respect to portability: to transfer the commuted value to an insurance company for the purchase of a deferred or immediate life annuity, to transfer the commuted value to another RPP, if the other RPP agrees to accept the transfer and to honour the locking in and certain other provisions of the original pension plan, or to transfer the commuted value to a tax-sheltered retirement savings vehicle, as prescribed by the applicable minimum standards legislation. This latter choice consists of options such as a locked-in RRSP, a LIRA, a LIF, a LRIF, or a prescribed RRIF. Chapter 14 provides additional details regarding each of these prescribed retirement savings vehicles.

Situations can arise where the amount that must be transferred in accordance with minimum pension standards legislation is greater than the maximum that may be transferred in accordance with the CRA's maximum transfer rules. This conflict is discussed further at ¶1743.

¶1314 Minimum Employer Contributions (the "50% Rule")

Under minimum standards reform, defined benefit pension plans that require employee contributions must provide that at least 50% of the benefit payable when an individual terminates, dies, or retires must be attributable to employer contributions. This 50% rule generally applies to post-reform contributions and benefits. In the case of younger employees who terminate or die, this usually results in an excess employee contribution, since the employee's post-reform contributions with interest often provide for more than 50% of the value of the post-reform benefit. This excess amount is refundable to the plan member, generally in cash.

Only Ontario and Nova Scotia require the excess amount to be refunded. Most jurisdictions allow the member the option to transfer the excess amount to another pension plan, a retirement savings plan such as an RRSP, or use the excess amount to purchase a deferred or immediate life annuity or to increase the amount of pension payable from the plan.

However, Quebec and the federal PBSA only permit the excess to be transferred to a LIRA or to another pension plan on a locked-in basis. The federal PBSA and British Columbia also provide that the 50% rule does not have to be applied if the plan provides indexing during the deferral period equal to 75% of the increase in the CPI, less 1%.

The determination of any excess employee contributions takes place when the individual exits from the plan through termination, death, or retirement, or upon plan termination. There is no ongoing calculation required while the individual is an active plan member, other than ensuring that the 50% rule is being appropriately handled in the ongoing actuarial valuations that are conducted from time to time (at least once every three years).

¶1315 Early Retirement

Minimum standards legislation requires that a pension plan member be permitted to take an immediate pension upon early retirement within 10 years of normal retirement age (i.e., generally at age 55) or, in some jurisdictions, within 10 years of the earliest age at which an unreduced pension is payable. As indicated at ¶1313, generally once the individual is entitled to an immediate pension, the plan is not required by legislation to offer portability of benefits, although portability may be offered, provided the pension plan document permits it.

The pension benefit payable at early retirement is normally reduced, either through the application of specific factors defined in the pension plan or on an actuarially equivalent basis. An example of the former would be a reduction in the benefit that would be payable at normal retirement age by ½ of 1% for each month that the retirement occurs prior to normal retirement age. Plan sponsors need to ensure, however, that when specified reduction factors are used, the actuarial value of the benefit payable on early retirement is not less than the value of the deferred benefit payable at normal retirement age.

Note that where an actuarial equivalent basis of reduction is used, the plan document must also specify that the resulting reduction will comply with the *Income Tax Act* (Canada), which allows early retirement benefits to be provided without reduction if certain criteria are met. If these criteria are not met, the early retirement benefit must be reduced by ¼ of 1% for each month that the retirement occurs prior to the date the member would have first met those conditions had he or she continued in employment (as discussed at ¶1720).

Phased Retirement

When older, experienced employees who are approaching early or normal retirement age work a reduced schedule for a period before finally retiring, this is usually referred to as phased retirement. In order to address Canadian employers' concerns regarding future shrinking workforces, certain jurisdictions have, in recent years, introduced phased retirement provisions.

Early forms of phased retirement were done on an informal and individual basis, whereby an employer would allow an employee to retire, begin receiving his or her defined benefit pension, and then return to work on a part-time contract basis. However, the resulting loss of seniority, job security, active member benefits (e.g., medical and dental), and discontinued pension accrual makes this a less than ideal employment situation.

More formal minimum standards provisions around phased retirement were hampered by a restriction under the *Income Tax Act* (Canada) that prohibits an individual from accruing a pension under an RPP while also being in receipt of a pension from the same plan. This restriction was seen as an impediment to encouraging workers to keep working, perhaps on a reduced schedule, without there potentially being a significant impact on their retirement benefit. It often simply made more sense, especially for an employee who belongs to a plan with generous early retirement provisions, to simply retire and move to another employer where the prohibition from receiving and accruing at the same time would not apply.

Although this *Income Tax Act* (Canada) impediment was resolved in October 2007 when Regulation changes were introduced to accommodate more beneficial phased retirement provisions (refer to ¶ 125 and ¶ 1775 for additional details), certain minimum standards jurisdictions had already introduced innovative ways to more or less achieve a phased retirement.

Quebec was the first jurisdiction to develop an approach to deal with the barriers by amending the SPPA to allow a phased retiree to continue to accrue a pension based on actual earnings while receiving a series of lump-sum payments from the pension plan rather than a monthly pension. There were certain restrictions in terms of the amount that could be received early from a pension plan in this manner. Alberta made similar changes to its pension legislation. Manitoba also included similar provisions in its updated 2005 legislation. New Brunswick introduced a program that applied narrowly to the nursing sector in that province.

Yet Quebec's innovative lump-sum approach had a very low take-up rate. There are several reasons for this, but the major reason is that the individual lost any early retirement subsidies that would have otherwise been available had full early retirement been chosen instead of electing to work part-time. The individual would select lump sums that are received annually during the phased retirement period and a pension of equivalent actuarial value is later offset against the normal retirement pension accrued to the date of final retirement. In a plan with a generous early retirement provision, this represented a huge potential loss.

Effective January 1, 2008, the *Income Tax Act* (Canada) was amended to permit phased retirement (i.e., the partial payment of pension benefits while still employed) under a defined benefit provision of a pension plan, provided one of the following criteria are met:

- the member must be at least age 55 and is entitled to receive an unreduced pension; or
- the member must be at least age 60.

These changes to the *Income Tax Act* (Canada) mean that a pension plan may provide a partial pension to a member of up to 60% of the member's accrued benefit that would be paid if the member retired. A member can continue to work and earn benefits while receiving this partial pension. There is no requirement that a member's working hours be reduced to qualify for this type of phased retirement.

To complete the picture, however, changes were also required to each jurisdiction's minimum standards pension legislation to accommodate these new *Income Tax Act* (Canada) Regulation changes. The first pension jurisdiction to introduce the necessary changes was the federal PBSA. The changes in that jurisdiction included:

- Phased retirement benefits could be offered to plan members who have reached normal retirement age or who qualify for early retirement under the terms of the pension plan;
- The plan member must enter into a written agreement with an employer who contributes to the plan from which the phased retirement benefits will be paid;
- The member continues to accrue a pension benefit during the phased retirement period. Pension benefits accrued during the phased retirement period are treated as vested without regard to conditions as to age, period of membership in the pension plan, or period of employment. The amount of the phased retirement benefit received is not taken into account when determining the immediate pension benefit to which a plan member is entitled or eligible to receive when they retire in full. This will ensure that the amount and value of the pension payable on complete retirement is not reduced or diminished because of the earlier phased retirement;
- Employees will still be considered plan members during a phased retirement period, will not be considered "retired" under the *Pension Benefits Standards Act*, and will be deemed not to be receiving an immediate pension benefit;
- The 50% minimum employer contribution rule (as discussed in greater detail at ¶ 1314) does not apply at the time of commencing a phased retirement period. Since the member on phased retirement is not considered to have retired, the 50% rule in a contributory plan would not apply until the member ceased employment with the employer;
- The phased retirement benefit can be paid to the member only, and there is no requirement to pay the benefit in a joint and survivor form if the member has a spouse when the phased retirement benefits begins;
- A member who passes away during the phased retirement period will be deemed to have retired for the purposes of the survivor benefit and to have chosen a joint and 60% survivor form of pension. As a result, the surviving spouse of that person will be entitled to the 60% survivor benefit commencing as of the death of the member; and
- Retirees may also take advantage of the phased retirement provisions provided that in the case of a retiree receiving a pension in the form of a joint and survivor pension, the spouse or common-law partner in question consents in writing to the cessation of the payment of the benefit. This ensures that the spouse or

common-law partner does not lose any rights to such joint and survivor pension without input. Once the phased retirement agreement is finished, there is no return to the formerly agreed-upon joint and survivor pension benefit. The initial election is rendered void and the retiree is required to make a new decision regarding any further pension benefits payable.

The above conditions are only relevant to members of federally regulated plans. Provincially regulated pension plans can only take advantage of the phased retirement rules once the relevant pension standards legislation is amended to accommodate the new phased retirement provisions now permitted under the Regulations.

Quebec has since made changes to its prior phased retirement provisions to coordinate with the Regulation changes. Alberta has not made any formal amendments to its legislation as it believes that its legislation currently permits the Regulation phased retirement changes. Other jurisdictions are in the process of making similar changes, or, where legislative changes are not formally needed, issuing policy statements about the application of the phased retirement provisions within the jurisdiction. This includes British Columbia, Nova Scotia, and Saskatchewan. Manitoba had also added provisions for phased retirement in its 2005 legislative changes, which are expected to be proclaimed on May 31, 2010. Eventually it is expected that the remaining minimum standards jurisdictions will follow suit and introduce appropriate phased retirement provisions.

In addition to the phased retirement provisions permitted under the *Income Tax Act* (Canada), Quebec offers another option for phased retirement.

This option allows a Quebec member to receive annually, a lump-sum benefit from his or her pension plan, to make up for a reduction in work hours. The member must be under 71 years of age and less than 10 years away from normal retirement age, and will receive the lowest of the following amounts:

(a) 70% of the income lost due to the reduced hours;

(b) 40% of the QPP's YMPE (which is the same as the YMPE for the CPP, or $47,200 for 2010); or

(c) the value of the pension benefits accumulated in the pension plan.

If the Quebec member belongs to a hybrid style of plan that has both defined benefit and defined contribution components, the annual lump sum will first be paid from the defined contribution account, for ease of administration, unless the plan provides otherwise. If the member belongs to a pure defined contribution plan, the lump sum is easily paid from the defined contribution account balance.

If the Quebec member belongs to a pure defined benefit plan, the pension received at the "full" retirement date will be actuarially reduced to reflect the phased retirement pension paid once the member commences to receive the regular pension benefit.

Depending upon the terms of the agreement with the employer, the member may either cease to be entitled to further accruals or continue to be an active member of the plan and continue to receive accruals. In neither case may the reduced salary be used in determining the pension accrued up to the effective date of the agreement to work reduced hours.

Temporary Pension

Provisions for temporary pensions also appear in Quebec legislation. A member or spouse who is entitled to a pension (deferred or immediate) may elect to replace all or a part of the lifetime pension to which he or she is entitled, with a temporary amount from the pension plan until the time when the individual is entitled to government benefits (i.e., age 65). In other words, the member may elect a bridge benefit from the plan even if the plan doesn't provide a bridge benefit in the traditional sense.

A temporary pension is available to a member or spouse who is entitled to receive a pension, but who is not yet in receipt of the pension (i.e., a deferred pensioner or a retiree). Generally, the member or spouse must be 10 years or less from normal retirement age (as set out in the pension plan, but in no case later than age 65) and must specify the amount of pension benefit before payment begins. The amount of the pension benefit cannot be greater than 40% of the QPP maximum pensionable earnings in the year payment begins. The limit is reduced by any other temporary benefits the member or spouse is entitled to under the plan (i.e., any traditional bridging benefits that the plan may provide). Quebec does allow plans to provide for earlier payment of a temporary pension but in this case, the maximum amount is directly related to OAS and CPP/QPP benefits, and is subject to other limits, namely the same 40% of QPP maximum pensionable earnings.

The temporary pension must end by the end of the month following the month in which the member or spouse turns 65 years of age. Only one temporary pension is permitted regardless of how many plans the member is entitled to receive a pension from (including locked-in vehicles that originated from RPP funds).

Similar provisions apply to a deferred vested member or retired member who elected to transfer his or her entitlement to an LIF.

Other Jurisdictions

In other jurisdictions, members may also elect to receive a temporary benefit in lieu of a part of the lifetime benefit of equal value, an option often referred to as "integration" or "level income". Limits may apply — the amount of the temporary benefit may be limited to the maximum government benefits payable. There may also be a minimum lifetime benefit, which must be retained.

The rules surrounding the payment of the temporary pensions and lump sums are extensive, and the above is only intended to provide background into the types of benefits provided under these rules.

¶1316 Postponed Retirement

When a pension plan member remains employed beyond normal retirement age, the pension plan generally allows the plan member to continue to accrue benefits (other than Quebec members of provincially regulated plans). The plan member then receives a benefit at postponed retirement age, calculated in a similar fashion to the benefits payable at normal retirement age, but based on service to the actual retirement date and, if applicable, final or best average earnings to that date. However, if the plan has service or benefit maximums, this may restrict longer-serviced employees from being able to continue to accrue benefits after the normal retirement age. Alternatively, the member may begin receiving the pension at the normal retirement date and there will be no further accrual of benefits or service.

Quebec requires that plans actuarially adjust benefits to reflect the postponement period. Quebec also allows members to receive payment of all or part of their normal pension during the postponement period but only to the extent necessary to offset any permanent reduction in remuneration during the postponement period. However, if the pension plan document permits, a member may receive all or part of his or her pension regardless of the limit under an agreement with his or her employer.

The amount of pension not paid during the postponement period shall be adjusted at the end of the postponement period. The adjustment shall be made to ensure that the pension payable at the end of the postponement period is actuarially equivalent to the value of the benefit that had accrued to the plan member's normal retirement date. If a member makes contributions during the postponement period, the member shall receive an additional pension equal to the value of the pension that could be purchased at the end of that period with the member's contributions paid during the period plus accrued interest.

¶1317 Pre-Retirement Death Benefits

Benefits payable in the event of death prior to retirement can be payable to a spouse, beneficiary, or the estate of the member.

The "spouse" of an individual for purposes of the *Income Tax Act* (Canada), includes a person to whom the member is married or a common-law partner who has been cohabiting in a conjugal relationship with the individual for at least 12 months, or who is a parent of a child of whom the individual is also a parent.

The terms of the RPP should include a definition for "spouse" and this definition is subject to provincial minimum standards. Therefore, an individual will not qualify as a spouse unless he or she meets the definition set out in the RPP.

Generally, a married spouse continues to have spousal status if there is no divorce. A few exceptions occur in Alberta (once the spouses have not been living together for three or more years), British Columbia (once the spouses have not been living together for two or more years), Ontario (once the spouses are not living together, the spousal status ceases) and, in Quebec (if the spouses are legally separated, spousal status ceases).

However, a married spouse, in certain provinces, may lose his or her spousal status for death benefit purposes when a member spouse establishes a common-law relationship.

To qualify as a common-law spouse, some jurisdictions require a longer period of cohabitation than the 12-month period specified in the *Income Tax Act* (Canada). The period of cohabitation is three years in Alberta, Manitoba, New Brunswick, Newfoundland and Labrador, Ontario, Prince Edward Island, and Quebec. The period of cohabitation is two years in British Columbia and Nova Scotia. The cohabitation period for the federal jurisdiction and Saskatchewan matches the one-year period under the *Income Tax Act* (Canada). There are exceptions in instances where common-law spouses have been cohabiting for one year but have a child together or where the common-law spouses are able to marry but choose not to.

Provincial legislation usually requires a minimum pre-reform benefit equal to a return of the member's own pre-reform contributions, if any, with interest. Beyond this, there is usually no specific requirement to provide a pre-reform pre-retirement death benefit.

In some jurisdictions, the minimum post-reform death benefit that is payable to a spouse (or beneficiary, if there is no spouse) on the death of a pension plan member before retirement is the commuted value of the post-reform benefit that would have been payable to the member if he or she had terminated service at the date of death. In some jurisdictions, the spouse has the right to waive entitlement to this death benefit.

There are exceptions to the post-reform rule. For example, Alberta's minimum pre-retirement death benefit for a member with a spouse is a pension to the spouse equal to the greater of 60% of the member's accrued pension benefit on and after January 1, 1987 and before January 1, 2000 and the member's contributions to the plan on and after January 1, 1987 and before January 1, 2000 with interest, plus 100% of the commuted value of the pension with respect to the deceased's membership on and after January 1, 2000.

Several jurisdictions require that only 60% of the commuted value of the post-reform benefit need be payable.

As well, a beneficiary who is not the member's spouse may not be entitled to the same benefits as the spouse. Some jurisdictions provide a commuted value to the spouse, but the non-spouse beneficiary is only entitled to contributions with interest.

The federal PBSA and Saskatchewan require that the commuted value of the post-reform benefit be paid to a surviving spouse if death occurs prior to becoming eligible for early retirement. However, where pre-retirement death occurs after eligibility for early retirement, the benefit payable is a spousal pension equal to 60% of the post-reform benefit the member would have been entitled to receive had he or she retired early. Some provinces, such as Alberta and British Columbia, require that the death benefit be in the form of a pension if the beneficiary is the member's spouse.

¶1318 Normal Form of Pension

The normal form of pension is a term that describes how the plan's normal retirement benefit is payable. It is the basis for calculating the commuted value of the pension, as well as the basis from which optional forms of pensions are determined.

Those jurisdictions that have enacted minimum standards legislation require that a joint and survivor pension be payable if a plan member has a spouse at termination or retirement, although a spouse is permitted to waive his or her joint and survivor pension entitlement. This mandatory form, as a general rule, requires a minimum of 60% to continue to the surviving spouse upon the member's death. The exception to this rule applies in the case of provincially regulated employees in Manitoba, which requires a minimum of 66⅔% of the initial benefit to continue to the surviving spouse. (Manitoba changed the mandatory normal form to 60% in legislation passed in April 2005 and expected to be proclaimed on May 31, 2010.)

The legislation in all jurisdictions permits the plan to reduce the initial pension payable to the member in order to finance the spousal pension.

Refer to ¶1317 for a discussion about who is considered to be a spouse for joint and survivor purposes. Although that section covers pre-retirement death benefits, the same principles apply in determining whether an individual has a spouse for the purposes of the required joint and survivor pension. All jurisdictions allow spouses to waive entitlement to the joint and survivor benefit with varying degrees of formality.

¶1319 Inflation Protection

Ontario is the only jurisdiction to legislate mandatory inflation protection of benefits after retirement. However, no indexation formula has been prescribed to date and, therefore, inflation protection is not yet formally required in any minimum standards jurisdiction in Canada. A significant number of companies, however, do provide inflation protection to retirees on an *ad hoc* (i.e., non-guaranteed) basis, typically with updates every two to three years. Many public sector pension plans and a few private sector plans provide inflation protection on a guaranteed basis.

Quebec, however, is the only jurisdiction that mandates a partial indexation of benefits during the deferral period in the event of termination prior to age 55. This partial indexation only applies to the benefits accruing on and after January 1, 2001 and is provided to the members in the form of an additional benefit, the value of which is the value of indexation during the deferral period of 50% of CPI between the age at termination and age 55.

Some provinces also require that in the event of the conversion of a plan from defined benefit to defined contribution, that salary escalation be reflected in conversion values.

¶1320 Eligibility

Eligibility requirements for entry into an RPP vary across the country. However, the common rule is that full-time employees must be permitted to join the pension plan after completion of two years of continuous employment. Part-time employees, generally, are required to be eligible to participate in the RPP upon completion of two consecutive calendar years of continuous employment during which they earned at least 35% of the YMPE in each of those years.

Ontario, Nova Scotia, and Saskatchewan also permit part-time employees to be eligible if they have worked 700 hours in each of the two consecutive calendar years immediately prior to membership. British Columbia and Alberta has a minimum 350 hours of work requirement in each of two consecutive years for members of certain MEPs, in addition to the requirement for 24 months of employment and earnings of 35% of the YMPE.

Quebec's eligibility requirements allow an individual, whether full-time or part-time, to be eligible for participation in the pension plan if the individual has earned 35% of the YMPE or worked 700 hours in the calendar year immediately prior to membership.

Manitoba requires that when an individual becomes entitled to participate in an existing pension plan, participation is, with certain exceptions, mandatory. Individual plan sponsors in other jurisdictions may choose to make membership in the pension plan mandatory for its employees once they have completed the eligibility requirements. However, no jurisdiction requires an employer to provide a pension plan.

¶1321 Surplus

Plan documents must stipulate how surplus is to be dealt with, both on an ongoing basis and in the event of the partial or full termination of the plan.

Surplus assets in an ongoing plan may be used by the employer to take a "contribution holiday" if the plan allows. Applicable minimum standards may stipulate that a certain level of assets remain in the plan after taking a contribution holiday. The employer may require approval from the applicable superintendent before taking a contribution holiday. In some jurisdictions, the employer must also notify its members that it is taking a contribution holiday.

Alternatively, surplus in an ongoing plan may be used to improve benefits for some or all existing members. However, care must be taken, depending on the situation and on the jurisdictions involved, where there are multiple types of employees with a variety of past service benefits, or where the current plan has resulted from the prior merger of two or several prior plans. It may be necessary to ensure that surplus attributable to or in respect of one or a few of the groups of employees is not used inappropriately to improve benefits for all groups of employees.

Generally, when a defined benefit RPP is terminated (either fully or partially), provisions must be made for handling any surplus assets that exist as at the date of the partial or full wind up. As a result of disputes over ownership of the surplus, there is often a time lag in the payment of the surplus in the case of a plan termination, resulting in the payment of the basic benefit entitlement, sometimes several years before the surplus is paid out. A surplus distribution can also arise at the time of a plan conversion from defined benefit to defined contribution.

Often, however, surplus ownership is in dispute and plan sponsors and members are increasingly turning to arbitration or the courts to resolve disputes involving surplus, to whom it is paid and when it is paid, when agreements cannot be made between the parties through surplus-sharing agreements. Certain jurisdictions stipulate that the disposition of surplus be dealt with first through an arbitration process.

Surplus, when paid to plan members at the time of a plan termination, is paid in one of the following forms:

- as a lump-sum cash payment;
- as additional lifetime benefits or ancillaries which can then be commuted and transferred to another tax-sheltered vehicle; however, this form of payment has implications both in the calculation of PSPA and in the calculation of the PAR; or
- as a combination of the above.

There are situations where the pension plan cannot satisfy both the *Income Tax Act* (Canada) and the requirements of the pension benefits supervisory authorities. For example, if a pension plan stipulates that the surplus assets are to be provided to members upon plan wind up, the minimum standards jurisdiction may require that the surplus be distributed to employees in the form of additional benefits, which are then locked-in. However, if this causes the total pension benefits to exceed the maximum pension permitted under the *Income Tax Act* (Canada), the CRA will require the excess assets to be distributed in the form of cash and included in the individual's taxable income in the year of distribution.

Another situation can arise when surplus is provided in the form of additional benefits but the additional benefits will create a PSPA that is required to be certified (as described in ¶1010). If some members have insufficient RRSP contribution room to accept the PSPA, or otherwise do not agree to have RRSP contribution room reduced because of the additional pension benefits, then the additional benefits will again be required to be distributed in cash for those members.

Surplus issues can also arise in plan merger situations. Plan sponsors at times find it necessary or desirable to merge pension plans for a variety of reasons to create a single, larger pension plan. Reasons for wanting to merge pension plans include bringing together groups of employees acquired through business transactions and the associated pension assets, or simply wanting to achieve economies of scale in the administration of one plan instead of several. The pension benefits supervisory authorities in some jurisdictions are concerned when assets in respect of a group of employees in one pension plan are merged with assets in respect of a group of employees in a separate pension plan as this could result in the use of surplus that existed at the time of plan merger in respect of the first group of employees to fund benefits of the second group of employees. By extension, the merger of two underfunded plans with different funding/solvency situations raises the same concerns. As a result, various pension benefits supervisory authorities have established policies around the merger, or commingling, of pension assets. Typically, if the two pools of assets are kept separate and apart from each other, then this will satisify the regulators. This segregation of assets can be "virtual" rather than an actual segregation: it is usually sufficient to track the two pools of assets separately in subsequent actuarial valuations.

¶1322 Interest on Employee Contributions

Minimum standards legislation sets the minimum rates that must be credited to employee contributions that are made to defined benefit plans. Typically, the plan sponsor must select either the investment return earned on the pension fund (net of investment expenses and administration costs) or the average of five-year personal term deposit rates. The plan sponsor generally cannot change which of these two rates is to be used without amending the plan and obtaining prior approval from the relevant pension benefits supervisory authority.

Quebec is the notable exception. Only the fund's rate of return may be used in determining the rate of interest to be applied to member contributions in a defined benefit plan, even if that rate results in a negative interest rate in a particular year.

For defined contribution plans or defined contribution accumulations within defined benefit or hybrid plans, the rate of return applied to contributions is the rate of return on the assets (less investment expenses and administration costs).

¶1323 Pension Credit Splitting Upon Marriage or Relationship Breakdown

The splitting of pension benefits upon marriage breakdown, either at the date of the breakdown or upon subsequent termination or retirement of the spouse who is the plan member, is subject to court orders or provincial legislation affecting matrimonial property in the provincial jurisdiction where the member resides. The minimum standards legislation in some jurisdictions limits the amount by which the member's pension benefits may be reduced.

Certain jurisdictions recognize common-law spouses for the purpose of property division upon marriage or relationship breakdown and other jurisdictions do not. Therefore, the entitlement of common-law spouses, opposite or same-sex, to receive a split of pension benefits is dependent on the jurisdiction involved.

¶1324 Quebec's Simplified Pension Plan and Member Funded Pension Plan

Quebec's SPPA includes provisions for two alternative types of pension plans that are designed to address employer issues of financial risk of running a pension plan and the corresponding administrative burden.

The simplified pension plan is a money purchase plan offered and administered by a financial institution and is designed to respond to the needs of small businesses. It combines elements of defined contribution pension plans, group RRSPs, and DPSPs.

Each participating plan member has two accounts: one locked-in and the other not locked-in. Employer contributions go into the locked-in account as well as any assets that the member transfers in from another locked-in source. Required employee contributions and transfers from DPSPs can, at the employer's choice, go into the locked-in or the not locked-in account. Other potential contributions are not locked-in (such as employee voluntary contributions and transfers from not locked-in sources).

This structure provides flexibility to the member at retirement since some of the funds are accessible as not locked-in funds. All assets must be transferred out of the simplified pension plan once the member ceases active membership, by way of a transfer to a tax-sheltered retirement vehicle, the purchase of an annuity or, for the not locked-in funds, in cash or as a transfer to an RRSP or RRIF. However, some of the locked-in assets may be accessed as early as age 55 even if the member has not ceased employment and can be transferred to a locked-in retirement savings vehicle. The not locked-in assets may be able to be transferred at any time without any age restriction.

In response to Quebec's simplified pension plan, the Registered Plans Directorate issued a newsletter (No. 98-1) setting out additional restrictions that would apply to similar plans introduced in jurisdictions outside Quebec (but not to simplified pension plans registered in Quebec).

The MFPP is a defined benefit plan structure that was introduced by Quebec in response to employer concerns about financial risk in defined benefit plans. Under an MFPP, the employer contribution is predetermined and the remaining contributions (including payments for any deficits) are paid by the members. Any surplus assets belong to the members.

This new type of defined benefit plan is seen as primarily for unionized workers. In fact, changes introduced to the Regulations under the *Income Tax Act* (Canada) in response to the introduction of the MFPP stipulate that an MFPP must be maintained pursuant to a collective bargaining agreement unless this requirement is waived by the Minister of National Revenue.

Several restrictions are in place to ensure that the members are not taking on undue financial risk, most notably that:

- The MFPP must have a career average or flat dollar benefit (i.e., not a final average benefit);

- The MFPP cannot provide for automatic indexing either before or after retirement (even though the funding requirements of the MFPP are determined by assuming that pensions are indexed to the CPI, to a maximum of 4%);
- The MFPP cannot have any defined contribution provisions, cannot be an insured plan, and cannot be a designated plan;
- The MFPP cannot be created by conversion of a traditional plan, cannot be amended to become a traditional plan, and divisions and mergers can only involve other MFPPs;
- The MFPP cannot have workers employed in other provinces or jurisdictions since it is recognized that the provisions of the MFPP do not meet the requirements of other minimum standards jurisdictions;
- The MFPP must be funded and solvent from inception; the plan must also be fully funded and solvent at the time the amendment takes effect, unless the amendment is statutorily required and such latitude in funding is not contemplated by the statute; this essentially means that any improvement in past service benefits can only be provided to the extent that there is available surplus to fund it; and
- Various other rules have been put into place to regulate how and when the plan can be amended or assets used for benefit improvements, how to deal with plan terminations and special minimum value rules to avoid penalizing a member for participating in the plan "at the wrong time".

Many of the other provisions of traditional defined benefit plans still apply to an MFPP, including the requirement for the MFPP to be administered by a pension committee (if there are at least 25 members of the MFPP). However, many of the minimum standards rules are not appropriate for this type of plan, such as the 50% rule or the ability of the employer to take contribution holidays.

In response to the introduction of the MFPP, changes were made to the Regulations under the *Income Tax Act* (Canada) setting out additional restrictions that apply to such plans. These are discussed further at ¶1815.

¶1400 TAX-SHELTERED RETIREMENT SAVINGS VEHICLES

¶1405 Introduction

The requirement to offer portability — the option for plan members to transfer the commuted value of their vested pension benefit out of their employer pension plan upon termination of employment — has been a reality for many years due to minimum standards pension legislation. Long gone are the days when a member's only option, with respect to his or her vested pension entitlement, was a deferred pension payable at retirement. Over the same period, the retirement savings vehicles available to receive these transfers have evolved from when the only option was a locked-in RRSP.

Portability is generally defined as the ability of a terminating pension plan member to transfer the commuted value of his or her vested benefit entitlement under the pension plan to one of the following:

- another pension plan in which the terminated member has become a member, provided the administrator of the pension plan agrees to accept the transfer of funds and to administer them in accordance with the applicable minimum standards legislation;
- an insurance company licensed to transact business in Canada, for the purchase of a deferred or immediate life annuity; or
- a tax-sheltered retirement savings vehicle that meets the requirements of minimum standards legislation.

The vast majority of terminating plan members elect the last of these three options — to transfer the commuted value to a tax-sheltered retirement savings vehicle.

There are now a variety of retirement savings vehicles available to individuals. Designed to meet the legislative requirements for portability, they continue to permit tax sheltering of pension benefits, while at the same time, ensuring the tax-sheltered funds retain certain characteristics underlying the original benefits defined by the originating pension plan.

This chapter outlines the regulations and structure of the various vehicles available in each minimum standards jurisdiction. Please note that the intent of this chapter is to provide an overview of the general provisions for locked-in RRSPs, LIRAs, LIFs, and LRIFs. Each minimum standards jurisdiction has specific rules regarding the tax-sheltered vehicles offered under the jurisdictions. Therefore, for more comprehensive information, please refer to the rules for each jurisdiction separately.

At the end of this chapter is a section covering the new TFSA, that was introduced effective January 1, 2009. The TFSA was not introduced strictly as a retirement savings vehicle, as it is intended to be a tax-sheltered vehicle to assist Canadians in saving for a variety of life events. However, as it does allow for additional tax-sheltering over and above the RRSP limits, some Canadians (and employers) may consider them to be an additional vehicle to be used for retirement savings.

¶1410 Non-Locked-In Retirement Savings Vehicles

Non-locked-in tax-sheltered savings vehicles include the RRSP and the RRIF. Both vehicles are sold by financial institutions and must follow the prescribed requirements for these vehicles under the *Income Tax Act* (Canada), including the types of investments that can be made with the assets.

Non-locked-in retirement funds include personal RRSP assets, assets from the transfer of a retiring allowance, and assets from a DPSP. In addition, there are certain circumstances, which assets from RPPs are not required to be locked in, such as:

- benefits payable to a member who terminates prior to being vested and locked in under minimum standards pension legislation;
- the commutation of small benefits not required to be locked in under the minimum standards legislation;
- in certain jurisdictions, unlocking of certain benefits upon termination, retirement, or other specific situations; and

- commuted values of RPP benefits that are in excess of the maximum transfer values (see ¶ 1743 for further details on the maximum transfer value) may be transferred directly to non-locked-in retirement savings vehicles provided the RPP member has sufficient available RRSP contribution room to make the direct transfer; alternatively, the excess maximum transfer value may be deposited indirectly (again, subject to available RRSP contribution room).

The contributions and investment earnings in both an RRSP and a RRIF are tax sheltered until they are withdrawn. Throughout the taxpayer's lifetime the assets can be transferred to another RRSP (but only up to age 71) or a RRIF at any time whether to consolidate retirement assets or improve investment returns. In addition, the assets in either can be accessed in cash at any time, in whole or in part, and are fully taxable at the individual's marginal tax rate in the year of withdrawal.

Under the existing RRSP rules, when individuals withdraw assets from their registered funds, financial institutions are required to withhold a certain amount of the funds for income tax purposes. The percentage of tax to be withheld at source depends on residency and on the amount withdrawn. For residents of Canada, the tax withheld is according to the following chart:

Amount Withdrawn	**Tax Withheld**
$5,000 or less	10% (21% in Quebec)
$5,001 to $15,000	20% (26% in Quebec)
$15,001 or more	30% (31% in Quebec)

For Quebec residents who withdraw registered funds, a 16% provincial tax is withheld in addition to the federal tax (5%, 10%, or 15% federally). For non-residents of Canada, withholding tax is 25% unless reduced by a treaty.

In addition to the taxes withheld at source, the total funds withdrawn are fully taxable at the individual's marginal tax rate. The financial institution is required to issue a T4A or Relevé 2 form to each taxpayer who withdraws registered funds. Therefore, additional tax may be assessed on the amount withdrawn when the individual files his or her next tax return.

As noted, funds in an RRSP can be accessed at any time, but must be removed by the end of the year in which the RRSP owner attains age 71. At that time (or earlier, if desired by the RRSP owner), the assets can be transferred to a RRIF, used to purchase an annuity (either a life annuity or a term-certain annuity which is payable for a fixed term only) from a life insurance company licensed to transact business in Canada, or taken in cash.

Two programs are available which permit individuals under certain situations to withdraw funds tax-free from their non-locked-in RRSPs provided they later repay the contributions to the RRSP.

The Lifelong Learning Plan permits the withdrawal of RRSP funds to finance training or education for the individual or his or her spouse or common-law partner. The maximum amount that can be withdrawn is $20,000 over a four-year period (and there is an annual withdrawal limit of $10,000). After the funds are withdrawn, they must be repaid over a period of up to 10 years. Amounts contributed to a spousal RRSP or transferred as a retiring allowance or amounts transferred into the RRSP from an RPP, a DPSP, another RRSP, or a RRIF are not considered eligible repayments.

The second program is the Home Buyers' Plan which permits withdrawals of up to $25,000 (for 2009 and subsequent years) to buy or build a first-time principal residence for the individual or to buy or build a home for a related person with a disability. The funds must be repaid within 15 years, with the first repayment due the second year following the year in which the withdrawal was made.

Assets can be transferred into a RRIF at any time; however, a percentage of the assets must begin to be removed every year starting with the year following the year in which the assets are deposited into the RRIF. The amount that must be withdrawn each year is a percentage of the assets in the RRIF, which varies by age according to the following chart:

Age	Percentage	Age	Percentage
70 or under	[1 - (90 - x*)]%	82	9.27
71	7.38	83	9.58
72	7.48	84	9.93
73	7.59	85	10.33
74	7.71	86	10.79
75	7.85	87	11.33
76	7.99	88	11.96
77	8.15	89	12.71
78	8.33	90	13.62
79	8.53	91	14.73
80	8.75	92	16.12
81	8.99	93	17.92
82	9.27	94 or older	20.00

* *Note: "x" is "age in whole years" on January 1 for calendar year of payout.*

Therefore, assets are generally only transferred to a RRIF when the taxpayer needs to begin receiving payments from the registered funds. The payments received from the RRIF are fully taxable at the individual's marginal tax rate in the year of receipt.

¶1415 Locked-In RRSPs and LIRAs

Locked-in RRSPs and LIRAs are simply RRSPs (as discussed at ¶1410 above) with certain additional restrictions on the use of the funds. RRSPs and LIRAs provide members with the same investment and tax sheltering abilities as non-locked-in vehicles; however, the flexibility with regard to distribution of the funds is more restrictive and is set by minimum standards legislation.

The minimum standards legislation, which resulted in portability becoming a right for all terminating plan members in lieu of leaving pension funds in the pension plan, generated a substantial market for financial institutions and therefore the need for a vehicle to accept these locked-in funds and to maintain certain minimum standards requirements. Prior to minimum standards pension reform, the only vehicle available to hold locked-in pension monies was the locked-in RRSP. Jurisdictions that introduced pension reform early in the process or who permitted portability prior to the minimum standards requirements to do so, offered the locked-in RRSP as its retirement savings vehicle portability option.

In order to assist financial institutions and plan members to distinguish between the locked-in and non-locked-in forms of the RRSP, Quebec introduced the LIRA, a new name for the locked-in RRSP. Some jurisdictions that originally offered locked-in RRSPs switched to LIRAs but others retained the term locked-in RRSP. There are no differences between LIRAs and locked-in RRSPs, other than differences due to specific jurisdictional requirements.

Most jurisdictions require financial institutions that offer transfer vehicles such as LIRAs to register with the minimum standards jurisdiction. A list of financial institutions that accept transferred funds is usually available on the Web site maintained by each jurisdiction. As specialized types of RRSPs, both locked-in RRSPs and LIRAs are subject to the *Income Tax Act* (Canada) provisions governing RRSPs.

The RPP provisions that carry forward as restrictions to the locked-in RRSP and LIRA include the following:

- The assets in the locked-in RRSP or LIRA must be used to provide retirement income (funds held in these vehicles must be withdrawn by the end of the year in which the plan holder turns 71) and cannot be cashed out, except under certain circumstances as prescribed by the minimum standards jurisdiction (such as shortened life expectancy, financial hardship, phased retirement or temporary pension situations, or in some jurisdictions, if the owner is no longer considered a resident of Canada under the *Income Tax Act*

(Canada). By age 71, the assets must either be transferred to an LIF or LRIF (see ¶1420) or used to purchase a life annuity from an insurance company licensed to transact business in Canada.

- The earliest date the member can commence receipt of retirement income from the locked-in RRSP or LIRA is confirmed when the transfer is completed and is specified based on the retirement eligibility rules of the originating pension plan (generally within 10 years of the normal retirement age).
- If the individual has a spouse at the date that the funds are used to provide a lifetime pension, then the pension must be payable in the form of a joint and survivor pension in which a minimum percentage (in accordance with the requirements of the minimum standards jurisdiction under which the pension funds originated) continues to the spouse after the death of the member. The minimum standards legislation of the jurisdiction defines the circumstances under which this mandatory form of pension can be waived and will outline the prescribed administrative rules to follow. The usual procedure is for both the member and the spouse to sign a waiver form.
- In the event of death prior to purchasing a life annuity, the spouse of the locked-in RRSP or LIRA owner is entitled to the assets in the locked-in RRSP or LIRA. The surviving spouse can maintain the tax-sheltered status of these funds by transferring the assets to an RRSP or LIRA in his or her name. If there is no spouse, a lump-sum payment, less withholding taxes as noted above, will be paid to the beneficiary or the estate of the owner of the locked-in RRSP or LIRA.
- In marriage or relationship breakdown situations, pension funds must be divided according to the legislative requirements in each jurisdiction. The former spouse or common-law partner may transfer his/her share of the locked-in RRSP or LIRA into another locked-in RRSP or LIRA, LIF or LRIF, if permitted in the jurisdiction. (LIFs and LIRAs are discussed at ¶1420.)
- If the termination benefit commuted value transferred in the locked-in RRSP was calculated using a unisex mortality basis and these funds are later converted into an annuity, the conversion must be done using unisex mortality. Note that there is no requirement to use the same unisex mortality basis that was originally used, simply that unisex mortality must be used.

The requirement to adhere to the above conditions is set out in a locking-in agreement signed by the financial institution accepting the assets. The locking-in agreement then forms part of the locked-in RRSP or LIRA contract.

As stated above, assets in a locked-in RRSP or LIRA are to be used to provide lifetime retirement income through the purchase of a life annuity from an insurance company. Alternatively, the funds can be transferred to:

- another locked-in RRSP or LIRA (up until age 71);
- an LIF (as discussed at ¶ 1420);
- an LRIF (as discussed at ¶ 1420), if one is available in the relevant minimum standards jurisdiction; or
- an RPP (up until age 71), provided the administrator of the pension plan agrees to administer the locked-in funds in accordance with the required minimum standards legislative provisions.

A notable exception to the requirement for the assets to be transferred into another locked-in vehicle is Saskatchewan with its prescribed RRIF, which is discussed in greater detail at ¶ 1425.

Most jurisdictions in Canada permit the immediate cash payment or a series of payments to be made to the holder of a LIRA (or any of the other retirement vehicles, if applicable), upon receipt of a physician's certification that the individual's life expectancy has been significantly shortened by either a mental or physical disability. The minimum standards legislation will specify if a spousal waiver form is required in such circumstances.

There are other situations in which the owner of a locked-in RRSP or LIRA may receive a lump-sum payment of the entire amount in the locked-in RRSP or LIRA. Various jurisdictions permit unlocking of funds where the balance in the LIRA is below a certain threshold, such as less than 20% of the YMPE, or higher if the owner is over age 65.

In several jurisdictions, locked-in funds are permitted to be withdrawn if the superintendent is satisfied that the conditions of "financial hardship" exist and approval is granted by the jurisdiction.

Finally, an owner of a locked-in RRSP or LIRA may also, depending on the jurisdiction, receive a lump-sum payment of the entire balance, if he or she is no longer considered a resident under the *Income Tax Act* (Canada) or has been outside Canada for a specified period of time.

Any of these immediate cash payment options may require the signing of a spousal waiver form, before the assets are released.

For more specific details on the common and unique features of the various locked-in retirement savings vehicles across Canada, refer to the chart in Appendix 3.

Despite the various restrictions outlined above for locked-in RRSPs and LIRAs, these retirement vehicles provide the advantages anticipated for portability, which include continued growth of funds on a tax-sheltered basis within any investments offered by the financial institution and within the provisions of the *Income Tax Act* (Canada).

The primary drawback to locked-in RRSPs and LIRAs is the requirement that funds held in these vehicles must be withdrawn by the end of the year in which the plan holder turns 71, to be used to purchase a life annuity with an insurance company. A life annuity requires periodic or annual withdrawals to be made, as prescribed under the *Income Tax Act* (Canada). Individuals wishing to tax shelter their pension assets as long as possible then became subject to whatever the annuity purchase rates applied at the time they purchased the annuity. Consequently, there could be significant variation in the lifetime annuity that could be purchased in periods of higher interest rates compared to periods of lower interest rates.

In order to purchase a life annuity with the locked-in funds, all of the funds have to be liquid at the time of purchase. Therefore, all of the investments in locked-in plans must be sold and converted into cash to pay the premium to the insurance company. This must take place regardless of the quality of the investments in the locked-in plans, or the level of interest rates at the time of purchase.

As a result, these limitations were unsatisfactory to those whose rate of return within a locked-in plan was substantially higher in comparison with the taxable income stream generated by the newly purchased annuity. Furthermore, the purchase of an annuity prevented the owner of a locked-in plan from using the funds to possibly generate further capital appreciation in a vehicle free of immediate tax consequences.

Therefore, the next generation of retirement savings vehicles evolved to reduce the limitations and inflexibility of these locked-in plans: the LIF and the LRIF. These are described in ¶1420.

¶1420 LIFs and LRIFs

An LIF offers more flexibility to plan members by allowing them to postpone the purchase of the annuity until age 80. Thus, an individual has a greater ability to take advantage of more beneficial interest rates by controlling the timing of the conversion of the funds in the LIF to an annuity contract. LIFs are available in all jurisdictions.

A variation on the LIF is the LRIF. Under the LRIF, there is no requirement to purchase an annuity by age 80. Several provinces now offer LRIFs in addition to LIFs. Further, certain jurisdictions changed their LIF rules so that the LIF does not need to be annuitized by age 80, making it unnecessary to offer both an LIF and an LRIF in a particular jurisdiction. Alberta (in 2006) and Ontario (in 2008) are two jurisdictions that have chosen to eliminate the LRIF and have revised the LIF rules to eliminate the annuitization requirement. However, as is generally the case in Canada, each pension benefits jurisdiction adopted one or more of the available portability options on different dates.

Both the LIF and the LRIF are forms of RRIFs that have been specially designed to hold locked-in pension funds. As such, they are both subject to the *Income Tax Act* (Canada) provisions governing RRIFs. For example, an LIF or LRIF is exempt from execution, seizure or attachment, and the funds inside the LIF or LRIF cannot be assigned. Investments inside the funds are governed in the same way. Further, as a form of a RRIF, payments from an LIF or LRIF to a person 65 years of age or over, are eligible for the pension tax credit. Payments to those under 65 years of age cannot be claimed for the pension tax credit.

In general, an LIF or LRIF allows more flexibility and investment options than a LIRA by deferring the purchase of an annuity until the end of the year in which the owner turns 80 years of age, or by completely removing the requirement to purchase an annuity.

Since payments out of an annuity are based on the type chosen as well as the interest rates available at the time of purchase, an LIF or LRIF provides its owner with more time to grow the capital tax-free within the plan, as well as providing its owner with more time in which to purchase a life annuity. Therefore, an LIF or LRIF owner may wait several years after the age of 71, if he or she believes that the combination of higher interest rates and greater capital appreciation will ultimately result in a larger monthly annuity payment, or decide to leave the funds within the LIF or LRIF and not purchase an annuity at all.

An LIF or LRIF may be the transfer vehicle chosen by individuals, generally within 10 years of normal retirement age or the early retirement age established by the pension plan from which the funds originated with some exceptions — e.g., Alberta's legislation permits the purchase of an LIF or LRIF at age 50), and can be held until the age of 80, or for the life of its owner by any of the following:

- retiring members of money purchase plans;
- retiring members of defined benefit plans (if the plan permits);
- individuals with funds in a locked-in RRSP or LIRA; or
- individuals with funds in another LIF or LRIF.

An LIF or LRIF is subject to the same spousal waiver restrictions as a locked-in RRSP or LIRA.

Upon marriage or relationship breakdown, pension funds must be divided according to the legislative requirements in each jurisdiction. The former spouse or common-law partner may transfer his/her share of the LIF or LRIF into a locked-in RRSP or LIRA, or another LIF or LRIF, if available, depending on the jurisdiction.

Upon the death of the owner, the balance of the LIF or LRIF is payable to the survivor in cash or into any transfer vehicle permitted under the *Income Tax Act* (Canada). If there is no survivor, the beneficiary or the estate will receive the balance of the funds in the LIF or LRIF.

Each jurisdiction has specific rules regarding the ability to unlock LIF or LRIF assets in various situations. For the most part, the same unlocking rules as apply to the locked-in RRSP or LIRA apply to LIF or LRIF assets.

For example, several juridisctions permit locked-in funds (LIRAs, LIFs, and LRIFs) to be withdrawn if conditions of "financial hardship" exist and approval is granted by the jurisdiction. Most jurisdictions permit unlocking in the event of shortened life expectancy. Several jurisdictions permit unlocking in the case of the owner no longer considered a resident for tax purposes under the *Income Tax Act* (Canada). In some jurisdictions (Alberta, for example), lump-sum payments are possible where the value of the LIF or LRIF is less than 20% of the YMPE, or if the owner is at least 65 years of age and the total value of all locked-in plans is less than 40% of the YMPE. Several jurisdictions permit a one-time unlocking of a substantial percentage of the assets in the LIF or LRIF (up to 50% depending on the jurisdiction).

For more specific details on the common and unique features of the various locked-in retirement savings vehicles across Canada, refer to the chart in Appendix 3.

Generally, assets may be transferred into an LIF or LRIF on or after January 1 of the year which is the calendar year prior to the year in which the LIF or LRIF owner is first eligible to retire under the terms of the registered pension plan from which the assets originated. Further, the LIF or LRIF payments are required to commence no later than the end of the second fiscal year of the fund. If the LIF or LRIF contains assets that originated in more than one RPP, then the earliest retirement date under any of the originating plans will generally determine the earliest age at which the LIF or LRIF payments must commence.

Since an LIF/LRIF is a form of a RRIF under the provisions of the *Income Tax Act* (Canada), the owner of the LIF or LRIF is required to make an annual minimum withdrawal. The annual minimum withdrawal is the same annual minimum withdrawal as is required under a RRIF, as set out at ¶ 1410. An LIF or LRIF must, therefore, have sufficient liquidity to fund the annual withdrawals. Payments out of an LIF or LRIF are fully taxable.

However, unlike a RRIF, LIFs and LRIFs have annual maximum withdrawal limits as well. This is because an LIF or LRIF is ultimately a vehicle to provide a steady income stream throughout the course of an individual's retirement. In other words, at the age of 80, there must be sufficient funds available in the LIF to purchase a life annuity for its owner where it is required, or in cases where it is not required (or for an LRIF), there must remain sufficient funds for the rest of the owner's life.

While the spouse's or common-law partner's age may be used to determine the minimum annual withdrawal limit, the LIF or LRIF owner's age must be used to calculate the maximum amount payable in the year.

The formula for the maximum annual withdrawal amount from an LIF is set by the minimum standards jurisdiction and is designed to ensure that a sufficient amount of money remains in the LIF for its remaining lifetime (i.e., either to age 80 or the LIF owner's lifetime, depending on the jurisdiction). Generally, the formula is the balance of the fund at the beginning of the fiscal year divided by the value of a guaranteed pension payable from the beginning of each fiscal year to the last day of the year during which the owner attains 90 years of age. In some jurisdictions, the maximum annual withdrawal amount in the first year is prorated according to the number of full or partial months in the period between the opening of the LIF and the calendar year end, divided by 12. Each jurisdiction annually publishes charts showing the maximum withdrawal percentage by age.

Generally, the formula to determine the maximum withdrawal each year uses an interest rate that is the greater of 6% and the interest rate under CANSIM series V122487 set out for the previous November for the first 15 years and 6% for the sixteenth and each subsequent year. CANSIM series V122487 is for Government of Canada long-term bonds.

Ontario's new LIF also permits the maximum to be based on the amount of investment earnings in the previous fiscal year, if this amount is greater than the prescribed maximum. This method of determining the maximum payment is similar to how the maximum payment is determined for an LRIF, as discussed later in this section.

Since the LIF still required conversion to a life annuity at age 80 in many jurisdictions, the LRIF was created in order to permit the potential of capital appreciation to be maintained for the life of its owner.

Therefore, the owner of the LRIF can exercise control over all investment decisions within the fund for his or her lifetime. Of course, the owner of the LRIF can always convert the fund into an annuity, or to an LIF (if the owner is under 80 years of age in jurisdictions that require the purchase of an annuity at age 80). Otherwise, the LRIF can exist until the owner's death.

As in the case of an LIF, an LRIF has an annual maximum withdrawal limit to ensure sufficient funds remain for the rest of the owner's life. However, the formula is different. Generally, the maximum annual withdrawal will be equal to the greatest of:

- the market value of the fund as of January 1, less the sum of all income paid to the owner from the LRIF, and if any funds were transferred from an LIF, the investment income earned by the LIF in its final fiscal year;
- the investment income earned by the LRIF during the immediately preceding fiscal year; and
- for the first two fiscal years, 6% of the fair market value of the fund. (In the first year, the amount must be prorated. After the first year, the fiscal year always begins on January 1.)

Although Ontario has now replaced its LRIF by a new LIF, that jurisdiction's LRIF contained a unique feature. If the owner of an LRIF elects to be paid an amount that is less than the maximum annual withdrawal amount for the fiscal year, the difference between the maximum amount and the amount paid in the year may be carried forward and paid out in a future fiscal year. However, this carry-forward feature was not extended to the new Ontario LIF.

¶1425 Prescribed RRIFs

As an exception to the requirements for locking in pension money described in this chapter, Saskatchewan introduced the prescribed RRIF in 2002. The prescribed RRIF is similar to a RRIF in that the assets are not locked in; however, there are still certain minimum pension legislation standards that apply, including:

- Assets are subject to division in the event of the breakdown of a spousal relationship;
- Assets may be attached for the purposes of enforcing an order for maintenance support;
- The beneficiary is the owner's spouse, unless the spouse signs a waiver; and

- Assets are subject to creditor protection in that they may not be assigned, charged, alienated, or anticipated and are exempt from execution, seizure, or attachment.

In Saskatchewan, money that is locked in under a pension plan, LIRA, LIF, or LRIF may be transferred directly to a prescribed RRIF if:

- The owner is at least 55 years of age (or if the plan from which money is to be transferred provides for retirement at an earlier age, the owner has attained that earlier age); and

- The owner's spouse has signed a prescribed consent form.

The funds in a prescribed RRIF are not locked in, and are not subject to annual maximum withdrawal limits. The owner of a prescribed RRIF may withdraw the entire amount in their prescribed RRIF at any time.

¶1430 Tax-Free Savings Accounts

The 2008 federal Budget introduced a new non-locked-in tax-sheltered savings plan: the TFSA. Canadian residents who are 18 years of age or older may make contributions to a TFSA each year up to certain limits and the investment earnings on the TFSA will remain tax sheltered during their lifetimes. The contributions to the TFSA are not deductible for tax purposes nor is interest on money borrowed to invest in the TFSA tax-deductible. However, any amounts withdrawn from the TFSA are withdrawn tax-free.

The maximum contribution to a TFSA for 2009 and 2010 is $5,000. This maximum limit will be indexed to inflation and rounded to the nearest $500 in future years. Unused TFSA contribution room can be carried forward to later years. Further, any withdrawal of contributions in a calendar year increases the amount, dollar for dollar, that can be contributed in a subsequent calendar year.

While not strictly speaking a retirement savings vehicle — the TFSA is intended to provide a mechanism for Canadians to save for a variety of life events, including retirement — the introduction of the TFSA represents an additional layer of tax sheltering over and above the limits in the various traditional retirement savings programs.

The TFSA will be especially useful in situations where members of existing retirement programs have reached the savings limits permitted under those programs. It is anticipated that some sponsoring organizations may set up group TFSAs with matching employer contributions in much the same way that group RRSPs exist within organizations.

Retirees with extra income will be able to take advantage of the less stringent rules governing TFSA contributions and withdrawals to build more savings, even past the age of 71, when contributions to RRSPs are no longer permitted.

Group TFSAs will likely be classified as capital accumulation plans (CAPs) where members are given choice regarding investments, and as a result, employers will have to ensure that the operation of a TFSA complies with the CAP Guidelines (as discussed at ¶140).

As with RRSP overcontribution penalties, an overcontribution to a TFSA will attract a penalty of 1% per month on the excess contribution amount.

Contributions may be made to a spouse's TFSA by an individual without affecting the individual's own TFSA contribution providing that the spouse has unused TFSA room. The income attribution rules which currently govern withdrawals from spousal RRSPs (as discussed at ¶430) do not apply.

One of the advantages of a TFSA is that amounts withdrawn are not included in income for certain government means-tested benefits such as the guaranteed income supplement and the OAS clawback.

In the event of the death of a TFSA holder, a spouse or common-law partner may assume the TFSA holder's plan provided the spouse or common-law partner has been designated as a "successor holder" on the TFSA. Alternatively, the TFSA holder may designate a beneficiary to receive the assets upon the holder's death.

The CRA has indicated that it will provide details each year on the amount of available contribution room for an individual on the individual's notice of assessment issued after filing each year's income tax return.

¶1500 PENSION PLAN VALUATION CONCEPTS

¶1505 Background

In addition to the minimum standards legislation described in Chapter 13 and the *Income Tax Act* (Canada) registration rules set out in other chapters of this book, the operation of pension plans (defined benefit plans in particular) is affected by various other sets of rules established by professional and regulatory bodies, including:

- standards of the Chartered Financial Analyst Institute that govern the reporting of investment performance;
- auditing and accounting standards of the Canadian Institute of Chartered Accountants that govern the preparation of plan financial statements that are filed annually with regulatory authorities;
- standards of the Canadian Institute of Actuaries (CIA) that govern the preparation of valuation reports, the calculation of commuted values and other actuarially equivalent benefits, and other aspects of defined benefit pension plan operations; and
- trust company and life insurance company regulations that govern the custody of assets.

For defined benefit plan sponsors, there are two areas in particular that require clear understanding of the rules and professional standards in order to make decisions that are appropriate to the long-term financial health of the pension plan and the plan sponsor:

1. funding of the defined benefit pensions (actuarial standards play a role); and

2. accounting for the cost of the pension promise in the financial disclosures of a plan sponsor (accounting standards and rules of securities regulators play roles).

The minimum standards jurisdiction is interested in the actuarial standards for funding of pension plans since pension legislation requires that employers pre-fund benefits. The Registered Plans Directorate of the CRA is interested as well since the contributions being made must be acceptable under the terms of the *Income Tax Act* (Canada) and Regulations. The accounting standards have little overlap with either the minimum standard rules or the *Income Tax Act* (Canada) rules, since the accounting valuation has no bearing on actual cash contributions being made to an RPP. Accounting standards govern disclosure of pension expense and pension plan obligations in a company's public financial statements. The only link to minimum standards and *Income Tax Act* (Canada) rules is to respect the benefit provisions and limitations set out in pension and tax legislation.

A thorough discussion of these topics is beyond the scope of this book. However, an overview is set out in this chapter to add context and additional framework to enable the reader to obtain a more complete picture of the relationship between the rules established under the *Income Tax Act* (Canada) and the rules established by the various other bodies.

¶1510 Fundamentals of Pension Plans Valuations

The commitment under a defined benefit plan involves the payment of benefits to members, surviving spouses, and beneficiaries at unknown time or times in the future. The amounts payable vary depending on a number of factors, including the plan formula, each plan member's service and earnings history to date, plus future unknowns, such as:

- future pay increases;
- whether the member will complete the future years of service required to qualify for retirement benefits;
- whether the member will terminate employment, or die, prior to completing the future years of service required to qualify for retirement benefits;
- retirement age; and
- age at death.

Moreover, if a fund is to be established, as is required under minimum standards legislation in order to be able to pay these future benefits from a registered defined benefit pension plan, the amounts to be deposited into the fund will depend upon future investment earnings of the fund.

These unknowns cannot be predicted accurately in advance. Nonetheless, some sort of estimate is essential in order to establish an orderly pattern of contributions and attribution of the cost of benefits. The balance between accumulated assets and an estimate of accumulated pension obligation is key to satisfying regulators, shareholders, and plan members as to the viability of the pension plan. An actuarial valuation of the pension plan is just such an estimate.

Actuaries are trained and experienced in the preparation of pension plan valuations. Only those actuaries recognized as Fellows of the Canadian Institute of Actuaries are permitted to prepare the valuations of registered defined benefit pension plans required by the *Income Tax Act* (Canada) and minimum standards pension legislation or to prepare valuations of employee future benefits accepted by Canadian auditors of the financial statements of public companies.

There are a number of different ways in which future obligations can be estimated. The methodology used and the set of economic and demographic assumptions depend on the purpose for which an estimate is required. Valuations are typically required in the following circumstances:

- The most common valuation of a defined benefit plan is one carried out for funding purposes, to determine the level of required employer contributions in order to meet the requirements set out in the *Income Tax Act* (Canada) and the applicable minimum standards pension jurisdiction. The funding valuation estimates the plan's obligations on a long-term going concern long-term basis, using assumptions and methods recommended by the actuary within the guidelines and constraints established by the CIA and the regulators. Funding valuations are discussed in greater detail at ¶ 1520.
- A solvency valuation is done in conjunction with a funding valuation, but the estimate is prepared as if the pension plan had been terminated and all obligations paid out as at the valuation date. Solvency valuations are required by minimum standards legislation, but not under the *Income Tax Act* (Canada) and the Regulations. However, the level of solvency contributions required must still be acceptable to the Registered Plans Directorate. Solvency valuations are discussed in greater detail at ¶ 1520.
- An accounting valuation is prepared for the purpose of determining the sponsor's pension expense and to inform financial statement users as to the status of the pension obligations, in accordance with generally accepted accounting principles (GAAP). In contrast to a

funding valuation, the actuarial assumptions used are "management's best estimates". Accounting valuations are discussed in greater detail at ¶ 1525.

- If the plan sponsor wishes to implement plan changes that will materially affect benefit costs (and therefore the rate of contribution required to fund the benefits), a determination of the value of the new benefits is required. For an RPP, a valuation of the new benefits is required both to provide information to the plan sponsor as to the value of the new benefits and for filing with the CRA and the minimum standards jurisdiction for approval to change the level of contributions to the plan. For a funded arrangement with surplus pension assets, a change in benefits may have no immediate impact on employer cash cost, but the value of the new benefits is still important to assess the new pension obligation being undertaken.

- In the event of a wind up or partial wind up of a pension plan either as a result of the sale of part or all of an organization, in the event of bankruptcy or where the plan sponsor makes a business decision to terminate the pension plan, appropriate valuation of the benefit obligations is required in order to pay out the benefits to entitled beneficiaries and for approval from the regulators to terminate the plan.

- In the event of an asset transfer in connection with a merger or the sale or disposition of a business unit, a valuation of the pension obligations, whether funded or unfunded, helps the purchaser and the seller to measure the value of the obligations being transferred and is one component in setting an appropriate purchase price for the business unit. Valuation work is often carried out as part of a due diligence exercise in order for the potential purchaser to determine whether the assets and obligations of the seller's pension plan(s) are appropriately represented.

- Valuations of certain parts of a plan may be carried out as part of a union negotiation process in order to assist the parties at the negotiating table in determining the overall cost of the negotiated benefit package.

- Valuation work is also sometimes carried out as part of a larger asset liability-modelling exercise to examine the risks of alternative investment policies, or the long-term viability of a particular combination of benefit design, funding policy, and investment policy.

Each of these types of valuations has unique requirements in areas such as:

- the degree of conservatism (if any) in actuarial assumptions;

- the actuarial method used to attribute future benefits to years of employment (e.g., whether salary increases should be anticipated or recognized in liabilities as they are granted);
- plan provisions, amortization methods, and supplementary disclosures stipulated by regulations or the sponsor; and
- the extent of disclosure required by the reader.

¶1515 The Valuation Process

The actuary prepares the valuation by taking into account the following:

- Membership data — Data on member's age, service, earnings, and other determinants of future pension benefits are maintained by the plan administrator and provided to the actuary at the beginning of the valuation process. Where there is missing data, or there is uncertainty as to a member's entitlement, the administrator will exercise judgment in deciding what data to provide to the actuary and whether to disclose the uncertainty. Where data inconsistencies are detected, the actuary relies on the plan administrator to investigate and correct the data. The degree to which steps are taken to investigate and correct the data depends upon the purpose of the valuation and the materiality of the data inconsistencies. Except in the case of a plan wind up, the actuary will not usually conduct a detailed audit of source records or insist upon 100% accuracy of all of the inputs and may make assumptions as to any missing data.
- Asset data — Asset values for actively traded securities are typically tracked by the fund's custodian. Other assets that must also be valued might include investments that are not actively traded, annuity contracts, outstanding contributions, and pending transfers from other pension funds. The valuation will include a reconciliation of changes in asset values since the last valuation and confirmation of consistency between contributions and benefit payments reported by the custodian and those indicated by the membership data. The purpose of this reconciliation is to permit an analysis of the sources of gains and losses and ensure that membership data has not been lost during the intervaluation period. It is not an exhaustive review to determine whether all contributions, and benefits have been paid correctly. In the course of reconciling the assets from a prior valuation to the current valuation, anomalies in investment returns or other areas of administration (including expenses) are sometimes uncovered that require additional analysis or explanation.

- Plan provisions — It would normally be expected that a valuation will reflect the terms of the pension plan documents that have been approved by the sponsor of the pension plan and filed with the regulators. The administrative or legal interpretations of an ambiguous or discretionary plan provision should be conveyed to the actuary as well so that the actuary may determine a value for a particular plan provision that accurately reflects the actual benefits that will ultimately be paid. Where there is a choice as to whether or not to include provision for amendments that will come into force after the valuation date, the alternatives should be discussed and the approach to be taken in the valuation should be specified and disclosed. Regulations may permit certain benefits (such as future inflation protection or benefits that are only payable under special circumstances) to be excluded in the determination of contributions. This is a funding policy decision of the plan sponsor.

- Actuarial assumptions — Expectations for contingent events that will occur in the future are called actuarial assumptions. These expectations may take the form of a single scenario (such as a fixed rate of investment return or a fixed retirement age), or a probability distribution of possible outcomes (such as a table of mortality rates). The contingencies that relate to individual plan members are broadly termed "demographic assumptions", while contingencies that relate to the financial operation of the sponsor, the pension trust fund, and the economy are termed "economic assumptions". The assumptions reflect current actuarial research and professional standards. They should also reflect the specific circumstances of the employer. The plan sponsor and administrator can assist the actuary in the development of actuarial assumptions by providing insight into recent and planned pay increases and employee turnover or other workforce management programs that may impact on total membership. The highest profile actuarial assumption is the expected rate of investment return — the valuation interest rate. This assumption has a powerful effect on all aspects of actuarial calculations, and must be thoroughly reviewed at each valuation date to ensure it continues to reflect current financial market conditions and expectations. In past, any margin for adverse deviations was expressed as a reduction in the valuation interest rate. More recently, however, there has been a movement towards using a margin for adverse deviations for each assumption, with the margin reflecting the uncertainty of that assumption, along with using sensitivity analyses to illustrate the affect of adverse deviations for valuations.

- An actuarial cost method — Benefits in a pension plan are earned during an employee's working career and payable many years later during retirement. A basic principle of RPPs is that benefits should be funded within the working lifetime of the member. An actuarial cost method is a set of rules for allocating the total projected future cost of benefits to individual years of employment.

- Constraints imposed by regulators and standards.
- The plan sponsor's internal policies — Plan sponsors may have pre-established policies on such items as margins of conservatism, amortization, periodic benefit upgrades, etc. (i.e., the plan sponsor's "funding policy", as discussed in greater detail at ¶ 1535).

The actuary will gather these inputs, assess their reasonability, resolve inconsistencies, and prepare the valuation, setting out two key results:

- the difference between the value of plan assets and the actuarial liability (a surplus if greater than zero or an unfunded liability if less than zero); and
- the normal cost (also known as current service cost).

The actuarial liability is the portion of the present value of future benefits allocated to pensionable service prior to the effective date of the valuation, while the normal cost is the portion allocated to the period immediately following the valuation. The normal cost might be expressed as a fixed dollar amount per year, a percentage of pay, a percentage of employee contributions, or a flat dollar amount per person, per hour, or per month of pensionable service, depending on the type of pension plan and the preferences of the plan sponsor, and the reasonableness of the approach in the specific situation (for example, a fixed dollar amount may not be appropriate if the membership group is increasing or decreasing).

¶1520 Funding Valuations

A funding valuation is carried out primarily for the purpose of establishing an appropriate level of contributions to an RPP that is acceptable to the Registered Plans Directorate and the minimum standards pension regulator.

The valuation method used most often for funding of defined benefit plans in Canada is the accrued benefit actuarial cost method, also known as the projected unit credit cost method. Under this method, the current service cost is the present value of the benefits attributable to service in the year following the date of the valuation, based on projected average earnings and pension eligibility service at retirement or other termination of active membership status. For any one individual, this present value will increase as retirement approaches, but the current service cost formula for the entire employee population will remain relatively constant as long as the demographic mix of the employee population (age, pension eligibility service, gender, and earnings relative to the YMPE) remains relatively constant.

The valuation actuary will determine and disclose:

- the minimum level of contributions, based on the requirements in the relevant minimum standards legislation;
- the maximum contributions permitted based upon the restrictions on employer contributions under the *Income Tax Act* (Canada), (as discussed at ¶ 1815); and
- a recommendation as to the level of contributions to be made, based on the plan sponsor's funding policy, if there is one; (see ¶ 1535 for a discussion on elements of funding policy).

In addition to establishing the level of contributions, the results of the funding valuation report may also affect:

- the frequency of future valuations and other monitoring activities by regulators — a significantly underfunded pension plan may be required to be valued more frequently or additional periodic reporting on the status of the plan may be required;
- Ontario Pension Benefits Guarantee Fund assessments — Ontario requires payment of premiums into an insurance plan to ensure certain minimum benefits are payable in the event of a bankruptcy;
- the transfer ratio of the plan, which is the ratio of solvency liabilities to available assets, which may result in restrictions on the ability of the plan sponsor to make lump-sum payments to plan members;
- benefit or indexing levels for pension plans in which benefits are not fully defined, but depend upon actual investment returns or other results; and
- plan member perceptions as to the security of their retirement income.

To the extent that the going concern actuarial liability exceeds the value assigned to the pension plan's assets, there is an unfunded liability. If the actuarial liability is less than the actuarial value of the assets, there is a surplus. This unfunded liability or surplus indicates that the contributions have fallen behind or crept ahead of schedule. When actual events turn out better than the economic and demographic assumptions of a previous valuation, an experience gain will arise, adding to a surplus or reducing the unfunded liability. Conversely, if actual events turn out worse than the assumptions, an experience loss will arise. These gains and losses will be reflected in adjustments to the contributions following each valuation.

For career average pension plans or plans with no guaranteed post-retirement indexing, deliberate conservatism in actuarial assumptions may be used to build reserves for future inflation protection. The CRA will generally permit an explicit allowance for future inflation protection, as long as there is pattern of past adjustments. In order to avoid creating a commitment to potential future improvements, sponsors of such plans are often reluctant to include explicit allowances or disclose the reason for conservatism in reports.

Where there is an unfunded liability, it is typically the employer (or employers) participating in the plan who will make additional contributions to make up the shortfall. If the plan is a shared-cost plan or negotiated-cost plan, either benefits or levels of employee contributions may be adjusted in addition to or instead of increased employer contributions.

When there is a surplus, employers are more constrained in terms of how that surplus can be utilized, as discussed at ¶ 1321. Typically, employers will reduce contributions or cease contributing to the plan (by taking a "contribution holiday") until the surplus has been reduced to levels where contributions are again permitted or required. Surplus can also be:

- used to improve benefits under the plan, for example, to provide an *ad hoc* improvement to pensions in payment or other such one-time improvements to benefits for active or retired members;
- paid out in cash to employees and employers, although this is very unusual unless a pension plan is being wound up;
- used to give employees a contribution holiday for a temporary period; or
- left in the pension fund to build a contingency reserve to offset possible future experience losses, subject to the limits discussed at ¶ 1321.

Solvency Valuations

The orderly accumulation and investment of pension plan assets is vital to the sustainability of a pension plan and stability of employer contributions. However, as long as the plan sponsor continues in business and remains prepared to fund any deficiencies that may arise, the exact balance between assets and going concern liabilities may not be very important to plan members and regulators. Full funding of pension benefits only becomes a real issue when a plan sponsor goes out of business and a pension plan is wound up. For this reason, actuarial standards require actuaries to include an estimate of the "hypothetical wind-up liability" of a pension plan in any actuarial valuation prepared for funding purposes.

A hypothetical wind-up valuation is an attempt to measure what it would cost to settle all of the guaranteed benefits of a pension plan as of a given point in time. For plan members who would have the right to receive a lump-sum settlement and would be expected to elect this option, the liability is computed using the prescribed basis for commuted values. For other plan members, the liability is an estimate of the price an insurance company would charge for immediate or deferred annuities equal to the plan members' accrued benefits. An estimate of the administration costs associated with settling the benefits is also included. If the hypothetical wind-up liabilities are more than the market value of the pension fund investments, it means that, as of the valuation date, all of the benefits promised by the plan could not have been replaced by insured benefits or lump-sums without further contributions by the employer. It does not necessarily mean that there is a problem with the long-term funding of the pension plan since, in normal circumstances, the plan members can rely upon the sponsor to continue to contribute to the plan and the plan investments can usually be expected to generate higher rates of return than the rates used to determine commuted values and annuity prices.

Minimum standards regulations place more emphasis on this type of settlement valuation than on the going concern valuation. However, detailed regulations specify the inclusion or exclusion of special benefits, such as those that are only payable at the discretion of the plan sponsor, or only payable as part of a major layoff or plant closure. The actuarial liabilities determined on this regulated basis are referred to as "solvency liabilities", and are often different from the hypothetical wind-up liabilities as described above.

In general, any solvency deficiency must be amortized over five years from the date of the valuation in which it is first reported, which is faster than the amortization period generally permitted to liquidate unfunded liabilities revealed in a going concern valuation. The Regulations explicitly permit funding on either a hypothetical wind-up basis or a solvency basis as an alternative to going concern funding (other than for designated plans). Designated plan funding rules are described at ¶1830, ¶1835, and ¶1840.

As a result of the economic downturn of 2008-2009, several minimum standards regulators introduced temporary solvency funding relief measures that permitted plan sponsors to extend the normal five-year amortization period to 10 years, as well as various other alternatives to assist plan sponsors in meeting cash flow constraints.

Finally, although the solvency valuation is currently only used to establish special payments in respect of benefits earned up to the valuation date, there is increasing interest from both the actuarial community and the minimum standards pension regulators towards the concept of a "solvency normal cost", whereby contributions for benefits arising in the current year will take into account both a solvency normal cost determined from the solvency valuation and the standard going concern normal cost.

Frequency of Valuations and Reporting

Routine funding and solvency valuations are required every three years for defined benefit RPPs. Minimum standards regulations may require valuations more frequently if the plan is significantly underfunded.

A full report is prepared and delivered to the provincial or federal minimum standards regulator, the Registered Plans Directorate, and where applicable, the union that represents the plan members. Once submitted to the regulator, it is available to plan members upon request. In some jurisdictions, key results, such as the solvency ratio, are also required to be disclosed in annual member statements.

A full valuation report contains not only information regarding the current financial position of the plan, but also information on the evolution of the assets and liabilities since the previous actuarial valuation, certifications as to the reliability of the membership and other data, a summary of the plan benefits being valued, a summary of the plan member data including a reconciliation of the plan membership since the last valuation and a breakdown of the membership into age and service bands, a detailed description of the economic, demographic, and any other assumptions used, and recommendations on the level of funding that is appropriate. The degree of detail provided in the valuation report should be sufficient for an independent actuary to be able to assess, using only the information provided in the report, whether the results of the valuation are reasonably accurate.

Administrators of larger pension plans will often choose to obtain valuation reports more often than strictly required under pension or tax legislation. This is because funding can go too far off target if the process of reviewing and updating the contribution rate is neglected for as long as three years. In some instances, an employer will choose to commission a full valuation earlier than required to obtain approval of a desired increase or decrease in contributions, or will commission a valuation report, and only choose to submit the report to the regulator if the results are supportive of the sponsor's funding policy. Some regulators restrict this practice of "strategic filing" by refusing to accept reports that are filed too long after the valuation date. With more minimum standards jurisdictions requiring more frequent valuations, especially for underfunded plans, the ability to do strategic filing is becoming more restricted.

Although it is the plan administrator who has a duty to obtain an actuarial valuation report, it is generally the participating employers who must actually make the actuarially determined contributions, and who are most immediately affected by the plan's funding policy and the valuation actuary's judgments. Funding policy (as discussed at ¶ 1535), which may be formally stated or as informal as selecting the contribution level within the range of minimum and maximum limits, is generally a prerogative of the plan sponsor in single employer pension plans.

¶1525 Accounting Valuations

An accounting valuation, while still an estimate of a plan's future obligations, is carried out for a very different purpose than a funding valuation. It is prepared for the sponsor for the purposes of determining the sponsor's pension expense and informing financial statement users as to the status of the pension obligations.

In contrast to a funding valuation report, the actuarial assumptions are described as "management's best estimates", meaning that corporate management takes responsibility for this aspect (and indeed all aspects) of the accuracy and reliability of corporate financial statements. However, there is less leeway with the discount rate, a key assumption. There are specific guidelines in the accounting standards as to how the discount rate is to be determined. The discount rate is developed by reference to market interest rates at the valuation date on high-quality debt instruments (i.e., corporate bonds) with cash flows that match the timing and amount of expected benefits payments. The objective of selecting the discount rate is to measure the single amount that, if invested at the measurement date in a portfolio of high-quality debt instruments, would provide the necessary pre-tax cash flows to pay the accrued benefits when due.

Rather than the restrictions of the *Income Tax Act* (Canada) and pension regulatory authorities, an accounting valuation is subject to restrictions imposed by the accounting profession and securities regulators.

The method of allocating future pension costs to the years in which service is rendered to the employer (and so to match costs with revenues) is prescribed by various accounting standards. The amortization of gains and losses and approaches to dealing with special events are also constrained by accounting standards. Amortization leads to differences between the net pension plan asset or liability recorded on the company's balance sheet and the surplus or unfunded liability reported in the accounting valuation. These differences have been severely criticized, and changes to accounting standards are being developed and implemented to ensure pension plans do not constitute hidden obligations (or assets). These changes are part of a larger trend in the accounting profession towards "market value accounting".

The applicable accounting standard depends upon the ownership structure of the company and, in the case of subsidiaries of foreign companies, the domicile of the parent company. The accounting standards are now in the process of transitioning to International Accounting Standards (IAS). In general,

- Canadian corporate tax returns should be in accordance with GAAP; for Canadian publicly accountable enterprises, transition to IAS will occur on January 1, 2011, with one comparative year to GAAP; for organizations that are not publicly accountable, new private enterprise standards are currently under development; Canadian non-profit companies (not in the public sector) are expected to be able to choose between the private enterprise standards that are being developed and IAS;
- companies with securities that trade in the United States must report under U.S. GAAP; companies may adopt IAS in 2009; adoption of IAS is required by 2014 for large U.S. companies, 2015 for medium U.S. companies, and 2016 for small U.S. companies;
- companies with securities that trade in the European Union must report under IAS;
- governments must report under Canadian public sector accounting standards; the applicability of IAS is to be determined by the Public Standards Accounting Board;
- companies with publicly traded securities (shares or bonds) must comply with more extensive disclosure requirements under Canadian GAAP than private and not-for-profit companies; and
- additional disclosure standards and restrictions on assumptions are imposed by the U.S. Securities and Exchange Commission and provincial securities regulators.

Although many of the principles underlying the different accounting standards are similar, there are subtle differences. Also, when an actuarial report is prepared under the accounting standards of a foreign jurisdiction (such as the U.S. Financial Accounting Standards Board rules), it is subject to the actuarial standards of that jurisdiction rather than Canadian actuarial standards.

Although the actuarial assumptions in an accounting valuation are "management's best estimates", in practical terms, the actuary is often involved in assisting in the selection of the assumptions, to varying degrees. Typically, the actuary will provide background information and pension accounting results on a range of scenarios (i.e., sensitivity issues), but will leave the final selection of key economic assumptions to the plan sponsor.

It is common for valuations for accounting and funding purposes to be prepared concurrently, and for the discussion of assumptions, methods, and preliminary results to be conducted in a single meeting. It is also common and efficient for the same data, benefit programming, actuarial methods, and demographic assumptions (but not key economic assumptions) to be used for both purposes. Although the employer representatives may be acting in their capacity as plan administrator when discussing the funding valuation and in their capacity as the plan sponsor when discussing the accounting valuation, the distinction is often obscure. Thus, although the accounting assumptions may be described as management's best estimates and the funding assumptions may be described as the actuary's provision for future benefits, the reality may be that a consensus has been reached on one or both of the sets of assumptions.

The actuary is often the individual most familiar with the accounting standards applicable specifically to pension plans and most capable of making the judgments required in their application to a particular pension plan design. However, actuaries will be less familiar with accounting policies dealing with acquisitions, discontinued operations, and other special events, and legal uncertainties around such matters as partial wind-up obligations and surplus ownership. The company's accountant and auditor will need to ensure treatment of these special events is consistent with overall accounting standards and choices the company has made concerning accounting for non-pension costs in these circumstances.

The timelines for financial statement reporting require that results are often based upon membership data assembled with an effective date months, or even years, prior to the measurement date. In order to meet tight timelines for quarterly and annual financial reporting, and to give sponsors good guidance for budgeting well in advance of the measurement date, actuaries are required to extrapolate results and make judgments as to whether corrections to extrapolations would be material to financial statement users.

Although the question of materiality arises in all actuarial work, it receives more attention and is discussed with the client and the auditor more frequently in the context of accounting valuations than of funding valuations. The frequency of reporting, the tight timelines, and the close working relationship amongst the actuary, the auditor, and the client also leads to streamlined reporting, in which detailed disclosure may be accomplished by reference to prior (or forthcoming future) accounting reports or funding valuation reports, rather than full reiteration in each instance.

Extrapolation should not be made to a measurement date more than three years after the date of the last full valuation. Whether or not a full valuation is needed sooner than this will depend upon an assessment of the materiality of the changes in plan membership and other events that have occurred in the interim.

¶1530 Other Valuations

In addition to the funding and accounting valuations, the valuation of a defined benefit plan's obligations is required in various other circumstances, such as a plan amendment that will materially affect benefit costs, a wind up or partial wind up of a pension plan, an offer to some or all of the plan members to convert defined benefit accruals to defined contribution, union negotiations, or an asset transfer in connection with a merger or the sale or disposition of a business unit.

For these non-recurring events, a special purpose report will be prepared, the contents of which will vary depending on the situation that has given rise to the need for the valuation. The special purpose report will contain additional information in support of the proposed transaction.

For example, in the case of an asset transfer, the pension regulator will want to ensure the transfer of assets and liabilities does not undermine benefit security for either the transferring plan members or the plan members remaining behind. Normally, the vendor's actuary will determine an asset transfer value and prepare an actuarial report that:

- complies with the terms of the purchase and sale agreement;
- demonstrates compliance with the specific policies of pension regulator and tax authorities;
- respects the interests of transferring and remaining plan members; and
- will stand up to scrutiny by the purchaser's actuary.

Special purpose reports may take the form of "supplementary actuarial valuation reports". That is, they may not entail a full valuation of all of the pension plan's obligations as of the date of the transaction. Instead, they may only restate the position as of the date of the most recent valuation with adjustments to reflect the impact of the transaction. This approach can be much easier to understand and more cost-effective, since only the benefits that are changing need to be analyzed. An actuary's supplementary valuation report can be much shorter than a full valuation report, since many of the required disclosures are covered by reference to the original report.

¶1535 Funding Policy

A funding policy, in basic terms, is a clearly articulated set of guidelines that describes the company's decision-making process for how and when and how much to contribute to the pension plan (within, of course, the limits set by the minimum standards jurisdiction and the *Income Tax Act* (Canada)). It forces a company to acknowledge its financial commitment to the pension plan and to understand how funding decisions can impact on the long-term financial health of the plan. This long-term funding policy is used to develop recommended contributions and as input to the evaluation of other pension plan policies such as the target asset mix.

In the past, most funding policies have been informal. However, with heightened scrutiny on all-around corporate governance and increased awareness of the potential for conflicts between the interests of owners and pension plan members, it has become more important for a company to have more formal funding strategies in place.

The pension plan funding policy adopted by a plan sponsor will depend on the weighting or priority the sponsor gives to several competing objectives. Different sponsors will emphasize different objectives, and this will lead to different decisions around such matters as:

- the actuarial cost method used to allocate the cost of benefits over the working lifetimes of their employees;
- the margins of conservatism in the actuarial assumptions;
- the asset valuation method;
- the actual contribution rates within the range of the minimum and maximum levels permitted by regulatory authorities (in particular, amortization of a surplus or deficit at a more rapid pace than required); and
- the frequency of valuations.

Some of the objectives used to establish a funding policy for a typical private sector pension plan are as follows:

- stability of contributions;

- maximizing or minimizing contributions;
- maximizing tax effectiveness and tax-sheltered funding;
- maximizing shareholder value;
- pre-funding possible future plan improvements;
- security of benefits;
- avoidance of regulatory intervention due to excessive under or overfunding;
- minimizing impact of pension plan accruals on the corporate balance sheet;
- the use of plan surplus and funding of deficits between plan sponsor and members;
- equity among generations of contributors and beneficiaries; and
- maintaining funding ratios comparable to competitors.

A well-thought-out and periodically reviewed funding policy will help an organization understand the risks and rewards with particular courses of action, will formalize the company's long-term goals with respect to the pension plan, and will also help to highlight whether the objectives around the pension plan are consistent with the company's overall business objectives.

Chapter 16

¶1600 REGISTRATION RULES FOR MONEY PURCHASE PLANS

¶1605 Introduction

A money purchase RPP, or a money purchase provision within an RPP, is also known as a defined contribution RPP or a defined contribution provision. "Money purchase provision" is defined in subsection 147.1(1) of the *Income Tax Act* (Canada). Money purchase provisions must have the following characteristics:

- provide for a separate account to be maintained for each member, where all contributions and other amounts allocated expressly for the member are deposited; and
- the only benefits payable to the member are those that can be provided from the amount in the member's account.

A defined benefit provision, as discussed in Chapter 17, is defined as a provision under which benefits are provided in any way other than as a money purchase provision.

The rules for obtaining and maintaining continued registration of a pension plan with the CRA can be found in Part LXXXV of the Regulations. These rules are more comprehensive than the previous registration rules set out in Information Circular 72-13R8.

This chapter covers the rules for stand-alone money purchase RPPs. These rules also apply to any money purchase provision in an RPP that contains both defined benefit and money purchase provisions (such as a defined benefit plan that allows additional voluntary contributions). However, there are some additional rules for RPPs that contain a combination of defined benefit and money purchase provisions, which are covered in Chapter 20. Additionally, special rules that cover benefits provided under MEPs are described separately in Chapter 21.

A money purchase provision may only provide benefits based on actual employer and employee contributions, the earnings on such contributions and a reallocation of forfeited amounts, if any. As discussed previously, these amounts make up the total amount in members' accounts. Ancillary benefits, such as bridging benefits, pre-retirement spousal pensions, or indexing, can only be provided to the extent that some of the assets in the member's account are applied for that purpose. Therefore, the benefits that are discussed at ¶1640, ¶1645, ¶1650, and ¶1655 can only be provided if the total value of all benefits provided to the member from the plan does not exceed the amount in the member's account.

¶1610 Registration of Plans

All RPPs containing money purchase provisions are required to comply with the registration rules set out in the Regulations.

A new plan must be submitted for registration in or before the calendar year in which the plan is effective. Thus, for a plan to take effect on, say, September 1, 2010, a complete application for registration must have been filed before December 31, 2010. The documentation that must be included with the application for registration is set out in ¶2210. An incomplete application will be returned to the submitter and the plan will not be deemed to be registered on the proposed effective date.

Administratively, however, we understand that the Registered Plans Directorate will accept an incomplete application for review in certain circumstances where documents are unavailable due to a pending transaction to purchase or sell a business. In situations where it is impossible to submit documents by the end of the calendar year, the Registered Plans Directorate will continue its practice of permitting such documents to be submitted early in the following calendar year provided the Registered Plans Directorate is sent written notice advising of the situation.

¶1615 Contributions

The discussions at ¶1616 to ¶1619 describe the limits on contributions and other allocations to member accounts in cases where benefits are determined exclusively on a money purchase basis.

¶1616 Employer Contributions

Conditions that apply to employer contributions are as follows:

- The contribution must be in accordance with the plan as registered.
- The contribution, together with any employee contribution and any forfeited amount (as discussed at ¶1618) reallocated to the member in the particular year, must not exceed the PA limit for the year. This is discussed in further detail below.
- The contribution must consist of amounts paid in respect of specific plan members and each amount must be allocated to the member in respect of whom it is made.
- The contribution cannot include amounts which represent foregone investment earnings. This could arise, for example, if an employer undercontributed by mistake for a particular employee or group of employees. When the contributions are later deposited to the members' accounts, it is not possible to make additional contributions in respect of lost investment earnings. Instead, lost earnings can be provided by temporarily changing the contribution level for the affected members, requiring a plan amendment and taking into account any minimum standards legislation requirements.
- The plan must not have a surplus. (In this context, surplus does not include any non-vested forfeited amounts, investment earnings on forfeited amounts, or investment earnings that will be allocated to members. Usually, there would only be a surplus under a money purchase RPP if surplus has been transferred from a pre-existing defined benefit RPP and if it was not allocated to members at the time of the transfer.)

Generally, an employer's contribution to a money purchase RPP is deductible in computing income for a taxation year if it was made within the year or within 120 days after the end of the taxation year. However, the contribution must not have been used as a deduction against income in a previous taxation year. Further, it must relate to the taxation year for which the deduction is claimed or to a previous taxation year.

The PA limit in any particular year is equal to the lesser of 18% of the member's compensation in that calendar year and the money purchase limit for that year.

Further, a member's PA in respect of a particular employer plus the member's PAs in respect of all other employers who do not deal at arm's length with that particular employer may not exceed the money purchase limit for the year. Note that the "18% of compensation" limit does not apply to this test.

The money purchase limit for each calendar year is defined as follows:

Year	Money Purchase Limit
2005	$18,000
2006	$19,000
2007	$20,000
2008	$21,000
2009	$22,000
2010	$22,450

Commencing in 2010 and in all future years, the money purchase limit is $22,000, indexed to the rate of increase in the average wage, with the result rounded to the nearest $10. If there is a decrease in the average wage, the money purchase limit will remain at the same level as the previous year.

A chart showing the money purchase limits in effect since 1990 is in Appendix 3.

Note that each year's RRSP dollar limit (as defined at ¶410) is equal to the money purchase limit for the immediately preceding year — for the same reason that the PA limit is based on 18% of the *current* year's compensation while the RRSP contribution limit is based on 18% of the *previous* year's earned income. Since, for example, the PA for 2009 affects RRSP contribution room for the year 2010, it follows that the 2010 RRSP dollar contribution limit should equal the money purchase limit for 2009.

¶1617 Minimum Employer Contribution

The Regulations state that contributions made by an employer under a money purchase RPP must be determined in a manner acceptable to the Minister of National Revenue. This provision allows the Minister to prescribe guidelines for minimum employer contributions. The Minister requires a minimum employer contribution of 1% of the total pensionable earnings of all active members under stand-alone money purchase RPPs. This requirement is stated in Pension Reform Update No. 91-4R.

Where a plan applies forfeitures (as defined at ¶1618) to reduce the employer's obligation to make contributions to a money purchase RPP and where the forfeitures are sufficient to fully reduce the employer's contributions, the employer will not be required to contribute the minimum 1% employer contribution. In addition, where a defined benefit RPP contains a supplementary money purchase provision (i.e., a combination plan), no minimum contribution to the money purchase provision of the plan will be required.

¶1618 Non-Vested Forfeitures

When a member who is not vested terminates from a money purchase RPP, the non-vested amount that remains after the member terminates is called a "forfeited amount". The rules require that amounts forfeited, plus all earnings of the plan reasonably attributed to such forfeited amounts, must be paid out to participating employers, reallocated to remaining plan members, or used to pay administrative, investment, or similar expenses incurred in connection with the plan. Such payment or reallocation must occur on or before December 31 of the calendar year immediately following the calendar year in which the forfeited amount arises. While the registration rules do not prohibit the payment of reallocated amounts directly to members rather than reallocation to members' accounts, plan sponsors and administrators should be aware that provincial minimum standards may not permit such an approach.

As discussed at ¶620, forfeited amounts that are allocated to the members' accounts must be included in the members' PAs.

A plan administrator may apply to the Minister of National Revenue for an extension on the time limit for the reallocation of forfeited amounts when the amount to be reallocated is greater than normal due to unusual circumstances. The extension on the time limit will only be granted when the forfeited amounts and related earnings are to be reallocated on a reasonable basis to the majority of plan members or are to be used to pay the expenses of the plan.

¶1619 Employee Contributions

Generally an employee's contribution to a money purchase RPP is deductible in computing income for a taxation year if it was made within the year. Other conditions that apply are as follows:

- The contribution must be made in accordance with the plan as registered; and
- The contribution, together with any employer contributions and any forfeited amounts (as explained at ¶1618) reallocated to the

member in the particular year, does not exceed the PA limit (as defined at ¶1616) for the year.

Current service additional voluntary contributions (AVCs, as defined at ¶205) may be made (and deducted from taxable income) if the plan allows, provided that the total contributions (inclusive of employee and employer contributions and forfeitures reallocated) do not exceed the PA limit for the year. AVCs in the context of a money purchase RPP would be employee contributions that are not required and that do not trigger an employer contribution.

¶1620 Permissible Distributions and Transfers Between Plans

In addition to permitting the payment of lifetime retirement and bridging benefits, the legislation specifically outlines other permissible types of distributions from an RPP, including limits on payments out of an RPP and, more particularly, controls on the tax-free transfer of funds between tax-sheltered arrangements.

All rules related to permissible distributions and transfers between plans are discussed in detail at ¶1740 to ¶1743. The most significant difference between a transfer from a money purchase RPP to an RRSP and a transfer from a defined benefit RPP to an RRSP is that there is no limit on the amount that may be transferred from a money purchase RPP. This is because the *Income Tax Act* (Canada) has already applied a control on the contributions to a money purchase RPP through the contribution dollar limits. Since these limits restrict the amounts paid into a money purchase RPP and allocated to individual member accounts, any benefit arising under a money purchase RPP may be transferred (including investment earnings on those contributions) and tax sheltered until eventual retirement or withdrawal.

¶1625 Leaves of Absence and Periods of Reduced Pay

The Regulations lay out a complex framework for the provision of benefits during periods of leave and reduced pay. There are also explicit rules describing the periods that may be considered pensionable service under a defined benefit plan. For a money purchase RPP, however, the accumulation of benefits during a period of leave or reduced pay is controlled by limits on contributions. No contributions may be made to a money purchase RPP by the employee or employer except where the employee is in receipt of "compensation" from an employer.

The Regulations prescribe notional amounts that may be included in a member's compensation in order to allow contributions to be made to the

RPP in respect of eligible periods of temporary absence and reduced pay. Without this prescribed compensation, contributions would exceed the PA limit set out at ¶ 1616 and the plan's registration would become revocable.

An eligible period of temporary absence is a period throughout which a member does not provide services to an employer due to a leave of absence, layoff, strike, lockout, or any other circumstance acceptable to the Minister of National Revenue. A temporary absence does not include any period in which the member is a connected person or during which the employee is disabled. (See ¶ 1630 for further information regarding periods of disability.)

An eligible period of reduced pay qualifies as such if:

- the employee, during such period, is not a connected person;
- the employee was employed by the employer for at least 36 months before the period; and
- the remuneration during the period is less than the remuneration that could reasonably be expected to have been received by the member had he or she worked on a regular basis at his or her rate of pay in effect before the period. Note that "regular basis" refers to the basis of employment before the period. For example, if the employee had never worked for the employer on a full-time basis, it would not be acceptable to determine reasonably expected remuneration during an eligible period of reduced pay by reference to employment on a full-time basis.

Examples of situations of reduced pay are a temporary reduction in hours of employment, phased retirement, or a temporary payment under an austerity program. Typically, these pay reductions are initiated by the employer. Another example is a salary deferral leave plan under which the employee elects to defer receipt of salary for tax purposes, thereby self-funding a sabbatical leave.

The prescribed amount that may be included in an individual's compensation for the purpose of determining the contributions during eligible periods of temporary absence or reduced pay (not including periods during which an individual works for another employer and participates in another RPP) is determined as the amount by which remuneration is reduced from its normal level. Compensation will not be prescribed, however, unless the period in question is a "qualifying period".

A period will be considered a qualifying period for the purposes of prescribed compensation under a money purchase RPP if:

- the period was an eligible period of reduced pay or temporary absence as discussed above;

- contributions were made by or on behalf of the member during the period and such contributions exceed the contributions that would otherwise have been made if they were based on services actually rendered and remuneration actually received by the member;
- such contributions are included in the member's PA for that year; and
- contributions are not made by or on behalf of the member to any other money purchase RPP or DPSP in which the employer does not participate.

In determining whether a period is a qualifying period, a contribution does not include amounts allocated to the member from forfeited amounts or surplus.

The total of prescribed amounts in respect of all eligible periods of temporary absence or reduced pay with a particular employer cannot exceed five years of equivalent full-time remuneration. An additional maximum of three years may be added to this limit in respect of periods of parenting. A period of parenting is defined as all or part of a 12-month period that commences at the birth or adoption of a child.

This cumulative limitation period of between five to eight years (depending on the periods of parenting) applies only with respect to a particular employer and any employers with which the employer operates at non-arm's length. Where an individual changes employers and the new employer is not a participating employer in the same RPP in which the former employer participated, a new five- to eight-year limit applies.

Leaves of absence and periods of reduced pay prior to January 1, 1991, are not subject to the prescribed compensation provisions set out above. Instead, these pre-reform periods of leave continue to follow the rules set out in Information Circular 72-13R8: paid leaves, sabbatical or education leaves, and maternity, parental, and adoption leaves are permitted without limit and periods of unpaid leave to a maximum of two years are generally permitted.

When a period of reduced pay is involved, an "additional compensation fraction" must be determined, as described in the example below.

Consider an individual who is on a temporary leave of absence for five months and, as a result, his or her expected compensation of $66,000 for the year is reduced by $27,500 to $38,500. Suppose the individual belongs to a money purchase RPP under which the total contribution rate is 12% of compensation and that provides for continued contributions during such leaves of absence. The total contributions for the year would be $7,920 ($66,000 × 0.12); however, based on actual earnings (before allowing for prescribed compensation), the PA limit would be $6,930 (18% of the individual's actual compensation of $38,500).

The prescribed compensation in respect of the leave would be $27,500, even though only an extra $5,500 is required to support the full contribution of $7,920 (($38,500 + $5,500) × 0.18). Therefore, the prescribed compensation is directly related to the amount by which remuneration is reduced from its normal level — there is no connection to the plan's contribution formula.

The prescribed compensation determined above is used in calculating the "additional compensation fraction", which is the ratio of the prescribed compensation to the normally expected remuneration, or 0.4167 years ($27,500/$66,000) in the example above. This is the amount by which the person's five-year limitation is reduced as a result of this period of reduced pay. After the first such period of leave, the individual in the example above would be left with 4.5833 years under the lifetime limitation, and the number of years remaining would continue to reduce as future leaves and/or periods of reduced pay occur.

Note that the reduction in this example is exactly equal to the period of the leave — the individual was on a five-month leave of absence and the additional compensation fraction in respect of this leave is 0.4167, which equals 5 divided by 12. Although the Regulations account for the balance of the lifetime five-year limit in terms of prescribed compensation, in most cases it works out to be the same as tracking the actual periods of leave.

The sum of all "additional compensation fractions" is referred to in the Regulations as the Cumulative Additional Compensation Fraction.

As mentioned above, up to three years may be added to the five-year limit in respect of periods of parenting. This three-year limit may actually cover more than three births depending on the terms of the RPP. If, for example, the RPP only allows continued contributions for six months of parenting leave, an individual could have leaves in respect of up to six children covered under this three-year extension. Also, once the three years of parenting leave have been used up, parenting leave may still be covered under the general five-year limit to the extent that this limit has not been used up by other leaves.

Salary deferral leave plans, under which an individual defers receipt of pay for tax purposes to self-fund sabbatical or other similar types of leaves of absence, are considered to be eligible periods of reduced pay for the purpose of the above rules. If the RPP allows, an individual generally may continue to accrue benefits based on his or her non-reduced pay during periods when salary is deferred under this type of arrangement, subject to the overall five-year limit.

Special rules apply where an employee is on "loan" to another employer (the "borrowing employer"). If the loaned employee continues to accrue benefits under the lending employer's RPP but is remunerated during this period by the borrowing employer, calculation of the prescribed amount is modified, resulting in a nil additional compensation fraction for the period. Therefore, while the period of loan is considered a period of temporary absence, it does not affect the employee's five-year limit on prescribed compensation.

Once the five-year and three-year leave periods have been used up, contributions may only be made in respect of actual compensation received; however, contributions may, of course, be made up to the PA limit for each year. In the example above, if the employee had used up the five-year/three-year leave period, the total contribution rate of 12% on actual remuneration of $38,500 would give rise to a total contribution of $4,620; however, total contributions of up to $6,930 (18% of $38,500) could be made, even though contributions in excess of $4,620 ordinarily would produce a reduction in the five-year/three-year leave period. In order to accomplish this, the contribution level in the RPP must be adjusted for this particular member. Note, however, that this may be contrary to minimum standards legislation.

¶1630 Periods of Disability

Contributions under a money purchase RPP may continue during a period of disability. For this purpose, the definition of "disabled" applies, which requires that the individual must suffer from a physical or mental impairment that prevents the individual from performing the duties of employment in which he or she was engaged before the commencement of the impairment. This type of definition is often referred to as an "own occupation" definition of disability. (Note that this definition differs from the definition of "totally and permanently disabled", which is more stringent and which generally applies in certain cases under defined benefit plans where extra disability-based benefits are being provided to the individual.)

To ensure that the PA limit is not exceeded, the Regulations allow a prescribed amount to be included in a disabled member's compensation. The prescribed amount is the remuneration that could reasonably be expected to have been paid to the individual during the period if the individual had not been disabled. This provision permits continued contributions to the RPP, even if the individual receives no remuneration (or a significantly reduced amount of remuneration).

In some cases, especially where the individual has been disabled for many years, it may be difficult, if not impossible, to determine the amount of remuneration that would have been paid to the individual for the year had his or her employment not been interrupted by the disability. In such cases, the CRA may permit the use of the individual's pre-disability earnings, increased by a reasonable inflation factor such as the increase in the average wage.

The maximum allowable contribution during the period of disability would then be based on the prescribed compensation — any lower amount of contributions would also be acceptable (for example, where contributions, according to the plan, are based on earnings in effect immediately before the onset of disability).

¶1635 Periods of Foreign Service

The extent to which contributions under a money purchase RPP may be made by or on behalf of an individual during a period of foreign service depends entirely on whether the individual has received compensation. Application of the "18% of compensation" PA limit means that an individual without any compensation in a year may not have any contributions made by, or on, his or her behalf in the year.

Normally, the definition of compensation excludes any amount of employment income that relates to a period throughout which the individual was not resident for tax purposes in Canada. However, compensation may include "an amount acceptable to the Minister in respect of remuneration received by the individual from any employer for a period in the year throughout which the individual was not resident in Canada. . .".

The Registered Plans Directorate's Pension Reform Update No. 93-2, dated October 29, 1993, amended by the Registered Plans Directorate Newsletter 00-1, dated February 7, 2000 states that, where the terms of the RPP permit contributions to be made by or on behalf of a member for a period when the member is employed outside Canada and is not resident in Canada for tax purposes, a request may be made to the CRA for the acceptance of the individual's remuneration for the period as "compensation" from the participating employer. Such requests will be considered on a plan by plan basis. Further, contributions may not be made by or on behalf of a member in respect of a period of foreign service without the prior written approval of the CRA.

The determination of the member's compensation from the participating employer rather than the foreign employer is important if the foreign employer does not participate in the RPP. In such cases, the contributions made by or on behalf of the member during the period of employment with the foreign employer must be attributed for PA purposes to the participating employer. Therefore, contributions that are dependent on the member's compensation from the participating employer might not be permitted unless the member's remuneration during this period is included in his or her compensation from the participating employer for that year.

If, during the period of employment with a foreign employer, the member continues to be employed by the participating employer and received remuneration from the participating employer, this remuneration will only be automatically included in the member's compensation from the participating employer in respect of periods when the member is resident in Canada. For periods when the member is not resident in Canada, a request must be made to the Minister of National Revenue to have such remuneration included in the member's compensation.

A member working for a foreign employer, a non-participating employer connected to the participating employer, or a non-participating employer who has entered into an arrangement with the participating employer outside of Canada may continue to participate in his or her home pension plan for up to five years. Under certain circumstances, the period of foreign service with the foreign or non-participating employer may also be considered a period of eligible temporary absence with respect to the participating employer. In such cases, amounts may be prescribed into compensation if the period of employment is a qualifying period as described in ¶1625.

¶1640 Pre-Retirement Death Benefits

On the death of a member prior to retirement, a money purchase RPP must provide for a pension to be paid to the surviving spouse using the assets accumulated in the member's defined contribution account. The "spouse" of an individual for purposes of the *Income Tax Act* (Canada) includes a person to whom the member is married or a common-law partner who has been cohabiting in a conjugal relationship with the individual for at least 12 months, or who is a parent of a child of whom the individual is also a parent and in a relationship of some permanence with the individual.

Refer to ¶1317 for a discussion regarding who is considered a spouse under minimum standards legislation, and is therefore entitled to receive the benefits described in this paragraph.

The pension paid to the surviving spouse under the terms of a money purchase RPP may be paid in any form that would have been permissible to pay to the member, such as a guarantee period of up to 15 years and/or bridge benefits, with one exception. A joint and survivor form of pension is not permissible since the pension may not be continued to a subsequent spouse of the surviving spouse in the event of the surviving spouse's death. Pension payments to the surviving spouse must commence by the end of the year in which the spouse attains age 71, or, if the spouse has already attained age 71 at the date of the member's death, within one year of the death of the member. The amount of the pension payable is equal to the amount that may be provided by the value of the member's account at the date of the member's death. On the death of the surviving spouse, any remaining guarantee payments may continue to the spouse's beneficiary or may be commuted by the beneficiary into a lump-sum payment.

Since benefits under a money purchase provision can be provided through the purchase of an annuity, as discussed at ¶1665 (unless the assets are transferred out to a tax-sheltered arrangement, as permitted at ¶1620), it is the purchased annuity which will pay the guarantee, not the money purchase RPP itself. However, more typically, the RPP will provide for a lump-sum payment to the spouse or beneficiary on the member's death. The amount of the lump-sum payment may not exceed the balance in the member's account. Only the spouse of the member is permitted to transfer the lump-sum death benefit to his or her RRSP. Note that minimum standards legislation generally requires death benefits to be paid to the member's spouse if he or she survives the member, rather than to a non-spouse beneficiary. Some provinces, however, permit the spouse of the member to waive his or her right to the pre-retirement death benefit.

The lump-sum payment must be made as soon as practicable after the date of the member's death. While the Regulations do not specify a time frame for payment, the payments must be made within the time frames specified by minimum standards legislation.

¶1645 Bridging Benefits

Bridging benefits may be paid to the member from retirement age to no later than the end of the month following the month in which the member attains age 65. Unlike defined benefit RPPs, there is no limit on the size of such benefits. However, since money purchase benefits are limited by the contributions and earnings in each member's account, these benefits may only be provided to the extent that assets are available in the account. Further, since retirement benefits under a money purchase provision are sometimes provided through the purchase of an annuity, as discussed at ¶1665 (unless the assets are transferred out to a tax-sheltered arrangement as permitted at ¶1620), it is the purchased annuity which will pay the bridging benefit, not the money purchase RPP itself.

¶1650 Post-Retirement Death Benefits

Where benefits under a money purchase provision are provided through the purchase of an annuity, as discussed at ¶1665 (unless the assets are transferred out to a tax-sheltered arrangement, as permitted at ¶1620), it is the purchased annuity which will pay the guarantee or survivor pension, not the money purchase RPP itself. Where the assets are transferred to a tax-sheltered arrangement, the rules governing the benefits payable on death for that particular vehicle will prevail.

Generally, the purchased annuity may be guaranteed for up to 15 years from the date of retirement. Alternatively, the purchased annuity may be a joint and survivor form in which a lifetime pension is paid to the surviving spouse of a member on the member's death (and minimum standards legislation would require this unless waived by the member and spouse). Continuing lifetime benefits may not be paid to a beneficiary who does not qualify as a spouse.

¶1655 Inflation Adjustments

If the retirement benefits are provided through the purchase of an annuity from an insurance company, the monthly payments may be adjusted in the same way as an annuity purchased from funds in an RRSP. The adjustments may be made by:

- a fixed annual increase of 4% *per annum* or less;
- adjustments that reflect changes in the CPI;
- adjustments linked to the rate of return on, or the value of, a pool of invested assets; or
- adjustments linked to increases or decreases in generally available Canadian market interest rates.

If the lifetime benefits are payable from the plan (as discussed at ¶1660) rather than purchased from an insurance company, any inflationary increases must be determined in a manner similar to the methods set out above and must be acceptable to the Minister of National Revenue.

¶1660 Variable Benefits

Retirement benefits under a money purchase RPP are to be paid directly from the member's account in the RPP if such benefits are paid in the form of variable benefits. This allows a defined contribution RPP to pay out benefits similar to how benefits are determined and payable from a RRIF. Variable benefits are retirement benefits provided to the member and, after the member's death, to one or more beneficiaries with the following conditions:

- the variable benefits are paid from the member's account;
- a minimum amount is payable each year based on the member's age or the spouse's age (permitting potentially a lower minimum benefit); in order that the minimum benefit not be required prior to the calendar year in which the member turns 70, the minimum benefit applicable prior to age 70 is zero;
- the variable benefits provided to the member or to the beneficiary upon the death of the member (except a beneficiary designated by the member under the provision as a "specified beneficiary") are payable for a period ending no later than the end of the calendar year following the calendar year in which the member dies;
- the member may designate the spouse (see ¶ 1640 to see who is considered to be a spouse) to be the specified beneficiary; such designation must be done in writing before the beginning of a calendar year in order to take effect in that calendar year; the amount then payable to the specified beneficiary will be adjusted upon the member's death to be based on the specified beneficiary's age; otherwise, the amount payable to the non-designated beneficiary remains the same as the benefit payable to the member;
- the variable benefits provided to the specified beneficiary of a member are payable for a period ending no later than the end of the calendar year following the calendar year in which the specified beneficiary dies; and
- the amount of variable benefits payable to the member and beneficiaries of the member for each calendar year is not less than the "minimum amount", as defined below, for the member's account under the provision for the calendar year.

Each year, the minimum amount payable to the member or beneficiary out of the member's account is equal to the balance of the member's account at the beginning of the year multiplied by the appropriate percentage set out in the year. The percentage is determined based on the minimum withdrawal factors set out in the Regulations for RRIFs. The result is that variable payments out of a money purchase RPP are paid out in a manner similar to a RRIF (as discussed at ¶ 1410).

¶1665 Pension Paid Directly from the Plan

With the exception of variable payments (as discussed at ¶1660), retirement benefits under a money purchase provision must be provided either:

- through the purchase of an annuity from a licensed issuer of annuities in Canada; or
- under an alternative arrangement acceptable to the Minister of National Revenue.

Self-insured arrangements which were in place prior to February 1993 continue to be acceptable to the CRA. However, after February 27, 2004 no further alternative arrangements will be considered acceptable by the Minister.

¶1670 Contributions After Retirement

As discussed at ¶1315, when older, experienced employees who are approaching early or normal retirement age work a reduced schedule for a period before finally retiring, this is usually referred to as phased retirement.

For defined benefit provisions, until recently, a Regulation existed under the *Income Tax Act* (Canada) that prohibited an individual from accruing a defined benefit pension under an RPP while also being in receipt of a defined benefit pension from the same plan. This impediment was resolved effective January 1, 2008 when Regulation changes were introduced to permit an employee to continue to work and earn pension benefits while in receipt of a partial pension under the same plan, provided certain conditions are met. Refer to ¶1775 for a discussion regarding the phased retirement rules for defined benefit provisions.

However, there were no such Regulation changes for defined contribution provisions since the same prohibition did not exist for money purchase provisions. It is possible to continue to make contributions to a money purchase provision for a member who is in receipt of benefits under either a money purchase provision or a defined benefit provision within the same plan. Further, since the Regulations allow for a lump-sum payment from a money purchase provision up to the full amount in the member's account, the member may transfer out the full amount of assets in the member account while remaining employed and while additional money purchase contributions are made by or on the member's behalf, provided this is permitted by under the applicable minimum standards legislation.

¶1675 Miscellaneous Registration Rules for Money Purchase RPPs

This section sets out miscellaneous rules for the registration and continuing compliance of money purchase RPPs.

The first seven of these rules also apply to defined benefit plans.

1. Designation of Administrator

Every RPP must have an administrator who is the person or body of persons that has ultimate responsibility for the administration of the plan. Unless otherwise permitted by the Minister of National Revenue, the administrator must be resident in Canada. The CRA must be advised in writing within 60 days of any change in administrator.

2. Primary Purpose of Plan

The RPP must be established with the purpose of providing lifetime retirement benefits to plan members in respect of service as employees. A plan would not qualify for registration if the intention is to terminate the plan shortly after registering it or it was established primarily for the purpose of receiving a transfer of assets and benefits from the RPP of a member's previous employer.

3. Equal Periodic Payments

Benefit payments must be in the form of equal periodic amounts (payable not less frequently than annually) except where they are adjusted for inflation or are reduced after the death of the member or the member's spouse. In connection with a money purchase RPP, this rule only applies in practical terms where the benefits are provided through the purchase of an annuity, as discussed at ¶1665.

4. Latest Start Date for Pension

Pension payments must commence to be paid by the end of the calendar year in which the member attains age 71.

5. Assignment of Rights

An RPP must include a provision that would prohibit benefits from being assigned, charged, anticipated, given as security, or surrendered. Note that the commutation of a benefit is not considered a surrender for this purpose, merely an alternative form of benefit. This provision does not prohibit the assignment of benefits pursuant to a court order or written agreement upon the breakdown of a marriage or conjugal relationship. Nor does it prohibit garnishment of pension benefits for maintenance support. It also does not prohibit the distribution of benefits by the legal representative of a deceased plan member.

6. Permissible Funding Media, Investments, and Borrowing

The arrangements under which the assets of the RPP are held must be acceptable to the Minister, and the RPP must not hold any prohibited investments.

Acceptable funding arrangements include those set out in paragraph 6(e) of Information Circular 72-13R8, as follows:

- a contract for insurance with a life insurance company authorized to carry out business in Canada;
- a trust governed by a written trust agreement under which the trustees are a trust company in Canada or are individuals, at least three of whom are resident in Canada;
- a pension corporation, which is a corporation incorporated and operated solely for the administration of an RPP, as accepted by the Minister, and used as a funding medium;
- an arrangement administered by the Government of Canada or one of the provinces; or
- a combination of the above.

Investments that cannot be held by an RPP are set out in the Regulations. A prohibited investment is a share of the capital stock of, an interest in, or a debt of any of a participating employer, a person connected with a participating employer, a member of the RPP, a person or partnership that controls a participating employer, or a person or partnership that does not deal at arm's length with a participating employer or a member of the RPP.

However, certain investments that would otherwise be prohibited are permissible, such as certain government bonds and other instruments, shares, and debt obligations of a corporation listed on a recognized domestic or international stock exchange; certain mortgages; and investments acquired before March 28, 1988.

In addition, the RPP may not hold any investments that are prohibited by applicable minimum standards pension legislation (or the *Pension Benefits Standards Act, 1985*, if there is no applicable minimum standards legislation).

An RPP is prohibited from borrowing money except in limited circumstances. Borrowing is permitted if the term of the loan is 90 days or less and property of the plan is not pledged as security for the loan. Borrowing is also permitted for the purpose of acquiring real property that is income-producing property. However, the amount borrowed cannot exceed the cost of the property and no plan assets (other than the real property being purchased) may be used as security for the loan.

7. Contributions by Unions and Employer Associations

In certain circumstances, a trade union or employee association may make contributions to an RPP that were originally received from an employer or employee. In such situations, the contributions are deemed to have been made directly by the employer or the employee. This prevents violation of the rules discussed at ¶ 1805 and ¶ 1815, which set out permissible employee and employer contributions to an RPP.

The balance of this section sets out additional rules that are applicable specifically to money purchase plans.

8. Payment of Expenses

In addition to the permissible distributions that may be made from an RPP as discussed throughout this chapter, an RPP may allow for the payment of reasonable administrative, investment, or similar expenses incurred in connection with the plan. As noted at ¶ 625, however, expenses generally may not be deducted directly from contributions made to the plan, since contributions to a money purchase RPP must be allocated to plan members. However, forfeited amounts and the earnings attributable to the forfeited amounts may be used for the purpose of paying such expenses.

9. Requirement for Return of Contributions To Avoid Deregistration

A provision must appear in the RPP document that requires a return of member or employer contributions in order to avoid the revocation of the registration of the plan. Normally this would occur where contributions have been made to the plan in excess of the money purchase limits set out at ¶ 1616, thereby causing the PA limits to be violated. Such excess contributions must be returned to the member and/or the plan sponsor, as applicable. However, permission still may be required from the provincial or federal pension supervisory authority for the return of these contributions.

10. Determination of Amounts

Any amounts determined in connection with the administration of the RPP must be determined using reasonable assumptions that are acceptable to the Minister and where actuarial principles are applicable in accordance with generally accepted actuarial principles. In connection with a money purchase RPP, this means, for example, that the amount of ancillary benefits that may be provided from the member's account (such as indexing or surviving spouse pensions) must be determined using generally accepted actuarial principles.

11. Commutation of Benefits

A lump-sum up to the amount in the member's account may be paid at any time prior to, upon, or after retirement. Minimum pension standards legislation generally requires a lump-sum payment to be paid upon termination of employment, death, or termination of the plan or pursuant to a court order or written agreement following the breakdown of a marriage or other conjugal relationship. The Regulations also allow the full commutation of the member's pension at any time after retirement, although generally this will not be allowed under minimum standards legislation. Note also that minimum standards legislation typically imposes restrictions on the portability of any lump-sum payments where the member is vested or locked-in.

12. Division of Benefits on Marriage or Relationship Breakdown

The splitting of pension benefits upon marriage breakdown either at the date of the breakdown or upon subsequent termination or retirement of the spouse who is a plan member is subject to court orders or provincial legislation affecting matrimonial property in the provincial jurisdiction where the member resides.

Certain jurisdictions recognize common-law spouses for the purpose of property division upon marriage breakdown and other jurisdictions do not. Therefore, the entitlement of common-law spouses, opposite or same-sex, to receive a split of pension benefits is dependent on the jurisdiction involved.

The Regulations allow for the payment of all or a part of the member's account to a spouse in the event of marriage or conjugal relationship breakdown, pursuant to a court order or legal separation agreement. This division of pension benefits, however, is subject to minimum standards legislation. Some provinces restrict the division of accrued pension benefits to not more than 50%.

In any event, the total of the benefits payable to both the member and the spouse may not exceed the benefits that would otherwise be payable to the member in the absence of such an order or agreement.

13. Allocation of Fund Earnings

Earnings (i.e., investment income) under a money purchase RPP must be allocated to plan members on a reasonable basis, no less frequently than annually.

¶1680 Special Rules for Connected Persons

Persons who are connected (as defined at ¶205) may not include any eligible periods of temporary absence or reduced pay in pensionable service and, therefore, may not contribute or receive employer contributions in respect of such periods of service.

Other than the restriction on eligible service described above, there are no other special restrictions on benefits that may be provided through a money purchase RPP to connected persons. As discussed previously, this is because maximum pension controls are applied to money purchase RPPs through the contribution limits.

Chapter 17

¶1700 REGISTRATION RULES FOR DEFINED BENEFIT RPPS — PERMISSIBLE BENEFITS

¶1701 Introduction

A defined benefit provision is defined in subsection 147.1(1) of the *Income Tax Act* (Canada) in an indirect way — a defined benefit provision is any provision that is not a money purchase provision. As discussed in Chapter 16, money purchase provisions must have the following two characteristics: a separate account must be maintained for each member, into which contributions and other amounts allocated expressly for the member are deposited, and all benefits payable to the member must be provided from this account. Therefore, a defined benefit provision is one that cannot be described as meeting both of these criteria.

This chapter covers the rules for stand-alone defined benefit RPPs. These rules also apply to defined benefit provisions in RPPs that contain both defined benefit and defined contribution provisions (such as a defined benefit plan that allows AVCs). However, there are some additional rules for RPPs that contain a combination of defined benefit and defined contribution provisions; these are covered in Chapter 20. Additionally, the rules that cover benefits provided under MEPs are covered separately in Chapter 21.

In this chapter, we have not attempted to cover all of the registration rules set out in the Income Tax Act *(Canada) and Regulations. We have, however, included the more important provisions that will affect most defined benefit RPPs.*

The information set out in this chapter is based on our understanding of the Regulations as of March 1, 2010 and includes information contained in the Registered Plans Directorate's Newsletters and Bulletins.

¶1705 Registration of New Plans

A new plan must be submitted for registration in or before the calendar year in which the plan is effective. Thus, for a plan to take effect on, say, September 1, 2010, a complete application for registration must have been filed before December 31, 2010. A complete application for registration includes the following documentation:

- a completed CRA application form (Form T510);
- a copy of the plan text;
- an initial actuarial valuation report;
- a copy of the funding agreement (typically a trust agreement or insurance contract); and
- a copy of any other relevant documentation such as a by-law or resolution that relates to any of the documents above.

The documents to be submitted must be originals or certified copies of originals. However, it is also acceptable to instead submit photocopies of the signed documents, although applicants who submit photocopies must make the documents with the original signatures available to the Registered Plans Directorate upon request.

Once a complete application for registration is filed, the RPP deemed to be registered from the effective date. While historically, the CRA has been somewhat lenient in enforcing the requirement for a completed package of documents within the year of the intended effective date, they are now enforcing that rule more strictly, although they have indicated the possibility of some flexibility if the effective date is late in the year due to a corporate takeover. See Registered Plans Directorate Newsletter 04-02 which confirms that the CRA will no longer accept incomplete applications and that an incomplete application will simply be returned to the submitter. The CRA's expressed intention is to issue deemed registration status within 60 days for any application that contains all the required documents.

The plan must also be submitted for registration in a minimum standards jurisdiction, as discussed at ¶1311. There may be additional filing documentation, as required by the minimum standards jurisdiction.

Refer also to ¶2210 for additional information on registering or amending a plan.

¶1707 Grandfathered Plans

A grandfathered plan is an RPP that contains a defined benefit provision and that was registered with the CRA on or prior to March 27, 1988, or an RPP for which an application for registration was made before March 28, 1988. A plan that has been established to replace defined benefits under another grandfathered plan is also considered to be a grandfathered plan.

A number of the new registration rules did not apply to grandfathered plans until 1992, and benefits accrued prior to 1992 under grandfathered plans are not subject to many of the new rules. The rules for obtaining and maintaining registration of an RPP were previously contained in Information Circular 72-13R8. Therefore, in many cases, pre-1992 benefits which comply with the rules set out in Information Circular 72-13R8 have been deemed to be acceptable to the Minister of National Revenue.

Throughout this chapter, reference is made to special rules for grandfathered plans, where appropriate.

Some additional considerations regarding the timing for the implementation of the current rules for grandfathered plans appears in Appendix 1, section 9A.

...m Lifetime Benefits

...ons set out three limits on the total lifetime benefits that ...ided to a member under a defined benefit provision:

- a limit on the maximum lifetime benefit, as discussed in this paragraph;
- a limit on the lifetime benefit that may be provided in respect of pre-1990 service, when such service is provided after June 7, 1990, as discussed at ¶1715; and
- a limit on the combined lifetime and bridge benefits payable before age 65, as discussed at ¶1726.

The interaction between the three limits may be complicated in certain situations, and all three limits must be viewed together with certain transitional rules for grandfathered plans that provide pre-reform service.

A defined benefit provision of an RPP must limit lifetime retirement benefits at the date of pension commencement to an amount equal to pensionable service multiplied by the lesser of:

- 2% of highest average compensation indexed to the year of commencement, as defined below; or
- the defined benefit limit in the year of commencement (which is currently set at $2,494.44 for 2010).

The $1,722.22 defined benefit limit that had been in place since 1990 was increased (in the 2003 and 2005 federal Budgets) according to the following schedule:

Year	*Defined Benefit Limit*
2004	$1,833.33
2005	$2,000.00
2006	$2,111.11
2007	$2,222.22
2008	$2,333.33
2009	$2,444.44
2010	$2,494.44
After 2010	Indexed in accordance with the average wage

Note that 2010 is the first year in which the defined benefit limit increased in accordance with the average wage. Prior to 2010, the limits were set by regulation changes.

This limit applies only for members who are not considered connected at any time after 1990. The limit that applies to connected persons is set out at ¶1790.

Note that in some circumstances the defined benefit limit is reduced by one-third. This is discussed at ¶ 1715.

Highest average indexed compensation is equal to the average of the best three non-overlapping 12-month periods of indexed compensation. For this purpose, monthly compensation is indexed to increases in the average wage from the calendar year in which the compensation was paid (or from 1986, if later) to the year of pension commencement. For example, suppose one is determining indexed compensation for an employee retiring in 2010 in respect of actual compensation received in February 2006 of $4,000. The average wage, based on the formula set out at ¶ 205, is $722.08 and $816.88 for 2006 and 2010, respectively. Indexed compensation in respect of February 2006 would therefore be equal to $4,525.15 (actual compensation × 2010 average wage divided by 2006 average wage, or $4,000 × $816.88 ÷ $722.08). To determine the best three non-overlapping 12-month periods of indexed compensation, a similar calculation would be performed for each relevant month of compensation.

This method of determining highest average compensation may be used for all service. In other words, service does not have to be split pre- and post-reform with different rules applying to each portion.

The Regulations set out two other rules with respect to compensation. For purposes of the maximum pension limit:

- bonuses and back pay may be treated as if they had been received in the year(s) in respect of which they are paid; and
- although the calculation of highest average indexed compensation requires the determination of the compensation paid monthly to a member, it is not necessary to keep track of monthly compensation — calendar year compensation may be prorated.

The 35-year limit on pensionable service that was in existence under Information Circular 72-13R8 for the purpose of determining the maximum lifetime benefit has been removed. A discussion on the effective date of the removal of this limit appears in Appendix 1, section 9A.

Any benefits payable under the 50% rule (as discussed at ¶ 1314) and Quebec's additional benefit (as discussed at ¶ 1319) can be paid on top of the limit on lifetime retirement benefits.

The limit on lifetime retirement benefits is an absolute amount without regard to the form in which that benefit is paid. This means that the maximum lifetime benefit permitted under a plan is not adjusted to take account of the form. (Adjustment is required, however, if the form of payment includes a post-retirement benefit in excess of 66⅔% or if the form of payment includes both a post-retirement benefit to the spouse and a guarantee of payments for more than five years.)

For example, consider a final average earnings plan that provides for an accrual rate of 2% per year and offers a normal form of life only. If the member has a spouse then the joint and 60% survivor form is actuarially equivalent to the life only form. A member whose final average earnings equaled $140,000 and who had accrued 20 years of service might well receive the same amount of benefit regardless of his or her spousal status.

The member's accrued pension would equal: 0.02 × $140,000 × 20 years = $56,000.

The maximum lifetime benefit for retirement in 2010 would equal: $2,494.44 × 20 years = $49,888.80.

Thus, the single member retiring at normal retirement age would receive an annual pension, limited by the maximum lifetime pension limits, of $49,888.80.

If that same member had a spouse at retirement and the actuarial reduction to account for the joint and 60% survivor form was 10% then the member's benefit under the plan would be determined as follows:

The member's accrued pension would equal: 0.02 × $140,000 × 20 years × 0.90 = $50,400.

The maximum lifetime benefit would still equal: $2,494.44 × 20 years = $49,888.80.

Therefore, the married member would also receive an annual benefit of $49,888.80 but payable in the form of a joint and 60% survivor benefit.

In general terms, the "defined benefit limit — 2% limit" is more generous than the limit that applied under paragraph 9(g) of Information Circular 72-13R8. The "defined benefit limit — 2% limit" limit may be applied retroactively, which will simplify plan administration for those organizations that were subject to the paragraph 9(g) limit prior to the introduction of the new rules.

Note that some organizations were previously exempted from the paragraph 9(g) limit because the plan text was actually a regulation (typically, organizations in the public sector). Although they must apply the new limit to post-1991 benefit accruals, they are not required to apply the limit to pre-1992 accruals. However, if pre-1990 past service benefits are being granted, the restriction discussed at ¶1715 will apply.

¶1715 Pre-1990 Past Service Benefit Restriction

The previous system for tax-assisted retirement savings permitted individuals to legitimately "double-dip" under certain circumstances. An employee who was not a member of an RPP or DPSP was permitted to make the higher maximum RRSP contribution of $5,500 up to 1985 and $7,500 from 1986 on, subject to a limit of 20% of earned income. On joining an RPP at a later date, such employee could receive past service under the RPP without any concern or penalty for any such higher maximum RRSP contributions already made during years when he or she was not a member of the RPP. This is despite the fact that, if this service had been provided on a current service basis under the RPP, the employee's maximum RRSP contribution would have been restricted to $3,500 (or less, if the RPP was a contributory plan).

A restriction exists under the Regulations that generally applies to any such pre-1990 past service that is credited on or after June 8, 1990. The defined benefit dollar limit in respect of such service is reduced to ⅔ of the defined benefit limit, or $1,150 if greater. For years up to and including 2004, this means a limit of $1,150. Indexing of this limit has commenced in 2005 as increases occur in the defined benefit limit.

This special limit is not applicable in the following situations:

- where the employee was entitled on or before June 7, 1990 (with documentation in writing) to be provided with the benefits;
- where all or part of the year being credited was previously pensionable service under a defined benefit provision of an RPP;
- where contributions were made by or on behalf of the individual to a defined contribution RPP or DPSP in respect of the year being credited; or
- where defined benefits accrued to the individual in respect of a year prior to the year being credited, but, because of a disability or leave of absence that had occurred, the plan did not credit service in the year that is now being credited.

It can be seen that, with the exception of the case where the individual had been on disability or a leave of absence, the special "⅔ of the defined benefit limit" rule applies only to pre-1990 service credited after June 7, 1990, where benefits in respect of such service were not previously provided under an RPP or DPSP. In other words, it generally applies only to pre-1990 service that has been credited to an individual after June 7, 1990, where the individual would have been eligible to make a maximum contribution of $7,500 or $5,500 before 1986 (subject to the old limit of

20% of earned income), regardless of whether the individual actually made this maximum RRSP contribution.

By reducing the maximum pension available in respect of pre-1990 service, the CRA has effectively limited pre-1990 "double-dipping". Post-1989 double-dipping is eliminated through the PSPA, as discussed in Chapter 10.

As a result of the introduction of this rule, where in the past only one maximum pension calculation was necessary, two may now be required. In such cases, it is necessary to keep separate records of pre-1990 service in cases where the special limit applies.

¶1720 Early Retirement Benefits

For most occupations (with the exception of employment in a public safety occupation as mentioned below), a lifetime retirement benefit upon early retirement may be paid to a member without reduction if one of the following conditions is satisfied:

- the member has attained age 60;
- the member has at least 30 years of early retirement eligibility service (as defined below); or
- the member's age plus years of early retirement eligibility service total 80.

Early retirement eligibility service includes pensionable service under the RPP, as well as any other periods of employment with that employer and any related predecessor employer that are not included in the member's pensionable service. The CRA interprets the reference to periods of employment to mean only periods where the member actually worked or for which the member was actually paid. This means that unpaid periods of absence, such as a layoff or a leave of absence, cannot be counted towards early retirement eligibility service unless they are actually credited as pensionable service.

If the member is employed in a public safety occupation (as defined at ¶205), the age 60 criterion is reduced to age 55, the 30-year eligibility criterion is reduced to 25 years, and the 80-point criterion is reduced to 75 points.

The lifetime retirement benefit of a member who retires early and who does not meet any of the above eligibility criteria must be reduced by 0.25% for each month prior to the date on which the member would have been entitled to an unreduced pension, had he or she remained in employment until that date. (Since "month" is not defined in this context, it is assumed that the calculation may be performed using completed months, thereby eliminating the need to prorate for partial months.)

The following example illustrates the above rules. A member retires on his or her fifty-eighth birthday with 20 years of early retirement eligibility service. If this member had remained in employment until age 59, he or she would have had 80 points (i.e., age 59 plus 21 years of service) at that time and would have been eligible for an unreduced pension. Since this member is retiring 12 months prior to the date on which he or she would have been eligible for an unreduced pension, the pension payable must be reduced by at least 3% (12 months × 0.25%).

Note that this early retirement reduction factor must be applied to the maximum lifetime limit determined pursuant to ¶1510 to determine the maximum lifetime benefit permitted on early retirement, regardless of the actual early retirement reduction factors applied to a member's pension under the plan. For example, the maximum pension payable to an individual retiring in 2010 under a plan that applies an early retirement reduction factor of 5% for each year that retirement precedes age 62, would be calculated as ($2,494.44 × years of pensionable service) and then reduced by 0.25% times the number of months prior to the date the individual would have been entitled to an unreduced pension. If the individual was aged 59 at the time of retirement, then the maximum lifetime benefit would be reduced by a factor of 3% (12 months × 0.25%). The result of this calculation would be compared with the individual's accrued pension reduced by the 15% reduction factor (i.e., 5% × 3 years prior to age 62) under the terms of the plan and the individual would receive the lesser of the two amounts.

The above early retirement reduction does not apply to members who retire as a result of total and permanent disability, as discussed at ¶1750 (nor do the "old rules", described at ¶1722, apply in this case).

Under Information Circular 72-13R8, plans could provide for a lower normal retirement age specifically for employees who were forced to retire as a result of automation or technological advancements. This permitted plans to give such employees an unreduced retirement pension even though they were actually taking early retirement. Under the current registration rules, plans cannot contain such provisions, nor could such a provision be grandfathered. However, the downsizing rules discussed at ¶1780 allow an employer to offer enhanced benefits in some cases where a minimum number of employees are affected by the reduction in the workforce.

¶1722 Transition Rules for Early Retirement Benefits

The rule at ¶1720 replaced the limits on early retirement benefits described in paragraphs 10(c) and 21 of Information Circular 72-13R8 (referred to below as the "old rules"). Non-grandfathered defined benefit plans apply the current rules in respect of all benefits. However, grandfathered plans need only apply the current rules to lifetime retirement benefits in respect of service after 1991 — the "old rules" may continue to be applied to benefits earned prior to 1992.

Under the old rules, a plan sponsor was required to apply a "maximum value" test to an early retirement pension commencing prior to age 60 (or normal retirement age, if earlier). Under this "maximum value" test, the value of a member's pension, payable at actual retirement date, including any excess bridging benefits (as discussed at ¶1725), could not exceed the value at age 60 (or normal retirement age, if earlier) of the maximum pension payable under paragraph 9(g) of Information Circular 72-13R8, and payable as a pension guaranteed for 10 years or as a joint and 60% survivor pension.

For convenience, the Minister of National Revenue allows sponsors of grandfathered plans to apply the current rules to a member's pension benefits earned prior to 1992. Applying the current rules retroactively may be more or less advantageous for an individual who wishes to retire before age 60, depending on the individual circumstances.

In many (though not all) situations, the current rules are more restrictive than those described in the Information Circular, as is shown by the following examples.

Consider a plan that offers a lifetime retirement benefit equal to 2% of the annual average of the member's final three years of earnings, less 0.7% of the average final three calendar years of YMPE under the CPP, multiplied by the member's years of pensionable service. The plan requires immediate participation upon hire, has a post-retirement pension guarantee of five years, and has a normal retirement age of 65. For the purpose of the following examples, we will assume that the member is male and that his pensionable service is the same as his early retirement eligibility service. (As assumptions, we have followed the 2009 CIA transfer value basis and have used the mortality table "UP94" projected to 2020 with a blend of 50% male rates and 50% female rates with an interest rate of 3.7% for 10 years and 5.3% thereafter.)

Example

A member is age 55 with 20 years of service and wishes to retire. The member's final three-year average annual earnings are $70,000 and the final three-year average YMPE is $46,300. His accrued pension under the plan is therefore $21,896 *per annum*, calculated as follows:

(0.02 × $70,000 - 0.007 × $46,300) × 20 years = $21,518.

Old Rules

Under the old rules, to determine whether this member's pension must be reduced for early retirement, the following test would be applied:

(a) The value, at age 60, of the maximum pension payable (assuming that $70,000 is also the average salary to be used to calculate the member's 2% maximum pension benefit) is calculated as follows:

Immediate guaranteed 10-year life annuity factor for a member age 60 = 15.0554

Maximum pension payable: 0.02 × $70,000 × 20 years = $28,000

Maximum value: $28,000 × 15.0554 = $421,551.

(Note that we have assumed that this member has no spouse at the date of retirement, and have therefore used a single life 10-year guarantee to determine the maximum value.)

(b) The value, at age 55, of the member's retirement benefit, payable as a single life pension guaranteed for five years, is calculated as follows:

Immediate guaranteed five-year life annuity factor for a member age 55 = 16.1890.

Value of member's pension: $21,896 × 16.1890 = $354,474.

Since the value in (b) is less than the value in (a), the retirement pension could have been paid without reduction under the old rules. Had the value in (b) been greater than the value in (a), then the pension payable would be the value of the maximum pension divided by the factor used in (b).

Current Rules

If the current rules are applied, the member's reduced pension on early retirement would be calculated as follows:

- Age plus service at date of retirement: 75
- Age at which he would have 80 points: 57.5
- Age at which he would have 30 years of service: 65.

Under the current rules, the early retirement pension is the lesser of the plan formula pension reduced by the early retirement reduction factors provided for under the plan and the maximum lifetime pension reduced by the early retirement reduction factors described at ¶1720.

In this example, assume that the plan's early retirement reduction factors are the same as the early retirement reduction factors described at ¶1720. Thus, the pension must therefore be reduced by 3% *per annum* for the period from age 55 to age 57.5 (i.e., 3% × 2.5 years = 7.5%).

His reduced pension at age 55 is, therefore, $21.896 × 0.925 = $20,253.80.

Therefore, the member would benefit if the old rules were applied to the portion of the benefit that accrued to the end of 1991 and if the current rules only apply to the balance of the early retirement benefit.

¶1725 Bridging Benefits

A bridging benefit is a temporary retirement benefit payable to a plan member who retires prior to age 65. Bridge benefits cease when the member attains age 65, and are generally used to "bridge" the gap in the total amount of retirement income payable to the member from both the RPP and from government-sponsored plans before and after the government benefits commence.

Normally, a bridging benefit cannot commence until lifetime retirement benefits commence to be paid. The exception to this rule is for members who are entitled to phased retirement benefits as discussed further at ¶1775.

As with lifetime retirement benefits, the legislation provides for a limit on the amount of bridging benefits that may be paid under a defined benefit RPP.

An RPP may provide a bridging benefit, payable up to attainment of age 65, to a plan member who is receiving lifetime retirement benefits. If the member has attained age 60 and has at least 10 years of pensionable service at the date of pension commencement, the maximum bridging benefit is equal to the total OAS plus CPP/QPP government benefits that the member would receive if he or she were age 65), for the month in which the bridging benefit commences.

For this purpose, the CPP/QPP benefit is equal to the maximum CPP/QPP benefit for the year of commencement, multiplied by the ratio (not to exceed one) of the member's highest three calendar years of earnings to the total YMPE for those three years. Also, it is assumed that the member is eligible for the maximum OAS benefit.

Once it has commenced, a bridging benefit may be indexed to reflect increases in the CPI, as discussed further at ¶1770. An RPP may also provide survivor benefits or a guarantee in respect of a bridging benefit but such survivor benefit or guarantee cannot provide for payment beyond the date when the member would have reached age 65. See ¶1765 for a general discussion of permissible survivor benefits and guarantee periods.

If a member is less than age 60 at pension commencement, the maximum bridging benefit is reduced by 0.25% for each month between the commencement date and the member's attainment of age 60. The maximum bridging benefit is also reduced, on a prorated basis, if the member has less than 10 years of pensionable service. However, these reductions do not need to be applied where the member is totally and permanently disabled, as discussed further at ¶1750.

The limit above describes the maximum bridging benefit that an RPP can provide without affecting the member's lifetime pension. The Regulations allow the provision of bridging benefits beyond the amount determined by the maximum limit discussed above if the portion of the bridging benefit that exceeds the amount determined under this maximum bridging benefit formula is provided in lieu of a part of the member's lifetime retirement benefit. The amount of reduction in the member's lifetime retirement benefit must be determined on an actuarially equivalent basis. However, the total bridging benefit may not exceed 40% of the YMPE for the year when the bridging benefit commences. The total bridging benefit in these circumstances used to be limited to the amount permitted to a member who had attained age 60 and who had earned at least 10 years of pensionable service, but the maximum that applies when additional bridging benefits are provided in lieu of lifetime pension was increased to a limit based on 40% of the YMPE, effective June 4, 1997, to accommodate the temporary pension provisions of the Quebec pension legislation. Any bridging benefits that are provided in lieu of part of the member's lifetime retirement benefit are not counted for purposes of the combined lifetime retirement benefit and bridging benefit limit set out at ¶1726 and ¶1727.

For example, assume a non-disabled member with eight years of pensionable service retired in September 2009 at age 57, with a spouse aged 54 and a lifetime retirement benefit of $675 per month, payable as a joint and 60% survivor pension. (Assume for simplicity that the transition rules set out in ¶1727 do not apply.) The maximum bridging benefit payable to a retiring member age 60 with 10 years of pensionable service is $1,425.71 per month in the third quarter of 2009 ($908.75 CPP/QPP plus $516.96 OAS). The maximum bridging benefit in our example would then be $1,037.92 per month, calculated as follows:

Reduction for less than 10 years of pensionable service:

$1,425.71 × 8 ÷ 10 = $1,140.57.

Reduction for retirement prior to age 60:

36 months of reduction at 0.25% per month = 36 × 0.25% = 9%.

Therefore, the maximum bridging benefit becomes $1,140.57 × 91% = $1,037.92.

This member could have received an increased bridging benefit of up to $1,543.33 (1/12 of 40% of the YMPE of $46,300 for 2009) as long as the lifetime retirement benefit is reduced by an amount equal in value to the value of the extra bridging benefit being paid out.

A bridge benefit need not be specifically defined in relation to the amount of government pension benefit a member will be entitled to receive. Where members are entitled to retirement benefits that are reduced at a specified age, for example, age 65, the CRA will consider the additional amount of benefit temporarily payable prior to this specified age to be a bridge benefit and acceptable only if the limits specified above and in ¶1726 are not exceeded. An example of this is a plan with a direct CPP offset where the offset is not applied until age 65 even though the member may retire earlier. The difference between the pre-age 65 and the post-age 65 benefits is considered to be the bridge benefit.

Note that while a bridge benefit may provide a temporary amount of benefit based on the amount of benefit to which a member would have been entitled from government-sponsored plans had he or she actually been age 65 at the time of retirement, this does not prohibit a member from applying for early payment of government benefits prior to age 65.

The Regulations contain a cross-plan restriction in respect of bridging benefits. The restriction, which is intended to prevent payment of an inappropriately large amount of bridging benefit, calls for the coordination of bridging benefits under all defined benefit provisions of an RPP and of other RPPs of the same employer or of associated employers. A member may, however, receive more than one maximum bridging benefit where he or she is receiving the additional bridging benefit from an RPP (or RPPs) sponsored by a completely independent employer.

¶1726 Combined Maximum Lifetime Retirement Benefits and Bridging Benefits

In addition to the limits on benefits discussed at ¶1710, another restriction applies to the total of a member's lifetime retirement benefit and bridging benefit in respect of pensionable service after 1991. A member's total retirement benefit payable before the member reaches age 65 may not exceed:

- the defined benefit dollar limit for the year of pension commencement (i.e., $2,494.44 for 2010) multiplied by pensionable service; plus
- 25% of the three-year average of the YMPE* (i.e., the maximum CPP benefit) multiplied by pensionable service (maximum 35 years) and divided by 35,

indexed from the year of commencement to the particular year in line with increases in the CPI.

Note that the formula is the same regardless of the actual age at retirement. In other words, the defined benefit limit is not reduced in the event of retirement prior to age 60.

This restriction severely limits the bridging benefits that may be paid to highly paid members whose lifetime retirement benefits are close to or at the maximum permitted, as well as other lower-income members with relatively short service. For an individual whose lifetime retirement benefit is at the defined benefit limit, the portion of the bridging benefit attributable to OAS benefits, for example, simply cannot be paid. Further, since the CPP/QPP component is spread over a full 35 years of pensionable service, in some cases, the maximum CPP/QPP component of the bridging benefit may not be able to be paid, even if the RPP were to provide for this to be paid after 10 years of pensionable service, in accordance with the maximum described at ¶ 1725. Accordingly, a highly paid individual needs 35 years or more of pensionable service before a "full" bridging benefit may be paid and, even in this case, the bridging benefit may only be based on CPP/QPP benefits, with no OAS benefits permitted.

In situations where this combined maximum applies, the result, from a practical and administrative point of view, is that the bridge benefit no longer follows a formula that relates to CPP/QPP or OAS benefits. The bridging benefit is simply the combined maximum benefit less the pre-age 65 lifetime benefit payable.

The restriction is not as severe for grandfathered plans, as discussed at ¶ 1727.

---

* Note that this formula appears to resemble the formula for determining the maximum CPP/QPP benefit; however, when the maximum CPP/QPP benefits were changed to be based on a five-year average of the YMPE, this formula was not correspondingly adjusted and the three-year YMPE average is still used.

¶1727 Transition Rule for Bridging Benefits

Some grandfathered plans may have contained bridging benefits for pre-reform service acceptable under Information Circular 72-13R8 rules which, however, exceed the current requirements. In some cases, an individual may have already been eligible for a full bridging benefit under the "old" rules, which would not currently satisfy the above restrictions as set out at ¶1725 and ¶1726.

The Regulations provide that, if a member was fully vested in a bridging benefit under a grandfathered plan on December 31, 1991 (i.e., the member had satisfied any age and/or service requirements under the plan), his or her benefit is exempt from the above rules, assuming the bridging benefit satisfied the old rules contained in the Circular. The old rules indicated that the bridging benefit must be "reasonable in the circumstances", which was generally interpreted to mean that a full bridging benefit (consisting of CPP/QPP plus OAS) could be paid to a member with 10 years of pensionable service.

In addition, under the old rules, bridge benefits could be based on the maximum benefits payable under the CPP/QPP, rather than the actual or a reasonable estimate of the actual amount an individual would be entitled to receive under the government pension plan.

In such cases, where pre-reform bridging benefits exceeded the limits imposed by the current legislation, plan sponsors needed to apply for a waiver from the Minister of National Revenue exempting the pre-reform benefits of the plan from paragraph 8503(2)(*b*) of the Regulations. If a wavier has not been granted, the grandfathered plan must state, with an effective date of January 1, 1992, that the bridging benefit will not exceed the amount of government pension benefit to which the member is entitled for all years of pensionable service.

Where a member of a grandfathered benefit with a pre-existing bridging benefit had not satisfied all eligibility requirements for that bridging benefit on December 31, 1991, the bridging benefit limit can be modified and applied as a weighted average of the old rules and the current rules in proportion to the member's pensionable service before and after January 1, 1992. In this situation, the maximum bridging benefit is to be determined as the sum of:

- the bridging benefit payable under the previous plan rules multiplied by pre-1992 pensionable service and divided by total pensionable service; and
- the maximum bridging benefit determined in accordance with the current rules, but based only on post-1991 pensionable service.

The limit on combined lifetime retirement benefits and bridging benefits discussed as ¶1726 only applies to lifetime retirement benefits and bridging benefits for post-1991 pensionable service.

¶1730 Postponed Retirement Benefits

Pension benefits may continue to accrue under an RPP after the member has attained the plan's normal retirement age. However, no further benefits can accrue after the end of the calendar year in which the member attains age 71 and payment of accrued benefits must commence by that date. The 1996 federal Budget reduced the age 71 limit to age 69; however, the 2007 federal Budget increased the age limit back to age 71. A later commencement date may be accepted by the Minister of National Revenue, provided that no benefits accrue after the end of the calendar year in which the member attains age 71, and no adjustment is made to the pension to reflect the delay in payment beyond that date.

Benefits that have accrued to age 65, however, may be increased on an actuarially equivalent (or less favourable) basis to take account of the period of postponement of payments after age 65 and prior to the end of the year in which the member attains age 71. In this case, the limits on lifetime retirement pensions, set out at ¶1710 and ¶1715, are applied when determining the pension payable at age 65. Thus, the actual pension payable at the postponed pension commencement age may exceed those limits because of the actuarial increase that is permitted after age 65.

¶1735 Maximum Accrual Rate

Where a member's pension benefit is dependent on the member's earnings, the benefit accrual rate for each year of pensionable service is limited to a maximum of 2% on any portion of pensionable earnings. This is true even in a career average plan whose accrual rate is presently in excess of 2% but whose overall benefit is still limited to 2% of final average earnings per year of pensionable service.

For example, a benefit formula which provides that a pension will be payable that is equal to 50% of the member's contributions will be subject to the maximum accrual rate limit if the member contributions are based on a percentage of earnings. In such a plan, therefore, if members make contributions to the RPP based on a formula of 5% of pensionable earnings, the benefit formula would not be permitted, as it would effectively result in a benefit accrual rate of 2.5%.

This rule is required to integrate properly with the PA-based retirement savings system under which the PA calculation does not distinguish between a career average plan and a final average plan.

The one exception to this accrual rate restriction was introduced in 2003. Effective August 2003, the benefit accrual rate for a plan member who is a firefighter may be as high as 2.33% if the benefit is integrated with the CPP/QPP. Effective January 1, 2005, this exception was extended to include members of all public safety occupations who are members of plans where the benefits are integrated with the CPP/QPP.

¶1740 Permissible Distributions and Transfers Between Plans

In addition to placing limits on the payment of lifetime retirement and bridging benefits, the legislation specifically outlines other permissible types of distributions from an RPP, including limits on payments out of an RPP and, more particularly, controls on the tax-free transfer of funds.

¶1741 Permissible Distributions

The following distributions may be made from an RPP:

- payment of benefits in accordance with the plan as registered, including a transfer on behalf of a member to an RRSP or another RPP (subject to certain limits, as discussed at ¶1742 and ¶1743) and a payment to a member's spouse on marriage breakdown;
- transfer of property (subject to certain conditions) from a defined benefit RPP to another defined benefit RPP (such as in the case where benefits are transferred from one to the other under a reciprocal agreement or where a plan is split into two or more plans) or surplus transfer from a defined benefit or defined contribution RPP to a defined contribution RPP to satisfy existing or future employer contribution obligations under the defined contribution plan;
- return of contributions to avoid revocation of the plan's registration, as discussed further at ¶1785 under number 9, "Requirement for Reduction of Benefits or Return of Contributions to Avoid Deregistration";
- refund of member contributions (with or without interest) pursuant to an amendment under which future member contributions are reduced or eliminated;
- refund of an individual's share of actuarial surplus;
- refund under a defined contribution RPP (such as a forfeited amount following a non-vested termination) to an employer; and
- a payment of a single amount that the plan is required to make because of the *Pension Benefits Standards Act, 1985* or a similar

law of a province, where the single amount is not transferred directly to another RPP, a RRSP, or a RRIF; this permissible distribution allows, for example, the payment of the Quebec 50% rule refund in the form of a lump-sum.

Other rules apply to the determination of amounts transferable to a defined contribution RPP or RRSP in respect of an individual, as noted at ¶1742 and ¶1743.

Generally, a person's share of an actuarial surplus is not transferable to another tax-sheltered vehicle. The only way to create an amount that could be transferred in respect of surplus is to use that surplus to provide additional lifetime retirement benefits and then to transfer the value of those benefits. To the extent that benefits in respect of pre-1990 service can be improved, "transfer room" is created for an individual and no RRSP contribution room is lost. However, as noted at ¶1746, Registered Plans Directorate Newsletter 99-1 outlines restrictions on the ability of a plan sponsor to improve pre-1990 benefits if this would result in a disproportionate amount of benefits being provided for pre-1990 service compared to post-1990 service. Thus, these proportionality conditions could affect the employer's ability to improve these benefits if the service was not credited beforehand or one of the other exceptions in the newsletter does not apply. If the improvement is in respect of post-1989 service (for example, where a member does not have any pre-1990 service), a PSPA may be created. Refer to Chapter 10 for further discussion on the subject of PSPAs.

In the administration of any defined benefit plan, there are sometimes situations where pension payments do not commence on time or where the pension has been underpaid in error and the plan sponsor wants to rectify these situations by making a retroactive lump-sum payment. The Regulations do not specifically allow for retroactive lump-sum payments to be made in such situations as the payment of these lump sums would violate the rules in two ways: the equal and periodic requirement, as described at ¶1675 and these corrective lump-sum payments are not permissible distributions in accordance with Regulation 8502(*d*), as described above. Nevertheless, for practical reasons, the Registered Plans Directorate has permitted requests to be made for one-time lump-sum payments in such situations and approval to make the lump-sum payments are granted on a case by case basis.

The Registered Plans Directorate Newsletter 09-1 sets out a more streamlined process that now permits administrators of defined benefit plans to make the necessary retroactive payments in certain situations without requiring pre-approval. Instead, the administrator files an annual report setting out a list of any such payments made along with details on the specific members to whom such payments were made and the reason for making the retroactive payment. The administrator is free to select any filing date as the annual reporting date.

Acceptable lump-sums that can be paid in this manner include the following:

- missed payments that otherwise should have been paid as of the member's retirement date (whether early, later, or normal retirement);
- catch-up payments following the approval by an provincial authority to restore benefits previously reduced;
- benefit underpayments caused by involuntary administrative errors or systemic problems in the calculation of the original benefits; and
- lump-sum payments to the member's surviving spouse or beneficiary that meet the above two criteria.

Note that applying interest to the outstanding payments is optional. If interest is applied, the rate used must be "reasonable", meaning either the rate of return on the pension fund or a rate determined in accordance with CANSIM series V122515, which is the rate typically applied to employee required contributions.

The details to be included in the annual report are as follows:

- member's name;
- member's date of birth;
- member's social insurance number;
- member's retirement date;
- deferred member's date of termination of employment (if applicable);
- period of missed payments;
- periodic pension amount;
- interest payable and rate used (if applied);
- date of lump-sum payment;
- total lump-sum retroactive amount paid; and
- reason for the delay in pension commencement.

The Registered Plans Directorate has noted that if the administrator has concerns as to whether a particular situation will not fit within the criteria where the lump-sum can be paid immediately, then the administrator may write to the Directorate with the information set out above in order to request confirmation in advance.

¶1742 Transfers Between Plans

The rules related to the transfer of assets between plans govern several different types of transfers, the most significant being the transfer from a defined benefit RPP to an RRSP, a DPSP, or a defined contribution RPP, which is addressed at ¶1743. Non-compliance with the transfer rules will be cause for revocation of the plan's registration.

Transfers are also permitted in the following situations:

- A transfer from one defined contribution plan (or provision) to another defined contribution plan (or provision), a DPSP, or RRSP — there is no limit on the amount that may be transferred.
- A transfer from a defined contribution plan (or provision) to a defined benefit plan (or provision) — this transfer would take place, for instance, where past service benefits are being provided under the defined benefit plan. The transfer of funds can occur to the extent that it does not exceed the cost of the defined benefits being provided.
- A transfer from one defined benefit plan to another defined benefit plan, where defined benefits become provided under the second plan to the individual.
- A transfer of a lump sum from one RPP to another or to an RRSP on behalf of a member's spouse or former spouse, pursuant to a court order or written property division agreement on marriage breakdown.
- A transfer of pre-1991 member contributions, including related interest, to an RRSP or a defined contribution RPP. (The rationale for allowing the continued tax sheltering of these contributions is the fact that pre-1991 member contributions generally served to reduce RRSP contribution room under the old system.) The transfer of post-1990 member contributions falls under the rules described at ¶1743.
- A transfer of a lump-sum death benefit payable to a member's spouse to an RRSP or a defined contribution RPP. A spouse who receives the death benefit through the member's estate may transfer in the same manner. Such transfers on behalf of beneficiaries other than the member's spouse are not permitted; however, a child may receive some tax relief through the purchase of a pension payable to age 18 in respect of a benefit payable on the death of a parent or grandparent.

In this paragraph and elsewhere in the book, a transfer to an RRSP may be read as including a transfer to a RRIF, subject, of course, to federal or provincial minimum standards legislation which may require that the transfer be made to a related locked-in arrangement.

RRSPs and RRIFs and their locked-in counterparts are discussed further in Chapter 14.

¶1743 Transfers — Defined Benefit to Defined Contribution or RRSP

The amount that may be transferred from a defined benefit plan (or provision) to an RRSP, a DPSP, or a defined contribution RPP is limited through the maximum transfer value factors. Generally, the amount eligible for transfer is equal to the amount of post-age 65 lifetime retirement benefit that is foregone or surrendered (the "normalized pension") multiplied by the maximum transfer value factor.

In addition, the following restrictions apply:

- actuarial surplus may not be transferred (unless the surplus is appropriately converted into plan benefits, as discussed at ¶1741); and
- the transfer value may not exceed the present value of the foregone benefits, determined using reasonable actuarial assumptions (i.e., assumptions that are acceptable to the Minister of National Revenue and determined using generally accepted actuarial principles). As discussed at ¶1785 (refer to number 12, "Indexing Included in Commuted Values"), this may include the value of future *ad hoc* pension increases.

The maximum transfer value factors are as follows:

Attained Age	Factor	Attained Age	Factor	Attained Age	Factor
Under 50	9.0	65	12.4	81	7.0
50	9.4	66	12.0	82	6.7
51	9.6	67	11.7	83	6.4
52	9.8	68	11.3	84	6.1
53	10.0	69	11.0	85	5.8
54	10.2	70	10.6	86	5.5
55	10.4	71	10.3	87	5.2
56	10.6	72	10.1	88	4.9
57	10.8	73	9.8	89	4.7
58	11.0	74	9.4	90	4.4
59	11.3	75	9.1	91	4.2
60	11.5	76	8.7	92	3.9
61	11.7	77	8.4	93	3.7
62	12.0	78	8.0	94	3.5
63	12.2	79	7.7	95	3.2
64	12.4	80	7.3	96 or over	3.0

Between ages 49 and 64, these factors are to be interpolated, based on the individual's exact age; otherwise, the factors are to be based on the individual's attained age.

The rules for determining the normalized pension for the purpose of determining "transfer room" are virtually the same as those described in Chapter 7 (e.g., the adjustment for variations in the form of benefit described at ¶745 is used both for PA and maximum transfer value purposes). In other words, whatever adjustments one would make to an individual's benefit accrual for PA purposes, one would also make to determine the amount of lifetime retirement benefit used in determining the maximum transfer value.

For example, assume that an individual who terminates service has a "normalized" pension of $20,000 and that the commuted value of the pension at the termination age of 61 is $246,000. Based on the above maximum transfer value factors, the maximum amount that may be transferred (to an RRSP or a defined contribution RPP) is $234,000 ($20,000 × 11.7). Thus, in this case, the individual could transfer $234,000 and the remaining $12,000 would, according to these rules, have to be paid to the individual in cash. Thus, the amount of tax deferral in respect of this transaction is limited, and the individual must either pay tax on the amount that is non-transferable or, provided the plan so allows, commute only part of the benefit and leave part (as a bridge benefit) to be payable to age 65 (since a bridging benefit is not a lifetime retirement benefit and therefore does not affect the calculation of the maximum transfer value).

Although in most cases, the benefit transferred would be fully locked-in under minimum standards legislation, most of the minimum standards jurisdictions made changes to legislation to permit any amounts in excess of that which can be transferred based on the maximum transfer value factors to be unlocked and paid in cash.

Where it is not practical or desirable to unlock excess amounts, there are two alternatives for amounts that cannot be transferred.

- Transfer all or a portion of the excess directly to the individual's RRSP; however, it is taken into income on the individual's tax return and then can be deducted from taxable income only to the extent that the individual has available RRSP contribution room. Also, because this "transfer" is treated like an ordinary RRSP contribution, the amount transferred may be sufficiently large that it causes the 1% per month penalty tax to be payable (on non-deductible RRSP contributions in excess of the lifetime limit of $2,000, as discussed at ¶435).

- Keep the non-transferable benefits in the plan and pay it out at early retirement as a bridging benefit, provided the maximum bridging benefits as set out at ¶ 1725 are not violated.

Note the following additional comments with respect to amounts that may be transferred:

- If the member is entitled to a "50% rule" excess member contribution, as discussed at ¶ 1314, or a lump-sum representing Quebec's additional benefit, as discussed at ¶ 1319, they can only be transferred to the extent that the total commuted value, inclusive of all ancillaries, falls within the maximum transfer value (other than the exception regarding pre-1991 50% rule refunds mentioned at the end of this section).

- Suppose, in the example above, where $12,000 was unavailable for transfer, that this was a contributory plan and that some or all of the $12,000 could be attributable to a "50% rule" excess member contribution. As mentioned at ¶ 1742, pre-1991 member contributions (with interest) may be transferred to an RRSP without limitation. Using this rule, that portion of excess member contributions that directly results from applying the minimum standards 50% rule to pre-1991 benefits may be transferred in addition to the maximum amount that may be transferred on behalf of lifetime retirement benefits. This is confirmed in Registered Plans Directorate Newsletter 98-2: the 50% rule excess member contributions in respect of pre-1991 service can be transferred over and above the limitations set out under this section.

- There is one further side effect of the connection that exists between the amount of lifetime retirement benefits being surrendered and the amount that may be made available for transfer to an RRSP. The ability to transfer excess member contributions is directly related to whether the member chooses to transfer the value of his or her deferred pension to an RRSP, since, if a deferred pension is elected, no lifetime retirement benefit is commuted and therefore the maximum transfer value is zero. However, as noted above, pre-1991 excess contributions may be transferred regardless. It is important to highlight this distinction in any communication material provided to a terminating member.

- Where the transfer is being made to the RRSP or defined contribution RPP of the spouse of a member payable as a death benefit in respect of a member, the amount that may be transferred is not limited by the maximum transfer value factors.

- The lifetime benefit "foregone" for the purposes of determining the maximum transfer value for a member does not include any benefits paid already, or to be paid, to the member's spouse or former spouse, pursuant to a court order or written property division agreement on marriage breakdown.

- Minimum standards legislation provides that, if the defined benefit plan is less than fully solvent, that the administrator may choose to transfer out a commuted value to the extent that it is funded and to pay the remaining portion of the transfer value within the following five years. The maximum transfer value determined at the time the initial payment is transferred out is based on the proportion of benefit paid at that time. For example, if the plan has a solvency ratio of 80% and the normalized pension for the purpose of determining the maximum transfer value is $15,000, then the lifetime retirement benefit forgone at that point is $12,000 and this is multiplied by the relevant maximum transfer value factor to determine the maximum transfer for the initial payment. Subsequent payments are each subject to a separate maximum transfer value test at each payment date, based on the amount of lifetime retirement benefit being paid at that point and using the factor based on the member's age at the subsequent payment date.

- The maximum lifetime retirement benefit, as described in detail at ¶1510, permits the maximum pension payable at retirement to a member to be based on the defined benefit limit in effect at the member's retirement date. For a member with high earnings who is terminating prior to retirement, this permits the commuted value of the retirement benefit payable to the member to take into account a projection of the defined benefit limit to the member's anticipated retirement age. However, since the rules for determining the maximum transfer value require a "normalized pension" approach which assumes that the member is retiring at age 65 at the end of the current year, projection of the defined benefit limit cannot be taken into account and the maximum transfer value will be based on the current defined benefit limit.

The form that facilitates the direct transfer of assets from an RPP to an RRSP (or another RPP) is the T2151 — Record of Direct Transfer of a "Single Amount". Although the CRA has indicated that the use of the form is not mandatory, it may be convenient to use it since it contains certain certifications that the CRA might look for in the event of an audit. Also, the T2151 form mentions locking-in under the applicable minimum standards legislation; however, a separate minimum standards compliant form should continue to be used to verify the locking-in requirements of transferred funds.

'inal note regarding the maximum transfer value factors is that, ..ctor of 9 used to determine pension adjustments (PAs), these factors are static. They have been based on assumptions consistent with those underlying the factor of 9. However, actual commuted values do fluctuate, mainly due to the influence of prevailing interest rates. When interest rates are low, commuted values are relatively high. Thus, the amount of pension that may be commuted will vary over time, whereas the maximum amount that can be transferred to an RRSP remains constant.

¶1744 Use of Registered Pension Assets To Purchase Annuity

Minimum standards legislation typically permits terminating plan members to elect portability, which generally means one of the following:

- transfer the commuted value to an RRSP;
- transfer the commuted value to another RPP; or
- transfer the funds to an insurance company for the purchase of a deferred or immediate annuity.

Rules setting out the treatment of transfers for the first two portability choices described above are set out in ¶1742 and ¶1743.

However, the *Income Tax Act* (Canada) does not permit the direct transfer from an RPP to an insurance company for the purchase of an annuity unless the annuity being purchased is considered not "materially different" than the benefits that would have been provided to the individual under the RPP. In other words, the annuity should provide the individual the same annual amount in the same form as the individual would have received had the individual drawn a pension from the plan. If the annuity purchased is materially different, then there could be significant tax consequences to the individual as the individual would have been considered to have received a distribution from an RPP and would be required to include the full amount of the annuity cost in income.

The taxation issue is avoided if the individual first transfers the commuted value to an RRSP and then purchases the annuity from the RRSP; however, the maximum transfer value limits, as set out at ¶1743, will still apply.

The Registered Plans Directorate has not provided any definitive guidance as to what features of the plan benefit must be preserved or what deviations from the plan benefit would be acceptable in order for the purchased annuity to be considered as not materially different from the plan benefit. However, the Registered Plans Directorate does acknowledge that often an individual will not be able to purchase an exact replicate of the pension that could have been paid from the plan, especially in the case of a plan that offers indexed benefits as there is only a very small market for indexed annuities in Canada.

Further, depending on market conditions at the time of the annuity purchase, it is possible that the available commuted value could be less than the premium required to purchase an exact replica of the plan benefit. In such cases either the plan sponsor could make up the difference or the annuity provisions are adjusted downward, that is, the plan member suffers a loss. However, this treatment may be contrary to minimum standards requirements. Under other market conditions, the commuted value may have been greater than the premium required to purchase the annuity. In those cases, an unintended windfall will have occurred and there is no mechanism for the excess to be refunded to the member.

Thus, the determination of whether a difference between what the member is entitled to under the plan and the annuity purchase is material can only be made after consideration of the specific circumstances of each case and after a quote for the annuity purchase has been obtained.

¶1745 Pensionable Service, Leaves of Absence, and Periods of Reduced Pay

Additional limits on the benefits under a defined benefit RPP are created by controlling the types of service, including leaves of absence, in respect of which benefits may be provided, as explained below.

¶1746 Pensionable Service

Lifetime retirement benefits may be provided in respect of the following periods:

- a period during which a member is employed in Canada by and receives remuneration from a participating employer or a predecessor employer to such an employer;
- an eligible period of temporary absence;
- a period of disability following a period of employment (but not for a connected person); or
- a period of pensionable service under another RPP, as long as the individual has ceased to be a member of that other plan (this provision accommodates transfers of service under a reciprocal transfer agreement or portability arrangement);

- a period of employment in Canada that was a waiting period for participation in another RPP;
- a period acceptable to the Minister of National Revenue throughout which the member is employed outside Canada (see ¶ 1755).

Note that only periods of service prior to the end of the calendar year in which the member turns age 71 can be included in pensionable service.

Often the nature of an industry will determine the way in which one full year of full-time service is accrued under the terms of the RPP. Typically, pensionable service is measured as the fractional period of service during which the member was employed or is based on completed calendar months during the year. It is common in unionized groups for a full year of pensionable service to be credited based on working a certain number of hours in a year (such as 1,800 or 2,000). If a certain industry sector, such as a trade, has a four-day workweek, this could be considered as full-time accrual of pensionable service. Conversely, if an industry sector has a five-day workweek, and an individual works four days a week, 80% of a full year would be accrued over a calendar year.

Where pensionable service is based on hours worked with an employer, and a set number of hours are used to determine whether a year of pensionable service has been accrued, this full-time number of hours must be reasonable given the circumstances. The Registered Plans Directorate would not, for example, accept one day a week or one day a month as being a full-time accrual of pensionable service.

In no event should the RPP provisions permit the accrual of more than one year of service in any calendar year.

Also, as discussed in greater detail at ¶ 125 and ¶ 1775, a member who is in receipt of a pension under a defined benefit RPP cannot also continue to accrue pension benefits (i.e., cannot continue to accumulate defined benefit pensionable service) under that same RPP, or the RPP of a related employer, unless the member has entered into a phased retirement agreement with the employer. The rules, however, do not restrict an individual from accruing pensionable service under one RPP while in receipt of a defined benefit pension from the RPP of another unrelated employer.

If an employee is notified of an upcoming termination of employment and the employee receives termination pay, pensionable service may be credited in respect of the severance period provided the employment continues during that period. One common indicator of this would be payment of the termination pay in the form of salary continuance and not as a retiring allowance. A retiring allowance is broadly defined as a payment in respect of a loss of office or employment or a payment upon or after retirement in recognition of long service. In certain circumstances, part of a retiring allowance may be able to be transferred tax-free to an RRSP (refer to ¶ 450 for further details). Regardless of whether any of the retiring allowance is transferred to an RRSP, none of it is permitted to be included in pensionable earnings for purposes of an RPP. Therefore, no additional pensionable service can accrue in respect of this form of severance.

However, if the severance is paid in the form of salary continuance for a period of time, say for the duration of the pre-termination leave with pay period, it may be possible to continue to accrue pension benefits in respect of the severance. In this case, the employer should be consistent in treating it as a period of employment (the payments reported as income from employment, withholding CPP contributions, Employment Insurance premiums, etc.) It should also be noted that generally employment standards legislation requires that the period of advance notice of the termination (the notice period) be included in service for most benefit purposes.

Members may only accrue service with a participating employer. However, a plan can recognize service with a predecessor employer and certain service with a former employer. A predecessor employer is an employer which has sold, assigned, or otherwise disposed of all or part of its business to another employer.

The rules regarding pensionable service permit employees who transfer employment between unrelated employers to have the service accrued under the former employer's RPP (Plan A) recognized under the terms of the new employer's RPP (Plan B).

There are a couple of scenarios where this type of situation could occur.

The first is where there is a corresponding transfer of assets and liabilities from Plan A to Plan B.

In other sale situations, there is no transfer of assets and liabilities from one RPP to another RPP. Instead, the benefit under the former employer's RPP (Plan A) is frozen and remains in Plan A. The benefit in the new employer's RPP (Plan B) is determined by calculating a benefit using all service, both pre-sale and post-sale, and the offsetting frozen benefit remaining in Plan B. This is commonly referred to as a "wraparound" benefit. In such a situation, Employer A is still considered to be a predecessor employer even though there has been no transfer of assets and liabilities.

As an alternative purchase and sale situation, sometimes there is no transfer of assets and liabilities from Plan A to Plan B, nor is there a wraparound type of benefit provided. Although Employer A is still considered a predecessor employer, pensionable service under Plan A is not recognized in any way under Plan B and therefore Plan A pensionable service is not considered to be recognized under Plan B. Note, however, that this does not prohibit Plan B from recognizing continuous service under Plan A for vesting and other eligibility purposes. In fact, most minimum standards jurisdictions would require that pre-sale service be recognized for eligibility purposes in Plan B (as well as post-sale service being recognized for eligibility purposes under Plan A).

A related situation in the case of a final average earnings plan is the ability of the employer to use pensionable earnings with the former employer in calculating the final average earnings in respect of the current plan. Generally, if the member's pensionable service includes service with the predecessor employer, then it is acceptable to use pensionable earnings from the predecessor employer in determining final average earnings. In the third sale scenario described above (where there is no recognition of Plan A's service in Plan B), pensionable earnings under Plan A could not be used to determine the final average earnings under Plan B, and therefore both pensionable service and earnings records start at the time of transfer to the new employer (with the exception being the use of continuous service under Plan A for eligibility purposes in order to meet the requirements of minimum standards legislation).

The converse is also restricted: Plan A is not permitted to recognize future earnings under Plan B, since Plan B does not recognize service under Plan A. In this case, Plan A is restricted to using earnings up to the transfer date, possibly indexed in accordance with increases in the average wage.

The Department of Finance has indicated that there is to be an amendment to the Regulations to clarify the use of predecessor employer earnings. Until the amendment is released, the Registered Plans Directorate will permit RPPs to be administered as described above.

Note, however, that in the case of an RTA, for example, where an individual has ceased to be a member of an RPP and has given up entitlement to pensionable service under the RPP in order to be credited with this same service under another RPP, it is not possible to use pensionable earnings under the former RPP when determining the benefits under the current RPP since the former employer in this situation is not considered to be a predecessor employer or a participating employer. In this case, the pensionable earnings used in the current plan can only be those earnings in respect of the employer who participates in the current RPP.

Generally a portability arrangement provides that where an individual has ceased to be a member of an RPP, pensionable service earned under that RPP may be recognized as pensionable service under another RPP. However, there is a conflict that arises in minimum standards jurisdictions that permit the transfer of assets under the portability arrangement to be made over a five-year period if the assets are transferring from an RPP that has a transfer ratio of less than 100% at the time of the transfer. In this situation, only a portion of the assets transfers initially (based on the transfer ratio) and as a result, the member has not fully ceased membership in the RPP yet. Since membership in the former RPP has not ceased, the Regulations do not permit any of the transferring service to be recognized until such time as the individual is no longer a member in the former plan (i.e., once all of the assets have been transferred).

As a final comment regarding RTAs, the tax rules permit eligible service to include a period of employment after January 1, 1991 with a former employer, subject to certain restrictions. To be eligible, the period of employment must be a period during which the member accrued benefits under the former employer's defined benefit pension plan, or during which contributions were made on the member's behalf by the former employer to a money purchase pension plan. A further condition is that the individual must no longer be a member of the former employer's pension plan, i.e., he/she must have terminated non-vested or transferred out a commuted value. This will allow, in some circumstances, the granting of a past service benefit for pensionable service with a former employer as far back as 1991 and to permit assets that have been transferred from the former RPP into a LIRA account (or other tax-sheltered retirement saving vehicle) to be transferred into the new employer's RPP to fund the service being provided. Even if no assets are transferred into the new RPP in respect of former employer service, double-dipping is prevented by the PSPA rules (as described at ¶ 1055) which ensure that service is only credited to the extent that the PSPA rules permit and to the extent that there is available RRSP contribution room. As discussed later in this section, pre-1991 service can only be credited if the amount necessary to fund the pre-reform benefit is transferred directly from an RRSP, DPSP, or another RPP.

Pre-1991 Service

The ability to provide benefits in respect of pre-1991 (pre-1992 for grandfathered plans) service continues to be governed by the rules outlined in paragraphs 8(e), (i), (ii), (iii), (iv), (v) and (vi) of Information Circular 72-13R8.

However, the RPP must indicate what, if any, pre-reform service is being included as eligible service. Additionally, where pre-reform service is credited after 1988 for new plans and after 1991 for grandfathered plans, this service also must comply with the eligible service requirements outlined in the Circular (or with the terms of the RPP if these terms are more restrictive).

Note that if members are allowed to commute pre-reform benefits in the manner described at ¶1785 (refer to number 11, "Payment of lump-sums and Commutation of Benefits"), the plan must state that the period of pre-reform service may not be credited again under that plan or under a successor employer's plan. Alternatively, the plan must state that if, at a later date, the member wishes to buy back that service, the service can only be credited again if the the amount necessary to fund the pre-reform benefit is transferred directly from an RRSP, DPSP, or another RPP.

Pre-1990 Proportionality Conditions

Initially under the tax reform rules, the strategy of improving pre-1990 benefits by crediting additional eligible pre-1990 service had been popular with plan sponsors since the tax reform rules were introduced, since such improvements do not give rise to PSPA and therefore do not impact on members' RRSP contribution room. However, the Registered Plans Directorate Newsletter 99-1 sets out limits regarding the extent to which pre-1990 benefits can be improved, in order to prevent a disproportionate amount of benefit being provided in respect of pre-1990 pensionable service, compared to post-1989.

The proportionality conditions focus primarily on those plans that are established exclusively to provide key employees with a fixed-dollar amount of pre-1990 past service benefits, without a corresponding commitment to provide ongoing pension benefits.

Under the proportionality condition, lifetime retirement benefits can only be provided or improved under a defined benefit provision in respect of pre-1990 service, if:

- the present value of all lifetime retirement benefits in respect of pre-1990 periods (other than certain lifetime retirement benefits that are excluded, as discussed below) do not exceed the present value of the lifetime retirement benefits provided to the individual under the provision before the improvement was granted, in respect of post-1989 periods; and
- the CRA has given written notice to the plan administrator that the lifetime retirement benefits are acceptable.

The present value is measured as at the date the benefit improvements are effective, based on the relative amounts of pre-1990 and post-1989 past service benefits.

There are three possible exceptions to the requirement to apply this proportionality condition:

1. It does not apply if the plan has at least 50 active members in the year in which the additional benefits are provided and the improvement is offered to all plan members.

2. It does not apply if the plan has less than 50 active members in the year in which the additional benefits are provided, the improvement is offered to all plan members, and the plan is not primarily for the benefit of key employees. Approval in writing is required from the CRA. For these purposes, key employees are considered to be connected persons or persons whose income for the year exceeds 2.5 times the YMPE (i.e., $118,000 for 2010).

3. It does not apply if the lifetime retirement benefits are considered "excluded". A defined benefit provision is considered "excluded" if any of the following apply:

   - The lifetime retirement benefits were provided under plan terms acceptable to the CRA before May 15, 1998, as long as the individual was a member of the plan on or before May 15, 1998.

   - The lifetime retirement benefits were provided under plan terms submitted to the CRA before May 15, 1998, as long as the individual was a member of the plan on or before May 15, 1998, and the plan complies with paragraph 18(b) and section 19 of Information Circular 72-13R8. Paragraph 18(b) of the Circular states that plans established to provide only past service benefits are not acceptable and section 19 sets out conditions generally requiring a reasonable proportionality of past service benefits to past service accrued.

   - The lifetime retirement benefits are exempted from the rules set out at ¶1715 restricting pre-1990 benefits to no more than two-thirds of the defined benefit limit.

   - The period in respect of which the lifetime retirement benefits are provided is a period in respect of which lifetime retirement benefits that were not subject to these proportionality conditions were previously provided to the individual under a defined benefit provision.

Plan administrators must be able to submit to the CRA sufficient information for the CRA to be able to judge whether the conditions have been met in order to be able to provide the pre-1990 benefits. Such information includes detailed calculations by individuals for the present value test specifying the years of service for which the benefits are being provided. As a minimum, this information is required to be included in the triennial actuarial valuation report when requesting approval for the employer contributions. The CRA has indicated that their approval of the valuation report, and the crediting of pre-1990 lifetime retirement benefits, will be given at the same time.

It is not expected that these proportionality rules will significantly impact benefits being provided under typical defined benefit plans and it will still be possible for a plan sponsor to make pre-1990 plan service improvements. As noted earlier, these conditions were introduced as a type of anti-avoidance rule.

One further change, introduced as part of pension reform, was to allow as eligible service a period of employment after January 1, 1991 with a former employer, subject to certain restrictions. To be eligible, the period of employment must be a period during which the member accrued benefits under the former employer's defined benefit pension plan, or during which contributions were made on the member's behalf by the former employer to a money purchase pension plan. A further condition is that the individual must no longer be a member of the former employer's pension plan, i.e., he/she must have terminated non-vested or transferred out a commuted value. This will allow, in some circumstances, granting of a past service benefit for service with a former employer as far back as 1991. Double-dipping is prevented by the PSPA rules: such past service benefit can only be granted if there is room to report a PSPA.

¶1747 Leaves of Absence and Periods of Reduced Pay

Some of the rules outlined at ¶1625 for money purchase plans apply equally under a defined benefit RPP.

As an example, consider an employee who is on a temporary leave of absence for five months and, as a result, expected compensation of $75,000 for the year is reduced by $31,250 to $43,750. Suppose that the individual belongs to a defined benefit plan with an annual benefit accrual rate of 1.5% of compensation and that the plan provides for automatic continued accrual of benefits during this particular leave of absence. The PA in respect of the entire year of benefit accrual is $9,525 ($75,000 × 0.015 × 9 - $600). Based on actual earnings, the PA limit would be $7,875 (18% of $43,750), but this limit is increased by virtue of the prescribed compensation of $31,250. As in the example at ¶1625, the additional compensation fraction is 0.4167, leaving 4.5833 years for future leaves of absence and periods of reduced pay (assuming this leave was the first to be tracked under the current rules after January 1, 1991).

At ¶1625, the rules are set out regarding when contributions may be made to a defined contribution RPP based on the level of earnings that existed prior to a reduction in pay. First, the period must comply with the definition of "eligible period of temporary absence" or "eligible period of reduced pay". Second, the "prescribed compensation" mechanism is used to determine how much of the five-year/three-year limit is used up by a particular period of absence or reduced pay — once the five-year/three-year limit has been reached, no further periods of absence may be treated as pensionable service with that employer, and no further contributions may be made based on the amount of the decrease in pay unless the plan's contribution formula is increased (as noted at ¶ 1625).

However, the rules operate differently for a defined benefit RPP. Any period of absence that complies with the CRA's definition of pensionable service (see ¶ 1746) may be included when determining credited service for benefit calculation purposes. The five-year/three-year limit serves to determine the portion of the benefit accruals that can be credited on a current service basis. Once the five-year/three-year limit has been used up, it would be possible to credit additional pensionable service for a temporary leave of absence on a past service basis, subject to PSPA reporting instead.

If such a period of absence is subject to the PSPA rules, the PSPA would be reported after the particular period has ended and service cannot be credited until the PSPA is certified (since this type of PSPA would require certification, as discussed at ¶ 1065) even though this may, in certain circumstances, conflict with employment standards legislation in some provinces. If a period of absence instead qualifies under the "prescribed compensation" mechanism and is recognized on a current service basis, PAs would be reported either during the particular period, or shortly after the period has ended, depending on the circumstances and timing (further details are provided at ¶ 775).

From the individual's perspective, the advantage of having a PA reported instead of a PSPA is that, as noted at ¶ 415, a PA for a year can have the effect of eliminating new RRSP contribution room that has been created for that year, but cannot create negative RRSP contribution room. In other words, a PA cannot use up any RRSP contribution room that had been carried forward from a previous year. However, a PSPA can have the effect of using up RRSP contribution room that has been carried forward, and can even leave the individual with a negative RRSP contribution room balance at the end of the year in which the PSPA arose. Where an individual's RRSP contribution room is negative, no further RRSP contributions may be made until new RRSP contribution room increases the balance to a positive amount. This is particularly important when a leave of absence is involved, because the new RRSP contribution room (being dependent on earned income) may be low or zero.

There is a further consideration regarding PSPAs. In virtually all cases of leaves of absence, any PSPA would be "non-exempt", which means that the applicable service may only be treated as pensionable service under the plan if the individual has sufficient RRSP contribution room to accommodate the PSPA (or is no more than $8,000 deficient). This is discussed in detail at ¶1065. It would appear, therefore, that in some circumstances it may not be possible for a leave of absence to be treated as pensionable service under an RPP, for example, where the individual is unwilling to deregister RRSP assets in order to create RRSP contribution room to permit the approval of the PSPA.

It should be noted, however, that any periods of leave taken prior to 1991 will not affect the prescribed compensation limit, nor will they use up the five-year/three-year limit for determining the portion of benefit accruals subjected to PA reporting.

¶1750 Benefits Following Disability

As indicated at ¶1746, an individual may be credited with pensionable service throughout a period of disability if he or she is disabled, as that term is defined at ¶205. This definition of "disabled" generally is referred to as an "own occupation" disability.

To allow benefits to accrue (i.e., to deem compensation for the purpose of ensuring that the PA limits are not violated), compensation is prescribed throughout the period of the disability.

Note, however, that the level of earnings used for the purposes of determining the amount of benefit accruing during a period of disability is not necessarily the same as the compensation that is deemed for the purposes of the PA calculations (as set out at ¶777).

For PA purposes, one is required to determine the amount that it is reasonable to consider would have been the individual's remuneration in the year for which the PA is being determined had the individual rendered services on a regular basis in that year.

However, for the purposes of determining the level of benefit accruing, the level of earnings used could be the prescribed compensation used for the PA calculations, but more typically is based on the level of earnings in effect immediately prior to the disability. In some cases, no earnings may be deemed for the period of disability at all, with the average earnings base used for benefit calculation purposes being frozen at date of disability.

In addition, a defined benefit RPP may provide an immediate pension in respect of an individual who is "totally and permanently disabled" (as defined at ¶205) where:

- the age and service reductions normally applicable to a bridging benefit may be waived;

- the reduction otherwise applicable on early retirement may be waived; and
- benefits may be provided on a projected basis, as described below.

An individual who is in receipt of a disability pension is not permitted to continue accruing benefits under the plan.

The maximum annual lifetime retirement benefit that may be paid to an individual who is totally and permanently disabled is equal to the greater of:

(a) the accrued benefits at the time of disability retirement, without reduction for early retirement; and

(b) the lesser of:

(i) the projected benefit that would be payable at age 65 if employment continued, assuming no increase in the rate of pay, and

(ii) the YMPE for the year of disability retirement.

The maximum YMPE limit above must be coordinated with other plans or provisions where similar benefits are being provided to the individual under a group of related plans. However, there are no published guidelines with respect to this cross-plan restriction and how this is coordinated with other plans or provisions is subject to Ministerial discretion.

It should be noted that before the CRA will accept a provision providing for the payment of the above benefits to a member who is totally and permanently disabled, the plan document must specify that a member will not be considered eligible for such benefits unless the plan administrator has received written certification from a medical doctor licensed to practice within Canada or within the country where the member resides that the member is totally and permanently disabled.

¶1755 Periods of Foreign Service

As indicated at ¶1746, pensionable service under a defined benefit RPP may include a period of employment outside Canada if it is acceptable to the Minister of National Revenue.

The Registered Plans Directorate released its Newsletter 93-2 in 1993. This newsletter sets out foreign service guidelines. Pursuant to Newsletter 93-2, the CRA will accept as eligible service any period during which a member renders services outside Canada while remaining employed by a participating employer resident in Canada, provided that the member is or has been resident in Canada. Where these conditions are met, any such periods will be considered eligible service regardless of whether the benefits for the period are provided on a current service or a past service basis.

Where a member renders services outside Canada while employed by a non-resident participating employer, a non-participating employer connected with a participating employer, or a non-participating employer under a special arrangement with a participating employer, the period of service outside Canada is accepted as eligible service, subject to the following conditions:

- the member must be, or was, resident in Canada;
- the member must have previously been employed by a resident participating employer; and
- the benefits for such period of foreign service must be provided on a current service basis.

The acceptance of such service as eligible service was originally limited to the first three years of foreign service; but this was increased to five years (see Registered Plans Directorate Newsletter 00-1 for announcement of change and transitional rules). However, the five-year limit may be renewed provided the member returns to Canada and renders service in Canada in the course of employment with a resident participating employer for a minimum 12-month period.

Benefits may only be provided for a period of temporary absence of a member employed outside Canada if the member is working for a resident participating employer.

Where a period of foreign service during which the member is employed by a resident participating employer is accepted as eligible service, the member's remuneration from the resident participating employer is accepted as "compensation" under subsection 147(1) of the *Income Tax Act* (Canada). The CRA will determine, on a case by case basis, whether past service benefits for such periods of eligible service will be excluded in calculating PSPAs. Generally, an exclusion will be permitted if the member's remuneration is not included in earned income.

Where a period of foreign service with a non-resident participating employer is considered eligible service, the member's remuneration from the employer is accepted as "compensation" from the employer. Where the employer is a non-resident, non-participating employer, the member's remuneration from the foreign employer, to the extent that such remuneration exceeds the amount, if any, included in the member's compensation from the participating employer, will be deemed to be compensation from the participating employer to whom the member's benefits for the period are attributed for the purpose of calculating the member's PA.

Grandfathered plans are exempted from the foreign service provisions in the Regulations for benefits provided for pre-1992 service. However, where a pre-1992 period of foreign service is to be credited as pensionable service after 1991, the period must be acceptable to the CRA. Where such a period of foreign service does not fall within any of the guidelines set out in Newsletter 93-2, the CRA will consider the acceptability of such periods as eligible service on a case by case basis.

¶1760 Pre-Retirement Death Benefits

If a member dies prior to retirement, a defined benefit RPP may provide for a lifetime pension to be paid to either the spouse of the member or another individual who was a dependant of the member. Pre-retirement death benefits may also be paid to other individuals or to the estate of the member in the form of lump-sum amounts. Paragraphs ¶1761 through ¶1765 cover the various types of benefits that may be paid to the spouse, dependant, beneficiary, or estate of a member upon the member's death prior to retirement.

¶1761 Pre-Retirement Survivor Pensions

If a member dies prior to commencement of retirement benefits, the RPP may provide for payment of a survivor pension to the deceased member's spouse or former spouse for his or her lifetime or to a dependant of the deceased member.

A spouse can include a same or opposite sex common-law partner.

A dependant can include a parent, brother, sister, child, grandparent, or grandchild, provided the individual was dependent on the member for financial support at the time of the member's death.

A survivor pension may be payable to a dependant for the "eligible survivor benefit period", which commences on the date of the member's death and ceases on the latter of the date when the individual ceases to be a full-time student or the end of the year in which the dependant attains age 18. If the individual is a dependant due to physical or mental infirmity, the eligible period is the full period of the infirmity.

A pre-retirement death benefit may also be paid to the spouse or former spouse of a deceased member in the form of a temporary bridging benefit, rather than a lump-sum. This feature was added to the Regulations to accommodate Quebec minimum standards legislation, which allows the spouse of a member to convert some or all of his or her pension entitlement into a temporary pension.

The total of all pre-retirement survivor pensions payable under a defined benefit provision of an RPP in respect of a deceased member may not exceed the member's projected lifetime retirement benefit calculated as of his or her date of death, adjusted to reflect increases in the CPI from the date of death. The amount payable to any one individual upon the member's death may not exceed $66\frac{2}{3}$% of the projected lifetime retirement benefit, plus CPI adjustments.

The member's projected lifetime retirement benefit at date of death is the greater of:

(a) the deceased member's lifetime retirement benefit accrued to his or her date of death (without any reductions related to early retirement); and

(b) the lesser of:

(i) the member's projected lifetime retirement benefit to age 65, calculated as though the member had continued in employment to that date and had received no increase in pay, and

(ii) one-and-a-half times the YMPE in effect in the year of the member's death.

If the member dies after attaining age 65 but before commencing retirement benefits, the projected lifetime retirement benefit is restricted to (a) above. This same restriction applies to a member who was connected at any time after 1990, regardless of the age at death, as discussed further at ¶1790.

For example, consider an RPP that provides a lifetime retirement benefit for each year of pensionable service equal to 1.3% of the final five-year average earnings up to the final five-year average YMPE, plus 2% of a member's final five-year average earnings in excess of the final five-year average YMPE. The normal retirement age under the plan is 65.

An employee, aged 40, died at the end of 2009 after completing five years of pensionable service under the plan. The member's final average earnings at the date of death was $65,000 and the final average YMPE was $44,966.67. The 2009 YMPE was $46,300. The member's annual rate of pay at the date of death was $70,000. The member's projected lifetime retirement benefit is the greater of:

(a) the accrued benefit at the date of death

$= [0.013 \times \$44,966.67 + 0.02 \times (\$65,000 - \$44,966.67)] \times 5 \text{ years} = \$4,926.17$; and

(b) the lesser of:

(i) the projected lifetime retirement benefit at age 65, assuming continued employment and no increase in pay, calculated as follows:

(1) Total pensionable service to age 65 = 30 years

(2) Projected final average earnings = $70,000 (earnings at the date of death)

(3) Projected final average YMPE = $46,300 (the YMPE for 2009).

The projected lifetime retirement benefit is therefore

$= [0.013 \times \$46,300 + 0.02 \times (\$70,000 - \$46,300)] \times 30$ years

= $32,277; and

(ii) one-and-a-half times the YMPE in the member's year of death

$= 1.5 \times \$46,300 = \$69,450$.

In this example, the maximum total survivor pension payable to all eligible beneficiaries would be $32,277 *per annum*. The maximum payable to any one eligible beneficiary would be 66⅔% of that amount, or $21,518.

As illustrated by this example, the Regulations permit a fairly generous survivor benefit to be payable after a member dies at an early age with only a short period of service. In addition, this benefit can be increased after commencement as discussed at ¶ 1770.

Minimum standards legislation sometimes requires that a surviving spouse be provided with a survivor pension that is equal in value to the value of the member's accrued pension. In certain circumstances, this benefit may be greater than the pension described above. To avoid this conflict with minimum standards legislation, an RPP may pay a survivor's pension to the spouse (or former spouse) of a deceased member that is greater than that determined above, provided that:

- the commuted value of the pension provided to the spouse is not greater than the commuted value of the deceased member's total benefits under the plan (including ancillary benefits) accrued up to his or her date of death; and
- the lifetime survivor pension commences before the end of the year in which the surviving spouse attains age 71, or, if later, within one year after the death of the member.

In the example above, a survivor pension equal in value to the commuted value of the member's accrued benefit to his or her date of death would be considerably less than the value of the maximum survivor pension permitted. However, this would not always be the case, as illustrated by the following example.

Consider the same plan as the one described in the example above. An employee dies at the end of 2009 at age 60 after 30 years of service and was eligible to retire with an unreduced pension as at that date, payable for his or her lifetime. The employee's final average earnings at the date of death were $65,000 and the annual rate of salary was $70,000. The final average YMPE was $44,966.67. The surviving spouse is age 64. The particular minimum standards legislation requires the use of unisex mortality rates to determine the commuted value of the pension.

The annual accrued pension under the plan at the date of death is

= [0.013 × $44,966.67 + 0.02 × ($65,000 - $44,966.67)] × 30 years

= $29,557.00.

Using the UP94 mortality table projected to 2020, based on a blend of 50% male rates and 50% female rates, and an interest assumption of 3.7% for 10 years and 5.3% thereafter, the commuted value of this pension is $29,557.00 × 14.7747 = $436,696.

If this lump-sum is converted to a survivor pension payable immediately to the surviving spouse, the annual amount of survivor pension would be $436,696 ÷ 13.5456 = $32,239.

Without this alternative rule, the maximum surviving spouse pension permitted by the CRA, using the projected lifetime retirement benefit approach, would be

= [0.013 × $46,300* + 0.02 × ($70,000 - $46,300)] × 35 years × 66⅔% = $25,104.

It should be noted that there is a cross-benefit/cross-plan restriction on the amount of survivor pension that may be paid from the RPP where other death benefits are payable under the same RPP or under another RPP. The purpose of this restriction is to avoid allowing an excessive or unreasonable death benefit from being paid. The "1.5 times the YMPE" limit must be reduced, to the extent that other benefits are payable. Each situation will be evaluated individually depending on the particular circumstances as there are no published guidelines with respect to this cross-plan restriction and how this is coordinated with other plans or provisions is subject to Ministerial discretion.

* The YMPE for 2009.

Minimum pension standards legislation in many jurisdictions requires that an RPP not restrict the payment of the spouse's pre-retirement death benefit to a survivor pension only. In many jurisdictions, the spouse is entitled to receive the commuted value of the pension accrued by the member prior to death, with the benefit payable in the form of a cash lump-sum or as a transfer to a registered retirement savings vehicle. For a full discussion of lump-sum death benefits, see ¶1763.

¶1762 Guarantee Period and Indexation of Pre-Retirement Survivor Pensions

Pre-retirement survivor pension payments to an individual who was the spouse or former spouse of the member at the date of the member's death may be guaranteed for up to 15 years. All pre-retirement survivor pension payments to a survivor (spouse or otherwise) may increase after commencement in line with increases in the CPI, either through automatic indexing under the terms of the plan or on an *ad hoc* basis.

¶1763 Lump-Sum Payments on Death

A pre-retirement death benefit may be paid in the form of a lump sum to one or more beneficiaries instead of a survivor pension, provided the lump-sum payment does not exceed the commuted value of the deceased member's total benefits under the RPP accrued up to his or her date of death. However, a contributory plan may guarantee that the total payments after the death of a member will not be less than the member's contributions accumulated with interest. For younger plan members, accumulated contributions with interest typically are greater than the commuted value of the accrued benefits.

Additionally, where minimum standards legislation requires, the Regulations also permit a contributory plan to provide members with an additional benefit in order to satisfy the 50% employer cost-sharing rule imposed by many of the jurisdictions. Under this 50% rule, a member's contributions to a contributory plan may not comprise more than 50% of the commuted value of the pension payable to the member from the plan. This 50% rule is generally extended to the determination of a person's commuted value on the member's death as well as at retirement.

A contributory plan may provide a lump-sum death benefit equal to twice the member's contributions to the fund (including interest), but only if no pre-retirement survivor pension is payable and only if that is the termination benefit the member would have received, had the member terminated service immediately prior to death. To provide this higher benefit, the limitation on the maximum contributions that may be made to the RPP by the member is reduced. This is discussed further at ¶1805.

As mentioned at ¶1640, payment of the lump-sum upon death must not be unduly deferred.

Lump-sum payments may be tax sheltered through transfer to an RRSP or a RRIF or to another RPP if the beneficiary is the deceased member's spouse. If the lump-sum is the commuted value of the pre-retirement survivor pension that would otherwise be payable to the spouse, the Minister's approval is required to transfer the lump-sum to another registered retirement savings vehicle and the Minister will not grant approval if such survivor pension was based on projected service.

Where a lump sum is received from an RPP as a consequence of the death of a plan member who was a parent or grandparent, an offsetting tax deduction is available to a financially dependent child or grandchild (as beneficiary) if he or she uses the proceeds to acquire an annuity for a fixed number of years, not exceeding 18 minus his or her age at the time when the annuity is acquired. The annuity must be acquired in the same year in which the lump-sum is included in the child's or grandchild's taxable income or within 60 days after the end of that year.

¶1764 Death Benefit Exemptions for Grandfathered Plans

The pre-retirement death benefits set out in ¶1761, ¶1762, and ¶1763 apply to both pre-reform and post-reform service. However, if the existing benefits payable under the terms of a grandfathered RPP exceeded the benefits set out in these paragraphs, it was possible for the plan administrator to submit a written request to the CRA in order to receive a waiver exempting benefits payable on behalf of pre-reform (i.e., pre-1992) service from the current rules. A written request by the plan administrator must be made to the CRA to obtain the waiver.

Exemptions on behalf of pre-1992 service have generally been granted in the following circumstances:

- existing survivor benefits are payable to beneficiaries other than the spouse or an eligible dependant;
- a joint and survivor pension in excess of 66⅔% as a normal form where the pension is actuarially equivalent to the maximum pension set out in paragraph 9(g) of Information Circular 72-13R8 based on a form of joint and 60% survivor; or
- the pre-reform death benefit associated with lifetime retirement benefits can be interpreted as complying with paragraph 9(f) of Information Circular 72-13R8, which provides that a pension can be payable to a spouse or other relative who is considered dependent on the member at the time of the member's death as long as the amount of pension is directly related to the pension accrued or is a "reasonable and moderate" amount of minimum pension.

¶1765 Guaranteed Period and Post-Retirement Survivor Pensions

Benefits paid in the form of a single life annuity may be guaranteed for up to 15 years after the commencement of the member's pension. Any remaining guaranteed payments after the member's death may continue to be paid to the beneficiary or may be commuted and paid in a lump-sum.

Periodic pension benefits may be paid after the death of a member to a survivor who is the spouse of the member or who was dependent on the member.

The maximum surviving spouse pension that may be paid without a reduction in pension is 66⅔% of the member's pension (including bridging benefits and inflation adjustments), with a maximum guarantee of five years (the guarantee period commencing at the member's pension commencement date) — this applies to both pre-reform and post-reform benefits. There is no requirement to reduce the initial pension payable to the member to reflect the value of these survivor benefits. Note that a grandfathered plan that provides a joint and survivor pension in excess of 66⅔% as a normal form could have applied to the CRA for a waiver with respect to pre-reform service. As mentioned in ¶1764 above, an exemption would generally have been given if the joint and survivor normal form is actuarially equivalent to the maximum normal form under the Circular.

More generous benefits may be provided to the surviving spouse, such as a higher percentage of the pension (up to 100% of the member's benefit) or a longer guarantee (up to 15 years), if the benefit payable to the member at pension commencement date is reduced accordingly. The member must forgo lifetime retirement benefits so that the value of the benefits payable to the member and surviving spouse do not exceed the value of the sum of the following:

(a) the lifetime retirement benefits payable to the member, ceasing at the member's death; and

(b) a 66⅔% survivor benefit payable to the member's spouse after the member's death, with a guarantee of five years of payments from the member's pension commencement date.

As an example, the RPP could provide a pension in which the full amount of the pension continues to the spouse after the member's death; however, the lifetime retirement benefits payable to the member must be reduced to reflect the amount by which the total value of the pension to the member and the subsequent pension to the surviving spouse exceeds the value described above (i.e., the joint and 66⅔% survivor pension).

Survivor benefit payments to an eligible spouse may continue for the spouse's remaining lifetime, whereas survivor benefit payments to a dependant may only continue for the eligible survivor benefit period of the dependant (which ends at the end of the year in which the individual attains age 18, or the time at which the individual ceases to be a full-time student, if later; however, if the individual is infirm, payments may continue for as long as the individual continues to be infirm).

Total monthly payments made to the spouse and any beneficiary after the survivor pension has commenced may not exceed the total monthly benefits (lifetime retirement benefits plus bridging benefits plus reasonable inflation adjustments) that would be payable to the member if the member were alive.

Note also that a plan may provide a guarantee that total payments in respect of a member will not be less than the member's contributions with interest.

¶1770 Inflation Adjustments

Lifetime retirement benefits payable after retirement, as well as survivor pensions payable on post-retirement death, may be adjusted periodically using one of the following approaches:

- a fixed annual increase of 4% *per annum* or less;
- adjustments that reflect changes in the CPI;
- adjustments based on an "excess earnings" approach whereby the increase is determined by reference to the rate of return on a specific pool of investment assets exceeding a specified base amount; or
- any combination of the above.

If the method used to provide the inflationary increases is either of the latter two, an additional restriction is placed on the amount of increase that may be paid. The actuarial present value of the additional pension that is provided (as determined at the pension commencement date) may not exceed the present value of the additional pension that would be provided under the greater of the first or the second method above.

However, there is a further restriction that overrides the above rules. After pension commencement, lifetime retirement benefits payable at any time must be limited to the maximum lifetime retirement benefit for the year of pension commencement, as discussed at ¶1710, adjusted to reflect increases in the CPI. Thus, if lifetime retirement benefits are automatically increased by a fixed rate of 4% *per annum*, for example, and the CPI is increasing at a lesser rate, a test may have to be conducted regularly to ensure that the pension payable in any year does not exceed this maximum limit.

Instead of automatic increases as described above, an RPP may be amended periodically to provide *ad hoc* increases up to the level of increase to reflect increases in the CPI. *Ad hoc* increases might be expressed as a fixed rate of increase but such increases must not exceed the cumulative rate of CPI increase over the relevant period.

After pension commencement, bridging benefits, pre-retirement survivor benefits, and the additional retirement benefits that may be paid to a member who is totally and permanently disabled may be increased in line with increases in the CPI.

Where limits on benefits depend on CPI increases, it is permissible to use any measure of the CPI that is substantially the same as the actual increases in the CPI. This rule exists for practical reasons, since the actual increase in the CPI from one point in time to another is not known until after the second point in time. This rule allows the increase to be determined, for example, by comparing the CPI for the third month prior to each of the points in time in order to implement an increase exactly on its effective date (typically January 1 of a particular year) rather than waiting until the exact CPI at January 1 is known (which typically would not be known until later in January).

Increases in excess of the limitations in the Regulations are permitted but must be done indirectly by restructuring the benefit formula to achieve the increase desired or through PSPAs. Refer to ¶ 1056 for additional details.

Increases may also be granted to accrued benefits prior to retirement. For the purposes of determining the maximum pension payable under the RPP, compensation is "indexed" as described in the definition of the highest average indexed compensation at ¶ 1710. Similarly, indexed compensation may be used for the purposes of the plan benefit formula provided the increases do not exceed the increase in the average wage (since increases in excess of the average wage will give rise to a PSPA) and benefits may be indexed during a pre-retirement deferral period. The CRA will accept indexation by either the CPI or the average wage as acceptable indexing adjustments. However, it should be noted that in any event, the benefit payable from the RPP is subject to the maximum pension test that must be applied at benefit commencement date, as set out at ¶ 1710.

¶1775 Benefit Accruals After Retirement

Unless a member has arranged to receive certain special benefits under a phased retirement program (as discussed below), a member may not accrue a benefit under a defined benefit provision of an RPP while in receipt of a pension under the same defined benefit provision or under any other defined benefit provision of the RPP or any other RPP of the employer or a related employer.

Phased retirement, meaning the ability to receive a partial pension from the plan while still accruing pension benefits under the same plan, became possible under the Regulations effective January 1, 2008. Certain minimum standards jurisdictions had previously introduced an "early benefit" which was available during the phase-in period prior to retirement (refer to ¶125 and ¶1315); however, these provisions were not seen as contravening this rule since the CRA considers these payments as partial commutations, rather than a retirement benefit or pension as the value of benefits received during the phased retirement period is later subtracted from the ultimate retirement benefit.

In the absence of a written phased retirement agreement with a member of a particular RPP, the existing rules regarding accrual of benefits from that RPP after commencing to receive a pension from the RPP are still in effect.

If an individual who is in receipt of defined benefit retirement benefits from an RPP is rehired, the individual's retirement benefits may be suspended to enable the individual to recommence accruals under the RPP. Wording in the RPP must specifically provide for this suspension of benefits. When the member retires for the second time, the RPP may then provide for the member's entire benefit (including accruals prior to the initial retirement and benefits in respect of the period of re-employment) to be redetermined by recalculating the early retirement reduction to take into account age and service at the second retirement date or to adjust the benefits to take into account any payments that would have been payable after age 65 under the first retirement if the individual had not become re-employed.

It should be noted that these rules are "same plan" rules meaning that a member cannot both accrue and receive a pension from the same RPP. However, there is nothing restricting the member from receiving a pension from one employer's RPP while accruing benefits under another RPP of an unrelated employer.

There is an exception to the general rule that benefits may not accrue while a pension is paid by the same employer. This exception occurs if the first retirement period commenced by virtue of a total and permanent disability and the member subsequently recovers and returns to work with the same employer. In this case, benefits may be credited on behalf of the period of disability even though a pension was paid during this period.

Another exception to the general rule is that the same restriction is not placed on the post-retirement accrual of benefits under a defined contribution provision. Therefore, after commencement of defined benefit retirement benefits, a member could start to accrue benefits under a defined contribution provision of a plan sponsored by the employer or a related employer.

As with many of the provisions in the Regulations, an anti-avoidance rule exists. If it can be shown that the primary reason for re-employing an individual after retirement was to allow the member to benefit from a subsequent recalculation of all benefits, the RPP's registration becomes revocable.

Phased Retirement

Effective January 1, 2008 the Regulations were amended to permit the payment of phased retirement benefits, allowing the partial payment of pension benefits to a member who is still employed and is still accruing benefits under a defined benefit provision of a pension plan. In order for a member to be eligible to receive these phased retirement benefits, the following criteria apply:

- the member must be at least age 55 and entitled to receive an unreduced pension; or
- the member must be at least age 60.

The member's "specified eligibility day" is generally the day the member first becomes eligible to retire under a phased retirement program in accordance with the above criteria.

These changes mean that a pension plan may provide a partial pension to a member of up to 60% of the member's accrued benefit (including bridging benefits) that would be paid if the member retired. A member can continue to work and earn benefits while receiving this partial pension. There is no requirement that a member's working hours be reduced to qualify for this type of phased retirement.

More specifically, subject to certain conditions, additional benefits may be provided under a defined benefit provision of an RPP while the eligible member continues to receive a partial pension under the RPP. The conditions that apply are as follows:

- The additional benefits accrue only in respect of a "qualifying period"; a qualifying period is defined as a period of post-pension commencement employment following the member's "specified eligibility day".

- The amount of retirement benefits payable to the member for each month in the "qualifying period" cannot exceed 60% of the monthly amount of retirement benefits accrued to the member to the beginning of the month, inclusive of bridging benefits that the member would be entitled to if fully retiring (both determined without any early retirement reduction).
- Alternatively, the member may be provided with stand-alone bridging benefits instead of the lifetime retirement pension; normally, bridging benefits are not permitted to be paid until a member commences to receive a lifetime pension under an RPP; however, for the purposes of the phased retirement rules, this requirement can be disregarded; however, if the member ceases employment, the stand-alone bridging benefits must cease unless the member commences to receive the lifetime pension at that time.
- The additional benefits accrue on a current service basis; however, they can subsequently be upgraded as long as the PSPA for the upgrade is nil or exempt from certification.
- The member was not at any time connected with a participating employer.
- The plan is not a designated plan.

The 60% limit does not apply to any month after which benefits cease to accrue to the member because of plan terms that restrict benefit accruals based on pensionable service (such as a 35-year cap), attainment of a certain age (such as age 71), or a combination of age and service.

Note that since the 60% limit is based on the amount of pension accrued to the individual at the beginning of the particular month, there is no restriction on the ability of the plan administrator to redetermine the amount of monthly pension that can be paid under the phased retirement rules to take into account higher earnings or additional pensionable service accrued since the beginning of the qualifying period.

When the member's qualifying period ends (i.e., the end of the phased retirement period) and the member commences to receive the regular retirement benefit, inclusive of the additional benefits accrued during the qualifying period, the maximum limits on lifetime pension and bridging benefits are those that apply as though the member first commenced to receive a pension at that time. In other words, the member's current age and service and the current defined benefit limit can be used to determine the maximum pension payable to the member and the maximum transfer value can be determined without regard to any benefits that were paid during the qualifying period.

Further, if the member were to die during the qualifying period, the Regulations provide that the guarantee period for survivor benefits can be determined without regard to the time that stand-alone bridging benefits or the partial lifetime pension had been paid.

These changes permit phased retirement under the income tax rules without regard to any other requirements or changes that may be necessary under minimum standards legislation. The changes required and the status of these changes in the various minimum standards jurisdictions is discussed further at ¶1315.

There is an anti-avoidance rule in order to prohibit the payment of the stand-alone bridging benefits or the partial lifetime pension and the additional accrual of benefits if the main reason for providing the phased retirement benefits is to enable the member to benefit from the phased retirement rules (for example, to permit the phased retirement in order to take advantage of later reflecting a higher defined benefit limit in the ultimate determination of the member's lifetime retirement pension). There are also cross-plan rules to be taken into account when the member participates in more than one defined benefit provision under the RPP or under other RPPs in which the employer is a participating employer or in RPPs with other employers that are not at arm's length from the employer. The cross-plan rules are important in determining whether the benefits payable under the phased retirement rules comply with the 60% limit set out above.

¶1780 Special Downsizing Benefits

The Regulations allow special additional benefits to be paid from a defined benefit RPP where an employer initiates a permanent workforce reduction. Additional benefits in excess of what may normally be provided under the *Income Tax Act* (Canada) and Regulations may be provided to individuals who terminate during an approved downsizing program, provided that the individuals were not at any time connected with the employer.

The Regulations do not set out what constitutes a workforce reduction. The Minister of National Revenue approves each specific downsizing situation by reference to internal guidelines that set out requirements with respect to staff reductions in each locality.

Registered Plans Directorate Newsletter No. 92-9 sets out the following guidelines:

- The program must result in a net reduction (i.e., terminated employees less employees hired), including part-time employees, of at least the greater of 50 employees and 10% of employees at a "locality". A locality generally means a region, such as a metropolitan area, a municipality, a remote work site, or an area as large as a province or all of Canada, or can mean distinct operating units such as plants, factories, or divisions which operate independently of the rest of the organization. (The CRA should be consulted to ensure that the "localities" affected by a particular downsizing are acceptable for the purposes of these downsizing rules.) This net reduction must occur during the period covered by the approved downsizing program, which is not to exceed two years.
- In the case of a voluntary downsizing program where eligible employees may choose to leave or to stay, the employer must provide information to the CRA on how the net reduction test will be met if the number of participants who elect to leave is not sufficient to meet the test. The CRA will look for a commitment from the employer that it will take steps to ensure that sufficient employees terminate to meet the net reduction test.
- Among the employees eligible to be part of the downsizing, not more than 35% may be in the "top earnings quartile" for the locality (or for the particular age group at which the downsizing is targeted, if preferred). The top earnings quartile means the 25% of all employees in the locality (or in the targeted age group at the locality, if applicable) with the highest remuneration.
- The program must be non-discriminatory, such that any benefit enhancements being provided within a given age or service profile may not be in favour of higher-paid employees, or those employees who participate in the RPP.

It can be seen that, to qualify as an approved downsizing program in order to gain access to the additional benefits as outlined below, a significant proportion of the organization's workforce must terminate or retire. If the workforce reduction qualifies for this purpose, the following rules apply:

- Additional lifetime retirement benefits not derived from a period of actual service may be provided to individuals age 55 or over at their termination date, subject to a maximum. This additional pension may only commence upon or after the individual's termination date. The maximum additional lifetime retirement benefit that may be provided is equal to the product of the number of years from the member's termination of employment to age 65 (to a maximum of seven years) and the lesser of the defined benefit limit (as defined at ¶205) for the year of commencement of the benefit and 2% of the member's highest average indexed compensation. Thus, the extra benefits provided under the downsizing are outside the normal maximum pension rules, as they are subject to their own rule. After commencement, these extra lifetime benefits may be increased to reflect increases in the CPI (the other indexing approaches discussed at ¶1770 are not permitted).

- No PSPA is generated in respect of the additional lifetime benefits.

In exchange for allowing the above-enhanced benefits, certain key conditions must be met, as follows:

1. Under an approved downsizing, retirement benefits must commence to be paid to the terminating individuals within a specified period of time (as set by the Minister of National Revenue, or, if not designated, within two years of the approval of the downsizing program).

2. Only those individuals who fall within the definition of "qualifying individuals" are eligible to receive enhanced retirement benefits under the downsizing program. A member will not fall into the class of qualifying individuals if it is reasonable to expect, at the time that that member's employment is terminated, that the member (or a corporation with which the member is connected) will become employed by or provide services to the employer or to an individual or entity that is not at arm's length with the employer. However, the Minister may waive this restriction provided that either the terminated member will not be involved in providing the services or the corporation with which the terminated member is connected will not provide services for a period greater than 12 months.

3. An individual retiring with additional benefits under an approved downsizing program may not commute any retirement benefits (either the additional or the regular benefits) into a lump-sum or as a transfer to an RRSP, unless the individual's life expectancy is significantly reduced.

4. An individual who is rehired subsequent to termination under an approved downsizing program is not required to cease or forfeit any of the enhanced downsizing benefits received as a result of the downsizing, provided that the individual suspends receipt of pension payments during the period of re-employment. In such cases, the Regulations provide that the additional lifetime benefit rule applicable to the enhanced downsizing benefits will continue to

apply to the individual as if he or she had not become re-employed and payment of the retirement benefits had not been suspended.

Under an approved downsizing program, the following additional rule changes may be applied:

- Unreduced early retirement may also be provided under the same terms as early retirement for employees in public safety occupations; that is, at age 55, or after 25 years of early retirement eligibility service (as defined at ¶1720), or after the total of age plus early retirement eligibility service exceeds 75. For early retirement before any of these three criteria is achieved, the reduction must be at least 0.25% for each month that early retirement precedes the earliest date of achieving any of the criteria. In this context, eligible service does not include any additional service granted under the downsizing. Further, this enhanced early retirement benefit does not apply to any benefits that are provided in respect of any periods after the individual has terminated employment under the downsizing program.
- The anti-avoidance rule that prohibits a plan member from agreeing to a reduced salary or retiring allowance in exchange for additional pre-1990 past service benefits (see ¶1785 — refer to number 17, "Past Service Benefits in Lieu of Earnings") is waived. Thus, if the member is entitled to a retiring allowance as part of the downsizing package, he or she may agree to waive that retiring allowance in exchange for enhanced pre-1990 benefits (to the maximum permitted).

¶1785 Miscellaneous Registration Rules for Defined Benefit RPPs

This section sets out miscellaneous rules for defined benefit RPPs that must be complied with upon registration of the plan and on an ongoing basis. A number of rules are identical to those pertaining to money purchase (defined contribution) provisions. Refer to ¶1675 in connection with the following rules:

1. **Designation of Administrator;**
2. **Primary Purpose of Plan;**
3. **Equal Periodic Payments;**
4. **Latest Start Date for Pension;**
5. **Assignment of Rights;**

6. Permissible Funding Media, Investments, and Borrowing; and

7. Contributions by Unions and Employer Associations.

Note under number 3, "Equal Periodic Payments", there are some additional considerations for defined benefit plans that do not apply in the case of defined contribution plans. The CRA does not permit "pop-up" benefits to be provided, except under certain circumstances. Pop-ups refer to provisions whereby a reduced pension amount pops-up to a higher pension amount once a triggering event occurs. For example:

- where an early retirement reduction is dropped upon attainment of the plan's normal retirement age; or
- where a member's spouse dies during the member's retirement, and the original pension amount had been reduced because the member was to receive the pension in the joint and survivor form.

The CRA had originally held the view that pop-ups were not permissible, because they contradicted the "equal and periodic rule". However, the Regulations were changed to permit pop-ups under various scenarios. To complete the picture, the Regulations also permit "pop-downs" (i.e., where the pension reduces instead of increases, such as would occur upon the death of member if a percentage of the pension is payable to the survivor).

Generally, the pop-up type benefits that are permitted are those in which the pop-up is merely restoring a benefit that could have been provided on an unreduced basis in the first instance. For example, suppose a plan imposes an early retirement reduction on a member who retires with 30 years or 85 points and this reduction is eliminated when the member reaches age 62. The plan could have provided an unreduced pension to this individual at the early retirement date instead of a pension with a reduction, but the unreduced pension is deferred to a later date, in this case, age 62. Thus, this is an example of a pop-up that is acceptable to the CRA.

The following are the exceptions permitted to the equal and periodic rule:

- An increase that takes place at a future specified date; for example, an SMEP amended January 1, 2010 by collective agreement to upgrade the benefit for all members in each of the next three years, regardless of whether the increases are warranted by cost-of-living increases.
- Elimination of the portion of an early retirement reduction that was not required to be made (refer to ¶ 1720).

- Elimination of an offset for disability benefits provided to the member under the CPP/QPP, workers' compensation or private insurance plans.
- Elimination of a joint and survivor reduction if it is determined that the survivor benefit will not be paid (either by virtue of the death of the survivor or by virtue of a marriage or relationship breakdown).
- Allowing a plan member who marries after pension commencement to take a reduced pension in exchange for spousal survivor benefits.
- Allowing a member of a pension plan who remains employed after normal retirement age to begin to receive a partial pension to reflect a reduction in earnings during the postponement period. The member is then entitled to a full pension when he or she eventually retires.

The remaining miscellaneous rules for defined benefit RPPs are described below.

8. Payment of Expenses

In addition to the permissible distributions that may be made from an RPP, as discussed throughout this chapter, an RPP may allow for the payment of reasonable administrative, investment, or similar expenses incurred in connection with the plan.

9. Requirement for Reduction of Benefits or Return of Contributions to Avoid Deregistration

A provision must appear in the RPP document that permits benefits to be reduced in order to avoid the revocation of the plan's registration. A provision must also be included to permit a return of member or employer contributions in order to avoid revocation.

These two provisions are necessary in order to be able to correct a situation in which contributions are in excess of those permitted under the registration rules, or where the maximum PA rule is violated. (See ¶510, ¶810, and ¶2015 for additional information regarding the maximum PA rule.)

However, note that, in certain jurisdictions, permission from, or a filing with, the pension supervisory authorities may be required to refund these contributions or reduce the accrued benefits. In such cases, an RPP may state that such return of contributions or reduction of benefits for the purpose of avoiding revocation of registration be subject to the approval of, or submission to, the minimum standards pension authority having jurisdiction over the RPP. Typically, where permission is required, the minimum standards jurisdiction will automatically grant permission to refund contributions or reduce benefits upon receipt of a letter from the CRA that such refund or reduction is required in order to avoid revocation.

10. Determination of Amounts

Any amounts determined in connection with the administration of the RPP must be determined using reasonable assumptions that are acceptable to the Minister of National Revenue and in accordance with generally accepted actuarial principles. In connection with a defined benefit RPP, this means, for example, that the calculation of the commuted value of a pension or other benefit (such as the value of indexation) must be determined using assumptions that are acceptable to the Minister for the particular situation, in accordance with generally accepted actuarial principles.

Registered Plans Directorate Newsletter No. 94-3R, updated to October 21, 2008, states that the CRA will accept the following assumptions in the calculation of the present value of benefits in connection with a defined benefit provision of an RPP:

- the assumptions contained in the standards of practice issued by the CIA for the computation of transfer values from registered pension plans, as in force at the relevant time.
- where mandated under the federal *Pension Benefits Standards Act, 1985* or a similar law of any province, the assumptions as specified in the applicable legislation.
- assumptions that are reasonable at the time they are used, provided that the present values produced do not exceed the present values that would have been produced using the assumptions set out in the applicable CIA standards of practice. Where assumptions produce present values in excess of those that would have been produced by the applicable standards of practice, the plan sponsor should provide the CRA with the actuarial reasoning to justify the use of these assumptions, to obtain its acceptance.

It should be noted that while any of various sets of assumptions are acceptable to the CRA in the calculation of a commuted value, the minimum standards legislations generally specify that a commuted value cannot be less that the value calculated using the most recent standards of practice in effect.

11. Payment of lump-sums and Commutation of Benefits

Subject to minimum standards legislation, which generally requires that benefits be locked-in once certain age and service conditions are fulfilled, a lump-sum equal to the present value of the member's benefits may be paid at any time prior to, upon, or after retirement if the provisions of the RPP provide for such commutation. This extends to benefits in respect of pre-reform service, again provided that the RPP specifically allows for such commutation. Where benefits are not indexed, or are only partially indexed, it is also permissible to determine the present value of the benefits on a fully indexed basis (see number 12 below). If this is the intention, then the RPP must also state that the calculation of the present value will include indexation assumptions. In calculating the present value of benefits for pre-reform service for connected persons where such commutation is permitted by the CRA, indexation assumptions may be used provided that the 50/50 present value test can continue to be met. Refer to ¶1790 for more information on the 50/50 present value test.

Minimum standards legislation may also require that the present value of benefits be subject to a minimum equal to the member's pre-reform contributions with interest, plus any benefits payable in respect of post-reform service in accordance with the "50% rule" (as explained at ¶1314). Generally, such a requirement will apply where a lump-sum amount is required to be paid on cessation of employment (whether by termination, retirement, or death), termination of the plan, or pursuant to a court order or written agreement following the breakdown of a marriage or other conjugal relationship.

As discussed at ¶1746, if the RPP permits members to commute pre-reform benefits, it must be specified in the plan that either the period of pre-reform service cannot be credited again under the RPP, or, alternatively, that if the member wishes to buy back the service, the amount necessary to fund those benefits must be transferred directly from an RRSP, a DPSP, or another RPP. The CRA will not, however, permit commutation of pre-October 1968 benefits, nor pre-reform benefits accrued under 1980 shareholder plans or which have been provided to partners or proprietors or their spouses for service while such individuals were employees.

It is permitted for an individual who terminates employment to receive (if the plan so provides) a refund equal to twice his or her contributions with interest. However, in this case, there is a special limit on the maximum member contributions to the plan, as described at ¶1805. Note that the ability to transfer the full amount to an RRSP, in this case, may be limited unless the "transfer room" available upon termination (as discussed at ¶1743) will permit this amount to be transferred. In other words, this provision may provide a potentially larger total benefit payable upon termination but the total amount that may be transferred to an RRSP must still fall within the requirements set out at ¶1743.

12. Indexing Included in Commuted Values

As discussed at number 11 above, a defined benefit RPP may provide for the commuted value of a benefit to be determined as if the benefit was partially or fully indexed, even if the plan does not provide for automatic partial or full indexing (although, as noted at number 11, the RPP should state that the commuted value is being determined including indexation). Such indexing may be based on average wage increases during the pre-retirement period and CPI increases during the post-retirement period.

The original purpose of this rule was to allow for commuted values payable on a member's termination to be increased to at least partially compensate for the fact that the sum of the PAs reported under a defined benefit RPP overstates the actual value of the benefit, in most cases, when an individual terminates employment prior to retirement.

Although this type of *ad hoc* indexing provides some equity for terminating members, it can be an expensive option, reducing considerably the experience gains resulting from individual terminations of employment. A plan sponsor may not be willing to absorb this entire cost and may prefer to share the extra cost with plan members in some way. This rule may be applied to benefits in respect of both pre-reform and post-reform service.

Further, the introduction of the PAR, which restores RRSP room upon termination that was "lost" due to the PA overstating the value of the benefits being accrued, somewhat alleviates the need to include this additional indexation in a member's termination benefit.

13. Pension Credits Must be Determinable and Not Inappropriately Low

To ensure that PAs can be calculated at the end of each calendar year, the Regulations require that the amount of retirement benefit under a defined benefit provision must be such that a pension credit (a component in the PA calculation, as explained at ¶ 520) is "determinable" at the end of each year. This replaced a similar clause in Information Circular 72-13R8, which required that defined benefits be in accordance with a formula set out in the plan. This would appear to be a somewhat subjective requirement, as there is no guidance as to what makes a pension credit "determinable".

An example of a benefit formula where the pension credit is considered to be not determinable is the greater of a defined benefit provision and a money purchase provision. Under this arrangement, the pension credit is deemed to be not determinable since it is not known whether the defined benefit or the money purchase provision prevails. The CRA requires such a plan to be described as a money purchase provision with a defined benefit top-up or a defined benefit provision offset by a money purchase provision. In respect of each year, the member's PA would be determined as the sum of (i) the money purchase contributions made in relation to the member, plus (ii) the difference, if positive, between the member's defined benefit pension credit and (i). Refer to ¶815 for further discussion regarding this type of formula.

There is a further general condition for a defined benefit provision: PAs and PSPAs determined in accordance with the plan must not be inappropriately low in comparison to the benefits actually provided. An extreme example of a formula with "inappropriately low" PAs is one in which the pension accrual is nil if final earnings are below $70,000 and 1% of final earnings for each year of service if final earnings exceed $70,000. Such a formula would be considered inappropriate since it will result in zero PAs in the early years when earnings are less than $70,000, and yet ultimately the final earnings will grow to produce a full benefit in respect of all service.

The Minister of National Revenue may waive this condition under certain circumstances, presumably where the level of "inappropriateness" is not significant or perhaps where there is an expectation that the formula will be amended from time to time to keep the PAs reasonably consistent with the benefits provided.

An extension of the rule requiring the benefit formula to result in PAs that are determinable and not inappropriately low is applicable in connection with plan formulae that are based on future earnings levels (i.e., final average earnings plans). In such cases, any increase in accrued benefits in accordance with the plan formula must result from an increase in the member's remuneration. This requirement is intended to control situations where a member's benefits increase due to an increase in the number of hours worked, and, as a result, such benefits are no longer appropriate in relation to the PAs reported. To comply with this provision, benefits on a final average earnings basis that are provided to employees who work on less than a full-time basis must be determined on the basis of annualized earnings and partial years of service. It would not be acceptable to credit 12 months of pensionable service in a year while deeming that year's pensionable earnings to be the actual earnings for the year (this applies after January 1, 1992 in a grandfathered plan).

14. Offset Benefits

A special rule applies in the situation where the benefit payable under a defined benefit provision is offset by the benefit payable under another defined benefit or money purchase provision or by the benefit payable under a DPSP. The rule requires that the offset be taken into account, regardless of the actual settlement in respect of the other RPP provision or DPSP.

For example, if the defined benefit is offset by the benefits payable under a DPSP and, at retirement, the DPSP benefit is taken in a lump-sum, the amount payable under the defined benefit formula must still be determined as though the DPSP benefit had not been taken as a lump-sum.

The purpose of this rule is similar to the rule set out above. The benefit ultimately provided under the defined benefit provision must be reasonable and appropriate in relation to the PAs that have been reported.

15. Anti-Avoidance Rule on Manipulation of Earnings

A further anti-avoidance rule prevents the use of RPP provisions in such a way as to provide a higher level of tax-sheltered retirement savings than is intended within the tax-assisted savings system. This rule concerns the manipulation of pensionable earnings in such a way as to create lower PAs that are inconsistent with the retirement benefits ultimately payable.

For example, suppose that bonus payments are excluded from the definition of pensionable earnings in a final average earnings plan. Until the beginning of the averaging period on which the final average earnings are based, suppose that a particular individual's compensation is largely comprised of bonuses, thereby artificially lowering the PAs, which are based on pensionable earnings. However, during the averaging period, the individual's bonuses are replaced by a significantly increased salary, which boosts the total pension payable in respect of all years of service while only increasing the PAs for a few years. This situation would jeopardize the plan's registration.

If it is determined that a member's remuneration is manipulated in this manner, the member is considered to have been connected with the employer (which leads to the use of the special maximum pension rules applicable to connected persons, as set out at ¶ 1790) and no earnings are deemed to be excluded from pensionable earnings. This means that any previously reported PAs would have to be amended.

16. Division of Benefits on Marriage or Relationship Breakdown

The Regulations allow for the payment of benefits to a spouse in the event of marriage or conjugal relationship breakdown, pursuant to a court order or legal separation agreement.

When determining whether the maximum pension or bridging benefit limits have been exceeded, the total benefit payable to both the member and the spouse must be taken into account.

An additional restriction is that the total of the benefits payable to the member and the spouse may not exceed the benefit (or the value of the benefit) that would be payable to the member alone if the marriage or relationship had not ended.

In addition, the Regulations state that a member who has lost benefits as a result of a division of benefits upon marriage or conjugal relationship breakdown may not later have any remaining benefits increased to replace the lost benefits.

17. Past Service Benefits in Lieu of Earnings

If a member of a defined benefit RPP agrees to reduced compensation or to a reduced retiring allowance in order to receive additional pension benefits on behalf of service prior to January 1, 1990, any employer contributions made to the RPP to fund the additional past service benefits could put the plan in a revocable position. This "salary sacrifice" rule is discussed in greater detail at ¶1820 and is intended to apply only in the situation where an individual employee agrees to the reduction in remuneration, and not in the situation where a union negotiates additional pre-1990 pension benefits on behalf of the employees in lieu of salary increases.

There is an exception to this rule in the case of an "approved downsizing", as described at ¶1780. In this case, it would be allowable to provide additional past service pension benefits in lieu of compensation or a retiring allowance to which the employee is entitled.

In some circumstances, it may be possible to arrange for an employee to choose between receiving some additional compensation or retiring allowance or being granted a pre-1990 pension improvement without contravening this rule. This could occur where the choice is offered before the employee is irrevocably vested in the additional compensation or retiring allowance, such as where a severance package is being offered to an employee who is being laid off. It would be best to obtain the CRA's approval before proceeding with such an arrangement.

¶1790 Special Rules for Connected Persons

The Regulations restrict or modify the benefits that may be provided to a member who is connected to an employer that participates in an RPP. For the purposes of the relevant regulations, a person is connected with an employer if he or she meets a specific test. Broadly speaking, the individual must own, directly or indirectly, 10% of any class of capital stock or otherwise does not deal at arm's length with the employer.

An employer is required to notify the CRA of a connected person's initial participation in the RPP within 60 days of the connected person becoming a member of the pension plan. Form T1007 is the form which must be filed with the CRA in respect of the connected person.

Generally, a connected person may only accrue benefits if he or she is receiving compensation. If such an individual's remuneration is completely in the form of, for example, dividend income, the individual may not accrue benefits under the RPP.

Provisions that are modified or restricted are as follows:

- The maximum pension limit discussed at ¶1710 is modified to be the sum of the following:
  - — the limit at ¶1710, but, in determining pensionable service, ignoring any year after 1990 in which the member is connected with the employer, plus
  - — for each year after 1990 in which the member is connected with the employer, the lesser of:
    - — 2% of "indexed compensation" for the year, and
    - — the defined benefit limit (as defined at ¶205) for the year, multiplied by the fraction of the year that is pensionable service.

  Indexed compensation, for this purpose, is the member's compensation for the year, adjusted to reflect increases in the average wage from that year to the year of pension commencement.
- Pre-retirement survivor benefits on behalf of a person connected at any time after 1990, as discussed at ¶1761, are limited to 66⅔% of lifetime retirement benefits (i.e., the projected lifetime retirement benefits that were discussed at ¶1761 may not be paid).
- Connected persons may not receive any additional benefits under an approved downsizing program, as discussed at ¶1780.
- Connected persons may not continue accrual of benefits during a post-1990 eligible period of reduced pay or temporary absence, since compensation is not prescribed for connected persons during these periods (see ¶1747).
- Increased benefits for a disabled member, as discussed at ¶1750, may not be paid to a person who was connected at any time after 1990, nor may an unreduced early retirement benefit on disability

be paid unless the employee has satisfied the non-disability eligibility requirements discussed at ¶ 1720.

- A period of disability does not qualify as eligible service for a connected person from 1991.
- Where benefits in respect of pre-1991 service are provided to connected persons, the Minister of National Revenue must be specifically notified in writing in order for such benefits to be acceptable.

The modification to the maximum pension rule is of particular note. A person who has one or more years in which he or she was a connected person and earned less than 50 times the defined benefit limit ($124,722 for 2010 based on a defined benefit limit of $2,494.44) will receive a reduced maximum pension. The maximum pension in respect of each of those years is unaffected by higher earnings in other years. On the other hand, a person who is not a connected person can receive earnings less than 50 times the defined benefit limit in some years, and still receive the maximum pension of the defined benefit limit multiplied by years of pensionable service, provided he or she has at least three non-overlapping periods of 12 consecutive months of earnings in excess of 50 times the defined benefit limit.

As pre-1992 service must be acceptable to the Minister and Information Circular 72-13R8 generally required that a defined benefit plan may not be primarily for the benefit of significant shareholders (the 50/50 Rule), the CRA continues to apply the 50/50 Rule with certain modifications. The test is determined on the basis of benefits accrued to December 31, 1990 (or December 31, 1991, for a grandfathered plan), where such benefits are based only on earnings to that date. Under this test, a pension plan is considered to be primarily for the benefit of significant shareholders if the present value of benefits purchased for or accrued to significant shareholders is in excess of 50% of the present value of the total benefits purchased for or accrued to active members under all RPPs of the employer.

Chapter 18

¶1800 REGISTRATION RULES FOR DEFINED BENEFIT RPPS — ELIGIBLE CONTRIBUTIONS

¶1805 Employee Contributions for Current Service

Employee contributions to a defined benefit provision of an RPP for current service, if made in accordance with the terms of the plan as registered, are fully deductible to the employee. In order to maintain control over tax revenues, the Regulations limit the amount of employee contributions that may be required under a defined benefit provision of a pension plan.

When a member is required to contribute to a defined benefit provision in respect of a calendar year after 1990, the contributions may not exceed the lesser of:

(a) 9% of the member's total compensation for the year from all employers that participate in the plan in the year; and

(b) the sum of $1,000 and 70% of the member's pension credit for the year under the particular defined benefit provision.

If the plan contains a provision stipulating a minimum benefit payable on termination of employment or pre-retirement death equal to two times the accumulated member contributions, with interest, the 70% figure in paragraph (b) above is reduced to 50%.

Note that whereas the offset in the PA calculation was reduced from $1,000 to $600 in 1997, as discussed in Appendix 1, section 5A, no comparable change was made to the $1,000 figure in the maximum contribution formula.

The following example describes the calculation of this limit using the 70% figure in the formula set out above:

Benefit formula: 1.5% of earnings to YMPE plus 2% of earnings in excess of YMPE

Earnings: $80,000

YMPE: $47,200 (for 2010)

Benefit entitlement: 0.015 × $47,200 + 0.02 × ($80,000 - $47,200)
= $1,364.

Pension credit: 9 × $1,364 - $600 = $11,676.

Maximum employee contributions are the lesser of (a) and (b), where:

(a) 9% of earnings (9% × $80,000) = $7,200; and

(b) 70% × $11,676 + $1,000 = $9,173.20.

Using this example, the maximum employee contributions are $7,200, representing 9% of earnings.

Now consider how this example changes for a member earning $300,000. As noted at ¶1710, the maximum benefit entitlement (i.e., the defined benefit limit) for 2010 is $2,494.44. This maximum — or a lower maximum set out in the plan — must be brought into the calculations:

Benefit entitlement: 0.015 × $47,200 + 0.02 × ($300,000 - $47,200)
= $5,764.

Defined Benefit Limit: $2,494.44

Pension credit: 9 × $2,494.44 - $600 = $21,849.96 (rounded up to $21,850).

Maximum employee contributions are the lesser of (a) and (b), where:

(a) 9% of earnings = $27,000; and

(b) 70% × $21,850 + $1,000 = $16,295.

In this revised example, for a member earning $300,000, the maximum employee contributions are $16,295, representing only 5.43% of earnings. If this particular plan requires employee contributions of 6% of earnings (or higher), this higher-income employee will be affected by the limit.

The impact of the maximum contribution limit becomes even more significant if the plan has a minimum termination benefit equal to twice the accumulated member contributions, with interest. In such case, the maximum contribution limit uses the 50% figure instead of 70%, and the limit becomes 50% × $21,850 + $1,000 = $11,925 representing an allowable contribution limit of only 4% of earnings for an individual earning $300,000. For an individual earning $80,000 per year, the contribution limit is reduced from $7,200 to $6,838, or 8.5% of earnings.

Member contributions in respect of a particular calendar year may not be paid prior to that year.

During a member's period of disability or an eligible period of reduced pay or temporary absence, the method for determining the limit on current service contributions must be consistent with that used for earlier years. However, the member may be permitted or required to make current service contributions, provided such contributions do not exceed the amount that may be reasonably determined as being necessary to fund the member's benefits in respect of the period of reduced service.

It is possible to apply for a waiver of these contribution limits from the Minister of National Revenue, where the employee contributions are determined in a manner acceptable to the Minister and it is expected that over the long-term the current service contributions made by members will fund no more than half of the related benefits.

The purpose of the limit on employee current service contributions is to prevent an abuse of the system that could occur if the benefit formula — and therefore the PA — is reduced while the employee's benefit is maximized using the minimum employer contribution rule (the 50% rule, discussed at ¶ 1314) to generate a refund of excess employee contributions.

The following types of plans will be affected by the maximum contribution limit:

- plans where the ratio of the employee contribution formula to the benefit formula is quite high;
- plans covering employees with very high incomes and which do not otherwise limit contributions at the stated percentage on the level of earnings that generate the maximum pension for the year;
- plans requiring employee contributions to continue after benefits have ceased to accrue — for example, if credited service is limited to 35 years — when benefits cease to accrue, the pension credit is nil; and

- plans featuring other, more complex, "career limits" that complicate the PA calculation (see ¶735), where employee contributions continue after the pension credit has been reduced to nil.

There are few solutions to the problem faced by plans that require employee contributions to continue beyond the point at which pension credits reduce to nil. However, the plan sponsor could consider the following:

- Impose a limit of $1,000 on required employee contributions once a member reaches the point at which the pension credit is reduced to nil (for example, after 35 years of credited service under the plan).
- Select a cap that can be applied to pensionable service under the plan (typically, at least 35 years, depending on the plan formula) that is low enough that the career limit that would otherwise reduce or eliminate PAs can be ignored.

¶1810 Employee Contributions for Past Service

Employee past service contributions for service after January 1, 1990 are permitted and are fully tax-deductible provided they are made in accordance with the terms of the plan as registered and do not exceed the actuarial cost required to fund the past service benefits being provided.

It should be noted that if additional lifetime benefits are being provided in exchange for the past service contributions, then a PSPA may arise (as discussed in Chapter 10).

If the past service being provided is being paid for through a direct transfer from another RPP, there is no issue regarding the tax-deductibility of such transfer since it is a direct plan to plan transfer. This situation typically arises through an RTA or portability arrangement where the member is purchasing past service in exchange for giving up that service under another RPP. In addition, the member may use other tax-sheltered assets, such as assets in a personal RRSP, in order to purchase the remainder of the service if the full amount of service could not be purchased through the RPP transfer. However, if the amount of the registered plan transfer(s) is insufficient to fully pay for the service being acquired and the member is required to make additional contributions to pay for the remainder of the service, then such contributions are fully tax-deductible to the member whether paid in a single lump-sum or periodically through payroll deduction or a combination of the two (provided the total amount paid does not exceed the actuarial cost of the past service benefits being provided in respect of the remainder of the service).

With respect to employee past service contributions for service before January 1, 1990, if the employee had made contributions to an RPP in the prior year under consideration (i.e., any RPP, not just the RPP in which the service is being purchased), then the service is considered "past service while a contributor". Otherwise, the service is considered "past service while not a contributor". The one exception to "service while a contributor" is for a period during which an employee had made past service contributions before March 28, 1988 or on or after March 28, 1988 pursuant to a written agreement entered into before that date — in this case, the period of service is considered to be past service while not a contributor.

For past service contributions in respect of years before 1990 in which the employee was not a contributor to an RPP, a maximum contribution of $3,500 may be deducted for each year in respect of contributions made for pre-1990 service. This deduction is subject to an overall limit of $3,500 times the number of years of pre-1990 past service (calculated on a calendar year basis, with partial years of past service counting as a full year for this calculation), less deductions previously claimed for those contributions and is in addition to any deduction for current or past service contributions for post-1989 service. Any contribution that exceeds the maximum deduction of $3,500 in a particular year may be carried forward and claimed in a subsequent year, subject to the same limitations.

However, if the total past service contribution for pre-1990 service while not a contributor exceeds the overall limit noted above, the excess may not be deducted at any time. Unless the plan sponsor is subsidizing the cost of past service, it may not be to the contributor's advantage to make non-deductible contributions to purchase past service benefits. Taxation of both the income used to pay the contributions and the full pension benefit will outweigh any advantage of tax-sheltered investing through a pension fund.

For past service contributions in respect of years before 1990 in which the employee was a contributor to an RPP (and the past service is considered to be past service while a contributor), the maximum deduction that an employee may claim in a year is equal to the lesser of:

(a) the amount of the contributions made by the employee in the year and in all previous years in respect of such years of service, minus deductions previously claimed for those contributions; and

(b) $3,500 minus the total amounts deducted for the year for current and post-1989 past service contributions, and pre-1990 past service contributions while not a contributor.

If an individual continues to make current service contributions that amount to at least $3,500, it can be seen that limit (b) above will be nil, and these past service contributions may not begin to be deducted. Any contributions that cannot be deducted due to this limitation can be carried forward indefinitely to be deducted in subsequent years as contribution room becomes available. Typically, this will not occur for many years, when the individual terminates service or retires, and even then, can only be deducted at the maximum rate of $3,500 per year.

As noted at ¶1785 (under 11, "Payment of lump-sums and Commutation of Benefits"), if the member wishes to buy back a period of pre-reform service that was previously commuted out of the plan, the amount cannot be credited again unless the amount necessary to fund the benefits is transferred directly from an RRSP, a DPSP, or another RPP.

It should also be noted that where an employee is entitled to carry forward a contribution for deduction in a subsequent year, the entitlement to the deduction is not dependent on the employment to which the contribution relates, or on employment status at all.

If a particular past service buy-back is being paid in instalments, the plan sponsor may charge interest separately (i.e., outside the plan). In general, the tax-deductibility for such interest charges was prohibited after November 12, 1981. There is one exception. A deduction is available for interest charges that relate to contributions required to be made under an obligation entered into before November 13, 1981.

Employees may not deduct interest and other financing costs incurred in borrowing money in order to make current service contributions to an RPP. There is an exception that applies to money borrowed by an employee to make past service contributions to an RPP after November 12, 1981 as a result of an obligation into which the employee entered prior to November 13, 1981.

Where a taxpayer dies after 1992, in computing the deceased's income for the year of death or the immediately preceding year, the tax rules permit unused past service contributions above the annual $3,500 limit to be deducted upon death, whether or not contributions were made in past years.

¶1815 Employer Contributions

A contribution made by an employer to a defined benefit RPP is an eligible contribution — and therefore may be deducted from taxable income of taxable organizations — if it complies with certain prescribed conditions described below. It must also be recommended by an actuary in whose opinion the contribution is required to be made in order that the plan has sufficient assets to pay its benefit liabilities under the defined benefit provision of the plan. The actuary's recommendation must be approved in writing by the CRA. Normally, employers should begin to make contributions in accordance with a new actuarial valuation as soon as the report has been sent to the CRA. Written approval of the valuation report may be subject to extended delays if there are outstanding plan amendments or there is a backlog in the CRA approval process.

In recent years, certain minimum standards jurisdictions have permitted or are considering permitting the use of an LOC in RPPs as a means of meeting an organization's funding requirements for solvency deficiencies. Refer to ¶2315 for a more complete discussion of the use of LOCs in the funding of supplemental pension plans.

In determining whether sufficient assets are available in the pension plan, the actuary may take into account, for purposes of the recommendation, anticipated cost-of-living increases and similar adjustments where the terms of the plan do not require such adjustments to be made but it is reasonable to expect that they will be made. This typically includes *ad hoc* increases for pensioners and increases in accrued benefits under career average earnings plans and flat benefit plans.

Special rules apply to the determination of required contributions to a designated plan (see ¶1830 to ¶1840).

The Regulations only permit contributions to be made to the pension fund if they are eligible contributions. Ineligible contributions are not only non-deductible; they also jeopardize the registration of the pension plan. Collective bargaining agreements or funding policies are not acceptable justifications for making contributions that are ineligible.

Contributions must be based on a valuation report with an effective date no more than four years prior to the date the contribution is made. Thus, if a triennial actuarial valuation report (normally required to be filed with the minimum standards regulator within six to nine months of the valuation date) is delayed until more than a year after the valuation date, the contributions must be suspended until the new valuation is complete. Note, however, that this suspension may not be permitted under the minimum standards jurisdiction.

Generally speaking, an eligible contribution is tax-deductible by the plan sponsor in a particular fiscal year if it was made in that year, or within 120 days after the end of the year, and if it was made in respect of periods prior to the end of the fiscal year.

The required content of an actuarial report is outlined in the Registered Plans Directorate Newsletter 95-3. For most pension plans, the key requirement is that the report be prepared by a qualified actuary in accordance with the Canadian Institute of Actuaries' Standards of Practice. Since these standards do not specifically address insured plans,

Newsletter 95-3 lists other requirements for an insured plan. In addition to all of the information required to be contained in an actuarial report under the standards of practice, actuarial reports must contain:

- details for connected persons relating to remuneration for connected persons for each year of pre-reform service credited after 1980 as well as a demonstration of compliance with the 50/50 rule discussed at ¶1830;
- a reasonable allocation of contribution requirements among participating employers; and
- tests demonstrating compliance with the proportionality rule, if that rule applies (as discussed at ¶1746 and Registered Plans Directorate Newsletter 99-1).

For plans in actuarial surplus, a certain portion of the surplus in a defined benefit plan may be disregarded in determining whether an employer may make eligible contributions. The amount that may be excluded is equal to the lesser of:

- 20% of the actuarial funding liabilities of the plan; and
- the greater of:
  - — two times the estimated current service contributions that are expected to be made by the employer and the employees during the 12 months immediately following the effective date of the actuarial valuation, determined as if there were no surplus, and
  - — 10% of the actuarial liabilities of the plan.

Actuarial surplus that exceeds this amount is referred to as "excess surplus" and must be used to reduce the amount of employer contributions that are otherwise required.

Note that excess surplus is defined differently for jointly sponsored plans, also known as shared funding arrangements, in which the responsibility for the governance of the plan is shared between the participating employers and the members of the plan. In such arrangements, the employer may continue to make eligible contributions in situations where there is surplus in excess of the levels set out above, on a sliding scale, such that up to 25% of required contributions can be made even if surplus is not more than 25% of the actuarial liabilities.

Further, under proposed pension reform changes announced on October 27, 2009, the 10% threshold set out above is to be increased to 25% for all defined benefit registered pension plans, including designated plans and jointly sponsored plans. It is believed that increasing the threshold will provide more flexibility to plan sponsors and will encourage employers to maintain a surplus cushion and should help to reduced the likelihood and severity of funding deficiencies in future. This new threshold is to apply in respect of employer contributions for 2010 and subsequent years.

Contributions to fund a solvency deficiency in accordance with the funding requirements of minimum standards legislation are permissible, even if not required on a going concern basis. Any other additional contributions required by minimum standards legislation are also permissible provided the requirement to contribute is supported by an actuarial report. For example, if the plan has an excess surplus on a going concern basis but has a deficiency on a solvency basis, contributions towards the windup deficiency are permitted to be made, up to and including the full amount of the deficit if it is funded in a single lump-sum. (The solvency deficiency differs from the windup deficiency in that the former may include certain permissible adjustments, depending on the jurisdiction, that would not apply in the event of a plan termination.) However, these minimum standards contribution requirements are not permitted for a designated plan (as discussed at ¶ 1830 to ¶ 1840).

If the plan's transfer ratio is less than 100%, there are restrictions that vary by minimum standards jurisdiction on the ability of the plan sponsor to pay out a full lump-sum termination benefit. Generally, the termination benefit that can be paid immediately is the proportionate amount based on the transfer ratio of the plan. However, if the plan sponsor makes an additional contribution to the plan in respect of the termination benefit in order to top-up the lump-sum, then the full termination benefit can be paid to the terminating plan member immediately and the top-up payment is an eligible contribution.

In light of the market turmoils in 2008 and 2009, the solvency position of most defined benefit plans deteriorated and many of the minimum standards jurisdictions introduced new rules requiring recognition of the lower transfer ratios when lump-sum benefits are paid out. Where the minimum standards regulator has established requirements for redetermining the transfer ratio of the plan, any additional contributions that the plan sponsor may make in the form of top-up payments as discussed above, must be supported by an actuarial report or interim cost certificate in order for those contributions to be considered eligible contributions.

Sometimes situations arise where a pensioner is overpaid in error and the plan administrator seeks to collect the overpayment in order to return it to the pension plan. While there are no restrictions under the tax rules that would require the plan administrator to recover the overpayment or that would prevent the plan administrator from recovering the overpaid benefits, the return of the payment into the pension plan would not be permitted since it is not considered an eligible contribution. The Registered Plans Directorate would not consider it appropriate to reduce the pensioner's monthly benefit until the overpayment has been recouped as this would place the plan in a revocable position since benefits are not being paid in accordance with the terms of the plan as registered. Nonetheless, there are situations where it would not be appropriate from a plan governance or minimum standards legislation point of view to not take steps to correct the overpayment. The Registered Plans Directorate recommends that the plan administrator seek to obtain an advance income tax ruling concerning any proposed payment into the plan to determine whether it would be considered an eligible contribution.

As discussed at ¶ 1321, it sometimes becomes necessary to merge two pension plans and the corresponding assets and to keep the two asset pools segregated. Minimum standards jurisdictions may require this in order to permit the plan merger or the plan sponsor may voluntarily agree to segregate the assets in order to facilitate the approval process for the plan merger. The segregation of assets, over time, can lead to one pool of assets being better (or worse) funded than the other, leading to different contribution requirements for each subfund within the single plan. Segregation of assets is not permitted under the *Income Tax Act* (Canada) as an employer cannot independently fund two segregated accounts within a single pension plan. Thus, there is no direct guidance as to whether a contribution to one account that is in a deficit will be considered as an eligible contribution if the second account is in a surplus position.

The requirement for segregation of assets is a relatively new development and the Registered Plans Directorate is still formulating policies around this. However, since it is becoming more common for this to be a requirement of the minimum standards regulators in order to approve the merger of two or more plans, the Directorate is considering requests to segregate assets on a case by case basis. Their present policy is generally to permit such segregation if it is required by either the minimum standards jurisdiction or a court order. Sometimes, an employer voluntarily offers to segregate assets in order to obtain approval for the merger in a timely fashion. For example, Ontario requires that the plan document (including all historical documentation) support the merger of assets. This typically can lead to a time-consuming and costly review of all historical plan documentation that may well result in an inconclusive result, leading the plan sponsor to offer to segregate assets in the absence of proof permitting the merger of the assets. The Registered Plans Directorate has indicated that voluntary segregation such as this is not permitted. However, they are continuing to monitor the nature and number of such cases. As noted at ¶ 1321, this segregation of assets can be "virtual" rather than an actual segregation: it is usually sufficient to track the two pools of assets separately in subsequent actuarial valuations.

As discussed at ¶1324, in 2008, Quebec introduced the concept of the MFPP. The MFPP is a defined benefit plan where the employer contribution is predetermined and the remaining contributions (including payments for any deficits) are paid by the members. Any surplus assets belong to the members. Such plans are permitted under the tax rules if maintained pursuant to a collective bargaining agreement unless this requirement is waived by the Minister of National Revenue.

One stipulation regarding the MFPP is that it must be fully funded and solvent from inception and also fully funded and solvent at the time the amendment takes effect unless the amendment is statutorily required and such latitude in funding is not contemplated by the statute; this essentially means that any improvement in past service benefits can only be provided to the extent that there is available surplus to fund it. As a result, a regulation change made to accommodate the MFPP is to permit an employer to make eligible contributions of up to 50% of the current service requirement even in situations of excess surplus.

¶1820 Employer Contributions for Pre-1990 Past Service

Where an employer makes a contribution to a defined benefit RPP for an employee for pre-1990 past service benefits and it is reasonable to conclude that the contribution is being made in lieu of a payment or benefit to which the employee would otherwise be entitled, registration of the plan becomes revocable.

This "salary sacrifice" rule was adopted by the CRA during the 1980s to prevent arrangements in which employees agree to reduced payment of a benefit owing to them — for example, in salary or wages or a retiring allowance — in return for employer contributions to fund pre-1990 service. Essentially, such contributions are employee contributions for past service and in certain circumstances could, if not for the existence of this rule, allow past service employee contributions that do not comply with the limits for past service contributions. An exemption to this rule may be obtained in certain approved downsizing situations, in order to permit the employer who is downsizing to offer employees enhanced pension benefits.

Note that the ability to provide and fund pre-1990 past service benefits is also restricted by the proportionality conditions adopted by the CRA in 1999, as set out in Registered Plans Directorate Newsletter 99-1 (refer to ¶1746 for additional information on these proportionality conditions).

¶1825 Other Permissible Contributions

Two other types of contributions qualify as permissible contributions to an RPP. A lump-sum transferred from another RPP in accordance with the transfer provisions relating to a transfer from an RRSP, a DPSP, or an RPP will also qualify as a permissible contribution. As well, an amount that is transferred to an RPP from a pension plan that is maintained for non-residents for services rendered outside of Canada may qualify as a permissible contribution if the amount is acceptable to the Minister of National Revenue.

¶1830 Designated Plan Rules

Employers maintaining designated plans should be aware of special limits on employer contributions to those plans. A designated plan is a defined benefit RPP that is not maintained pursuant to a collective bargaining agreement and in which more than 50% of the total pension credits or PAs for the plan members are either for connected persons or for persons whose income for the year exceeds 2.5 times the YMPE (i.e., $118,000 for 2010). Typically, plans established for senior management only or single person plans for CEOs or owner-managers will fall within the designated plan definition.

Note that the income limit is based on aggregate remuneration from all participating employers, not pensionable earnings. In some instances, plan members will exceed the earnings limit because of non-pensionable bonuses or overtime.

For designated plans, eligible contributions must be determined on the basis of a separate maximum funding valuation for which the Regulations specify certain benefits regardless of the plan's actual benefit provisions and actuarial assumptions. (See ¶1835 and ¶1840.) Contributions to the designated plan must not exceed the amount determined pursuant to the designated plan rules.

Thus, regardless of the plan's benefits and the actuary's usual actuarial assumptions and methods adopted for the funding valuation, the designated plan rules apply an artificial cap on employer contributions.

Additionally, member contributions for past service, if made when the plan is a designated plan and which would not be an eligible contribution if made by the employer, are not permitted. Such contributions will make the RPP a revocable plan.

¶1835 Definition of Designated Plan

As stated at ¶1830, a designated plan is a defined benefit RPP that is not maintained pursuant to a collective bargaining agreement and in which more than 50% of the total pension credits or PAs for the plan members are either for connected persons or for persons whose income for the year exceeds 2.5 times the YMPE. This test can only be applied once the PAs and income for all the plan members is known. Thus, there are rules to delay the change to and from designated plan status.

An RPP will not be considered a designated plan for a particular calendar year if the plan was not a designated plan in the prior year and for the current year, the 50% test is replaced with a 60% test. This exemption allows for slight changes in circumstances in the composition of the pension credits or PAs of a plan without the plan qualifying as a designated plan, unless the changed circumstances continue for more than a year.

Generally, a plan that was a designated plan in the immediately preceding calendar year will remain a designated plan for the current calendar year. However, if the plan would otherwise not be a designated plan, the plan sponsor may apply for the Minister of National Revenue to waive the application of the previous year rule.

A number of exemptions exist under which a plan may escape qualification as a designated plan. A plan with more than nine active members may be exempted from the definition of a designated plan by the Minister if the plan is a "normal" defined benefit plan, rather than simply a series of individual plans for each member. A "normal" defined benefit plan is a plan in which:

- the benefit formula does not vary by member;
- there is no member involvement in the decision regarding the amount of contribution made in respect of the member;
- there is no member control over the investment of any portion of the plan assets; and
- surplus is not tracked individually for each member.

¶1840 Maximum Funding Valuation for Designated Plans

A maximum funding valuation is the actuarial valuation prepared for the purpose of determining eligible contributions made to a designated plan. The actuarial methods and assumptions are specified in the Regulations. In addition, deemed benefit provisions are substituted for certain actual plan benefits.

A maximum funding valuation is required to use the "projected accrued benefit" actuarial cost method. This method, also known as the "projected unit credit" actuarial cost method, is widely used in Canada to value defined benefit pension plans. Under this method, the projected cost of benefits is allocated to individual years of service using the plan's benefit formula. Expected future salary increases are used to determine the projected cost of benefits.

The assumptions applicable to pensions currently in pay are:

- a valuation interest rate of 7.5%;
- a rate of inflation of 4%; and
- 80% of the rates in the 1983 Group Annuity Mortality Table (sex-distinct).

The past service liability and current service cost for plan members whose pensions are not yet in pay depends on future salary increases, retirement age, marital status at retirement, and pre-retirement death benefits.

For these "restricted funding members", special assumptions and deemed plan provisions apply, as follows:

- a valuation interest rate of 7.5%;
- salaries and average wages increase by 5.5% *per annum*;
- a rate of inflation of 4%;
- deemed cost-of-living adjustments will occur at the rate of 3% per year (i.e., 1% less than the rate of inflation), regardless of the actual cost-of-living adjustments provided by the plan;*
- the member is assumed to have a spouse who is the same age as the member on the date benefits commence to be paid;
- the pension will be payable monthly in advance, regardless of the actual form of pension;
- the normal form of pension will be a pension for the lifetime of the member with a five-year guarantee, and with two-thirds of the member's pension continuing after death for the lifetime of the spouse, regardless of the actual normal form of pension;*
- the member is assumed to retire at age 65;*

---

* Alternatively, the actual normal form, indexing, and early retirement provisions can be used for pre-1991 accruals (along with an appropriate early retirement assumption). This alternative is intended to grandfather the funding of early retirement benefits that became provided before 1991.

- it is assumed that no pre-retirement deaths or terminatic employment occur;
- mortality after retirement for both the member and the spouse is 80% of the average of the rates for males and females from the 1983 Group Annuity Mortality Table (i.e., a unisex table, 50% male and 50% female); and
- the member will elect a pension rather than a lump-sum portability benefit.

The most important restriction is the assumption that the member will retire at age 65 — effectively preventing the pre-funding of early retirement subsidies, other than as noted in the footnote on the previous page for pre-1991 accruals.

Surplus (using the market value of assets) may be ignored in the determination of contributions, according to the same rules as outlined at ¶ 1815 above.

If it were to turn out that a standard going concern funding basis would require a lower contribution requirement than that resulting from the prescribed maximum funding valuation basis, then the funding requirements would follow the going concern basis. However, more typically (and more probably given a "designated plan" is typically a plan for executives or other high earners), the minimum required contributions, determined in accordance with a "normal" funding valuation that would be acceptable to a minimum standards jurisdiction, would exceed the maximum permissible contributions. If this is the case, the plan sponsor is not able to make contributions that would otherwise be required to fund the benefits in accordance with the minimum standards jurisdictions (and in accordance with the CIA standards of practice). When this occurs, the plan is faced with a "deficit" on a typical going concern basis and yet the benefits underlying the deficit must eventually be paid to the plan beneficiaries.

However, the designated plan rules permit terminal funding of these benefits in certain situations. If the designated plan is being partially wound up or if a commuted value is being transferred from the plan as a result of a termination of employment, there is no ability to "terminally fund" the shortfall that has crystallized as a result of the partial wind up or commuted value transfer. However, if the designated plan is being fully wound up, terminal funding of the full deficit is permitted. Minimum standards legislation, however, generally does not allow terminal funding. Therefore, plan sponsors must keep both the minimum standards requirements as well as the designated plan rules in mind when establishing the benefits to be provided under such a plan.

¶1845 Return of Contributions

All RPPs must contain a provision permitting the reduction of benefits provided under a defined benefit provision in order to avoid revocation of plan registration. Similarly, a provision is also required that permits a return of contributions to either an employer or an employee where such a refund is necessary to avoid revocation of registration. Registration of a plan will become revocable, for example, when employer contributions exceed eligible contributions; in such cases, this required provision in the plan permits the non-compliance to be remedied.

If it is discovered, within the same calendar year, that excess contributions have been made (either by the employer or the employee), then it is straightforward to make an adjustment to the next required contribution to correct the overcontribution. However, more typically, it is not known until a subsequent calendar year that an overcontribution has been made. In this case, steps must be taken to remove the excess contributions from the plan and refund them to the employer or employee as appropriate — the CRA does not consider it appropriate to reduce required contributions in the current calendar year to correct an overcontribution in a prior calendar year. Because the minimum standards jurisdictions are concerned with plan funding and removal of surplus (whether perceived or real), a withdrawal of contributions may require permission of the relevant pension benefits supervisory authority. The approval process to remove the contribution varies from jurisdiction to jurisdiction. The plan administrator may be required to obtain a letter from the CRA stating that the plan's registration is in jeopardy and the plan is in a revocable position. It may also require permission of the relevant pension benefits supervisory authority.

It should be noted that in the event that there is a refund to an employee or employer as a result of an overcontribution made in error, the employee or employer may be subject to double taxation. The amount of the refund will be included in income (and therefore taxed) in the year in which it was paid out but the amount may never have been permitted as a deduction when originally contributed to the plan. An exception will be made in the case of an excess contribution made by an employee as a result of "reasonable error" and the error is identified by the plan administrator and steps are taken as quickly as possible to remove the excess contribution. In such a case, the Registered Plans Directorate considers each individual case in order to resolve the situation in a fair and equitable manner.

¶1900 REGISTRATION RULES FOR DPSPs

¶1905 Background

The registration rules for DPSPs are set out in section 147 of the *Income Tax Act* (Canada) and amplified in Information Circular 77-1R5. A DPSP is a savings vehicle to which employer contributions in respect of all or a designated group of employees are made out of or determined by reference to profits from the employer's or a non-arm's length corporation's business. The plan must be registered with the CRA using a T2214 form.

Employer contributions to a DPSP, and any income earned on the contributions, are not taxed in the hands of a beneficiary until actually paid out of the plan. The employer may, for a given tax year, deduct all contributions made during or within 120 days of the tax year.

The registration rules for DPSPs include the following main features:

- Vesting in post-1990 employer contributions must occur after no more than two years of plan membership.
- Members are not allowed to contribute.
- Contributions made by the employer are normally calculated by reference to profits as defined in the plan and expressed as a percentage of profits for the year. Profits can be defined either as profits for that particular year or of previous years that have not yet been allocated from the business of the employer and corporations with which the employer does not deal at arm's length.
- There is no minimum contribution requirement for DPSPs as there is with a stand-alone defined contribution plan (as discussed at ¶1617); employer contributions may be made at the employer's discretion, or contingent on prerequisites (such as an employee's performance).

- The maximum employer contribution limits for a year are equal to the lesser of 18% of compensation (as defined at ¶205 except that no compensation is prescribed for an unpaid absence) and one-half the money purchase limit for the year (as defined in ¶1616). Thus, the current schedule of dollar limits is as follows:

Year	Maximum DPSP Employer Contribution
2005	$ 9,000
2006	$ 9,500
2007	$10,000
2008	$10,500
2009	$11,000
2010	$11,225
2011	(indexed in accordance with the average wage)

A chart showing the DPSP limits in effect since 1990 is in Appendix 3. Note that 2010 is the first year in which the DPSP limit (that is, the money purchase limit) increased in accordance with the average wage. Prior to 2010, the limits were set by Regulation changes.

- Excess employer contributions are not permitted (i.e., employer contributions in excess of the maximum deductible limits).
- All contributions made to a DPSP must be allocated to members in the year received by the DPSP trustee. It is not possible for the plan administrator's expenses to be paid out of contributions made to the fund, prior to allocating the balance of the contributions amongst the members — instead, they have to be made directly by the employer to the administrators, taken out of the investment income (if possible), or taken directly out of the members' account balances.
- Forfeitures must be reallocated to members, refunded to the employer, or used by the employer to offset future contributions by December 31 of the following year, or such later time as permitted by the Minister of National Revenue.
- Contributions (including any reallocated forfeitures) are reported as a PA and these contributions cannot be so large that the PA for an employee in a given year exceeds the maximum permissible PA (refer to ¶630 and ¶655 for details).
- No person who is related to the employer is allowed to become a beneficiary under a DPSP.

- No loan may be made to a participating employee or a beneficiary.

- A member's right or interest under the DPSP is not capable of surrender or assignment, in whole or in part (draft amendments to take effect after March 20, 2003, are to draw exceptions in cases of spousal breakdown orders, distributions of a deceased member's estate, and to prevent revocation of the plan's registration; as of the date of writing of this book, these amendments have not yet passed; however, the Registered Plans Directorate has indicated that the DPSP may be administered as though the amendments were in effect).

- All payments made under the plan to the trustee to the benefit of members must be allocated by the trustee to the individual members in the year in which the payments are received.

- The trustee must inform all new members in writing of their rights under the DPSP.

- No part of the trust fund may be invested in notes, bonds, debentures, or similar obligations of an employer making payments to the plan.

- All income and all capital gains and losses sustained by the trustee must be allocated to the members under the plan within 90 days after the end of the trust year in which they were earned.

- There is no prescribed compensation for a DPSP and therefore employer contributions may not be made to a DPSP during an unpaid leave of absence. However, with respect to an employee working abroad, the employer may only continue to contribute to a DPSP if the Minister so permits. The Minister will generally apply the same criteria as apply to the continued payment of contributions to a money purchase pension plan, as discussed at ¶645, ¶646, and ¶647.

¶1910 Distribution of Benefits

The member's vested DPSP account must be distributed no later than the earliest of the following:

- 90 days after the member ceases to be employed by an employer participating in the DPSP;

- 90 days after the termination of the DPSP;

- 90 days after the member's death; and
- the end of the year in which the member attains age 71.

Note that the 1996 federal Budget reduced the age 71 limit to age 69; however, the 2007 federal Budget increased the age limit back to age 71.

These distributions may be made in cash or in equal instalments, not less frequently than annually, over a period of up to 10 years, or may be used to purchase an annuity from an insurance company. A rollover may also be made on a tax-free basis to an RPP, RRSP, or another DPSP by a member. Draft amendments, to be effective after March 20, 2003, would also permit the RRSP transfer of benefits to a spouse or former spouse in the event of the member's death or as a result of a court order regarding marriage or relationship breakdown. The draft amendments will also permit the transfer of funds to the member's RRIF. Although these draft amendments have not yet passed, the Registered Plans Directorate has indicated that the DPSP may be administered as though the amendments were in effect.

In addition, if the plan text permits, the DPSP may allow members to withdraw all or a portion of their vested DPSP account at any time while continuing in employment. Again, the portion representing the employer's contributions may be rolled over to an RPP, RRSP, or another DPSP.

Except after a plan member's death, transfers from a DPSP to an RPP, RRSP, or another DPSP must be direct. Furthermore, the only occasions when the amount may be transferred to a spouse's RPP, RRSP, or DPSP are following a plan member's death or marriage breakdown. However, a tax-free transfer may be indirect in the case of a deceased plan member's spouse who receives a lump-sum through the estate of the deceased and contributes it to an RRSP, for example.

Chapter 20

¶2000 REGISTRATION RULES FOR COMBINATION PLANS AND HYBRIDS

¶2000 Introduction

A hybrid plan is an RPP that provides benefits under more than one type of benefit provision — the hybrid plan typically combines a defined benefit provision with a defined contribution or money purchase provision. Such plans are known as combination plans and both terms will be used interchangeably in this chapter.

Two main types of hybrid plans exist:

- A "stacked" plan in which the benefit is the sum of the benefits provided under separate defined benefit and money purchase provisions in the plan (including a defined benefit plan where AVCs are permitted).
- An integrated plan where the defined benefit and money purchase provisions are linked. For example, a defined benefit provision that is offset by a defined contribution provision, or a defined contribution provision with a top-up to a defined benefit formula.

Special registration rules apply to hybrid RPPs. These rules deal primarily with maximum benefits and maximum contribution rules that must be met in order to ensure that PA limits are not exceeded.

In addition to compliance with the rules set out in this chapter, each of the defined contribution and defined benefit provisions in the hybrid plan must also meet the registration requirements set out in Chapters 16 and 17 respectively.

¶2010 Contributions to Defined Contribution Component

Unlike a stand-alone defined contribution plan, there is no requirement for a minimum employer contribution of 1% of pensionable earnings to the defined contribution component of a hybrid plan.

The employee contribution limits to the money purchase component are described in Chapter 16.

¶2015 Maximum PA Rule

As discussed at ¶510, the *Income Tax Act* (Canada) requires that benefits provided under any RPP must not provide total pension credits exceeding the lesser of the money purchase limit for the year and 18% of compensation. This rule becomes particularly important for a hybrid plan. For example, in a two-tiered defined benefit/defined contribution plan, the contributions under the defined contribution tier must be limited to an amount that, when added to the defined benefit pension credit, will not exceed the lesser of the money purchase limit for the year and 18% of compensation.

The maximum PA rule came into effect with the 1991 calendar year. For hybrid plans, this rule essentially replaced the maximum benefit rules applicable under Information Circular 72-13R8. Under the prior tax registration rules, benefits payable under both the defined contribution components and the defined benefit components of a hybrid plan had to comply with a combined maximum benefit limit. Under the Regulations, the maximum PA rule is the mechanism that provides a cap on total benefits payable from a hybrid plan and the money purchase elements of the hybrid plan no longer need to be subject to the maximum benefit limitations. However, the maximum PA rule only applies to limit post-reform benefits; thus, pre-reform benefits payable from a hybrid plan — both defined contribution and defined benefit components — continue to be subject to the old maximum pension rules.

Refer to ¶810 for additional information on how the maximum PA rule works.

¶2020 Maximum Benefit Limitations

As discussed at ¶2015, under Information Circular 72-13R8, the total retirement benefit payable under a hybrid plan — that is, the total of the benefit available under both the defined benefit and the money purchase elements — was subject to the old maximum pension rules.

Under the *Income Tax Act* (Canada) and Regulations, the maximum pension rules no longer apply to the total benefit payable out of a hybrid plan. The maximum PA rule, discussed at ¶2015, works as the mechanism limiting the total benefits payable under the hybrid RPP for post-reform service.

Under the tax rules, only the post-reform defined benefit provision is subject to the maximum pension test. This entails the separation of the benefits payable under the defined benefit elements of the hybrid plan from the money purchase benefits. Additionally, the new maximums apply only to post-reform benefits. Since the total pre-reform benefits payable from a hybrid plan — both money purchase and defined benefit — continue to be subject to the old maximum pension rule, benefits therefore must also be separated into pre-reform and post-reform portions.

This split of the benefits payable under a combination plan for purposes of applying pre-reform and post-reform maximums can cause complexities for plan administration. Certain practical problems arise as a result of this pre-reform/post-reform split of benefit accruals. For example, in order to apply the maximum benefits test correctly to both pre-reform and post-reform accruals, the money purchase accumulations arising from pre-reform contributions must be maintained separately from the accumulations in respect of post-reform contributions. This special accounting is in addition to the separate accumulations that in many circumstances already must be maintained as a result of federal or provincial minimum standards legislation. As well, the reform dates of the applicable minimum standards legislation will likely differ from the reform dates of the maximum pension rules.

¶2025 Treatment of Pre-Reform AVCs

Pre-reform AVCs are not taken into account when comparing the accrued benefits for pre-reform service with the maximum pension limit under Information Circular 72-13R8. It should be noted that the CRA definition of an AVC is not the same as the definition of an AVC under minimum provincial standards. Because of this, certain employee contributions that might be included as AVCs for minimum standards purposes may nevertheless be excluded from the pre-reform maximum pension calculation. This potentially increases the overall benefit a member might receive.

Under the *Income Tax Act* (Canada), an employee contribution is considered to be an AVC if it is used to provide benefits on a money purchase basis and if it is not required as a general condition of membership in the RPP. For example, in a plan where members are automatically covered under a defined benefit tier, employee contributions to a defined contribution tier where the employer contributes 50% of the member's contribution will likely fall within this definition of an AVC, provided the member has the option — but is not required — to contribute to this defined contribution tier. In this situation, the pre-reform member contributions to the defined contribution tier may be excluded in the maximum pension calculation for purposes of the previous rules under Information Circular 72-13R8. Note, however, that the employer matching contributions to the defined contribution tier in this example do not fall within the definition of an AVC and therefore the benefit derived from these contributions must be included in the maximum pension calculation.

¶2030 Grandfathering and Timing for Compliance

As with stand-alone defined benefit plans and stand-alone defined contribution plans, certain special pre-reform rules apply to a grandfathered combination plan. For a definition of grandfathered plans, see ¶1707.

Special rules for hybrid plans focus primarily on the maximum PA rule, discussed at ¶2015, and the maximum benefit rule, discussed at ¶2020. These rules serve to provide a cap on benefits payable from a hybrid plan and permit the application of pre-reform and post-reform maximums. Other rules in Chapters 16 and 17 that have an impact on the defined benefit or money purchase provisions of the hybrid RPP take effect from the effective date of the particular rule.

For a grandfathered hybrid RPP that was amended effective January 1, 1992 to comply with all of the new registration rules, the defined benefit and money purchase components may only be separated, for the purpose of applying the maximum benefit rules to the defined benefit portion, as described in ¶2015, for benefits accruing on and after January 1, 1992, the effective date of the amendments to the plan for compliance with the tax rules. If the plan was amended to comply completely with all of the registration rules effective from an earlier date than January 1, 1992, the defined benefit provision may be separated from the money purchase elements for the purpose of applying the maximum pension rule from the effective date of the amendment, but not earlier than January 1, 1990. All benefit accruals prior to the date of the compliance amendments of a grandfathered RPP must continue to comply with the maximum pension limits under Information Circular 72-13R8.

For non-grandfathered hybrid RPPs, benefits accruing prior to the effective date of the new registration rules — the "pre-reform accruals" — must also continue to comply with the maximum limits under the old rules.

Regardless of whether a plan is grandfathered, different maximums apply to limit benefits accruing pre- and post-reform.

If a hybrid plan is not a grandfathered plan, the post-reform benefit limitations described at ¶2020 apply to all service. For all plans, the maximum PA rule discussed at ¶2015 applies from January 1, 1991.

Chapter 21

¶2100 REGISTRATION RULES FOR MULTI-EMPLOYER PLANS

¶2105 Additional or Adjusted Requirements

An MEP and an SMEP are exempt from some of the registration rules that apply to other RPPs (which are described in Chapters 16 and 17):

- The special restrictions ordinarily applicable to connected persons are not applicable to benefits earned by connected persons under an MEP or an SMEP. These special restrictions are set out at ¶1790.
- Members of defined benefit RPPs are not permitted to continue accruing benefits after retirement benefits have commenced to be paid (as set out in ¶1775) unless the retirement benefits being paid are phased retirement benefits. This restriction also applies where more than one pension plan in which the employer participates is involved. For MEPs and SMEPs, this cross-plan referencing is not applicable; in other words, if a member has commenced receipt of a pension under a regular RPP of his or her employer, the individual is not prevented from continuing to accrue benefits under an MEP or SMEP to which the employer is contributing on his or her behalf.
- Similarly, the cross-plan restrictions (set out at ¶1725) with regard to the payment of bridging benefits are not applicable, provided a member is not receiving bridging benefits from more than one defined benefit provision of the MEP or SMEP.

Another exemption applies to those MEPs or SMEPs sponsored by non-taxable organizations (typically in the public sector) that had been exempted from application of the maximum pension rules in Information Circular 72-13R8. For these plans, there is no maximum limit on the pension payable in respect of pre-1992 service (except for the special limit on pre-1990 benefits described at ¶1715). Thus, for example, a high income member of such a plan could retire in 2010 with a benefit of $3,000 per year of pre-1992 service, plus $2,494.44 per year of post-1991 service.

Additional exemptions apply if the MEP is an SMEP:

- Provided employer contributions are made in accordance with the plan as registered, the restrictions on contributions where there is a build-up of actuarial surplus (as set out at ¶ 1815) do not apply; however, the total contributions to be made each year must reasonably be expected not to exceed 18% of the total compensation of plan members. This requirement must continue to be satisfied whenever new contribution rates are established.
- SMEPs are not required to ensure that PAs are determinable, nor that benefits are appropriate in relation to PAs, which would be a requirement for other defined benefit RPPs (as set out at ¶ 1785 — refer to "13. Pension Credits Must Be Determinable and Not Inappropriately Low").
- SMEPs are exempt from the maximum pension rule set out at ¶ 1710, and from the rules related to the tracking of the five-year/three-year periods in respect of leaves of absence (set out at ¶ 1625 and ¶ 1747).
- SMEPs are also exempt from the offset rules discussed at ¶ 1785 — refer to "14. Offset Benefits".
- Employee contributions to an SMEP are not subject to the maximum limits described at ¶ 1805.

Employers and union negotiators should take particular note of the "18% of total compensation" rule on each occasion that the issue of pension contributions is brought to the bargaining table. Typically, contributions to SMEPs are determined by reference to a "cents per hour" formula. Therefore, the amount of contribution as a percentage of each member's total compensation is not immediately obvious, although, of course, it can be easily determined.

Additional hours of credit may be "purchased" by a member of an SMEP in a year during which he or she does not work on a full-time basis, as long as benefits under the plan are determined by reference to a member's employment hours and the plan permits a member to purchase such hours up to a reasonable measure of full-time hours that could have been worked. This differs from regular defined benefit RPPs, where additional service may be purchased only to the extent that the member has eligible service that is not already covered as pensionable service or has available "room" within the five-year/three-year leave of absence rules.

MEPs and SMEPs must comply with all of the other registration rules set out in Chapters 16 and 17, as applicable.

¶2200 FILING REQUIREMENTS FOR RPPS

¶2205 Introduction

This chapter sets out the requirements for filing with the Registered Plans Directorate of forms and documentation related to the initial and/or continuing registration of RPPs, in addition to the requirement for provision of information to certain parties. The procedures for reporting PAs and PSPAs are also summarized in this chapter. In addition, Appendix 2 lists the CRA forms used for RPPs, RRSPs, and DPSPs. Copies of some of the more frequently used forms are also reproduced. In addition, of course, there are filings to be made with the relevant pension benefits supervisory authority in order to meet the minimum standards legislation compliance requirements. However, a detailed discussion regarding these filings is beyond the scope of this book.

¶2210 Registration of a New RPP

To establish a new RPP, the plan administrator must apply for the registration of the RPP by filing certain documents within the calendar year of the plan's effective date. The following documents are required for registration of the RPP:

- a completed Application to Register a Pension Plan (Form T510) signed by the plan administrator;
- the plan document and any other documents that contain the terms of the plan;

- the trust deeds, insurance contracts, and other documents relating to the funding of benefits under the plan (not required for a non-insured pension plan registered in Quebec, British Columbia, Newfoundland and Labrador, or Saskatchewan which is required to establish a pension committee, if documentary evidence is provided to the CRA of the particulars of the pension committee members); and
- resolutions and by-laws relating to the plan and the pension fund.

The documents to be submitted must be originals or certified copies of originals. However, it is also acceptable to instead submit photocopies of the signed documents, although applicants who submit photocopies must make the documents with the original signatures available to the Registered Plans Directorate upon request.

The above documents must be sent by registered mail to the following address:

Canada Revenue Agency
Registered Plans Directorate
Ottawa, ON K1A OL5

or by courier to:

Information Holdings Operation Section — Pensions
Registered Plans Directorate
Canada Revenue Agency
875 Heron Road, A-200
Ottawa, ON K1A 1A2

The effective date of the plan may not be any earlier than January 1 of the calendar year in which a complete application is made. Once a complete application for registration is filed, the RPP is deemed to be registered from the effective date. While historically, the CRA has been somewhat lenient in enforcing the requirement for a completed package of documents within the year of the intended effective date, they are now enforcing that rule more strictly. See Registered Plans Directorate Newsletter 04-02 which confirms that the CRA will no longer accept incomplete applications and that an incomplete application will simply be returned to the submitter. The CRA's expressed intention is to issue deemed registration status within 60 days for any application that contains all the required documents.

The Registered Plans Directorate has, however, indicated that administratively they will accept an incomplete application in the case of a pending transaction to purchase or sell a business. They will continue to permit such filings if documents are submitted in the following year provided written advice is provided indicating that the documents required for a complete application will not be available until the following year and that the effective date of the plan will be the closing date of the transaction.

The plan must also be submitted for registration with the relevant minimum standards jurisdiction. There may be additional filing documentation, as required by the minimum standards jurisdiction.

¶2215 Amending an RPP

To amend an RPP, the plan administrator must apply for approval of the amendment by filing the following documents:

- a completed Application to Amend a Registered Pension Plan (Form T920); and
- amendment, plan revision, or change in funding media.

These documents must be sent by registered mail or courier within 60 days after the effective date of the amendment to the address shown at ¶2210. The Registered Plans Directorate will return incomplete applications to amend the RPP.

As with the filings required for the registration of a new RPP, the documents to be submitted must be originals or certified copies of originals. However, it is also acceptable to instead submit photocopies of the signed documents, although applicants who submit photocopies must make the documents with the original signatures available to the Registered Plans Directorate upon request.

¶2220 Other Filings

In the past, there was a separate annual information return to be prepared for the tax authorities in addition to the annual information return required by the minimum standards province of registration. However, all minimum standards jurisdictions have now harmonized their annual information return (AIR) with the CRA's Form T244, requiring the plan sponsor to file just one form with the minimum standards jurisdiction, within the time frames required by that jurisdiction. The harmonized return contains a schedule for the information required by the CRA (the jurisdiction is responsible for forwarding the completed schedule to the CRA).

When an RPP is terminated, the CRA does not require returns to be filed after the plan year in which the RPP became inactive. However, plan administrators are required to inform the CRA, in writing and within 60 days of the final distribution of the funds, of the date of the final distribution of the assets and the method of settlement.

Recently, two new forms have been introduced to assist in the identification, processing, and updating of contact information and submissions with respect to RPPs. Form T2011, Registered Pension Plan Change of Information Form, allows a plan sponsor to notify the Registered Plans Directorate of a change in the address or contact information for the plan sponsor, the consultant, or the trustee or insurer. Form T2014 is the Registered Pension Plan Priority Identification Form and is designed to assist in categorizing the nature of the request to facilitate its processing. Neither form is mandatory.

¶2225 Actuarial Reports

An actuarial report must be filed with the CRA whenever the Minister of National Revenue's approval is sought with respect to employer contributions to be made in connection with a defined benefit provision of an RPP. The actuary's recommendations must be contained in the actuarial report. The actuarial report must also contain all of the information set out in Registered Plans Directorate Newsletter 95-3. For a defined benefit plan, written approval for an employer contribution must be based on an actuarial valuation prepared as of a date that is not more than four years before the day on which a contribution is made.

Actuarial reports are not required for SMEPS or money purchase provisions. Generally, the CRA does not require an actuarial report for a defined benefit provision if an employer will not be making contributions to the provision. This could occur, for example, if the employer is taking a contribution holiday because of surplus. Another example would be in the case of a wind up of a defined benefit plan or provision: if no funding approval is required, then it is not necessary to submit a wind-up valuation report. However, such reports may still be required to be filed if requested by the Registered Plans Directorate. In any event, the minimum standards jurisdiction likely requires the report in question to be filed and typically the plan sponsor files the report with both the Registered Plans Directorate and the applicable pension benefits supervisory authority.

Various other forms relating to the actuarial valuation are also required by the applicable pension benefits supervisory authority. For example, the Actuarial Information Summary (AIS — Form T1200), must also be filed with reports submitted for RPPs which are registered with the Financial Services Commission of Ontario or the Office of the Superintendent of Financial Institutions Canada. It is expected that the AIS will also be required to be filed in the future for RPPs registered with other minimum standards jurisdictions.

In addition, the Regulations also give the Minister the right to request an actuarial report at any time.

It should be noted that contributions to a defined benefit RPP must be based on a valuation report with an effective date no more than four years prior to the date the contribution is made. Even if a triennial actuarial valuation report (normally required to be filed with the minimum standards regulator within six to nine months of the valuation date) is delayed until more than a year after the valuation date, the contributions must continue until the new valuation is complete. In such a situation, approval for an extension of the filing of the valuation report would normally be required from the minimum standards regulator if the usual six to nine months filing deadline is missed.

¶2230 Additional Requirement for Plans with Connected Members

Whenever a connected person becomes a member of an RPP, the employer is required to file a Connected Person Information Return (Form T1007) within 60 days after the member joins the plan or commences to accrue lifetime retirement benefits under a defined benefit provision of the RPP.

¶2235 Reporting of Pension Adjustments, Past Service Pension Adjustments, and Pension Adjustment Reversals

¶2236 Pension Adjustments

PAs are reported in Box 52 of the T4 slip, or in Box 34 of the T4A slip (for PAs accrued during a period of leave or reduced services) by the employer (or in the case of certain MEP situations, by the administrator). In addition, the registration number for the RPP must be reported in Box 50 of the T4 slip or in Box 36 of the T4A slip. The T4 or T4A slip for an individual for a particular calendar year must be filed on or before the last day of February immediately following the calendar year. Two copies of either the T4 or T4A slip are to be mailed to the individual's last address or delivered in person at the same time as they are filed with the CRA.

PAs are not required to be reported when they are nil (a PA cannot be less than zero) or in the year of the death of the individual.

Where benefits are retroactively provided to members in respect of a leave of absence, for example, and redetermined PAs are to be reported (as discussed at ¶635, ¶778, and ¶779), the revised T4 or T4A slip containing the revised PA must be reported within 60 days of the decision to provide the benefits (or the decision to make the additional contributions, in the case of a defined contribution plan). All information on the original T4 or T4A slip must be reproduced on the replacement.

If a PA has been incorrectly reported, an amended PA must be reported. An amended PA does not have to be reported if the difference between the previously reported PA and the amended PA is less than $50. However, this administrative rule does not apply if an employee wants his or her PA to be accurately reported or the CRA requests that the amended PA be reported.

The process for reporting an amended PA differs depending on whether the amended PA is in respect of one of the immediately preceding four tax years or whether the amended PA is for an earlier period (or whether it is a combination of the two). Refer to ¶560 for additional details on the processes.

There is no official deadline for refiling the corrected PA, but it should be done as soon as practicable after the error is discovered. All information on the original form must be reproduced on the replacement, the word "amended", and the tax year for which the correction is being made, should also be shown.

Refer to ¶515, ¶525, and ¶560 for additional information regarding the reporting of PAs.

¶2237 Past Service Pension Adjustments

PSPAs are reported by the plan administrator, which is generally the employer for most single employer plans.

The method of reporting PSPAs depends on whether the PSPA is exempt from certification. Chapter 10 provides information on when a PSPA is created and how to determine if a PSPA is exempt from certification.

If a PSPA is exempt from certification (see ¶1060 for the conditions under which a PSPA will be exempt), the administrator must file a completed T215 return, and distribute to members, within 120 days of the date of the past service event. If the return is not filed within the 120-day deadline, a late-filing penalty could be applied of a minimum of $100 and a maximum of $2,500 for each return. The T215 return consists of the following forms:

- T215 Supplementary: This form must be completed for each plan member whose PSPA is greater than nil. One copy is mailed to the Ottawa Technology Centre (see address listed at ¶1070), one copy is given to the member, and one copy is kept by the administrator.

- T215 Summary: This form reports the totals of certain information appearing on the T215 Supplementaries. One copy is attached to the T215 Supplementaries and mailed to the Ottawa Technology Centre and the other copy is kept by the administrator.

- T215 Segment: This form is required if more than 100 sheets or 300 separate T215 Supplementaries are filed. A T215 Segment is attached to each group of 100 sheets or 300 separate T215 Supplementaries and is mailed to the Ottawa Technology Centre.

If the administrator is filing more than 500 T215 Supplementaries, the return must be filed electronically. The electronic filing must be done either using the CRA's secure Internet file transfer (XML) service or on electronic media (CD, or DVD). If the administrator fails to file electronically, a penalty of $2,500 may be applied on first offence. For each subsequent offence, a penalty in increments of $2,500 may be applied.

If a PSPA is not exempt from certification (see ¶1065 for conditions under which PSPAs must be certified), the administrator must complete the form Applying for the Certification of a Provisional Past Service Pension Adjustment (Form T1004) for each member affected and mail three copies to the Ottawa Technology Centre. There is no deadline for filing this form; however, the benefit improvement may not be paid until the PSPA is certified by the CRA. Once the application is approved, two copies of the form are returned to the administrator, who must send a copy to the member within 60 days of the date on which the certification is received.

If the PSPA cannot be certified unless the member designates a qualifying withdrawal (as discussed at ¶1065), the member must complete the form Designating an RRSP Withdrawal as a Qualifying Withdrawal (Form T1006). The member may choose to have Form T1006 filed together with Form T1004. Otherwise, the member must file Form T1006 within 30 days of notification from the CRA that such a form is required. One copy must be mailed to the Ottawa Technology Centre and one copy is kept by the member. The member must include with the Form T1006 a copy of the T4RSP slip proving that the withdrawal was made. If the RRSP issuer has not yet provided a T4RSP slip, the RRSP issuer must complete Part IV of the form within 30 days of being requested to do so.

A PSPA that is less than $50 need not be reported unless the affected individual or the CRA so requests.

Refer to ¶1070 for details on how to correct, amend, or delete a previously reported PSPA.

¶2238 Pension Adjustment Reversals

PARs are reported by the plan administrator, which is generally the employer for most single employer plans, but could instead be a pension committee (for example, in Quebec). In the case of DPSPs, PARs are reported by the plan trustee. However, in this latter situation, the employer can be deemed to be a trustee for the purpose of reporting the PAR.

PARs are required to be reported on a quarterly basis, as follows:

For specified distributions taking place during:	*To be reported to CRA by:*
January 1 – March 31	May 30
April 1 – June 30	August 29
July 1 – September 30	November 29
October 1 – December 31	January 31

Note that, for terminations in the first three quarters of each year, the PARs are to be reported within 60 days of the end of the calendar quarter. However, for the final quarter, PARs are to be reported no later than the end of January in order to give individuals the opportunity to make additional RRSP contributions before the RRSP deadline and to be able to deduct the contributions from taxable income arising in the previous calendar year.

If there have been no terminations during a quarter that give rise to a PAR, then the plan administrator or DPSP trustee need not report anything for that calendar quarter.

If the calculation of the PAR results in a nil PAR (which would occur if the specified distribution is greater than the total of all relevant PAs and PSPAs previously reported in respect of the distribution), then there is no PAR reported.

Further, if the PAR to be reported is less than $50, there is no need to report the PAR. This could arise in two situations:

- the actual PAR calculates to be less than $50; or
- a PAR is being amended as a result of more accurate information or correction of an error and the resultant difference between the original and amended PARs is less than $50.

However, the terminating plan member has the right to request that the PAR be reported accurately, and the CRA may request it, in which case, the administrator or trustee is obligated to do so.

PARs are reported on the T10 return form, consisting of:

- a T10 Summary;
- T10 slips; and
- in certain situations, where there are more than 100 sheets or 300 T10 slips to be reported, T10 Segment forms where each group of T10 slips is grouped together into groups of 300 slips or 100 sheets.

A copy of the T10 form is forwarded to both the CRA and the affected plan member. The plan administrator or DPSP trustee fulfils his obligations by mailing the T10 form for the plan member to the individual's latest known address. If the form is returned as a result of a change of address that the administrator/trustee is unaware of, there is no further obligation on the part of the administrator or trustee since the CRA is also provided with a copy of the T10 and will advise the employee of the increased RRSP room in the next notice of assessment.

While there is a requirement to file PSPAs electronically if there are more than 500 PSPAs being reported, there is no similar requirement to file PARs electronically.

There is a late filing penalty that may be levied which is equal to the greater of:

- $100; and
- $25 for each day late, to a maximum of 100 days late (i.e., $2,500).

If a PAR is to be amended, than another T10 slip must be filed for the plan member and the Box 5 "Amendment" should indicate "yes". The amended T10 slip should contain the full amount of the revised PAR, not simply the difference between the original and revised PAR amounts. As noted above, if the calculation of the amended PAR is within $50 of the original PAR, there is no need to report a revised PAR amount, unless requested to do so.

¶2240 Provision of Information

If an individual requires information from another individual to complete the reporting of PAs, the information must be provided within 30 days of the written request if the return is to be filed in the calendar year in which the request is made. Otherwise, the information must be provided by January 31 of the year following the year of the request.

Information required by the administrator to determine the amount of a provisional PSPA must be provided within 30 days of the written request.

In reciprocal transfer or portability situations, a PA transfer amount is to be reported by the importing plan in order for the exporting plan to correctly calculate the PAR. (Refer to ¶1165.) Generally, the importing plan administrator will calculate the PA transfer amount and provide it to the exporting plan administrator. The importing plan administrator is required to advise the administrator of the exporting plan administrator within 30 days of the transfer that there will be a PA transfer amount to be reported. The importing plan administrator must then report the PA transfer amount to the exporting plan administrator within 60 days of the transfer.

Information required by the administrator to complete the Annual Information Return must be provided within 30 days of the written request.

The Minister of National Revenue may require information relating to the determination of PAs, PSPAs, and PARs or relating to the determination of whether the registration of an RPP may be revoked. Such request will be served personally or by registered or certified mail and will state the time period within which the information must be provided.

¶2300 PENSIONS FOR THE HIGHLY PAID

¶2305 Pensions for the Highly Paid

Not all retirement income provided by companies for its employees is from traditional registered retirement savings vehicles such as RPPs, DPSPs, or RRSP arrangements. For various reasons, most notably in the case of highly paid employees, a company may decide that that it needs to provide retirement income from outside a registered vehicle, either in whole or supplemental to a registered vehicle.

Registered arrangements are those that are registered under the *Income Tax Act* (Canada) in order to receive preferential tax treatment (tax-deductible contributions and tax sheltering of investment income), and include RPPs (defined benefit and defined contribution), RRSPs, LIRAs, LIFs, and other similar vehicles.

Until 2005, the limit on defined benefit pensions payable from RPPs had been frozen at effectively the same level for close to 30 years (that is, $1,715 per year of service in 1976 and $1,722 per year of service in 2003), impacting members of a 2% defined benefit plan who earned roughly $86,000 per year or more. The limit was increased stepwise starting in 2004 through to 2009. Starting in 2010, the limit will increase in accordance with the increases in the average wage. Thus, in 2010, with the defined benefit limit set at $2,494.44, members of a 2% plan with earnings over $124,722 will be impacted by the limits.

The maximum amount that can be contributed to a defined contribution RPP (employer and employee contributions combined) is set at 18% of earnings up to certain fixed dollar amounts. These fixed dollar amounts are also increasing along with the defined benefit limit increases. For 2010, the maximum dollar amount that may be contributed to a defined contribution plan is set at $22,450, with this maximum level reached at earnings of $124,722 and over.

Although the limits are increasing, they are still lower than the comparable limit in most other countries with which Canadian organizations compete for executive and professional talent. Many organizations, therefore, feel the need to "bridge the gap" by providing a non-registered arrangement on top of the registered plan for their higher income employees, for competitive reasons.

While the registered plan limits once impacted only the top level of executives, a much broader group of management and other highly skilled employees are now often affected, and it has become more common to offer non-registered pension benefits to top-up the RPP for any employee impacted by the limits. It has also become more common for the non-registered plan to match the ancillary benefits and the other terms of the employer's RPP. Thus, termination benefits and lump-sum options have become more common.

The non-registered portion of the pension promise may be provided through a number of different vehicles. Individual executives within an organization might negotiate different arrangements, depending on their particular situation and on their position within the organization.

Non-registered arrangements, or SERPs, can be unfunded, pre-funded, secured, or a combination of all three.

It should be noted that the CRA has, in the past couple of years, taken the viewpoint that excessively generous SERP benefits, whether unfunded, pre-funded, or secured, could be treated as salary deferral arrangements and therefore subject to the salary deferral rules under the *Income Tax Act* (Canada). If the benefit provided by the supplemental program essentially mirrors the terms of the underlying RPP, except for limits that are required in the RPP under the tax rules, then such benefits would generally be considered reasonable and not subject to salary deferral rules. Examples of unreasonable benefits would be credit for multiple years of service or salary which are inappropriate when compared to the use of actual years of service or salary. Similarly, a vesting schedule that is less than the vesting schedule under the RPP would not likely be appropriate. A salary deferral arrangement is a plan or arrangement whereby a person has a right to receive an amount in a future year in lieu of salary or wages, where one of the main purposes is to postpone payment of tax on such amount. The *Income Tax Act* (Canada) treats the deferred salary and wages as employment income in the year the employee earns the amount rather than in the year the amount is paid. The CRA viewpoint does not definitively apply this treatment to all enhanced SERP benefits, but it does increase the burden on the employer to demonstrate that there is no intent to defer taxes.

Unfunded defined benefit arrangements are simply pay-as-you-go arrangements where the benefit payments are paid from general revenues as they come due. Unfunded defined contribution arrangements typically take the form of notional accounting of contributions and investment income.

Secured arrangements provide a degree of benefit security to the SERP members by having the plan sponsor enter into an arrangement with a financial institution, such as a bank, so that in exchange for paying a relatively small annual fee, the financial institution will deposit funds equal to the benefit promise into a trust in the event the plan sponsor defaults on a pre-agreed set of conditions.

Pre-funding may not be attractive from the employer's viewpoint (for a defined benefit arrangement and from the employee's viewpoint for a defined contribution arrangement), because the same tax advantages are not available for non-registered arrangements as are available for the registered portion. The most common type of pre-funding for defined benefit SERPs is through the use of an RCA, a tax vehicle introduced in 1998 specifically for the pre-funding of such types of benefits. The most common type of pre-funding for defined contribution SERPs is an after-tax savings account. These are discussed in greater detail at ¶2315 and ¶2320.

¶2310 Maximizing the Defined Benefit Registered Pension Plan Benefits

The registered portion of most pension arrangements for the highly paid is a defined benefit plan with benefits close to or at the maximum allowed.

It should be noted that if a SERP is established to top-up pension amounts that are restricted by the limits under the *Income Tax Act* (Canada), the SERP is generally exempt from pension standards legislation. However, if there is no underlying RPP and/or the underlying RPP does not provide benefits at the maximum, the SERP may not be exempt from pension standards legislation and therefore may be subject to funding rules. For this reason, most SERPs are designed to top-up benefits from an RPP.

To the extent that a registered defined benefit plan is used for the benefits up to the maximums permitted under the *Income Tax Act* (Canada), there are special funding rules for "executive only" pension plans. If the total of the PAs of benefits for "connected persons" and highly paid employees exceeds 50% of the total PAs of the plan, limitations on funding must be taken into account. Highly paid, in this context, refers to employees who are earning in excess of 2.5 times the YMPE. Thus, in cases where the executives belong to the same RPP as other employees, these special rules generally do not apply. Refer to ¶1830 to ¶1840 for more information on "designated plans".

It is common for a non-registered SERP to be provided in conjunction with an RPP, in such a way that the non-registered arrangement acts as a top-up that brings the total benefits under the registered and non-registered plans to a desired target income. In this situation, the tax effectiveness and security of the combined arrangement can be enhanced by maximizing the value of the benefits payable from the RPP, thereby minimizing the benefits needed to be payable under the non-registered arrangement. The most obvious technique for achieving this is to ensure that the RPP provides the maximum permitted benefits at normal and early retirement. A secondary reason for maximizing the benefits under the RPP, or at least to provide benefits that are no less generous than those under the SERP, is to avoid the situation discussed at the end of ¶2305, whereby the SERP benefits could be viewed as excessively generous.

Another technique that can be used to maximize benefits from the RPP is in the situation where the "target benefit" does not have guaranteed inflation protection after retirement. In this case, the RPP benefit is increased each year by the maximum indexing permitted under the *Income Tax Act* (Canada), as discussed at ¶1770. Over time, the RPP benefit will increase and eventually "catch up" to the level of the target benefit. Thereafter, no SERP benefit needs to be paid. This technique has benefits to both the employer and the member. The employer can fund the increases under the RPP in a tax-effective manner. From the employee's perspective, the employee has greater benefit security, as eventually the full pension becomes provided under the RPP.

A flexible pension plan may also be used to maximize the value of a defined benefit plan (see ¶120). Under this approach, the employee (and possibly the employer as well) makes additional contributions to a defined contribution side account that can be used at the time of retirement to purchase ancillary benefits (partial or full indexing or bridging benefits, for example). If this cost-sharing approach is taken, it may be beneficial to offer less generous ancillary benefits from the RPP to provide room for the executive to later purchase these ancillaries using the flex contributions; such a strategy would also afford the employer the opportunity to provide more generous supplemental benefits from the non-registered plan.

¶2315 Funded or Secured Defined Benefit SERPs

It is increasingly common for defined benefit SERP promises to be funded (either partially or fully) through the use of an RCA or to be secured through an LOC.

Funding Through a Retirement Compensation Arrangement

As noted at ¶2305, the most common way to pre-fund a defined benefit SERP is through an RCA.

The *Income Tax Act* (Canada) defines an RCA to be any arrangement under which contributions are made by an employer to provide for benefits to be received after employment has terminated, other than an arrangement that qualifies as something else. In other words, if it looks like a pension fund but it is not an RPP, it is probably an RCA. The language in the *Income Tax Act* (Canada) with respect to RCAs is designed to cover all attempts to secure post-employment compensation in any manner, other than those arrangements contemplated elsewhere in the *Income Tax Act* (Canada), such as RPPs and RRSPs.

An RCA is created when contributions are made to a custodian (e.g., a trust company), thereby keeping the RCA assets separate from the employer's other assets. A book entry in the employer's account or a separate investment fund that does not place the SERP ahead of the other creditors does not create an RCA.

Whenever contributions are remitted to an RCA, an equal amount of "refundable tax" must be remitted to the CRA by the SERP plan sponsor. The tax is refunded, without interest, to the custodian when benefits are actually paid out to the beneficiaries.

At the end of each calendar year, the RCA custodian must compute and remit additional amounts to the CRA so that the accumulated refundable tax account equals 100% of the contributions made to date to the trust plus 50% of the realized investment earnings on the fund, less 50% of benefit disbursements to date. The fund is not afforded any favourable capital gains or dividend tax treatment. The effect is to produce an effective rate of return on the total contributions to the RCA trust and to the corresponding refundable tax account with the CRA of about half the actual rate of return that could be achieved on registered investments.

Despite these negative tax consequences compared to an RPP, some organizations do establish fully funded RCAs to secure their SERP obligations. An RCA trust provides security comparable to an RPP, as long as the trustee is empowered to act without direction from the employer (just as a government regulator can assume administration of an RPP). RCAs probably receive more attention than other pre-funded or secured arrangements because there is a build-up of assets and a greater perceived degree of security than other approaches.

An RCA may provide for tax-deductible employee contributions in addition to employer contributions, provided the employer contributions equal or exceed the employee contributions, the plan is a pension plan, and a Canadian custodian is used. This is the only viable funding option for tax-deductible employee contributions in excess of the maximum permissible employee contributions to an RPP.

In an RCA, the fund, rather than the employee, is taxed. If the employee terminates employment before vesting, the employee does not suffer any adverse tax consequences. When the benefits become payable, the refundable tax is returned to the fund after the end of the year at the rate of 50% of the benefit actually paid. When an RCA is wound up, the employer may need to make a temporary loan to the trust in order to pay out all of the benefits due. The employer is repaid when the refund from the CRA becomes available the following year.

The 50% refundable tax is applied to contributions and realized investment gains during the year (net of benefit and expense payments during the year). Note that since unrealized investment gains are not subject to the 50% refundable tax, it may make sense to use a different investment policy than what would be used for an RPP. Therefore, the refundable tax would have less of an impact on a high-growth, low turnover portfolio as compared to a portfolio that regularly realizes all of its investment gains.

As with an RPP, there are various CRA reporting requirements. These filings are related to amounts paid to or from the refundable tax account and are normally completed by the RCA custodian. There is no requirement to report on the value the benefits promised under the SERP.

Securing Through a Letter of Credit

LOCs provide third-party protection with little current cash outlay on the employer's part. Under a typical LOC, a financial institution such as a bank agrees to pay the beneficiary of the LOC in the event that the company should default on its payments or in other predetermined circumstances. When an LOC is used to secure supplementary pensions, it is generally held by a corporate trustee in an RCA trust. The employer makes a contribution to the trust equal to the bank's fee for the LOC, plus the trustee's expense charges, thereby creating an RCA, and makes a matching RCA refundable tax remittance to the CRA. The employer can take a current tax deduction for both payments.

The CRA's position is that the LOC must be unsecured: if it is secured, then they will deem the full face amount to have been contributed to an RCA, which in turn would require a corresponding refundable tax payment by the employer.

Under the terms of the trust, the trustee is required to demand payment from the bank by calling the LOC in the event the employer fails to make a supplementary pension payment as it falls due or if the employer fails to arrange for renewal of the LOC prior to its expiry date. In some cases, the LOC may also include a provision that it will be called in in the event of a change of control of the employer. It should be noted that the CRA deems the calling of an LOC to be a contribution to the RCA so that half of the face amount must be paid by the trustee as a refundable RCA tax. As a result, 50% of the LOC proceeds will be unavailable until the first half of the benefits have been paid or the plan is wound up.

The employer must contribute an amount to the RCA trust sufficient to allow it to purchase the LOC from the bank each year, and the employer must also pay the corresponding refundable RCA withholding tax to the CRA. If the LOC is the only asset of the trust, then the refundable tax account is not recoverable from the CRA until the arrangement is wound up. However, if the RCA is partially funded, then the cost of the LOC might serve to offset the refundable tax on investment income that would otherwise be payable. Typically, for administrative reasons, one RCA is created for all the eligible employees and only one LOC is issued, rather than having individual RCA accounts with corresponding individual LOCs.

The fee for an LOC is comparable to the fee charged by the bank for a line of credit, and any LOC will reduce the available line of credit. The fee and maximum line of credit depends on the credit worthiness of the corporation, but an annual fee of 1% of the guaranteed amount is currently typical for an unsecured LOC. The LOC is usually renewed annually with the face amount together with the refundable tax account and any assets in the RCA being sufficient to cover the cost of settling the SERP benefits one year hence, based on the advice of an actuary.

While the cost of the LOC is usually relatively low at the outset, it tends to increase over time and is non-refundable. The LOC annual renewal cost will increase when an employer's finances become unstable, at which point full funding may become the only viable option from an employee security point of view (but the employer may not have the necessary cash to fund the plan at the time it is most needed).

While an LOC can provide security to employees at substantially less cost than a fully funded RCA, especially for a financially secure tax-exempt employer, it may be difficult to unwind an LOC arrangement at a future date other than by fully funding the benefits and by securing consent from all the beneficiaries. An LOC can prove to be more expensive than other options if maintained indefinitely as the refundable tax account will grow to a significant portion of total plan liabilities.

Interestingly, LOCs have also been attracting more interest in recent years in the funding of RPPs. A few minimum standards jurisdictions have permitted or are considering permitting the use of LOCs to meet an organization's funding requirements for solvency deficiencies.

¶2320 Alternatives to RCAs and LOCs

The methods described in ¶2315 best lend themselves to defined benefit SERPs. There are other approaches that can be considered for defined benefit SERPs, as discussed in this section. Further, while the RCA and LOC concepts can be extended to defined contribution SERP promises, there are other alternatives to consider for those types of SERPs as well. The most appropriate solution, or combination of solutions, for a particular plan sponsor, can only be determined after a complete review of the plan sponsor's financial position, funding philosophy, and its objectives with respect to meeting the SERP retirement promise.

Unfunded Pay-As-You-Go Arrangements

Unfunded defined benefit arrangements are simply pay-as-you-go arrangements where the benefit payments are paid from the general revenues of the company as they come due. Such arrangements, while administratively simple, provide no security to the SERP members since there are no assets, no safeguards, and no external oversight.

A subset of a pay-as-you-go arrangement is used commonly for defined contribution SERPs. Under this type of arrangement, the defined contribution SERP balances are notional accounts. The "deemed" contributions are accumulated with notional investment credits and the account balance is tracked notionally to determine an amount of lump-sum benefit to be paid at retirement. The plan sponsor must decide on an appropriate methodology to use to determine the notional investment income to be credited to the member's "account balance". If the objective is for the arrangement to mirror an underlying defined contribution RPP, then logical choice is to credit the notional account with the same rate of return that the member is earning on the RPP's investment funds. Other possibilities include using a fixed rate of return, a return linked to bond yields (with or without the addition of a fixed spread representing a partial equity risk premium) or a phantom fund consisting of a mixture of investments with rates of return measured against specific benchmarks. Although it is normal to think that the member is bearing the risk in a defined contribution arrangement, in an unfunded defined contribution SERP, the employer is liable for notional investment returns, which could be higher or more volatile than expected, and the employer generally does not have the actual investments with returns to offset this liabililty. For this reason, some employers choose more stable rates of notional investment returns and avoid linking the notional returns to equity market returns.

Annuities

Immediate annuity purchases can be a practical way to settle and secure a SERP at retirement. The cost of providing this security may not be excessive in comparison to pay-as-you-go funding on an after-tax present value cash flow basis for tax-paying entities. This is due to the fact that the full cost of the annuity purchase is immediately deductible by the employer, whereas pay-as-you-go benefits are only deductible when they are paid. At the same time, the annuity premiums are taxable to the retiring employees when paid to the insurer (unless the annuity policy is owned by the employer, in which case an RCA is created) and a portion of the annuity payments is also taxable each year as interest income. As a result, when arranging for an annuity purchase in lieu of SERP benefit payments, the employer typically needs to pay somewhat more than the accrued SERP liability in order to make the retiring employee whole on an after-tax basis. This approach is usually referred to as a "grossed-up prescribed annuity". The monthly annuity payment is less than the monthly SERP payment to reflect the fact that it is not fully taxable, but the lump-sum payment is "grossed-up" for the taxes the employee has to pay on the annuity purchase. The interest portion of the annual annuity benefit is favourably taxed in a fixed manner for the employee's lifetime, as prescribed by Regulation 300 under the *Income Tax Act* (Canada) provided the prescribed conditions are met.

Life Insurance

If life insurance is used to pre-fund retirement income benefits, it is taxed like an RCA, with the plan sponsor assumed to be the custodian. Thus, the plan sponsor must not only pay the annual premium, but must also send an equal amount to the CRA. However, the build-up in the underlying cash value of a qualifying policy is on a tax-sheltered basis, hence, no RCA tax is required on the investment income being credited.

Life insurance policies purchased with after-tax dollars provide another alternative for funding non-registered plans on a tax-effective basis. As the investment return inside the cash value of a policy is only taxable to the life insurance company, policies with high cash values can be tax-effective. The employer may not deduct the premiums for income tax purposes. The policy must be maintained in force until the death of the insured to maintain the tax-free status of benefits.

When reviewing the appropriateness of the life insurance approach, key elements should be analyzed. Often the commissions and expenses associated with these policies outweigh the tax advantage. In addition, life insurance policies only pay out on death, not on retirement. Therefore, when a policy is taken out on an individual, premiums are paid for as long as required under the terms of the policy. After the individual retires, his or her pension benefits must be paid out of the employer's cash flow, although loans against the policy cash values could be utilized for this purpose. Under one possible life insurance strategy, the death benefit is paid to the employer and is theoretically used to repay the employer for all the benefits and premiums it has already paid out; however, this may not occur until decades after the individual's retirement. Plan sponsors considering the use of insurance policies should be wary of illustrations showing the death of the individual conveniently at the time when insurance policy proceeds exactly match the face value of the loan. Consideration should also be given to the consequences of a change in circumstances, such as termination of employment or (if the insurance is designed to pre-fund surviving spouse benefits) divorce.

After-Tax Savings Plan

Another arrangement that can be used to pre-fund retirement benefits for an individual is an after-tax savings plan sometimes also referred to as an employee savings plan. Under this approach, the employer makes contributions on the employee's behalf into a non-tax-sheltered account. The payment is tax-deductible by the employer as compensation, which means that it will also attract payroll and other taxes. The payment is included as taxable income to the employee. Any resulting investment income and realized capital gains or losses are treated as if they are earned directly by the individual. Vesting is immediate. Relative to an RCA, this approach is advantageous when the employee's marginal tax rate is less than 50%. In addition, capital gains and dividends receive preferential tax treatment, instead of being taxed at the 50% RCA refundable tax rate.

After-tax savings plans are commonly used as defined contribution SERPs although plan sponsors that have after-tax savings plans as one component in their retirement program do not typically think of the after-tax savings plan as a SERP. Where the employee's earnings result in a level of contribution that is higher than that permitted to defined contribution RPPs under the *Income Tax Act* (Canada), the excess contributions are directed to an after-tax savings plan so that the member is kept whole in terms of the amount of contribution made as a percentage of pay. However, the underlying RPP benefit need not be a defined contribution benefit; any type of top-up benefit for high earners could be funded through the use of an after-tax savings plan and an appropriate level of contribution.

Tax-Free Savings Accounts

In 2008, the federal government introduced TFSAs for Canadians 18 and over. The TFSA allows taxpayers to contribute up to $5,000 per year in after-tax funds to a designated account. While TFSA contributions are not tax-deductible, withdrawals are tax-free and investment income (including interest, capital gains, and dividends) is tax sheltered. Withdrawals result in restored contribution room in subsequent tax years. Unused contribution room can be carried forward into subsequent years, and the yearly maximum contribution will be indexed to inflation (rounded to the nearest $500). TFSAs are available as of the 2009 taxation year. While not strictly created for use as a retirement savings vehicle (they are intended to help Canadians save for a variety of life events, including retirement), it is anticipated that TFSAs will be used in conjunction with after-tax savings plans to provide some tax sheltering not otherwise offered under the after-tax savings plan.

Employees Profit Sharing Plan (EPSP)

The EPSP rules are set out in section 144 of the *Income Tax Act* (Canada). Employer contributions are made either from current or accumulated profits. For this reason, an EPSP does not lend itself to non-profit organizations, public sector employers' or companies with negative retained earnings. Employer contributions must be allocated contingently or absolutely to the participants each year. Although the employer may not permit a distribution from the trust fund until the individual's retirement or termination of employment, the individual is taxed each year on the share of the employer contributions and trust earnings allocated to him or her as if in immediate receipt of such amounts, regardless of any vesting requirements. The individual's allocated share of net capital gains (or losses) realized by the trust fund is subject to capital gains tax treatment. If an individual forfeits an EPSP benefit on termination or retirement due to the plan's vesting rules, he or she can claim a tax deduction for the employer contributions that were taxed in previous years.

Company Stock

There are a variety of long-term incentive plans available, usually for senior employees, the most typical varieties being stock option plans and stock purchase plans. Although these are not usually regarded as a primary means of providing retirement income (their real value lies in their application as a long-term incentive plan), they are a means of providing employer monies or subsidies to individuals in advance of retirement to assist them in building an estate and, if significant, can provide a material source of income in retirement.

Any of these vehicles for pre-funding or securing future retirement income may be appropriate, depending on the circumstances, and are often used in combination with each other and with and in conjunction with the RPP.

Appendix 1

TRANSITION AND HISTORICAL RULES

TRANSITION AND HISTORICAL RULES

The main body of the book is concerned with the rules as they apply for 2010 and later years. While many of these rules applied equally for the years 1990 through 2009, there are a number of transitional rules and exceptions for certain situations, particularly with respect to the rules for determining PAs, PSPAs and PARs. These transition rules and exceptions have been set out in this Appendix for reference and historical purposes.

1. Conceptual Overview of RRSP Contribution Rules (Chapter 3)

A. One Year Lag

The one year lag in the system (i.e., RRSP contribution room in a particular year is based on plan membership in the prior year) had one further consequence in addition to those set out at ¶310. This consequence resulted in a slight element of unfairness in 1990. If an individual had no earned income in 1990, he or she was not able to make an RRSP contribution in either 1990 or 1991, because the contribution limit for both years was based on earned income in 1990 — the 1990 contribution limit was determined under the previous set of rules, based on the current year's earned income.

B. $8,000 Overcontribution Threshold Reduced to $2,000

As outlined at ¶310, there is a threshold of excess RRSP contributions above which a penalty tax will apply. Originally this threshold was established at $8,000 on a lifetime basis. However, in the February 1995 federal Budget, this threshold was reduced from $8,000 to $2,000 applicable to the 1996 and subsequent taxation years.

2. Detailed RRSP Contribution Rules (Chapter 4)

A. Earned Income

Until the end of 1989, it was possible for a pensioner to include his or her pension income, net of any transfers of pension income to the pensioner's RRSP, for the purpose of calculating earned income on which

RRSP contributions are based. However, for 1990 and subsequent taxation years, the definition of earned income was amended to exclude all benefits received from registered pension plans, RRSPs, registered retirement income funds (RRIFs), DPSPs (including amounts from revoked plans), retiring allowances (even the portion not transferable to an RRSP), RCAs, the Canada Pension Plan (CPP), the Quebec Pension Plan (QPP), and Old Age Security (OAS). It was also amended to exclude death benefits, as well as Canadian-source income (or losses) for people who are not residents of Canada for tax purposes.

In the February 1992 federal Budget, the Minister of Finance expanded the definition of earned income, effective for 1991, to include CPP/QPP disability pensions, for the purpose of determining eligible RRSP contributions for the 1992 and subsequent taxation years.

B. RRSP Contribution Room before 1990

Until and including 1990, the RRSP contribution limit for a year equalled the lesser of 20% of that year's earned income and a dollar limit. The dollar limit equalled:

- $7,500 for individuals who were not active members of a pension plan or DPSP;
- $3,500 for employees for whom the employer made a DPSP contribution during the year (even if only in respect of the previous year); or
- $3,500 less any employee RPP contributions for members of a pension plan who, in general terms, accrued benefits under the plan in respect of pensionable service in the year.

C. Adjustments to RRSP Contribution Limits from 1990 to 1992

The RRSP contribution room available at any point in time after January 1, 1991 is set out at ¶415. Two further adjustments applied as follows:

- Unused RRSP contribution room that was carried forward from an earlier calendar year excluded any portion of the RRSP contribution limit for 1990 or earlier years that was not utilized.
- RRSP contribution room is reduced by any PSPA that has become effective during a particular calendar year. However, as a result of a February 14, 1992 Press Release from the Department of Finance, PSPAs in respect of 1990 or 1991 had no impact on RRSP contribution room until 1992. Thus, 1992 RRSP contribution room is also reduced by any PSPA that arose in respect of past service events that occurred in 1990 or 1991.

D. Transfer of Annuity/Pension Income to RRSP

From January 1, 1990, periodic annuity and pension income was no longer permitted to be transferred directly into an individual's own RRSP.

However, as an interim measure, transfers of pension payments or annuity income from an RPP or DPSP could be made to a spousal RRSP until and including the 1994 taxation year, up to an annual limit of $6,000, without reducing RRSP contribution room. This did not apply to income received from Old Age Security or the Canada/Quebec Pension Plan, nor to annuity income from another RRSP (even if that annuity income was derived from funds that had previously been transferred to the RRSP from an RPP).

The special attribution rule which applies to spousal RRSP contributions (as described at ¶ 430) applied equally to these transfers of annuity and pension income into a spousal RRSP.

E. RRSP Contribution Carry-Forward

Prior to the March 6, 1996 federal Budget, there was a mechanism in place for limiting the amount of RRSP contribution room that may be carried forward. The carry-forward was generally seven years; however, because of how the carry-forward limit was calculated, that limit would have affected a much smaller number of people than was commonly presumed. Thus, for most individuals, it was possible to have a carry-forward longer than this. The March 6, 1996 Notice of Ways and Means Motion eliminated the limit and, as a result of that change, all individuals may carry forward all unused RRSP contribution room indefinitely into the future.

F. Impact of Alternative Minimum Tax

Prior to 1998, an individual who made a large RRSP contribution in a calendar year could have caused the Alternative Minimum Tax to be triggered where it might not otherwise be applicable. This was occurring with increased frequency in the 1990s due to an increase in the number of large RRSP contributions being made from severance packages. As a result of this unintended inequity, the February 24, 1998 federal Budget removed RRSP contributions from the Alternative Minimum Tax calculation. There were also some retroactive measures introduced for the years 1994 through 1997.

G. Expansion of Definition of Spouse for Spousal RRSPs

Prior to 1993, a spousal RRSP contribution could only be made to the RRSP of a legally married spouse. With effect from 1993, the definition of "spouse" was expanded to include certain common-law relationships. Effective January 1, 2001, the definition was also expanded to include same-sex partners living in common-law relationships.

H. Penalties for Excess RRSP Contributions

Under the rules that were in effect before 1990, if an individual made an RRSP contribution of more than $5,500 (or the amount that may be deducted from taxable income, if greater) in a year, a penalty tax arose. The penalty tax of 1% was applied monthly to the amount of the excess existing in the RRSP at the end of the month. This rule for determining penalty taxes continued to apply to excess contributions that were made before 1991 (excluding contributions made in the first 60 days of 1991 in respect of 1990).

Under the rules for determining the penalty taxes for contributions made after 1990 (including contributions made in the first 60 days of 1991 in respect of 1990), as discussed at ¶435, there was a penalty-tax-free lifetime allowance of $8,000. However, this allowance was reduced from $8,000 to $2,000 in the February 27, 1995 federal Budget.

3. Introduction to Pension Adjustments and General PA Rules (Chapter 5)

A. PAs Greater than Money Purchase Dollar Limits

The 1996 federal Budget reduced and froze defined contribution dollar limits without a corresponding change to the rules in calculating PAs (i.e. the transition rules discussed at ¶720); a situation could have arisen from 1996 to 2003 where high-income earners exceeded the reduced defined contribution dollar limits, thereby violating the "maximum PA rule" described at ¶510. In most situations, exceeding the "maximum PA rule" causes an RPP to become revocable. In order to avoid revocation, transitional provisions ensured that under such circumstances, an otherwise acceptable defined benefit RPP would not become revocable. The transitional provisions stated that if a plan member's PA exceeded the dollar limit in any year from 1996 to 2003, the portion of the PA that was more than the dollar limit, but less than $15,500 was disregarded.

B. PA in Year of Non-Vested Termination

When a member of an RPP (other than a specified multi-employer plan and a multi-employer plan, as discussed at ¶910 and ¶915) or a DPSP terminates from all RPPs and DPSPs of an employer, prior to becoming vested, and does not subsequently acquire a right to vested benefits under the RPP or DPSP later in the year of termination, a special PA rule applied for the year of termination, if the year of termination was during 1990 to 1996, inclusive.

For the years 1990 to 1996, these special rules were as follows:

- For defined contribution plans, the PA equaled the employee contributions made to the plan during that final year — any interest that is credited to employee contributions is not included in the PA. If the plan was non-contributory, the PA equaled zero.
- For defined benefit plans, the PA equaled the lesser of the employee contributions made to the plan during the final year (not including interest on those contributions and excluding any contributions to purchase past service benefits) and the PA that would have applied had the individual been vested. Generally, the result equaled the employee contributions made to the plan that year, unless the employee terminated service early in the year or the plan formula was relatively poor. Again, if the plan was non-contributory, the PA equaled zero.
- For a DPSP, that final year's PA equaled zero.
- If a member of an RPP or DPSP terminates when only partially vested, the PA rules for a fully-vested termination apply (e.g., based on a partial year of service for a defined benefit plan, or including the full employer contribution for that year in the case of a defined contribution RPP or DPSP).

Beginning in 1997, these special rules were eliminated as a result of the introduction of PARs (see Chapter 11). The final-year PA for a member of an RPP or DPSP who terminates and is not vested, is now calculated in the usual manner.

It should be noted, however, that there are certain past service pension adjustment situations that require the PA calculated using these special year of non-vested termination rules to be taken into account in order to properly calculate the PSPA, as a result of the introduction of the PAR. Refer to ¶ 1037 for further details.

C. PA for a Specified Retirement Arrangement

As set out in ¶ 545, there are special rules to determine the PA for a specified retirement arrangement. An amount is determined in accordance with the following:

the lesser of

- 18% of the individual's compensation from that employer less the PA offset, and
- the money purchase limit for the year less the PA offset.

For years prior to 1997, the PA offset used in this calculation is $1,000 and from 1997 on, the PA offset used is $600.

For the years 1996 through 2003, $15,500 is used as the money purchase limit for the year instead of using the actual money purchase limit.

If the PAs reported with respect to other plans that the member may have been participating in is less than 85% of this calculated amount, then a special PA must be reported in respect of the specified retirement arrangement. The special PA is equal to the above calculated amount, less the actual PA reported under an RPP, DPSP or foreign pension plan, if the member was also a member of such plan.

There was a further adjustment in the specified retirement arrangement PA calculation for the years 1996 to 2003: the actual reported specified retirement arrangement PA (before subtracting the actual PA reported in respect of the other plans) is the lesser of:

- 18% of the resident compensation from that employer less the PA offset; and
- the money purchase limit for the year (note that the PA offset is ignored at this point).

D. Prescribed Amounts for a Government Sponsored Retirement Arrangement

As set out at ¶ 545, the Regulation prescribed amounts which reduced the amount an individual, who is a member of a government sponsored retirement arrangement (GSRA), can contribute to his or her RRSP. The reduction first applied in 1994, based on participation in a GSRA in 1993. For 1994 to 1996, the prescribed amount for a GSRA is equal to the money purchase limit minus $1,000. For years after 1996, the prescribed amount for a GSRA is equal to the preceding year's money purchase limit.

4. Pension Adjustments for Money Purchase Plans (Chapter 6)

A. Employer Contributions for 1989

As discussed at ¶ 610, the PA for a defined contribution RPP for a year includes all employer contributions made during the year or made in respect of the year by the end of February of the following year. This means that employer contributions made by the end of February 1990 in respect of 1989 were not included in any PA. However, there was no such exception for those contributions that were made after the end of February 1990, in respect of 1989 — these were to be included in the PA for the year in which those contributions were made, in spite of the fact that they covered pre-1990 service.

B. Additional Voluntary Contributions; Optional Employee Contributions to Defined Contribution Provision

As mentioned at ¶ 610, any additional voluntary contributions (AVCs) made on a money purchase basis to an RPP are included in the PA. However, a special rule excluded them from the 1990 PA.

In certain situations, this exclusion of 1990 AVCs from the 1990 PA was extended to optional employee contributions to a defined contribution provision of an RPP. This occurs where an individual belongs to a two-tiered RPP, under which employees who are covered by the basic tier (whether on a defined benefit or defined contribution basis) are permitted to contribute to an optional upper tier, which is in the form of a defined contribution provision. Employees may choose to contribute to the upper tier, but are not required to do so. Since an AVC, for purposes of determining whether it was to be included in the 1990 PA, is defined in subsection 248(1) of the *Income Tax Act* (Canada) as a contribution made by a plan member, that is used to provide benefits under a money purchase provision of the plan, and is not required as a general condition of plan membership, any employee contributions to the upper tier would be classified as AVCs and therefore would have been excluded from the 1990 PA. Note, however, that all 1990 employer contributions were to be included in the 1990 PA, using the usual rules discussed at ¶ 610.

Consider a defined contribution RPP under which members may contribute 1%, 2% or 3% of their pay and the employer will match these contributions. Assume that this is the only plan provision under which members are covered (i.e., in this case, the defined contribution provision is not supplementary to another defined benefit or defined contribution tier). Clearly, membership in the plan requires the employee to contribute at least 1% of pay. Therefore, the first 1% of pay does not fall within the definition of an AVC, since it is required as a general condition of plan membership. However, any employee contributions in excess of 1% of pay do fall within the definition, and therefore the excess over 1% of pay would have been excluded from the 1990 PA.

C. Reallocations of Non-Vested Forfeitures

As mentioned at ¶ 620, if a defined contribution RPP reallocates forfeitures among other active plan members, the amount of any forfeiture allocated to an individual plan member must be included in that member's PA for the year in which it is reallocated. This rule includes any employer contributions made prior to 1990 that were subsequently reallocated. However, any amounts forfeited by members who terminated before 1990 that were reallocated in 1990 were not included in the 1990 PA.

D. Foreign Plan Rules — Services Primarily in Canada — Prescribed Contribution Conditions for 1992, 1993 and 1994

The conditions that a contribution made to a foreign plan must meet in order to be classified as a "prescribed contribution" depend on the year in which the contribution is made. For contributions made since 1991, two sets of conditions are stipulated:

- for contributions made in 1992, 1993, or 1994; and
- for contributions made after 1994.

Some of the conditions are aimed at foreign non-profit organizations, which are defined as non-profit organizations that have their main place of management outside Canada and that carry on their activities primarily outside Canada. For years before 1995, the definition also included non-profit organizations whose assets are situated primarily outside Canada throughout the year. A typical example is an international union.

Contributions made in 1992, 1993, or 1994 were classified as "prescribed contributions" if all of the following conditions were satisfied:

(a) the contributions were paid to a "qualifying entity" (a non-resident trust, corporation, or other entity that is tax-exempt or is permitted a reduced rate of tax or other favourable tax treatment in the country in which it is resident and whose principal purpose is to provide benefits under a retirement plan or other employee benefit plan);

(b) the employer has elected to have all such contributions treated as "prescribed contributions" (i.e., the employer has elected to make the foreign plan exempt from taxation as an RCA). This election must be made in writing to the Minister of National Revenue, in the form of a signed letter from the employer, within the time frame described earlier (under the description for the second category of contribution). The employer may, with the Minister's permission, revoke any such election at any time, in which case future contributions will fall into categories 1 or 3 as described at ¶ 646 (if the circumstances remain as described in the first paragraph of ¶ 646);

(c) in the case of an employer other than a foreign non-profit organization, the individual is not a member of an RPP (other than a specified multi-employer plan (SMEP)) or a DPSP in which the employer or a related employer participates; and

(d) either the employer is:

(i) a non-resident corporation,

(ii) a partnership that is the employer of the individual and that participates in the foreign plan primarily in respect of services rendered outside Canada by its non-resident employees, or

(iii) a foreign non-profit organization,

or

the individual was a non-resident at some previous time and became a member of the foreign plan before the end of the month after the month in which the individual became a Canadian resident.

If the contribution is made after 1994, the contribution is classified as a "prescribed contribution" if the conditions set out at ¶ 646 are satisfied.

PA Rules

Having decided whether the contributions to a foreign plan on behalf of Canadian resident employees are to be subject to RCA taxation, the employer is then in the position of determining any PAs. Suppose that

(i) the employee earned benefits under the foreign plan in a particular year in respect of services rendered to the employer while a Canadian resident;

(ii) the employee remains entitled to benefits under the foreign plan at the end of the year; and

(iii) at least one contribution made in the year in respect of the employee was not subject to the RCA tax or, alternatively, no contributions were made in the year on behalf of the employee.

In that case, for 1992 to 1994, the PA, inclusive of any PA otherwise determined for the employee by virtue of membership in any RPP or DPSP with which the employer is involved, equaled the lesser of two amounts:

- the money purchase limit for the year (as defined at ¶ 205), minus $1,000 (the PA offset applicable for those years), and
- 18% of the individual's "compensation" for the year from the employer, minus $1,000 (the PA offset applicable for those years). In this context, "compensation" means compensation as defined in subsection 147.1(1) of the *Income Tax Act* (Canada) but without including prescribed amounts and amounts in respect of periods of non-residency that are permitted by the Minister of National Revenue to be included in compensation for other purposes.

If the employer adopts this "default PA" calculation method, no PSPA can arise in the future if benefits are retroactively increased.

If the employer prefers to calculate a PA in a different manner (for example, in a manner that is more consistent with the PA rules applicable to RPPs), the employer may write to the Minister of National Revenue — the Minister's approval is effective only if it is in writing.

It should be noted that if benefits for post-1991 service are retroactively increased in a later year, the use of such an alternative PA calculation method may mean that PSPAs will have to be reported, as noted at ¶1085.

The PA rules after 1994 are the same as those set out above in respect of the period from 1992 to 1994, with two exceptions. The PA offset for years after 1996 was $1,000 instead of $600. In addition, after 1994, the PA is not inclusive of any PA that is otherwise determined for the individual by virtue of membership in any RPP or DPSP with which the employer is involved — that PA must be added to the foreign plan PA to obtain the total PA that the employer must report on behalf of the individual.

Further, as noted at ¶646, for the period from 1996 to 2003, there was another adjustment in the PA calculation to take into account the delay in the retirement savings system reaching full maturity (i.e. the delay in the maximum RRSP contribution reaching $15,500). For that period, the PA, exclusive of any PA otherwise determined for the employee by virtue of membership in any RPP or DPSP with which the employer is involved, equaled the lesser of the following two amounts:

- the money purchase limit for the year (as defined at ¶205), and
- 18% of the individual's "compensation" (as defined earlier) for the year from the employer, minus the PA offset.

Therefore, for years after 2003, the PA, exclusive of any PA otherwise determined for the employee by virtue of membership in any RPP or DPSP with which the employer is involved, equals the lesser of the following two amounts:

- the money purchase limit for the year (as defined at ¶205) minus the PA offset, and
- 18% of the individual's "compensation" (as defined earlier) for the year from the employer, minus the PA offset.

However, as with the pre-1995 PA rules, an alternative PA calculation method may be accepted by the Minister, although, again, this introduces the risk that if benefits for post-1991 service are later increased retroactively, PSPAs may have to be reported, as noted at ¶1085.

E. Foreign Plan Rules — Services Outside Canada — For 1994, 1995 and 1996

Since January 1, 1993, Canadian resident employees who participate in a foreign plan may have to report an amount similar to a PA that will reduce their RRSP deduction limit in the following year. The purpose is to reduce the amount of RRSP contribution room available to members of foreign pension plans so that their tax-assisted savings for retirement is equivalent to that available to Canadian resident employees who are members of registered pension plans.

The reduction applies for a particular calendar year after 1992, if

(i) the Canadian resident rendered services outside Canada at any time in the particular year; and

(ii) the individual's employment did not relate to a business carried on in Canada; and

(iii) the individual continued to be entitled, either absolutely or contingently, to benefits under the foreign plan at the end of that particular year.

This reduction in RRSP contribution room is not achieved through the use of PAs, and employers are not required to report the amount of the reduction. Instead, each individual taxpayer is responsible for ascertaining whether their RRSP contribution room is to be reduced on account of participation in the foreign plan.

The first year for which RRSP contribution room was affected in this manner was 1994, based on participation in a foreign pension plan in 1993.

For calendar years from 1994 to 1996 inclusive, the prescribed reduction for a year is the lesser of two amounts:

(i) the money purchase limit for the particular year, minus $1,000 (the PA offset prior to 1997); and

(ii) 10% of the portion of the individual's "compensation" (as defined earlier) for the year the services were rendered outside Canada.

For calendar years after 1996 (and before 2005), the amount in (i) above is the money purchase limit in the particular year — the PA offset is not factored in. The amount in (ii) is unchanged.

For calendar years after 2004, as described at ¶ 647, the amount in (i) above is reduced by the PA offset (i.e. $600) instead of reduced by $1,000 (the PA offset in effect prior to 1997). The amount in (ii) is unchanged.

The amount prescribed for a year in respect of an individual is subtracted from the individual's new RRSP contribution room for the year, in exactly the same way as if it were a PA. Thus, if the prescribed amount exceeds the new RRSP room for the year (for example, if the individual has relatively low earned income for RRSP purposes), no new RRSP room is created that year — but there is no impact on any unused RRSP room carried forward from the previous year.

F. Back Pay or Bonus Included in Pensionable Earnings

As mentioned at ¶ 650, there are rules for determining the extra PA in respect of additional contributions that are made as a result of an employer retroactively increasing an employee's compensation in respect of an earlier year or paying a pensionable bonus after the end of a calendar year. There was an exception to this rule if the contribution in question was made before March 1, 1990, in respect of 1989, in which case it was not included in the 1990 PA.

G. Deferred Profit Sharing Plans

As noted at ¶ 655, the PA for a deferred profit sharing plan (DPSP) equals the total of all employer contributions made on behalf of an individual. In 1990, it was possible for employees to contribute to a DPSP (this was no longer possible from January 1, 1991), and any such 1990 employee contributions were not to be included in the 1990 PA.

5. Pension Adjustments for Defined Benefit Plans (Chapter 7)

A. Offset to PA formula

The formula for determining the PA for a defined benefit plan is:

PA = (9 × Benefit Entitlement) - $600

However, prior to 1997, the offset was $1,000. The February 1997 federal Budget changed the offset for PAs for 1997 and subsequent years to $600, resulting in a higher PA and thus lower RRSP contribution room than previously. The reason for the change was to attempt to keep the RRSP system tax-neutral as a result of additional RRSP contribution room provided through the Pension Adjustment Reversal (PAR), which was also introduced in the February 1997 federal Budget. PARs are described in more detail in Chapters 11 and 12.

B. Special PA Transition Rules for Higher Income Employees

For the years 1990 through 1994, there were some PA transition rules for higher income employees who belonged to earnings-related defined benefit plans. In determining the Benefit Entitlement for PA purposes, a portion of the individual's pensionable earnings during the year was excluded (known as the "earnings carve-out") and then a cap was applied (known as the "benefit accrual ceiling"). The earnings carve-out and the benefit accrual ceiling varied year by year.

Both the earnings carve-out and the benefit accrual ceiling had the effect of decreasing the PAs and therefore increased the individual's RRSP contribution room in the following year. They acted as an additional component of equity in the system during the early transition years, by providing for consistency between lower and higher income employees, as well as consistency from year to year as one tracked the PAs for one individual from 1990 (the start of the PA system) until 1996 (when the system was scheduled, at one time, to be mature).

The earnings carve-out and the benefit accrual ceiling were in effect for the years 1990 through 1994.

(a) Earnings Carve-Out

Specifically, the portion of pensionable earnings that was excluded under the earnings carve-out is set out in the following table:

Year	*Pensionable Earnings Excluded*
1990	$63,889–$86,111
1991	$69,444–$86,111
1992	$69,444–$86,111
1993	$75,000–$86,111
1994	$80,556–$86,111

From 1995, the earnings carve-out no longer applied.

Originally, the earnings carve-out was to apply for the years 1990 through 1993. The above table reflects the one-year delay that was proposed by the Minister of Finance in the February 1992 federal Budget, as confirmed in the draft amendments to the Income Tax Regulations that were released on June 19, 1992.

This earnings carve-out could not be applied where the defined benefit formula could reasonably be considered to have been established or modified in order to take advantage of this special rule. For example, amending a defined benefit plan to increase the benefit formula that applied only on earnings above $70,000 could have had this effect.

(b) Benefit Accrual Ceiling

The benefit accrual ceiling that is applied for PA purposes is set out in the following table:

Year	*Benefit Accrual Ceiling for PA Purposes*
1990	$1,277.78
1991	$1,388.89
1992	$1,388.89
1993	$1,500.00
1994	$1,611.11

As with the earnings carve-out discussed in *(a) Earnings Carve Out*, above, this table reflects the proposed changes included in the June 19, 1992, draft amendment to the Income Tax Regulations.

From 1995, these artificial ceilings no longer apply. However, it should be noted that one must take into account any maximum benefit provisions that apply under the pension plan. For example, defined benefit plans are limited in 2010 to the defined benefit limit of $2,494.44 per year of service, and the limit for each year must be taken into account when determining PAs. It is also important to note that even if the PA for a particular year is over the RRSP limit for the subsequent year, the full PA should be reported for those years (1995 to 2002) where it was possible for that to occur, as described in ¶ 720.

The benefit accrual ceiling was also adjusted for 1990 and 1991 PA purposes in the case of defined benefit plans whose pension formula was higher than 2% of pensionable earnings. For such plans, the benefit accrual ceiling set out above was subject to a maximum of 2% of taxable compensation for the year (possibly adjusted if the individual's earnings were reduced due to a leave of absence, layoff or disability).

Note that for years after 1994, there were further modifications to the rules, introduced in subsequent federal budgets, which delayed the complete transition into the new system until 2004, when the maximum RRSP contribution room finally reached $15,500.

As a result of these delays, for years after 1994 until the system matured in 2004, there were situations for high earners where the calculated PA was actually higher than the maximum RRSP dollar limit for the following year. As discussed at ¶ 510, the CRA required that the higher PA be reported; however, there was no impact on RRSP contribution room by the reporting of a PA higher than the maximum RRSP contribution limit, since new RRSP contribution room generated in a particular year can never be less than zero (as indicated at ¶ 325). It should be noted that for the calculation of the PAR, the administrator must ensure that the lower of the reported PA and the relevant maximum dollar limit be used, as discussed further at ¶ 1130. However, unlike the situation just described for PARs, the actual reported PA, regardless of the fact that it exceeds the maximum RRSP contribution room, is used in the calculation of a PSPA.

C. Greater of Career Average and Final Average/Best Average Formula

For 1990 and 1991 PA purposes, a special rule applied in the case of plans whose benefit was the larger of a career average earnings formula and a final average or best average earnings formula. In these cases, if the final average/best average earnings formula was lower than the career average earnings formula and if both formulae were in place before March 28, 1988, an interim rule was applied when determining the 1990 and 1991 PAs. Under this rule, the final average/best average formula was to be utilized for PA purposes if there was a reasonable expectation that more than 75% of members would retire under that formula. If there was no such reasonable expectation, the Benefit Entitlement was based on the greater of the two pension formulae in the usual way (as was the case from 1992).

Example

Consider a defined benefit plan whose formula per year of credited service is:

- 1% of final average salary up to the YMPE; plus
- 1.8% of final average salary in excess of the YMPE.

There is a minimum benefit under this plan in the form of a career average earnings formula, as follows:

- 1.2% of salary below the YMPE; plus
- 2% of salary in excess of the YMPE.

If regular upgrades of the past service benefits under the minimum career average earnings formula are granted under the plan from time to time, it is probably reasonable to assume that many plan members will retire under the career average earnings formula. However, if regular career average upgrades are not expected in the future, it may be possible to argue that more than 75% of members will retire under the final average earnings formula. In that case, the 1990 and 1991 PAs would have been based on the lower final average earnings formula instead of the minimum career average earnings formula. Starting in 1992, the PAs were based solely on the career average earnings formula.

D. Back Pay in 1990

As noted at ¶770, in the case of an employer who retroactively increases an employee's pensionable earnings in such a way that an earlier year's PA would have increased had it been based on that higher level of pensionable earnings, the extra benefits based on that increase in pensionable earnings form part of the Benefit Entitlement for the year in which the back pay was actually paid.

A special rule existed for back pay in 1990. If the pensionable back pay was paid in 1990 and retroactively increased compensation levels for 1989 or an earlier year, this back pay was only to be included in the 1990 Benefit Entitlement for PA purposes if the individual had any credited service in 1990. Under this rule, if the individual had no 1990 credited service (for example, if the individual terminated service or retired before 1990), no extra PA arose.

6. Pension Adjustments for Combination Plans and Hybrids (Chapter 8)

A. PAs for 1990 and 1991

On March 13, 1991, the Director of the CRA's Registered Plans Directorate, wrote a general letter to the pension industry regarding "Combination Plans and Determination of the Pension Adjustment". The letter described the method of calculating PAs for 1990 and 1991 under plans providing benefits on the basis of either the greater of a defined benefit promise and a money purchase component or the sum of a defined benefit promise and a money purchase component. The letter pointed out that the limits under paragraph 9(*g*) of Information Circular 72-13R8, which applied to pre-1992 service under "grandfathered plans" (defined benefit plans in existence on March 27, 1988), should be taken into account when determining PAs for 1990 and 1991.

Since that letter was published after the deadline for reporting 1990 PAs, it is likely that a number of employers with this type of pension arrangement may have reported incorrect 1990 PAs. However, the CRA did not intend that, in those situations, employers would have to correct those PAs. Rather, the CRA gave employers the option of reporting a corrected PA for 1990, but stipulated that the correct method was to be used for the 1991 PAs.

The methodology to be applied based on this March 13, 1991 letter, was quite complex and differed in its application to the 1990 and 1991 PAs. This is because the "maximum PA rule" (discussed at ¶510, ¶655 and ¶810) came into effect on January 1, 1991. The methodology set out in the March 13, 1991 letter, no longer applied from 1992 because the limits under paragraph 9(*g*) of the Information Circular do not apply to benefits accruing after January 1, 1992.

Further complexity was added by the fact that it is not always obvious whether any employee contributions under a money purchase tier within a combination plan fall under the definition of an additional voluntary contribution (AVC) under subsection 248(1) of the *Income Tax Act* (Canada), as discussed at Section 4B of this Appendix. If any employee contributions were AVCs, they were to be ignored in determining the 1990 PAs and also excluded when applying the limit under paragraph 9(*g*) of the Information Circular for both the 1990 and 1991 PAs. However, if they were not AVCs, they could not be ignored in the 1990 PAs and were limited by paragraph 9(*g*).

In determining the 1990 PA for two-tiered plans in existence on March 27, 1988, where the pre-1992 benefits under a defined benefit tier and the benefits under a money purchase tier are jointly subject to the paragraph 9(*g*) limit, the approach set out in the CRA's March 13, 1991 letter led to the following methodology:

(1) Determine the Benefit Entitlement under the defined benefit tier, allowing for the earnings carve-out.

(2) Determine the employee and employer contributions under the money purchase tier to be included in the 1990 PA, excluding any AVCs.

(3) Divide the amount in (2) above by 9 and add it to the amount determined in (1). This represents the Benefit Entitlement before allowing for the paragraph 9(*g*) limit.

(4) Determine the Benefit Entitlement as if the plan formula was instead equal to the paragraph 9(*g*) limit, allowing for the earnings carve-out.

(5) Determine the lesser of (3) and (4) and ensure that this amount does not exceed the benefit accrual ceiling ($1,277.78 in 1990).

(6) Multiply (5) by 9 and subtract $1,000 to obtain the 1990 PA.

In some circumstances, the more long-winded "normalized pension" approach may have to be followed, as discussed at ¶ 735.

For the above type of two-tiered combination plan, the 1991 PA follows exactly the same approach, except that a final stage must be added:

(7) Add to (6) any 1991 AVCs to produce the final 1991 PA amount.

Because the maximum PA rule came into effect for 1991, it may have been necessary to compare this final 1991 PA amount against the PA limit for the year, namely the maximum amount that could have been contributed instead to a defined contribution plan on behalf of the employee in 1991. If it turns out that the 1991 PA exceeded this PA limit, then, as discussed at ¶ 1675 (refer to "9. Requirement for Return of Contributions to Avoid Deregistration"), it may have been necessary to refund excess

AVCs in order that the final PA determined at stage (7) above did not exceed the PA limit for the year.

B. PAs for Pre-1999

A complex transitional rule applied for each year up to and including 1999, provided that:

- the defined benefit minimum formula had been in place since January 1, 1981, and has not been substantially changed since December 31, 1989;
- the employer contributions under the defined contribution had, for each and every member, never exceeded $3,500 in each year before 1990; and
- the plan is not a multi-employer plan (MEP) or a specified multi-employer plan (SMEP).

If these conditions were met, the transitional rule operated by reducing the pension credit under the defined benefit provision by an amount equal to the lesser of:

(a) $2,500; and

(b) 10% of [**A - (B** × **C)**], where:

A equaled the balance in the member's defined contribution account at December 31, 1989;

B equaled the member's pensionable service under the defined benefit provision up to the end of 1989; and

C equaled the defined benefit pension credit that would have applied for 1989 as if the PA rules had existed in that year, ignoring the earnings carve-out and benefit accrual ceiling and ignoring the defined contribution provision.

Example

Consider a defined contribution plan to which the employee and employer each contribute 5% of salary. Benefits under the plan are subject to a minimum defined benefit guarantee equal to 1.5% of final average salary per year of credited service. (Although, as mentioned, the Regulations require this minimum to be expressed as a second tier that is provided in addition to the defined contribution first tier.)

Consider an individual whose 1989 salary was $36,000 and whose 1992 salary was $40,000. Suppose the individual had five years of pensionable service under the defined benefit provision to the end of 1989 and the balance in his or her money purchase account at December 31, 1989, was $25,000. The individual belonged to the pension plan throughout 1992.

The 1992 pension credit under the defined contribution provision equaled 10% of 1992 salary, i.e., $4,000.

The 1992 Benefit Entitlement under the defined benefit formula before allowing for the transitional rule, was 1.5% × $40,000. This is compared to the $1,388.89 benefit accrual ceiling at this stage of the calculation — clearly, the benefit accrual ceiling can be ignored.

Therefore, the pension credit in respect of the defined benefit for 1992, before allowing for the transitional rule, was: (9 × $600) - $1,000 = $4,400.

To determine the offset under the transitional rule, we begin by determining what the 1989 pension credit would have been under the defined benefit formula had the PA rules existed for 1989. Based on the 1989 salary of $36,000, the 1989 Benefit Entitlement under the defined benefit formula would have been 1.5% × $36,000, or $540, and the 1989 pension credit under the defined benefit formula would have been: (9 × $540) - $1,000 = $3,860.

Therefore, the transitional rule offset for each year from 1990 to 1999 was equal to the lesser of:

(a) $2,500; and

(b) 10% × [$25,000 - (5 × $3,860)] = $570.

After applying the transitional rule offset, the adjusted 1992 pension under the defined benefit formula became $4,400 - $570, or $3,830.

The 1992 PA was equal to the larger of the pension credit under the defined contribution formula ($4,000) and the adjusted pension credit under the defined benefit formula ($3,830).

Therefore, the 1992 PA equaled $4,000.

It can be seen that, if it were not for the transitional rule, the larger of the two pension credits would have been $4,400, which is the pension credit under the defined benefit formula. The transitional rule has allowed for the fact that the individual had accumulated a significant amount of assets under his or her defined contribution account at the end of 1989, and the PA rules are effectively assuming that, because of this, the individual will probably end up retiring with a pension based on the defined contribution accumulation rather than the defined benefit minimum. Therefore, the defined benefit pension credit was artificially reduced.

Note that once the transitional offset applicable to the defined benefit pension credit was determined for 1990 (the first year for which PAs were reported), the amount of this offset remained the same throughout the transitional period, although the defined benefit pension credit before application of the transitional offset changed from year to year. The fact that the transitional offset remained static made the year by year calculations associated with this rule somewhat simpler than one might initially expect.

7. Pension Adjustments for Multi-Employer Plans (Chapter 9)

As noted at ¶ 910, there are a number of exceptions to the rule that requires the PA for a specified multi-employer plan (SMEP) to be treated using the rules for defined contribution plans. One of those exceptions is that any employee contributions made to the plan in a particular calendar year in respect of pensionable service for that year, or in respect of pensionable service for a plan year ending in that year, are to be included in the PA for the calendar year in which the contribution is made. However, for 1990 PA purposes, an individual's PA was not to include the portion of an employee contribution that was in respect of a period before 1990.

8. Past Service Pension Adjustments (Chapter 10)

A. Reporting Deadlines for 1990 and 1991 Exempt PSPAs

Exempt PSPAs are to be reported within 60 days of the past service event. Improvements made in 1991, as well as 1990 improvements which, for PSPA purposes, the Regulations consider to have been made effective January 1, 1991, generated "special 1991 PSPAs". The reporting deadline for these was March 16, 1992. Therefore, no RRSP room was lost in 1990 or 1991 due to a PSPA.

B. PSPAs for Flat Benefit Plans under Binding Commitment Made Prior to 1992

As discussed at ¶ 1017, benefit improvements in flat benefit plans can be increased within certain limits without creating a PSPA; however, if the benefit improvement occurred because of a binding commitment made prior to 1992, the benefits could be increased by a higher amount than described at ¶ 1015 without creating a PSPA, provided the rate of increase was not substantially in excess of the rate of increase in the average wage.

C. PSPA Rules Prior to Introduction of PARs

As discussed at ¶ 1035, ¶ 1036 and ¶ 1037, the rules for calculating PSPAs were changed once the pension adjustment reversal (PAR) was introduced in 1997.

Set out below are the rules for determining PSPAs that were in effect prior to the introduction of the PAR, under both the basic and the modified methods.

Basic Calculation Method

The basic process for calculating the PSPA involved four steps, as follows:

(1) Calculate the redetermined pension credit as of the time of the past service event. This amount is essentially the sum of the pension credits (each rounded to the nearest dollar) that should have been reported, covering all prior years of post-1989 credited service but excluding the year of the past service event, had the benefit improvement always been in place. In calculating the redetermined pension credit, various exclusions are taken into account, such as the exclusions for flat benefit plans as described in Chapter 10.

(2) Calculate the total redetermined pension credit as of the time immediately prior to the past service event. In an earnings-related plan, this amount is essentially the sum of the pension credits and PSPAs that have already been reported for prior years on behalf of the individual over the period of time to which the past service improvement applies. In a flat benefit plan, this amount would be based on the benefit level in effect immediately prior to the past service event — adjusted for exclusions as described in Chapter 10.

(3) The amount in step (1) is reduced by the amount in step (2) and by any qualifying transfers.

(4) If the amount in step (3) is greater than zero, it is the PSPA; otherwise, the PSPA is nil.

This basic approach was used primarily in those situations where benefits were being credited for the first time or where benefits were being improved under an existing defined benefit provision and no assets were being transferred from the replaced defined benefit provision to an RRSP or a money purchase RPP provision in respect of the individual. It can be seen that the benefits in respect of current service in the year of the past service event are ignored in calculating the PSPA under this approach. Those current service benefits are included when determining the PA for that year.

For these purposes, qualifying transfers are as described at ¶ 1036; however the restriction that only that portion of the transfer that can reasonably be considered to be required or used to fund post-1989 benefits is considered as a qualifying transfer did not come into effect until June 26, 1998. Thus, prior to June 26, 1998, qualifying transfers that included funds in respect of pre-1990 service were able to be used to reduce the amount of the PSPA.

Modified Calculation Method

Modifications to the basic approach have to be made in more complex situations. Where the service was not pensionable service under the plan immediately prior to the past service event, the "modified" approach must be used. Therefore, the "modified" approach was used in a reciprocal transfer or portability situation, where an employee changed employers and the employers had a reciprocal transfer agreement or portability arrangement whereby the service from the old employer's pension plan would be treated as pensionable service under the new employer's plan. In addition, this "modified" approach was applied where the employee was applying for reinstatement of benefits which had already been foregone — for example, as a result of a previous termination of employment.

The steps were similar to the basic PSPA calculation approach, but there were some material differences:

(1) As in step (1) under the basic approach, the redetermined pension credits are calculated in respect of the service being credited, but rather than being calculated to the end of the year prior to the year of the past service event, they are calculated covering service up to the date of the past service event.

(2) As in step (2) under the basic approach, the total of the PAs and PSPAs that were previously reported (or will be reported) is calculated in respect of the service being credited, but these must cover service up to the date of the past service event. Where part of the service being credited is not for a complete calendar year, this may entail recalculating the PA for that partial year (unless, of course, the original PA for that year was based on the same partial year of credited service).

Note that in steps (1) and (2) the individual is assumed to be vested — the "year of non-vested termination" rule (discussed in more detail below) is ignored.

(3) An adjustment must be made for the "year of non-vested termination" rule that applies to pension plans that are not multi-employer plans. As discussed at Section 9B of this Appendix (for terminations occurring prior to 1997), the PA in the year of non-vested termination is calculated as the lesser of the pension credit determined as if the individual were vested and the member's contributions for the year. If this rule had been applied to the individual when his or her PA was determined for a year that is part of the period covered in step (2), the PSPA now being determined must be increased by the amount by which that PA was actually reduced because of the application of the "year of non-vested termination" rule.

For example, if the individual should have had a PA of $1,000 in the earlier year of termination had he or she been vested at that time, but only $400 was reported as the PA because this was the employee contribution in the year of termination and the employee was not vested, then an additional $600 must be added to the PSPA to reflect this special adjustment.

(4) An amount also must be added to the PSPA representing any money purchase transfer from the previous defined benefit provision that is attributable to post-1989 service. For example, if under the previous defined benefit plan an amount was transferred to the individual's RRSP upon termination of employment, the portion of this amount which is attributable to post-1989 service must be added to the PSPA.

(5) The amount in step (1) is reduced by the amount determined in step (2) and by any qualifying transfers. To this is added the amounts determined in steps (3) and (4).

(6) If the amount in step (5) is greater than zero, it is the PSPA; otherwise, the PSPA is nil.

The intent of this "modified PSPA" approach was to recognize that there could be a duplication of benefits in reciprocal transfer, portability and reinstatement situations. In a reinstatement, for example, the member may have already received the benefit of a tax-sheltered transfer to an RRSP in respect of the service being reinstated. The reinstatement of service could potentially give rise to additional tax-sheltered benefits in respect of the same period of service — this "double-dipping" in respect of post-1989 service was prevented by the modified PSPA calculation.

D. Timing of filing of Exempt PSPAs

As noted at ¶1060, the plan administrator submits the T215 Summary, along with individual PSPA forms (T215 Supplementary), within 120 days of the past service event. This 120-day deadline became effective May 18, 2005; previously this form was required to be filed within 60 days of the past service event, but was extended to allow employers more time to obtain all the information required for the forms.

E. Timing of when Exempt PSPA reduces RRSP Contribution Room

As discussed at ¶1060, an exempt PSPA reduces RRSP room in the year following the year of the past service event. However, this timing was set out in a technical amendment to the Regulations on April 18, 2000. Prior to that, an exempt PSPA reduced an individual's RRSP contribution room by the amount of the PSPA in the current year, once the PSPA was reported (which is required to be done within 60 days of the past service event). The technical amendment changed this to the current timing for past service events after 2000. This change was introduced to ensure that an exempt PSPA would not affect the deductibility or RRSP contributions that were made before the occurrence of a past service event on the expectation that these contributions would be deductible.

F. Pre-1998 PSPAs and Special Rule for 1997 Modified PSPAs

The revisions to the methods for calculating PSPAs were effective January 1, 1998. However, the rules for reporting PARs came into effect for terminations occurring after 1996. Thus, for 1997, the PSPA calculations in the rare situation involving a termination of employment in 1997 (after the introduction of the PAR) and reinstatement of service later in 1997 (prior to the new PSPA rules coming into effect) required a unique approach. The PSPA Guide indicates that in this situation, the modified method that was in effect prior to 1998 was to be used to calculate the PSPAs in this situation.

Generally, for past service events that occurred prior to 1998, there was no change in the PSPA reporting rules. In other words, if a particular situation occurred in 1997 that required reporting of a PSPA and a modified PSPA (under the old rules) would have been reported, then a modified PSPA (under the old rules) would continue to be reported. If a regular PSPA (under the old rules) would have been reported for that past service event, the regular PSPA reporting rules (in accordance with the old rules) would continue.

9. Pension Adjustment Reversals (Chapter 11)

A. Special 1997 PA Transfer Amount

If an individual ceased in 1997 to be entitled to benefits under a defined benefit provision of an RPP and buys back those same benefits in the same year, there was a special PSPA transitional rule for 1997 past service events, as set out at Section 6E of this Appendix 1. The 1997 PSPA in this situation would have been calculated using the modified PSPA rules that were in existence before the introduction of PARs. These "former" modified PSPA rules reduced the PSPA to take into account PAs already reported. However, now that a PAR is being reported for this 1997 event, the deemed PA value of the buy-back must be included in the PAR to ensure that such PAR is not overstated. This "deemed PA value" that is offset from the PAR is known as the "Special 1997 PA Transfer Amount".

B. Changes to the PA Calculation as a Result of the Introduction of the PAR

When the PAR was introduced in 1997, this necessitated some changes to the methodology for calculating pension adjustments. This included the following:

- The offset in the PA formula for defined benefit plans was reduced from $1,000 to $600 effective with the PAs reported for 1997. There was no requirement to revise any PAs reported for years prior to 1997 since no PARs are reportable for benefits paid out prior to 1997.
- There is a change in the calculation for the year of termination. Previously, the PA reported for the year of termination was the lesser of the calculated PA and the member's contributions for the year. For example, for a non-vested termination under a non-contributory plan, the PA, previously, would always be zero for the year of termination. Since the PAR calculation takes into account specified distributions up to the date the employee ceases entitlement, a regular PA for the final year of employment must now be reported, although effectively, the PAR cancels out this final year PA. This change in methodology took place for PAs reported in respect of 1997 and subsequent years.

C. Reporting Requirements for 1997 and 1998 PARs

Since the Regulations covering the PARs were not introduced until mid-1998, the first PARs did not have to be reported by plan administrators until December 31, 1998. The earliest deadline for RPP administrators and DPSP trustees to file PAR information returns was December 31, 1998. PARs for individuals who received a specified distribution in 1997 were added to their RRSP deduction room in 1998. Thereafter, PARs were required to be reported on a quarterly basis, as set out in ¶1160.

10. Registration Rules for Defined Benefit RPPs — Eligible Benefits (Chapter 17)

A. Grandfathered Plans

Some grandfathered plans (as defined at ¶1707) were amended to comply with the new registration rules under Part LXXXV with an effective date prior to January 1, 1992. The CRA accepted plan amendments to existing plans for compliance with the new rules prior to this date, as long as the amended provisions did not have an effective date prior to January 1, 1990, and as long as the plan was amended with respect to all of the new registration requirements as of the earlier effective date.

Consider, for example, a defined benefit RPP where a member had already reached the 35-year limit specified under the Circular. In order to credit additional years of service in excess of that limit, the plan sponsor could either have amended the plan effective January 1, 1992, the date on which all plans were required to comply with the new legislation, or could have considered amending the plan in all respects to comply with the new rules with an effective date retroactive to a date as early as January 1,

1990, the earliest date that the plan could permit accrual of service beyond 35 years. Note, however, that the retroactive crediting of post-1989 service would have given rise to a past service pension adjustment (PSPA), as discussed in Chapter 10.

However, service in excess of 35 years cannot be included in the calculation of the benefit in respect of service prior to January 1, 1992 (or as early as January 1, 1990, as discussed above). Thus, if the plan member had more than 35 years of service as at January 1, 1992 (or as early as January 1, 1990, as discussed above), a gap in credited service can exist between the date where 35 years of service was attained and the date when the plan was amended to include service in excess of 35 years.

B. Maximum Accrual Rate

The maximum accrual rate under an RPP cannot exceed 2% per year of pensionable service. There was a transition rule in effect that applied to a plan that was an RPP on January 15, 1992: the 2.0% maximum accrual rate described at ¶ 1735 only applied to benefits accruing after 1994.

C. Transfers — Defined Benefit to Defined Contribution or RRSP

As noted at ¶ 1743, the amount that may be transferred from a defined benefit plan (or provision) to an RRSP or a defined contribution RPP is limited through the maximum transfer value factors. With few exceptions, the amount eligible for transfer is equal to the amount of post-age 65 lifetime retirement benefit that is foregone or surrendered (the "normalized pension") multiplied by the maximum transfer value factor. Two exceptions are the transfer before 1993 (or later with Ministerial approval) of benefits in respect of a pre-1989 plan wind-up or pre-1989 replacement of a defined benefit plan by a defined contribution plan, and the transfer of a minimum of a member's contributions with interest.

The T2151 — Record of Direct Transfer of a "Single Amount" form is used to facilitate the direct transfer of assets from an RPP to an RRSP (or another RPP). This form replaced the previously used TD2 form. When the TD2 form was used, a transferred amount was both included in income and treated as a deduction on the individual's tax return, whereas the T2151 form used direct plan-to-plan transfers without income inclusion and deduction. Accordingly, separate reporting of the lump sum on a T4A Supplementary is no longer required.

Periods of Foreign Service

An exception to the rules set out at ¶ 1755 for periods of foreign service exists where the defined benefit RPP provides for the crediting of foreign service and was submitted for registration on or before October 29, 1993. In such cases, periods of foreign service that are credited on a current-service basis are acceptable as eligible service, providing the following conditions are met:

- the foreign service terms of the RPP must have been submitted on or before October 29, 1993;
- the CRA accepted the terms either by registering the RPP or registering any amendments to the RPP containing such foreign service terms; and
- the terms do not credit the service dependant on obtaining the CRA's approval or on the service being acceptable under an administrative position taken by the CRA. An example of the latter would be a term that refers to the acceptance of the foreign service under the Circular. Where the above two conditions are met, but the crediting of the service in the RPP is dependant on the CRA's approval or on acceptability under the CRA's administrative policies, a request may be made to the CRA to consider the acceptability of periods of foreign service as eligible service.

E. Inflation Adjustments under Information Circular 72-13R8

Under Information Circular 72-13R8, inflation adjustments could not be provided prior to age 60. Where retirement occurred before age 60, the pension could increase at age 60 to reflect inflation since the date of retirement, provided that the total lifetime retirement pension payable at age 60 did not exceed the limitation set by paragraph 9(*g*) (the maximum pension rule). For retirements on and after January 1, 1992, this limitation was removed and a maximum pension could be fully indexed from the date of pension commencement, in respect of both pre-reform and post-reform service with no age restrictions. The RPP must, however, contain wording providing for this.

11. Registration Rules for Defined Benefit RPPs — Eligible Contributions (Chapter 18)

A. Employee Contributions

As discussed at ¶ 1805, the maximum contribution that may be made to a defined benefit provision by a member in respect of a calendar year after 1990 cannot exceed the lesser of:

(a) 9% of the member's total compensation for the year from all employers that participate in the plan in the year; and

(b) the sum of $1,000 and 70% of the member's pension credit for the year under the particular defined benefit provision.

If the plan contains a provision stipulating a minimum benefit payable on termination of employment or pre-retirement death equal to two times the accumulated member contributions, with interest, the 70% figure in paragraph (b) above is changed to 50%.

For years where an earnings carve-out or benefit accrual ceiling were in effect, this pension credit was calculated without reference to the benefit accrual ceiling and earnings carve-out outlined in Section 2 of this Appendix 1.

B. Employee Contributions for Past Service

Teachers employed by Her Majesty or by a tax-exempt employer such as a school board, were allowed additional deductions for past service contributions. The $3,500 deduction for past years was allowed even if the teachers were contributors to the plan for the 1991 to 1994 taxation years, inclusive. This rule expired in 1994.

Transition Rules for Excess Surplus

As set out at ¶1815, "excess surplus" must be used to reduce the amount of employer contributions that are otherwise required. However, there was a transition rule in effect that permitted excess surplus to be taken into account uniformly after 1990 and before 1995 for employers who still wished to contribute in spite of a large surplus or who were required to make contributions pursuant to a collective agreement or the plan's terms.

Appendix 2

TAX FORMS

TAX FORMS

This appendix lists Guides issued by the Canada Revenue Agency that are relevant to Registered Pension Plans (RPPs), Registered Retirement Savings Plans (RRSPs), and Deferred Profit Sharing Plans (DPSPs). It also lists the more frequently used forms associated with RPPs, RRSPs, DPSPs and TFSAs.

The lists are followed by the most current versions of certain forms that are in use at the time of publication: Forms T4, T4A, T215, T10, T1004, T1006, T2151 and T920.

Guides

Name	*Form No.*	*Purpose*
Registered Pension Plan Guide	T4099	Explanation of procedures and forms to be completed to register a new plan or an amendment to an existing plan, as well as how to complete an Annual Information Return
Pension Adjustment Guide	T4084	Examples of calculation of pension adjustment and reporting procedures
Past Pension Service Adjustment Guide	T4104	Past service pension adjustments and reporting procedures
RRSPs and Other Registered Plans for Retirement, 2008	T4040	Explanation of different types of pension plans, contribution limits, and RRSP contribution room
Pension Adjustment Reversal Guide	RC4137	Explanation of calculation of pension adjustment reversals and reporting procedures
Tax-Free Savings Account (TFSA) — Information Sheet	RC4466	Explanation of how a TFSA works, how to set up a TFSA, contribution limits and investments

Forms

Application Forms and Information Returns

Name	*Form No.*	*Completed by*	*Filing Deadline*	*Purpose*
Application to Register a Pension Plan	T510	Plan administrator	Within 60 days of plan establishment	To apply for registration of a new pension plan. CRA has updated this form. Applicants must use the new version of T510 for all plan registrations and amendments submitted after May 11, 2009. As of September 1, 2009, CRA will not accept applications that use a previous version of T510.
Application to Amend a Registered Pension Plan	T920	Plan administrator	Within 60 days of date amendment is made	To request acceptance of an amendment to a registered pension plan. CRA has updated this form. Applicants must use the new version of T920 for all plan registrations and amendments submitted after May 11, 2009. As of September 1, 2009, CRA will not accept applications that use a previous version of the T920.
Employees' Pension Plan Income Tax Return	T3P	Trustee	Annually within 90 days of fiscal year-end	To provide current information on trust governed by a pension plan

Name	*Form No.*	*Completed by*	*Filing Deadline*	*Purpose*
Connected Person Information Return	T1007	Employer	Within 60 days after individual becomes a member of an RPP	Notification to the CRA of connected person's RPP participation
Application for Registration as a Deferred Profit Sharing Plan	T2214	Employer and trustee	Prior to plan effective date	To apply for registration of a deferred profit sharing plan
Registered Pension Plan Priority Indentification Form	T2014	Plan Sponsor	To be filed with relevant request	To be attached to certain submissions to the Registered Plans Directorate including requests for a waiver, an interpretation, a review of a draft submission or a review of a specimen plan. Form is not to be used to submit an application to register a pension plan or an amendment to a pension plan.
Registered Pension Plan Change of Information Form	T2011	Plan Sponsor	To be filed upon change of information	To advise the Registered Plans Directorate of a change of address or contact person for plan sponsor, plan administrator or consultant.
PSPA Forms				
Applying for the Certification of a Provisional PSPA	T1004	Plan administrator	None — however, benefit improvement cannot be made unless certification is granted	To request certification of non-exempt PSPA

Name	*Form No.*	*Completed by*	*Filing Deadline*	*Purpose*
Designating an RRSP Withdrawal as a Qualifying Withdrawal	T1006	Employee (and RRSP issuer, if necessary)	Within 30 days of notification from the CRA	To designate an amount of RRSP withdrawal to enable certification of a provisional PSPA
Past Service Pension Adjustment (PSPA) Exempt from Certification	T215	Plan administrator	Within 60 days of past service event	To report exempt PSPAs for each individual affected by a benefit improvement
T215 Segment	T215 Segment	Plan administrator	Within 60 days of past service event	To accompany each T215 return when more than 300 PSPAs are reported
Summary of Past Service Pension Adjustments (PSPA) Exempt from Certification	T215 Summary	Plan administrator	Within 60 days of past service event	To report the totals of certain information from the T215 slips
PAR Forms				
Pension Adjustment Reversal (PAR)	T10	RPP Administrator or DPSP Trustee	No later than 60 days after the end of the calendar quarter in which the termination occurs (no later than 31 days after the end of December for the last calendar quarter)	The reported PAR amount will result in an increase in the taxpayer's RRSP deduction limit for that year
T10 Segment	T10 Segment	RPP Administrator or DPSP Trustee	No later than 60 days after the end of the calendar quarter in which the termination occurs (no later than 31 days after the end of December for the last calendar quarter)	To accompany each group of T10 slips when more than 300 PARs are reported

Name	*Form No.*	*Completed by*	*Filing Deadline*	*Purpose*
Summary of Pension Adjustment Reversals (PARs)	T10 Summary	RPP Administrator or DPSP Trustee	No later than 60 days after the end of the calendar quarter in which the termination occurs (no later than 31 days after the end of December for the last calendar quarter)	To report the totals of certain information from T10 slips
Transfer Forms				
Direct Transfer Under Subparagraph 60(1)(v)	T2030	Taxpayer, transferor, and transferee	By transfer date	To transfer certain eligible amounts from an RRSP or RRIF to an RRSP, RRIF, or annuity
Direct Transfer Under Subsection 146.3(14.1) or Paragraph 146(16)(a) or 146.3(2)(e)	T2033	Employee, transferor, and transferee	By transfer date	To record a direct transfer of amounts from an RRSP or RRIF to another RRSP, RRIF, or RPP
Direct Transfer of a Single Amount Under Subsection 147(19) or Section 147.3	T2151	Taxpayer, transferor, and transferee	By transfer date	To record a direct transfer of a single amount from an RPP or DPSP to an RPP, RRSP, RRIF or DPSP, if permitted
Transfer from an RRSP or RRIF to Another RRSP or RRIF on Breakdown of Marriage or Common-Law Partnership	T2220	Annuitant and spouse (including common law partner), transferor, and transferee	By transfer date	To transfer RRSP or RRIF amounts on marriage or relationship breakdown pursuant to court order or separation agreement
Other Forms				
T1 Adjustment Request	T1-ADJ	Taxpayer	Whenever a change to a tax return occurs	To request an adjustment to an individual tax return

Name	*Form No.*	*Completed by*	*Filing Deadline*	*Purpose*
2009 Individual Tax Return for RRSP Excess Contributions (*Note: there is a separate form for each calendar year*)	T1-OVP T1-OVP_S (*simplified version*)	Taxpayer	By March 31 of the year following the year in which excess RRSP contributions are subject to tax	For payment of tax on excess RRSP contributions
Statement of Remuneration Paid	T4	Employer	Annually by February 28	To report employment income, tax and other amounts deducted from income, and the pension adjustment
Statement of Pension, Retirement, Annuity, and Other Income	T4A	Employer or plan administrator	By February 28 following year of payment	To report pension, retirement, annuity, and other income and/or a pension adjustment in certain cases
Statement of Distributions from a Retirement Compensation Arrangement	T4A-RCA	Employer	Annually by February 28	To report payments made from a retirement compensation arrangement to employers and beneficiaries
Statement of RRSP Income	T4RSP	RRSP trustee	Annually by February 28	To report amounts paid in a calendar year from an RRSP
Statement of Income from a Registered Retirement Income Fund	T4RIF	RRIF trustee	Annually by February 28	To report amounts paid in a calendar year from a RRIF
Statement of Contributions Paid to a Custodian of a Retirement Compensation Arrangement (RCA)	T737-RCA	Employer	Annually by February 28	To report contributions made to an RCA and refundable tax deducted

Name	*Form No.*	*Completed by*	*Filing Deadline*	*Purpose*
Calculating Your Deduction for Refund of Unused RRSP Contributions	T746	Taxpayer	When filing tax return for the year in which the refund was made	To calculate the deduction for withdrawn unused contributions made to taxpayer's own, or to his/her spouse/common-law partner's RRSPs
Statement of Qualifying Retroactive Lump-Sum Payment	T1198	Payer of retroactive lump sum	When filing tax return for the year in which the refund was made	To apply for special tax treatment when the taxpayer receives a qualifying lump sum representing more than one year's worth of periodic payments
Death of a RRSP Annuitant — Refund of Premiums	T2019	Taxpayer's legal representative and beneficiary	When filing tax return for the year in which the refund was made	To designate an amount withdrawn from a deceased taxpayer's RRSP as a refund of premiums
Election Under Subsection 147(10.1) in Respect of a Single Payment Received From a Deferred Profit Sharing Plan	T2078	Beneficiary of DPSP	Within 60 days of end of the taxation year in which the payment was received	To determine the amount received from the DPSP that can be excluded from income
Amounts from a Spousal or Common-Law Partnership RRSP or RRIF to Include in Income for__________ (Year)	T2205	Annuitant of RRSP or RRIF	When filing tax return	To determine amounts to be included in income when amounts are withdrawn from spousal RRSP or RRIF
Tax Deduction Waiver on a Refund of Your Undeducted RRSP Contributions Made In . (Year)	T3012A	Contributor, annuitant, RRSP issuer, and CCRA	After notice of assessment is received	To request that refund of unused RRSP contributions not be subject to withholding tax

Name	*Form No.*	*Completed by*	*Filing Deadline*	*Purpose*
Required Amendments for Deferred Profit Sharing Plans	EF97-10	Sponsor of DPSP	To be filed with relevant amendment, including plan termination	To advise CRA of an amendment to a DPSP that uses generic wording or to confirm that a DPSP has been terminated
Application for Tax-Free Savings Account (TFSA) Identification Number	RC236	Issuer of TFSA	Prior to TFSA effective date	For set up of TFSA and request for issuance of TFSA identification number

Forms No Longer Used

Name	*Form No.*	*Comments*
Registered Pension Plan Annual Information Return	T244	This form was used by the plan administrator to provide current information on the registered pension plan; however, all jurisdictions have now incorporated the requirements of this form into their minimum standards annual information return and one form is filed by the plan administrator and the minimum standards jurisdiction reports relevant information to the Canada Revenue Agency
Tax Deduction Waiver in Respect of Funds to be Transferred	TD2	A letter containing the information previously requested in the TD2 form should be sent to the district tax services office. Contact a Canada Revenue Agency office if more information is required.
Identification of Amounts Transferred to an RRSP for 19______	T2097	The form was used by taxpayers when filing tax returns to identify eligible amounts transferred to an RRSP.
Calculation of Earned Income for 19______	T1023	This form was used by the taxpayer to determine earned income for a particular taxation year
Notice of Purchase of Annuity with "Plan Funds"	T2037	This form was used to to transfer funds from an RPP, DPSP or RRSP to an insurance company for the purchase of an annuity other than an annuity which falls under Form T2030.

Employer's name – Nom de l'employeur

Canada Revenue Agency Agence du revenu du Canada

Year Année

T4

STATEMENT OF REMUNERATION PAID
ÉTAT DE LA RÉMUNÉRATION PAYÉE

Employment income – line 101 / Revenus d'emploi – ligne 101 — 14

Income tax deducted – line 437 / Impôt sur le revenu retenu – ligne 437 — 22

Payroll Account Number (15 characters) / Numéro de compte de retenues (15 caractères) — 54

Province of employment / Province d'emploi — 10

Employee's CPP contributions – line 308 / Cotisations de l'employé au RPC – ligne 308 — 16

EI insurable earnings / Gains assurables d'AE — 24

Social insurance number / Numéro d'assurance sociale — 12

Exempt – Exemption — 28 — CPP/QPP, EI, PPIP / RPC/RRQ, AE, RPAP

Employment code / Code d'emploi — 29

Employee's QPP contributions – line 308 / Cotisations de l'employé au RRQ – ligne 308 — 17

CPP/QPP pensionable earnings / Gains ouvrant droit à pension – RPC/RRQ — 26

Employee's name and address – Nom et adresse de l'employé

Last name (in capital letters) – Nom de famille (en lettres moulées) First name – Prénom Initials – Initiales

Employee's EI premiums – line 312 / Cotisations de l'employé à l'AE – ligne 312 — 18

Union dues – line 212 / Cotisations syndicales – ligne 212 — 44

RPP contributions – line 207 / Cotisations à un RPA – ligne 207 — 20

Charitable donations – see over / Dons de bienfaisance – voir au verso — 46

Pension adjustment – line 206 / Facteur d'équivalence – ligne 206 — 52

RPP or DPSP registration number / N° d'agrément d'un RPA ou d'un RPDB — 50

Employee's PPIP premiums – see over / Cotisations de l'employé au RPAP – voir au verso — 55

PPIP insurable earnings / Gains assurables du RPAP — 56

Other information (see over) / Autres renseignements (voir au verso)

Box – Case	Amount – Montant	Box – Case	Amount – Montant	Box – Case	Amount – Montant
Box – Case	Amount – Montant	Box – Case	Amount – Montant	Box – Case	Amount – Montant

T4 (09)

Employer's name – Nom de l'employeur

Canada Revenue Agency Agence du revenu du Canada

Year Année

T4

STATEMENT OF REMUNERATION PAID
ÉTAT DE LA RÉMUNÉRATION PAYÉE

Employment income – line 101 / Revenus d'emploi – ligne 101 — 14

Income tax deducted – line 437 / Impôt sur le revenu retenu – ligne 437 — 22

Payroll Account Number (15 characters) / Numéro de compte de retenues (15 caractères) — 54

Province of employment / Province d'emploi — 10

Employee's CPP contributions – line 308 / Cotisations de l'employé au RPC – ligne 308 — 16

EI insurable earnings / Gains assurables d'AE — 24

Social insurance number / Numéro d'assurance sociale — 12

Exempt – Exemption — 28 — CPP/QPP, EI, PPIP / RPC/RRQ, AE, RPAP

Employment code / Code d'emploi — 29

Employee's QPP contributions – line 308 / Cotisations de l'employé au RRQ – ligne 308 — 17

CPP/QPP pensionable earnings / Gains ouvrant droit à pension – RPC/RRQ — 26

Employee's name and address – Nom et adresse de l'employé

Last name (in capital letters) – Nom de famille (en lettres moulées) First name – Prénom Initials – Initiales

Employee's EI premiums – line 312 / Cotisations de l'employé à l'AE – ligne 312 — 18

Union dues – line 212 / Cotisations syndicales – ligne 212 — 44

RPP contributions – line 207 / Cotisations à un RPA – ligne 207 — 20

Charitable donations – see over / Dons de bienfaisance – voir au verso — 46

Pension adjustment – line 206 / Facteur d'équivalence – ligne 206 — 52

RPP or DPSP registration number / N° d'agrément d'un RPA ou d'un RPDB — 50

Employee's PPIP premiums – see over / Cotisations de l'employé au RPAP – voir au verso — 55

PPIP insurable earnings / Gains assurables du RPAP — 56

Other information (see over) / Autres renseignements (voir au verso)

Box – Case	Amount – Montant	Box – Case	Amount – Montant	Box – Case	Amount – Montant
Box – Case	Amount – Montant	Box – Case	Amount – Montant	Box – Case	Amount – Montant

T4 (09)

Report these amounts on your tax return

- 14 **Employment income** – Enter on line 101.
- 16 **Employee's CPP contributions** – See line 308 in your tax guide.
- 17 **Employee's QPP contributions** – See line 308 in your tax guide.
- 18 **Employee's EI premiums** – See line 312 in your tax guide.
- 20 **RPP contributions** – Includes past service contributions. See line 207 in your tax guide.
- 22 **Income tax deducted** – Enter on line 437.
- 37 **Employee home-relocation loan deduction** – Enter on line 248.
- 39 **Security options deduction 110(1)(d)** – Enter on line 249.
- 41 **Security options deduction 110(1)(d.1)** – Enter on line 249.
- 42 **Employment commissions** – Enter on line 102. This amount is already included in box 14.
- 43 **Canadian Forces personnel & police deduction** – Enter on line 244.
- 44 **Union dues** – Enter on line 212.
- 46 **Charitable donations** – See line 349 in your tax guide.
- 52 **Pension adjustment** – Enter on line 206.
- 53 **Deferred security option benefits** – See Form T1212.
- 55 **Provincial Parental Insurance Plan (PPIP)** Residents of Quebec, see line 375 in your tax guide. Residents of provinces or territories other than Quebec, see line 312 in your tax guide.
- 72 **Section 122.3 income – Employment outside Canada** – See Form T626.
- 73 **Number of days outside Canada** – See Form T626.
- 74 **Past service contributions for 1989 or earlier years while a contributor**
- 75 **Past service contributions for 1989 or earlier years while not a contributor** – See line 207 in your tax guide.
- 77 **Workers' compensation benefits repaid to the employer** Enter on line 229.
- 78 **Fishers gross earnings**
- 79 **Fishers net partnership amount**
- 80 **Fishers shareperson amount**

  See Form T2121. **Do not** enter on line 101.
- 81 **Placement or employment agency workers**
- 82 **Drivers of taxis and other passenger-carrying vehicles**
- 83 **Barbers or hairdressers**

  Gross earnings. See Form T2125. **Do not** enter on line 101.
- 84 **Public transit pass** – See line 364 in your tax guide.
- 85 **Employee-paid premiums for private health services plans** See line 330 in your tax guide.

Do not report these amounts on your tax return – **Canada Revenue Agency use only**
(Amounts in boxes 30, 32, 34, 36, 38, and 40 are already included in box 14.)

- 30 **Board and lodging**
- 31 **Special work site**
- 32 **Travel in a prescribed zone**
- 33 **Medical travel assistance**
- 34 **Personal use of employer's automobile or motor vehicle**
- 36 **Interest-free and low-interest loans**
- 38 **Security options benefits**
- 40 **Other taxable allowances and benefits**
- 70 **Municipal officer's expense allowance**
- 71 **Status Indian employee**

Veuillez déclarer ces montants dans votre déclaration d'impôt

- 14 **Revenus d'emploi** – Inscrivez à la ligne 101.
- 16 **Cotisations de l'employé au RPC** Lisez la ligne 308 de votre guide d'impôt.
- 17 **Cotisations de l'employé au RRQ** Lisez la ligne 308 de votre guide d'impôt.
- 18 **Cotisations de l'employé à l'AE** Lisez la ligne 312 de votre guide d'impôt.
- 20 **Cotisations à un RPA** – Comprend les cotisations pour services passés. Lisez la ligne 207 de votre guide d'impôt.
- 22 **Impôt sur le revenu retenu** – Inscrivez à la ligne 437.
- 37 **Déduction pour prêts à la réinstallation d'employés** Inscrivez à la ligne 248.
- 39 **Déduction pour options d'achat de titres 110(1)d)** Inscrivez à la ligne 249.
- 41 **Déduction pour options d'achat de titres 110(1)d.1)** Inscrivez à la ligne 249.
- 42 **Commissions d'emploi** – Inscrivez à la ligne 102. Ce montant est déjà compris dans la case 14.
- 43 **Déduction pour le personnel des Forces canadiennes et des forces policières** – Inscrivez à la ligne 244.
- 44 **Cotisations syndicales** – Inscrivez à la ligne 212.
- 46 **Dons de bienfaisance** – Lisez la ligne 349 de votre guide d'impôt.
- 52 **Facteur d'équivalence** – Inscrivez à la ligne 206.
- 53 **Report des avantages liés aux options d'achat de titres** Consultez le formulaire T1212.
- 55 **Régime provincial d'assurance parentale (RPAP)** – Résidents du Québec, lisez la ligne 375 de votre guide d'impôt. Résidents des autres provinces ou territoires, lisez la ligne 312 de votre guide d'impôt.
- 72 **Revenu selon l'article 122.3 – emploi hors du Canada** Consultez le formulaire T626.
- 73 **Nombre de jours hors du Canada** – Consultez le formulaire T626.
- 74 **Services passés pour 1989 et les années précédente pendant que l'employé cotisait**
- 75 **Services passés pour 1989 et les années précédente pendant que l'employé ne cotisait pas** – Lisez la ligne 207 de votre guide d'impôt.
- 77 **Indemnités pour accidents du travail remboursées à l'employeur** Inscrivez à la ligne 229.
- 78 **Pêcheurs – Revenus bruts**
- 79 **Pêcheurs – Montant net d'un associé de la société de personnes**
- 80 **Pêcheurs – Montant du pêcheur à part**

  Consultez le formulaire T2121. **N'inscrivez pas** ce montant à la ligne 101.
- 81 **Travailleurs d'agences ou de bureaux de placement**
- 82 **Chauffeurs de taxi ou d'un autre véhicule de transport de passagers**
- 83 **Coiffeurs pour hommes ou dames**

  Revenus bruts. Consultez le formulaire T2125. **N'inscrivez pas** ce montant à la ligne 101.
- 84 **Titres de transport en commun** Lisez la ligne 364 de votre guide d'impôt.
- 85 **Primes versées à un régime privé d'assurance-maladie** Lisez la ligne 330 de votre guide d'impôt.

Ne déclarez pas ces montants dans votre déclaration d'impôt. À l'usage de l'Agence du revenu du Canada seulement.
(Les montants des cases 30, 32, 34, 36, 38 et 40 sont déjà inclus dans la case 14.)

- 30 **Pension et logement**
- 31 **Chantier particulier**
- 32 **Voyages dans une zone visée par règlement**
- 33 **Aide accordée pour les voyages pour soins médicaux**
- 34 **Usage personnel de l'automobile ou du véhicule à moteur de l'employeur**
- 36 **Prêts sans intérêt ou à faible intérêt**
- 38 **Avantages liés aux options d'achat de titres**
- 40 **Autres allocations et avantages imposables**
- 70 **Allocation de dépense versée à un conseiller municipal**
- 71 **Employé indien inscrit**

Canada Revenue Agency / Agence du revenu du Canada

Year / Année

T4A

STATEMENT OF PENSION, RETIREMENT, ANNUITY, AND OTHER INCOME
ÉTAT DU REVENU DE PENSION, DE RETRAITE, DE RENTE OU D'AUTRES SOURCES

16 Pension or superannuation Prestations de retraite ou autres pensions	18 Lump-sum payments Paiements forfaitaires	20 Self-employed commissions Commissions d'un travail indépendant	22 Income tax deducted Impôt sur le revenu retenu	24 Annuities Rentes	26 Eligible retiring allowances Allocations de retraite admissibles	27 Non-eligible retiring allowances Allocations de retraite non admissibles
28 Other income Autres revenus	30 Patronage allocations Répartitions selon l'apport commercial	32 Registered pension plan contributions (past service) Cotisations à un régime de pension agréé (services passés)	34 Pension adjustment Facteur d'équivalence	36 Plan registration number Numéro d'agrément du régime	40 RESP accumulated income payments Paiements de revenu accumulé d'un REEE	42 RESP educational assistance payments Paiements d'aide aux études d'un REEE
46 Charitable donations Dons de bienfaisance	12 Social insurance number Numéro d'assurance sociale	38 Footnote codes Codes de notes	13 Account Number (15 characters) Numéro de compte (15 caractères)	14 Recipient's number Numéro du bénéficiaire	61 Payer's Account Number (15 characters) Numéro de compte du payeur (15 caractères)	
				Payer's name – Nom du payeur		

Recipient's name and address – Nom et adresse du bénéficiaire

Last name (in capital letters) – Nom de famille (en lettres moulées) First name – Prénom Initials – Initiales

Footnote code explanation
Also complete box 38

Explication des codes de notes
Remplissez aussi la case 38

T4A (09)

Canada Revenue Agency / Agence du revenu du Canada

Year / Année

T4A

STATEMENT OF PENSION, RETIREMENT, ANNUITY, AND OTHER INCOME
ÉTAT DU REVENU DE PENSION, DE RETRAITE, DE RENTE OU D'AUTRES SOURCES

16 Pension or superannuation Prestations de retraite ou autres pensions	18 Lump-sum payments Paiements forfaitaires	20 Self-employed commissions Commissions d'un travail indépendant	22 Income tax deducted Impôt sur le revenu retenu	24 Annuities Rentes	26 Eligible retiring allowances Allocations de retraite admissibles	27 Non-eligible retiring allowances Allocations de retraite non admissibles
28 Other income Autres revenus	30 Patronage allocations Répartitions selon l'apport commercial	32 Registered pension plan contributions (past service) Cotisations à un régime de pension agréé (services passés)	34 Pension adjustment Facteur d'équivalence	36 Plan registration number Numéro d'agrément du régime	40 RESP accumulated income payments Paiements de revenu accumulé d'un REEE	42 RESP educational assistance payments Paiements d'aide aux études d'un REEE
46 Charitable donations Dons de bienfaisance	12 Social insurance number Numéro d'assurance sociale	38 Footnote codes Codes de notes	13 Account Number (15 characters) Numéro de compte (15 caractères)	14 Recipient's number Numéro du bénéficiaire	61 Payer's Account Number (15 characters) Numéro de compte du payeur (15 caractères)	
				Payer's name – Nom du payeur		

Recipient's name and address – Nom et adresse du bénéficiaire

Last name (in capital letters) – Nom de famille (en lettres moulées) First name – Prénom Initials – Initiales

Footnote code explanation
Also complete box 38

Explication des codes de notes
Remplissez aussi la case 38

T4A (09)

Canada Revenue Agency / Agence du revenu du Canada

Year / Année

T4A

STATEMENT OF PENSION, RETIREMENT, ANNUITY, AND OTHER INCOME
ÉTAT DU REVENU DE PENSION, DE RETRAITE, DE RENTE OU D'AUTRES SOURCES

16 Pension or superannuation Prestations de retraite ou autres pensions	18 Lump-sum payments Paiements forfaitaires	20 Self-employed commissions Commissions d'un travail indépendant	22 Income tax deducted Impôt sur le revenu retenu	24 Annuities Rentes	26 Eligible retiring allowances Allocations de retraite admissibles	27 Non-eligible retiring allowances Allocations de retraite non admissibles
28 Other income Autres revenus	30 Patronage allocations Répartitions selon l'apport commercial	32 Registered pension plan contributions (past service) Cotisations à un régime de pension agréé (services passés)	34 Pension adjustment Facteur d'équivalence	36 Plan registration number Numéro d'agrément du régime	40 RESP accumulated income payments Paiements de revenu accumulé d'un REEE	42 RESP educational assistance payments Paiements d'aide aux études d'un REEE
46 Charitable donations Dons de bienfaisance	12 Social insurance number Numéro d'assurance sociale	38 Footnote codes Codes de notes	13 Account Number (15 characters) Numéro de compte (15 caractères)	14 Recipient's number Numéro du bénéficiaire	61 Payer's Account Number (15 characters) Numéro de compte du payeur (15 caractères)	
				Payer's name – Nom du payeur		

Recipient's name and address – Nom et adresse du bénéficiaire

Last name (in capital letters) – Nom de famille (en lettres moulées) First name – Prénom Initials – Initiales

Footnote code explanation
Also complete box 38

Explication des codes de notes
Remplissez aussi la case 38

T4A (09)

IMPORTANT

For instructions on how to complete this slip, see the reverse.

Les instructions sur la façon de remplir ce formulaire se trouvent au verso.

HOW TO COMPLETE THIS SLIP

Complete this form using the instructions in Guide RC4157, *Deducting Income Tax on Pension and Other Income, and Filing the T4A Slip and Summary.*

If you file by Internet file transfer (XML), through My Business Account, or on electronic media, visit the following Web pages: **www.cra.gc.ca/file-xml**, **www.cra.gc.ca/electronicmedia**, or **www.cra.gc.ca/mybusinessaccount**.

If you file your T4A slips on paper:

- Use one sheet for three different recipients for the copy you are sending to the CRA. Do not separate the slips when you send them with your T4A Summary.
- Use a separate sheet for the two copies you are giving to the recipient and the copy you are keeping in your records. Do not print your Payer Account Number (box 61) on the recipient copies.

COMMENT REMPLIR CE FEUILLET

Remplissez ce formulaire selon les directives indiquées dans le guide RC4157, *Comment retenir l'impôt sur les revenus de pension ou d'autres sources et établir le feuillet T4A et le Sommaire.*

Si vous produisez vos feuillets T4A par transfert de fichiers par Internet (XML), à partir de Mon dossier d'entreprise ou sur support électronique, visitez, selon le cas, les pages suivantes de notre site Web : **www.arc.gc.ca/fichiers-xml**, **www.arc.gc.ca/supportelectronique** ou **www.arc.gc.ca/mondossierentreprise**.

Si vous produisez vos feuillets T4A sur papier :

- Utilisez une page pour trois bénéficiaires distincts pour la copie que vous envoyez à l'ARC. Ne séparez pas les feuillets avant de nous les envoyer avec le T4A Sommaire.
- Utilisez une page distincte pour les deux copies que vous remettez à chaque bénéficiaire et la copie que vous gardez dans vos dossiers. N'indiquez pas votre numéro de compte du payeur (case 61) sur les copies du bénéficiaire.

Report these amounts on your tax return.

Box 16, Pension or superannuation: Enter this amount on line 115. It **may** qualify for the pension income amount (see line 314 in your tax guide).

Box 18, Lump-sum payments: Enter this amount on line 130. Lump-sum payments out of a registered pension plan (RPP) or deferred profit-sharing plan (DPSP) that you cannot transfer (code 08) and amounts from an unregistered plan (code 09) will be identified in the footnote codes area.

Box 20, Self-employed commissions: Enter your gross commissions income on line 166 and your net commissions income on line 139.

Box 22, Income tax deducted: Enter this amount on line 437.

Box 24, Annuities: See line 115 in your tax guide. Deferred profit-sharing plan (DPSP) annuity or instalment payments (code 15) will be identified in the footnote codes area.

Box 26, Eligible retiring allowances: Enter this amount on line 130. You may be able to transfer part or all of this amount into a registered retirement savings plan or registered pension plan. See line 130 in the *General Income Tax and Benefit Guide.*

Box 27, Non-eligible retiring allowances: Enter this amount on line 130.

Box 28, Other income: See the footnote codes area for the type of payment.

Enter on line 104:

- research grants (code 04)
- payments from a wage-loss replacement plan (code 07)
- medical premium benefits (code 18)
- premiums paid to a group term life insurance plan (code 19)
- veterans' benefits (code 27)
- Wage Earner Protection Program (code 32)

Enter on line 125:

- registered disability savings plan (code 31)

Enter on line 130:

- death benefits (code 06)
- periodic payments from an unregistered plan (code 09)
- medical travel assistance (code 16)
- loan benefits (code 17)
- payments from a revoked DPSP (code 23)
- disability benefits paid out of a superannuation or pension plan (code 25)
- scholarships, bursaries, fellowships, artists' project grants, and prizes (code 05). See line 130 in your tax guide.
- tax deferred cooperative share (code 29). See line 130 in your tax guide.
- apprenticeship incentive grant (code 30)
- apprenticeship completion grant (code 30)
- Tax-Free Savings Account (TFSA) taxable amount (code 34)
- variable pension benefits (code 33). **See line 115** in your tax guide.

Box 30, Patronage allocations: Enter this amount on line 130. Do not report the amount if it was for goods or services you consumed and for which you cannot deduct the cost when you calculate your income. This amount does not qualify for the federal dividend tax credit.

Box 32, Registered pension plan contributions (past-service): Enter the amount you can deduct on line 207 (see guide T4040, *RRSPs and Other Registered Plans for Retirement*). Pre-1990 past service contributions (code 26) will be shown in the footnote codes area.

Box 34, Pension adjustment: Enter this amount on line 206. This amount is not income or a deduction.

Box 40, RESP accumulated income payments: Enter this amount on line 130 and complete Form T1172, *Additional Tax on Accumulated Income Payments from RESPs.*

Box 42, RESP educational assistance payments: Enter this amount on line 130. For details, see the Information Sheet RC4092, *Registered Education Savings Plans (RESPs).*

Box 46, Charitable donations: See line 349 in your tax guide.

Déclarez ces montants dans votre déclaration de revenus.

Case 16, Prestations de retraite ou autres pensions – Inscrivez ce montant à la ligne 115. Vous **pourriez** avoir droit au montant pour revenu de pension (lisez votre guide d'impôt à la ligne 314).

Case 18, Paiements forfaitaires – Inscrivez ce montant à la ligne 130. Les paiements provenant d'un régime de pension agréé (RPA) ou d'un régime de participation différée aux bénéfices (RPDB) qui ne peuvent pas être transférés (code 08), ainsi que les montants d'un régime non agréé (code 09), sont indiqués dans l'explication des codes de notes.

Case 20, Commissions d'un travail indépendant – Inscrivez le montant brut de vos revenus de commissions à la ligne 166 et le montant net de vos revenus de commissions à la ligne 139.

Case 22, Impôt sur le revenu retenu – Inscrivez ce montant à la ligne 437.

Case 24, Rentes – Lisez la ligne 115 de votre guide d'impôt. Les paiements d'une rente et les versements selon un régime de participation différée aux bénéfices (RPDB) (code 15) sont indiqués dans l'explication des codes de notes.

Case 26, Allocations de retraite admissibles – Inscrivez ce montant à la ligne 130. Ce montant peut être transféré en partie ou en totalité dans un REER ou dans un régime de pension agréé. Lisez la ligne 130 du *Guide général d'impôt et de prestations.*

Case 27, Allocations de retraite non admissibles – Inscrivez ce montant à la ligne 130.

Case 28, Autres revenus – Lisez l'explication des codes de notes pour connaître le genre de paiement.

Inscrivez à la ligne 104 :

- les subventions de recherche (code 04)
- les paiements reçus d'un régime d'assurance-salaire (code 07)
- les avantages pour primes de soins médicaux (code 18)
- les primes payées pour une police d'assurance-vie collective temporaire (code 19)
- les prestations pour anciens combattants (code 27)
- le Programme de protection des salariés (code 32)

Inscrivez à la ligne 125 :

- régime enregistré d'épargne-invalidité (code 31)

Inscrivez à la ligne 130 :

- les prestations consécutives au décès (code 06)
- les paiements périodiques d'un plan qui n'est pas agréé (code 09)
- aide financière pour voyages pour soins médicaux (code 16)
- les avantages liés à un prêt (code 17)
- les paiements provenant d'un RPDB dont l'agrément a été retiré (code 23)
- les prestations d'invalidité payées à même un régime de prestations de retraite ou d'autres pensions (code 25)
- les bourses d'études, de perfectionnement et d'entretien, les subventions reçues par un artiste pour un projet et les récompenses (code 05). Lisez la ligne 130 de votre guide d'impôt.
- la part de votre coopérative à imposition différée (code 29). Lisez la ligne 130 de votre guide d'impôt.
- la subvention incitative aux apprentis (code 30)
- la subvention à l'achèvement de la formation d'apprenti (code 30)
- le compte d'épargne libre d'impôt (CELI) montant imposable (code 34)
- les prestations de retraite variables (code 33). **Lisez la ligne 115** de votre guide d'impôt.

Case 30, Répartitions selon l'apport commercial – Inscrivez ce montant à la ligne 130. Ne déclarez pas ce montant s'il concerne des produits de consommation ou des services dont vous ne pouvez pas déduire le coût dans le calcul de votre revenu. Ce montant ne vous donne pas droit au crédit d'impôt fédéral pour dividendes.

Case 32, Cotisations à un régime de pension agréé (services passés) – Inscrivez le montant que vous pouvez déduire à la ligne 207 (consultez le guide T4040, *REER et autres régimes enregistrés pour la retraite*). Les cotisations pour périodes de services avant 1990 (code 26) sont indiquées dans l'explication des codes de notes.

Case 34, Facteur d'équivalence – Inscrivez ce montant à la ligne 206. Ce montant n'est ni un revenu ni une déduction.

Case 40, Paiements de revenu accumulé d'un REEE – Inscrivez ce montant à la ligne 130. Vous devez aussi remplir le formulaire T1172, *Impôt supplémentaire sur les paiements de revenu accumulé de REEE.*

Case 42, Paiements d'aide aux études d'un REEE – Inscrivez ce montant à la ligne 130. Pour en savoir plus, consultez la feuille de renseignements RC4092, *Les régimes enregistrés d'épargne-études (REEE).*

Case 46, Dons de bienfaisance – Lisez la ligne 349 de votre guide d'impôt.

Canada Revenue Agency / Agence du revenu du Canada

PAST SERVICE PENSION ADJUSTMENT (PSPA) EXEMPT FROM CERTIFICATION
FACTEUR D'ÉQUIVALENCE POUR SERVICES PASSÉS (FESP) EXEMPTÉ D'ATTESTATION

T215

See the back of this slip for information – Lisez les renseignements au verso

1 Date of past service event (YY - MM - DD) (AA - MM - JJ) Date du fait lié aux services passés	2 PSPA amount Montant du FESP	3 Registered pension plan registration number Numéro d'agrément du régime de pension agréé	4 Social insurance number Numéro d'assurance sociale	5 Amendment or deletion Modification ou annulation

Employee's last name (Please Print), first name, initials, and address
Nom de famille (en lettres moulées), prénom, initiale et adresse de l'employé

Plan administrator's name and address
Nom et adresse de l'administrateur du régime

Privacy Act personal information bank number CRA/P-PU-005
Loi sur la protection des renseignements personnels – Fichier de renseignements personnels ARC/P-PU-005
T215 (07)

Return with T215 Summary
À retourner avec le formulaire T215 *Sommaire*

1

Canada Revenue Agency / Agence du revenu du Canada

PAST SERVICE PENSION ADJUSTMENT (PSPA) EXEMPT FROM CERTIFICATION
FACTEUR D'ÉQUIVALENCE POUR SERVICES PASSÉS (FESP) EXEMPTÉ D'ATTESTATION

T215

See the back of this slip for information – Lisez les renseignements au verso

1 Date of past service event (YY - MM - DD) (AA - MM - JJ) Date du fait lié aux services passés	2 PSPA amount Montant du FESP	3 Registered pension plan registration number Numéro d'agrément du régime de pension agréé	4 Social insurance number Numéro d'assurance sociale	5 Amendment or deletion Modification ou annulation

Employee's last name (Please Print), first name, initials, and address
Nom de famille (en lettres moulées), prénom, initiale et adresse de l'employé

Plan administrator's name and address
Nom et adresse de l'administrateur du régime

Privacy Act personal information bank number CRA/P-PU-005
Loi sur la protection des renseignements personnels – Fichier de renseignements personnels ARC/P-PU-005
T215 (07)

Employee copy
Copie de l'employé

2

Information for the employee

- The PSPA amount in box 2 will decrease your RRSP deduction limit for the year following the year shown in box 1.
  Example: If the year shown in box 1 is 2006, the amount in box 2 will decrease your RRSP deduction limit for 2007.
- Do not send a copy of this slip to us. We will adjust your RRSP deduction limit based on the original T215 slip submitted by your registered pension plan administrator.

Renseignements pour l'employé

- Le montant du FESP indiqué à la case 2 réduira votre maximum déductible au titre des REER pour l'année suivant l'année indiquée à la case 1.
  Exemple : Si l'année indiquée à la case 1 est 2006, le montant indiqué à la case 2 réduira votre maximum déductible au titre des REER pour 2007.
- Ne nous envoyez pas de copie de ce feuillet. Nous modifierons le maximum déductible au titre des REER selon le feuillet T215 original produit par l'administrateur de votre régime de pension agréé.

Canada Revenue Agency / Agence du revenu du Canada

PAST SERVICE PENSION ADJUSTMENT (PSPA) EXEMPT FROM CERTIFICATION
FACTEUR D'ÉQUIVALENCE POUR SERVICES PASSÉS (FESP) EXEMPTÉ D'ATTESTATION

T215

See the back of this slip for information – Lisez les renseignements au verso

1 Date of past service event (YY - MM - DD) (AA - MM - JJ) Date du fait lié aux services passés	2 PSPA amount Montant du FESP	3 Registered pension plan registration number Numéro d'agrément du régime de pension agréé	4 Social insurance number Numéro d'assurance sociale	5 Amendment or deletion Modification ou annulation

Employee's last name (Please Print), first name, initials, and address
Nom de famille (en lettres moulées), prénom, initiale et adresse de l'employé

Plan administrator's name and address
Nom et adresse de l'administrateur du régime

Privacy Act personal information bank number CRA/P-PU-005
Loi sur la protection des renseignements personnels – Fichier de renseignements personnels ARC/P-PU-005
T215 (07)

Plan administrator copy
Copie de l'administrateur du régime **3**

Instructions for the plan administrator

- An exempt past service pension adjustment (PSPA) is one that satisfies the conditions in section 8306 of the *Income Tax Regulations.*
- Complete a T215 slip whenever the cumulative total of the exempt PSPA of an employee is equal to or greater than $50 for an original information slip. Also, you have to report an amended PSPA for a plan member when the difference between the previously reported PSPA and the amended PSPA is equal to or greater than $50.
- Enter in box 2 the amount rounded to the nearest dollar.
- Write **yes** in box 5 only if this PSPA is an amendment or deletion of a previously reported PSPA. Otherwise, leave it blank.
- For more information on the date of the past service event and on the calculation of the PSPA amount, see Guide T4104, *Past Service Pension Adjustment Guide.*

Distribution of copies

Copy 1: Send it to us no later than 120 days after the day on which the past service event occurs.

Copy 2: Mail it to the employee's last known address no later than 120 days after the day on which the past service event occurs.

Copy 3: Keep it for your records.

Printed in Canada

Instructions pour l'administrateur du régime

- Un facteur d'équivalence pour services passés (FESP) exempté d'attestation est un FESP qui satisfait aux conditions indiquées à l'article 8306 du *Règlement de l'impôt sur le revenu.*
- Remplissez un feuillet T215 lorsque le total cumulatif du FESP exempté d'attestation d'un employé est égal ou supérieur à 50 $ pour un feuillet de renseignements original. Vous êtes aussi tenu de déclarer un FESP modifié lorsque la différence entre le nouveau FESP et celui qui a été déclaré est égale ou supérieur à 50 $.
- Inscrivez le montant dans la case 2, arrondi au dollar le plus près.
- Inscrivez **oui** dans la case 5 seulement si vous modifiez ou annulez un FESP qui a déjà été déclaré. Autrement, laissez la case en blanc.
- Pour obtenir des précisions sur la date du fait lié aux services passés et sur le calcul du montant du FESP, consultez le guide T4104, *Guide du facteur d'équivalence pour services passés.*

Distribution des copies

Copie 1 : Envoyez-nous cette copie au plus tard 120 jours après la date du fait lié aux services passés.

Copie 2 : Postez-la à l'employé, à sa dernière adresse connue, au plus tard 120 jours après la date du fait lié aux services passés.

Copie 3 : Conservez-la pour vos dossiers.

Imprimé au Canada

Canada Revenue Agency / Agence du revenu du Canada

PENSION ADJUSTMENT REVERSAL (PAR)
FACTEUR D'ÉQUIVALENCE RECTIFIÉ (FER)

T10

See the back of this slip for information – Lisez les renseignements au verso

1 Year of PAR	2 PAR amount	3 Plan registration number	4 Social insurance number	5 Amendment
Année du FER	Montant du FER	Numéro d'agrément du régime	Numéro d'assurance sociale	Modification

Employee's name and address – Nom et adresse de l'employé
Last name (Print) – Nom de famille (en lettres moulées) First name – Prénom Initials – Initiales

→

Name and address of RPP administrator or DPSP trustee
Nom et adresse complète de l'administrateur du RPA ou du fiduciaire du RPDB

Privacy Act Personal Information Bank number CRA PPU 005
Loi sur la protection des renseignements personnels, Fichier des renseignements personnels ARC PPU 005

T10 (09/08)

CRA copy
Copie de l'ARC

1

Canada Revenue Agency / Agence du revenu du Canada

PENSION ADJUSTMENT REVERSAL (PAR)
FACTEUR D'ÉQUIVALENCE RECTIFIÉ (FER)

T10

See the back of this slip for information – Lisez les renseignements au verso

1 Year of PAR	2 PAR amount	3 Plan registration number	4 Social insurance number	5 Amendment
Année du FER	Montant du FER	Numéro d'agrément du régime	Numéro d'assurance sociale	Modification

Employee's name and address – Nom et adresse de l'employé
Last name (Print) – Nom de famille (en lettres moulées) First name – Prénom Initials – Initiales

→

Name and address of RPP administrator or DPSP trustee
Nom et adresse complète de l'administrateur du RPA ou du fiduciaire du RPDB

Privacy Act Personal Information Bank number CRA PPU 005
Loi sur la protection des renseignements personnels, Fichier des renseignements personnels ARC PPU 005

T10 (09/08)

Employee copy
Copie de l'employé

2

Canada Revenue Agency / Agence du revenu du Canada

PENSION ADJUSTMENT REVERSAL (PAR)
FACTEUR D'ÉQUIVALENCE RECTIFIÉ (FER)

T10

See the back of this slip for information – Lisez les renseignements au verso

1 Year of PAR	2 PAR amount	3 Plan registration number	4 Social insurance number	5 Amendment
Année du FER	Montant du FER	Numéro d'agrément du régime	Numéro d'assurance sociale	Modification

Employee's name and address – Nom et adresse de l'employé
Last name (Print) – Nom de famille (en lettres moulées) First name – Prénom Initials – Initiales

→

Name and address of RPP administrator or DPSP trustee
Nom et adresse complète de l'administrateur du RPA ou du fiduciaire du RPDB

Privacy Act Personal Information Bank number CRA PPU 005
Loi sur la protection des renseignements personnels, Fichier des renseignements personnels ARC PPU 005

T10 (09/08)

Administrator or trustee copy
Copie de l'administrateur ou du fiduciaire

3

For information on how to complete this form, see the back.

Les renseignements sur la façon de remplir ce feuillet se trouvent au verso.

Distribution of copies

Copy 1: Send it no later than 60 days after the end of the calendar quarter in which the termination occurs (no later than 31 days after the end of December for the last calendar quarter) to the Canada Revenue Agency - Ottawa Technology Centre, Pension Section, 875 Heron Road, Ottawa ON K1A 1A2. Attach all required T10 Summary and T10 Segment forms.

Copy 2: Mail it to the employee's last known address no later than 60 days after the end of the calendar quarter in which the termination occurs (no later than 31 days after the end of December for the last calendar quarter).

Copy 3: Keep it for your records.

Note For the definition of "calendar quarter" and more information on filing requirements, see Guide RC4137, *Pension Adjustment Reversal Guide.*

Distribution des copies

Copie 1 : Envoyez-la au plus tard 60 jours après la fin du trimestre de l'année civile où le retrait a lieu (au plus tard 31 jours après la fin de décembre pour le dernier trimestre) à l'Agence du revenu du Canada - Centre de technologie d'Ottawa, Section des pensions, 875, chemin Heron, Ottawa ON K1A 1A2. Incluez tous les formulaires T10 *Sommaire* et T10 *Segment* tel que requis.

Copie 2 : Postez-la à l'employé, à sa dernière adresse connue, au plus tard 60 jours après la fin du trimestre de l'année civile où le retrait a lieu (au plus tard 31 jours après la fin de décembre pour le dernier trimestre).

Copie 3 : Conservez-la pour vos dossiers.

Remarque Pour connaître la définition du terme « trimestre de l'année civile » et obtenir plus d'information sur les exigences de production, consultez le guide RC4137, *Guide du facteur d'équivalence rectifié.*

Information for the employee

- We, at the Canada Revenue Agency, will take into consideration the PAR amount reported in box 2 to determine your RRSP deduction limit for the year indicated in box 1. This will result in an increase of your RRSP deduction limit for that year.
- This copy is for your information. Do not send it to us. Your plan administrator will send us a copy that we will use to adjust your RRSP deduction limit.
- For more information on PAR, refer to Guide T4040, *RRSPs and Other Registered Plans for Retirement.*

Renseignements pour l'employé

- Nous, à l'Agence du revenu du Canada, tiendrons compte du montant du FER indiqué dans la case 2 afin d'établir votre maximum déductible au titre desREER pour l'année indiquée dans la case 1. Ceci aura pourconséquenced'augmenter votre maximum déductible au titre des REER pour cette année-là.
- Cette copie du feuillet vous est fournie à titre de renseignement Ne nous la soumettez pas. Nous modifierons votre maximum déductible au titre des REER selon la copie produite par l'administrateur de votre régime.
- Pour obtenir plus d'information sur le FER, consultez le guide T4040, *REER et autres régimes enregistrés pour la retraite.*

Instructions for the RPP administrator or DPSP trustee

- A pension adjustment reversal (PAR) is an amount that is calculated under section 8304.1 of the *Income Tax Regulations.*
- For information about calculating the PAR amount, see Guide RC4137, *Pension Adjustment Reversal Guide.*
- Enter the amount rounded to the nearest dollar in box 2.
- Insert **Yes** in box 5 only if this PAR is an amendment or deletion of a previously reported PAR. Otherwise, leave it blank.

Instructions pour l'administrateur du RPA ou le fiduciaire du RPDB

- Un facteur d'équivalence rectifié (FER) est un montant qui est calculé en vertu de l'article 8304.1 du *Règlement de l'impôt sur le revenu.*
- Pour obtenir des précisions sur le calcul du FER, consultez le guide RC4137, *Guide du facteur d'équivalence rectifié.*
- Inscrivez le montant dans la case 2, arrondi au dollar le plus près.
- Inscrivez **Oui** dans la case 5 seulement si vous modifiez ou annulez un FER qui a déjà été déclaré. Autrement, laissez la case en blanc.

Canada Revenue Agency / Agence du revenu du Canada

APPLYING FOR THE CERTIFICATION OF A PROVISIONAL PSPA

- Complete this form if you are a registered pension plan (RPP) administrator and are requesting certification of a plan member's provisional past service pension adjustment (PSPA) for post-1989 past service benefits provided under a defined benefit provision of an RPP.
- The PSPA amount will decrease the plan member's RRSP deduction limit for the year in which we certify the PSPA.
- If the provisional PSPA requires certification, you cannot fund the past service benefits until you complete this form and file it with us. You cannot pay the past service benefits to the member until we issue the certification.
- For more information, see the back of this form and Guide T4104, *Past Service Pension Adjustment Guide.*

Part 1 – RPP member information (print)

First name and initial	Last name		Social insurance number
Address			
City	Province or territory	Postal code	

Part 2 – RPP information

RPP's name			RPP registration number
RPP administrator's name			
Mailing address			
City	Province or territory	Postal code	
Contact person's name	Phone number		

Part 3 – Provisional PSPA

Amount .... $ ______________ A

Part 4 – RPP administrator's certification

I certify that the information given on this form is, to the best of my knowledge, correct and complete.

RPP administrator or authorized officer's signature ______________ Date ______________

Part 5 – To be completed by the Agency **Please do not write in this area.**

The provisional PSPA amount on line A of this form for the plan member specified in Part 1 is:

☐ Approved ☐ Denied

Authorized signature ______________

Date ______________

CRA stamp

Privacy Act Personal Information Bank number CRA/P-PU-005

T1004 E (08) (Vous pouvez obtenir ce formulaire en français à **www.arc.gc.ca** ou au **1-800-959-3376**.)

Canada

Additional Information for RPP Administrators

We use the following calculation to approve or deny an application for certification of a provisional PSPA.

The formula is for your information only. **You do not have to complete the calculation.**

Step 1 – Add:

$ 8,000	$ 8,000	
The RPP member's unused RRSP deduction room at the end of the immediately preceding year (see note 1)	+	
The total of all qualifying withdrawals made in the year (see note 2)	+	
The total of all qualifying withdrawals made for this past service event (see note 3)	+	
The RPP member's total pension adjustment reversal for the year	+	
Total	=	1

Step 2 – Subtract from line 1:

Member's accumulated PSPA for the year (see note 4)	–	2
Line 1 **minus** line 2	=	3

Step 3 – Compare line 3 with:

The provisional PSPA amount from line A on the front of this form		4

If line 3 is greater than or equal to line 4, we will approve the application for certification. If line 3 is less than line 4, we will deny the application. If we cannot approve the application, the RPP member may be able to increase the amount on line 3 by designating eligible RRSP withdrawals as qualifying withdrawals. See note 3 below for more details.

Note 1: The unused RRSP deduction room can be a positive or a negative amount. The RPP member can get this amount by calling our Tax Information Phone Service (T.I.P.S.) at **1-800-267-6999**, from general enquiries at **1-800-959-8281**, or by visiting our Web site at **www.cra.gc.ca**.

Note 2: This amount is the total of all qualifying withdrawals made by an individual for purposes of any previous PSPA that was certified in the current year.

Note 3: An RPP member can create more "room" to get approval of an application for certification by designating eligible RRSP withdrawals. The member has to complete Form T1006, *Designating an RRSP Withdrawal as a Qualifying Withdrawal.* Form T1006 has information on the minimum and maximum amounts that can be designated. The member can get more information on qualifying withdrawals in Guide T4040, *RRSPs and Other Registered Plans for Retirement*, which is available on our Web site at **www.cra.gc.ca**, or he or she can also order it by calling **1-800-959-2221**.

Note 4: This amount is the total of:

- any PSPA exempt from certification in the previous year (total amounts from all T215 slips for that year); and
- any previous PSPA that was certified in the current year (total amounts from all T1004 forms that we approved in the current year).

Complete this form and keep a copy for your records. Send three copies to:

Pension and RRSP Processing Group
Ottawa Technology Centre
875 Heron Road
Ottawa ON K1A 1A2

We will indicate our approval or denial of the application in Part 5 of the form and return two copies to you.

Canada Revenue Agency / Agence du revenu du Canada

DESIGNATING AN RRSP WITHDRAWAL AS A QUALIFYING WITHDRAWAL

- This form has to be used if a member of a defined benefit registered pension plan (RPP) designates an amount withdrawn from a registered retirement savings plan (RRSP) as a qualifying withdrawal in connection with the certification of a provisional past service pension adjustment (PSPA).
- See the back of this form for instructions and information on RRSP qualifying withdrawals. For more information on qualifying withdrawals, see Guide *T4040, RRSPs and Other Registered Plans for Retirement*, which is available on our Web site at **www.cra.gc.ca**, or you can also order it by calling **1-800-959-2221**.
- Sections, subsections, and paragraphs referred to on this form are from the *Income Tax Act*.

Part 1 – RPP member information (print)

First name and initial	Last name		Social insurance number
Address			RPP registration number
City	Province or territory	Postal code	

Part 2 – Calculating amounts that have to be designated to certify the provisional PSPA

Total of:

Provisional PSPA for the past service event .... $ ______

+ accumulated PSPA for the year (see **note 1** on the back of this form) .... + ______ ▶ $ ______ A

Minus the total of:

Unused RRSP deduction room at the end of the immediately preceding year .... $ ______

+ pension adjustment reversal (PAR) for the year .... + ______

+ PSPA withdrawals for the year (see **note 2** on the back of this form) .... + ______ ▶ – ______ B

Line A **minus** line B: This is the maximum amount that you can designate as a qualifying withdrawal
(If the amount on line C is zero or negative, you cannot designate an amount as a qualifying withdrawal.) .... $ ______ C

Minus .... – **8,000** D

Line C **minus** line D: This is the minimum amount that you can designate as a qualifying withdrawal
(If the amount on line E is greater than zero, you have to designate at least that amount, or we will not certify the provisional PSPA.) .... $ ______ E

Part 3 – Calculating RRSP withdrawals eligible for designation as qualifying withdrawals

You have to give proof of the amount on line F below. Attach a photocopy of the T4RSP slip issued for the withdrawal. If the T4RSP slip has not yet been issued, have the RRSP issuer(s) complete Part 4 of this form.

Amounts withdrawn from RRSPs under which you are the annuitant .... $ ______ F
(These amounts must have been withdrawn in the current year or in either of the two preceding calendar years.)

Subtract from line F above the total of the following amounts that:

(i) were transferred directly to another RRSP, to a registered retirement income fund (RRIF), or to an issuer to purchase an eligible annuity under which you are the annuitant and for which a deduction was claimed, or can be claimed, under paragraph 60(l) .... $ ______

(ii) were claimed as a deduction under subsection 146(8.2) for a refund of undeducted RRSP contributions or amounts claimed under subsection 147.3(13.1) of the *Income tax Act* ....

(iii) were claimed as a deduction under section 60.2 as a refund of undeducted past service additional voluntary contributions .... + ______

(iv) have been designated by you for any other PSPA certification .... + ______

Total of lines (i), (ii), (iii), and (iv) .... $ ______ ▶ – ______ G

Line F **minus** line G: This is the amount eligible to be designated as a qualifying withdrawal .... $ ______ H

If the amount on line H is less than the amount on line E, you will have to withdraw additional amounts from your RRSPs to have the provisional PSPA certified. If you do not want to withdraw additional amounts from your RRSPs, you do not have to file this form. However, the provisional PSPA will not be certified and the past service benefits to which the provisional PSPA relates cannot be provided to you.

If the amount on line H is equal to the amount on line E, you have to designate the full amount entered on line H.

If the amount on line H is more than the amount on line E, you have to designate an amount that is at least equal to the amount on line E. However, you can designate any amount up to the amount on line C or the amount on line H, whichever is less.

I designate $ ______ as a qualifying withdrawal for the provisional PSPA shown in Part 2 of this form.
I certify that the information given on this form is, to the best of my knowledge, correct and complete.

______ RRSP annuitant's signature ______ Date

Part 4 – To be completed by RRSP issuer (print)

RRSP issuer's name			RRSP plan number
Address			
City	Province or territory	Postal code	Annuitant's social insurance number
Annuitant's name	Amount of RRSP withdrawal less redemption fees $		Date of RRSP withdrawal
Name of authorized person	Telephone number		

I certify that the information given in this area is correct and complete.

______ Date ______ Signature of authorized person

Privacy Act personal information bank number CRA/P-PU-005
T1006 E (08)
Printed in Canada

(Vous pouvez obtenir ce formulaire en français à **www.arc.gc.ca** ou au **1-800-959-3376**.)

Canada

General Information

Registered Retirement Savings Plan (RRSP) Qualifying Withdrawals
In general, a qualifying withdrawal is an amount that you withdraw from your RRSP so that you can receive post-1989 past service benefits under a defined benefit provision of your employer's registered pension plan (RPP). The value of the RPP benefits is measured and is called a past service pension adjustment (PSPA).

The RRSP withdrawal has to be included in your income for the year you receive it. It also has to meet the conditions shown on the front of this form. If these conditions are met and you designate an amount as a qualifying withdrawal, we can certify your PSPA. Our certification allows your RPP administrator to credit you with past service benefits under the RPP. Use this form to designate the withdrawn amount.

Information for RRSP Issuers and Annuitants
All RRSP withdrawals have to be reported on a T4RSP slip for the year it is received. Please refer to T4079, *T4RSP and T4RIF Guide*, for additional information.

If we cannot certify your PSPA because it is more than the allowable amount, we will send you a qualifying withdrawal letter and another Form T1006. The letter will ask if you want to designate an RRSP qualifying withdrawal so that we can certify your PSPA.

If you designate a qualifying withdrawal, complete the form and send us a copy. We will then determine if we can certify the PSPA.

If you do not designate a qualifying withdrawal, we will not approve the certification request. We will tell the RPP administrator that the past service benefits related to the PSPA cannot be provided to you.

Note
When your RPP administrator requests that we certify Form T1004, *Applying for the Certification of a Provisional PSPA*, the administrator may already know that the past service benefits cannot be certified unless you designate an RRSP qualifying withdrawal. In this case, your administrator may ask if you want to designate an RRSP qualifying withdrawal. If you choose to make this designation, the administrator may also ask you to complete this form so that he can send it to us with the certification request. If this happens, we will not send you a qualifying withdrawal letter or ask you to complete another Form T1006.

Additional information for completing Part 2

Note 1.

This amount is the total of:

- any PSPA exempt from certification in the previous year (total amounts from all T215 slips for that year); and
- any previous PSPA that was certified in the current year (total amounts from all forms T1004 that we approved in the current year).

Note 2.

This amount is the total of all qualifying withdrawals made by an individual for purposes of any previous PSPA that was certified in the current year.

Instructions for completing this form

We will complete Parts 1 and 2 of this form before we send it to you. Use Part 3 to calculate the amount of your RRSP withdrawal that is eligible to be designated as a qualifying withdrawal. In some cases, your RPP administrator may ask you to complete this form before the administrator sends us Form T1004. If this is the case, complete Parts 1, 2, and 3.

In either case, attach copies of the T4RSP slips related to the amounts you designate in Part 3 as a qualifying withdrawal. If you have not received your T4RSP slips, ask your RRSP issuer to complete Part 4 of the form before you send the completed form back to us. The issuer has to complete the form and return it to you no later than 30 days after he receives your request to complete Part 4.

Where to send this form
If we ask you to complete this form, return a copy to the address shown on the request. If your RPP administrator asks you to complete this form, return it to the administrator, who will send it to us. In both cases, keep a copy for your records.

Canada Revenue Agency / Agence du revenu du Canada

DIRECT TRANSFER OF A SINGLE AMOUNT UNDER SUBSECTION 147(19) OR SECTION 147.3

You can use this form to record a direct transfer. Tick the boxes that apply to you, and see the back of this form for instructions and definitions.
Legislative references on this form are from the *Income Tax Act*.

Area I – Applicant

Name ____ Social insurance number ____ Telephone ____

Address ____

If the transfer is from a deferred profit-sharing plan (DPSP), complete Parts A, C, and D below.
If the transfer is from a registered pension plan (RPP), complete Parts B, C, and D below.

Part A – Transfer from a DPSP

☐ I am an employee or former employee who is a beneficiary of the DPSP.

☐ I am a current or former beneficiary spouse or common-law partner requesting a transfer because of the death of an employee or former employee who was the beneficiary of the DPSP.

☐ I am a current or former beneficiary spouse or common-law partner of an employee or former employee who was the beneficiary of the DPSP requesting a transfer because of a breakdown of our marriage or common-law partnership.

Canada Revenue Agency's DPSP registration number ____ Employer's name ____

Plan number ____ Employer's address ____

Part B – Transfer from an RPP

☐ I am a member of the RPP.

☐ I am a current or former beneficiary spouse or common-law partner requesting a transfer because of the death of a member of the RPP.

☐ I am the RPP member's current or former spouse or common-law partner requesting a transfer because of a breakdown of the marriage or common-law partnership.

Canada Revenue Agency's RPP registration number ____ Employer's name ____

Plan number ____ Employer's address ____

Part C – Description of amount to be transferred

☐ Please transfer my whole entitlement under the plan identified in Part A or B.

☐ Please transfer $ ____, which is my partial entitlement under the plan identified in Part A or B.

Part D – Identification of the RRSP, RRIF, RPP, or DPSP the funds are being transferred.

☐ Please transfer the RPP or DPSP single amount to my registered retirement savings plan (RRSP).

Individual plan number ____ Name of plan and approved specimen plan number ____

☐ Please transfer the RPP or DPSP single amount to my registered retirement income fund (RRIF).

Individual fund number ____ Name of fund and approved specimen fund number ____

☐ Please transfer the RPP or DPSP single amount to my account as a member of this RPP.

☐ Please transfer the DPSP single amount to my account as a beneficiary under this DPSP.

Employer's name ____ Canada Revenue Agency's registration number of RPP or DPSP ____

Transferee's address ____

Date ____ Applicant's signature ____

Area II – Transferor's certification

1. The $ ____ transferred is the applicant's ☐ whole or ☐ partial entitlement under:
   ☐ the DPSP identified in Part A of Area I, or ☐ the RPP identified in Part B of Area I.
2. We have transferred $ ____ according to:
   ☐ subsection 147(19) (a DPSP lump-sum transfer to an RPP, an RRSP, a RRIF, or another DPSP); or
   ☐ one of the following subsections: 147.3(1) to (8) (an RPP lump-sum transfer to an RRSP, a RRIF, or another RPP).
3. A lock-in provision applies to $ ____ of the amount we transferred from the RPP identified in Part B of Area I, under the *Pension Benefits Standards Act* or a provincial pension benefits act (specify the act). ____ ☐ Does not apply
4. We did not transfer $ ____ of the RPP single amount indicated in item 1 according to one of the following subsections: 147.3(1) to (7). We will report this amount as the applicant's income on a T4A slip.

I certify that the information given on this form is, to the best of my knowledge, correct and complete.

Transferor's name ____

Date ____ Authorized person's signature ____

Area III – Transferee's certification

1. We have received $ ____, and we have credited it to:
   ☐ the applicant's RRSP identified in Part D of Area I;
   ☐ the applicant's RRIF identified in Part D of Area I;
   ☐ the applicant's account as a member of the RPP identified in Part D of Area I; or
   ☐ the applicant's account as beneficiary under the DPSP identified in Part D of Area I.
2. The plan to which the single amount has been transferred is registered under the *Income Tax Act*.
3. We will administer the amount indicated in item 3 of Area II as a locked-in amount under the recipient fund or plan.
4. We will issue a receipt for the amount indicated in item 4 of Area II.

I certify that the information given on this form is, to the best of my knowledge, correct and complete.

Transferee's name ____

Date ____ Authorized person's signature ____

T2151 E (08) (Vous pouvez obtenir ce formulaire en français à **www.arc.gc.ca/formulaires** ou au **1-800-959-3376**.)

Copy 1 – For the transferor (all areas completed)

Canada

Copy 2 – For the applicant (all areas completed)
Do not attach this copy to your income tax return

Copy 3 – For the transferee (all areas completed)

Copy 4 – For the transferor (Areas I and II completed)

Instructions

Who can use this form?

If you are a DPSP trustee or an RPP administrator, you can use this form to record the direct transfer of a single amount for an applicant.

- As a DPSP trustee, you can make a direct transfer to another DPSP, an RPP, an RRSP, or a RRIF.
- As an RPP administrator, you can make a direct transfer to another RPP, an RRSP, or a RRIF.

Note

If you do not use Form T2151 to document this transfer, ensure that you, as the transferor, provide the transferee with the information required to correctly complete the transfer.

Who completes this form?

Area I

The plan member or beneficiary requesting the transfer (the applicant) completes and signs Area I. All copies have to be given to the DPSP trustee or the RPP administrator from which the amount is to be transferred (the transferor).

Area II

The transferor completes and signs Area II. The transferor keeps copy 4, and sends copies 1, 2, and 3 to the DPSP trustee, the RPP administrator, the RRSP issuer, or the RRIF carrier to which the single amount is to be transferred (the transferee), along with the amount being transferred.

Area III

The transferee completes and signs Area III of copies 1, 2, and 3. The transferee keeps copy 3, and returns copy 1 to the transferor and copy 2 to the applicant.

Transfers from a DPSP

As the transferor, you can transfer a single amount for an employee or former employee who participated in the plan as described in subsection 147(19). You can transfer the amount to an RPP for that person's benefit, to an RRSP or a RRIF under which that person is the annuitant. Also, you can transfer the amount to another DPSP for that person's benefit, **if it can reasonably be expected that the recipient DPSP will have at least five beneficiaries throughout the year in which you make the transfer.**

Similarly, you can transfer a single amount for the current or former spouse or common-law partner of the employee or former employee, if that person is entitled to the amount:

- because the employee or former employee died; or
- because the marriage or common-law partnership with the employee or former employee breaks down. In this case, the transfer has to result from a decree, order, or judgment of a competent tribunal, or from a written separation agreement that relates to a division of property in settlement of rights arising out of, or on the breakdown of, the marriage or common-law partnership.

Do not include the amount that you transfer under subsection 147(19) in the income of the person for whom you made the transfer. Also, that person cannot deduct the amount transferred. Do not issue a T4A slip or a receipt for the amount.

Do not withhold income tax from an amount you transfer under subsection 147(19).

Transfers from an RPP

As the transferor, you can transfer a single amount for a plan member to another RPP for the member's benefit, or to the member's RRSP or RRIF. See section 147.3 for the details of such transfers.

You can transfer a single amount for the member's current or former spouse or common-law partner, if that person is entitled to the amount:

- because the member dies; or
- because the marriage or common-law partnership with the member breaks down. In this case, the transfer has to result from a decree, order, or judgment of a competent tribunal, or from a written separation agreement that relates to a division of property in settlement of rights arising out of, or on the breakdown of, the marriage or common-law partnership.

In certain cases, the rules in section 147.3 limit the amount that you can transfer without tax consequences. If part of an amount transferred does not meet the rules of the subsection under which you transfer, that part is considered to have been paid to the applicant as a pension benefit. In such cases, you have to report that part as the applicant's income on a T4A slip. That part is also considered to have been contributed by the applicant to the RRSP or to the other RPP, whichever applies. The transferee should give the applicant a receipt for the amount.

Similarly, if you transfer the single amount to a RRIF, the excess part is considered to have been contributed to an RRSP. In such cases, you have to report the excess part as the applicant's income on a T4A slip. The transferee should give the applicant an RRSP receipt for the excess part.

Do not include the amount that you transfer under any of subsections 147.3(1) to (8) in the income of the person for whom you make the transfer. Also, that person cannot deduct the amount transferred. Do not issue a T4A slip or a receipt for the amount.

Do not withhold income tax from the amount you transfer under section 147.3.

Definitions

Annuitant – The person who is entitled to receive payments from an RRSP or a RRIF.

DPSP trustee – A corporation named as a trustee under the plan, that is resident in Canada, and licensed or otherwise authorized under Canadian law to carry on in Canada the business of offering to the public its services as a trustee. A DPSP trustee can also mean a group of at least three individuals who are resident in Canada, and who are named as trustees under the plan.

Individual plan number or **individual fund number** – The individual account, contract, certificate, or other identifier number that the RRSP issuer or RRIF carrier assigns.

RPP administrator – The person or organization that is responsible for administering the RPP.

RRIF carrier – A person described in subsection 146.3(1), with whom an annuitant has an arrangement that is a RRIF.

Single amount – An amount that is not part of a series of periodic payments.

RRSP issuer – A person described in subsection 146(1), with whom an annuitant has a contract or arrangement that is an RRSP.

Transferee – The administrator, issuer, or trustee of the plan, or the carrier of the fund to whom the amount is transferred.

Spouse or common-law partner – You can find the definition of these terms in most of the income tax guides or pamphlets we publish.

Transferor – The administrator or trustee of the plan from whom the amount is transferred.

Printed in Canada

Canada Revenue Agency / Agence du revenu du Canada

Application to Amend a Registered Pension Plan

- As the pension plan **administrator**, you must fully complete this form when you request acceptance of an amendment to a registered pension plan under subsection 147.1(4) of the *Income Tax Act.*
- All questions on the form must be answered unless you are instructed otherwise. Incomplete forms will be considered incomplete applications and will be returned to the submitter.
- You do not have to file this form if the amendments you are submitting are solely in response to the Registered Plans Directorate's request for an amendment to the plan. Please use Form T2011, **Registered Pension Plan Change of Information** instead, if the changes relate **only** to the contact person and/or address of the plan sponsor, pension plan administrator, trustees, insurance carrier and/or consultant.
- Send us a completed copy of this form and include a **certified copy** of the amendment, plan revision, or change in funding medium no later than 60 days from the date on which the amendment was made, as required by subsection 8512(2) of the *Income Tax Regulations.* For plans required by law to establish a pension committee, see **Registered Plans Directorate Newsletter no. 04-2**.
- Should you require more space to provide us with information, please use **Appendix A** located at the end of this form, or attach the information on additional sheets, using the same format.

Send the documents by registered mail to: Canada Revenue Agency, Registered Plans Directorate, Ottawa ON K1A 0L5.

Throughout the form, certain words have been linked to a glossary. You can also obtain more information from the **Registered Pension Plan Guide T4099E** or by calling us at 613-954-0419 or 1-800-267-3100.

(Ce formulaire existe en français.)

Canada

Canada Revenue Agency / Agence du revenu du Canada

Protected B when completed

Application to Amend a Registered Pension Plan

(Please print or type)

Section 1 – Plan identification

(a) Registration number – Enter the seven-digit registration number assigned by the Canada Revenue Agency. This number begins with zero or one. | Registration number

Prior to this amendment, the plan was a (check all that apply):

☐ **defined benefit plan** ☐ **money purchase plan** ☐ **combination plan** ☐ **multi-employer plan**
☐ **specified multi-employer plan** ☐ **designated plan** ☐ **flexible pension plan**

(b) Name of the pension plan – Enter the official name of the plan (**prior** to this amendment): ______

(c) Has the name of the pension plan changed? ☐ Yes ☐ No

If yes, please provide the **new** name of the plan: ______

(d) Has the plan's fiscal year end changed? ☐ Yes – New fiscal year end: M M D D **or** ☐ No

Section 2 – Administrator information

If the pension plan is administered by an employer, complete Section 2, part (a)(i). If the pension plan is required by law to establish a pension committee or is administered by a board of trustees, complete Section 2, part (a)(ii) by inserting the name of the pension committee or board of trustees in the "Care of" field. For language of correspondence, indicate the language in which the person named prefers to receive correspondence. Under "Contact," enter the name and telephone number of an individual to whom we can direct general enquiries.

(a) Provide the name and current address of the plan **administrator**:

(i) Name of the plan administrator ______

Address

City	Province	Postal code	Telephone
Contact	Telephone Ext.	Language of correspondence ☐ English ☐ French	

OR

(ii) Care of ______

Address

City	Province	Postal code	Telephone
Contact	Telephone Ext.	Language of correspondence ☐ English ☐ French	

(b) Is this a change of plan administrator? ☐ Yes ☐ No

Subsection 147.1(6) of the *Income Tax Act* requires the administrator of a pension plan to be resident in Canada or to have received permission from the Minister in writing to be non-resident.

(c) Has the plan **administrator** changed to a person who is not resident in Canada? ☐ Yes ☐ No

If yes, please complete the following:
As an **authorized representative** of the administrator of this pension plan, I, ______ *(please print)*, confirm the ability and commitment of the administrator to perform the duties and obligations of an administrator and to comply with all of the conditions required or imposed by the Canadian *Income Tax Act and Regulations* with respect to a registered pension plan, including the filing of information returns, actuarial valuation reports, pension adjustments, past service pension adjustments and pension adjustment reversals, as required.

I also confirm that the administrator will retain and make available, upon request, the books and records for examination by the Canada Revenue Agency (CRA), either by submitting them to a tax services office or by assuming the travel costs incurred by a CRA officer to visit the location of such books and records.

Date ______ Signature ______ Title ______ Telephone ______

T920 E (09/12) (Ce formulaire existe en français.) Canada

(d) Has the mailing address where you would like us to send **all** pension plan correspondence changed?

☐ Yes ☐ No ☐ Same as plan administrator

If yes, please provide the new mailing address:

Company name			
Address			
City	Province	Postal code	Telephone
Contact	Telephone Ext.	Language of correspondence ☐ English ☐ French	

(e) Has the **delegated administrator** changed?

☐ Yes ☐ No ☐ No delegated administrator

If yes, please provide the name of the firm or the individual to whom the plan **administrator** has delegated to perform the duties indicated.
Note: If the name of a firm is provided, any representative of that firm may perform the delegated duties.

Name of the delegated administrator			
Address			
City	Province	Postal code	Telephone
Contact	Telephone Ext.	Language of correspondence ☐ English ☐ French	

(f) Have the duties of the **delegated administrator** changed?

☐ Yes ☐ No ☐ No delegated administrator

If yes, please indicate the following:	Delegated?
Receipt and submission of Form T244 or other annual information return	☐ Yes ☐ No
Signing of all other forms (such as Form T920)	☐ Yes ☐ No

Signature of the administrator ______________________
Signature

(required if changes have been made with respect to the delegated administrator)

Section 3 – Amendment identification

(a) Effective date of the amendment
Note: If the amendment includes several effective dates, write the earliest chronological date in the space below

| Y | Y | Y | Y | M | M | D | D |

(b) Amendment number (if applicable) ______________________

Section 4 – Employer information

(a) Has the name of the **plan sponsor** changed? ☐ Yes ☐ No

From ______________________ To ______________________

(b) Has any **participating employer** been added to, or removed from the plan? ☐ Yes ☐ No

If yes, please provide the name of every participating employer added or removed from the plan.
For each of them, enter the first 9 digits of the Business Number (i.e. the number under which the employer deducts employer contributions to the registered pension plan and remits payroll deductions to the Canada Revenue Agency).

Participating employer	Business Number	Added	Removed
______________	_ _ _ _ _ _ _ _ _	☐	☐
______________	_ _ _ _ _ _ _ _ _	☐	☐
______________	_ _ _ _ _ _ _ _ _	☐	☐

List additional **participating employers** added or removed in **Section II of Appendix A**, if necessary.

Section 5 – Funding information

(a) Has the **funding medium** changed? ☐ Yes ☐ No

If yes, please identify how the benefits are to be funded, as a result of the amendment (check all that apply):

☐ insured insurance policy number ______________

☐ trusteed

☐ other (specify) ______________

(b) Has the name or address of the financial institution or trustee for the funding medium changed? ☐ Yes ☐ No

If no, go to Section 6.

If yes, please complete the following. If individual trustees, list the address of the trustee to whom correspondence should be directed.

(i) Name			
Address			
City	Province	Postal code	Telephone
Contact	Telephone Ext.	Language of correspondence ☐ English ☐ French	

Name of second individual trustee (if applicable) ______________

Is this trustee resident in Canada? ☐ Yes ☐ No

Name of third individual trustee (if applicable) ______________

Is this trustee resident in Canada? ☐ Yes ☐ No

Complete Section 5, part (b)(ii) only if the plan is now funded by two separate funding media.

(ii) Name			
Address			
City	Province	Postal code	Telephone
Contact	Telephone Ext.	Language of correspondence ☐ English ☐ French	

Section 6 – Plan details

(a) How many members are currently accruing benefits under the plan (**active members**)? ______________________

Does this amendment:

(b) change the defined **benefit accrual rate** or formula?	☐ Yes	☐ No	☐ No **defined benefit** provision
(c) change the **money purchase contribution rate**?	☐ Yes	☐ No	☐ No money purchase provision
(d) add or remove a **defined benefit** provision?	☐ Adds	☐ Removes	☐ N/A
(e) add or remove a **money purchase** provision?	☐ Adds	☐ Removes	☐ N/A
(f) cause a full or partial plan **conversion**?	☐ Yes	☐ No	
(g) result in a plan **merger**?	☐ Yes	☐ No	
If yes, please provide the registration number of the other affected pension plan:	_ _ _ _ _ _ _		
(h) result in a plan **split**?	☐ Yes	☐ No	
If yes, please provide the registration number of the other affected pension plan:	_ _ _ _ _ _ _		
(i) add or remove the ability to make **additional voluntary contributions** ("AVCs")?	☐ AVCs added	☐ AVCs removed	☐ No change
(j) add or remove **bridging benefits**?	☐ Added	☐ Removed	☐ No change
(k) add or remove **optional ancillary benefits** under a **flexible pension plan**?	☐ Added	☐ Removed	☐ No change or not a flexible pension plan
(l) add or remove the post-retirement indexing of benefits? (for this question, ignore ad hoc indexing)	☐ Added	☐ Removed	☐ No change
(m) change the definition of **pensionable service**? (if the plan contains a **defined benefit** provision)	☐ Yes	☐ No	☐ No defined benefit provision
If yes, please answer (i), (ii) and (iii) below:			
(i) Has past service been added or upgraded?	☐ Yes	☐ No	☐ N/A
(ii) Has pre-1990 service been added or upgraded?	☐ Yes	☐ No	☐ N/A
(iii) Has **foreign service** been added or upgraded?	☐ Yes	☐ No	
(n) change the definition of **earnings** on which the contributions and/or the **defined benefits** are based?	☐ Yes	☐ No	
(o) make the plan a **multi-employer plan**?	☐ Yes	☐ No	
(p) make the plan a **specified multi-employer plan**? If yes to (p), submit the portion(s) of the collective agreement relevant to the pension plan.	☐ Yes	☐ No	
(q) make the plan a **designated plan**?	☐ Yes	☐ No	

Section 7 – Connected persons

(a) Are new **connected persons** participating in the plan? ☐ Yes ☐ No
If no to (a), go to Section 8.

(b) Provide the following details:

Participating employer	Person connected	Social insurance number
____________	____________	_ _ _ _ _ _ _ _ _
____________	____________	_ _ _ _ _ _ _ _ _
____________	____________	_ _ _ _ _ _ _ _ _

If more space is required, please provide the information in **Section I of Appendix A**.

Section 8 – Plans based on an approved specimen

(a) Prior to the amendment, did the plan text and/or **funding medium** conform to an approved specimen? ☐ Yes ☐ No

(b) Further to the amendment, has the plan text and/or funding medium changed so that it now conforms to an approved specimen? ☐ Yes ☐ No
If no, go to Section 9.

Complete the following if the specimen to which the plan text and/or **funding medium** now conforms to has changed:

I certify that, except for the details of the permitted variables submitted with the application, the plan text and the funding medium conform in all respects to the specimen numbered

____________-P ____________-F ____________-SP
(specimen plan text) (specimen funding document) (specimen plan text and funding document)

Name of the company that secured the approval of the specimen(s) ____________

Name of an **authorized representative** of that company ____________
(Please print)

____________ ____________ ____________ ____________
Date Signature Title Telephone

Section 9 – Cessation / termination of plan

(a) Has the plan become **inactive**? ☐ Yes ☐ No
If no, go to Section 10.

If yes, please specify the date the plan became inactive: Y Y Y Y M M D D

(b) Have all of the funds been disbursed from the plan? ☐ Yes ☐ No
If no, go to Section 9, part (c).

(i) Date of final distribution of funds from the plan: Y Y Y Y M M D D

(ii) Manner of final distribution of funds from the plan (check all that apply):

☐ annuity purchases ☐ transfers under section 147.3 of the *Income Tax Act* ☐ cash payment to members ☐ cash payment to employers

(c) Does this amendment provide additional benefits to members on **windup**? ☐ Yes ☐ No

Section 10 – Certification

The plan **administrator** or the delegated administrator (where that task has been delegated) must sign the certification before we can approve the plan amendment.

As an **authorized representative** of the administrator of this pension plan, I, ______________________________,
(Please print)

certify that the information given on this application is, to the best of my knowledge, correct and complete. I also certify that, to the best of my knowledge, the plan complies with and is being administered according to sections 147.1, 147.2, 147.3 and 147.4 of the *Income Tax Act* and related *Regulations*, and where copies of documents are attached, they are **true copies of the originals**.

Date	Signature	Title	Telephone

Section 11 – Documents attached

- ☐ Pension plan text
- ☐ Trust document
- ☐ Insurance contract
- ☐ Amendment
- ☐ Board resolution or bylaw
- ☐ Collective agreement (**SMEP**)
- ☐ Specimen variable sheet
- ☐ Other (please specify) ______________________________
- ☐ Actuarial valuation report
  - ☐ **Proportionality test**
  - ☐ **50/50 demonstration**
  - ☐ **Cost certificate**
- ☐ Evidence of **reasonable remuneration** in respect of pre-reform service for connected persons
- ☐ Employee booklet (**flexible pension plan**), if any

Appendix A

Section I – Additional connected persons

Use this area to list additional members who are **persons connected** with a participating employer if the space provided in Section 7, part (b) is not sufficient:

Participating employer	Person connected	Social insurance number

Attach a separate sheet providing any additional information in the same format if necessary.

Section II – Additional participating employers

Use this area to list additional **participating employers** if the space provided in Section 4, part (b) is not sufficient:

Participating employer	Business Number	Added	Removed
		☐	☐
		☐	☐
		☐	☐
		☐	☐
		☐	☐
		☐	☐
		☐	☐
		☐	☐
		☐	☐
		☐	☐
		☐	☐
		☐	☐

Attach a separate sheet providing any additional information in the same format if necessary.

Appendix 3

REFERENCE DATA

This Appendix sets out the various statistics referred to throughout this book.

1. RRSP/DC/DPSP Contribution Limits (1984 to present)

1984 to 1990						
Year	RRSP Dollar Limit		DC / Money Purchase Dollar Limit		DPSP Dollar Limit[2]	
	RPP participant (reduced by RPP or DPSP contribution)	RPP non-participant	Employer	Employee	Employer	Employee
1984	$3,500	$5,500	$3,500	$3,500	$3,500	$5,500
1985	$3,500	$5,500	$3,500	$3,500	$3,500	$5,500
1986	$3,500	$7,500	$3,500	$3,500	$3,500	$5,500
1987	$3,500	$7,500	$3,500	$3,500	$3,500	$5,500
1988	$3,500	$7,500	$3,500	$3,500	$3,500	$5,500
1989	$3,500	$7,500	$3,500	$3,500	$3,500	$5,500
1990	$3,500	$7,500	New rules – see below		$3,500	$5,500

1991 to Present						
Year	DB Max PA[4]	MP Limit	RRSP Dollar Limit[3]	DPSP Dollar Limit[2]	Maximum DB PA for PAR calc[4]	Max DB Pension
1990	$10,500	$11,500	Old rules – see above	Old rules – see above	$10,500	$1,722.22
1991	$11,500	$12,500	$11,500	$6,250 [2]	$11,500	$1,722.22
1992	$11,500	$12,500	$12,500	$6,250	$11,500	$1,722.22
1993	$12,500	$13,500	$12,500	$6,750	$12,500	$1,722.22
1994	$13,500	$14,500	$13,500	$7,250	$13,500	$1,722.22
1995	$14,500	$15,500	$14,500	$7,750	$13,500	$1,722.22
1996	$14,500	$13,500	$13,500	$6,750	$13,500	$1,722.22
1997	$14,900	$13,500	$13,500	$6,750	$13,500	$1,722.22
1998	$14,900	$13,500	$13,500	$6,750	$13,500	$1,722.22
1999	$14,900	$13,500	$13,500	$6,750	$13,500	$1,722.22
2000	$14,900	$13,500	$13,500	$6,750	$13,500	$1,722.22
2001	$14,900	$13,500	$13,500	$6,750	$13,500	$1,722.22
2002	$14,900	$13,500	$13,500	$6,750	$14,500	$1,722.22
2003	$14,900	$15,500	$14,500	$7,750	$14,900	$1,722.22
2004	$15,900	$16,500	$15,500	$8,250	$15,900	$1,833.33
2005	$17,400	$18,000	$16,500	$9,000	$17,400	$2,000.00
2006	$18,400	$19,000	$18,000	$9,500	$18,400	$2,111.11
2007	$19,400	$20,000	$19,000	$10,000	$19,400	$2,222.22
2008	$20,400	$21,000	$20,000	$10,500	$20,400	$2,333.33
2009	$21,400	$22,000	$21,000	$11,000	$21,400	$2,444.44
2010	$21,850	$22,450	$22,000	$11,225	$21,850	$2,494.44
2011	Indexed[5]	Indexed[5]	$22,450	Indexed[5]	Indexed[5]	Indexed[5]

Notes:

(1) The maximum contribution, as a percentage of earnings, for the years 1984 to 1990 inclusive was 20% of current year's earned income. For years on and after 1991, the maximum contribution is 18% of prior year's earned income.

(2) As a result of DPSP registration rules that came into effect on January 1, 1991, employee contributions were no longer allowed and maximum employer contribution limits were revised. For "1991 to Present", limits shown are employer only.

(3) The RRSP Dollar Limit is prior to reduction by previous year's PA.

(4) For the years 1990 to 1994 inclusive, there were certain earnings exclusions and benefit accrual ceilings in effect for the PA calculations only. See Appendix 1 for additional information about how these exclusions and ceilings were applied. The exclusions and limits were as follows:

Year	Benefit Accrual Ceiling	Earnings Exclusions	Maximum Earnings Excluded
1990	$1,277.78	Earnings from $63,888.89 to $86,111.11	$22,222.22
1991	$1,388.89	Earnings from $69,444.44 to $86,111.11	$16,666.67
1992	$1,388.89	Earnings from $69,444.44 to $86,111.11	$16,666.67
1993	$1,500.00	Earnings from $75,000.00 to $86,111.11	$11,111.11
1994	$1,611.11	Earnings from $80,555.56 to $86,111.11	$5,555.56

(5) Indexation will be annual, in accordance with increases in the average wage.

2. Average Wage Information (1984 to present)

Average Wage for Calendar Year				
	1980, SIC Base		NAICS Base	
Year	Average Wage	Percent Increase over Previous Year	Average Wage	Percent Increase over Previous Year
1984	371.66		388.28	
1985	391.82	5.42%	409.34	5.42%
1986	405.13	3.40%	423.25	3.40%
1987	419.39	3.52%	438.15	3.52%
1988	431.98	3.00%	451.30	3.00%
1989	451.43	4.50%	471.62	4.50%
1990	471.13	4.36%	492.20	4.36%
1991	494.93	5.05%	517.07	5.05%
1992	518.87	4.84%	542.08	4.84%
1993	538.60	3.80%	562.34	3.74%
1994	554.39	2.93%	579.31	3.02%
1995	562.70	1.50%	587.35	1.39%
1996	571.33	1.53%	596.04	1.48%
1997	577.81	1.13%	603.09	1.18%
1998	594.67	2.92%	619.74	2.76%
1999	602.71	1.35%	628.22	1.37%
2000	606.90	0.70%	635.37	1.14%
2001	618.38	1.89%	647.70	1.94%
2002			656.97	1.43%
2003			663.28	0.96%
2004			681.64	2.77%
2005			700.72	2.80%
2006			722.08	3.05%
2007			746.69	3.41%
2008			771.60	3.34%
2009			800.37	3.73%
2010			816.88	2.06%

The NAICS Base has superseded the SIC Base from January 1, 2001. Refer to Notes below for additional discussion regarding the derivation of the average wage numbers.

Notes:

(1) Average wage — For a calendar year, average wage is the sum of wage measures over a period of 12 months ending on June 30 of the immediately preceding calendar year, divided by 12. For example, the 2009 average wage is determined by summing all of the wage measures from July 2007 to June 2008 inclusive, and then dividing the total by 12.

(2) Wage measure — Wage measure is a monthly measure of the average weekly wages and salaries of the industrial aggregate in Canada as published by Statistics Canada. Of all the aggregates that Statistics Canada compiles, the one that corresponds to wage measure is the monthly industrial aggregate in Canada representing the average weekly earnings for all employees, including overtime. Statistics Canada publishes the monthly industrial aggregate in Catalogue 72-002 called *Employment, Earnings and Hours.*

(3) Industry Classifications — The SIC basis (Standard Industry Classification — CANSIM Series v250529; formerly CANSIM Series L57711) was used until December 2000 to determine the average wage. As of January 2001, the NAICS basis (North America Industry Classification Standard — CANSIM Series v1558664; formerly CANSIM Series L172126) has replaced the SIC basis. The NAICS rates were retroactively determined back to 1991 by Statistics Canada (i.e. the 1993 average wage in the chart above is the average of the NAICS average wage numbers for the period July 1, 1991 through June 30, 1992). For years from 1984 through 1992, inclusive, Statistics Canada has advised to artificially determine the rates by using the increases in the SIC basis for the same period.

(4) Data Revisions — From time to time, Statistics Canada makes revisions to the monthly and weekly earnings data, requiring a recalculation of prior years' average wage figures. Most recently, revisions were made in March 2009 covering the period from January 2001 to December 2008. Note, therefore, that PSPAs may have previously been calculated and reported using average wage data that slightly differs from the above.

3. CPP/QPP/YMPE Benefits and Contributions (1966 to present)

Year	Year's Maximum Pensionable Earnings (YMPE)	Year's Basic Exemption	Maximum Contributory Earnings	Maximum Employee's or Employer's Contribution		Maximum Self-Employed Contribution		Maximum Retirement Pension
				Rate	Amount	Rate	Amount	
	$	$	$	%	$	%	$	$
1966	5,000	600	4,400	1.8	79.20	3.6	158.40	
1967	5,000	600	4,400	1.8	79.20	3.6	158.40	104.17
1968	5,100	600	4,500	1.8	81.00	3.6	162.00	104.86
1969	5,200	600	4,600	1.8	82.80	3.6	165.60	106.25
1970	5,300	600	4,700	1.8	84.60	3.6	169.20	108.33
1971	5,400	600	4,800	1.8	86.40	3.6	172.80	110.42
1972	5,500	600	4,900	1.8	88.20	3.6	176.40	112.50
1973 (CPP)	5,600	600	5,000	1.8	90.00	3.6	180.00	114.58
1973 (QPP)	5,900	700	5,200	1.8	93.60	3.6	187.20	116.66
1974 (CPP)	6,600	700	5,900	1.8	106.20	3.6	212.40	122.92
1974 (QPP)	6,600	700	5,900	1.8	106.20	3.6	212.40	125.00
1975 (CPP)	7,400	700	6,700	1.8	120.60	3.6	241.20	136.11
1975 (QPP)	7,400	700	6,700	1.8	120.60	3.6	241.20	138.19
1976	8,300	800	7,500	1.8	135.00	3.6	270.00	154.86
1977	9,300	900	8,400	1.8	151.20	3.6	302.40	173.61
1978	10,400	1,000	9,400	1.8	169.20	3.6	338.40	194.44
1979	11,700	1,100	10,600	1.8	190.80	3.6	381.60	218.06
1980	13,100	1,300	11,800	1.8	212.40	3.6	424.80	244.44
1981	14,700	1,400	13,300	1.8	239.40	3.6	478.80	274.31
1982	16,500	1,600	14,900	1.8	268.20	3.6	536.40	307.65
1983	18,500	1,800	16,700	1.8	300.60	3.6	601.20	345.15
1984	20,800	2,000	18,800	1.8	338.40	3.6	676.80	387.50
1985	23,400	2,300	21,100	1.8	379.80	3.6	759.60	435.42
1986	25,800	2,500	23,300	1.8	419.40	3.6	838.80	486.11
1987	25,900	2,500	23,400	1.9	444.60	3.8	889.20	521.52
1988	26,500	2,600	23,900	2.0	478.00	4.0	956.00	543.06
1989	27,700	2,700	25,000	2.1	525.00	4.2	1,050.00	556.25
1990	28,900	2,800	26,100	2.2	574.20	4.4	1,148.40	577.08
1991	30,500	3,000	27,500	2.3	632.50	4.6	1,265.00	604.86
1992	32,200	3,200	29,000	2.4	696.00	4.8	1,392.00	636.11
1993	33,400	3,300	30,100	2.5	752.50	5.0	1,505.00	667.36
1994	34,400	3,400	31,000	2.6	806.00	5.2	1,612.00	694.44
1995	34,900	3,400	31,500	2.7	850.50	5.4	1,701.00	713.19
1996	35,400	3,500	31,900	2.8	893.20	5.6	1,786.40	727.08
1997	35,800	3,500	32,300	3.0	969.00	6.0	1,938.00	736.81
1998 (CPP)	36,900	3,500	33,400	3.2	1,068.80	6.4	2,137.60	744.79
1998 (QPP before July 1)	36,900	3,500	33,400	3.2	1,068.80	6.4	2,137.60	750.69
1998 (QPP as of July 1)	36,900	3,500	33,400	3.2	1,068.80	6.4	2,137.60	744.79
1999	37,400	3,500	33,900	3.5	1,186.50	7.0	2,373.00	751.67
2000	37,600	3,500	34,100	3.9	1,329.90	7.8	2,659.80	762.92
2001	38,300	3,500	34,800	4.3	1,496.40	8.6	2,992.80	775.00
2002	39,100	3,500	35,600	4.7	1,673.20	9.4	3,346.40	788.75
2003	39,900	3,500	36,400	4.95	1801.80	9.9	3,603.60	801.25
2004	40,500	3,500	37,000	4.95	1831.50	9.9	3,663.00	814.17
2005	41,100	3,500	37,600	4.95	1861.20	9.9	3,722.40	828.75
2006	42,100	3,500	38,600	4.95	1,910.70	9.9	3,821.40	844.58
2007	43,700	3,500	40,200	4.95	1,989.90	9.9	3,979.80	863.75
2008	44,900	3,500	41,400	4.95	2,049.30	9.9	4,098.60	884.58
2009	46,300	3,500	42,800	4.95	2,118.60	9.9	4,237.20	908.75
2010	47,200	3,500	43,700	4.95	2,163.95	9.9	4,326.30	934.17

Notes:

(1) Prior to 1998, the Maximum Retirement Pension was based on a 3-year average of the YMPEs. For 1998, the Maximum Retirement Pension for CPP was based on a 4-year average. For 1998, the Maximum Retirement Pension for QPP was based on a 3-year average for the first half of the year and on a 4-year average for the last half of the year. Subsequent years are based on a 5-year average for both CPP and QPP.

(2) Contribution rates are currently scheduled to remain at the rates shown above until 2016. The actual contributions, however, will increase as the YMPE increases.

CPP Rates
http://www.sdc.gc.ca/en/isp/pub/factsheets/rates.shtml

4. OAS Benefits (1966 to Present)

Old Age Security Pension (OAS)				
Year	January	April	July	October
	$	$	$	$
1966	75.00	75.00	75.00	75.00
1967	75.00	75.00	75.00	75.00
1968	76.50	76.50	76.50	76.50
1969	78.00	78.00	78.00	78.00
1970	79.58	79.58	79.58	79.58
1971	80.00	80.00	80.00	80.00
1972	82.88	82.88	82.88	82.88
1973	82.88	100.00	100.00	105.30
1974	108.14	110.09	112.95	117.02
1975	120.06	123.42	125.76	129.28
1976	132.90	135.43	137.06	139.39
1977	141.34	143.46	147.05	150.43
1978	153.44	156.66	159.79	164.74
1979	167.21	170.39	174.82	179.02
1980	182.42	186.80	191.28	196.83
1981	202.14	208.20	214.86	221.74
1982	227.73	232.97	239.73	246.92
1983	251.12	254.13	256.67	260.52
1984	263.78	266.28	269.74	272.17
1985	273.80	276.54	280.14	282.94
1986	285.20	288.34	291.51	294.43
1987	297.37	300.34	303.64	308.19
1988	310.66	313.15	315.97	320.08
1989	323.28	325.87	330.43	337.04
1990	340.07	343.13	347.93	351.41
1991	354.92	362.37	369.62	373.32
1992	374.07	374.44	376.31	378.19
1993	378.95	381.60	383.51	384.66
1994	385.81	387.74	387.74	387.74
1995	387.74	388.52	392.41	394.96
1996	394.76	395.55	397.92	399.91
1997	400.71	403.51	405.12	406.34
1998	407.15	407.15	408.78	410.82
1999	410.82	411.23	413.70	417.42
2000	419.92	420.34	424.12	428.79
2001	431.36	433.52	436.55	442.66
2002	442.66	442.66	443.99	449.32
2003	453,36	456.08	461.55	461.55
2004	462.47	463.39	466.63	471.76
2005	471.76	473.65	476.97	479.83
2006	484.63	484.63	487.54	491.93
2007	491.93	491.93	497.83	502.31
2008	502.31	502.31	505.83	516.96
2009	516.96	516.96	516.96	516.96
2010	516.96			

CPP and OAS Stats Book

http://www.sdc.gc.ca/en/isp/statistics/statbook.shtml

5. Consumer Price Index (1966 to Present)

Consumer Price Index, Canada, All items, 2002=100									
Year	CPI (v41690973)	Annual Increase	Annual Average (v41693271)	Annual Average Increase	Year	CPI (v41690973)	Annual Increase	Annual Average (v41693271)	Annual Average Increase
	(2002=100)	%	(2002=100)	%		(2002=100)	%	(2002=100)	%
1966	17.7	3.5	17.5	4.2	1988	72.3	3.9	71.2	3.9
1967	18.4	4.0	18.1	3.4	1989	76.1	5.3	74.8	5.1
1968	19.2	4.3	18.8	3.9	1990	79.9	5.0	78.4	4.8
1969	20.1	4.7	19.7	4.8	1991	82.9	3.8	82.8	5.6
1970	20.3	1.0	20.3	3.0	1992	84.7	2.2	84.0	1.4
1971	21.3	4.9	20.9	3.0	1993	86.1	1.7	85.6	1.9
1972	22.4	5.2	21.9	4.8	1994	86.3	0.2	85.7	0.1
1973	24.5	9.4	23.6	7.8	1995	87.8	1.7	87.6	2.2
1974	27.6	12.7	26.2	11.0	1996	89.7	2.2	88.9	1.5
1975	30.2	9.4	29.0	10.7	1997	90.4	0.8	90.4	1.7
1976	31.9	5.6	31.1	7.2	1998	91.3	1.0	91.3	1.0
1977	34.9	9.4	33.6	8.0	1999	93.7	2.6	92.9	1.8
1978	37.9	8.6	36.6	8.9	2000	96.7	3.2	95.4	2.7
1979	41.6	9.8	40.0	9.3	2001	97.4	0.7	97.8	2.5
1980	46.2	11.1	44.0	10.0	2002	101.1	3.8	100.0	2.2
1981	51.8	12.1	49.5	12.5	2003	103.2	2.1	102.8	2.8
1982	56.6	9.3	54.9	10.9	2004	105.4	2.1	104.7	1.8
1983	59.2	4.6	58.1	5.8	2005	107.6	2.1	107.0	2.2
1984	61.4	3.7	60.6	4.3	2006	109.4	1.7	109.1	2.0
1985	64.1	4.4	63.0	4.0	2007	112.0	2.4	111.5	2.2
1986	66.8	4.2	65.6	4.1	2008	113.3	1.2	114.1	2.3
1987	69.6	4.2	68.5	4.4	2009	114.8	1.3	114.4	0.3

Source:

Statistics Canada, CANSIM database. CPI: CANSIM Series v41690973, 2002 = 100, Monthly (December); CANSIM Series v41693271, 2002 = 100, Annual Average.

6. Interest on Employee Contributions (1969 to present)

Chartered Bank - 5 year Personal Fixed Term			
Year	Annual Average (Jan.-Dec.)	Year	Annual Average (Jan.-Dec.)
	%		%
1969	7.52	1989	9.71
1970	7.63	1990	10.33
1971	6.48	1991	8.10
1972	6.88	1992	6.58
1973	7.88	1993	5.29
1974	8.81	1994	6.79
1975	8.27	1995	6.70
1976	9.31	1996	5.33
1977	7.79	1997	4.56
1978	8.79	1998	4.25
1979	10.02	1999	4.68
1980	11.25	2000	5.22
1981	14.90	2001	3.90
1982	12.94	2002	3.78
1983	8.40	2003	2.99
1984	11.02	2004	2.72
1985	9.63	2005	2.46
1986	8.25	2006	2.91
1987	7.17	2007	3.09
1988	7.94	2008	2.81
		2009	1.76

Source:

Statistics Canada, CANSIM database. Chartered bank — 5 year Personal Fixed Term (percent): CANSIM series v122515 (formerly B14045).

7. Interest Rates used for Commuted Values (1993 to Present)

The following are the interest rates used to determine commuted values of pensions in various scenarios. Refer to the Notes at the end of the tables for additional information.

Period	7 Year Gov't of Canada Bench mark Bond	Long Term Gov't of Canada Bench mark Bond	Avg. Long Term Gov't of Canada Real Return Bond	PCV 1-10 (see Notes)	PCV 10+ (see Notes)	PCV real 1-10 (see Notes)	PCV real 10+ (see Notes)	QSV 1-10 (see Notes)	QSV 10+ (see Notes)
	V122542	*v122544*	*v122553*	*2009 Standard*					
Jan-93	7.90	8.51	4.60						
Feb-93	7.35	8.13	4.57						
Mar-93	7.39	8.18	4.53						
Apr-93	7.41	8.15	4.44						
May-93	7.53	8.17	4.39						
Jun-93	7.26	8.01	4.33						
Jul-93	7.00	7.85	4.31						
Aug-93	6.68	7.47	4.24						
Sep-93	6.86	7.57	4.07						
Oct-93	6.48	7.41	4.09						
Nov-93	6.80	7.56	3.96						
Dec-93	6.34	7.28	3.78						
Jan-94	6.04	7.16	3.52						
Feb-94	6.72	7.53	3.79						
Mar-94	7.80	8.33	4.10						
Apr-94	7.81	8.22	4.16						
May-94	8.26	8.58	4.29						
Jun-94	9.04	9.27	4.70						
Jul-94	9.23	9.46	4.70						
Aug-94	8.52	8.87	4.69						
Sep-94	8.68	9.07	4.63						
Oct-94	8.88	9.36	4.67						
Nov-94	8.97	9.26	4.80						
Dec-94	9.08	9.13	4.92						
Jan-95	9.30	9.40	5.03						
Feb-95	8.65	8.87	4.79						
Mar-95	8.44	8.76	4.77						
Apr-95	8.14	8.52	4.59						
May-95	7.67	8.26	4.43						
Jun-95	7.56	8.19	4.42						
Jul-95	8.04	8.66	4.86						
Aug-95	7.78	8.41	4.68						
Sep-95	7.68	8.27	4.73						
Oct-95	7.68	8.28	4.92						
Nov-95	6.93	7.63	4.48						
Dec-95	6.99	7.63	4.42						
Jan-96	6.77	7.64	4.57						
Feb-96	7.30	8.08	4.88						
Mar-96	7.41	8.14	4.90						
Apr-96	7.51	8.26	4.99						
May-96	7.40	8.09	4.80						
Jun-96	7.44	8.17	4.81						
Jul-96	7.28	8.06	4.85						
Aug-96	6.96	7.83	4.74						
Sep-96	6.73	7.75	4.58						
Oct-96	6.02	7.12	4.14						
Nov-96	5.68	6.75	3.97						
Dec-96	6.02	7.09	4.09						
Jan-97	6.27	7.38	4.19						
Feb-97	5.99	7.08	4.13						

Mar-97	6.27	7.24	4.25						
Apr-97	6.37	7.18	4.24						
May-97	6.30	7.15	4.34						
Jun-97	5.76	6.73	4.19						
Jul-97	5.51	6.32	3.95						
Aug-97	5.73	6.63	4.21						
Sep-97	5.38	6.26	4.01						
Oct-97	5.20	6.05	4.02						
Nov-97	5.34	5.96	4.05						
Dec-97	5.48	5.95	4.14						
Jan-98	5.23	5.81	4.11						
Feb-98	5.35	5.78	4.06						
Mar-98	5.20	5.70	4.03						
Apr-98	5.39	5.76	3.95						
May-98	5.27	5.61	3.90						
Jun-98	5.33	5.52	3.85						
Jul-98	5.46	5.61	3.87						
Aug-98	5.69	5.83	4.10						
Sep-98	4.84	5.32	4.02						
Oct-98	4.79	5.45	4.07						
Nov-98	5.11	5.47	4.17						
Dec-98	4.82	5.23	4.11						
Jan-99	4.87	5.23	4.10						
Feb-99	5.28	5.43	4.13						
Mar-99	5.05	5.36	4.16						
Apr-99	5.12	5.41	4.09						
May-99	5.44	5.58	4.08						
Jun-99	5.48	5.63	4.03						
Jul-99	5.63	5.74	4.02						
Aug-99	5.57	5.68	4.03						
Sep-99	5.75	5.91	4.05						
Oct-99	6.28	6.36	4.05						
Nov-99	6.04	6.10	4.04						
Dec-99	6.18	6.23	4.01						
Jan-00	6.45	6.27	4.02	7.00	7.10	4.90	5.00	6.00	6.10
Feb-00	6.32	5.83	3.92	7.20	7.30	4.90	5.00	6.00	6.10
Mar-00	6.16	5.84	3.80	7.50	7.20	5.10	4.90	6.30	6.00
Apr-00	6.20	5.92	3.64	7.30	6.60	5.20	4.70	6.20	5.60
May-00	6.19	5.63	3.81	7.20	6.70	4.90	4.60	6.00	5.60
Jun-00	6.06	5.61	3.77	7.20	6.80	4.70	4.50	6.00	5.60
Jul-00	6.01	5.55	3.65	7.20	6.30	5.10	4.60	6.20	5.40
Aug-00	5.92	5.51	3.67	7.10	6.40	5.00	4.60	6.00	5.40
Sep-00	5.82	5.67	3.60	7.00	6.30	4.90	4.40	5.90	5.40
Oct-00	5.80	5.61	3.52	6.90	6.30	4.90	4.50	5.90	5.40
Nov-00	5.62	5.51	3.51	6.80	6.60	4.60	4.50	5.70	5.50
Dec-00	5.34	5.56	3.42	6.80	6.50	4.60	4.40	5.70	5.40
Jan-01	5.20	5.72	3.36	6.60	6.40	4.50	4.40	5.50	5.40
Feb-01	5.14	5.66	3.39	6.30	6.70	4.20	4.40	5.30	5.50
Mar-01	5.30	5.79	3.45	6.20	7.00	4.00	4.40	5.10	5.70
Apr-01	5.52	5.97	3.61	6.10	6.90	4.00	4.50	5.00	5.70
May-01	5.86	6.03	3.58	6.30	7.00	4.10	4.50	5.20	5.80
Jun-01	5.63	5.89	3.53	6.50	7.20	4.30	4.70	5.40	5.90
Jul-01	5.64	5.94	3.66	6.80	7.10	4.40	4.60	5.60	5.80
Aug-01	5.23	5.67	3.68	6.60	7.00	4.30	4.50	5.40	5.80
Sep-01	5.00	5.86	3.68	6.60	7.10	4.40	4.70	5.50	5.90
Oct-01	4.54	5.31	3.60	6.20	6.90	4.30	4.80	5.30	5.80
Nov-01	5.10	5.59	3.68	6.00	7.30	4.10	4.90	5.00	6.10
Dec-01	5.13	5.69	3.76	5.50	6.70	4.00	4.80	4.70	5.70
Jan-02	5.11	5.68	3.73	6.10	6.80	4.30	4.80	5.20	5.80
Feb-02	5.00	5.69	3.73	6.10	7.00	4.30	4.90	5.20	5.90
Mar-02	5.58	5.98	3.68	6.10	7.00	4.30	4.90	5.20	5.90
Apr-02	5.35	5.92	3.63	6.00	7.00	4.20	4.90	5.10	5.90
May-02	5.21	5.78	3.54	6.60	7.20	4.40	4.70	5.40	5.90
Jun-02	5.00	5.74	3.42	6.30	7.20	4.20	4.70	5.30	6.00
Jul-02	4.75	5.73	3.45	6.20	7.10	4.10	4.60	5.10	5.80
Aug-02	4.84	5.58	3.40	6.00	7.10	3.90	4.60	4.90	5.80

Sep-02	4.59	5.43	3.25	5.70	7.20	3.80	4.70	4.70	5.90
Oct-02	4.76	5.63	3.45	5.80	6.90	3.90	4.60	4.80	5.70
Nov-02	4.79	5.58	3.43	5.50	6.80	3.70	4.40	4.60	5.60
Dec-02	4.47	5.42	3.33	5.70	7.10	3.80	4.70	4.80	5.80
Jan-03	4.62	5.49	3.22	5.70	7.00	3.90	4.60	4.80	5.80
Feb-03	4.54	5.46	3.06	5.40	6.90	3.70	4.60	4.50	5.70
Mar-03	4.79	5.58	3.08	5.60	6.90	3.60	4.40	4.60	5.60
Apr-03	4.53	5.41	3.13	5.50	6.90	3.50	4.20	4.50	5.60
May-03	4.09	5.12	3.00	5.70	7.00	3.60	4.20	4.60	5.60
Jun-03	3.92	5.03	2.99	5.50	6.80	3.50	4.30	4.50	5.60
Jul-03	4.23	5.40	3.15	5.00	6.60	3.30	4.20	4.20	5.40
Aug-03	4.41	5.44	3.15	4.90	6.60	3.20	4.20	4.00	5.40
Sep-03	4.27	5.23	3.08	5.20	7.00	3.40	4.40	4.30	5.70
Oct-03	4.48	5.38	3.00	5.40	6.90	3.50	4.40	4.40	5.60
Nov-03	4.45	5.29	2.91	5.20	6.70	3.40	4.30	4.30	5.50
Dec-03	4.30	5.20	2.79	5.40	6.80	3.40	4.20	4.40	5.50
Jan-04	4.17	5.23	2.57	5.40	6.70	3.40	4.10	4.40	5.40
Feb-04	3.94	5.09	2.56	5.20	6.60	3.20	4.00	4.20	5.30
Mar-04	3.83	5.04	2.39	5.10	6.70	3.00	3.80	4.00	5.20
Apr-04	4.26	5.31	2.46	4.90	6.60	2.90	3.80	3.90	5.20
May-04	4.38	5.32	2.32	4.80	6.60	2.70	3.60	3.70	5.10
Jun-04	4.46	5.33	2.37	5.20	6.80	2.90	3.60	4.00	5.20
Jul-04	4.45	5.29	2.31	5.30	6.80	2.80	3.40	4.10	5.10
Aug-04	4.40	5.15	2.22	5.40	6.70	2.90	3.50	4.10	5.10
Sep-04	4.30	5.04	2.32	5.40	6.70	2.90	3.40	4.10	5.00
Oct-04	4.23	5.00	2.28	5.30	6.50	2.80	3.30	4.10	4.90
Nov-04	4.14	4.90	2.17	5.20	6.40	2.90	3.40	4.10	4.90
Dec-04	4.08	4.92	2.11	5.20	6.40	2.80	3.40	4.00	4.80
Jan-05	3.87	4.74	2.03	5.10	6.20	2.70	3.30	3.90	4.70
Feb-05	3.96	4.76	2.07	5.00	6.30	2.70	3.20	3.80	4.70
Mar-05	4.12	4.77	2.08	4.80	6.10	2.60	3.10	3.70	4.60
Apr-05	3.84	4.59	1.92	4.90	6.10	2.60	3.20	3.80	4.60
May-05	3.74	4.46	1.86	5.10	6.10	2.70	3.10	3.90	4.60
Jun-05	3.49	4.29	1.87	4.80	5.90	2.50	3.00	3.60	4.40
Jul-05	3.63	4.31	1.93	4.70	5.80	2.50	2.90	3.60	4.30
Aug-05	3.57	4.12	1.73	4.40	5.60	2.40	3.00	3.40	4.30
Sep-05	3.74	4.21	1.64	4.60	5.60	2.50	3.00	3.50	4.30
Oct-05	3.99	4.37	1.70	4.50	5.30	2.40	2.80	3.40	4.00
Nov-05	3.94	4.18	1.65	4.70	5.40	2.40	2.60	3.50	4.00
Dec-05	3.87	4.02	1.44	4.90	5.50	2.50	2.70	3.70	4.10
Jan-06	4.03	4.20	1.54	4.90	5.20	2.50	2.60	3.70	3.90
Feb-06	4.05	4.15	1.44	4.80	5.00	2.30	2.40	3.50	3.70
Mar-06	4.19	4.23	1.59	5.00	5.20	2.40	2.50	3.70	3.80
Apr-06	4.45	4.57	1.79	5.00	5.10	2.30	2.40	3.60	3.70
May-06	4.39	4.50	1.83	5.10	5.20	2.50	2.50	3.80	3.80
Jun-06	4.58	4.67	1.90	5.40	5.60	2.70	2.70	4.00	4.10
Jul-06	4.31	4.45	1.80	5.30	5.50	2.70	2.80	4.00	4.10
Aug-06	4.06	4.20	1.61	5.50	5.70	2.80	2.80	4.10	4.20
Sep-06	3.92	4.07	1.66	5.30	5.50	2.70	2.70	3.90	4.10
Oct-06	4.11	4.24	1.78	5.00	5.20	2.50	2.50	3.70	3.90
Nov-06	3.87	4.02	1.63	4.90	5.10	2.50	2.60	3.70	3.80
Dec-06	3.98	4.10	1.73	5.10	5.30	2.60	2.70	3.80	4.00
Jan-07	4.12	4.22	1.79	4.80	5.00	2.50	2.60	3.60	3.80
Feb-07	3.98	4.09	1.75	4.90	5.10	2.60	2.70	3.70	3.90
Mar-07	4.03	4.21	1.77	5.10	5.20	2.70	2.70	3.80	4.00
Apr-07	4.12	4.20	1.76	4.90	5.10	2.60	2.70	3.80	3.90
May-07	4.50	4.39	2.02	5.00	5.20	2.60	2.70	3.80	4.00
Jun-07	4.63	4.56	2.15	5.10	5.20	2.60	2.70	3.80	3.90
Jul-07	4.59	4.49	2.09	5.50	5.30	3.00	2.90	4.20	4.10
Aug-07	4.33	4.44	2.15	5.60	5.50	3.10	3.00	4.30	4.20
Sep-07	4.34	4.50	2.15	5.50	5.40	3.00	3.00	4.30	4.20
Oct-07	4.24	4.38	2.05	5.30	5.40	3.00	3.10	4.10	4.30
Nov-07	3.97	4.23	2.14	5.30	5.50	3.00	3.10	4.10	4.30
Dec-07	4.02	4.18	1.99	5.20	5.40	2.90	3.00	4.00	4.20
Jan-08	3.66	4.19	1.98	4.90	5.30	2.90	3.10	3.90	4.20
Feb-08	3.55	4.18	1.94	5.00	5.20	2.80	2.90	3.90	4.10

Mar-08	3.13	3.96	1.67	4.60	5.40	2.60	3.00	3.60	4.20
Apr-08	3.22	4.08	1.72	4.50	5.40	2.60	3.00	3.50	4.20
May-08	3.49	4.12	1.57	4.10	5.30	2.20	2.80	3.10	4.00
Jun-08	3.55	4.05	1.45	4.10	5.50	2.30	2.80	3.20	4.10
Jul-08	3.57	4.16	1.60	4.40	5.40	2.20	2.60	3.30	4.00
Aug-08	3.25	4.01	1.53	4.50	5.20	2.20	2.40	3.30	3.80
Sep-08	3.41	4.13	2.06	4.50	5.40	2.30	2.60	3.40	4.00
Oct-08	3.27	4.27	2.49	4.20	5.30	2.10	2.60	3.10	3.90
Nov-08	2.87	3.94	2.68	4.30	5.40	2.60	3.20	3.50	4.30
Dec-08	2.13	3.45	2.10	4.20	5.70	2.80	3.70	3.50	4.70
Jan-09	2.42	3.72	2.26	3.80	5.40	2.90	4.00	3.30	4.70
Feb-09	2.31	3.69	2.19	3.00	5.00	2.20	3.40	2.60	4.20
Mar-09	2.16	3.74	2.00	3.30	5.30	2.40	3.60	2.90	4.40
Apr-09	2.26	3.82	2.01	3.20	5.30	2.30	3.50	2.70	4.40
May-09	2.84	4.19	2.34	3.10	5.50	2.10	3.30	2.60	4.40
Jun-09	2.82	3.91	1.91	3.20	5.50	2.10	3.30	2.60	4.40
Jul-09	2.91	4.05	1.89	3.80	5.80	2.50	3.60	3.10	4.70
Aug-09				3.70	5.40	2.30	3.10	3.00	4.20
Sep-09				3.80	5.60	2.30	3.10	3.00	4.30
Oct-09				3.70	5.40	2.20	3.00	2.90	4.20
Nov-09				3.70	5.30	2.20	2.90	3.00	4.10
Dec-09				3.90	5.40	2.10	2.70	3.00	4.10
Jan-10				3.70	5.40	2.00	2.70	2.80	4.00
Feb-10				4.00	5.50	2.10	2.60	3.00	4.00
Mar-10				3.70	5.50	2.00	2.70	2.90	4.10
Apr-10				3.80	5.60	2.00	2.70	2.90	4.10

Notes:

CANSIM figures quoted are as of the last Wednesday of each month, unless indicated otherwise. Please note that as of September 2001 the CANSIM numbering system was revised. The old CANSIM databank numbers were replaced by CANSIM II series numbers (e.g., B14070 is now called v122542).

Pension Commuted Value and Québec Supplemental Value (2009 Standard)

PCV (Pension Commuted Value) is the discount rate for the computation of commuted values as recommended by the Canadian Institute of Actuaries, effective April 1, 2009. For non-indexed pensions, the select $PCV_{1\text{-}10}$ rate is to be applied to the first 10 years; thereafter, the PCV_{10+} rate is used. For fully indexed pensions, the select $PCVreal_{1\text{-}10}$ (Pension Commuted Value "real") is to be applied to the first 10 years; thereafter, the $PCVreal_{10+}$ is used. For deferred pensions partially indexed under Quebec Bill 102, the $QSV_{1\text{-}10}$ (Quebec Supplemental Value — Select Rate) is to be applied to the first 10 years; thereafter, QSV_{10+} is used during the deferred period up to 10 years prior to normal retirement age.

APPLICATION Used for determining commuted values with a calculation date on or after April 1, 2009. All commuted values with a calculation date prior to April 1, 2009 and on or after February 1, 2005, except those in Quebec, should be determined using the 2005 Standard. Quebec commuted values with a calculation date on or after April 14, 2005 should be determined based on the 2005 Standards, unless the plan document requires otherwise. Commuted values with a calculation date prior to February 1, 2005, except those in Quebec, should be determined based on the 1993 Standard. Quebec commuted values with a calculation date prior to April 14, 2005 should be determined based on the 1993 Standard, unless the plan document requires otherwise.

CANSIM RATES USED

v122542 — Government of Canada Benchmark Bond Yields: 7 Year (formerly B14070).

v122544 — Government of Canada Benchmark Bond Yields: Long Term (formerly B14072).

v122553 — Government of Canada Benchmark Bond Yields: Real Return Bonds, Long Term (formerly B14081).

FOR NON-INDEXED PENSIONS

$PCV_{1\text{-}10}$ Select interest discount rate for the first 10 years following the computation date. This rate is CANSIM Series v122542 for the second month (first month effective from February 2011) preceding the month in which the computation falls, adjusted by i) converting the nominal rate, which is based on semi-annual compounding, to the equivalent effective annual rate (this interim rate is referred to as "i_7"); and ii) adding 0.9%. This un-rounded rate of interest (referred to as "$i_{1\text{-}10}$") is rounded to the nearest multiple of 0.10%.

PCV_{10+} Ultimate interest discount rate after 10 years following the computation date. This rate is CANSIM Series Number v122544 for the second month (first month effective from February 2011) preceding the month in which the computation falls, adjusted by i) converting the nominal rate, which is based on semi-annual compounding, to the equivalent effective annual rate (this interim rate is referred to as "i_L") and ii) adding 50% of the difference between i_L and i_7; and iii) adding 0.9%. This un-rounded rate of interest (referred to as "i10+") is rounded to the nearest multiple of 0.10%.

FOR FULLY INDEXED PENSIONS

$PCVreal_{1\text{-}10}$ Select interest discount rate for the first 10 years following the computation date. This rate is calculated by i) multiplying rL by the ratio i7 / iL; and ii) adding 0.9%. This un-rounded rate of interest (referred to as "r1-10") is rounded to the nearest multiple of 0.10%.

$PCVreal_{10+}$ Ultimate interest discount rate after 10 years following the computation date. This rate is CANSIM Series Number v122553 for the second month (first month effective from February 2011) preceding the month in which the computation falls, adjusted by i) converting the nominal rate, which is based on semi-annual compounding, to the equivalent effective annual rate (this interim rate is referred to as "r_L"); and ii) adding 50% of the difference between r_L and r_7; and iii) adding 0.9%. This un-rounded rate of interest (referred to as "r_{10+}") is rounded to the nearest multiple of 0.10%.

FOR DEFERRED PENSIONS PARTIALLY INDEXED UNDER SECTION 60.1 OF THE QUEBEC SUPPLEMENTAL PENSION PLANS ACT

$QSV_{1\text{-}10}$ Select interest discount rate for the first 10 years following the computation date. This rate is based on the implicit inflation rate and is calculated as follows: i) calculate the implicit inflation rate between $i_{1\text{-}10}$ and $r_{1\text{-}10}$ and ii) calculate the indexing rate by multiplying the implicit inflation rate by 50% and limit the result to not less than 0% and not more than 2% (un-rounded) and iii) calculate the resulting rate for a partially indexed pension based on $i_{1\text{-}10}$ and this indexing rate. This un-rounded rate is then rounded to the nearest multiple of 0.10%.

QSV_{10+} Ultimate interest discount rate after 10 years following the computation date. This rate is based on the implicit inflation rate and is calculated as follows: i) calculate the implicit inflation rate between i10+ and r10+ and ii) calculate the indexing rate by multiplying the implicit inflation rate by 50% and limit the result to not less than 0% and not more than 2% (un-rounded) and iii) calculate the resulting rate for a partially indexed pension based on i_{10+} and this indexing rate. This un-rounded rate is then rounded to the nearest multiple of 0.10%.

Information regarding Prior Standards

2005 CIA Standard Used for determining commuted values with a calculation date prior to April 1, 2009 and on or after February 1, 2005 (on or after April 14, 2005 for Quebec members).

1993 CIA Standard Used for determining commuted values with a calculation date on or after September 1, 1993 but prior to February 2, 2005 (prior to April 14, 2005 for Quebec members, unless plan document requires otherwise).

1988 CIA Standard The first set of recommendations was formally introduced effective November 14, 1988 after a two year initial trial period

The interest rates associated with these bases have not been included in the above chart due to space considerations.

8. Summary of Portability Options In Each Jurisdiction

Jurisdiction[1]	Locked-in RRSP/LIRA	LIF	LRIF
Common in All Jurisdictions	▪ One or the other vehicle is available in all jurisdictions ▪ Funds must be withdrawn by the end of the year in which the owner turns 71 and used to purchase a life annuity, or transferred to a LIF or LRIF, if permitted in the jurisdiction. ▪ Spousal waiver forms are usually required upon any transfer. ▪ Survivor benefits or, if no survivor, a lump sum payment will be paid to the beneficiary or the estate of the owner. ▪ Funds may not be assigned, charged, alienated or anticipated, and are exempt from execution, seizure or attachment. ▪ Upon breakdown of the marital or common-law relationship, funds must be divided in accordance with legislative requirements. ▪ Commutation of small amounts permitted. ▪ Early withdrawal payable in lump sum or a series of payments where a physician certifies owner has an illness or disability that is likely to considerably shorten owner's life expectancy.	▪ Funds must be withdrawn by the end of the year in which the owner turns 80 and used to purchase a life annuity (with exceptions noted below), or transferred to an LRIF where permitted. ▪ Spousal waiver forms are usually required upon any transfer. ▪ Survivor benefits or, if no survivor, a lump sum payment will be paid to the beneficiary or the estate of the owner. ▪ Funds may not be assigned, charged, alienated or anticipated, and are exempt from execution, seizure or attachment. ▪ Upon breakdown of the marital or common-law relationship, funds must be divided in accordance with legislative requirements. ▪ Commutation of small amounts permitted. ▪ Early withdrawal payable in lump sum or a series of payments where a physician certifies owner has an illness or disability that is likely to considerably shorten owner's life expectancy. ▪ Subject to minimum and maximum annual withdrawal amounts.	▪ Funds can remain in the plan for the owner's lifetime (no requirement to annuitize the funds at age 80). ▪ Spousal waiver forms are usually required upon any transfer. ▪ Survivor benefits or, if no survivor, a lump sum payment will be paid to the beneficiary or the estate of the owner. ▪ Funds may not be assigned, charged, alienated or anticipated, and are exempt from execution, seizure or attachment. ▪ Upon breakdown of the marital or common-law relationship, funds must be divided in accordance with legislative requirements. ▪ Commutation of small amounts permitted. ▪ Early withdrawal payable in lump sum or a series of payments where a physician certifies owner has an illness or disability that is likely to considerably shorten owner's life expectancy. ▪ Subject to minimum and maximum annual withdrawal amounts.

[1] Prince Edward Island is not included in the above chart as its *Pension Benefits Act* has not yet been proclaimed into force.

Jurisdiction[1]	Locked-in RRSP/LIRA	LIF	LRIF
Federal	▪ Locked-in RRSP is available vehicle. ▪ Withdrawal of locked-in funds permitted for non-residents who have been outside Canada for more than two calendar years ▪ Withdrawal of locked-in funds may be permitted in conditions of "financial hardship". ▪ Unlocking of locked-in funds permitted at age 55 if total value in all locked-in funds does not exceed 50% of the YMPE.	▪ LIF owners not required to purchase a life annuity at age 80. ▪ Withdrawal of locked-in funds permitted for non-residents who have been outside Canada for more than two calendar years. ▪ Withdrawal of locked-in funds may be permitted in conditions of "financial hardship". ▪ At age 55 or later, individuals are permitted a one-time transfer of up to 50% of balances in LIF and LRIF into a RRIF. ▪ Unlocking of locked-in funds permitted at age 55 if total value in all locked-in funds does not exceed 50% of the YMPE.	▪ Not available
Alberta	▪ LIRA is available vehicle. ▪ Withdrawal of locked-in funds may be permitted in conditions of "financial hardship". ▪ Withdrawal of locked-in funds permitted for non-residents of Canada. ▪ Unlocking of locked-in funds if total value in the LIRA is less than 20% of the YMPE. Funds over 20% of the YMPE cannot be subdivided to create funds containing less than 20% of the YMPE. ▪ Unlocking of locked-in funds if over age 65 and the total value in the LIRA is less than 40% of the YMPE. Funds over 40% of the YMPE cannot be subdivided to create funds containing less than 40% of the YMPE. ▪ Unlocking of up to 50% of account value permitted, if owner is at least 50 years of age and is transferring the balance to a LIF or using it to purchase an annuity.	▪ Purchase permitted after age 50. ▪ LIF owners not required to purchase a life annuity at age 80. ▪ Withdrawal of locked-in funds may be permitted in conditions of "financial hardship". ▪ Withdrawal of locked-in funds permitted for non-residents of Canada. ▪ Unlocking of locked-in funds if total value in the LIF is less than 20% of the YMPE. Funds over 20% of the YMPE cannot be subdivided to create funds containing less than 20% of the YMPE. ▪ Unlocking of locked-in funds if over age 65 and the total value in the LIF is less than 40% of the YMPE. Funds over 40% of the YMPE cannot be subdivided to create funds containing less than 40% of the YMPE. ▪ At age 50 or later, one-time unlocking of up to 50% of the balance in a LIRA when transferred into a LIF or used to purchase an annuity. ▪ Superintendent's List provides names of the financial institutions eligible to accept funds.	▪ No longer permitted after August 10, 2006; Replaced by LIF with new features.

Jurisdiction[1]	Locked-in RRSP/LIRA	LIF	LRIF
British Columbia	▪ Locked-in RRSP is available vehicle. ▪ Unlocking of locked-in funds if total value in the locked-in RRSP is less than 20% of the YMPE. Funds containing less than 20% of the YMPE cannot be subdivided. ▪ Unlocking of locked-in funds if over age 65 and total value of all B.C. regulated locked-in RRSPs, LIFs and DC pension plans is less than 40% of the YMPE. ▪ Withdrawal of locked-in funds permitted for non-residents of Canada.	▪ LIF owners are not required to purchase a life annuity at age 80. ▪ Unlocking of locked-in funds if total value in the LIF is less than 20% of the YMPE. Funds containing less than 20% of the YMPE cannot be subdivided. ▪ Unlocking of locked-in funds if over age 65 and total value of all B.C. regulated locked-in RRSPs, LIFs and DC pension plans is less than 40% of the YMPE. ▪ Withdrawal of locked-in funds permitted for non-residents of Canada. ▪ Superintendent's List provides names of financial institutions eligible to accept funds.	▪ Not available.
Manitoba	▪ LIRA is available vehicle. ▪ Withdrawal of locked-in funds permitted for non-residents of Canada. ▪ Unlocking of funds permitted if total value of all LIFs, LIRAs and LRIFs (plus future interest calculated at 6% PA up to the account holder's age 65) is less than 40% of the YMPE.	▪ Current policy permits transfer to LIF irrespective of age. ▪ Withdrawal of locked-in funds permitted for non-residents of Canada. ▪ Unlocking of funds permitted if total value of all LIFs, LIRAs and LRIFs (plus future interest calculated at 6% PA up to the account holder's age 65) is less than 40% of the YMPE. ▪ Individuals are permitted a one-time transfer of up to 50% of balances in LIF and LRIF into a RRIF. ▪ Superintendent's List provides names of financial institutions eligible to accept funds.	▪ Current policy permits transfers to LRIF irrespective of age. ▪ Withdrawal of locked-in funds permitted for non-residents of Canada. ▪ Unlocking of funds permitted if total value of all LIFs, LIRAs and LRIFs (plus future interest calculated at 6% PA up to the account holder's age 65) is less than 40% of the YMPE. ▪ Individuals are permitted a one-time transfer of up to 50% of balances in LIF and LRIF into a RRIF. ▪ Superintendent's List provides names of financial institutions eligible to accept funds.

Jurisdiction[1]	Locked-in RRSP/LIRA	LIF	LRIF
New Brunswick	▪ LIRA is available vehicle. ▪ Withdrawal of locked-in funds if not Canadian citizen and not a resident for tax purposes ▪ Withdrawal are permitted if the adjusted commuted value (ACV) of the LIRA is less than 40% of the YMPE. The ACV is determined as follows: ACV = V x 1.06^ (65-n) Where V = commuted value of benefit N = age of member on December 31 of year when employment terminated or plan would up (cannot be greater than 65) ▪ Withdrawals to reduce penalty tax permitted, but withdrawn funds must be placed in a non-registered sub-account.	▪ LIF owners not required to purchase a life annuity at age 80. ▪ Individuals who begin their LIF in the middle of a calendar year may withdraw the maximum amount for an entire year. ▪ An owner of an LIF is permitted to make a one-time withdrawal of the lesser of 25% of the value of the fund at the beginning of the year or three times the annual LIF withdrawal. ▪ Withdrawal of locked-in funds if not Canadian citizen and not a resident for tax purposes ▪ Withdrawals to reduce penalty tax permitted, but withdrawn funds must be placed in non-registered sub-account. ▪ Province provides list of financial institutions eligible to accept funds.	▪ Not available.
Newfoundland and Labrador	▪ LIRA is available vehicle ▪ Province provides list of financial institutions eligible to accept funds.	▪ Province provides list of financial institutions eligible to accept funds.	▪ Province provides list of financial institutions eligible to accept funds.
Nova Scotia	▪ LIRA is available vehicle. ▪ Unlocking of locked-in funds if over age 65 and total value of all Nova Scotia regulated LIRAs, LIFs and DC pension plans is less than 40% of the YMPE. ▪ Withdrawal of locked-in funds may be permitted in conditions of "financial hardship".	▪ LIF owners not required to purchase a life annuity at age 80. ▪ Unlocking of locked-in funds if over age 65 and total value of all Nova Scotia regulated LIRAs, LIFs and DC pension plans is less than 40% of the YMPE. ▪ Withdrawal of locked-in funds may be permitted in conditions of "financial hardship". ▪ Superintendent's List provides names of financial institutions eligible to accept funds.	▪ Not available.

Jurisdiction[1]	Locked-in RRSP/LIRA	LIF	LRIF
Ontario	▪ LIRA is available vehicle. ▪ Withdrawal of locked-in funds may be permitted in conditions of "financial hardship". ▪ Withdrawal of locked-in funds permitted for non-residents who have been outside Canada for more than two years ▪ Withdrawal of locked-in funds permitted at age 55 if total value of all locked-in funds does not exceed 40% of the YMPE.	▪ Effective January 1, 2008, a new LIF was introduced to replace existing LIFs ▪ No new funds may transfer into old LIFs after December 31, 2008. ▪ New LIF owners not required to purchase a life annuity at age 80. ▪ New LIF permits unlocking or cash payment of up to 50% of the assets transferred into the new LIF from an old LIF, LRIF, LIRA or an RPP within 60 days of establishing the new LIF. ▪ Withdrawal of locked-in funds may be permitted in conditions of "financial hardship". ▪ Withdrawal of locked-in funds permitted for non-residents who have been outside Canada for more than two years ▪ Withdrawal of locked-in funds permitted at age 55 if total value of all locked-in funds does not exceed 40% of the YMPE.	▪ No longer permitted after December 31, 2008. ▪ Replaced by new LIF with new features which was introduced effective January 1, 2008. ▪ Existing LRIFs permitted to continue without change (except for certain windows to permit unlocking of up to 50% of assets).
Quebec	▪ LIRA is available vehicle. ▪ Withdrawal of locked-in funds if not residing in Canada for at least two years. ▪ Unlocking of locked-in funds if over age 65 and total value of all LIRAs, LIFs and DC pension plans is less than 40% of the YMPE. ▪ Province provides list of financial institutions eligible to accept funds.	▪ LIF owners not required to purchase a life annuity at the age of 80. ▪ Withdrawal of locked-in funds if not residing in Canada for at least two years. ▪ Unlocking of locked-in funds if over age 65 and total value of all LIRAs, LIFs and DC pension plans is less than 40% of the YMPE. ▪ Annuitants under age 54 can elect to receive a special bridge benefit until no later that age 54; annuitants within 10 years of normal retirement can elect to receive special bridge benefits for a lifetime pension. ▪ Province provides list of financial institutions eligible to accept funds.	▪ Not available.

[1] Prince Edward Island is not included in the above chart as its *Pension Benefits Act* has not yet been proclaimed into force.

Jurisdiction[1]	Locked-in RRSP/LIRA	LIF	LRIF
Saskatchewan	▪ LIRA is available vehicle.	▪ LIF is no longer available; instead funds can be transferred into a Prescribed RRIF in which there are minimum withdrawals but no maximum withdrawal requirements; assets can be transferred from an existing LIF into a Prescribed RRIF.	▪ LRIF is no longer available; instead a Prescribed RRIF is offered in which there are minimum withdrawals but no maximum withdrawal requirements, assets can be transferred from an existing LRIF to a Prescribed RRIF.

Appendix 4

CROSS-REFERENCE TO INCOME TAX ACT (CANADA) AND REGULATIONS

CROSS-REFERENCE TO INCOME TAX ACT (CANADA) AND REGULATIONS

Cross-references between various chapters of this book and the legislation are provided below. The chapters that are cross-referenced are those containing detailed tax rules — Chapters 4 to 10, and 14 to 22.

aragraph in Book		Section in Income Tax Act	Section in Regulations/ Other Reference
¶ 400 DETAILED RRSP CONTRIBUTION RULES			
¶ 405	Definition of Earnings for RRSP Purposes	146(1)	
¶ 410	New RRSP Contribution Room for the Year	146(1)(g.1), (g.2), 146(2)(*b*.4)	
¶ 415	RRSP Contribution Limit and Carry-Forward	146(1)(g.1), (*l*)	8301, 8303, 8308(2)
¶ 420	RRP Tax Deduction and Carry-Forward	146(1), 146(5)	
¶ 425	Spousal RRSP Contributions	146(1)(*k*), (*l*), 146(2)(*b*,4) 146(5.1), 146(8.2)	
¶ 430	Special Attribution Rule	146(8.3), 204.1, 204.2	
¶ 435	Excess RRSP Contributions	146(8.2), 204.1, 204.2	
¶ 440	Deregistered RRSP Assets		8307(3)
¶ 445	Transfer of Retiring Allowance to RRSP or RPP	60(*j*.1)	
¶ 470	RRSP Contribution Following Death	146(5.1)	
¶ 500 INTRODUCTION TO PENSION ADJUSTMENTS AND GENERAL PA RULES			
¶ 505	Introduction		830(1) to (4), (6), (8)
¶ 510	Use of a Pension Adjustment	147.1(8)	8503(4)(*a*)
¶ 515	PA Reporting		8301(1), (12), (13), 8305(1) 8401(2), (4), 8409
¶ 520	Pension Credit		8301(1)
¶ 525	Rounding		8310
¶ 530	Circumstances Where No Pension Credit Arises		8301(3), (8), 8302(3)(*n*), 8401(5)
¶ 535	PA Upon Re-Employment After Downsizing		8505(3)(*d*), (5)
¶ 540	First Year PA for Connected Person		8308(2)

Paragraph in Book		*Section in Income Tax Act*	*Section in Regulations/ Other Reference*
¶ 545	PA for a Specified Retirement Arrangement (SRA)		8308.3(2), (3)
¶ 550	Prescribed Amounts for a Government Sponsored Retirement Arrangement (GSRA)		8308.4
¶ 555	Prescribed Amounts and PAs for Foreign Registered Pension Plans		8308.1 8308.2
¶ 560	Correcting an Earlier PA		8308(4), (5), 8401(6)
¶ 600 PENSION ADJUSTMENTS FOR DEFINED CONTRIBUTION RPP AND DPSP			
¶ 610	General PA Rules for Defined Contribution RPPs		8301(4), (11)
¶ 620	Reallocations of Non-Vested Forfeitures		8301(4)*(b)*
¶ 630	Timing of Contributions	147(5.1), 147.1(8)	8301(11)
¶ 635	Contributions to Defined Contribution RPP Following Leave of Absence		8308(5), (6)
¶ 640	Employees Borrowed from Another Employer		8308(7)
¶ 645 to ¶ 647	Employees Working Abroad and Foreign Pension Plans Services Primarily in Canada or Primarily With a Business in Canada Services Outside Canada, Not Related to a Business in Canada	207.6(5)	6804 8308.1 8308.2
¶ 650	Back Pay or Bonus Included in Pensionable Earnings		8308(3)
¶ 655	General PA Rules for DPSPs	147(5.1), 147(5.11)*(b)*	8301(2), 8301(3)

Paragraph in Book		*Section in Income Tax Act*	*Section in Regulations/ Other Reference*
¶ 700 PENSION ADJUSTMENTS FOR DEFINED BENEFIT PLANS			
¶ 710	Basic PA Rules		8301(6), 8302(3)
¶ 720	Special PA Transition Rules for Higher Income Employees Prior to 2005		8302(2)(*b*) 8302(3)(*g*)
¶ 725 to ¶ 730	PA Examples for a Full Year of Credited Service; PA Rules and Examples for a Partial Year of Credited Service		8302(3)(*a*), (*g*)
¶ 735	Situations Requiring the Calculation of Normalized Pensions		8302(2)
¶ 740 to ¶ 742	Government Benefits Offsets; CPP/QPP Offset Not Prorated		8302(3)(*j*)
¶ 744	Offset Based on Old Age Security Benefits		8302(3)(*k*)
¶ 745	Adjustments Due to Special Normal Forms and Optional Forms of Pension		8302(3)(*o*) 8302(4)
¶ 750	Normal Retirement Age Less Than 65		8302(3)(*a*), (*b*), (*o*)
¶ 755	Adjustments for Members Still Employed Beyond Normal Retirement Age		8302(3)(*b*), (*n*), (o)
¶ 760	Minimum Benefits		8302(8)
¶ 770	Back Pay and Bonuses		8302(3)(*f*), 8308(3)
¶ 775 to ¶ 777	Pensionable Leaves of Absence and Disability; Service Automatically Credited During the Leave		8507(2)

Paragraph in Book		*Section in Income Tax Act*	*Section in Regulations/ Other Reference*
¶ 778 to ¶ 779	Service Credited After the Leave, Contingent on Returning to Work; Service Granted Retroactively (Not Automatically) After Returning to Work		8308(4)
¶ 780	Employees Borrowed from Another Employer		8308(7)
¶ 785	Employees Working Abroad and Foreign Pension Plans	207.6(5)	6802
¶ 790 to ¶ 793	Crediting Extra Service; Waiting Period with Automatic Crediting of Past Service; Reciprocal Transfer Agreement; Future Years of Service Credited at Retirement		8308(11)
¶ 795	Sale of a Company or Division		8308(8)
¶ 800 PENSION ADJUSTMENTS FOR COMBINATION PLANS AND HYBRIDS			
¶ 810	Two-Tiered Plans	147.1(8)	8506(2)(*d*)
¶ 815	Greater of Defined Benefit and Defined Contribution Formulae		8301(10) 8302(2)(*c*)
¶ 900 PENSION ADJUSTMENTS FOR PLANS WITH SEVERAL PARTICIPATING EMPLOYERS			
¶ 910	Specified Multi-Employer Plans		8301(5), 8510(2)
¶ 915	Multi-Employer Plans Other Than SMEPs		8301(7), (9)
¶ 920	Several Participating Employers		8301(6), 8302(1)

Paragraph in Book		Section in Income Tax Act	Section in Regulations/ Other Reference
¶ 1000 PAST SERVICE PENSION ADJUSTMENTS			
¶ 1005	Introduction		8402
¶ 1010	The General Process		8306, 8307(2), 8402
¶ 1012	Precise Use of Terminology		8303(1) to (3)
¶ 1014	Effective Date		8300(1)
¶ 1017	Excluded Benefits – Flat Benefit Plans		8303(5)(*g*) to (*i*)
¶ 1018	Excluded Benefits – Increases in Flat Rates (Including Increases in the Flat Dollar Maximum Pension)		8303(5)(*f*), 8303(5)(*f.1*) 8303(5)(*f.2*)
¶ 1019	Job Category or Rate-of-Pay Change Resulting in Benefit Increase		8303(5)(*i*)
¶ 1020	Updating the Pensionable Earnings Base		8302(3)(*e*), 8303(5)(*d*)
¶ 1021	Ancillary Benefits		8303(5)
¶ 1023 to ¶ 1024	Breaks in Service; Past Service in the Current Year		8308(4)
¶ 1026	Reciprocal Transfers Between Similar Plans		8304
¶ 1028	Increases to Pensions in Payment and Increases in Pensions during Deferral Period		8303(5)(*j*) to (*l*)
¶ 1032	Special Downsizing		8308(11)
¶ 1033	Increases in Foreign Service from 3 to 5 Years		RPD Newsletter 00-1
¶ 1036	The Basic Calculation Method		8303(4) to (7)
¶ 1037	The Modified Calculation Method		8304(5) to (7)
¶ 1040	Mid-Year Past Service Event		8304(3), (4)
¶ 1051	PSPA Calculation for Earnings-Related Plans		8303
¶ 1052 to ¶ 1053	Flat Benefit Plans – Special Treatment; Escalating Flat Dollar Benefits		8303(5)(*f*), (*g*)

Paragraph in Book		*Section in Income Tax Act*	*Section in Regulations/ Other Reference*
¶ 1054	Transfers from Flat Benefit Plan to Earnings-Related Plan		8303(5)
¶ 1055	Transfers Between Pension Plans		8304(5) to (8)
¶ 1057	PSPA with No Change in Benefit Formula		8301(7), 8302(3) 8303(5)(*d*)
¶ 1060	Exempt PSPA Approval Process		8306
¶ 1065	Non-Exempt PSPA Approval Process	204.2(1.1)	8307
¶ 1075	PSPAs for Specified Retirement Arrangements		8308.3(4), (5)
¶ 1080	PSPAs for Government Sponsored Retirement Arrangements		8308.4
¶ 1085	PSPAs for Foreign Pension Plans		8308.1(5), 8402(2)
¶ 1100 PENSION ADJUSTMENT REVERSALS			
¶ 1105	Introduction		8304.1(2)
¶ 1115	Basic PAR Rules		8304(3), (4), (7), (10) 8300(11), 8300(12)
¶ 1120	The Specified Distribution		8304.1(8)
¶ 1125	PARs for Defined Contribution Plans and DPSPs		8304.1(3), (4)
¶ 1130	PARs for Defined Benefit Plans		8304.1(5), (6), (7), (8)
¶ 1140	PARs for Defined Benefit Plans with Related Provisions		8300(11)
¶ 1145	PARs and Surplus Distributions		8304.1(8)(*d*)
¶ 1150	PARs and Marriage Breakdown		8304.1(15)
¶ 1155	PARs and PSPAs and Reciprocal Transfer Agreements		8304.1(10)
¶ 1160	Reporting Requirements		8402.01
¶ 1165	Special Timing Issues When There is a PA Transfer Amount		8401.01(4)

Paragraph in Book		*Section in Income Tax Act*	*Section in Regulations/ Other Reference*
¶ 1200 PSPA AND PAR FOR MULTI-EMPLOYER PLANS			
¶ 1210	Specified Multi-Employer Plans	147.1(9)	8303(8), (9), 8304(9)
¶ 1215	Multi-Employer Plans Other Than SMEPs	147.1(9)	8510
¶ 1600 REGISTRATION RULES FOR MONEY PURCHASE PLANS			
¶ 1610	Registration of Plans	147.1, 147.1(11), (12), (13)	8512 RPD Newsletter 04-2
¶ 1616	Employer Contributions	147.2(1)	8506(2)(*a*) to (*c*)
¶ 1617	Minimum Employer Contribution		8506(2)(*a*)
¶ 1618	Non-Vested Forfeitures		8506(3)
¶ 1619	Employee Contributions	147.2(4)(*a*)	
¶ 1625	Leaves of Absence and Periods of Reduced Pay		8308(7), 8500(1), 8507, 8508
¶ 1630	Periods of Disability		8507(1)
¶ 1635	Periods of Foreign Service	147.1(1)	RPD Newsletter 93-2 RPD Newsletter 00-1
¶ 1640	Pre-Retirement Death Benefits	147.3(7)	8506(1)(*e*), (*g*) 8506(2)(*h*)
¶ 1645	Bridging Benefits		8506(1)(*b*)
¶ 1650	Post-Retirement Death Benefits	147.3(7)	8506(1)(*c*), (*d*), (*i*)
¶ 1655	Inflation Adjustments		8506(1)(*a*)
¶ 1660	Variable Benefits		8506(1)(*e.1*) 8506(5), (6), (7)
¶ 1665	Pension Paid Directly from the Plan		8506(2)(*g*)
¶ 1670	Contributions after Retirement		8506(1)(*f*), (*h*)

Paragraph in Book		Section in Income Tax Act	Section in Regulations/ Other Reference
¶ 1675	1. Designation of Administrator	147.1(6), (7)	
	2. Primary Purpose of Plan		8502(*a*)
	3. Equal Periodic Payments		8506(1)(*a*)
	4. Latest Start Date for pension		8502(*e*)
	5. Assignment of Rights		8502(*f*)
	6. Permissible Funding Media		8502(*g*) to (*i*)
	7. Contributions by Unions		8501(6)
	8. Payment of Expenses		8502(*d*)
	9. Requirement for Return of Contributions		8506(2)(*d*)
	10. Determination of Amounts		8502(*j*)
	11. Commutation of Benefits		8506(l)(*f*), (*h*)
	12. Division of Benefits		8501(5)
	13. Allocation of Fund Earnings		8506(2)(*e*)
¶ 1680	Special Rules for Connected Persons		8507
¶ 1700 REGISTRATION RULES FOR DEFINED BENEFIT RPP – PERMISSIBLE BENEFITS			
¶ 1705	Registration of New Plans	147.1(3)	8512 RPD Newsletter 04-2
¶ 1707	Grandfathered Plans		8500(1), 8509
¶ 1710	Maximum Lifetime Benefits		8504(1), (2)
¶ 1715	Pre-1990 Past Service Benefit Restriction		8504(6)
¶ 1720	Early Retirement Benefits		8503(3)(*c*)
¶ 1725	Bridging Benefits		8503(2)(*b*), (*l*), 8503(2)(*1*.1) 8503(3)(*k*), 8504(8), 8509(4)(*b*)
¶ 1726	Combined Maximum Lifetime Retirement Benefits and Bridging Benefits		8504(5) 8509(7)

Paragraph in Book		*Section in Income Tax Act*	*Section in Regulations/ Other Reference*
¶ 1727	Transition Rule for Bridging Benefits		8509(2), (4), (7)
¶ 1730	Postponed Retirement Benefits		8502(*e*), 8504(10)
¶ 1735	Maximum Accrual Rate		8503(3)(*g*)
¶ 1741	Permissible Distributions	147.3(3), (8)	8502(*d*)
¶ 1742	Transfers Between Plans	147.3(1), (2), (5) to (7)	
¶ 1743	Transfers – Defined Benefit to Defined Contribution or RRSP	147.3(4), (12)	8517
¶ 1744	Use of Registered Pension Assets to Purchase Annuity	147.3(4) 147.4(1)	Compliance Bulletin #3
¶ 1746	Pensionable Service		8500(1), 8503(3)(*a*), (*e*) 8509(3) RPD Newsletter 99-1
¶ 1747	Leaves of Absence and Periods of Reduced Pay		8507
¶ 1750	Benefits Following Disability		8503(3)(*d*), 8504(8)
¶ 1755	Periods of Foreign Service	147.1(1)	RPD newsletter 93-2 RPD Newsletter 00-1
¶ 1761	Pre-Retirement Survivor Pensions		8503(2)(*e*), (*f*), 8503(2)(1.1) 8504(8)
¶ 1762	Guarantee Period and Indexation of Pre-Retirement Survivor Pensions		8503(2)(*c*), 8503(2)(*g*)
¶ 1763	Lump Sum Payments on Death		8503(2)(j), (*n*) 8503(4)(*d*)
¶ 1764	Death Benefit Exemptions for Grandfathered Plans		8509(4)
¶ 1765	Guaranteed Period and Post-Retirement Survivor Pensions		8503(2)(*c*), (*d*), (*k*)
¶ 1770	Inflation Adjustments		8503(2)(*a*), (12) 8504(l)(*b*), 8504(13)
¶ 1775	Benefit Accruals After Retirement		8503(3)(*b*), (9), (11), (16) to (25)

Paragraph in Book		*Section in Income Tax Act*	*Section in Regulations/ Other Reference*
¶ 1780	Special Downsizing Benefits		8308(11), 8505
¶ 1785	Miscellaneous Registration Rules for Defined Benefit RPPs		
	8. Payment of Expenses		8502(*d*)
	9. Requirement for Reduction of Benefits		8503(4)(*c*)
	10. Determination of Amounts		8502(*j*), RPD Newsletter 94-3
	11. Payment of Lump Sums		8503(2)(*h*), (*m*)
	12. Indexing Included		8503(2)(*m*)
	13. Pension Credits Determinable		8502(*l*), 8503(3)(*f*), (*h*), (*i*)
	14. Offset Benefits		8503(3)(*j*)
	15. Anti-Avoidance Rule		8503(14)
	16. Division of Benefits		8501(5), 8503 (3)(*l*)
	17. Past Service in Lieu		8503(15)
¶ 1790	Special Rules for Connected Persons		8500(1), 8500(7) 8503(2)(*b*), (*e*) 8503(3)(*a*), (*c*) to (*e*) 8504(1), 8505(2) 8507, 8509(3)
¶ 1800 REGISTRATION RULES FOR DEFINED BENEFIT RPP – ELIGIBLE CONTRIBUTIONS			
¶ 1805	Employee Contributions for Current Service	147.2(4)	8503(2)(*h*), 8503(4)(*a*) 8503(5)
¶ 1810	Employee Contributions for Past Service	147.2(4)(*b*), (*c*) 147.2(5)	
¶ 1815	Employer Contributions	147.2(1), (2), (7)	8510(9) 8516(3), 8516(4) RPD Newsletter 95-3 RPD Newsletter 99-1

Paragraph in Book		*Section in Income Tax Act*	*Section in Regulations/ Other Reference*
¶ 1820	Employer Contributions for Pre-1990 Past Service	147.1(10)	8503(15) RPD Newsletter 99-1
¶ 1830 to ¶ 1840	Designated Plan Rules Definition of Designated Plan Maximum Funding Valuation for Designated Plans		8515
¶ 1900 REGISTRATION RULES FOR DPSP			
¶ 1905	Background	147	8301(2) Information Circular 77-1R5
¶ 1910	Distribution of Benefits	147(19) to (22)	
¶ 2000 REGISTRATION RULES FOR COMBINATION PLANS AND HYBRIDS			
¶ 2015	Maximum PA Rule	147.1(8)	
¶ 2020	Maximum Benefit Limitations	248(1)	
¶ 2100 REGISTRATION RULES FOR MULTI-EMPLOYER PLANS			
¶ 2105	Additional or Adjusted Requirements		8510
¶ 2200 FILING REQUIREMENTS FOR RPP			
¶ 2210	Registration of a New RPP	147.1(2) 147.1(3)	8512(1) RPD Newsletter 04-02
¶ 2215	Amending an RPP	147.1(4)	8512(2)
¶ 2220	Annual Information Return		8409
¶ 2225	Actuarial Reports	147.2(2), (3)	8410
¶ 2230	Additional Requirement for Plans with Connected Members		8404(2) 8403

Paragraph in Book		Section in Income Tax Act	Section in Regulations/ Other Reference
¶ 2235	Reporting of Pension Adjustments, Past Service Pension Adjustments and Pension Adjustment Reversals		8401(1), (5), (6) 8402, 8402.01, 8404 8407
¶ 2240	Provision of Information		8406(1) to (3), 8408

TOPICAL INDEX

(References are to Paragraphs)